Acknowledgements

This book is dedicated to all my friends and subscribers on YouTube® who have given me great feedback on the video tutorials that I have produced for this and for many other cameras. Your encouragement and constructive comments have helped to develop the idea to create this book and other tutorial material.

About Me

With more than 40 years' experience in the photographic industry, teaching photography at a local adult education college and as a product specialist and European trainer with Kodak Limited I have been fortunate to learn many aspects of photography and photographic science.

I have been passionate about my own photography for many years striving always to achieve the highest standards at photographic club level and with my own private images.

I have evolved with this as a hobby, developing my own black and white and transparency material and then migrating to digital photography as the first of the digital cameras were commercially available.

I was fortunate to see the first hybrid camera with the Eastman Kodak sensor in a Nikon F3 body, the Kodak DCS100 digital professional camera with a massive 1.3 mega-pixel KAF1300 sensor.

This camera had a CCD back where the traditional film plane would be and a tethering cable to a display and digital storage unit. How technology has developed since 1991.

Through my YouTube® channel www.youtube.com/user/ghough12 and this guide book I hope to be to pass on some of this information and hopefully encourage others to take more rewarding images with their FZ1000 camera.

Graham Houghton
Manchester, UK
March 2019

The FZ1000 User's Guide - Disclaimer

The reference to any manufacturer's product is done purely to illustrate an example and does not imply that I endorse, or have been sponsored by them to promote the product! This guide has been a "labour of love" taking many hours to photograph the illustrations, write the content and check the validity of the adjustment etc.
I don't have a whole production and publishing team to help me format and professionally typeset it however I do hope it doesn't affect your enjoyment of the content.

The opinions expressed within this booklet are my own and derived through extensive use with this camera. There may be some areas that may contain references which may generate some discussion however I hope that these don't detract from the overall aim of the book which is to offer sensible reference material for this camera.

All images are from my own library (except where stated otherwise) and used to illustrate functions or settings etc.

The menu items and features are current as of firmware version 2.2

No responsibility is assumed from any settings or adjustments made to the camera or use of third party accessories mentioned in this book. All reasonable precautions have been made to highlight any material or adjustment which may result in damage to the camera or result in personal injury.

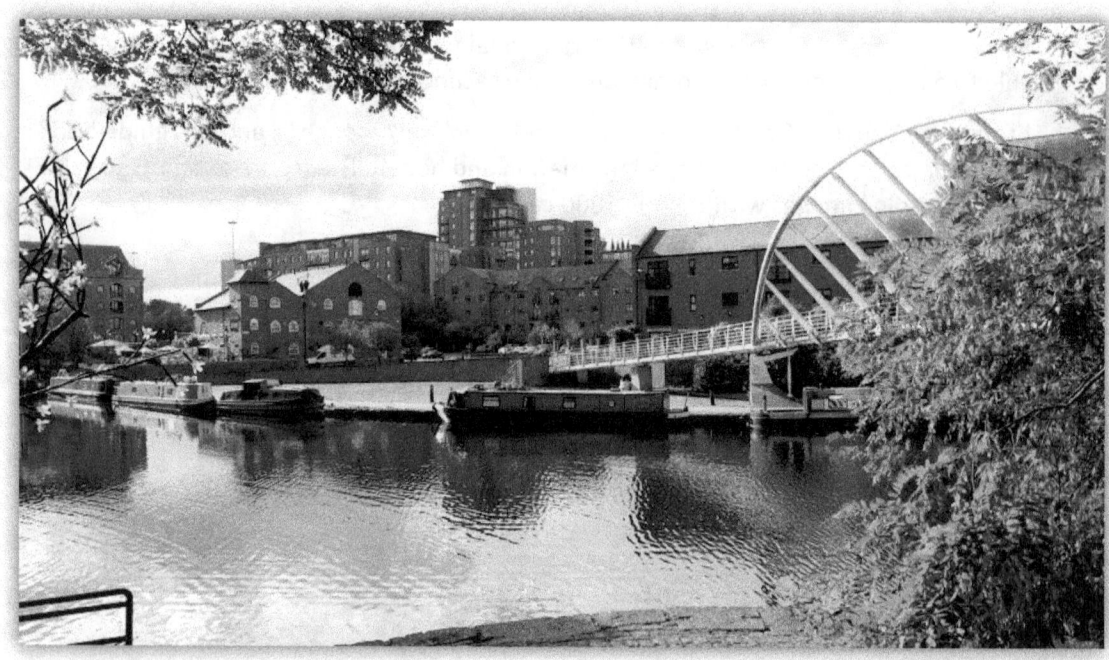

Preface

You don't want excellent pictures from your Panasonic Lumix F1000 – you *demand outstanding pictures*, after all your Panasonic Lumix FZ1000 is one of the most advanced, 4K enabled, digital bridge cameras that Panasonic have produced.

The Panasonic Lumix FZ1000 boasts many features 20.1-megapixel type 1"- sized sensor 25-400mm equiv. F2.8-4 "Leica" lens 5-axis lens-based image stabilization. Burst rate shooting at 12 frames per second shooting mode and 30 frames per second using the electronic shutter. The Panasonic Lumix 1000 has enough customisable features to satisfy the most avid of amateur photographers. This fantastic piece of opto-mechatronics is only let down by the hard to read documentation that comes with the camera in the form of the basic user's manual or the advanced guide found on the accompanying CD-ROM.

You know what you want to find out is in there, however it is so hard to find and you don't know where to start. Furthermore, the "official" manual doesn't offer very much information regarding the basics of digital photography or photography in general.

This is where this field guide about the Panasonic Lumix FZ1000 will help. It explains the purpose of each of the Panasonic Lumix FZ1000 functions and controls, how you should use them and, more importantly, why. The official manual contains a lot of useful information however trying to use it as a reference book is almost impossible.

From the start, there should be some information regarding the file formats, aspect ratios, image size, the priority shooting and autofocus modes. Many like to dash out with their new camera and shoot off a few hundred pictures and then come back later to review these things. So why isn't there a section in the official manual which summarises this important, foundational knowledge in its opening chapters and presenting lots of illustrations showing what your results will look like when you alter each of these settings?

So, if you can't understand what basic settings to set up your camera with, because you don't understand, for example, how changing ISO or focus default method will affect your images, then you need this guide.
I don't assume any superior knowledge; I just offer you experienced advice. This guide isn't packed with pages and pages of check lists on how to take travel pictures, wedding pictures, sports pictures etc., but will endeavour to give you the information that you will need to take great images on your own.

The first step is to familiarise yourself with the camera, the first chapters of this guide will ensure you will do that. As you gain more experience and new skills you'll be eager to know how to improve your exposures, fine tune the colour balance and use some of the essential tools of photography such as using the pop up electronic flash correctly and how to use the camera in a wide range of photographic lighting conditions.
The Panasonic Lumix FZ1000 is not only very easy to use, it's also easy to *learn* to use if you have my little guide book to help you along the way.

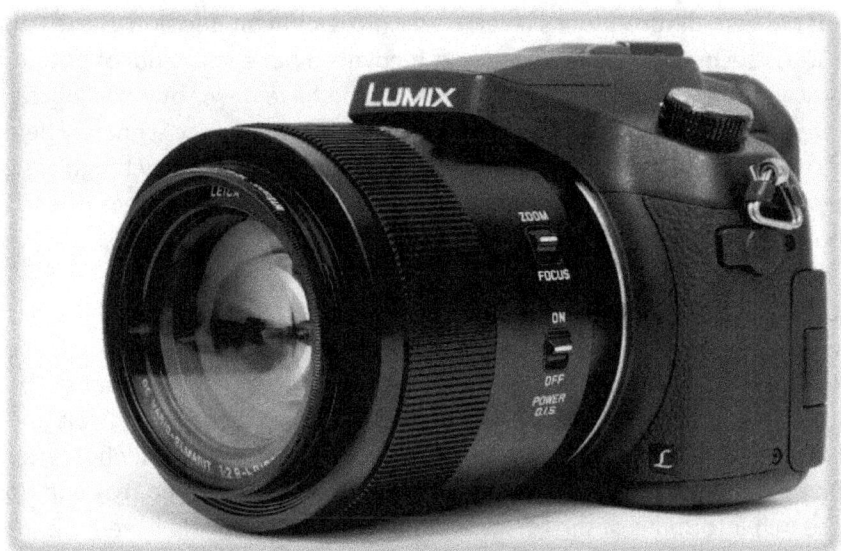

Figure 1 The Panasonic Lumix FZ1000 Camera

About You the Reader

Whilst I was in the process of putting this guidebook together I tried to consider exactly who would be benefiting from its contents. Indeed, I made repeated visits to the comments section of the featured videos on my YouTube® channel to see the sort of questions being asked.
It is by reviewing those which led me to the style and format of this guide book. I don't cover all the basic steps like attaching the neck strap or lens retaining cord.

I prefer to show you the set ups and adjustments to allow you to take great pictures with this camera.
From a skills level, you may fall broadly into one of the following categories:

- An amateur photographer who already knows all the photographic science needed to take great pictures and simply wants to use the Panasonic Lumix FZ1000 as a simple "out and about" camera without the need to carry a huge bag of lenses needed to fulfil his or her needs.

- Individuals who want to get better images than can be afforded from just basic compact digital cameras or smartphones.

- Those who want to strive to get better, professional looking images for their business or website and feel the Panasonic Lumix FZ1000 will give them that facility.

- Corporate workers who may want to produce higher quality images for inclusion in some of their company presentations, reports or other applications.

Considering the very different skills levels was a more difficult decision as the Panasonic Lumix FZ1000 is such a fantastic camera that it covers a huge spectrum of potential people who will buy and use it, from absolute beginners who have never owned a digital camera before to the advanced amateur with years of shooting experience who may be using the Panasonic Lumix FZ1000 as a backup camera. I decided it was a pretty tough assignment to provide something for everybody, so I will be trying to cover the needs of each of the following groups and their skill levels:

- Complete beginners to digital photography: if you have only used the basic of compact cameras, or have worked only with film based cameras in the past then you are to be congratulated on the choice of camera you have made. This guide to the Panasonic Lumix FZ1000 will help you to understand the controls and features that this camera provides and help you to progress into digital photography with the minimum of concerns. If you get keen, then you may find that additional research into some of the topics that I will explore will help speed this journey.

- Advanced point and shooter who is upgrading: There are many technically well specified cameras out there in the market place. Panasonic has an extensive range of models to suit consumer lifestyles. Models like the LX series and TZ (ZS) series do have many user definable options and settings and it is quite possible you have a lot of technical expertise with these cameras. You may have recognised some of the inherent problems associated with this class of camera like slow autofocus or shutter lag and sometimes the restricted aperture or zoom range available on them. The possibility of using more powerful, external flash units, external microphones to record better sound for your video clips and simple things like the facility to employ filters to modify the light entering the camera or provide creative effects may be another reason you have decided to purchase the Panasonic Lumix FZ1000.

- Traditional film users new to the digital era: You probably know all about photography, you understand f-stops, shutter speed and ISO which make up the components of the "exposure triangle". You may even have had one of the more sophisticated film cameras which also employ some pretty slick electronics like autofocus and metering modes. All you need is the relevant information on using the digital specific features of the Panasonic Lumix FZ1000 and how to match, or exceed the capabilities of your previous film based camera.

- Advanced Users: I expect you to be the most discerning readers who have already extensive working knowledge of digital photography and the associated digital work flow. I cannot teach you much more about digital photography but hopefully allow you to experience the joys of shooting digital images with the Panasonic Lumix FZ1000. You might feel, like I do, that the Panasonic Lumix FZ1000 will provide a tool to capture great images in a variety of situations without the added hassle of a DSLR and lenses so providing you with a very quick, lightweight and feature rich tool to do it with.

Getting a new camera, and I'm sure it will be the same for you, is exciting.
It's tempting to install the battery, insert a memory card and dash out shooting a variety of subjects in varying lighting conditions just to see what the image quality is like.
Let me advise you against this. Whilst you may be pleased with the image quality that the camera has delivered for you there will be some images that are not quite up to your expectations as no camera is 100% perfect in achieving either correct exposure, correct focus point or colour rendering.
So how would you go about analysing why those few images were failures. You need to be well disciplined in your methodology when testing new pieces of gear. Note taking, I find is essential. I might think that I can recall how I took the shots however in many case I find that I cannot.
A simple notepad and pen, or increasingly I'm now using my smartphone to either jot down a note, a simple record photo of the scene or an audio note if the testing is a little more complex.
Getting to know the camera is, in my opinion, key to getting consistently good images without any 'nasty' surprises. I guess we all hate user manuals and consider it almost a failure if we must resort to looking something up in them. However, in this guide I will be attempting to add extra dimensions to what is in the advanced user guide supplied on DVD-rom, or download, with the camera in the form of actual user examples to illustrate the more advanced features which does make the FZ1000 a very capable imaging device.

If you are new to the Panasonic camera range then you will need to familiarise yourself with the ways of navigating through the menu system, the use of the control buttons and dials to access and change settings. If you have owned previous Panasonic compact cameras, then this should be very easy as the menu access and setting is consistent across nearly all the camera range. It would be impossible in a book of this nature to cover every menu option, adjustment procedure or shooting option however I have endeavoured to cover all the main options.
The Panasonic Advanced Manual is the complete reference for this camera.

ftp://ftp.panasonic.com/camera/om/dmc-fz1000_en_adv_om.pdf

Procedures like adjusting the eyepiece dioptre adjustment to enable a sharp view of the EVF (electronic viewfinder) should be done, especially if you wear spectacles.
Although not essential to do immediately, there are some adjustments that can be made within the menus to enhance the information presented on the EVF or the LCD screen.
Elements that you may not have considered may affect the type of images that you can record with the camera, such as the speed and capacity of the memory card that you will be using. What aspect ratio and image size and format will you be shooting the images at?
Let's begin by looking at what you will need to consider when purchasing and using memory cards for use with the FZ1000.

The memory card that the Panasonic Lumix FZ1000 utilises is referred to as the SD standard. This "secure digital" card format is an industry standard in terms of size and shape but unfortunately the way in which the memory "write" speeds are disclosed, leaves some room for improvement and causes a great deal of confusion with buyers.

Often cards are purchased on the advice of camera shop sales persons who, in many cases, do not understand this system either!

Let me break this down as simply as I can to prevent you making expensive buying mistakes with future purchases.

Basically, the SD format card is available in two packages, one is the first-generation card and referred to as SD and is generally available in capacities of 2MB to 2GB.

Although these cards can be used I would like to persuade you not to use them as they usually have a slower "write" time and with video recording limit the time you have available considerably.

It is better to start your collection of addition memory with the second generation of card, the SDHC (secure digital high capacity).

You can tell the difference by the logo on the card.

The SDHC compact memory card, identified with the SDHC logo on the face of the label.

I would generally recommend at least a class 6 rating card if you are shooting stills or AVCHD video, however, with the advent of higher video recording bit rates in MP4 format – especially the 4K UHD video we need to consider a totally different variety of memory card the SDXC – secure digital extended capacity for 64GB and above.

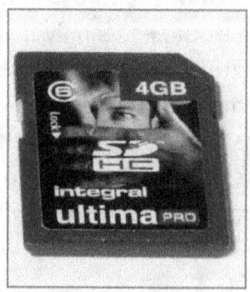

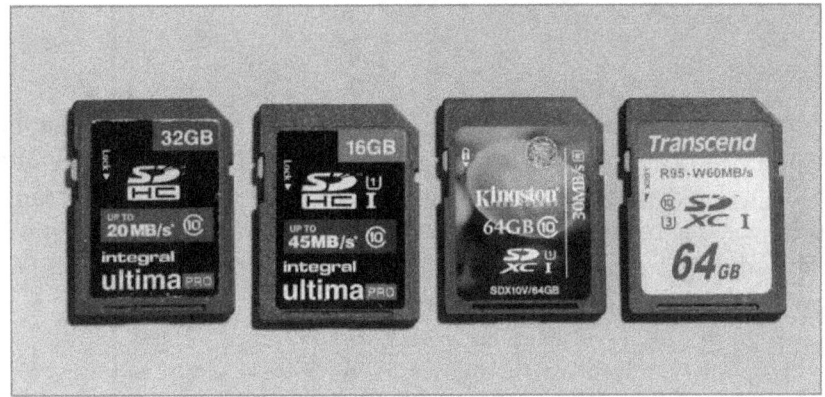

Recommended SD Memory cards

In the illustration above you can see my recommendations for memory cards suitable for use with the Panasonic Lumix FZ1000.

The two cards on the left are the SDHC cards suitable for all photographic stills shooting plus AVCHD or MP4 video at 1080p.

On the right the two SDXC memory cards with the new U1 and the faster U3 ratings code. The two cards are required for reliable shooting in both 4K photo and video modes. SDXC cards also have the advantage that they are not constrained by the 4GB fat32 file system limit so longer video clips are not fragmented.

If you are shooting video, then the highest capacity card is advisable as the files can become quite large and fill smaller cards quite quickly.

One tip I can offer you here is to use the micro SDXC cards in their supplied SD adaptor. Not only are they the same electronics in a smaller profile but are about half the cost of their equivalent SD card. Their functionality is the same as their full size equivalent.

Keep them in their adaptor when you use them in your pc or external card reader.

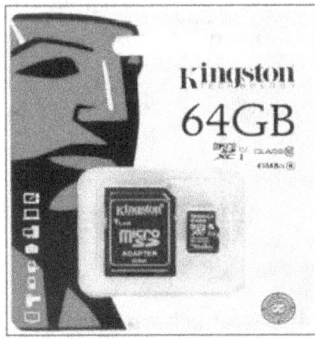

a typical micro SD card and adaptor

Formatting Memory Cards

Formatting the cards in camera is the best option after they have been used a few times, and especially if you share them across a range of cameras. This has the advantage of recovering the file system and structure and thus overcoming some of the fragmentation which occurs if you delete files either from within the camera or later when the card is in your pc card reader. This process allows the camera buffer to write to the card faster and hence allowing it to clear quickly. This is essential when shooting in the burst modes of the camera.

Batteries and Chargers for the Panasonic Lumix FZ1000

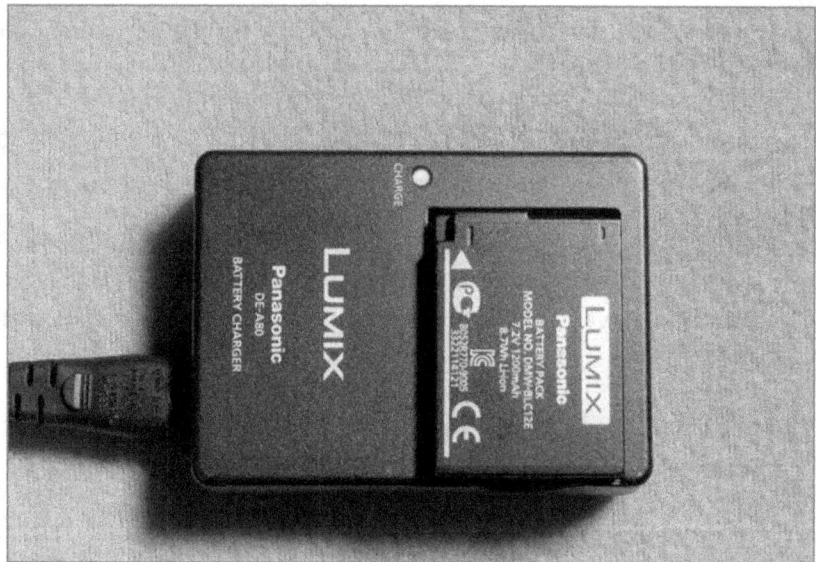

The Official Charger DE-A80 and DMW-BLC12E Battery

There has been much written, and debated, about the use of third party batteries in Panasonic Lumix cameras.
Fears of fires and explosions either during the charging phase or the subsequent use in the camera have been circulation around the camera forums now for years.

It's obvious to see why third party batteries are so much in demand as they can be as little as one fifth of the price of an OEM battery.

In my, opinion, I see absolutely no reason why not to use these batteries if you take a few sensible precautions.

I do recommend using the original DE-A80 charger from Panasonic as it has a few useful checking features to prevent such accidents occurring during the charging phase. It will, however, only work with Panasonic OEM batteries and not third party ones.

Let's examine why batteries catch fire or explode during charging.

During the charging process, there are several checks made by the charger to ensure that it is safe to apply a charging voltage to the lithium ion cell.

During charging the internal resistance of the cell causes heat, created as a by-product of the charging process, to increase the temperature of the cell. If the temperature continues to rise, unchecked, the cell can develop thermal runaway with catastrophic results.

The cell has 4 terminals marked +, -, T and D. It's the + and – terminals that are used during charging and discharging and the T terminal is the one which notifies the charging device or discharging device (i.e. the camera) that there is a problem. The usual strategy for dealing with this is to immediately discontinue charging or discharging.

The Panasonic charger will not charge a third-party battery which does not have the "T" terminal connected internally to a protection integrated circuit within the cell. It will also very quickly cease charging if the charging current causes heating of the cell to occur.

The camera has similar protection circuitry to prevent the battery becoming too hot due to heavy current demands such as those seen during video recording where the camera internal heat can build up by the processor generating heat also.

If your charger only has two contacts which align with the + and – terminals only, the charger is relying upon the battery terminal voltage to regulate the charging voltage. It is with these chargers that potential problems of overcharging can occur.

If you notice that the battery become too hot to hand hold during charging, then it is likely the charger is not calibrated correctly and you should discontinue using it.

Lithium-ion batteries should never be allowed to completely discharge and if the cell voltage drops below 2 volts the chances are that copper shunts will have formed within the cell and it may become dangerously hot if recharged.

Many of the travel chargers or those intended for use in vehicles fall into this category and you should monitor the battery case temperature for signs of overheating. Alternative chargers are discussed in the accessory chapter.

To add to this, it is always wise not to charge the batteries in a high ambient temperature or cover the battery during charging.

Similarly, lithium-ion batteries should not be stored where the ambient temperature may become excessively hot (50C/120F).

Allow batteries that have been removed from the camera to cool before charging again. If the DE-A80 charging LED is flashing this indicates that there is a problem with the battery that is being attempted to be charged.

The battery temperature may be too high or too low or the contacts dirty.

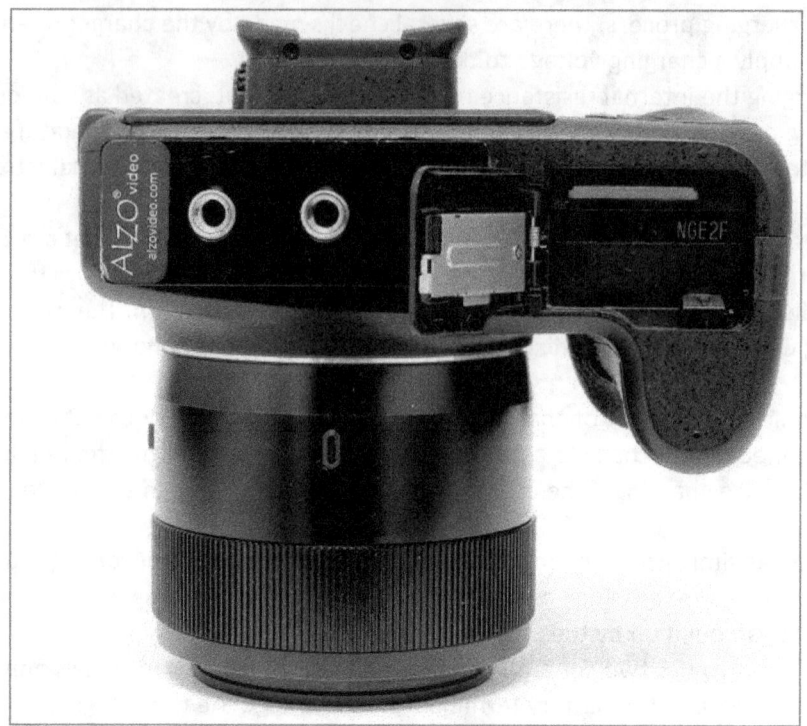

The battery and memory card compartment of the FZ1000

A tripod adaptor plate, manufactured by ALZOVIDEO.com allows standard quick release plates to be fixed to it and allow access to the battery compartment if the camera is mounted on a tripod or in a camera rig. Product code is 1649-PAN

As usual a dummy battery adaptor (the DMW-DCC8) can be inserted into the battery compartment where the connection cable is brought out though a small rubber flap in the side of the camera case. It is used with a suitable ac power adaptor.

In terms of battery performance, the Panasonic CIPA (Camera & Imaging Products Association) results for the cameras suggest that around 360 images or 180 minutes of recording time when using the LCD to view the images.

These values are reduced to 300 images and 150 minutes if you use the EVF (which is surprising!)

Estimated Images Stored on Memory card

The number of images that can be stored on a capacity of memory card will depend upon the image size and quality.

Aspect ratio is set to 3:2 and Quality is set to JPEG Fine

Image Size	8 GB card	32 GB card	64 GB card
L (20M)	720	2910	5810
EX M (10M)	1310	5310	10510
EX S (5M)	2270	9220	17640

Aspect ratio is set to 3:2 and Quality is RAW + JPEG Fine

Image Size	8 GB card	32 GB card	64 GB card
L (20M)	220	920	1840
M (10M)	260	1070	2140
S (5M)	290	1170	2340

Recording Time for Video Clips

Recording format is AVCHD

Rec Quality	8 GB card	32 GB card	64 GB card
FHD/28M/50p	35m00sec	2h30m	5h00m
FHD/17M/50i	55m00sec	4h05m	8h15m
FHD/24M/25p	40m00s	2h50m	5h50m
FHD/24M/24p	40m00s	2h50m	5h50m

Recording format is MP4

Rec Quality	8 GB card	32 GB card	64 GB card
4K/100M/25p	8m00sec	40m00sec	1h20m
4K/100M/24p	8m00sec	40m00sec	1h20m
FHD/28M/50p	34m00sec	2h25m	5h00m
FHD/20M/25P	45m00sec	3h15m	6h40m
FHD/10M/25p	1h25m	6h20m	12h45m
VGA/4M/25p	3h15m	13h00m	26h00m

When recording AVCHD recording stops when the time exceeds 29mins 59sec.
(tax implications for any camera able to record longer than this)
If recording in MP4, recording will stop at 29mins and 59sec or when the file size exceeds
4GB (depends upon scene content)
If recording 4K video MP4 recording stops at 29mins and 59secs however, this will be
made of several 4GB clips (separate files). With SDXC and EXFat file system this is
overcome and files are not fragmented into 4GB clips.

However, the continuity of recording is maintained during the creation of the individual
clips. These can be recombined in a video editing program seamlessly.
During recording the number of still images, or the remaining recording time is shown at
the lower right hand side of the LCD screen.

The Camera Controls and Functions

A look at some of the main user controls and features of the FZ1000.

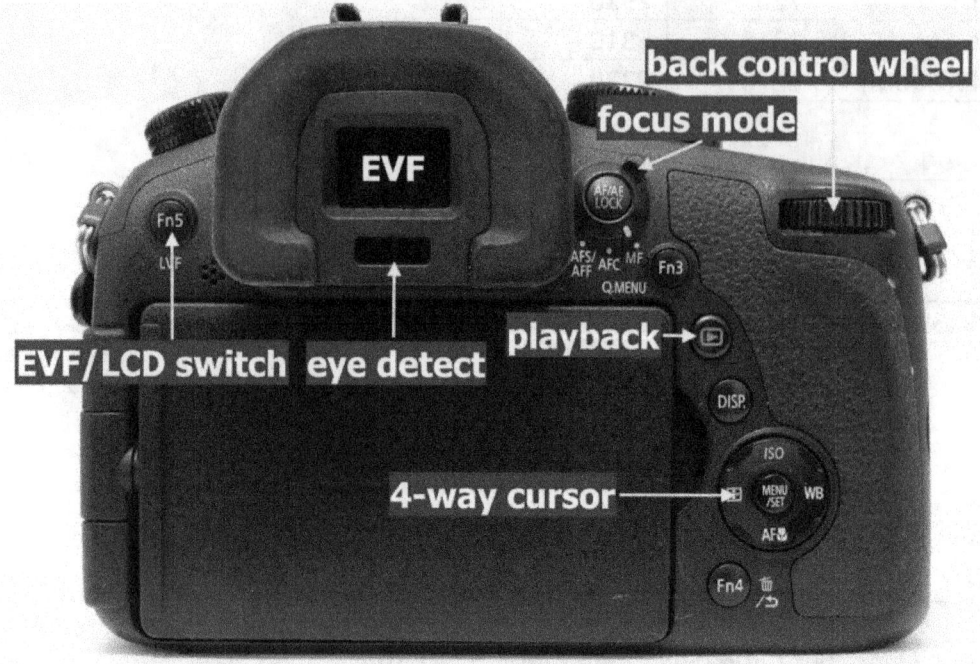

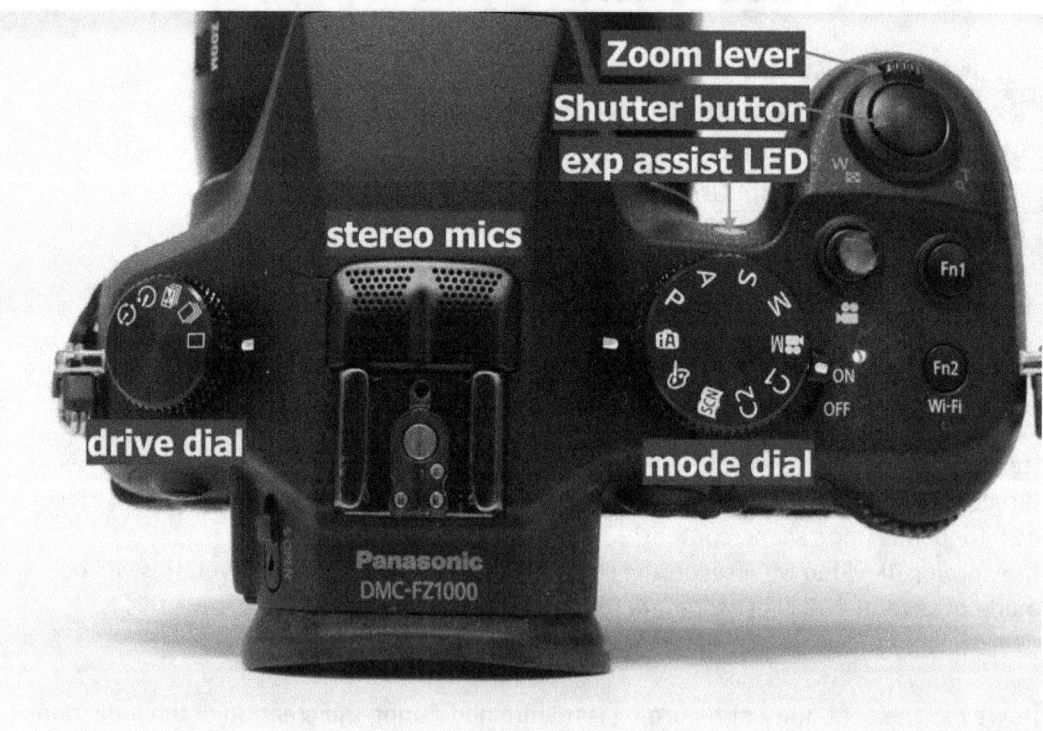

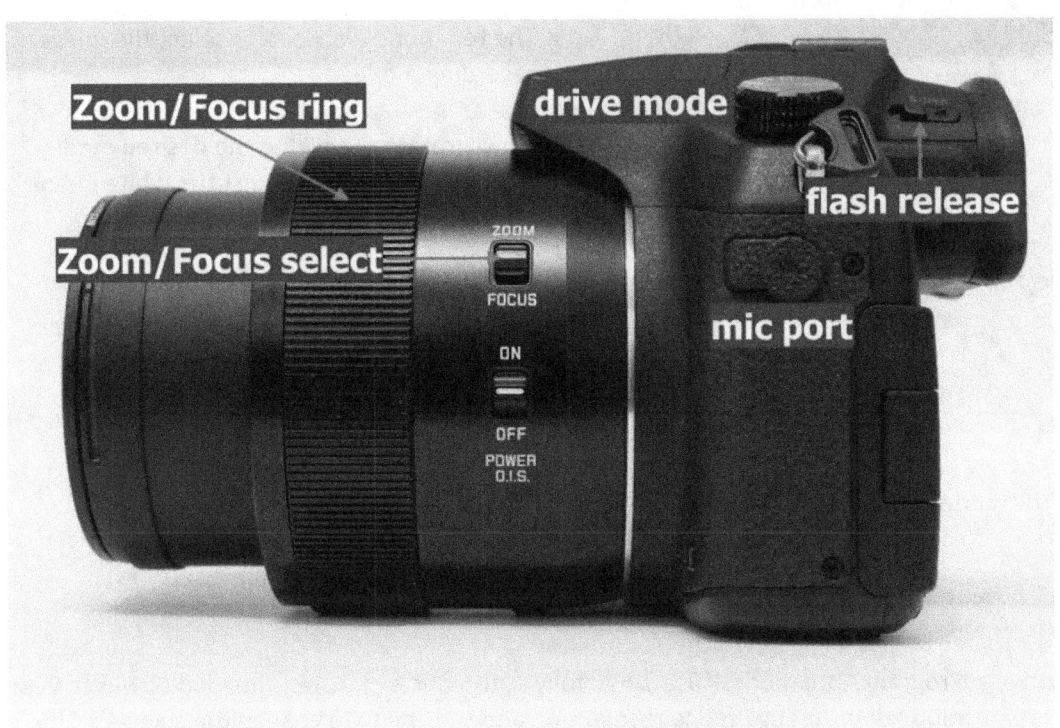

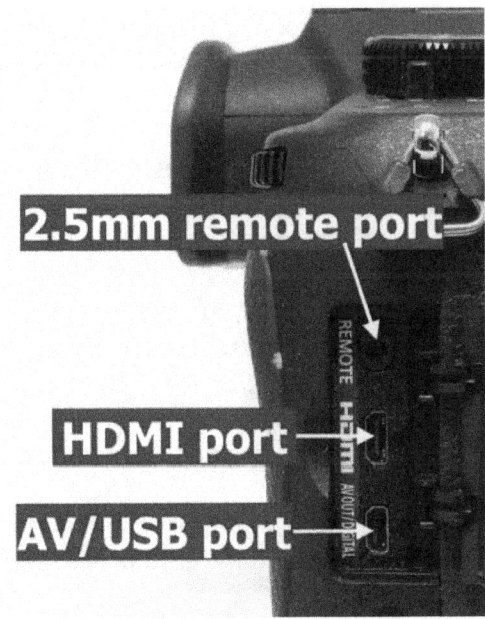

remote/HDMI/AV-USB ports on the camera

On the right-hand side, the communication, HDMI and wired remote input socket are located behind the rubber cover.

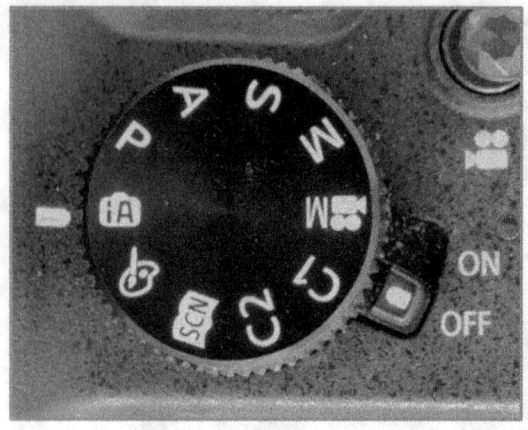 The top mode dial used to select the image recording mode.

Slowly rotate the dial to the desired mode aligning the symbol against the white index mark adjacent to the flash head.

The dial can be rotated in either direction and is fitted with strong detents to ensure that the mode isn't accidentally changed when slipping the camera in a bag, for example.

The modes are set as follows:

iA   Intelligent Auto Mode – used to take images with fully automatic settings.

P   Program Auto mode – use when fully automatic exposure is needed however this mode does not use scene recognition and the ability to change the selected aperture/shutter speed combination is available via the program shift option.

A   Aperture priority mode – use when depth of field (DOF) is the main requirement in the image.

S   Shutter priority mode – use when it is necessary to select a specific shutter speed. For example, a fast shutter speed to eliminate subject motion blur or a slow shutter speed to create effects like silky running water or streaking clouds.

M   Manual exposure mode – use when you want to select a specific aperture for DOF and a shutter speed for motion effects. Use the ISO to control the exposure.

M   Creative Video Mode – used to select the recording mode for video capture using the same P/A/S/M options depending upon requirements.

C1,2   Custom mode – allows the recall of pre-set conditions for image capture after they have been registered to one of the custom mode settings

SCN   Scene mode – use this mode to select one of the pre-set scene modes which have been created to optimise the image under these specific scene types or lighting situations.

CCM   Creative Control Mode – use to create images using one of several image effects from a list of 22 pre-set filters.

Several of the FZ1000's most important functions are controlled by physical push buttons, control dials, switches or levers. The only feature this camera lacks, I feel, is a touch screen which would have been a nice feature (now available on the FZ1000 mk2).

I thought that I would write an explanation of all the controls here in this section so they are available as a future reference.

Let's start with the top of the camera:

THE SHUTTER BUTTON
Arguably this is the most important control on the camera. Set with its default operating mode lightly pressing the button until you feel a little resistance (called the half-way point) checks and sets focus and exposure.
Fully depressing the button fully completes the image taking process.
In the creative video mode, it starts and stops the video recording process. (Note however whilst in this mode you cannot use the shutter button to capture still images – this is a feature that can only be done when the FZ1000 is being used with the red button recording mode).
Additionally, if the camera has "gone to sleep" in its energy conservation mode then you can half depress the shutter button to "wake" it up again.
The shutter button is also used to exit to the shooting mode from a recording or playback menu screen.
When the shutter speed is set to "B" (bulb) in Manual Exposure mode press and hold the shutter button down for as long as you want the exposure to last (up to 120 seconds).
There are several ways in which the functionality of the shutter button can be programmed using the options in the Custom menu.
The half way focus operation can be disabled by setting Shutter AF to OFF in the option on page 1 of the Custom menu.
Whilst you are in this Custom menu, on page 2/8 you can set the half way point to release the shutter button – this can be useful if you are setting the camera up for Back Button Focus – which I detail later in the book.

ON/OFF SWITCH
Situated adjacent to the Mode Dial, sliding the switch to the front of the camera to turn the camera power on and pulling it back towards the rear of the camera to power it off. Power on is indicated by a small green LED adjacent to this switch.
To conserve precious battery life the ECO (Economy) mode of the camera will automatically power off if the Sleep Mode option is set to one of the intervals available (1,2,5 or 10 minutes) however using this option and setting the Sleep mode to Off the camera will not power down – which can be useful in some situations.

ZOOM LEVER
This is a small plastic ring with a finger grip which surrounds the shutter button.
It has the basic function of changing the focal length of the lens ranging from the wide angle setting of 25mm (35mm equiv) to the telephoto setting of 400mm (35mm equiv).

From its central, default, position pushing the lever to the left causes the camera to move the focal length towards the wide-angle setting (W) and pulling it right will cause the lens to move towards the telephoto setting (T).

This lever can be programmed to provide a "stepped" zoom rather than the smooth change. To achieve this the option is changed with the option in the Custom menu on page 7/8.

The Zoom lever can also be programmed to alter the Exposure Value compensation rather than using the back-control dial.

By using the zoom control ring on the lens barrel and the zoom lever set to exposure compensation gives a very quick and convenient way to make the usual changes that you might want to do when setting up a photographic composition.

When using the playback feature of the camera the zoom lever can be used to enlarge the image displayed if you move it to the right and will cause the camera to display various options of thumbnails if you move push it to the left.

The zoom lever can additionally be used to move from page to page whilst in the menu screens either forwards or backwards.

MODE DIAL

The knurled black Mode dial is screen printed with icons representing each of the cameras shooting modes:

Intelligent Auto, Program Auto, Aperture priority, Shutter priority, Manual, Creative video, Custom Mode C1, Custom Mode C2, Scene type and Creative filter.

The Mode dial preselects the features available for shooting and how some of the other controls perform.

Still images can be captured by just depressing the shutter button fully in any of the modes available other than in the Creative Video mode (where the camera will start or stop a video recording as you press the shutter button).

You can record a video clip in any mode by pressing the red video recording button.

For the most basic "point and shoot" operating mode turn the mode dial to the iA position.

VIDEO RECORD BUTTON

This red button is located adjacent to the Mode dial. Its only function is to start and stop recording a video clip.

FN1 (FUNCTION BUTTON #1)

This button is one of the five physical buttons (Fn1, Fn2, Fn3, Fn4, Fn5) which can be programmed to your own preference thus enabling you to set the camera to suite your photography needs.

In its default, programmed mode, the Fn1 button is set the allow quick access to the camera's "photostyles".

FN2 (FUNCTION BUTTON #2)

In its default, programmed mode, the Fn2 button is set the allow quick access to the camera's "Wi-Fi" connection. When Wi-Fi is enabled a small blue LED is illuminated adjacent to this button.

The final control located on the top of this camera is the Drive Mode Dial and it is located at the top left hand side of the camera. Like the Mode control it has five icons screen printed on it. These denote the five possible positions which select the relevant drive mode for the camera.

Single frame:

Starting with the white rectangular icon this is the "single frame" mode followed by Burst mode shooting, Bracketing mode, Self-timer and, finally, Interval timer mode. Some of these modes conflict with other camera operations such as HDR and Intelligent zoom so if you are having problems setting some operations try setting the drive mode to single frame to see if this helps.

Burst shooting:

The second position on this dial activates burst mode shooting (also referred as continuous mode shooting). With this mode selected the camera will take a series of images if you hold the shutter button depressed.

With this mode selected you may find this useful for sports or action photography or in children's portraiture where there is a good chance to capture a good facial expression.

The FZ1000 can shoot a continuous series of images at different speeds.

These are labelled H, M and L referring to High, Medium and Low.

The actual Burst Rate is set in the Recording set up menu page 1. The actual rate at which the images will be capture also depends upon the Focus Mode selected (detailed later) however, in the Autofocus single mode the High speed will be 12 frames per second, Medium will be 7 frames per second and Low will return 2 frames per second.

During shooting with the High speed setting the camera will not update the Live view display.

If the focus mode is set to either Manual focus or AFS the exposure and the white balance settings will be locked at the first exposure.

If you have selected AFF or AFC both the exposure and white balance will be adjusted as the camera adjusts the focus.

When the Medium or Low setting, the camera will be shooting at 7 or 2 frames per second respectively and irrespective of the AFS/AFF/AFC setting and the live view is updated during shooting with white balance and exposure adjusted with each shot.

With any of the burst speed settings the setting of the image Quality will heavily impact on the sustained rate as the internal camera buffer needs to write is file to the SD memory card.

The larger the file, as generated when using RAW quality, will cause the burst rate to slow down after several shots are taken.

If RAW files are not selected the speed will slow down much later and is limited only by the capacity of the memory card.

If you half depress the camera shutter button with one of the detailed information screens displayed it will show the letter "r" followed by the number of images that the camera can capture in a continuous burst sequence.

With all burst mode shooting the actual frames per second will also be affected by the shooting conditions.

For example, if the ambient lighting is dark then this might force the camera to use longer exposure times – this will alone slow down the rate at which the images are captured.

With all these variables affecting the actual burst mode achievable my recommendation is to select the M or L modes when you don't need super-fast shooting.
For example, when shooting child portraiture, we don't need to "freeze the action" just capture the subtle change in facial expression.
If shooting sports or action, then you can use the High-speed mode to increase the chances of getting a few frames in focus or at the right point in the action.

You will find that there are several limitations on the use of burst mode shooting.
For example, it cannot be used with flash shooting and some of the creative filter effects such as Star filter and soft focus.
Additionally, it cannot be used with some of the other special settings like Multiple Exposure, White Balance Bracket, Hand Held Night Shot and during motion picture recording using the red button.

When you release the shutter button during burst mode shooting you may see the red icon at the left-hand side of the screen indicating that the camera buffer is still writing to the SD memory card. Whilst this is happening you should not remove the memory card or removing the battery otherwise some of the images may not be written to the memory card.

Auto Bracketing Mode:
This mode position is used in conjunction with the Single/Burst settings, Step and Sequence in the Rec Setting menu under Auto Bracket.
It is used to automatically take a series of images with varying exposures ranging from under exposure to overexposure.
Its use varies from ensuring that you have at least one correct exposure when the lighting situation may be tricky or when you want to create a series of images for combining to produce an image with an expanded or higher dynamic range – HDR.

Self-timer:
The next icon on this dial is the Self-timer option.
With this you can activate the camera self-timer and hence set a delay between the full depress of the shutter button and the completion of the exposure. The camera can be programmed for a two or ten seconds' delay. The ten second delay is useful if you have the camera on a tripod when pressing the shutter button and then running back for a self-portrait or inclusion in a group shot.
The two second timer is useful to prevent camera shake when hand holding the camera for close-ups where pressing the shutter release may cause a change in camera position or induce movement in the image.
To select the delay time that you use, this mode is used in conjunction with the Self-timer option in the Rec Set up menu.
During the self-timer count down the Focus Assist LED acts as an indicator and the camera will beep until the final exposure is made.

During the final second of the delay, when the ten second delay mode is set, the beeps and flashes of the LED speed up to indicate that the exposure is imminent.

During the two second count down the camera beeps four times and the LED flashes five times.

If you select the ten second delay with three images at two second interval the camera will delay for ten seconds and then make the first exposure, delay for two seconds and then complete the second exposure, wait again for two seconds and then complete the third and final exposure of the sequence.

During the countdown period, you can cancel it by pressing the Menu/set button.

You cannot use the self-timer in conjunction with any auto bracketing or multiple exposure. You cannot use it at all during recording video clips.

Interval Timer:

The Interval Timer allows setting of the camera's Time lapse or Stop Motion Animation features.

To change the settings of either of these features you select either option in the Time Lapse/Animation from the recording menu page 2/7.

Full details of both operations on page 120.

Controls on the camera back:

AFS/AFF/AFC/MF SELECTOR:

When you choose the AFS/AFF position of this switch the camera will use the autofocus system along with other focus related settings such as the AF mode, AFF/AFS selection choice and others.

The camera will allow autofocus from its closest working distance of 11.8 inches (30cms) to infinity at the wide angle setting in the normal AF mode and from 1 inch (2.5cms) to infinity at the wide angle setting and macro AF setting.

When you zoom to full 400mm EFL the focus distances become 6 feet 6 inches (2metres) at normal AF and three feet 3 inches (1metre) at macro AF setting.

If you choose AFC, the camera continues to focus even if the subject is not moving.

Using this mode consumes more battery power than AFS or AFF.

AFC is good for subjects which continuously change focus position whereas AFS is a better choice for static subjects. Further details are discussed later in this guide.

Manual Focus (MF):

If you move the mode lever to the MF position, then providing that the side switch on the lens barrel is also set to Focus, the large control ring on the lens will adjust the focus position.

To select the area used for manual focus assist press the Left navigation button (unless you have set Manual Focus assist to include operation of the Focus ring in the Custom Set Up menu page 3/8) this will then bring up an enlarged view so that you can accurately set the focus point.

Rotating the ring to your left focus towards infinity (the on-screen focus guide moves towards the mountains icon) and turning the ring to the right moves the focus point closer (towards the flower icon on the on-screen focus guide).

When manual focus is engaged if you want the camera to set the focus quickly for you press the AF/AE Lock button, then you can use the focus ring to fine tune the actual focus point, if needed.

Additionally, another focusing aid called "focus peaking" can also be activated and I detail this later in this manual.

THE AF/AE LOCK BUTTON:

This button, located in the centre of the focus mode lever, is hard programmed to perform either a Focus Lock, Exposure Lock, Both or to provide the AF on feature.
These choices are assigned in the Custom menu page 1/8 under AF/AE Lock.
By default, the button is set to provide Exposure Lock only.
In this mode, pressing and holding the button will lock the current camera exposure in all the shooting modes except in the Manual Exposure and the iA modes.
If you desire you can have this exposure locked on depressing this button by setting the value of the AF/AE Lock Hold button to ON. You will find this option in the same menu setting page 1/8.
To release the lock, press the AF/AE Lock button again. (the loch hold does not work when the button is assigned as the AF-On mode).

THE FN3 BUTTON:

The Fn3 button, in its default programmed state, is assigned as the Q.menu button. If you wish, this can be programmed to other functions with the Function Button Set option on page 7 of the Custom menu although as this has the silk screen printed Q.menu on the camera body I recommend leaving this set to that function.
The Q.menu is a useful button as, in the recording mode, it pops up an abridged version of the camera's main menu system allowing you to choose settings for various options without having to search through all of the main menu pages.
Fn3 also has one hidden option as Fn3 is also programmed to set the pattern that you may assign to the Custom Multi option of the 49 AF point selection.
You press Fn3 to lock the highlighted desired points which are then saved for the AF points for this mode.

PLAYBACK BUTTON:

This button which has the green arrow symbol silk screen printed on it is located below the Fn3 Q.menu button.
Pressing this button puts the camera into the image/video playback mode.
The lens will retract automatically after about 15 seconds as it is not needed to be extended during playback operations.

THE DISPLAY BUTTON:

This button, located in the centre of the camera back adjacent to the 4-way navigation dial, has several functions depending upon its current context.

It has the main function of allowing you to switch through several display screen options for both the LCD screen and the EVF. This is for both the recording and playback modes.

When you are in the recording mode the allowable choices are:

Full display. With all the available shooting information displayed which includes Battery status, focus mode, AFS/AFF mode, recording quality, picture size, video quality and format, flash status, Photostyle, current shooting mode, metering mode, aperture set, shutter speed, exposure compensation, ISO (if you have this set to a specific value), white balance mode and the remaining number of images or video recording time available on the memory card that is currently inserted in the camera.

Blank display. In this mode, the whole LCD or viewfinder has no overlaid shooting information apart from the aperture, shutter speed and exposure compensation. This information is only briefly displayed for about 10 seconds when you half depress the shutter button. During this time, it will also show the focus frame if you have selected a mode which uses one (such as the 1-area AF or AF Tracking)

Level Display. In this screen, all the shooting information is displayed plus a "level gauge". This allows you to check that the camera is level in both horizontal and vertical planes

Shooting information without live view. In this mode, all the relevant shooting information is displayed on the LCD/EVF on a black background.

Two display areas will show the current aperture and shutter speed when you half depress the shutter button.

Additionally, any control that is highlighted in yellow text can be adjusted by using the back-control wheel. If you are in Aperture priority mode, (A) on the mode dial, then Aperture can be adjusted with the dial.

If you are in Shutter priority mode, (S) on the mode dial), then the shutter speed can be adjusted. In the Program Auto Mode, (P) on the mode dial, the camera selected Aperture and Shutter speed values are shown.

In this mode turning the back-control wheel to the left with invoke the "program shift" feature whereby you can change the combination pair to suit your need for the image that you are taking.

This could be a higher shutter speed for sports or action for example.

In the Manual Mode, (M) on the mode dial, the current values for Aperture and Shutter speed are displayed and the back-control wheel can be used to adjust either. Pressing in the back-control wheel alternates between the two settings. The cameras exposure meter will be displayed in the central area plus any current exposure compensation value that you may have previously set.

Totally Off. The final screen is totally black as the screen is turned off.

If you are in the Playback mode, the functions of this button are as follows:

Full shooting information. When in the playback mode the default screen shows all the information that was gathered during the time that the image/video was captured.

It displays the current image number/total images on the memory card, the quality of the image (Raw/JPEG), the aspect ratio, flash status, the shooting mode, the aperture and shutter speed used, any exposure compensation used, the ISO used and the white balance.

Shooting info plus thumbnail. The second press of the Display button brings up a display which details the main shooting information for that image plus a thumbnail view. It additionally adds the following information in the lower third of the screen; the image stabilisation mode used, details about Intelligent Dynamic and Intelligent Resolution used, the time and date the image was captured, the actual image number and the colour space that was used to record the image.

Image Histogram. This screen displays the image pixel data in a graphical form. It shows you the Red, Green, Blue and Illuminance values (brightness) with the X axis denoting the shadow to highlight range which have digital value of 0 (zero) to 255. The Y axis denotes the count of the number of pixels at each of the values from 0 – 255. The higher the peak the more the number of pixels in this band.
As discussed later this information can be used to allow you to capture images which are more accurately exposed.

Image Only. The final display is the image only with no overlays at all so that the image can be fully inspected. In this mode, you can use the shutter button zoom lever to increase the zoom level.
Operating the lever to the right (T) will increase from x1 to x2, x4, x8 and finally x16. Turning it towards the (W) will decrease the magnification if you are already using an enlarged display or, if you are at x1 will bring up a thumbnail view of the images on the memory card.
Another press towards (W) will show more thumbnails but smaller and then finally bring up a calendar view where you can select images that were taken on a specific date.
The Display button shows similar views when you have selected a video clip plus an up-arrow icon to indicate how to play back the recorded clip.

   Menu/Set and Navigation Buttons:
One of the most important groupings of buttons that are arranged in a compass style around a central button. Each of the buttons has on it a silk screen printed icon on it which denotes its default operation. The central button is marked Menu/Set and can be likened to the OK button on other devices such as remote TV controllers etc. It generally sets the option and closes the menu.
In this guide, I will usually refer to the direction, or navigation, buttons as Up, Down, Left or Right as these are the directions that the menu option move as you press these buttons.

THE UP BUTTON: ISO – This button, in the default mode, allows you to access the menu to be able to set the cameras sensitivity to light – the ISO control. Again, in the default state the camera sensitivity is from ISO 125 to ISO 12800. It is always best to select the lowest ISO value as this is where the camera will produce the best image quality but requires more light.
Using higher ISO values, it allows you to capture images in lower light levels but with more image noise in this situation.
The ISO setting is only available when it is set to one of the semi-automatic modes including the PASM, Panorama and Creative Video. In the default camera mode (or after a camera reset function) the default values are 125,200,400,800,1600,3200 and 12800.

If you change the ISO increments in the Rec Menu page 5/7 you can set the increment to be 1/3 EV (f-stop).

In all modes except the iA/iA+ modes there is the option to select Auto ISO or iISO (intelligent ISO). These two features automatically set the ISO depending upon the exposure conditions up to the ISI Limit.

The ISO limit is useful if you don't want to exceed the value at which you are no longer happy with the quality of the images produced.

For example, I set an upper limit of 800 as I feel that this is the threshold at which I accept the noise increase on these higher ISO images.

If you are post processing RAW files you may extend this a little.

If you select iISO then the camera not only uses the exposure conditions but also tries to evaluate any subject motion so that it can set a high enough shutter speed to prevent blur in the subject. It is for this reason that iISO cannot be used with shutter priority mode only the P and A modes will allow you to select iISO.

In addition to ISO Limit set there is the option to use extended ISO.

This adds extra values which you can select (LO or ISO 80) and (Hi or 25600).

These values are extrapolated values.

The particularly LO setting of ISO may appear useful in getting even less image noise but this value is a computed value and is reported to reduce the overall dynamic range (or the ability to record a full range of image tones) and highlight detail loss has also been reported. I would advise not to use this value for these reasons.

In the playback mode, this UP button is used to start video playback and act as the play/pause button during video playback.

THE RIGHT BUTTON: WHITE BALANCE. The Right button invokes the menu to select a White Balance operating point.

White balance is needed when recording JPEG images for the camera to record accurately the colours of the objects in the scene that you are about to capture.

Now colour temperature is expressed in degrees Kelvin (K) and an illuminating light source with a low colour temperature such as 2700K produces a redder or "warmer" image tone. Conversely images captured using a much higher temperature like 8000K appear to be bluer or "colder".

Daylight and electronic flash have a colour temperature of around 5600K.

If you capture an image using the wrong camera white balance, then the faithfulness of the colours in the image will be compromised.

Most, if not all, digital cameras have an Auto White Balance mode which does appear to operate quite well in all but extreme lighting scenarios.

The white balance setting is available in all modes except the two intelligent auto modes and in the creative control mode.

Besides the option to use the Auto white balance mode the camera has several preset white balance settings.

These are Daylight (sun icon); Cloudy; Shade, Incandescent, Flash, White set 1 - White set 4 and the final option of manual Kelvin temperature set.

If you want far more accurate rendering of the subject colours in your image it is recommended to "calibrate" the camera by using a piece of white or neutral grey card in one of the 4 manual presets.

This procedure and the option to fine tune any of these white balance operating points is detailed later in this guide book.

THE LEFT BUTTON: AF FOCUS POSITION. **The Left button** is silk screen printer with a focus frame rectangle with 4 direction arrows.
In the default mode, this button accesses the AF mode choices of:
Face/eye detection, AF tracking, 49 Area, Custom Multi, Single area and Pinpoint.
To make the choice you can either use the Left/Right navigation button or the back-control wheel. In all modes, except the AF Tracking mode, using the Down navigation key brings up the control for setting both the size and position of the focus area target.
In the Pinpoint AF mode, the size of the area that you select will dictate the magnification of the target when you half depress the shutter button.
The target is defined by a yellow cross-hair.

THE DOWN BUTTON: AF MACRO & MACRO ZOOM SELECTION.
The Down button, with the AF and flower silk screen printed on it, activates the Macro mode choices menu.
This allows you to select the option for shooting objects which are close-up to the camera lens. The menu choices are AF Macro, Macro Zoom (JPEG images only) and OFF.
   AF Macro.
 The camera can focus as close as 1.2 inch or 3cms (just inside the lens hood) when the camera is set to its widest-angle setting.
At the longest focal length setting the nearest focus distance becomes 3.3 feet or 1 metre.
   Macro Zoom.
With this choice of AF macro mode, the camera can same close-up distances as the AF Macro mode with the additional option of using Digital Zoom at a magnification factor of up to three times.
As you move the zoom lever in this mode the image becomes enlarged however the lens will not change position. The image is being magnified by image quality reducing, digital zoom only.
You may see this option unavailable if you have selected any Quality mode which has the RAW file format selected as the zoom is based solely on the JPEG image processed.
Also, preventing Macro Zoom are Multiple exposure, Panorama mode and some of the Art Filters choices such as Toy effect, Toy pop, Impressive art or Miniature modes.
As well as the primary function of selecting the AF Mode it also is used in secondary menu operations like selecting the AF area in the AF Focus modes, selecting the option for fine tuning the white balance operating point in the white balance menu and for selecting options in the Q.menu mode.

FN5 LVF: LIVE VIEW BUTTON.
This button allows you to cycle through the three possible choices for this button, in its default programmed operating mode.
In the camera default mode, If the LCD monitor is illuminated at the time the LVF (live view finder) button is pressed the LCD turns off and the EVF (EVF and LVF are the same i.e. electronic viewfinder) is turned on.
Pressing the LVF button again will return the display back to the LCD screen but this now locks out the inbuilt auto eye sensor.

This can be a useful feature if you are adjusting some control and your hand triggers the EVF detection and blanks out the LCD.

Pressing the button once again returns the camera to default with the auto eye detection sensor turned on again.

A Live View display takes its image from the real-time readout coming from the image sensor. This has a huge advantage in that not only does it display 100% of the image you are about to capture, but any effects that you have applied through settings, or any shooting aids the camera offers, can also be seen – overlaid on the image and all before you take the shot itself.

These things can, of course, be displayed on the larger built-in display LCD screen, but the EVF has the advantage that it is not affected by bright sunlight and is therefore easier to see in all conditions. Another advantage is that because the camera is held closer to your face when you are using the EVF, this traditional shooting style can be more comfortable and help you to keep the camera steadier as you are effectively adding a third point of mechanical stabilisation to the camera grip.

The EVF also has an inbuilt auto eye sensor that detects when the viewfinder is held near your eye and switches the Live View image accordingly.

Also, situated on the left-hand side of the EVF is the dioptre adjustment dial and this is useful if you wear glasses as you may be able to adjust the setting so that you can use it without wearing glasses. Set the best focus by setting it when the EVF is displaying a menu choice and not the camera scene view.

Taking images using the Fully Auto iA/iA+ Modes

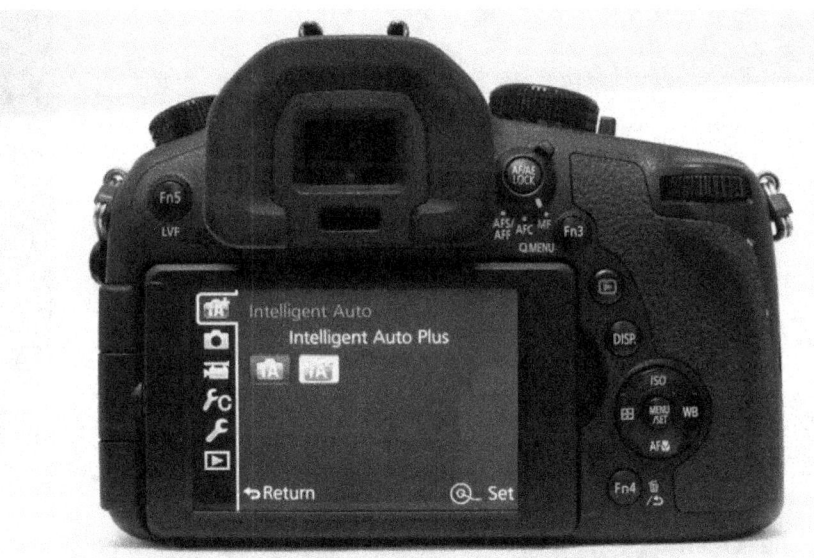

This, fully automatic, mode is recommended for those users new to the camera or simply want to use the camera in a "point and shoot" mode.

The camera uses "scene" type recognition and automatic exposure determination to expose the images. By default, the camera is factory set to the more advanced iA+ mode. The basic iA is available via the REC set up menu however I recommend that you keep the iA+ menu options.

This enhanced mode allows you the user to adjust the exposure (effectively exposure compensation) and the hue or tint of the image to apply either a warming or cooling tint to the image.

Begin by rotating the top mode control dial to the iA position, aligning the iA symbol against the white index on the flash head.

When you point the camera at the subject the image processor will attempt to determine what type of scene that the lens is imaging on the sensor. It looks for colour and light intensity patterns and facial features to set the optimal exposure conditions.

You can see the scene type that has been selected by looking at the top left hand side of the LCD (or EVF if enabled). Initially the icon will be displayed with a blue colour for about two seconds and then will turn red.

It is advised to check that the scene being captured is correctly interpreted by the camera. Sometimes the scene recognition software incorrectly determines the scene being imaged.

If this is the case switch to the SCN scene mode and select the most applicable scene type for the scene being photographed.

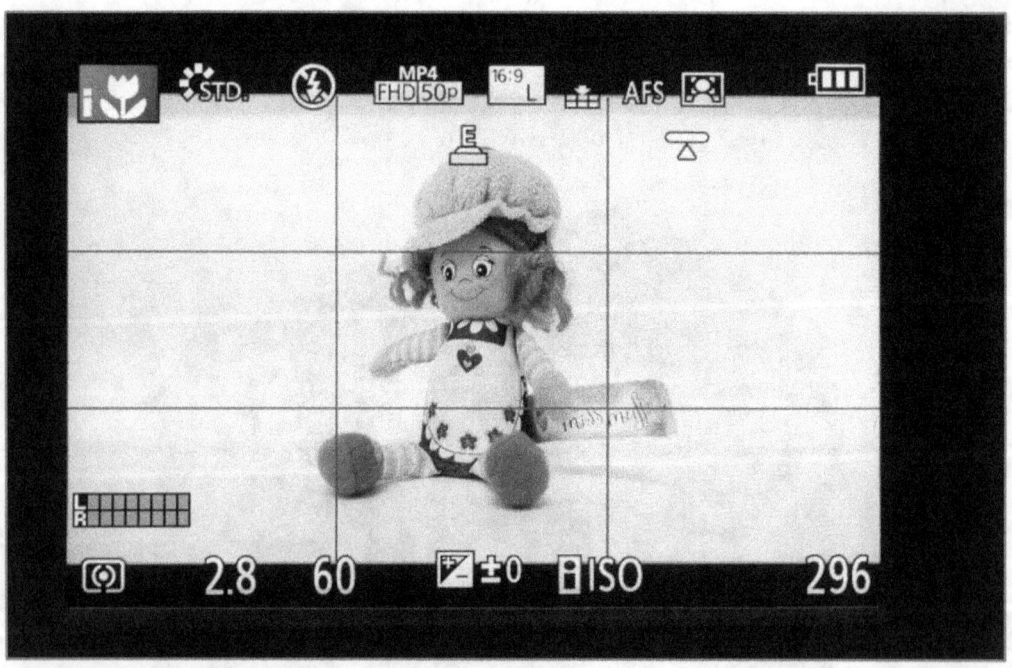

This is how the screen will look when the camera is set up in the iA+ mode.

The upper left icon displays the selected scene type that the camera has determined is the most appropriate for this capture. In this case, it has recognised the scene as a close-up one.

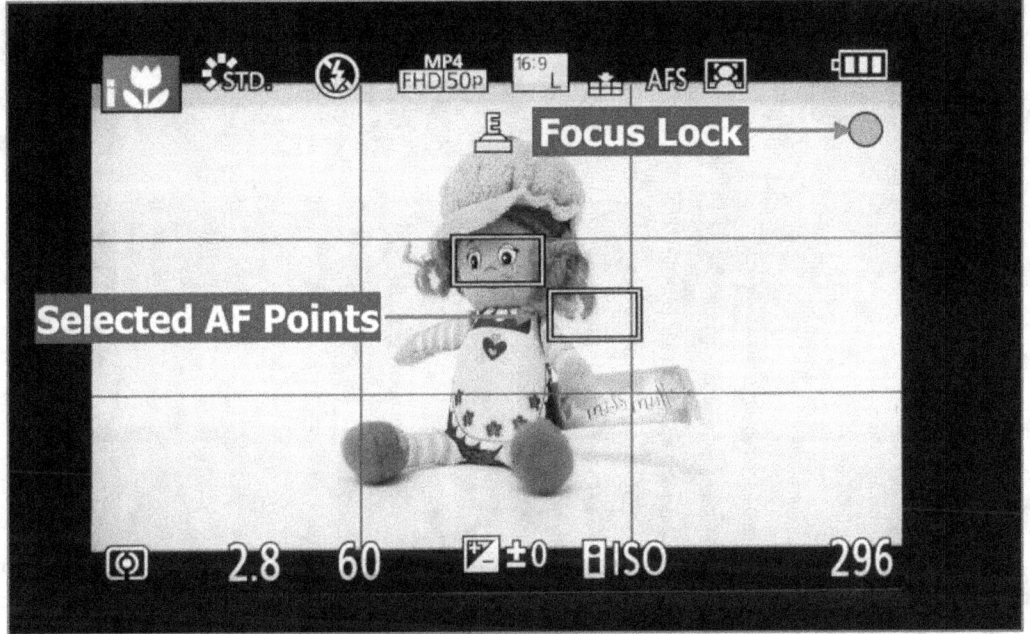

Half depressing the shutter button shows the area selected for focus and the focus lock green indicator (and audible beep) confirm that focus has been achieved.

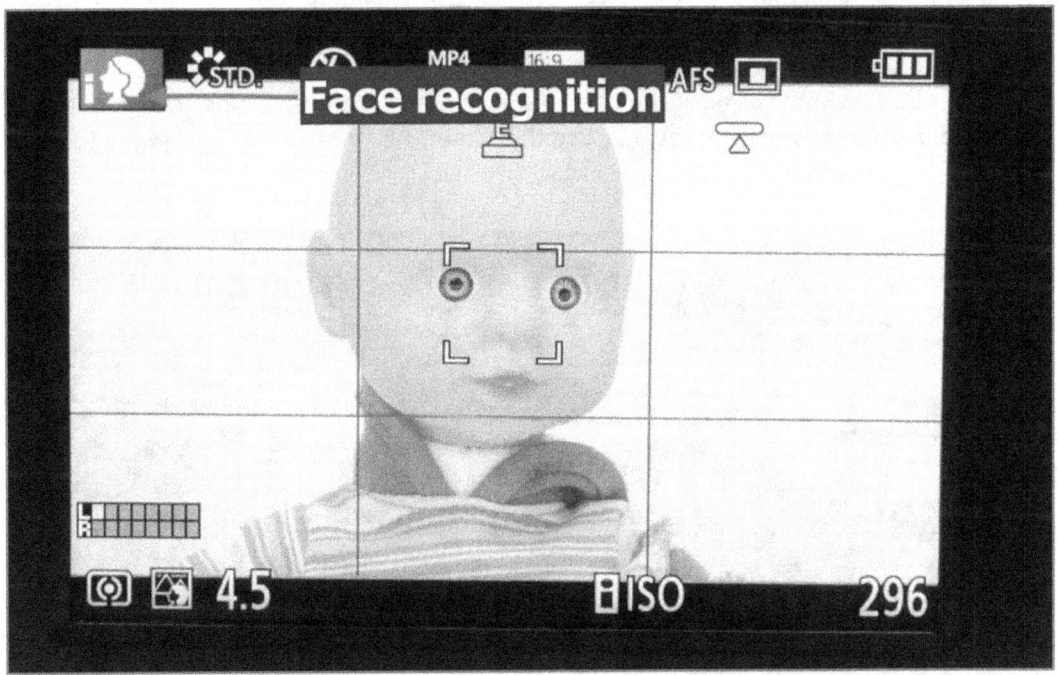

If the camera recognises a face, then the icon displayed will be the "portrait" icon.

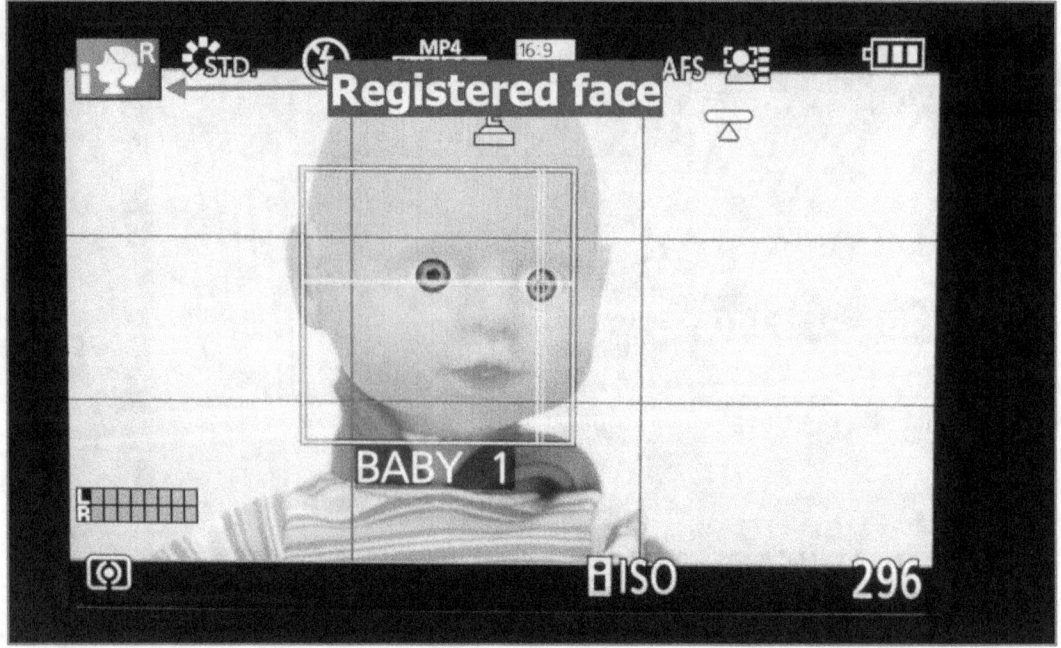

If the face detected has been previously added to the face recognition gallery then the name of the person will be displayed, the "portrait icon" will also show the addition of the "R" symbol signifying that this is a "registered" face. The camera will then switch to eye detection mode to set the point of focus on the most critical area for portraits – the eyes. Face recognition is detailed later in this guide book.

The iA mode is the most basic of the two fully automatic shooting modes however, it allows very little adjustment to be made to the camera settings. These are limited to the following two screens.

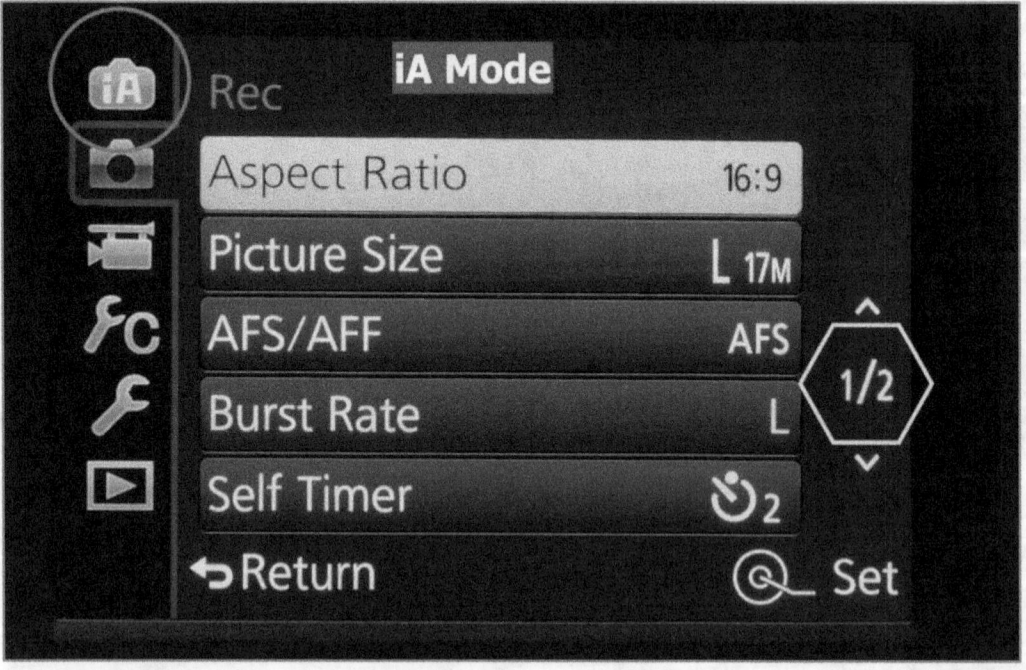

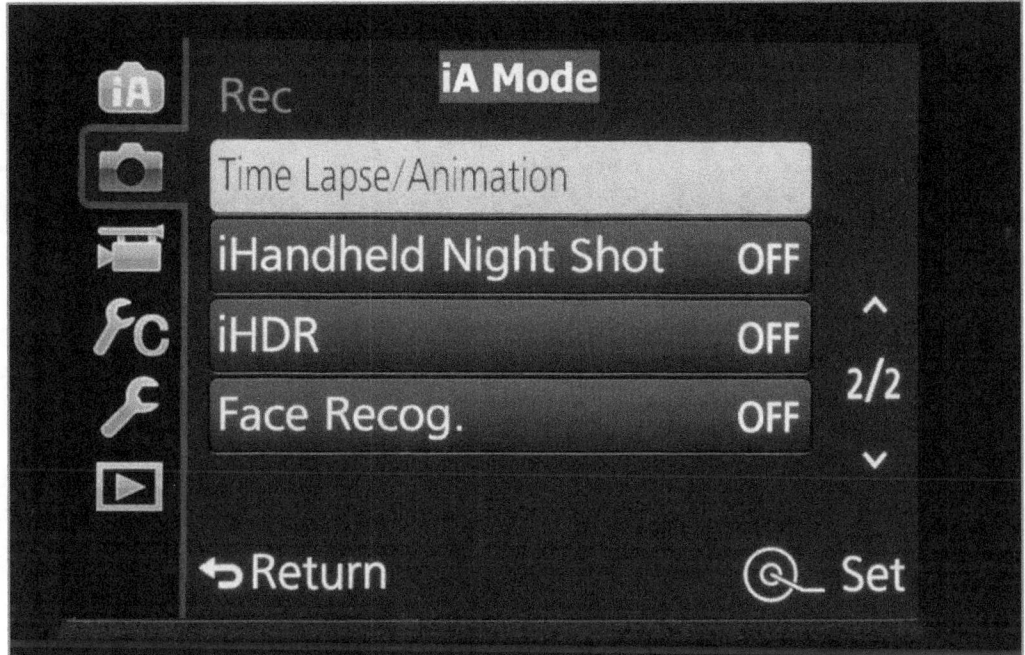

The basic adjustments available in the iA mode of the FZ1000

The iA+ mode is a far more advanced feature of this camera and allows the user to make more adjustments to the shooting parameters.

It is the mode that I recommend that you select if you want to use this camera in a point and shoot mode only until you gain more familiarity with its operation.

iA+ mode is selected from the iA set up menu when the mode control dial is rotated so that the iA icon is aligned with the index mark on the camera top plate.

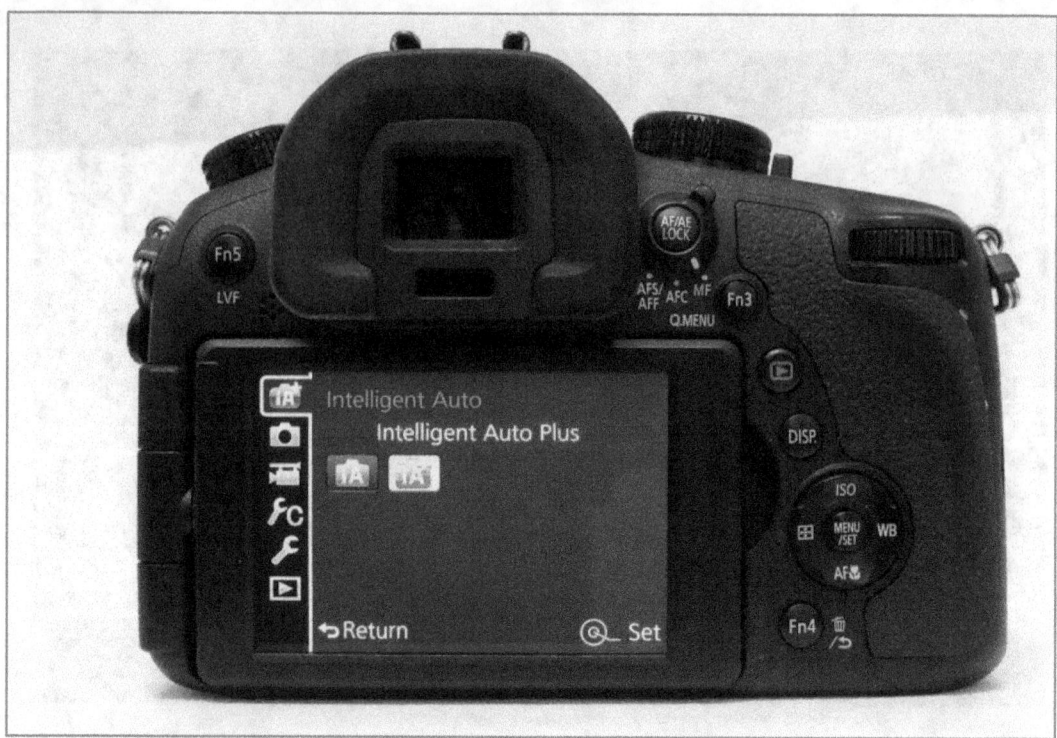

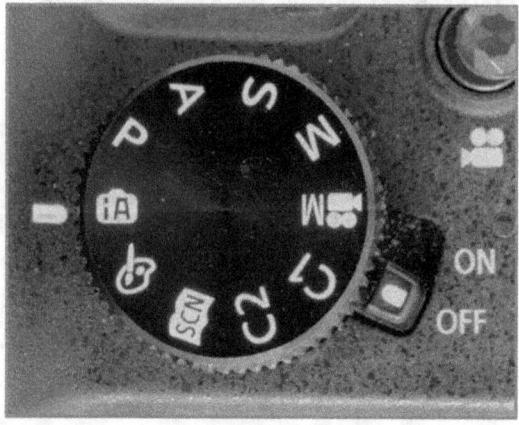

Selection of the iA mode is made by rotating the Mode Dial to the iA icon aligning it with the white index mark on the top plate of the camera.

The dial may be rotated in either direction and has sufficient resistance to prevent it from inadvertently being changed to a different setting.

The iA+ mode opens the options on seven set up menus and allows the user to select quite a few advanced features that are normally not available in a "bridge camera". The opportunity to shoot in the camera RAW mode is one such facility.

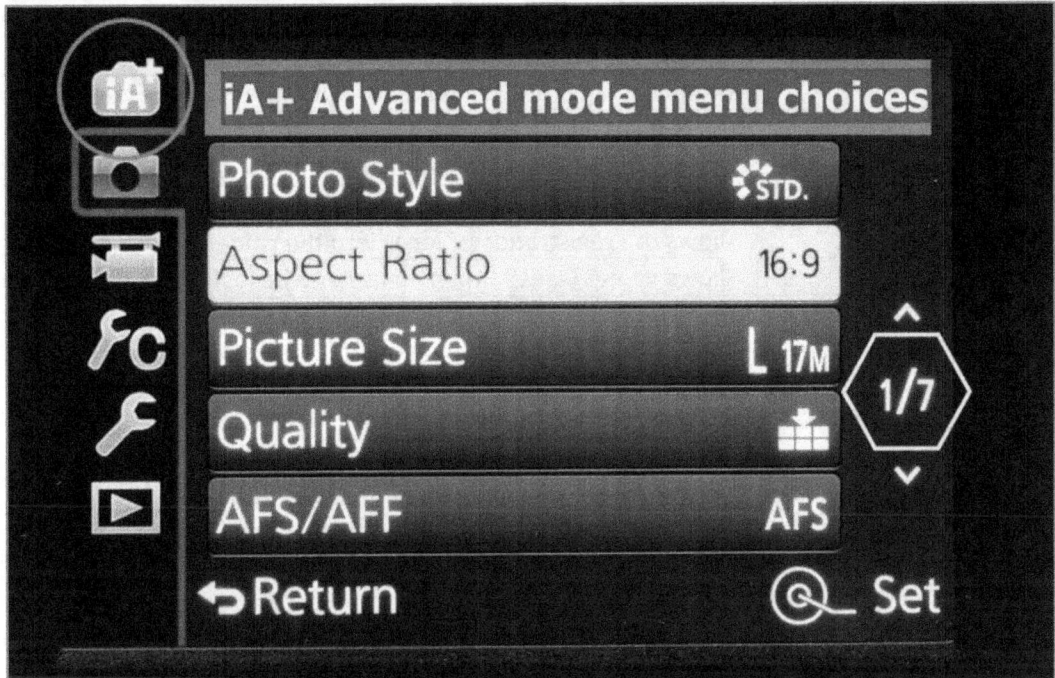

This is a summary of the menu choices in the two modes.

iA MODE

Menu item	Feature adjusted with the camera
Aspect Ratio	Width to Height proportions – select to match output
Picture Size	Sets the number of recorded pixels in the image
AFS/AFF	Sets the AF mode on the Focus Mode Lever
Burst rate	Sets the rate at which images are captured
Self Timer	Allows 2 or 10 second delay or 3 shots at 10 second interval
Time Lapse Animation	Allows a series of images to be captured and make a video
iHandheld Night Shot	Shoots multiple images and combines into 1 improved image
iHDR	Multiple images and combine for optimum brightness range
Face Recognition	Allows the registration of faces into the camera memory.

iA+ MODE

Menu item	Feature adjusted with the camera
Photo Style	Choice of Colour or Black & White
Aspect Ratio	Width to Height proportions – select to match output
Picture Size	Sets the number of recorded pixels in the image
Quality	Allows selection of RAW, JPEG or both formats
AFS/AFF	Sets the AF mode on the Focus Mode Lever
Burst rate	Sets the rate at which images are captured
Auto Bracket	Allows a series of exposures at set exposure increment
Self Timer	Allows 2 or 10 second delay or 3 shots at 10 second interval

Time Lapse Animation	Allows a series of images to be captured and make a video
iHandheld Night Shot	Shoots multiple images and combines into 1 improved image
iHDR	Multiple images and combine for optimum brightness range
Shutter Type	Selection of Electronic or Mechanical Shutter
Colour Space	Set format for PC or professional printing
Stabiliser	Options for image stabiliser mode
Face Recognition	Allows the registration of faces into the camera memory.
Profile Setup	Allows names/ages for baby or pets to be included

The **Photo style** option allows the user to select either colour (Standard) or monochrome However, it does not allow the individual adjustment of the operating parameters such as sharpness, saturation contrast and noise reduction.

The **Quality** option allows selection of JPEG images with either fine (double blocks ===) or coarse compression (single blocks ---) or RAW image format. Additionally, you can select to record the RAW format plus one of the JPEG formats simultaneously.
The RAW format needs special software, or the in-camera processing option to "develop" the image. The camera produces the JPEG using the RAW file and your set options for the JPEG files such as Photostyle, aspect ratio, image size, white balance etc.

The **Auto bracket** option allows the user to set up the number of exposures in a series of exposures and the exposure increment between each of them. Up to 7 images can be captured with either 1/3, 2/3 or full EV increments (F-stops) between each exposure. Auto bracketing is covered fully, later in this guide.

The **Shutter type** allows selection of the mechanical shutter which allows the camera to use shutter speeds from $1/8^{th}$ second to 1/4000th sec. If the silent electronic shutter is selected the camera select a shutter speed from $1/8^{th}$ to $1/4000^{th}$ second. In the AUTO mode, the camera will select the most appropriate type per the ambient light level.

The **Colour Space** option allows the selection of the standard sRGB, which is the colour space used by most electronic displays, or the ADOBE RGB colour space which has a wider colour range and usually used for producing files for printing.

The **Stabiliser** option allows the user to select the normal full stabilising of all camera motion or the mode which allows the camera to ignore any horizontal movement so that the camera can be used for "panning" operations. Image stabiliser is turned ON or OFF by the slide switch on the lens barrel.

The **Profile Setup** allows the user to enter the name and age of 1 pet and 2 babies in order that they are displayed when face recognition is enabled. These will appear on prints made from programs which read the camera EXIF (extended information file) such as the PhotofunStudio software supplied with the camera.

The detected **Scene Type** is determined by the processor in the camera and can set the camera in one of the following modes when the camera is set for still image capture:

i-Portrait, i-Scenery, i-Macro, i-Night Portrait, i-Night Scenery, i-Hand Held Night shot (*if set to ON in the REC set up menu*), i-Food, i-Baby, i-Sunset and the defaults to the iA mode when neither of these scene types are determined. If shooting 4K still the scene detection works in the same way as recording video clips.

When recording video, the camera will automatically select one of the following scene types:
i-Portrait, i-Scenery, i-Low Light, i-Macro and the default iA when none of the scene types are recognised.

Auto Focus, Face/Eye Detection and Face Recognition

When shooting in the fully automatic mode (iA or iA+) the camera will select the most appropriate focus method.
In this mode, face detection is active (as shown in the image below) and eye detection software attempts to locate and focus on the eye closest to the camera.

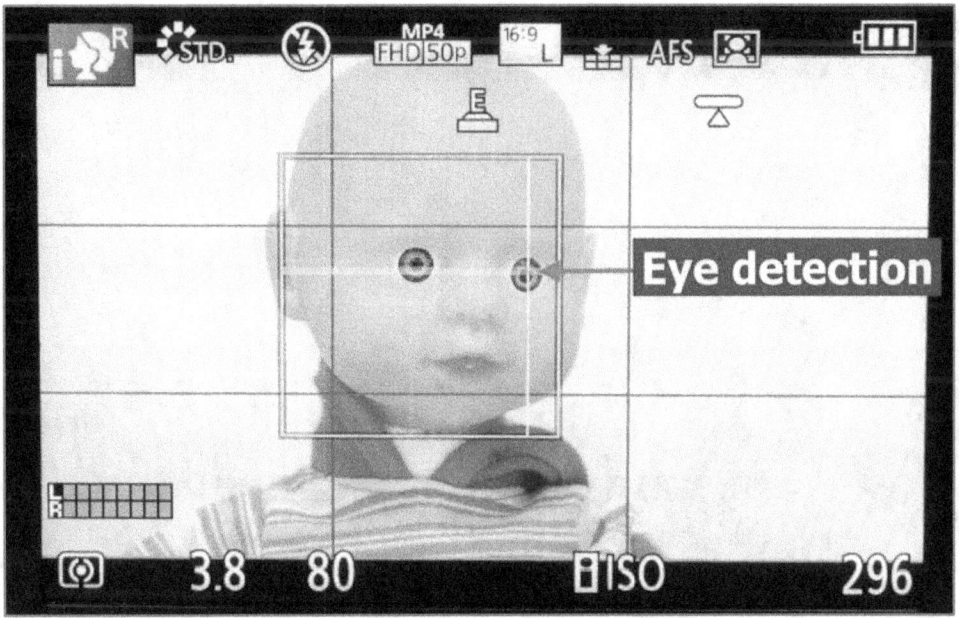

Face detection and eye detection in operation on the FZ1000.

This eye detection mode is automatic and focusses on the nearest eye to the camera. This method cannot be changed.
When in this mode the camera adjusts the exposure to give the best image based upon the metering from the face.
If face recognition has been turned on and faces have been registered if the camera detects a subject which has been previously registered, then an "R" is displayed on the upper right corner of the display.

The icon could be the i-Portrait, i-Night Portrait or the i-Baby icon depending upon the subject recognised.

Face recognition is further detailed later in this guide book.

If you experience some of your images not being recorded as you saw them at the time of shooting or images of a similar subject appear to be recorded differently to each other then it is worth having a look at how the iA/iA+ method recorded them.

Panasonic do state that, in some scene types, you should watch the indicated icon when you shoot in this mode and if the wrong scene type is detected then you should select the most appropriate mode from the SCN mode dial setting and menu choice.

To see how the image was detected by the camera, with the memory card still inserted in the camera, select the green playback button on the back of the camera body.

Using the left or right navigation buttons of the 4-way controller scroll through to the image in question.

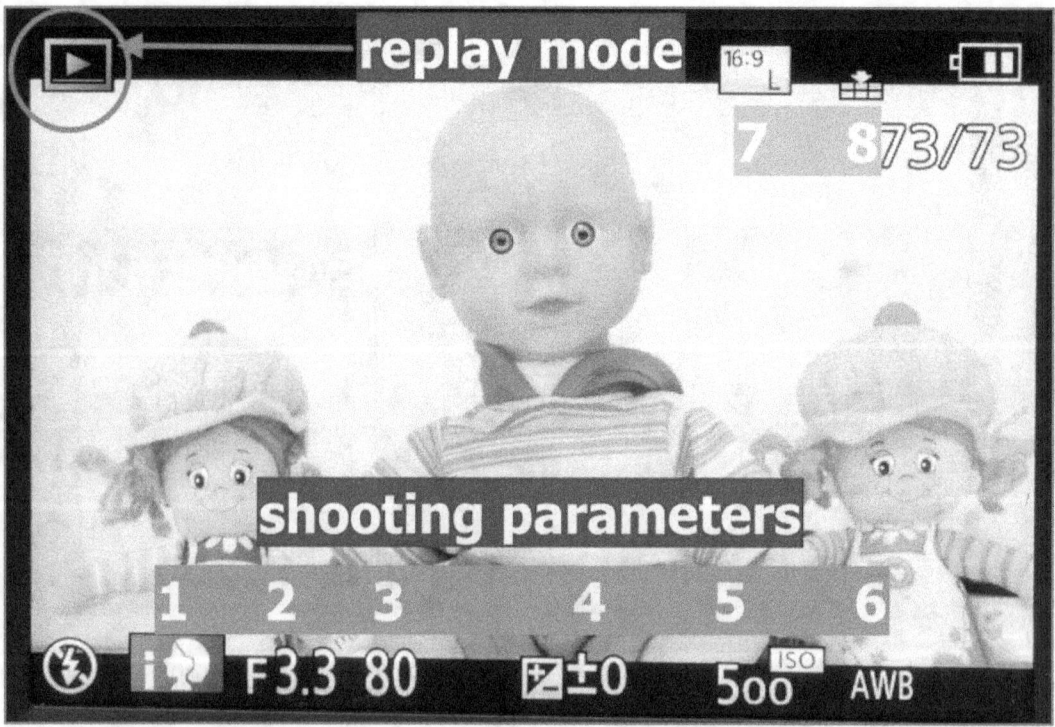

An image selected in the replay mode showing some of the available image information that was used to capture it.

The parameters on the image are:

Number on illustration	Image parameter
1	Scene type detected (portrait)
2	Aperture used (f3.3)
3	Shutter speed used (1/80th second)
4	Exposure compensation (none)
5	ISO used (500)
6	White balance (AWB) auto white balance
7	Aspect ratio + size (16:9) Large
8	Quality (fine JPEG)

During the replay mode the way in which the image is presented on the screen can be changed by pressing the DISP key.

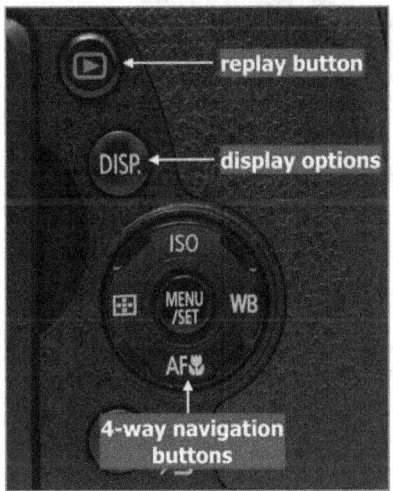

The replay button (green arrow)

The Display Options button

4 Way navigation and Menu/set button

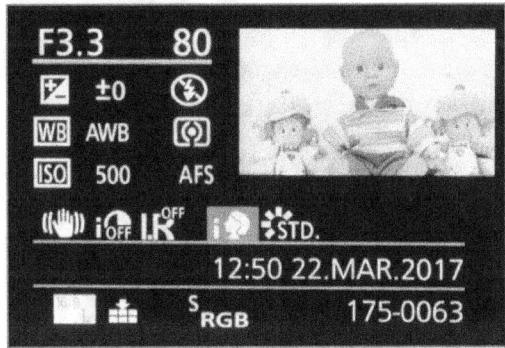
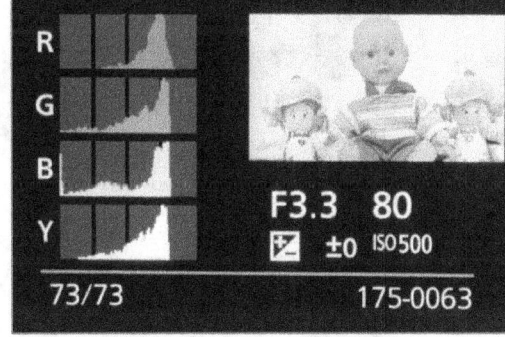

Two of the other displays available on the cyclical display DISP button. The extended shooting information and the Histogram of Red, Green, Blue and Luminance (brightness).

There is also a screen which is uncluttered and just the image with no information overlaid on it. The final screen is a black, blank screen.

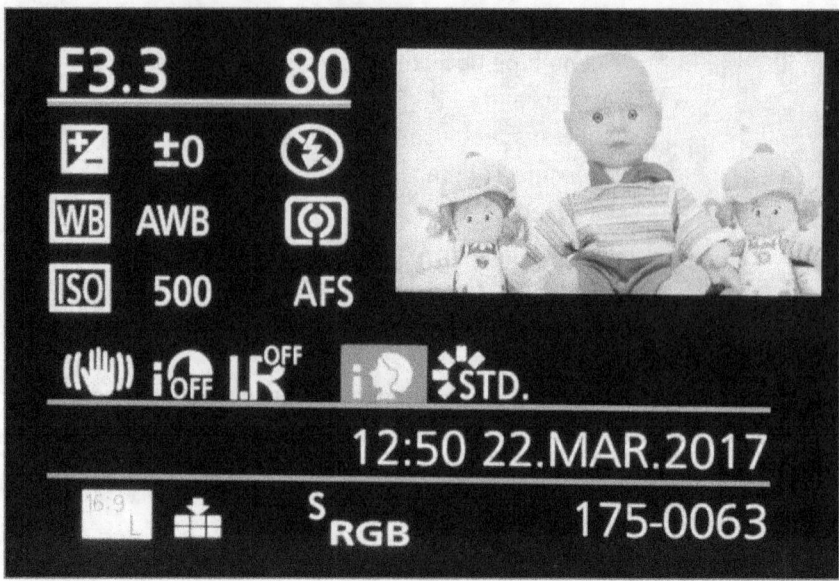

This is the extended shooting information screen showing the basic details about Aperture, Shutter Speed, Exposure Compensation, White Balance mode and ISO. It also shows detail about the Scene Mode, The Photo style used, the Autofocus mode, the status of i.Dynamic and i.Resolution. The Date and Time the image was captured, the Image Number, the Aspect Ratio/Image Size, the Colour Space used and Image Quality.

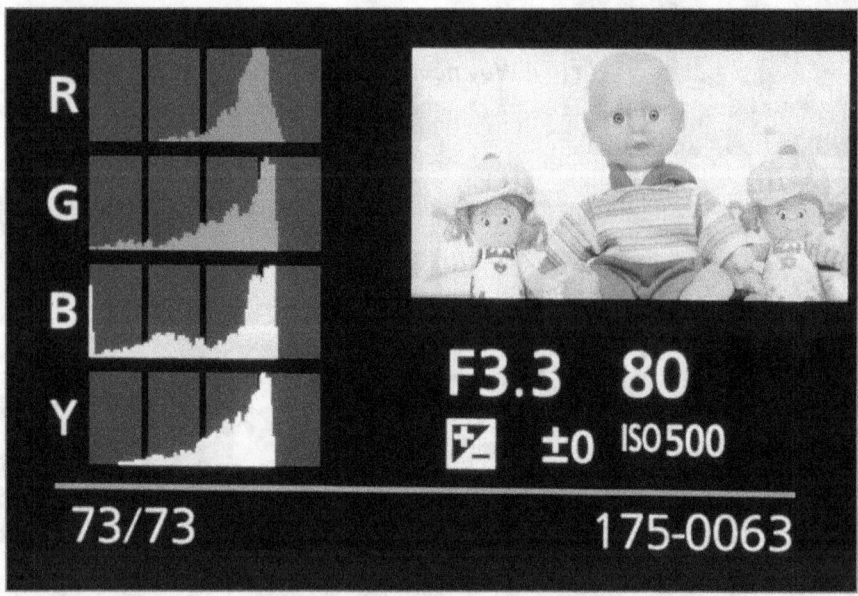

The Histogram shows the basic exposure detail plus the distribution of the brightness of each primary colour and the overall illuminance levels. More details later in this guide. In the next image illustrated, the camera correctly identified the i-Landscape mode whilst setting optimal parameters for this scene such as enhancing greens and blues.

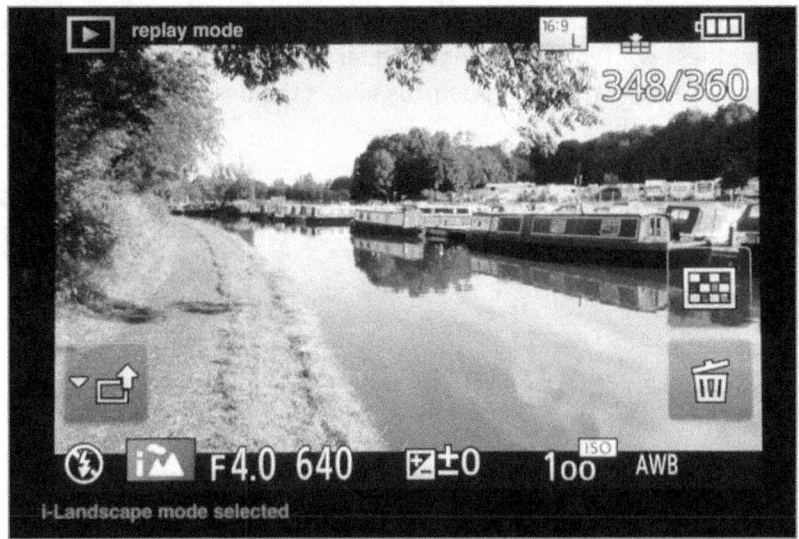

If the camera doesn't recognise a scene type, then it reverts to a default setting and determines the exposure without adjusting other parameters such as saturation of colour or aperture. (actual image from FZ300 but illustrates the scene mode icon).

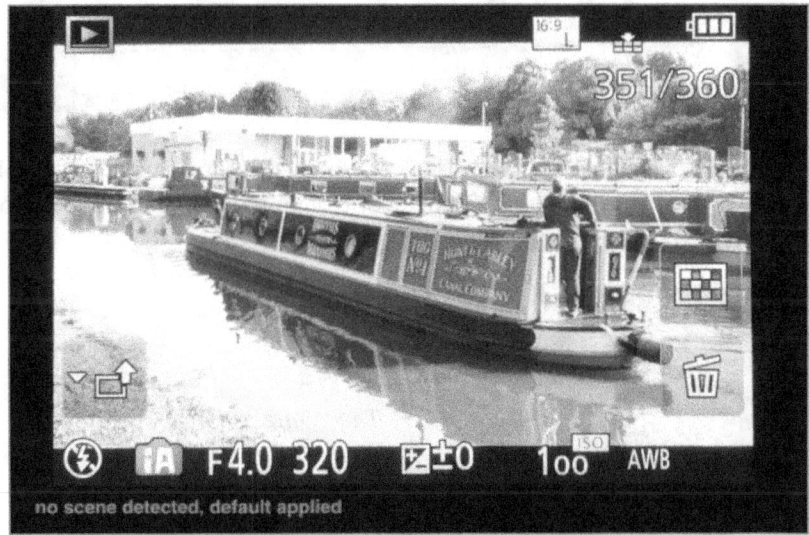

(image from FZ300 but illustrates the scene mode icon)

A lot of thought has gone into the automatic scene detection algorithms and they are becoming very reliable in selecting the correct scene type for the image being recorded. If the subject is being photographed where there is light shining behind the subject, which would cause the subject to be recorded with a dark appearance, the camera applies backlight compensation to lighten the recorded image.

In the superior iA+ mode there are also three other controls which are exposed to the user:

Colour tint: which allows the tone of the image to be changed from neutral to either a warming or cooling tone.

Exposure compensation: which allows the image to be adjusted when subject to background brightness is affecting the correct operation of the camera metering circuit. **Aperture control:** cited as background defocus allows the user to select the most appropriate aperture for the scene.

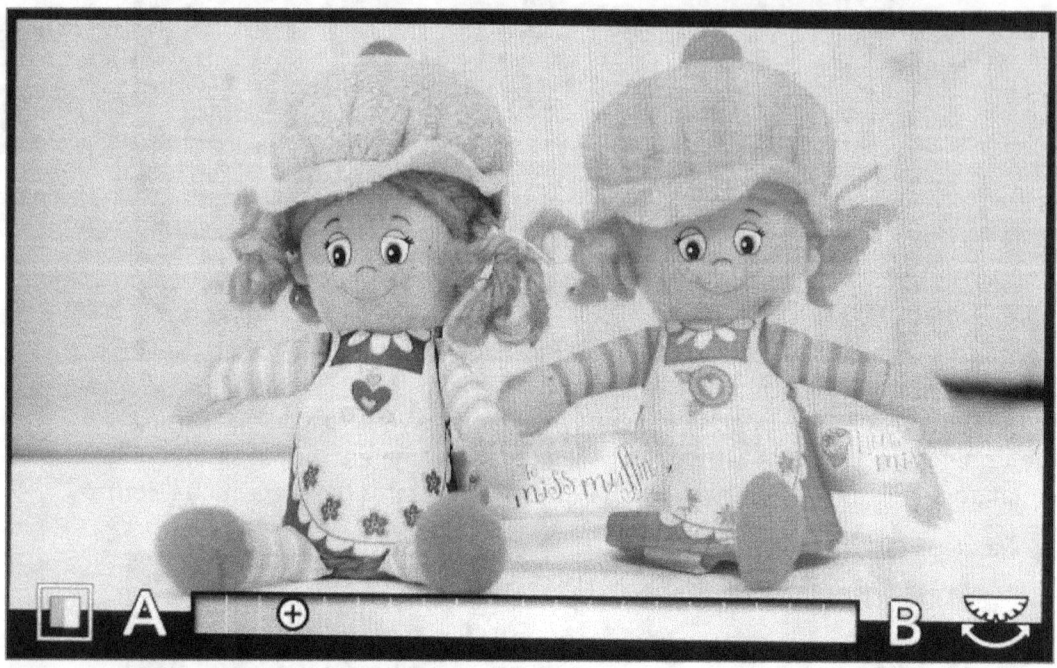

The colour tint control is accessed in the iA+ mode by depressing the WB (white balance) button on the 4-way navigation pad. The back-control wheel can then be used to adjust the tint from neutral to a slightly warming tone to a cooling tint.

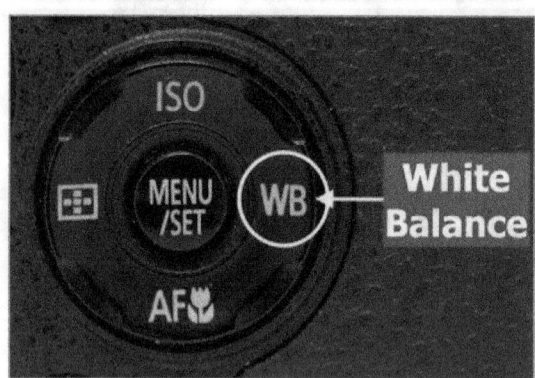

The White Balance button on the 4-way navigation control is used to access the colour tint adjustment in the iA+ mode.

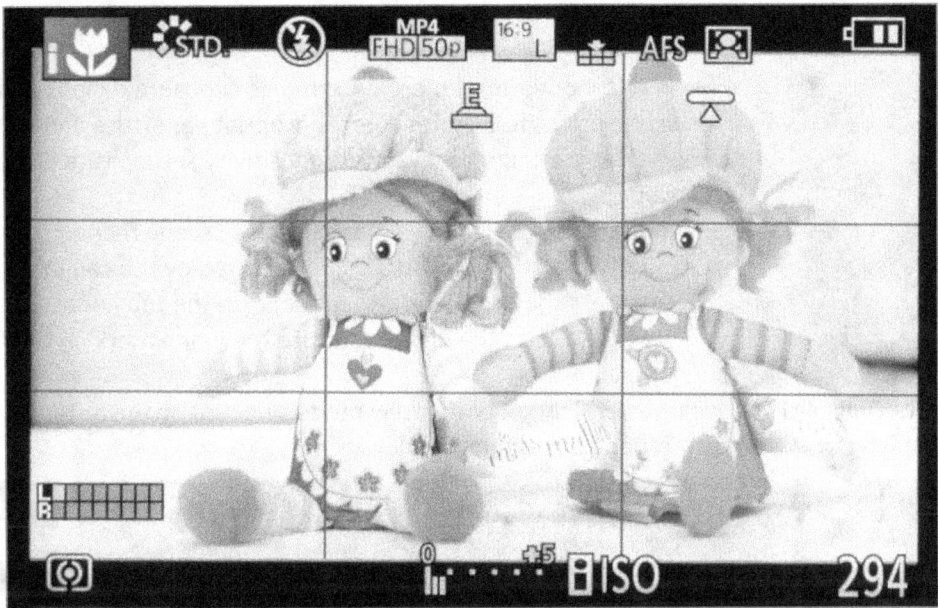

Exposure compensation is invoked by depressing in the back-control wheel in towards the camera body. Once clicked in the indicator at the lower centre of the LCD display will turn yellow indicating that adjustment is now possible by rotating the same back-control wheel. Up to +/- 5 EV (F-stops) of adjustment is possible.

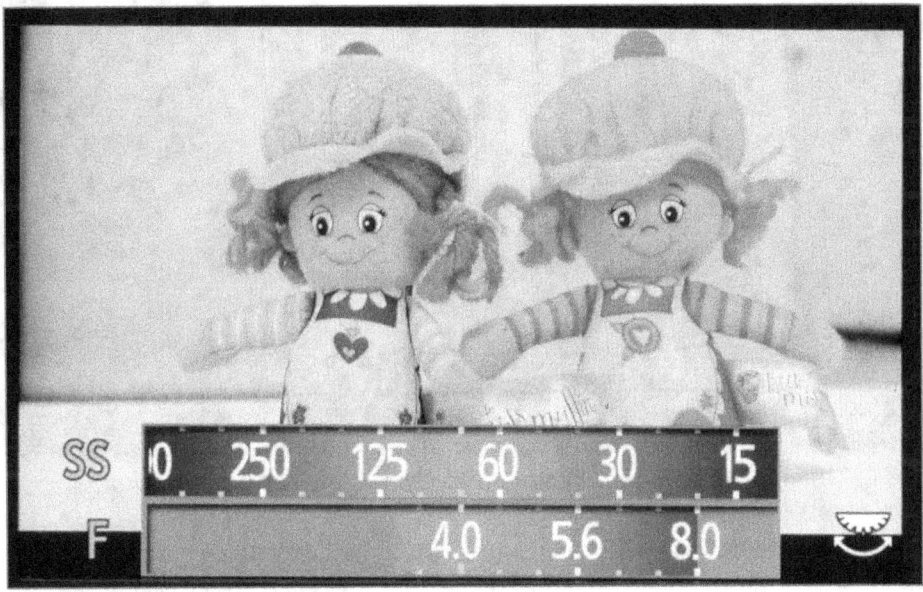

The same back-control wheel allows access to changing the Aperture value. The process of depressing in towards the camera body is a two-state operation between Exposure Compensation and Aperture control.

The aperture can be set and the camera adjusts the ISO and then shutter speed to achieve the correct exposure.

Taking Images using the Program Auto Mode: "P" mode

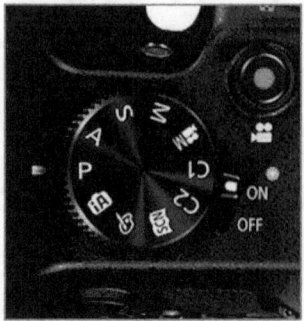

In this mode, the camera determines exposure by looking at scene brightness and sets an appropriate aperture and shutter speed based upon the camera sensitivity setting (the ISO value).

Unlike the iA/iA+ modes it does not use scene recognition to modify the basic exposure as determined by the camera.

To access the Program Auto mode, turn the top control dial until the "P" on the dial is opposite the white mark on the flash housing.

On the LCD display you will see verification of the new mode selected by the letter "P" being indicated at the top left hand side of the display.

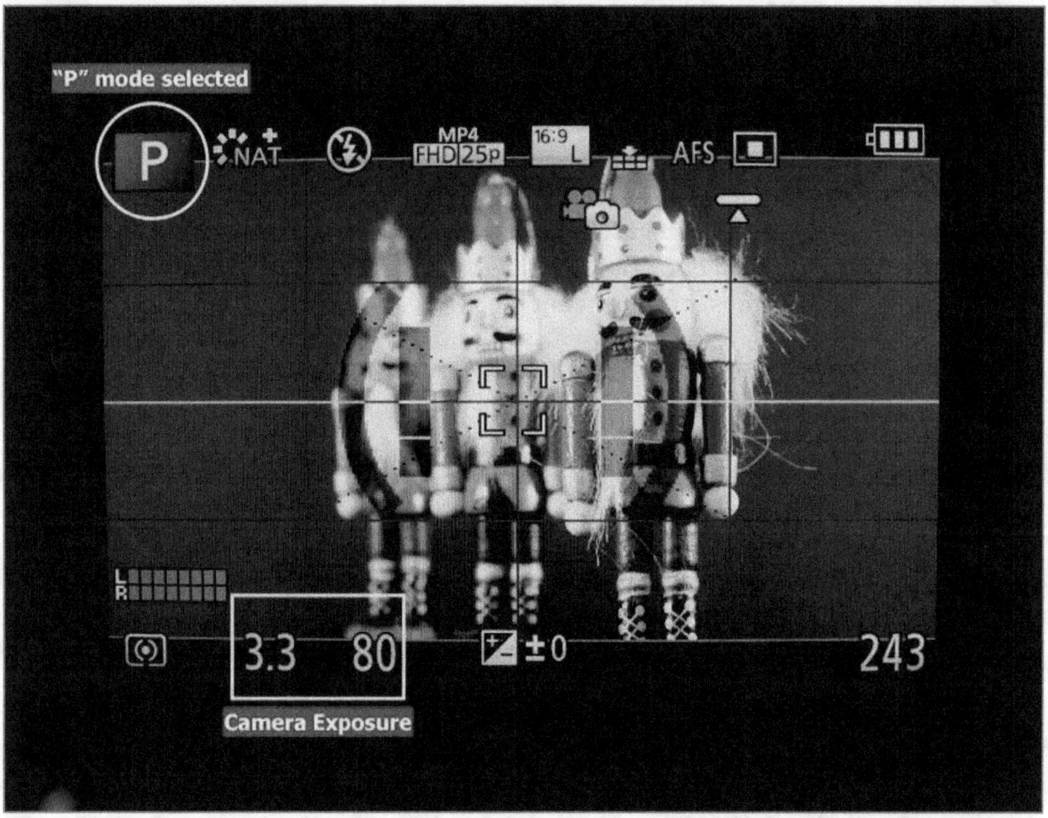

Half depressing the Shutter Button shows the camera exposure

To capture an image, first depress the shutter button half way down and this will display the exposure that the camera has set per scene brightness and the ISO value set.

If you judge the exposure conditions to be suitable then recompose and take the shot again, this time fully depress the shutter button once you have set focus at the half way point of the shutter button travel.

If you determine that the exposure would not give you the image that you want, then the facility of "Program Shift" allow you to change the combination of the selected aperture and shutter speed combination.

A reason to change this would be to the depth of field (DOF) you wanted in your image or to control the amount of subject motion.

To engage Program Shift, half depress the shutter button to bring up the aperture/shutter speed indication and then whilst these are on screen turn the back-control wheel to the left. This will display the new aperture/shutter speed values with a double headed arrow. This could be intentionally creating blur by selecting a slower shutter speed or arresting (freezing) any subject motion by choosing a faster shutter speed.

For example, if the camera determined that the correct exposure would be 1/125 sec at f2.8 with the ISO set to a value of 200 then if you wanted to include more of the image to be in focus by having a larger depth of field (created using a smaller aperture value) then you could use Program Shift to change the Aperture value/Shutter speed combination so that the aperture value (i.e. the bigger number) is aligned to the centre of the display. This is illustrated below.

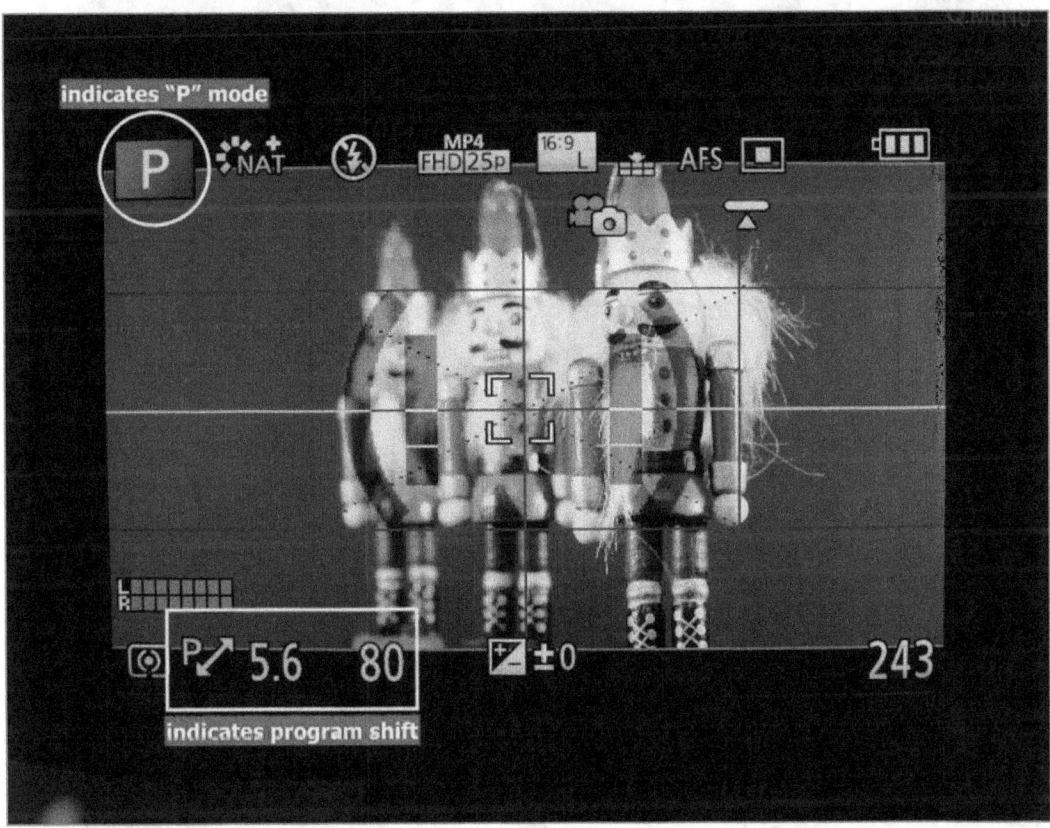

In this example. I selected F5.6. The shutter speed stays the same because auto ISO is set.

If you have a fixed ISO set, then the shutter speed will change as illustrated in the next images. Essentially the control works like it was in Aperture priority mode adjusting shutter speed as the aperture changes.

With the iISO setting selected then you will not be able to enter the Program Shift mode.

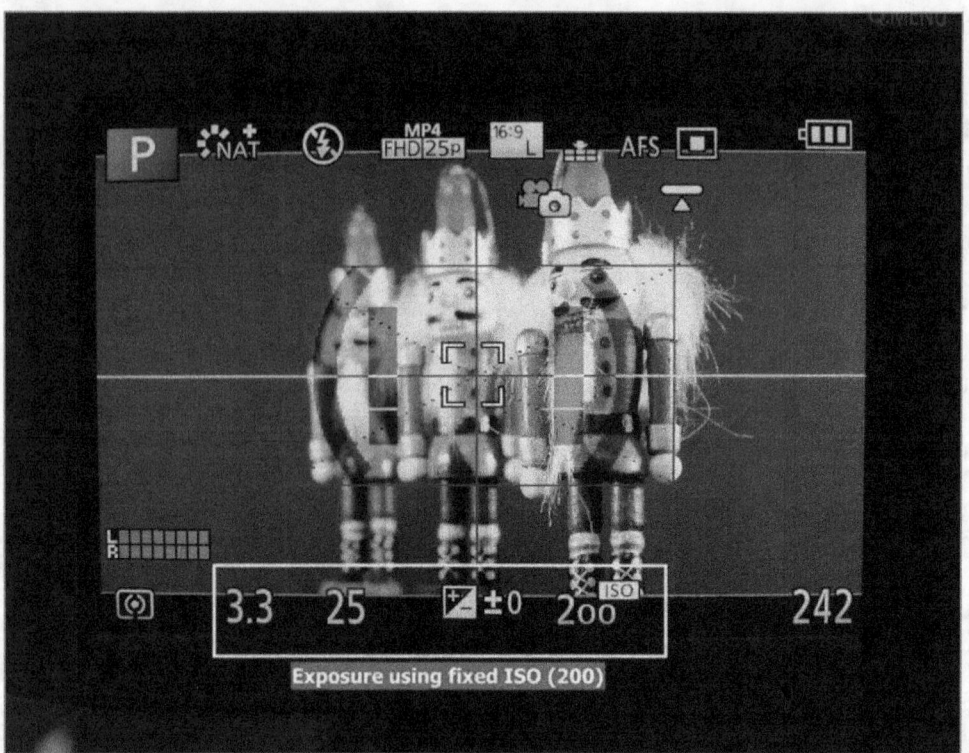

Exposure using fixed ISO (200)

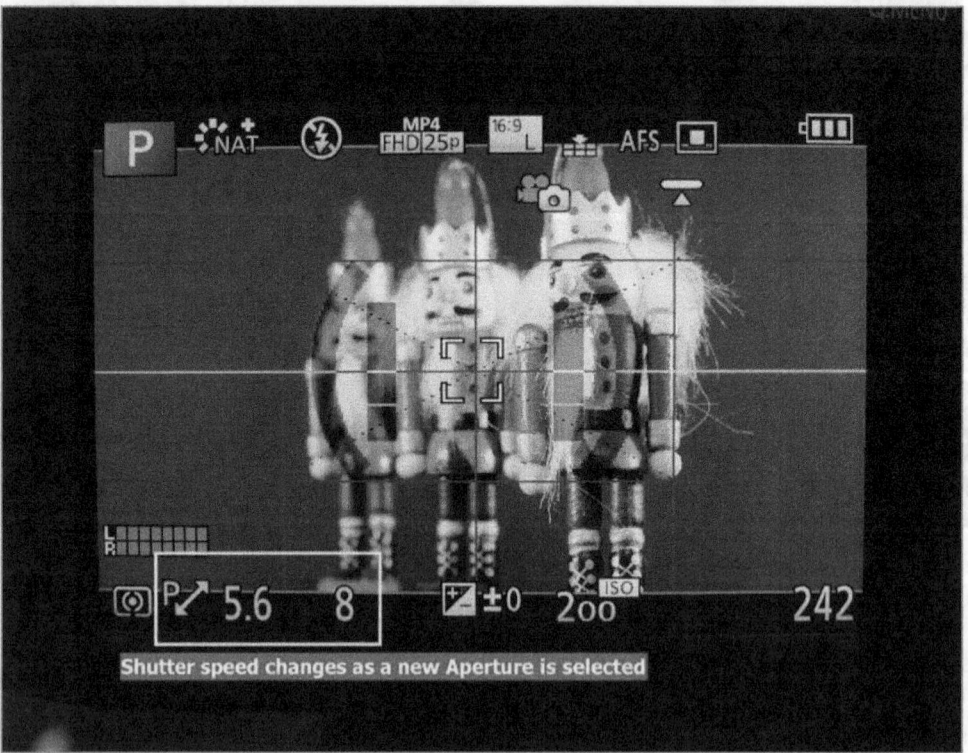

Shutter speed changes as a new Aperture is selected

In summary in the Program Auto Mode, the camera fully automates both aperture and shutter speed, changing both together depending upon the measured subject light.

For brighter subjects the camera gradually closes the aperture and sets higher speeds, reaching the smallest F8 only for very high speeds at or above 1/1000sec.

For lower light levels the camera gradually opens the aperture and sets slower speeds. Once the maximum aperture of F2.8 (or the minimum aperture determined by the zoom setting) has been reached with a shutter speed of 1/100sec, then if the subject is still too dark for this exposure, the "program" keeps the F2.8 aperture while decreasing shutter speed.

If the you set ISO to Auto, the camera will give priority to increasing the ISO sensitivity before setting too slow a speed.
As with all camera metering systems, they can be fooled by large areas of bright or dark foreground or background.
Such scenes might be beach or snow scenes or backlit portraits for example.
In my example, here the black background is forcing the camera to overexpose the image slightly. The background looks a dark grey rather than black as I see it.
To compensate for this, it is possible to use exposure value compensation (EV) to adjust for this as shown below.
Using −VE values of EV shorten the exposure making the background (and subject) darker.

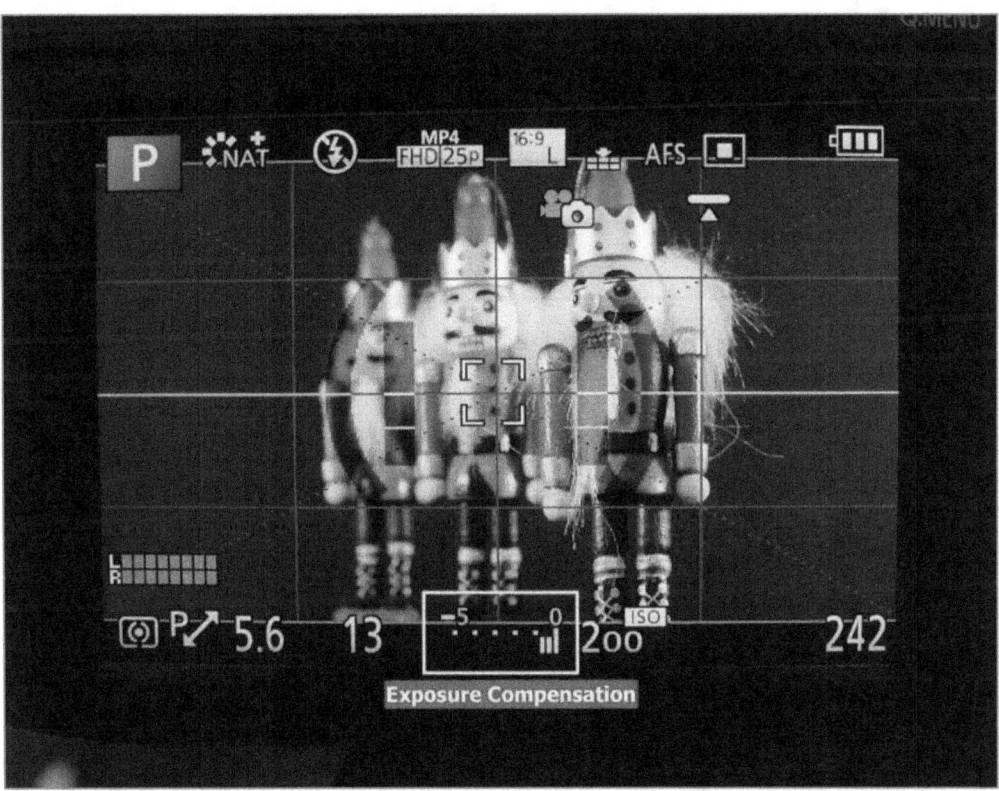

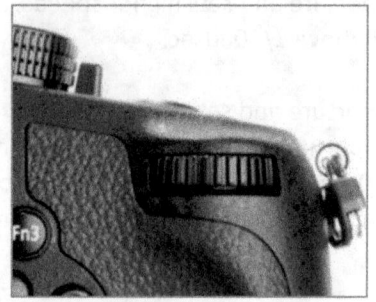

To use exposure compensation, it is necessary to press in the back-control wheel.
Doing so changes the operation from aperture to EV adjustment.

You can adjust the exposure by up to 5 F-stops for either the under or over exposed images.

To change back to controlling the exposure press in the back-control wheel once again. Program shift will stay set even if you turn to a new shooting mode and then back again. To cancel the program shift it is necessary to turn the back-control wheel to the right until the double headed arrow disappears from the screen.

Taking Images Using the Aperture Priority Mode: "A" mode

Aperture priority is selected by the user when the main exposure driving reason is one of the need for depth of field (DOF). Selecting a wide aperture (like F2.8) produces a shallow depth of field and conversely selecting a small aperture (like F8.0) will give deeper depth of field.

Selecting a large aperture, a long focal length and placing the subject close to the camera with the subject far from the background is the usual way to produce images with great differentiation of subject from background. This can be used to great advantage in portraiture and wildlife.

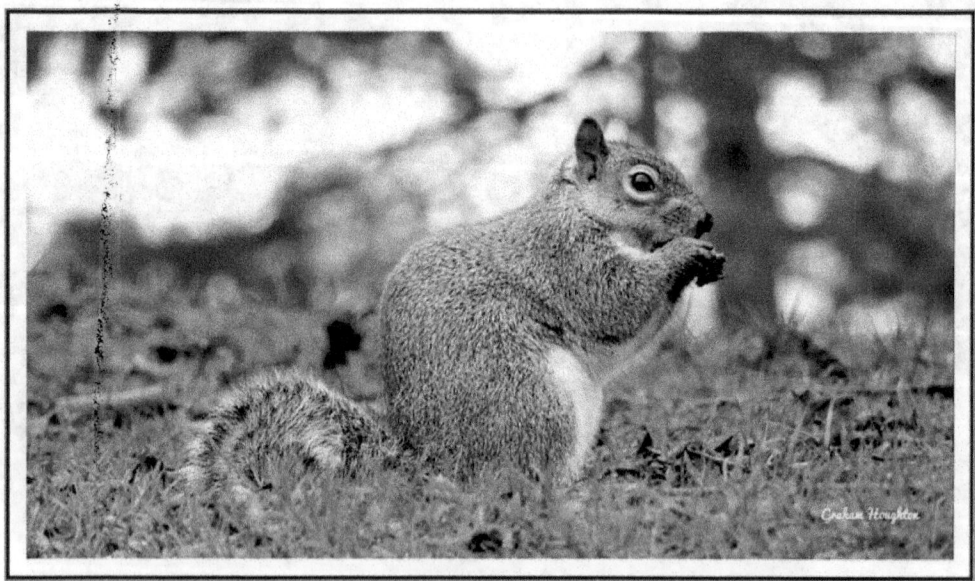

Selecting a large aperture (small f-number) for reduced depth of field

Aperture priority is selected by rotating the top mode control dial to the "A" position aligned to the white marker on the flash housing.

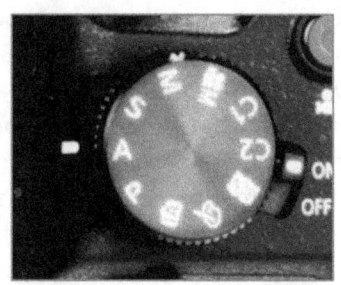

The range of adjustment is from F2.8 to F8.0 however the lens aperture quickly drops from f2.8 to f3.2 once you leave the 25mm (equivalent focal length) setting and reaches F4 from 200mm (equivalent focal length).

indicates Aperture Priority Mode

selected Aperture

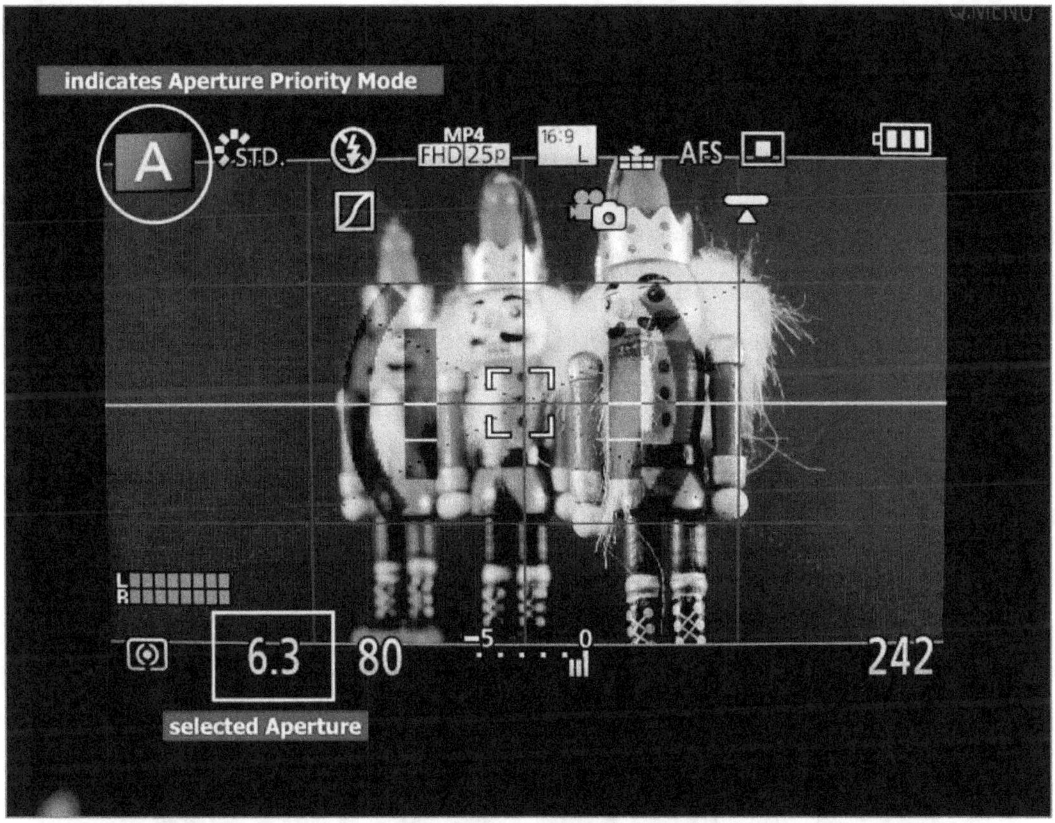

Aperture is adjusted by rotating the back-control dial. As with the "P" mode if you need at apply any exposure value compensation (EV) you need to push in the back-control wheel to set the control to the EV adjustment – at which point the exposure compensation scale will be highlighted in yellow as shown below. To adjust the aperture again depress the back-control wheel. The Aperture value will now be highlighted yellow.

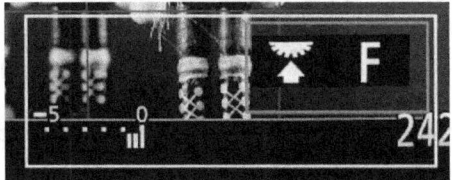

In Aperture Priority mode, the camera will set the shutter speed automatically depending upon the subject brightness and the camera ISO setting.

The range of control is from 60 seconds to 1/4000 sec with the mechanical shutter selected and 1 second to 1/16000 sec with the electronic shutter selected however, this will be set by the zoom setting as this affects the aperture value as well.

If none of these results in a "normal" exposure the aperture and shutter speed values on the LCD screen will flash in red.

If this situation occurs you need to adjust aperture, ISO (or both), change shutter type or increase/decrease the subject lighting.

So, in summary the main reason to select Aperture Priority mode is when you want to have control over the amount of depth of field that will be created in an image.

In practice because of the range of aperture values, at best, is F2.8 to F8 there is not much change in the image and consequently the ability to produce dramatic shallow depths of field is considerably reduced.

To achieve shallow depth of field it is important to select a small aperture number, use a medium to long telephoto setting and the try to keep the subject close to the camera and as far from the background as possible.

The other option to achieve a blurred background is to focus on the subject at a very close distance. The depth of field will be minimal and the background will have a blurred appearance.

With either of these techniques you must accept the other effects that using a specific setting imposes.

For instance, a telephoto shot or a close-up shot which may not be practical for the image you are creating.

As an example, a portrait might be better suited to using a wider aperture and a landscape a smaller aperture.

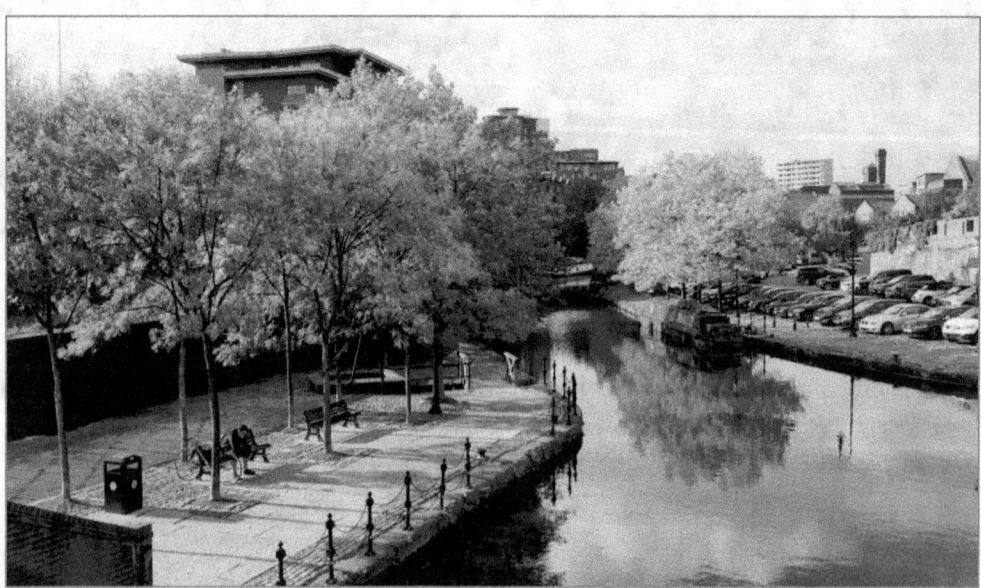

For this landscape shot a combination of a wide angle setting and small aperture were used to get as much of the image as sharp as possible.

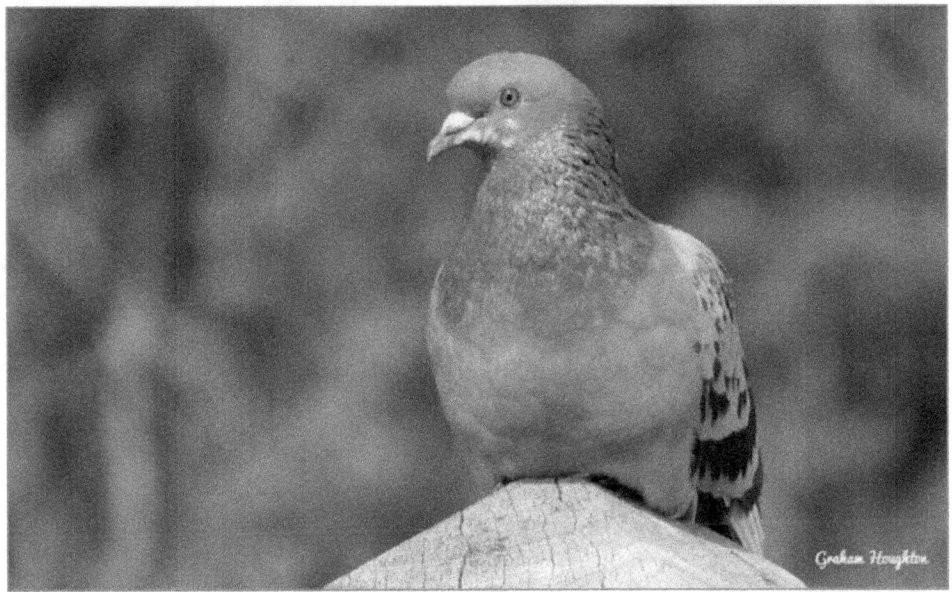

In this example of a pigeon I used a longer focal length and a wider aperture to create the blurred background so that the bird stood out distinctly against the background.
This is a useful technique if your background contains a lot of distracting clutter.

Aperture, Focal Lengths and Equivalences

I've found in my years of teaching photography that one of the hardest concepts for new users of digital cameras is understanding how the sensor size in the camera directly affects the physical size of any lens attached, the focal length of the lens and the amount of depth of field that the combination delivers.
It is because of these, hard to grasp facts, that a system was devised which allowed the smaller than 35mm full frame sensors to be compared to the full frame sensor.
The system relies upon the ratio of the diagonal size of the camera sensor compared to that of the diagonal of 35mm full frame sensors.

For a 35mm full frame sensor and the FZ1000 type 1 inch sensor the dimensions are;

Sensor Size	Aspect Ratio	Height x width	Diagonal mm	Area mm^2
Full Frame 35mm	3:2	24x36	43	864
FZ1000 type 1 inch	3:2	8.8x13.2	15.9	116

By dividing the 35mm diagonal by the FZ1000 sensor diagonal we have 43/15.9 = 2.704 This mathematical result is called the "Crop Factor" and is key to understanding all the equivalents quoted.

A 100mm *equivalent* lens zoom setting on the FZ1000 will give the same framing and the same perspective as an *actual* 100mm lens does on a full frame camera, because they are *equivalent*.
This assumes that you shoot the image from the same physical position.

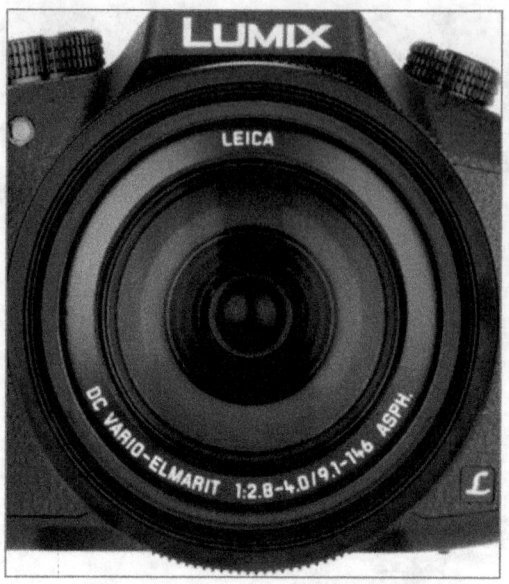

So, what about the lens of the FZ1000? Well you can see from the lens marking that it is a lens which has an aperture of F2.8 which reduces to F4.0 (1:2.8-4.0) as the lens focal length changes from 9.1mm to 146mm.

The 9.1mm to 146mm is the *native* focal length of this lens and this is where the *equivalence* in focal length is used to make this more meaningful for comparison of lens fields of view.

By multiplying the native focal length and the crop factor of the image sensor together you will arrive at the equivalent full frame focal length.

So, with the FZ1000 we have 9.1mm x 2.704 to 146mm x 2.704 which gives us the 25mm to 400mm when rounded up to the nearest focal length.

Now this explains how we get the equivalent lens focal lengths but sensor size and crop factor also affect the lens depth of field and the noise recorded with the sensor.

It also turns out, the relationship between sensor size and aperture is like that between focal length and sensor size.

It's the physical size of the aperture that defines depth-of-field, not its F-number.

The F number is a relationship derived by dividing the lens actual focal length by the diameter of the lens aperture.

So, for example a lens which has an actual focal length of 100mm and a lens aperture size of 25mm would give an aperture of F4 (100/25).

Similarly, an actual 50mm lens with an aperture of 25mm would have an aperture of F2 (50/25).

If, for a moment, we could remove the FZ1000 zoom lens allowing us to place a full frame lens at the same physical position that would still allow it to focus to infinity we can see how this helps to explain the effect of aperture and depth of field.

Firstly, the image circle created by the full frame lens would be much larger as it needs to cover the whole size of the sensor.

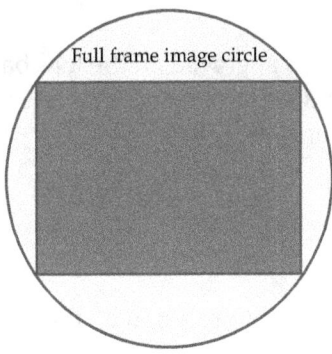
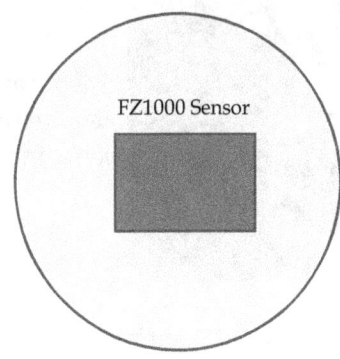

As you can see from the two illustrations the relative sizes of the FZ1000 compared to a full frame sensor and shows that the "total light" gathered by the full frame sensor is much more than the FZ1000 sensor. This is proportional to the area of the sensor, 864 mm^2 versus 116mm^2 a factor of 7.5 times.

The actual light reaching the sensor would be the same (after all that is determined by the lens aperture) however the one thing that should be most obvious is the fact that the image that would be captured by the FZ1000 sensor with this full frame lens would have a much narrower field of view, in other words it would look as though this image was taken with a longer focal length lens.

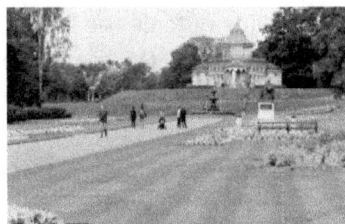
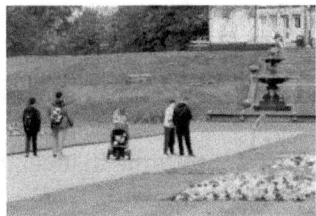

Full frame image(left) and the image from the FZ1000 sensor(right)

What this means is that to produce an image of the same field of view as the full frame sensor we would have to use a lens with a much wider field of view. In fact, this lens would be exactly 2.704 times shorter in terms of focal length.

So, in the example above if the scene was captured using a 50mm lens with a full frame camera to get the same view on the FZ1000 camera with its physically smaller imaging size we would need a lens of 18.5mm focal length.

With the FZ1000, in a departure from the usual way in which Panasonic indicates zoom with their bridge cameras, the equivalent focal length is indicated on both the LCD screen and on the lens barrel as it extends.
Previously they indicated zoom by a zoom factor.
For example, when the lens was at 25mm it would show x1 and at 50mm it would show x2 and all the way up to the x16 zoom that the FZ1000 is capable of.

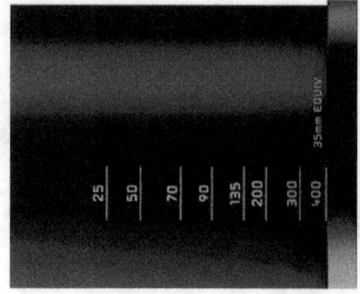

The focal length of the lens engraved on the lens barrel to denote the effective (or 35mm full frame equivalent) focal length that the lens is currently set to.

The depth of field (DOF), diffraction, and total amount of light projected on the sensor are all intimately related to the aperture diameter.
The DOF is the distance between the near and far points from the focal plane that appear to be in critical focus and is key in the amount of detail rendered in an image. It is also important not to confuse DOF with background blur or "Bokeh".

Only a small portion of the image is in critical focus (at the focal plane), but as our eyes and brain cannot see with infinite precision, the focal plane is perceived to have some depth. As we enlarge the image, we can more clearly see that less and less of the image is within focus, and this is how the DOF changes with enlargement.

Of course, no lens is perfect, and the focal plane is not a plane at all, but rather a curved surface. In some instances, the curvature of the focal plane can be extreme enough that what appears to be edge softness is actually a flat surface falling outside the focal 'plane'. In addition, the focus falloff is gradual, the closer the parts in the scene are to the focal surface, the sharper they will appear.

The DOF is the depth from an ideal focal plane in which we consider elements of the scene to be "sharp enough".
As we close the aperture of the lens, i.e. moving from a small f-number to a larger one, we reduce its effective diameter. This not only reduces the amount of light reaching the sensor but it also increases the amount of depth of field recorded in the image.

In "stopping down" the aperture it not only increases the depth of field but also reduces some of the lens aberrations (imperfections) that all lenses have.

However, because of the nature of light is in the form of light rays of the three primary colours of RED, Green and Blue these wavelengths are "disturbed" as they pass through the aperture blades.
The longer wavelength of red is most impacted by this phenomenon and the effects upon the image captured is one of image softening. This in a physical sense is called "diffraction".
This is referred to as aperture limited softening or more commonly described as Diffraction Limited Resolution and progressively increases as the lens aperture is decreased.

In the FZ1000 diffraction starts as early as F5.6 and by F8 it is becoming noticeable.

Therefore, the lens aperture range on this camera is restricted from F2.8 to F8. However, putting this into full frame equivalent context this aperture range gives the same DOF as F8 to F16 on a full frame sensor camera.

What is sometimes not appreciated is the fact that the "crop factor" not only affects the equivalence of focal length and the effect on depth of field but it also impacts on the ISO equivalence for noise in an image.

You can also use crop factor to estimate the total image noise different sensors will have at a specific ISO.

Simply multiply the ISO of the smaller sensor by the crop factor twice:

Smaller Sensor ISO * Crop Factor * Crop Factor = Full Frame ISO

So, in the FZ1000 having the 2.704 crop factor setting an ISO of 200 would produce an image which has the same noise as a full frame sensor camera with the ISO set to ISO 1250 (the nearest value to the calculation which is ISO 1400 which is 200 x 2.70 x 2.70)

Taking Images using the Shutter Priority Mode: "S" mode.

Shutter priority mode is usually selected when the main exposure driving reason is one of controlling subject motion. By selecting a fast shutter speed (like 1/2000 sec) subject motion may be completely frozen whilst conversely selecting a longer exposure (like 1/8 sec) will allow a degree of subject motion blurring such as you might see in images of flowing water or clouds streaking across a skyscape image.

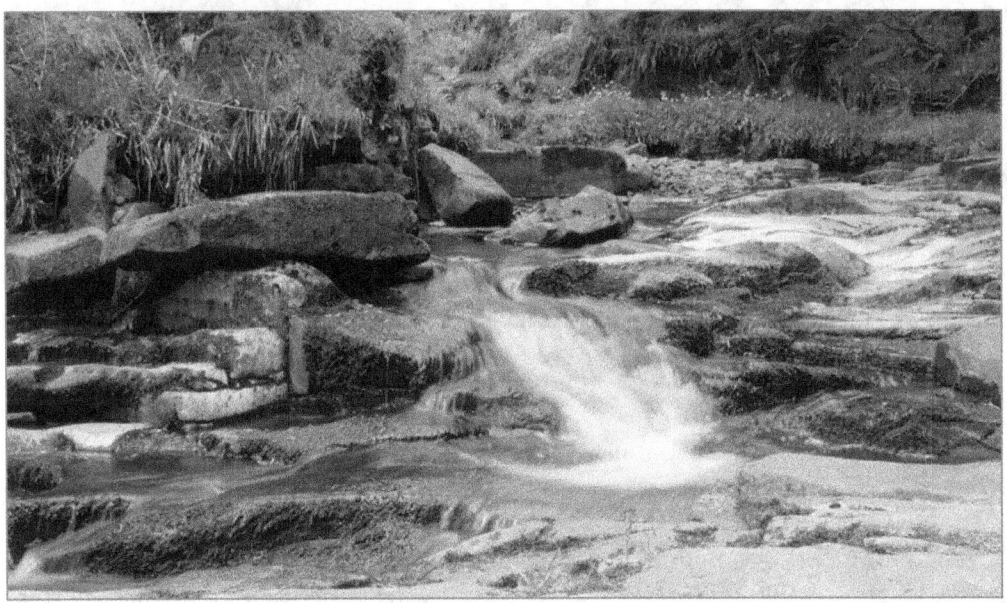

A longer exposure allows some subject motion blur

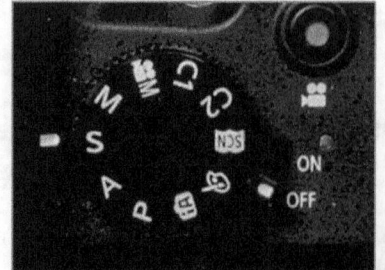

Shutter priority is selected by rotating the top mode control dial to the "S" position to align it against the white index mark.

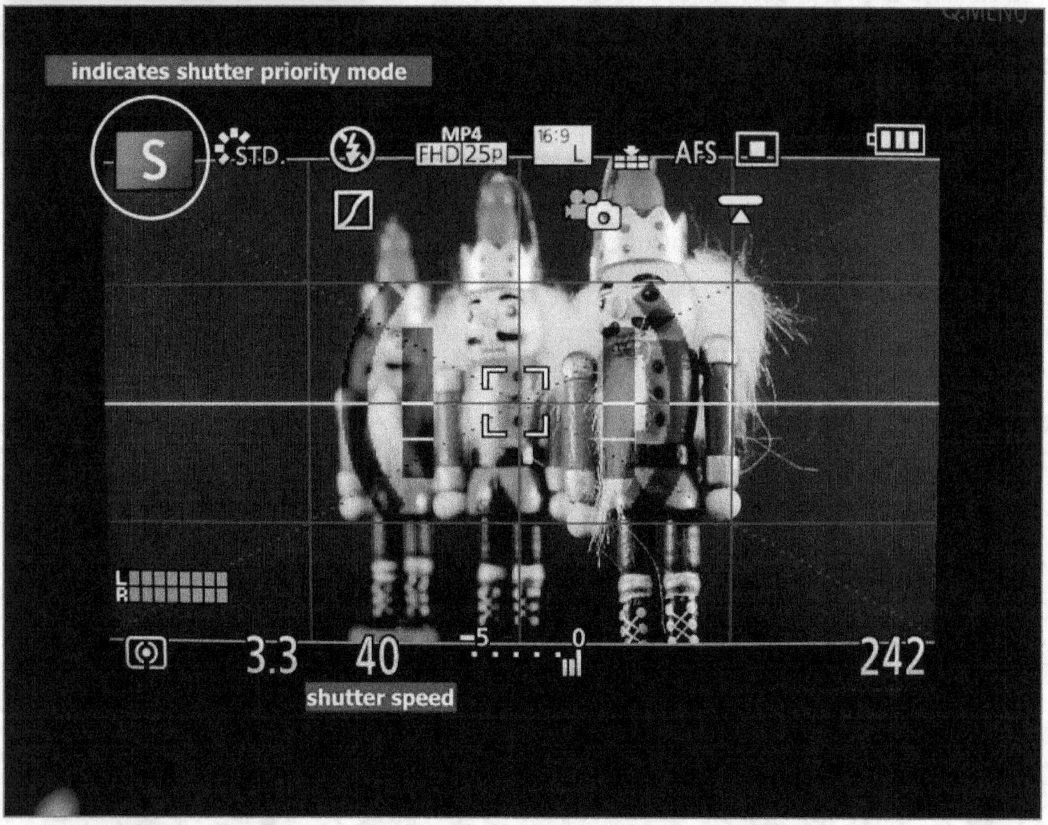

indicates shutter priority mode

S .:STD. FHD 25p 16:9 L AFS

shutter speed

The range of adjustment is from 1 second to 1/16000 sec if the electronic shutter is used and 60 seconds to 1/4000 sec when the mechanical shutter is used.

The camera automatically adjusts the aperture to give the correct exposure (and possibly ISO if Auto ISO is selected).
You cannot however use the iISO function as this will automatically set the ISO to Auto ISO.

As in the Aperture priority mode exposure compensation can be used to correct for any metering failures. Pushing in the rear control wheel switches between controlling shutter speed and exposure compensation.

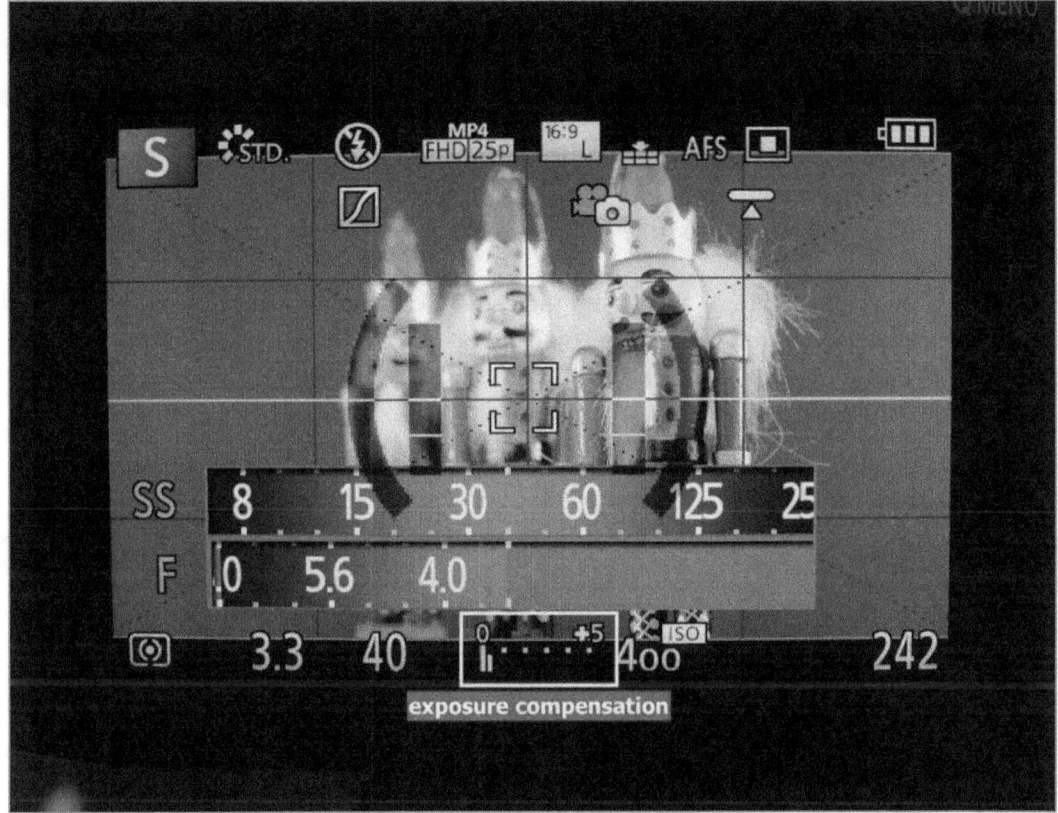

If the camera cannot set an aperture to result in a normal exposure, the shutter speed and aperture values will flash in red.

One of the confusing aspects of the way in which shutter speeds are displayed is the situation when the shutter speed exceeds 1 second.

Longer shutter speeds are displayed with what resembles double quotation marks e.g. 4" means 4 seconds.

Fractional seconds can also confuse new users. Speeds like 1/2.5 and 1/3.2 which will be 0.4 seconds and 0.3 seconds respectively are a little hard to get your head around initially.

Although optical image stabilisation can eliminate or reduce hand shake (by allowing shutter speeds at least 3 f-stops slower than without) it does not reduce any subject motion blur if the subject is moving. Subject motion blur is often the cause of sports or action images that do not look "sharp".
To ensure that you capture images with the least amount of this subject motion it is necessary to use a shutter speed which is fast enough to arrest the motion.
One rule that is often quoted is to use a shutter speed which is at least the reciprocal of the lens focal length. So, for example if the lens is extended to give an equivalent focal length of 200mm the shutter speed should be set to 1/200sec.

Although this is a "one size fits all" rule it does help to reduce the subject motion blur however, the amount of reduction will also depend upon the speed, direction and distance from the camera at which the subject is moving.

A subject moving at a walking pace close to the camera, or with a telephoto setting on the lens, will require a faster shutter speed than one in which the subject is moving at the same speed but further away.

Similarly, the angle at which the subject moves relative to the camera will also affect the amount of blur.

A subject moving parallel to or away from the camera can be captured with a slower shutter speed than one that is moving diagonally towards the camera.

With sports and action type photography it is often necessary to use 1/500 sec exposure to ensure that subject motion is frozen, or reduced.

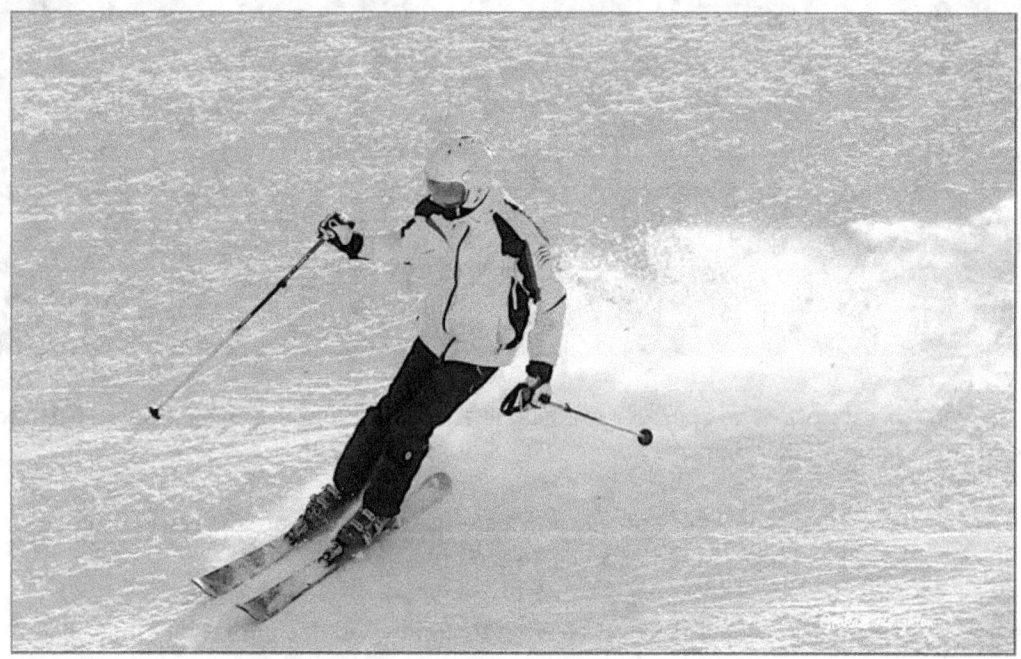

With a telephoto setting and moving towards the camera needed 1/1000 sec to capture

In some low ambient light this may mean that even at the widest aperture setting the exposure may need a high ISO for this shutter speed to be used.

This is the necessary compromise in this situation, better a slightly noisy image that can be post processed than one without noise but with subject motion blur that makes the image less pleasing.

On the other end of the scale sometimes we need to make long exposures to either capture the shallowest depth of field available or to purposely introduce subject motion blur such as capturing flowing water, light trails from moving vehicle head/tail lights or light painting.

To achieve the longer shutter speeds in daylight even using an aperture of F8 and an ISO of 80 (in the extended ISO mode) it may be necessary to attenuate the light entering the camera using a ND filter.

ND filters are available as 62mm filter rings in both fixed value and "variable" types.

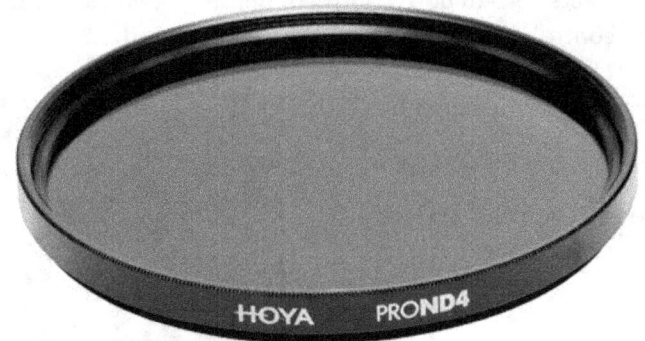

The fixed types of the ND filter are available in different attenuation. They range from ND2 (one stop attenuation) to ND1000 (10 stops attenuation)

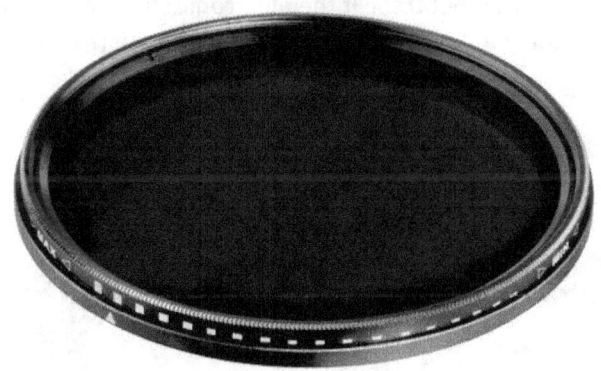

The variable ND filters are constructed from 2 polarising filters and the reduction in light will depend on the angle of each of the filters to the other. One filter is static in the mount and the other rotates. They vary from ND4 to ND400 however can suffer image degradation and colour shift.

Neutral density filters are supposed to attenuate all colours equally however some filters may introduce some slight colour shift, especially the higher density ones.

It is worth investing in a good make, like the Hoya Pro range which are excellent at maintaining neutral images.
The variable ND filters also can reduce image quality as they have four air to glass transitions and hence do add the possibility of image quality loss though flair when shooting towards any light source.
At the higher attenuation settings, they also show a very dark "X" shaped cross on the image.
Being polarising filters as well may introduce some "cut" to any reflections on water or foliage or darken skies.
There are also square filters and filter mounts which are designed for the graduated filter that is sometimes used by landscape photographers to reduce the lighting difference between skies and foreground.
They do however have limited application in this respect if the horizon is also interrupted by skies or mountains which can look unrealistically darkened by the filter if they enter the harder parts of the transition zone of the filter.

Taking Images using the Manual Mode: "M" mode.

Manual exposure mode is normally selected when both control of depth of field using the aperture control and subject motion control using the shutter speed is required.

Manual mode is selected by rotating the top mode control dial to the "M" position.

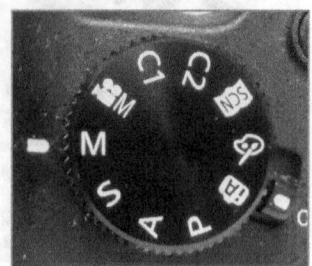

Use the Fn1 button, adjacent to the top control wheel to alternate the choice of adjustment by alternating between aperture and shutter speed.

By using the top-control wheel, you can change the value of the selected control.
The range of adjustment is from 1 second to 1/16000 sec if the electronic shutter is used and 60 seconds to 1/4000 sec when the mechanical shutter is used and the aperture can be adjusted from F2.8 to F8.0.

Exposure is indicated by the exposure meter at the centre, bottom of the LCD display screen. +/- 0 being the correct exposure (as in the image below)

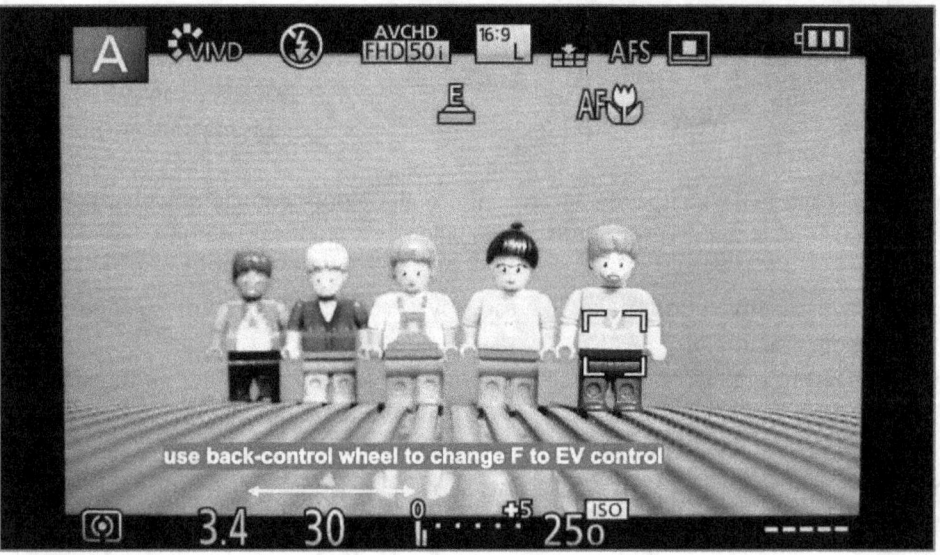

If shutter speed and aperture values have been set for image condition reasons, as mentioned previously, then ISO is used adjust the exposure to give a "0" meter indication.
It is important to recognize that this 'exposure meter' is an estimate of the exposure recommended by the camera metering system.

The metering mode and subject type will affect the outcome of the image and as such it is import to also understand how and when adjustments should be applied to correct for the situations.

For example, it may be necessary to set the exposure meter to read with a few of the indicator bars (which are 1/3 F-stop increments) on the plus side if shooting scenes where the background has a higher brightness than the principal foreground subject. Snow or beach scenes would be a classic example of this type of scene.

A useful feature now incorporated into the FZ1000 is the ability to have the ISO adjust automatically to give the correct exposure.
This allows you to change camera position without the additional worry of resetting the ISO to give the correct exposure.
If you have set iISO in the aperture priority mode, then this will become Auto ISO in the manual mode.
One element of manual exposure that I feel needs to be clarified and that is in the case of what is referred to as "Bulb" or "B" mode.

With traditional film based cameras it was possible to engage this mode and lock the shutter open for an indefinite period. Originally pneumatic control (hence the term bulb from the rubber bladder used to compress air to the shutter release mechanism) and then latterly with a wired solid cable type release. This was useful for night time images and astro-photography and some medical based imaging.

With the FZ1000 Panasonic have introduced a "Bulb" mode which is accessible through the manual exposure settings. In this mode, it is possible to hold the shutter button open by keeping the shutter button fully depressed or the use of an external wired remote switch such as the DMW-RSL1.
To access the "B" mode the camera must be in the "M" mode and then with the back-control wheel set to adjust the shutter speed rotate the back-control wheel to adjust the shutter speed so that you see the shutter speeds decrease and move into the seconds of exposure. When you reach 60 seconds the next increment on the wheel is the "B" position

What is not clear is that the period that the shutter can be set open is limited to 120 seconds. The camera will close the shutter even if you keep the shutter button, or wired release, depressed.
There is no exposure indication so your exposure must be done by trial and error methods or by use of an external, hand held exposure meter.
A tripod, or other method of holding the camera rigid is essential for this type of photography.

Using the Constant Preview Mode in Manual Mode

When recording images in the manual mode the image on the LCD screen (or EVF) is automatically adjusted by the camera to give an image of 'normal' brightness for you to be able to view it.
There is however a mode, the "constant preview mode" which can be set which enables you to see the result of the ISO, aperture and shutter speed combination – a real time view of the depth of field and the affect that the shutter speed has on image motion. This mode is set to "ON" in the Custom Set Up menu (spanner + C) on page 5/8 under

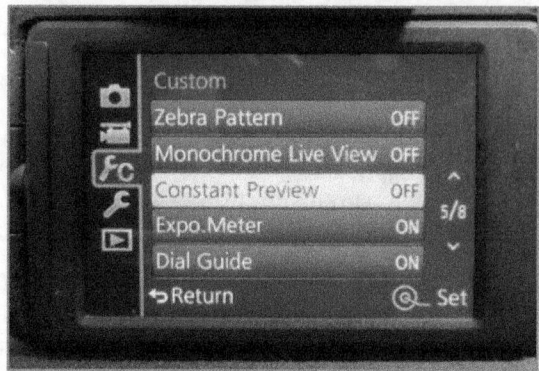

When this mode is enabled you will see any changes you make to any one of these parameters. This is useful to be able to preview the effect of changing the controls on your image.

The caveats are that if you set ISO to AUTO you will not see any change as the camera will adjust ISO every time you make a change to aperture or shutter speed and you cannot use this in the pre-burst mode of 4K photo mode.

If you assign PREVIEW to Fn1 button you can use this function more easily.

Once you have the preview mode turned on you can use the Fn1 button to see the effects of the shutter speed that has been set.

You can preview the subject motion blur that the current aperture setting will give. This is achieved when the Shtr Speed Effect ON is displayed and you press the Fn1 button.

To see the effects of the shutter speed control with the Shtr Speed Effect OFF is displayed and you press the Fn1 button.

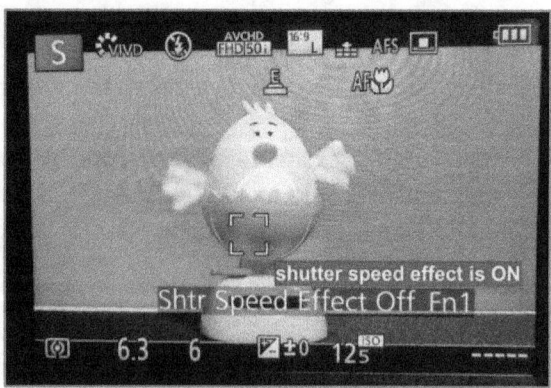

The range for shutter speed effect check is 60 seconds to 1/16000th of a second.

One Push Auto Exposure

This is useful feature If you would like the camera to quickly set the correct exposure or you if a situation where you get the RED exposure warning blinking on the LCD.

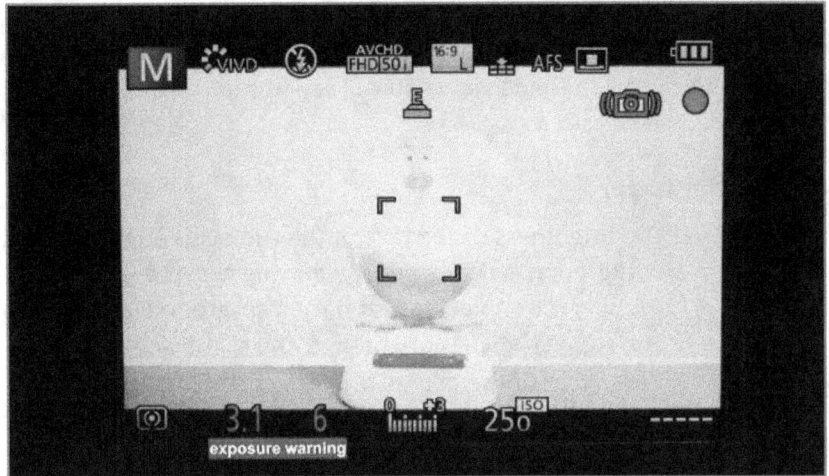

To do this you need to re-program one of the Fn Buttons to achieve this. Fn1 is a good candidate (if you didn't set PREVIEW as described before).

Re-program Fn1 to One Push Auto exposure and if you get the red exposure warning just press the Fn1 button and the camera will try to correct it (if possible).

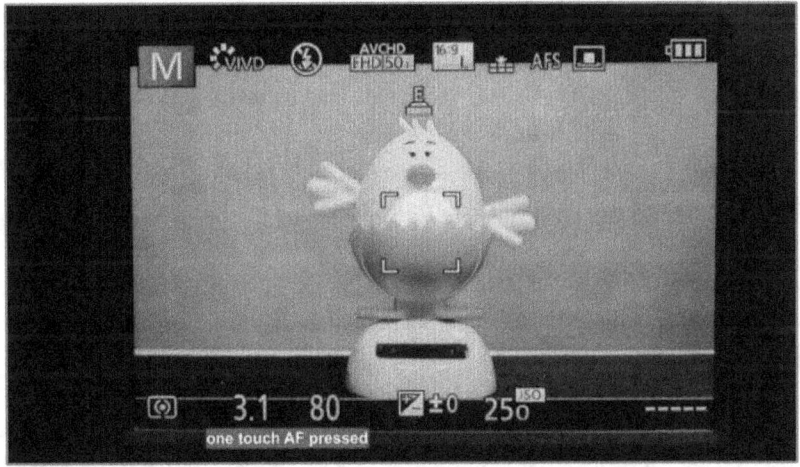

It may not correct when the subject is extremely dark and it is not possible to achieve adequate exposure by changing the aperture value or shutter speed or recording using the flash.

Taking Images that Match the Scene Being Recorded

In the iA and iA+ modes the camera attempts to identify the scene type however if the camera does not identify it correctly Panasonic recommend that you switch to the SCENE mode (SCN) and select the appropriate one from the available types.

To select a suitable scene type, turn the top mode dial to SCN and then use the left/right navigation buttons to scroll through the options. Confirm your selection by pressing Menu/Set.

You can use the DISP button to switch the LCD display of the menu options. The button operates in a cyclical way showing a Normal view, Guided view and finally a List view. When the menu choice is set to Guide view you will see tips for creating suitable picture effects

SCENE TYPE	EFFECTS
Clear Portrait	The brightness of the face of the subject is adjusted and the background is defocused. By moving close to the subject and keeping the subject far from the background improves the result.
Silky Skin	The subjects face is brightened and slightly de-saturated
Backlit Softness	When backlit the overall brightness is increased by diffuse light applied to the whole scene
Clear in Backlight	Outdoors the flash is enabled to illuminate the subjects face.
Relaxing Tone	A warm colour tone is applied to the whole image.
Sweet Childs Face	Slight background defocus and skin tones added saturation
Distinct Scenery	Increased green and blue saturation
Bright Blue Sky	On a sunny day, the overall scene brightness is increased to create a vibrant blue sky.
Romantic Sunset Glow	Purple tones have increased saturation
Vivid Sunset Glow	Red tones have increased saturation
Glistening Water	Highlights are brightened and toned slightly blue
Clear Nightscape	The saturation of the sky is increased to accentuate the sky
Cool Night Sky	Blue tones in the sky are enhanced to create a cooler image
Warm Glowing Nightscape	A warm colour is applied to the whole image.
Artistic Nightscape	The camera sets a slow shutter speed for light trail images etc
Glittering Illuminations	Image has star filter applied to the point light sources
Hand Held Night Shot	Camera captures multiple images and combines them to minimise blur and noise when hand holding for night scenery
Clear Night Portrait	Camera uses fill flash and a longer exposure to capture better portraits set against a nightscape
Soft Image of Flower	Camera applies diffuse soft focus to image.
Appetising Food	Overall image brightness is increased
Cute Dessert	Overall image brightness is increased more.
Freeze Animal Motion	Camera selects a faster Shutter speed to prevent subject motion blur
Clear Sports Mode	Camera selects a faster Shutter speed to prevent subject motion blur
Monochrome	Images created have monochromatic look

Creating an Automatic Panorama Shot

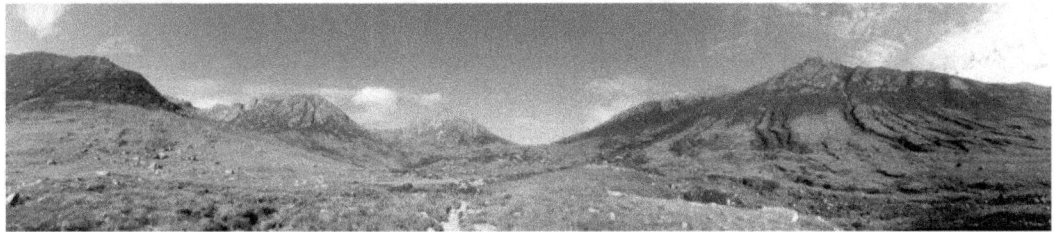

In the Panorama Mode, consecutive images are captured as the camera is moved to build a single image.

To begin capturing a panoramic image with the FZ1000 turn the top mode dial so that the SCN icon aligns to the white mark on the flash housing and then select #25 from the SCN menu.
The panorama can only be constructed from a landscape orientated camera.
The camera direction is set from left to right and cannot be changed.

Press the shutter halfway down to lock the focus and exposure and then fully depress the shutter button and then pivot your body about your waist slowly and at a constant speed.
Keep the horizontal guideline parallel to the horizon.
If you attempt to move the camera too quickly or too slowly the camera may not create the image.

As the arrow on the images progresses across the screen you will have an indication of how much time remains during the capture phase.
You can press the shutter button again to end the sequence or the camera will automatically stop at the end of the time limit.

If you pause during the capture process the recording will also stop.
During the panorama mode, the camera is set to wide angle and exposure and focus is fixed at the time that the shutter button is half depressed.
You can set the exposure from a suitable point on the image sequence and then recompose and fully depress the shutter button to begin recording.

Setting Up Your Camera to Meet Your Photographic Needs

Everyone's preferences will be different as to how to set up the controls of the FZ1000 to make the camera ideally suited to your style of photography.
Panasonic have created several programmable buttons and controls to enable specific adjustments to be created to meet your needs.
In most cases function buttons, can be re-assigned from their default operation to one where you would gain greater advantage.
The Fn1 button is one where you have the greatest degree of freedom as to which function to assign to it.

It maybe that you want to use this button to quickly access the facility to move the AF area and set its size or you may want to use this button as the switch to a monochrome live view in the EVF.

The Fn5 button, normally assigned to switching from EVF to LCD, is also one where greater benefit could be achieved for switching to other features.

These re-assignments are made in the Custom (spanner + C) menu under the Fn Button Set option on page 7/8.

Cursor Buttons, Menu/Set Button Operation

The 4-way cursor button is used to navigate through menus, either up/down or left/right. Selection is made by depressing the Menu/Set button in the middle of the cursor control.

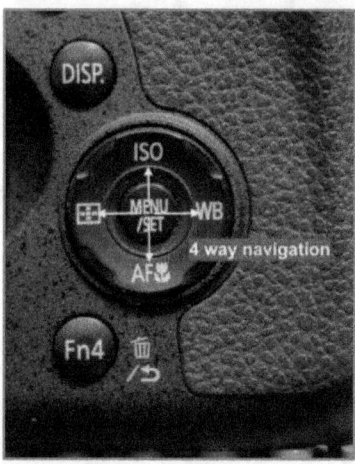

DISP Button Operation

The DISP (display) button can be used to cycle the content of the LCD or EVF through four different screen displays for the LCD and four displays for the EVF.

Each depress of the button steps the display on by one screen.

The four LCD display screens (shown next) which are displayed in the image recording mode; when Monitor Info Disp is set to ON (page 6/8 Custom set up menu).

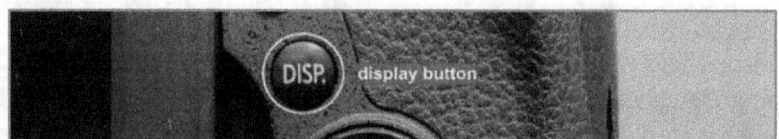

use the display button to cycle through the options

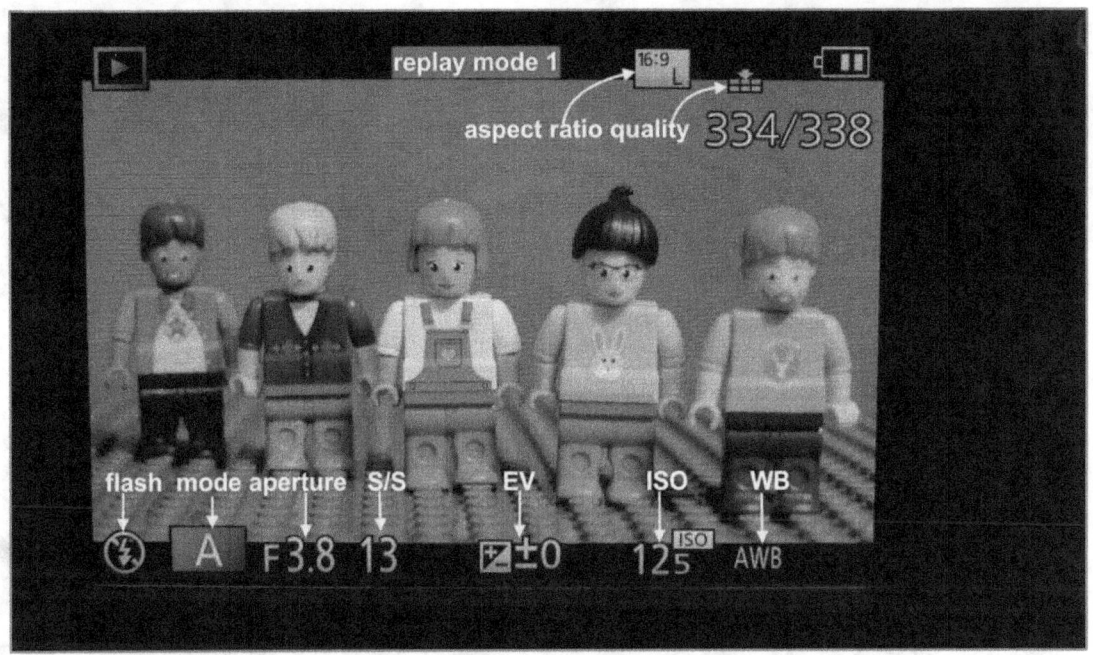

replay mode 1

aspect ratio quality

334/338

flash mode aperture S/S EV ISO WB

A F3.8 13 ±0 125 AWB

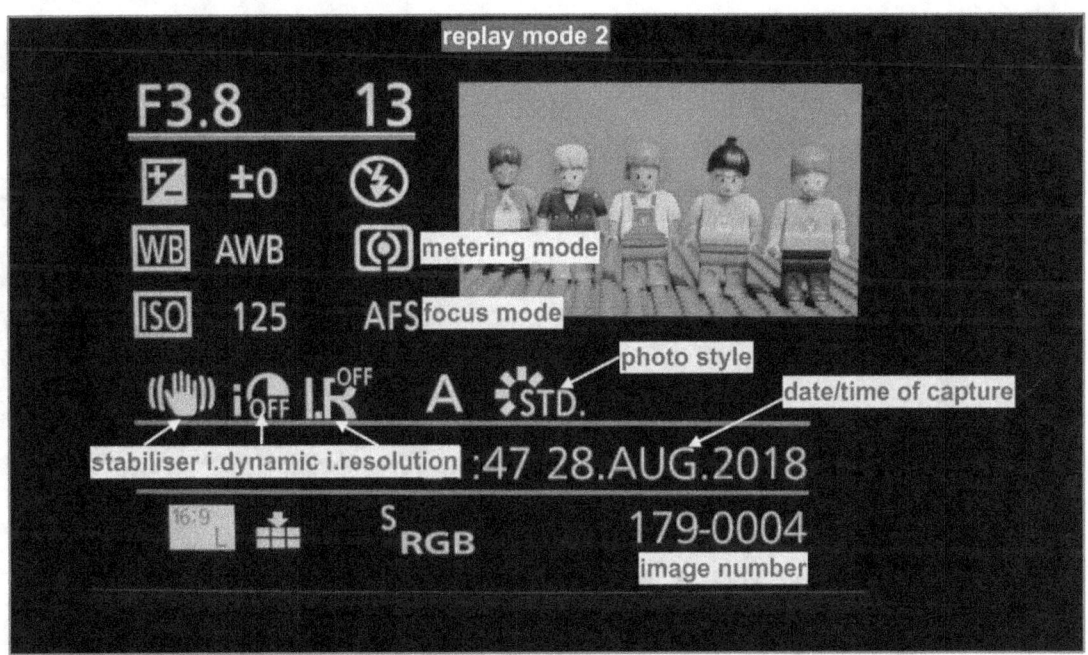

replay mode 2

F3.8 13

±0

WB AWB metering mode

ISO 125 AFS focus mode

photo style

i.OFF I.R OFF A STD. date/time of capture

stabiliser i.dynamic i.resolution :47 28.AUG.2018

RGB 179-0004

image number

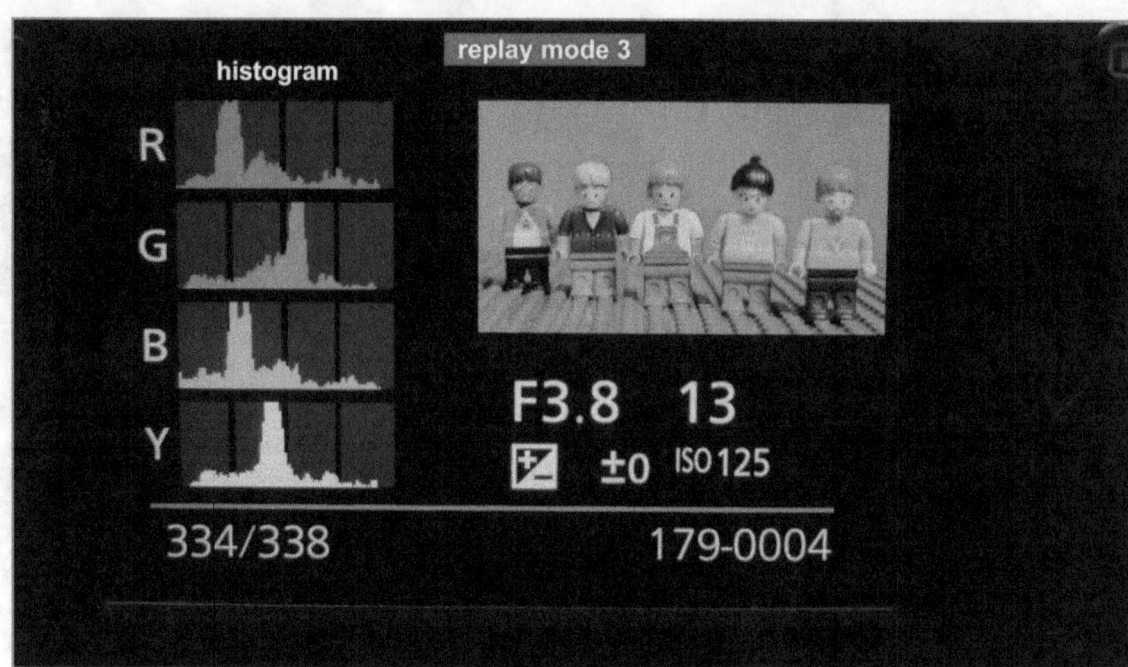

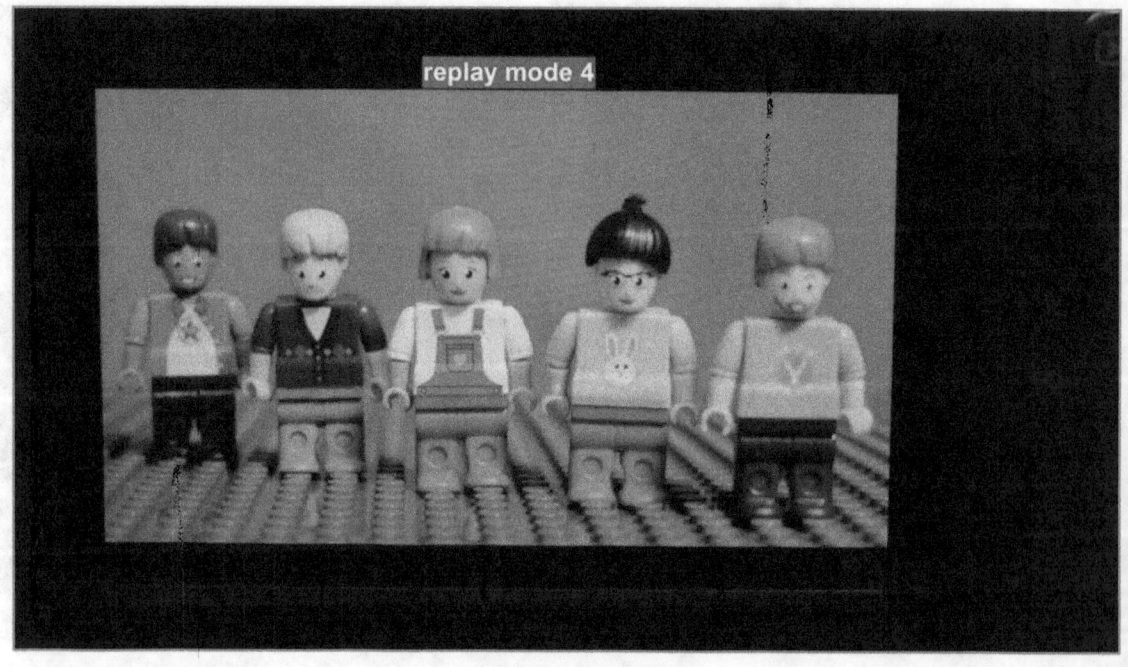

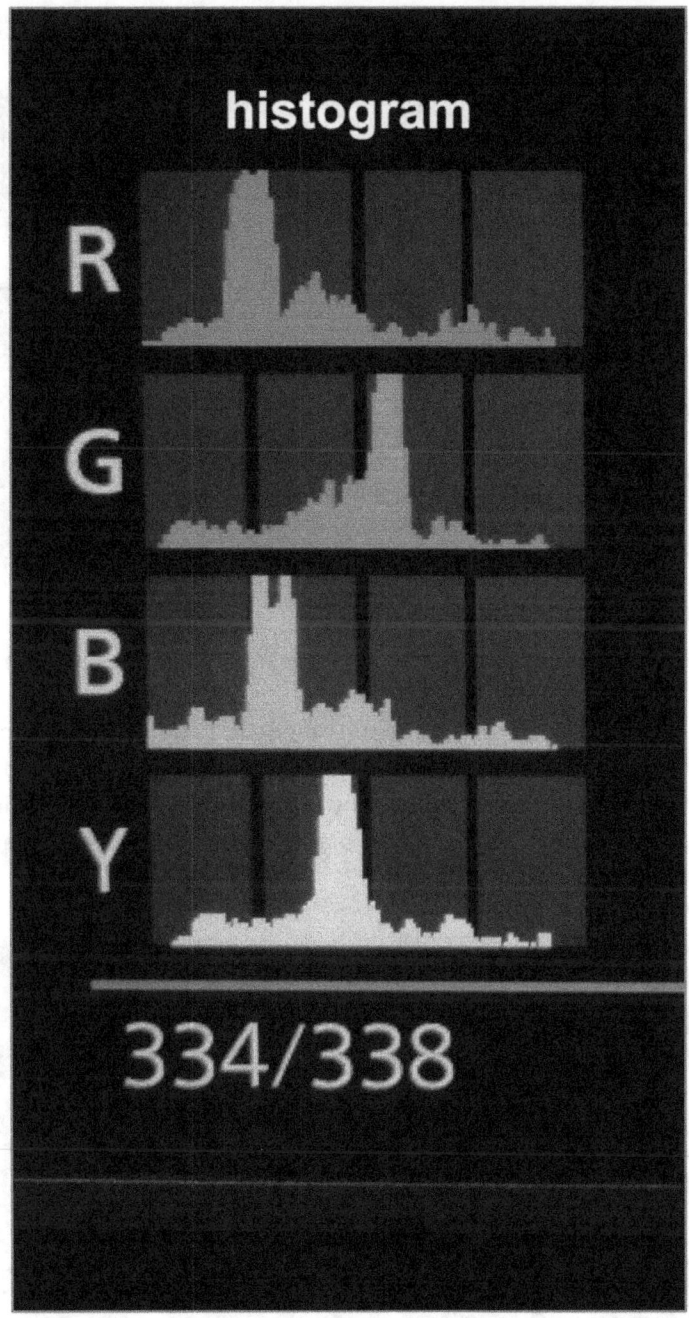

The histogram is a pictorial representation of the number and distribution of pixels in the image. On the left-hand side of the graph are the dark (shadow areas) and on the right the light (highlight areas). The height of the bars represents the number of pixels of that value. The shadows represent a digital value of 0 (zero) whilst the highlights have a digital value of 255. Thus, each colour has a range of 256 discrete brightness values.
An image will have a maximum tonal range of 256 Red, 256 Green and 256 Blue values giving 16777216 colour values, commonly referred to as "true colour".

The distribution pattern will give an indication on the exposure. A correct exposure will have bars in the highlight and shadow area and a peak or cluster of bars about halfway representing the mid-tones. R(ed), G(reen), B(lue) and Y is the illuminance (or brightness).

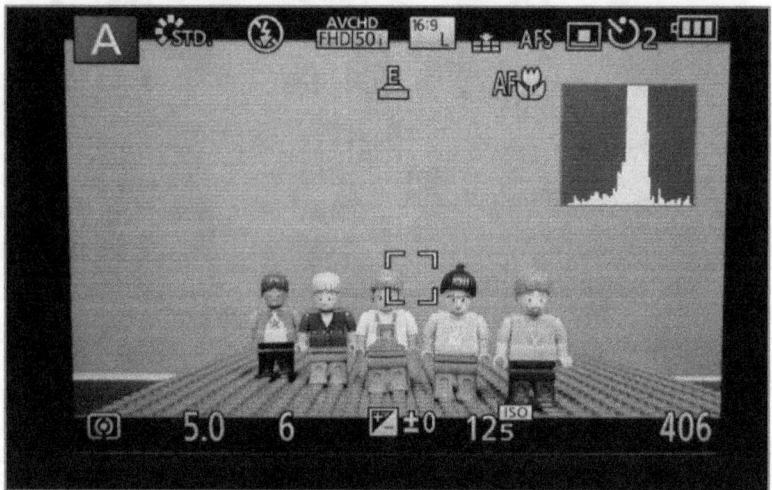

The playback histogram is more useful, in my opinion than the on-screen histogram available during shooting as this only shows the tonal range of the image, not how it will be recorded.

Brightness histogram displayed during shooting mode (if enabled in Custom Menu (4/8)
The brightness values can be seen in the two examples of images shown above. There is a grouping of bars around the central area of the graph which indicates the neutral grey background has many recordable pixels. The blacks of the image (0) value are visible as well as the highlight pixels with a value of 255.

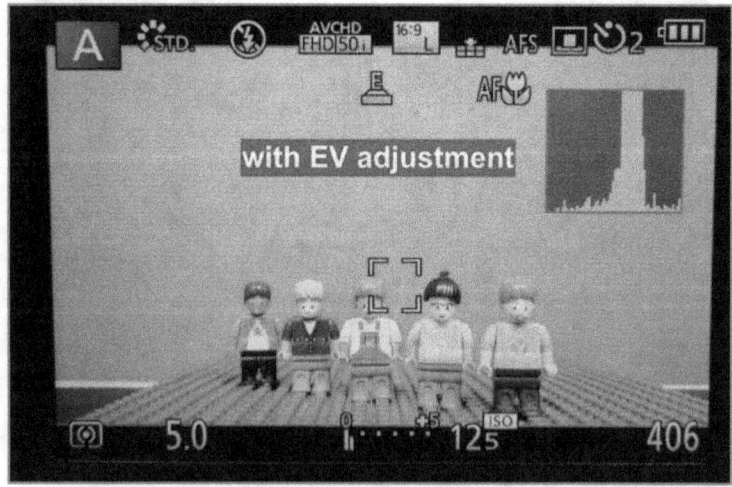

when EV is applied, the histogram will be shown in yellow
This histogram feature can be turned on in the custom (Spanner +C) menu on page 4/8.

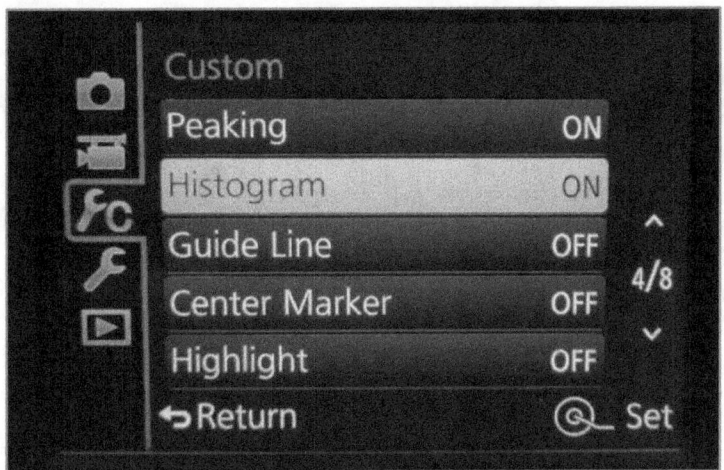

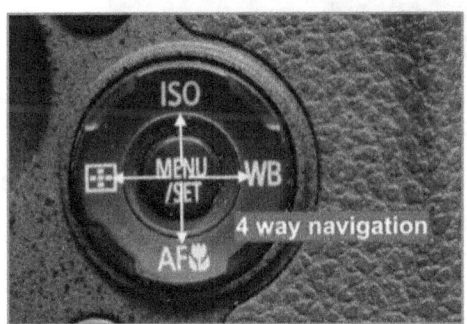

When set to ON its position on the LCD screen can be positioned on the LCD screen by using the 4-way navigation button.

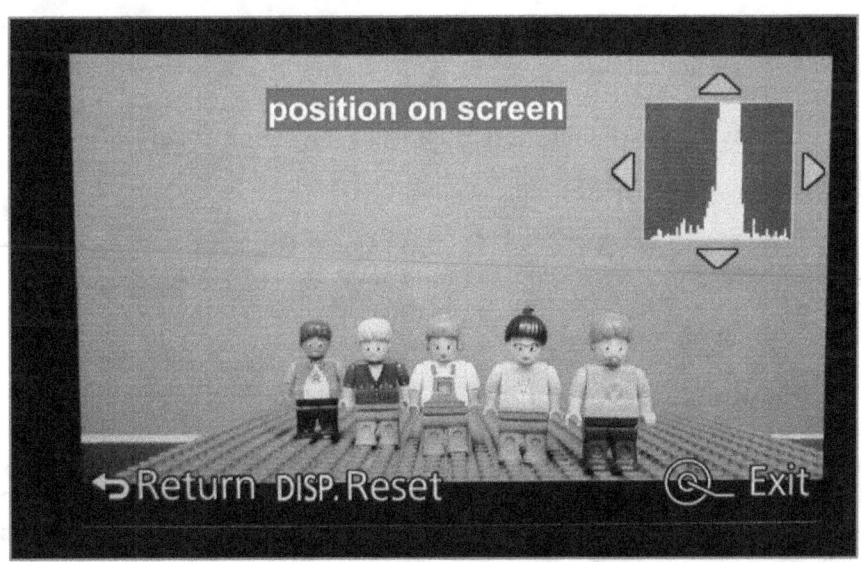

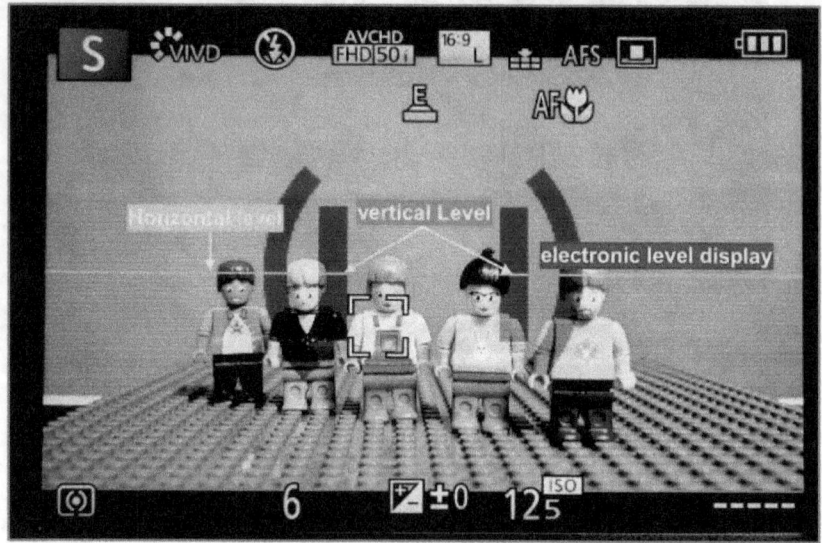

The electronic level is useful when you want to ensure that the camera is either level horizontally, vertically or both. This may be for landscape images or buildings to ensure that there are no converging verticals.

Note that both the level lines are "green" when the camera is level in both plains, there could be an error of up to +1 /- 1 degree in the system.

The level lines are yellow when the camera is tilted outside this 1 degree of inclination of either plain.

Electronic Viewfinder Dioptre Adjustment

Because people's eyesight is different from person to person the optics of the electronic viewfinder (EVF) are adjustable in order that you can sharply focus the image on this display.

To adjust the lens of the viewfinder there is a small adjustment wheel at the side of the viewfinder.

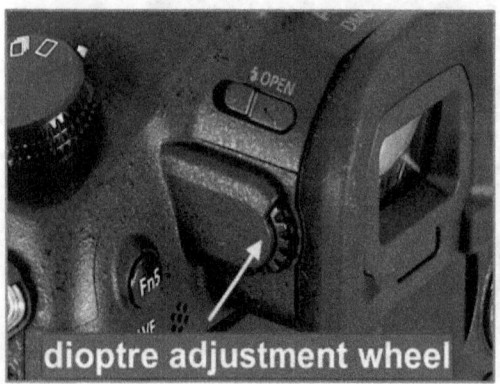

dioptre adjustment wheel

For this adjustment, it is preferable to use a camera generated image, such as a menu display, as this has very well defined pixels. Press Menu/Set, to display the main menu, and then use your left-hand thumb placed on this adjustment wheel to adjust the focus as you bring the camera viewfinder up to your eye. The wheel will move either direction so it is best to find the focus point then slightly overshoot it and then return to the exact point. If you normally wear spectacles adjust it whilst wearing them.

Associated with the EVF are a couple of adjustments which can be made to affect the way that this operates.

It can be set so that its sensitivity is slightly reduced so that the display doesn't switch over to the EVF inadvertently such as when you place your hand near the touch screen. This is adjusted from the Custom set up menu page 8/8. Sensitivity can be Low or High.

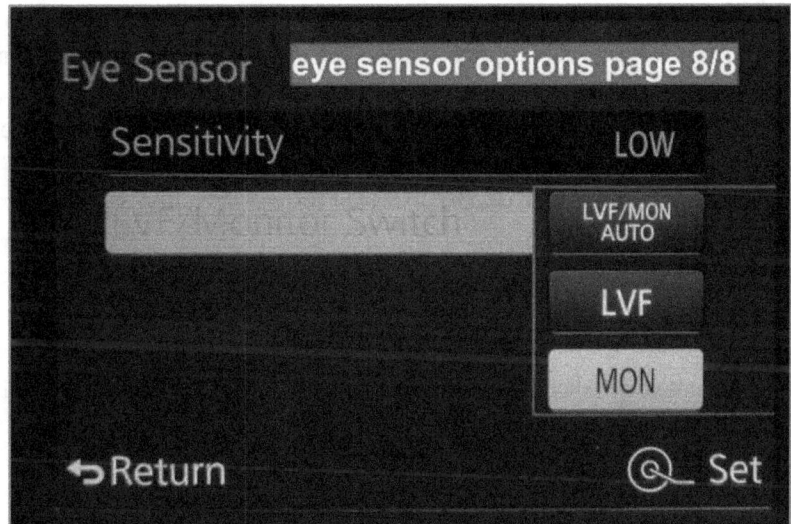

Adjusting the sensitivity of the EVF eye sensor

The second option is for the auto focus to begin to operate as you bring the camera up to your eye. This can help to get the focus quickly acquired when situations may require it. The focus does not activate the beep until focus is locked with the half depress of the shutter release button.

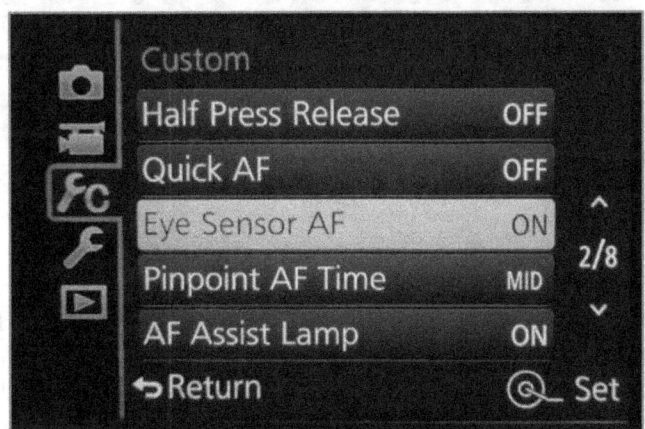

Auto Focus begins with eye sensor activation

Image Size and Quality Choices

Setting up your camera for your photographic requirements will require careful consideration of the elements which, when combined, produce the final image.

The first consideration is one of choosing the aspect ratio for your images.

What is aspect ratio?

Aspect ratio describes the relationship between the width and height of an image.

It's written as a figure, in this form – width:height (width always comes first).

The aspect ratio that you select is just down to what kind of image you are trying to create.

4:3 a common format for digital compact cameras as this matches standard TV and monitor aspect ratios.

3:2 is the original standard for 35mm film shooting, many DSLRs continue to use this ratio and many compact digital cameras support this as an option too.

16:9 is widescreen TV or the newer HDTV/UHD (4k) format and most personal computer displays now.

1:1 is just a square format and matches the older 6x6 cms film format.

If you have a requirement to display on a TV/monitor, go 4:3.

If you have a requirement to display on a widescreen HDTV/HD monitor go for 16:9.

If you need to print to match a frame you may find it easier to take at the correct ratio rather than cropping in an image editing program, later.

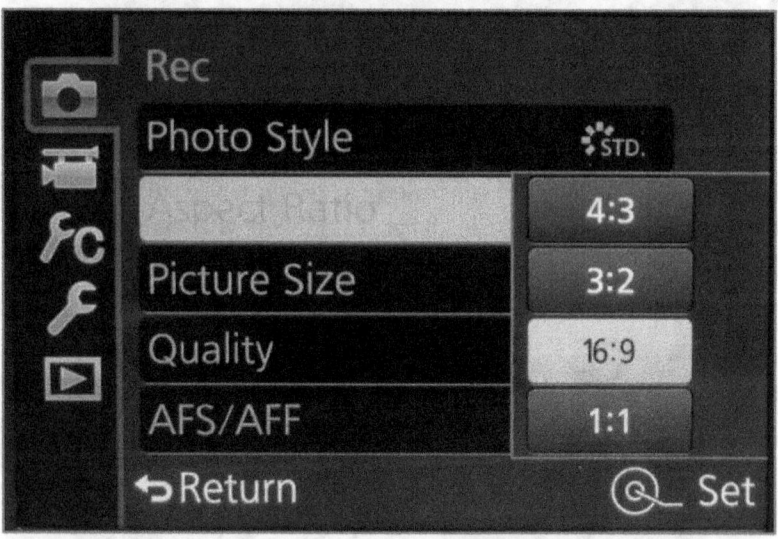

Most printing companies offer at a minimum both 6 x 4.5 inch (to match 4:3 ratio images) and 6 x 4 inch (to match 3:2 ratio images) so you are unlikely to have any problems printing at either ratio.

You'll find that most modern basic albums and frames you buy on the high street will probably be 4:3 as they cater for the general consumer market which is largely digital now, but there's plenty of 3:2 frames around though.

Other than that, just choose whatever suits your subject/shot/composition the best.

In the table below you will find the most common print/photo frame dimensions.
To ensure that any picture taken will not result in part of the image being cropped when printed it is essential to match the image aspect ratio with the standard print sizes.
To do this take your aspect ratio and if it will scale up to a standard size then no cropping will occur.
For example, a 3:2 aspect ratio image scales to a 6x4 inch print exactly but will be cropped at all other print sizes.
A 4:3 aspect ratio image scales perfectly at 6 x 4.5 inches, 40x30cms and 16x12 inch however is cropped at all other sizes
These dimensions for print sizes assume that the pixel density used to produce the image is 300 ppi (pixels per inch). This is the standard requirement required by most commercial printing labs/photo booths etc.
So how many pixels are required to produce standard sized prints and how does this relate to the megapixels captured by the sensor in the FZ1000

Image Resolution and Sensor Pixels

We have seen that printing requires a pixel density of 300 pixels per inch (ppi) so taking, for example, a standard print dimension of 6 x 4 inch it would require the image sent to your photo lab (or desktop printer with direct sd-card printing facility) for printing to be 1800 x 1200 pixels.

A Sizes	Cm	Inches		
A6 (148 x 105mm)	24 x 30cm	5" x 3.5"	10" x 10"	20" x 16"
A5 (210 x 148mm)	30 x 40cm	5" x 4"	10" x 12"	24" x 18"
A4 (297 x 210mm)	40 x 50cm	6" x 4"	14" x 10"	24" x 20"
A3 (420 x 297mm)	50 x 50cm	5" x 7"	14" x 11"	30" x 20"
A2 (594 x 420mm)	50 x 60cm	10" x 4"	16" x 12"	30" x 24"
A1 (841 x 594mm)	50 x 70cm	9" x 7"	18" x 14"	36" x 24"
A0 (1,189 x 841mm)	60 x 80cm	8" x 8"		30" x 30"
		10" x 8"		48" x 30"
				48" x 36"

If the image is to be printed directly from the memory card, where the image was captured by the camera, then it is essential that the image is captured with sufficient pixels to allow this to happen if you don't want the image to appear pixelated.

With the FZ1000 set to the 4:3 aspect ratio (giving the exact match for a 6 x 4.5 inch print) the available options from the Picture Size menu are as follows when JPEG only is selected:
L 4864 x 3648 (17.5M) pixels allowing up to A3 (14 x 11 inch)
Ex M (9M) 3465 x 2592 pixels allowing up to A4 (10 x 8 inch)
Ex S (4.5M) 2432 x 1824

These image sizes suggested in the camera menu assume a printing density of just 200 ppi which, in my opinion, is insufficient to produce the stated size of prints.

Whilst larger format prints can be printed with lower ppi they require the images to be viewed from greater distances.
So, what size should we select, why not just shoot at the largest image size the camera can produce, in this case the 4864 x 3648 or 17.5 Megapixel size.
If memory card size isn't a restraint, then shooting at the full resolution has the advantage that a degree of post cropping might be useful in achieving a better composition for example.
If you want to achieve the effect of a longer focal length, then you can use one of the Extended Optical Zoom settings.

This is really 'marketing talk' as it isn't optical zoom that is being extended here.
The effective increase in focal length is achieved by cropping into the image formed on the sensor once the x16 optical zoom limit has been reached.

Up to this the image is downscaled to the set pixel dimensions. If the image is cropped more than the set dimensions, then it is scaled up back to these dimensions.

By doing this 'in camera crop' the image size is reduced and therefore more images may be recorded on the memory card.
This down sampling of the image does have some additional advantages.
 It reduces the amount of image noise by about the same factor as the image size reduction and, surprisingly, in my tests the actual sharpness of the resulting JPEG image is higher with the Ex M image than the L image.
You can see in the following images that the EX M image appears to have a higher resolution at the same degree of enlargement.

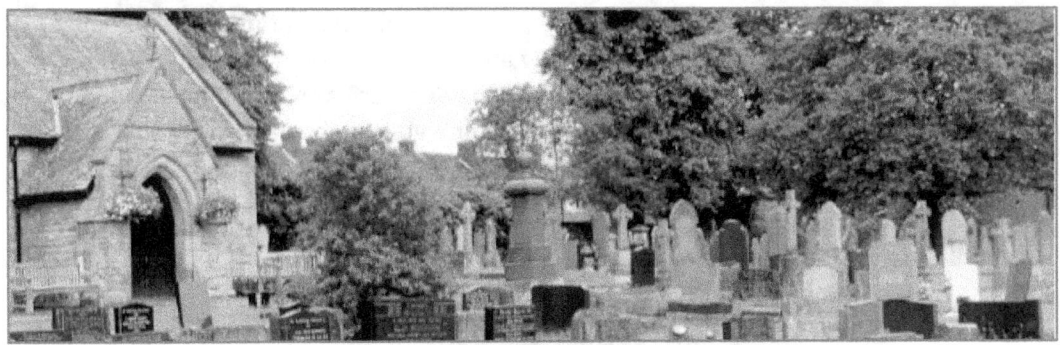

12M image crop from 16:9 aspect ratio

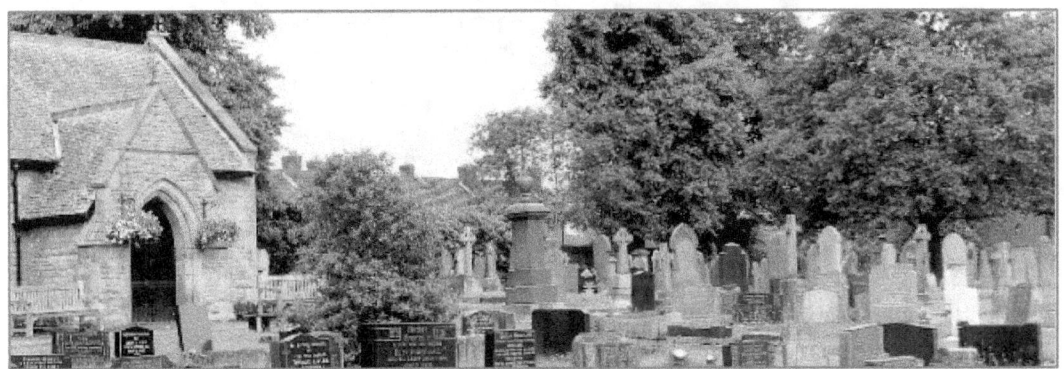

8M EZ image crop from 16:9 aspect ratio

So far we have chosen the aspect ratio and the image size. There is also one more important consideration, the recording image format.

This can be either a "RAW" file format which is just the sensor data.
This data must be "developed" by an image editing application like Silkypix (which is supplied with the camera on CD-rom) or a program like Lightroom or Photoshop from Adobe.
There are other development programs which are compatible with the Panasonic camera RAW format, like RawTherapee (http://rawtherapee.com/downloads) and Zoner photo studio (https://www.zoner.com/en/download-request)
The other, most commonly used format is the JPEG file format. JPEG is one of the world's most popular image formats and is used to provide a 'straight out of camera' (SOOC) image.
This image can then be uploaded to websites, social media platforms or used to produce prints from the images.

The FZ1000 additional supports the simultaneous recording of both a RAW and a JPEG file and with this camera you can now shoot RAW in the iA/iA+ mode!
There are some advantages in using a RAW format.
It has an extended colour depth over the 8 Bit JPEG format. If the RAW image is developed as a TIFF image it can be a 16-bit able to hold much more tonal data. The downside of using TIFF is that for most applications such as printing and web page viewing it must be converted into an 8-bit JPEG image.

RAW format does however have much more processing options during 'development' such as the ability to 'pull' detail from shadow areas.

Multiple JPEG images can be extracted with varying degrees of highlight and shadow detail being developed and then these images combined to give a higher dynamic range image.

The choice of image quality is selected from the REC set up menu.

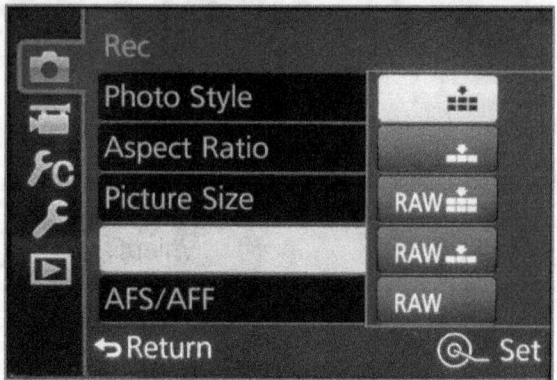

image quality setting

For each of the RAW or JPEG options there are two choices.

The double row of bars or the single row of bars. The double row provides the highest level of image quality.

If the RAW option alone, or a RAW plus JPEG option is selected then some image options may not be available in other menus. These will be those which are only available to JPEG processed images. For instance the i.Zoom, digital zoom, EX zoom and i.Exposure will not be available.

When shooting with the RAW file format the resulting image is quite large (over 20 Megabytes) and can take up to 5 times longer to write the image to the memory of the camera buffer, and the subsequent writing of the file to the SDHC memory card, compared with the JPEG file.

This might not be a consideration, depending upon your shooting requirements. However, in operations like burst mode shooting this will dictate the number of images that can be captured at the stated burst speed before the camera begins to slow down because of the camera buffer to SDHC card writing delay.

If you do want to use the RAW file mode and use the higher burst speeds, then it essential to use a SDHC/SDXC memory card with the fastest write speed such as the U3 rated cards which has a claimed write speed of 96MB/sec.

Sometimes these cards are annotated with a comparative speed to the CDROM drive and in that case, you will need to purchase one showing x633, at least. X1000 cards are also now available however they are quite expensive.

Later you will see that it is possible to shoot in the RAW file format and subsequently process these files "in camera" using the same JPEG processing engine which produces the JPEG image if you were to shoot only in that mode.

RAW format does have the advantage that you can alter the processing options 'after the shot has been taken' thus giving a lot more flexibility than just relying on the one JPEG processing set up that you have.

When you shoot in JPEG mode only the image processing uses several of your set up options in the way that the image is finally produced.

This is a single write operation and as a lot of information is discarded it is important that the camera exposure is as near to perfect out of the camera as possible as subsequent post processing is limited.

If you have elected to shoot in the iA/iA+ mode then a lot of the decision making has been made for you and your manual intervention is limited to the Photo style (but no fine adjustment available), exposure tint, exposure compensation and iHDR if you use the iA+ mode.

The main benefits of shooting in JPEG mode are only realised when you shoot in one of the non-iA modes such as the PASM selections where you gain more control of the options.

These processing parameters allow the camera to process the RAW camera data and apply some standard image processing to each image produced.

The camera also supports in-camera RAW processing (more later in this guide).

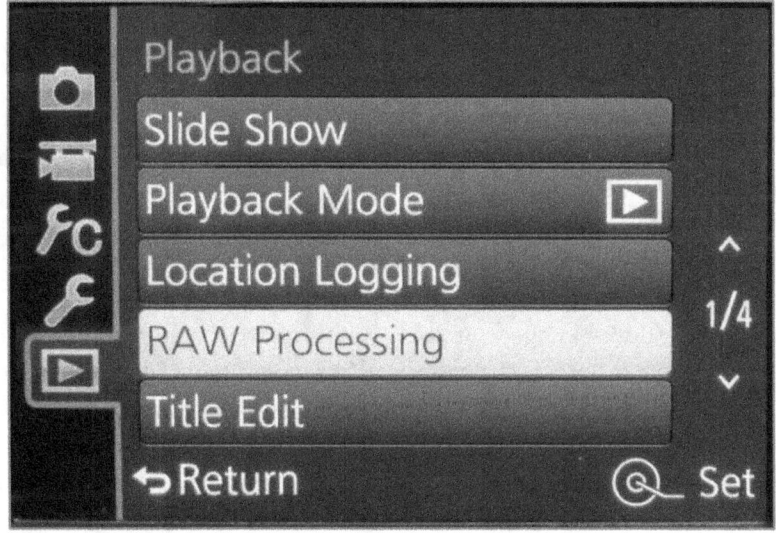

The first main choice to make is in the selection of the **Photo style**.
The Photostyle selection is made from page 1/7 in the REC set up menu screen

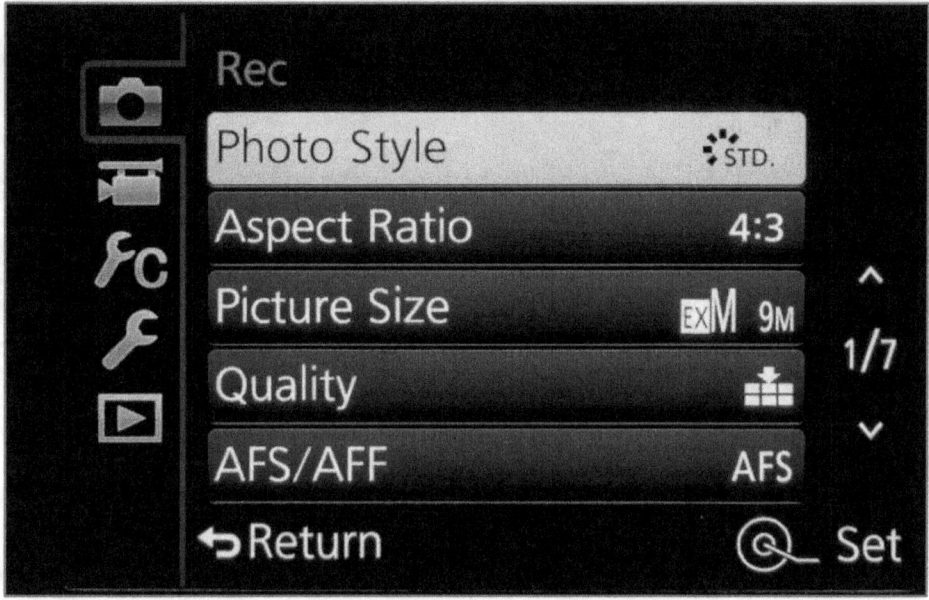

The way in which the Photostyle affects JPEG image quality is tabled below.

Photo Style	Image Effect
Standard	Basic Setting
Vivid	As the basic setting with slightly more image contrast/saturation
Natural	As the basic setting with slightly less contrast
Monochrome	Produces an image with shades of grey (black and white)
Scenery	Produces images with richer saturation in blue and greens
Portrait	Images have slightly reduced sharpness and slightly increased red
Custom	Uses your adjustments made to one of the photo styles

If you are shooting in the iA/iA+ mode, the selection is limited to just Standard and Monochrome with no adjustment available of the individual parameters.

If you are shooting in a semi-automatic mode (PAS) or in manual (M), then you have the option to choose any of the available photo styles, and additionally, adjust the parameters of the one chosen.

Photo styles applied to the same scene:

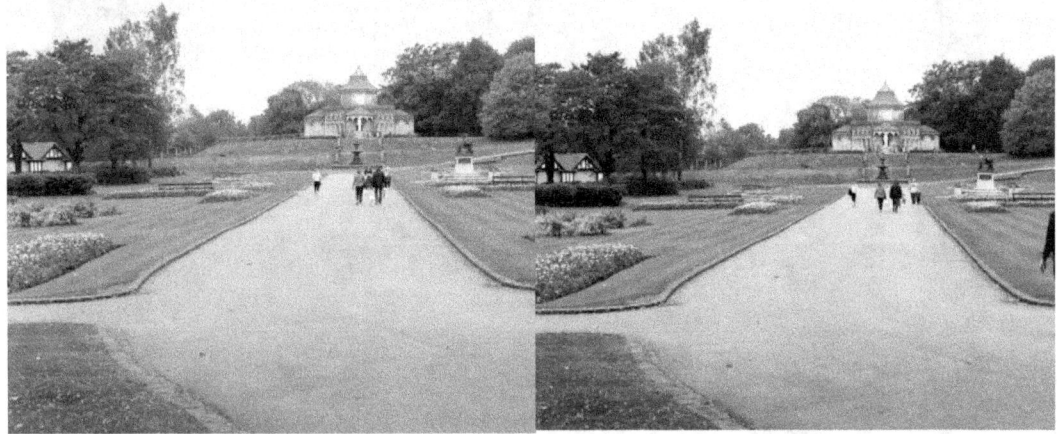

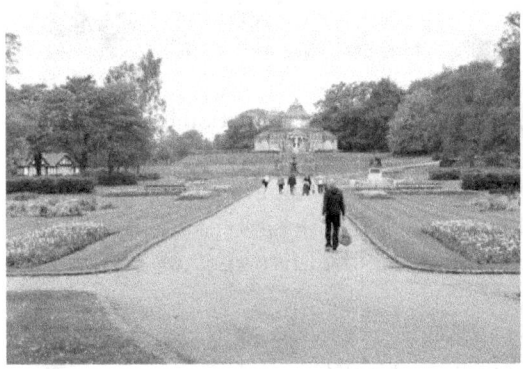

standard

vivid

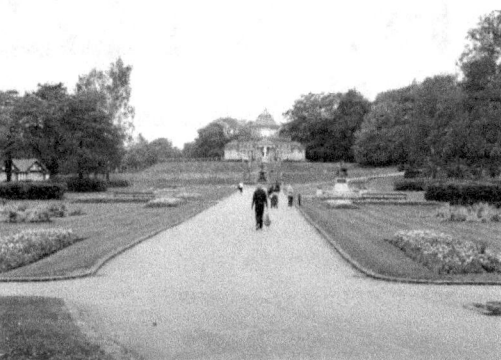

natural

monochrome

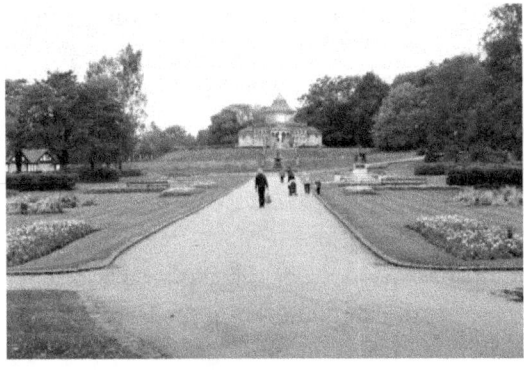

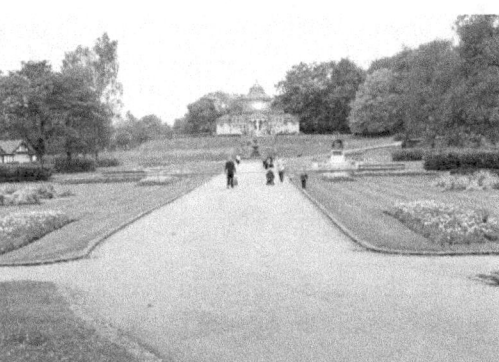

scenery

portrait

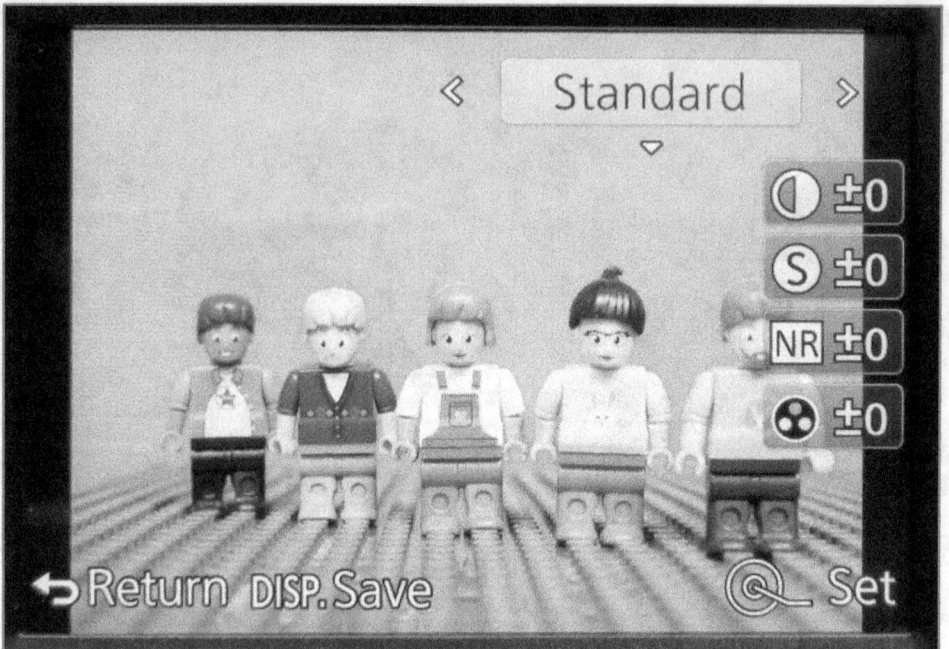

Individual parameter adjustment of Contrast, Sharpening, Noise reduction or Saturation is a personal choice.

If you want to perform your own post processing of the out of camera images it may be advisable to reduce sharpening and noise reduction to -5 in both cases to reduce the amount of JPEG artefacts and loss of fine detail that is found with the default setting (0). The adjustment is +/- 5 units.

They only affect images shot in the JPEG only modes not RAW.

There are some benefits in making a "Custom" set up and saving this as your own photo style for your commonly used picture taking situations. You may want, for instance, to have less noise reduction set up in the photo style.

This which will increase the amount of fine detail that may, under some circumstances, be reduced by the standard default level applied by the photo style that you may have selected.

You can then apply some noise reduction in your final image processing software so that you can see the amount of detail removed versus the noise remaining in the image.

If the day is very bright and strong shadows are being cast by the sun it might be worth reducing the contrast to -5 setting to preserve some of the highlights from "blowing out." Again, in post processing you can adjust the contrast back to your individual need for that image taking note of the image detail in the shadow areas, for example.

You may arrive at a photo style adjustment which suits your photographic need. For example, if you want to use the camera images without any additional post processing you may find that increasing the sharpness parameter to +2 and reducing the noise reduction to -3 may produce crisper looking images by enhancing fine details.
You can make these adjustments in any of the photo styles and then save them as the Custom photo style so it is available for selection just as if it was a regular choice of photo style.

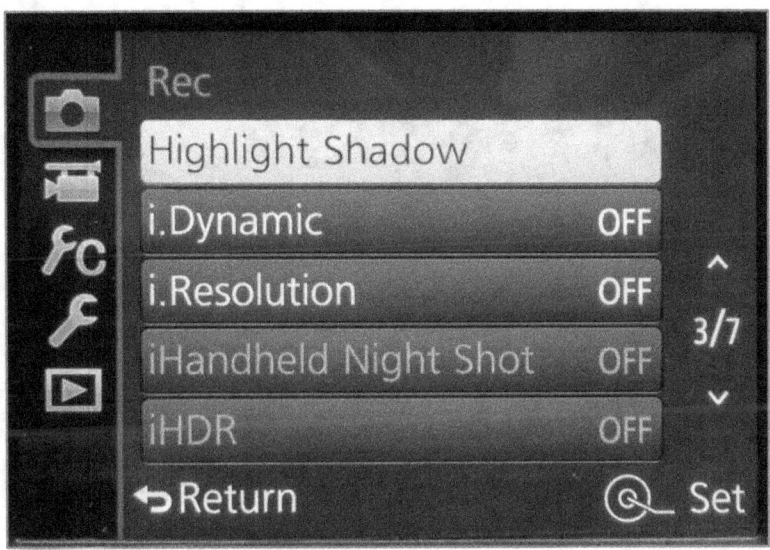

If the contrast adjustment within the photo style doesn't have the right effect, then there is another adjustment in the REC set up menu Highlight/Shadow which allows you adjust the upper (highlight) or lower (shadow) portion of the contrast curve.

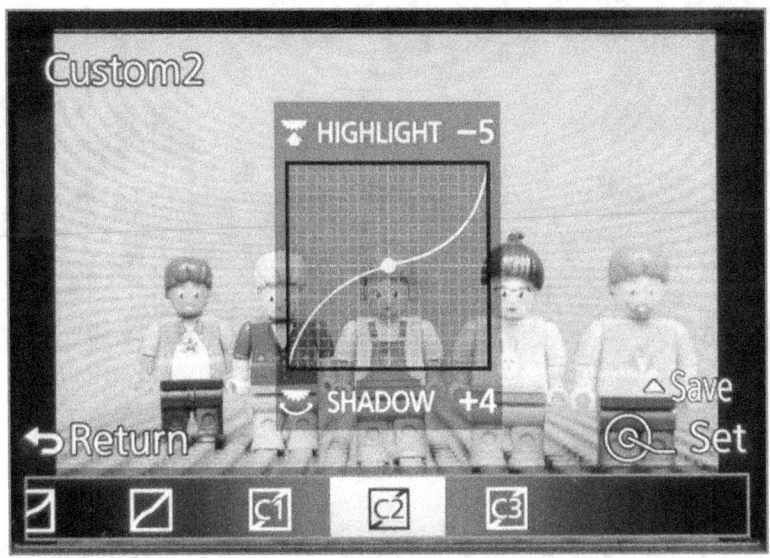

increasing the contrast

With the side and the top wheels the curves can be boosted or suppressed to add or reduce contrast to either area.

Additionally, these adjustments can be saved as one of three presets by using the up (ISO) button of the 4-way controller. If any of the preset curves are adjusted they will be restored to the camera defaults when the camera is turned off.

The adjustments are available in the PASM modes and can be used in the creative video mode to alter the contrast of any recorded video clips.

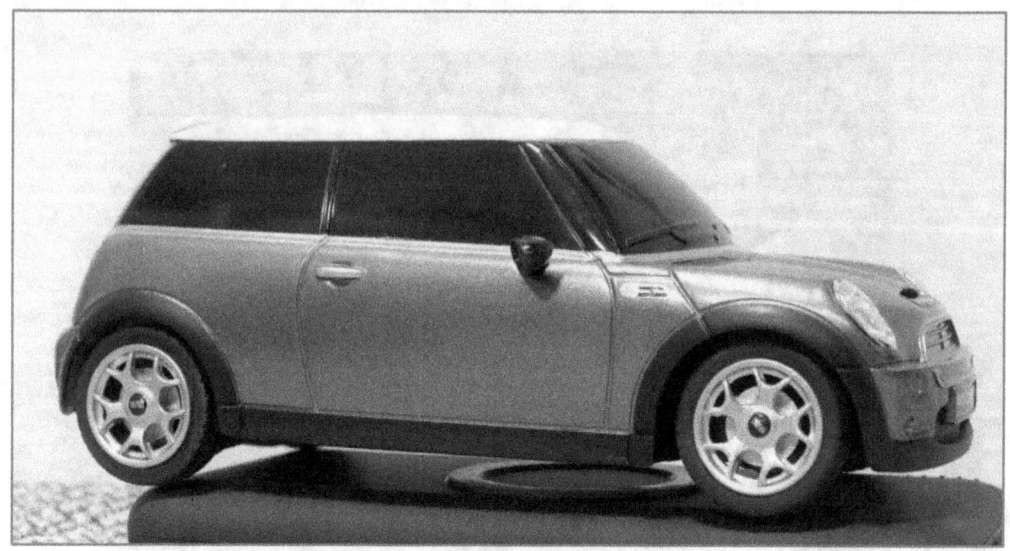

normal image

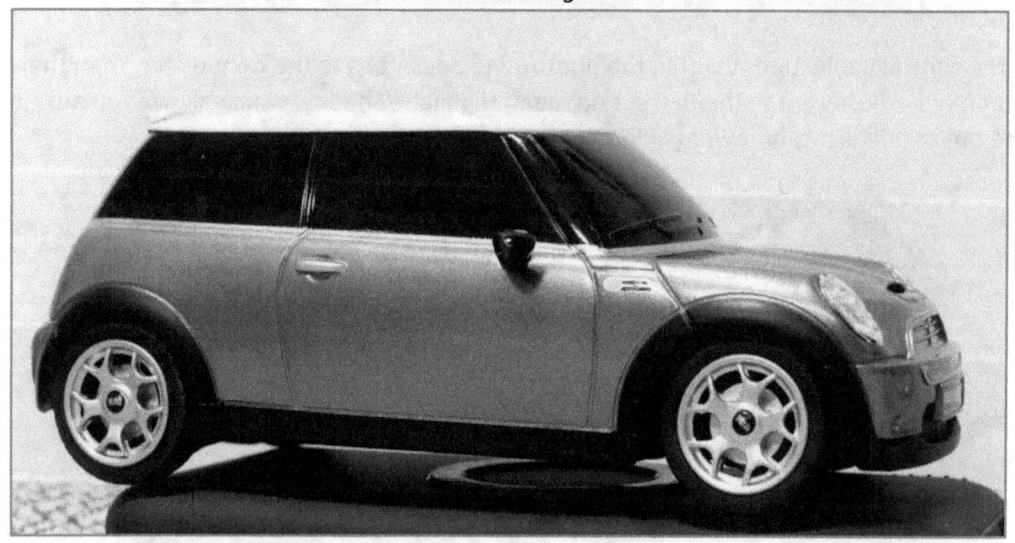

image with highlight -3 and shadow +3 (increased contrast)

White Balance

White balance is a method used by the camera to ensure that the recorded image matches closely to the one we perceive when taking that image. Our eyes can very quickly establish colours in a variety of different lighting types.

For instance, if we take an object into sunlight, then into shade and then into artificial light our eyes can adjust to these different "colour temperatures" and the object looks, to a very large degree, the same in each lighting situation.

The digital camera sensor does not have a way to do this. It has a response to light which is fixed. Within the cameras processing software there is a program called "auto white balance" (AWB) which corrects for different colour temperatures of the lighting in a recorded scene.

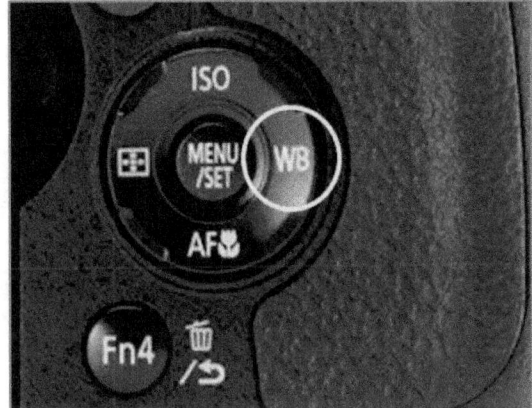

Selection of the white balance is made by depressing the WB control button on the four- way pad.

My understanding of how this process works is based upon my work in the colour photographic printing industry and may not be absolutely accurate for digital colour science however it serves to give some understanding of how it works, and more importantly why sometimes AWB gives the wrong colours (or a colour bias) when we shoot in the JPEG mode with the camera.

The camera software will look for the brightest areas of the image, normally the highlights, and then assume that these should be the white areas of the image.
It will then take the values of the Red, Green and Blue components of this pixel area and then adjust the gain of the two lower value channels to match the highest value.

At this point the measured area plus all the other pixels in the image have been adjusted by the same amount and thus will have, in theory, removed any colour cast created by the light source having different energy levels in the RGB values.

The camera can do this with a continuous range of adjustment values and so the resulting image should be very close to a "neutral" white balance point.

If the light source is of a mixed nature, for example there is a mixture of both daylight and artificial light in the image the camera may determine the white balance operating point from the brightest area which may not be the area of interest in your final image.

In these situations, it is often more useful to either use one of the camera preset white balance operating points or use the manual Kelvin temperature adjustment scale found in the white balance control.

The FZ1000 has 4 custom presets which you can record your own white balance operating point in the procedure detailed later.

Auto white balance may not provide the correct operating point if the scene is either too bright or too dark or there is a predominance of one colour in the image.

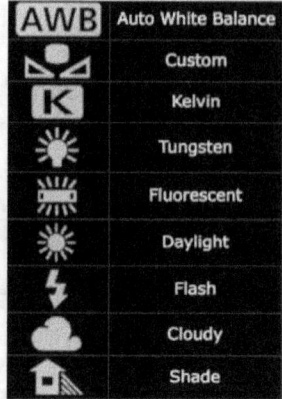

The preset values available within the camera white balance control.

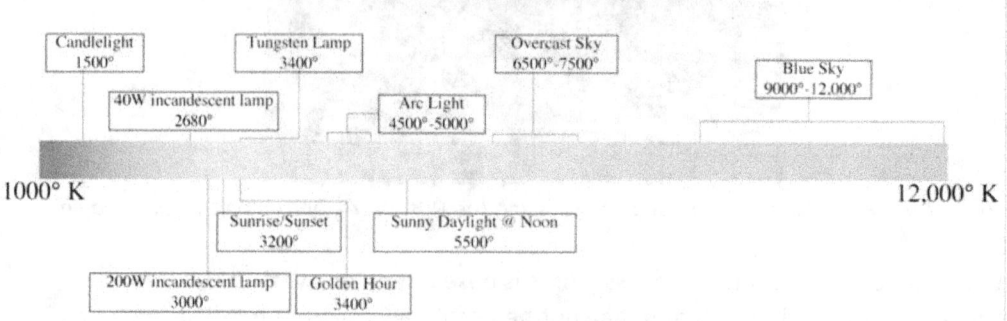

The colour temperature scale with typical light sources indicated

The default camera choice is to set the camera to use Auto White Balance (AWB) and in most situations, will give neutral colour tone to your "out of camera" JPEG images.

If there is a mixture of light sources in your intended image source, then it may be advisable to select the white balance preset which is appropriate for the most predominant light source in that image.

Indoors that might be tungsten lighting if there is weaker daylight coming through a window, for example.

Setting White Balance

To calibrate the camera to the correct white operating point to shoot your images or video we either need to choose one of the camera preset white balances or preferably carry out a manual white balance set procedure.

Selection of the white balance is made by depressing the WB control button on the four-way pad. The default camera choice is to set the camera to use Auto White Balance (AWB) and in most situations, will give neutral colour tone to your "out of camera" JPEG images.

If there is a mixture of light sources in your intended image source, then it may be advisable to select the white balance preset which is appropriate for the most predominant light source in that image.

Indoors that might be tungsten lighting if there is weaker daylight coming through a window, for example.

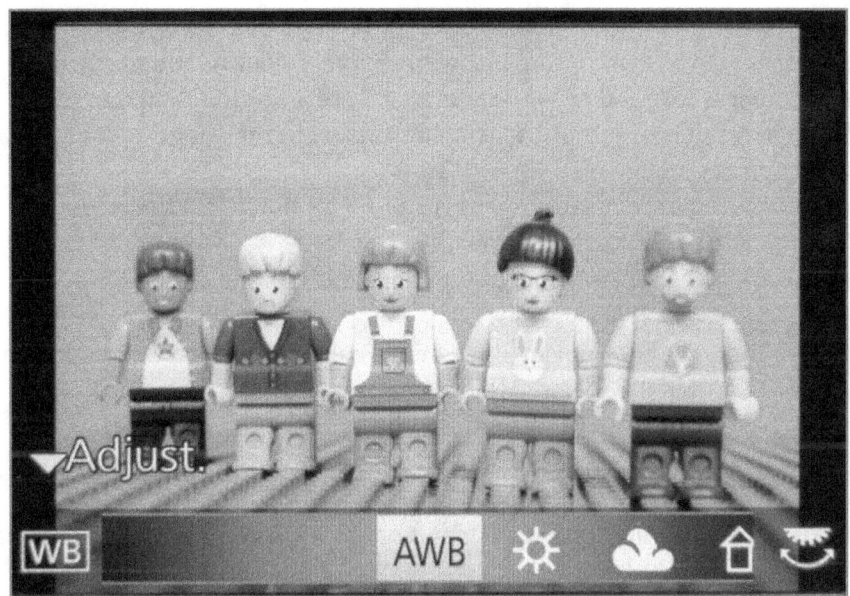

The white balance preset selection screen, here Auto is selected

To select this preset value again use the WB button to access the list of presets and then use the cursor buttons (left and right) to select the required preset control from this on-screen list, pressing menu/set to exit this procedure.
If you want consistent colour in images shot in the same lighting conditions, then the selection of the most appropriate preset can help here.

For example, outdoors in full sunshine where your subject is under clear sky with large areas of blue sky and white clouds then selecting the "sun" symbol preset will keep the camera white balance consistent at 5600K, the normal daylight setting.

If you find that you are shooting in an overcast, cloudy sky then if you were to select the "cloud" symbol then the camera will raise the colour temperature to 7000K and the result will be warmer" looking images than these shot with the "sun" symbol which will look much cooler in this light.

If the subject is in shade with the main light being sunlight, then if you select the "shade" symbol it will again raise the colour temperature to offset any blueness often recorded in these scenes.
The tungsten preset white balance is for use under tungsten filament lights at about 2700K (normal domestic household lamps).

The electronic flash symbol will set an operating point suited to this type of illumination and reduces the slight blueness often generated by xenon flash.

Auto white balance can correct for scenes illuminated from this 2700K preset to cloudy sky setting at around 7000K.

You can use the presets creatively.

Selecting a preset with a temperature below the actual colour temperature will result in a scene with a coolness to it and conversely setting a preset higher than the actual temperature will result is a warming tone being applied to the image.

As well as the white balance presets, there is also the option to set the colour temperature using the Kelvin colour temperature slider.
If the actual degree Kelvin is known, it can be selected from the sliding scale.

Again, a picture becomes cool looking if the actual colour temperature is higher than the one selected or reddish if it is lower than the one selected.

There is provision with each of the preset controls to adjust the operating point if you wish to bias the colour in one direction.
This can be used to set an accurate white point or use it to create a special colour bias.

There are four manual white balance presets in the FZ1000 menu which can be used to store four lighting set ups in terms of their colour temperature.

They are set individually by using the WB control, pointing the target at either a white piece of paper or grey card such that it completely fills the target area and then pressing the shutter button.

This will record and set this operating point.

Examples of the White Balance Presets on One Scene.

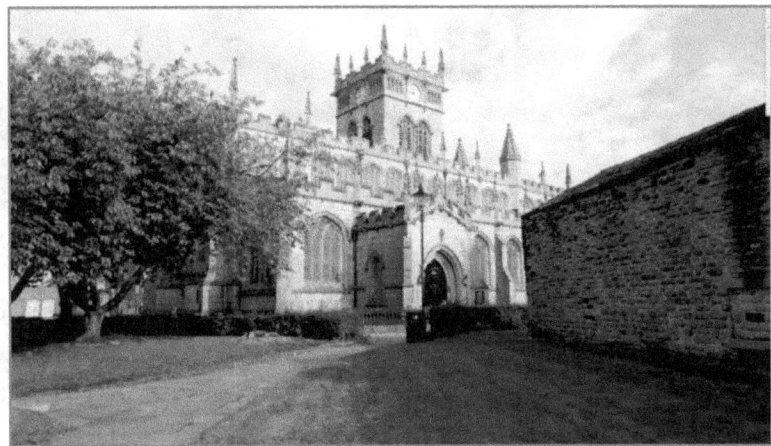

Auto White Balance

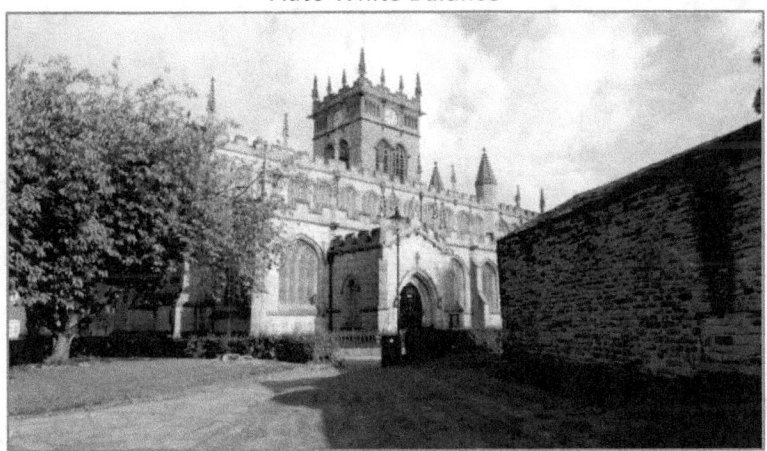

Sunny Preset

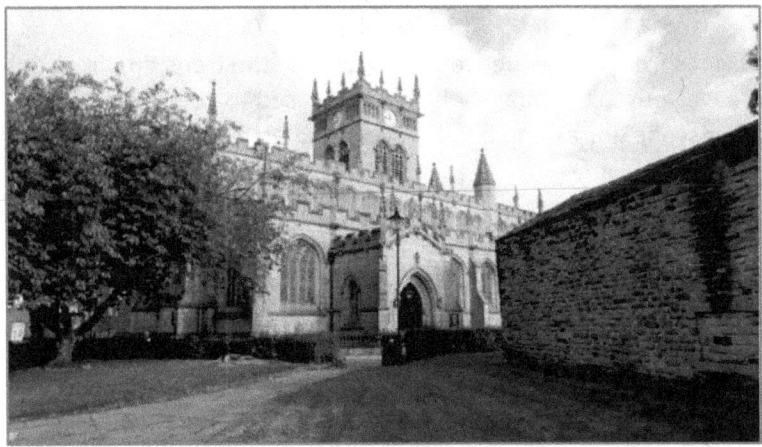

Cloudy Preset

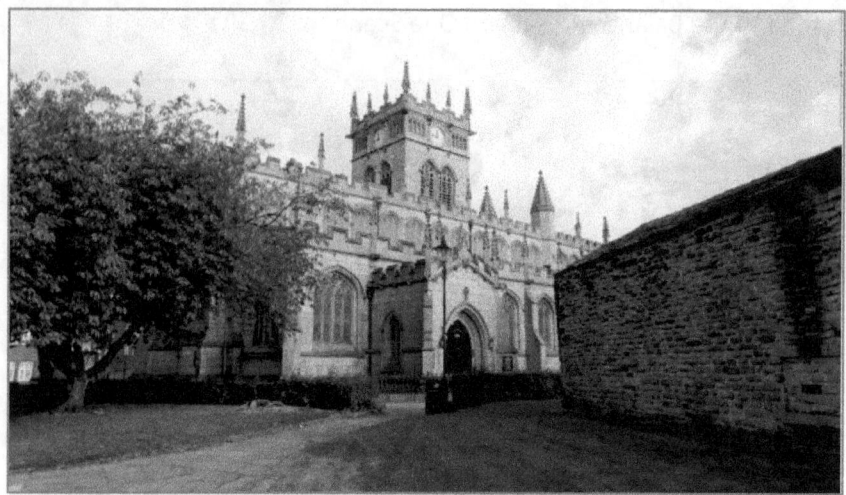

Shade Preset

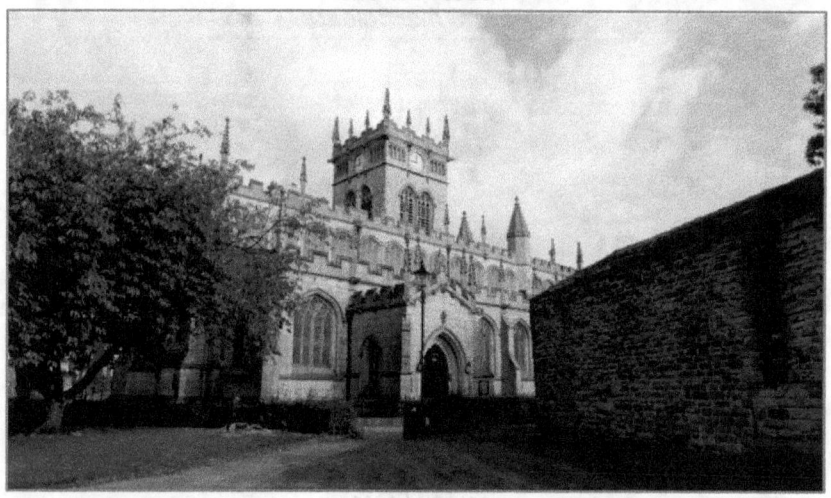

Using the Tungsten Preset in Daylight

It should be obvious from the sequence of images that the transition from Sunny through to shade adds a warmth to the image which can be used to your advantage if you want to warm up a colder scene, for example if it is raining selecting shade will warm the scene up.

Performing a Custom (Manual White Balance)

Manual white balance set procedure allows the camera to set the correct white operating point given a white (or neutral grey) target as the reference.

To set a manual white balance operating point we can choose any one of the four custom white balance presets by depressing the WB button on the 4-way controller.

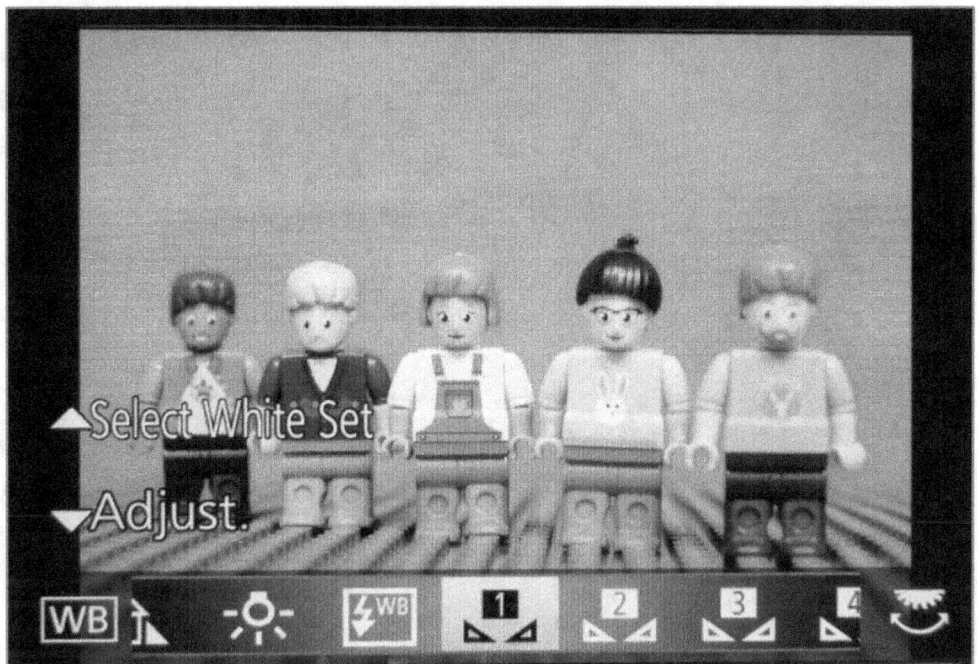

select one of the 4 custom settings and press Select White Set

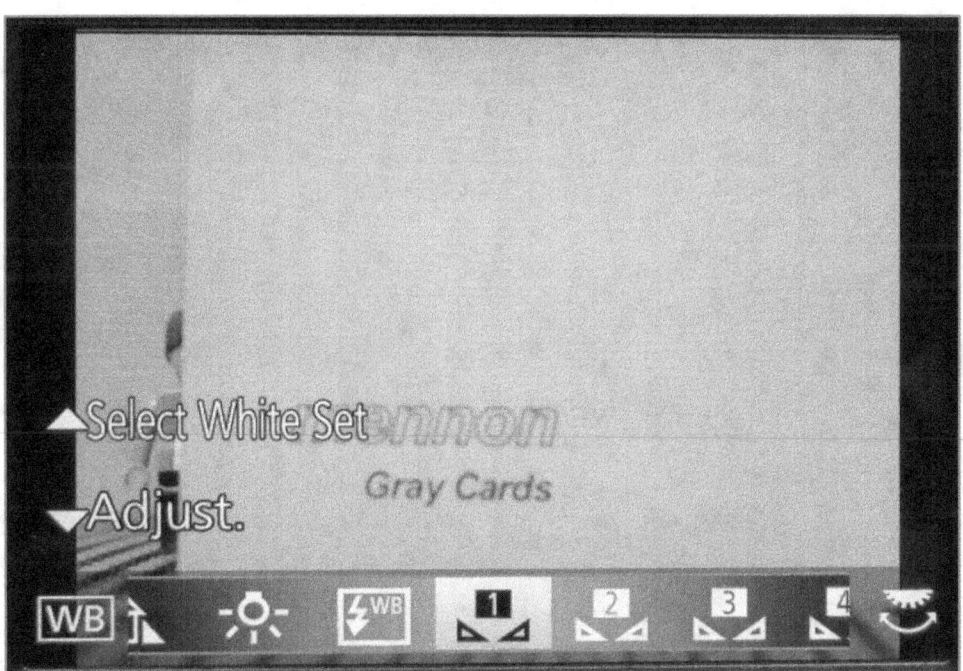

place white or neutral grey card in frame and press Select white set

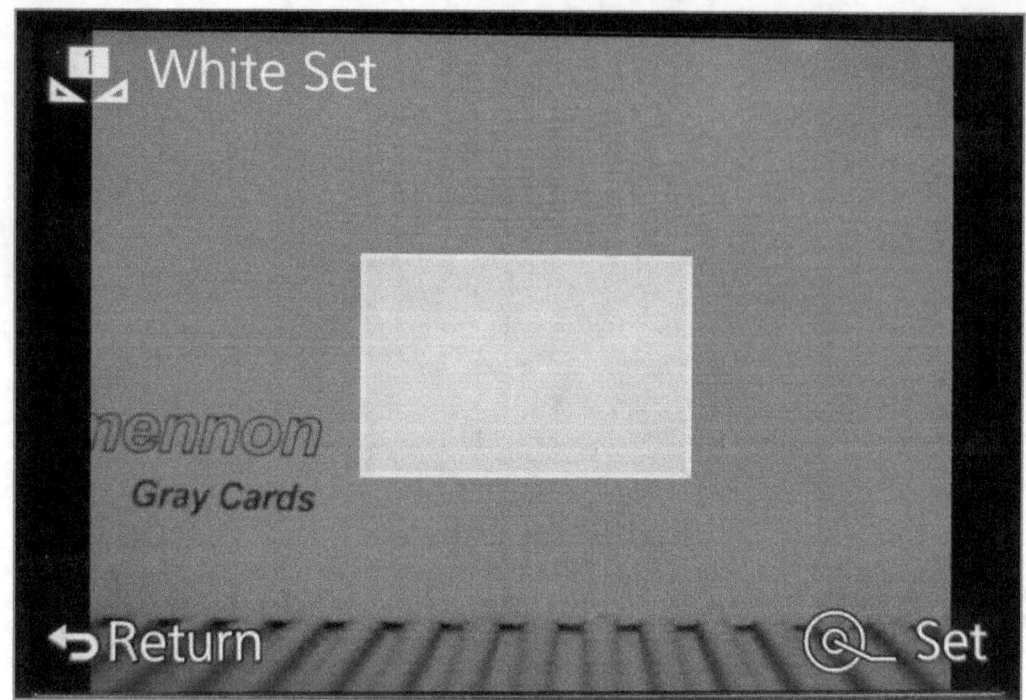

ensure target is covered and press Set

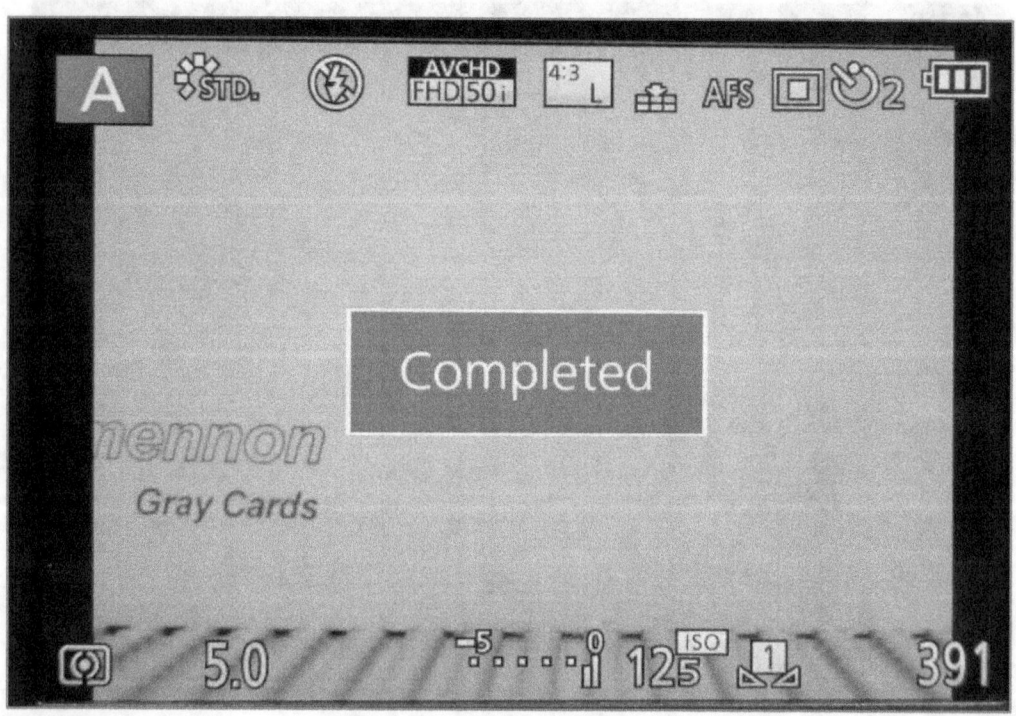

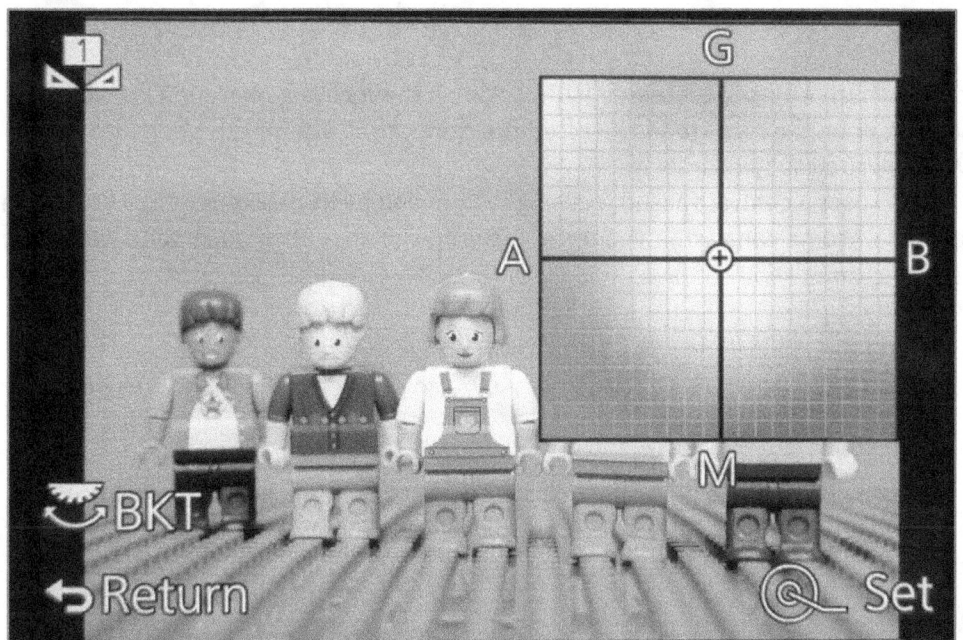

fine tuning the operating point

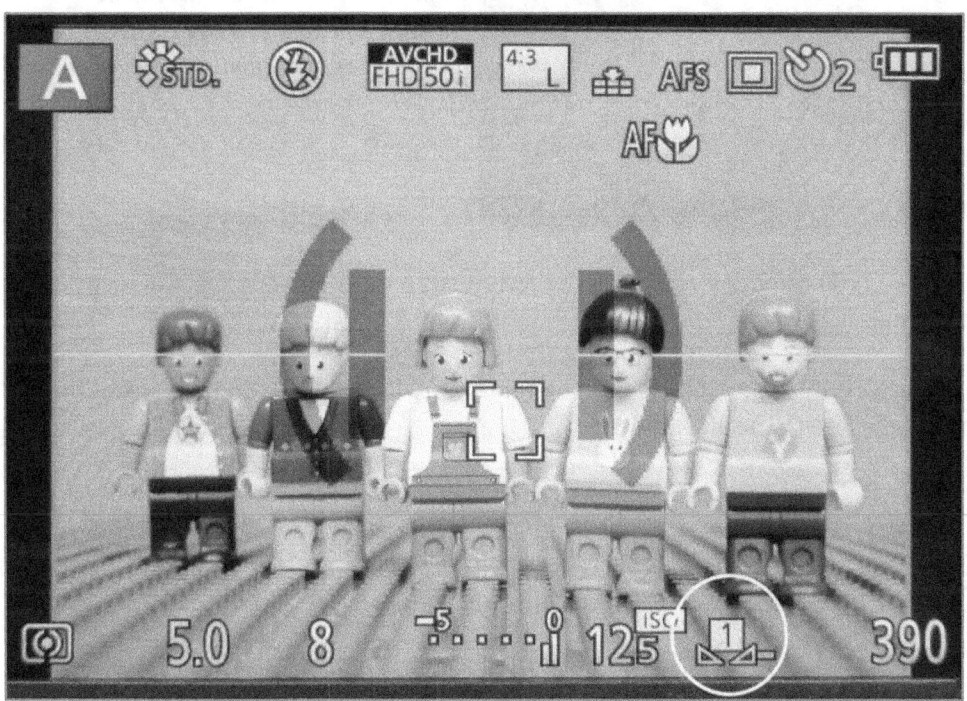

once the process ends you will see Completed on the LCD

Auto Focus Modes

When the shutter button is pressed halfway down the focusing operation is invoked. Depending upon the focus mode selected the camera will attempt to bring into sharp focus the desired subject area.

The FZ1000 uses a contrast based focusing system and by its nature requires the image to have areas of some contrast. If you try to focus on a plain area of equal tone without any texture the camera will not be able to "lock focus."

It's essential then to include some visual contrast for the camera to "see" and focus on. Especially so in low light where the camera will also struggle to find the focus point.

For this reason, the camera does have a built-in orange led light (the focus assist light), which can be disabled (it's on by default) if you don't want the light to be illuminating whenever the light level is low, which provides enough illumination to assist the camera to focus.

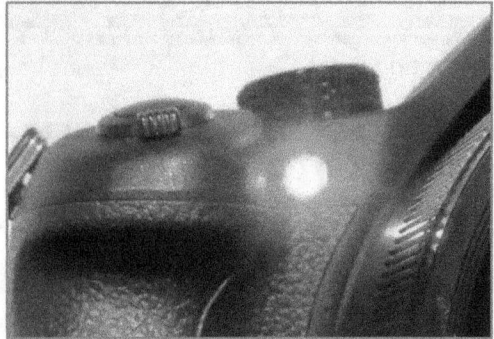

The Focus assist LED illuminating when the light entering the lens would be insufficient to allow the contrast based focus system to operate effectively.

With the FZ1000 camera there are three autofocus modes and one manual focus mode that can be selected.

These modes are initially selected by the rear rotary lever switch on the back of the camera, adjacent to the viewfinder.

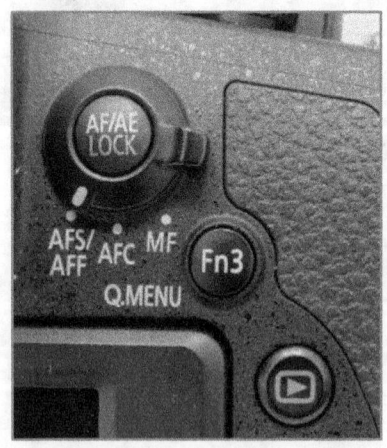

The rotary Focus Mode Selector Switch This allows the user to select between the:

Single Shot / Flexible Auto Focus (AFS/AFF)
Continuous Autofocus (AFC)

Manual Focus (MF)

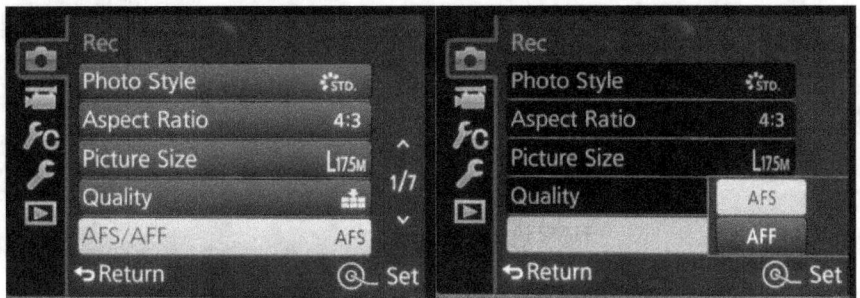

AFS/AFF initial selection   *AFS or AFF selection*

The initial choice is made via the rotary switch however the option to select either the AFS or the AFF mode is made in the REC set up menu (page 1/7)

AFS is an abbreviation for Auto Focus Single and focus is acquired, and set, once the shutter button is pressed to the half-way point in its travel distance.
If the camera can focus at the distance that the subject is from the camera there will be an accompanying "beep" and solid green indicator and the focus target area shown on the LCD screen will also be green.

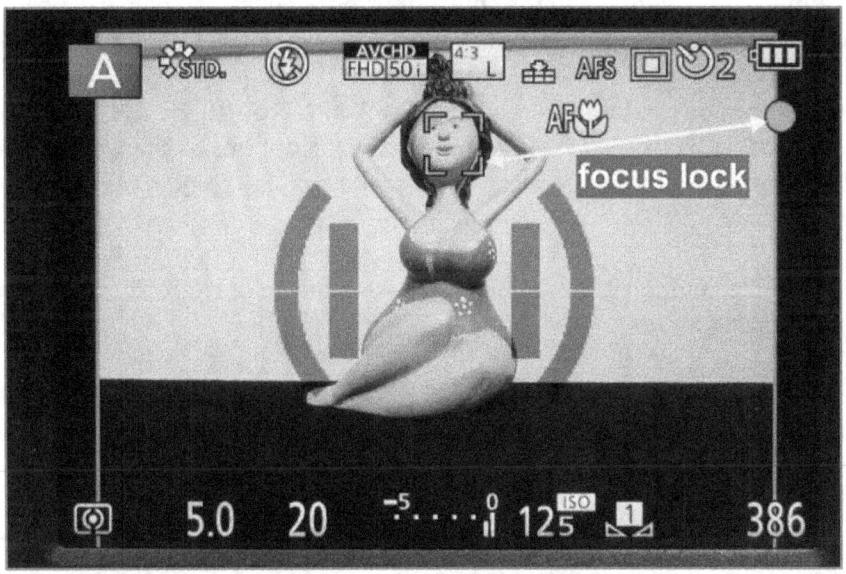

The green indicator and audible beep confirm focus lock

If the subject is too close, (or too far away if you are using close-up lenses attached to the camera) the camera will not focus and there will be four rapid beeps from the camera, the green indicator dot will be flashing on the LCD screen and the allowable focus distance will be displayed in red text on the LCD screen and the focus target area marker will also be in red.

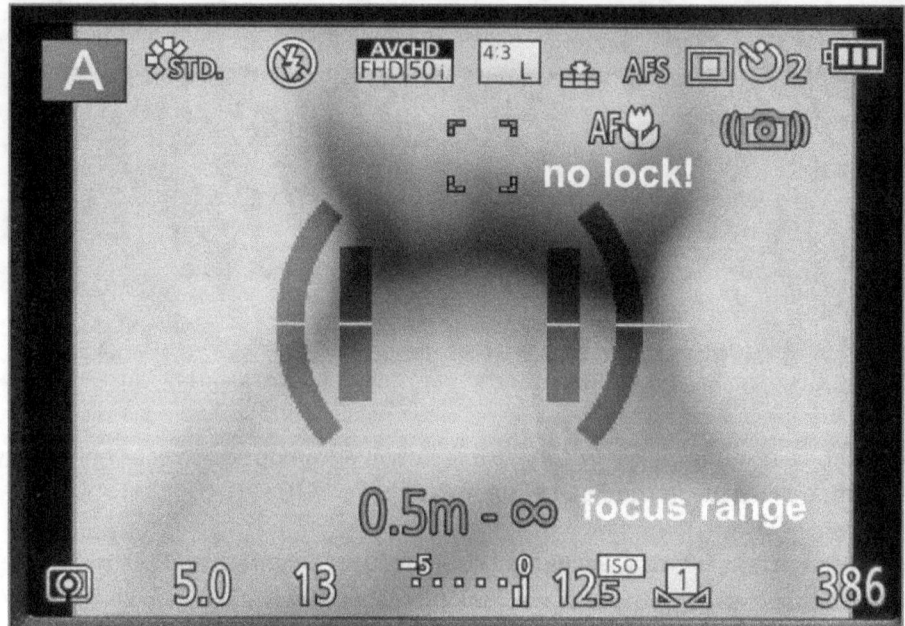

focus lock has not been achieved

AFF is an abbreviation for Auto Focus Flexible and has been designed to allow the camera to follow subject movement when the shutter button is depressed half way down.
In contrast to AFS where focus is locked at the half way point AFF continues to follow the movement of the subject.
This movement can be random in direction which contrasts with the **AFC** (Auto Focus Continuous) mode which uses movement prediction algorithms to change the focus point. AFC mode performs the focus operation again at the halfway point in the shutter button travel.

It is ideally suited to motion which is moving consistently in one direction such as trains, aircraft and sporting events.

It appears to work best when the direction of travel is parallel to the camera and less able to re-focus quickly when the subject is moving in a diagonal fashion either towards or away from the camera.

Birds in flight is an area where gaining and keeping focus lock is extremely difficult and burst mode shooting with a lot of image rejections are to be anticipated is the most popular method used here. Lighting is important.

If the camera "can't see", it can't find differences in the scene and will just hunt for the focus point. If the subject you are trying to focus on is of less contrast than the background or other nearby objects, it may choose to leave your subject out of focus.

In terms of the AF areas, there are six options:
Face and Eye detection, Focus Tracking, 49 Area, Custom Multi, Single Area and Pinpoint.

Face and Eye detection look for a human face and if one's spotted, it focuses on the closest eye, and if not, reverts to a single AF area. Up to 15 faces can be recognised. Tracking lets you place crosshairs over a subject, which is then confirmed with a half press of the shutter release. After this the crosshairs follow it quite effectively as you recompose, or as it moves across the frame.

The 49 Area mode lets the camera choose from a 7x7 array spread across most of the frame. Custom Multi mode allows you to select a subset of the 49 areas arranged in a diamond configuration, a single row or column, or a user defined pattern.

In the Single Area Mode, this lets you position a single AF area anywhere on the frame, even right up to the edge.
It also lets you choose from eight different sizes.

The Pinpoint Mode allows you to position a tiny AF point accompanied by a magnified view for confirmation.
In either mode, you can reposition the AF area using the navigation keys.

Out of the box, or after a factory reset the left-hand cursor button is used to allow access to the choice of AF mode.

Face detection will look for any faces and if one or more are detected will attempt to switch to eye detection on the nearest face.
If a face which has be previously "registered" is detected in a group of faces, then this face will receive a higher focus priority.

You may find the 49 Area mode sets focus on areas that you may not want to be the principal focus and it is then best to select either the Custom/multi-mode or more preferably the single (1-area) mode.

Here you can set the size and positon of the focus target area.
There is the option in the Custom (spanner+C) menu to set Direct Area Focus to ON.

With this option set the navigation buttons now allow the positioning of the focus target area. However, you then lose the ability to set ISO, white balance, AF mode and Self timer.

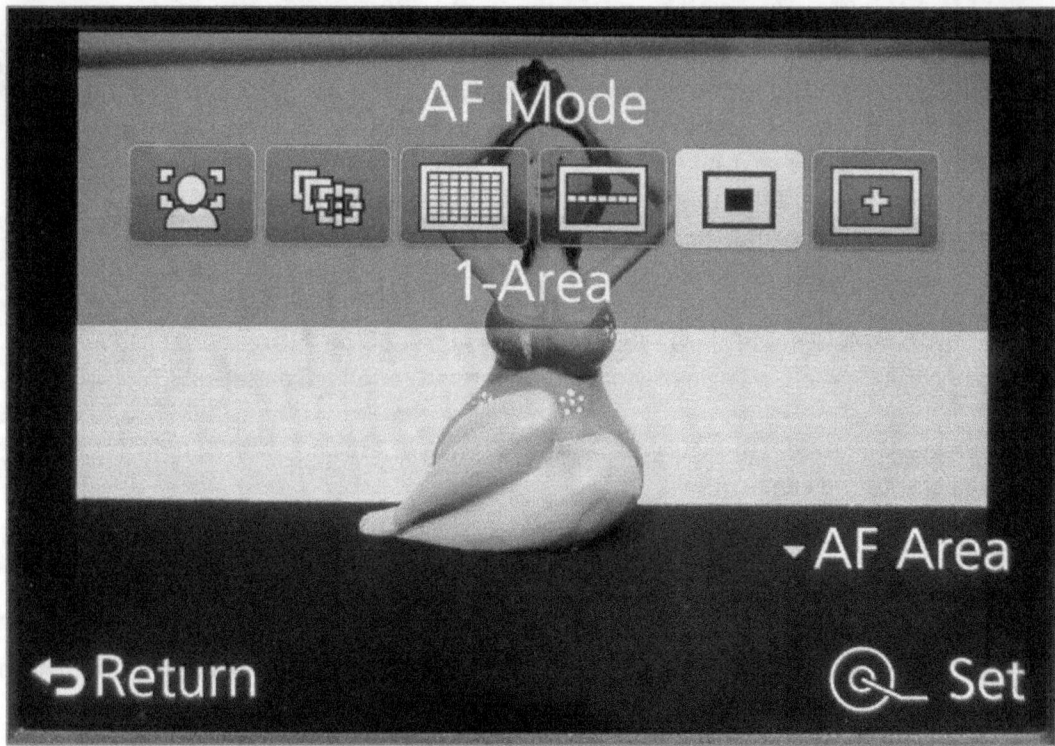

The six AF modes

The FZ1000's AF system now works reliably in lower light levels right down to -3EV and it also supports Panasonic's new Depth by Defocus technology to deliver a quicker response and better continuous AF.

Ordinarily, contrast detect AF systems in models like the FZ1000 adjust the focus to try and achieve higher contrast in edge detail.

But it's difficult to determine which way to go - is the current focus position in front of or behind the subject?

The latest DFD (depth from de-focus) technology uses the out of focus lens profile to assist in providing direction however it is far from perfect at the current implementation and sometimes you may find that the camera will confirm focus with a steady green icon on the screen and the focus target is green however the actual image is way out of focus.

You may find that even attempting to re-focus will result in a similar situation. The only workaround that I have found to work in this situation is to force the camera to re-focus on an entirely different position and then go back and attempt the shot again!

Contrast detect AF systems also find it difficult to know when the optimum focus point is reached, so they often go past the best focus position before returning to it.

Depth by defocus profiles the out-of-focus characteristics of the lens to help overcome these problems, resulting in faster more confident focussing.

Why would you want to use manual focus when we know that this camera has a super-fast and mostly accurate automatic focussing system?

Well there may be situations when it is not possible for the AF system to acquire focus. Low light levels and subjects beyond the range of the focus assist led will make it difficult for the AF to lock on.

Subjects behind glass or are small compared to the background will also confuse the AF system, for instance, a thin blade of grass standing in a wider landscape.

The camera will most likely focus on the background totally ignoring your intended focus point. It is under these situations that the manual focus system can come to your aid.

Manual focusing is selected with a three-position switch on the rear panel to the right of the viewfinder which is also used to choose between continuous and single or flexible AF. The focus is then adjusted using the large ring on the lens barrel when the Zoom/Focus slide switch set to Focus.

For manual focus the FZ1000 offers the usual array of focusing assistance methods including a distance scale, MF assist (which you can choose to display as a picture-in-picture inset or full-screen), magnification and peaking.

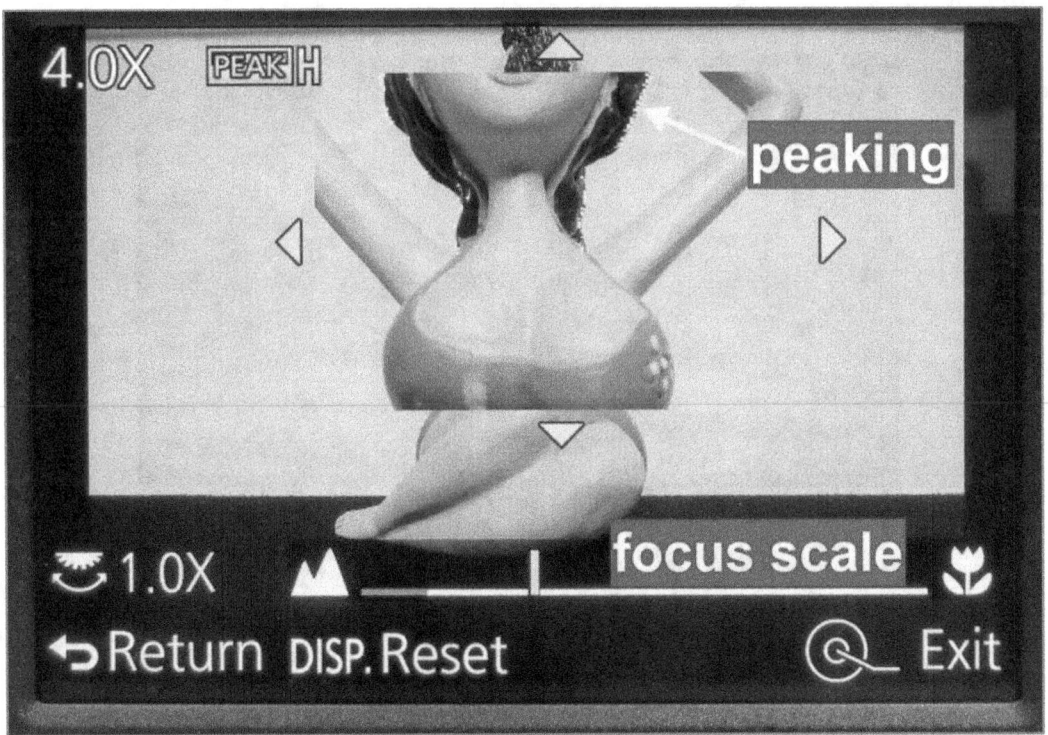

The manual focus options, back control wheel adjusts magnification of PIP

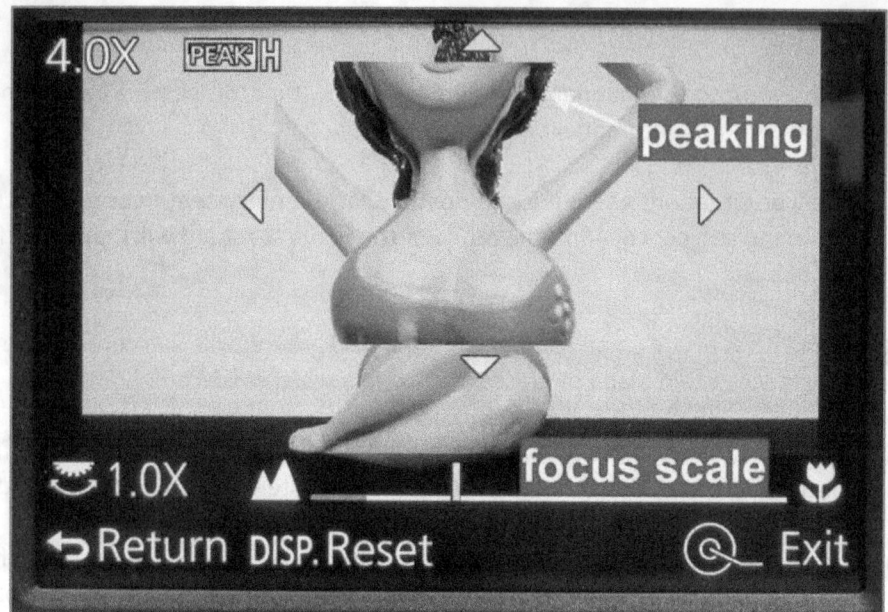

The focus ring on the lens barrel is used to adjust focus

The Manual Focus Assist screen (set from page 3/8 in custom set up) allows you to set whether you have picture in picture or whole screen view and pop up when you move the focus ring or move the 4-way navigation buttons (L/R), you can also invoke Focus peaking from the same menu page.

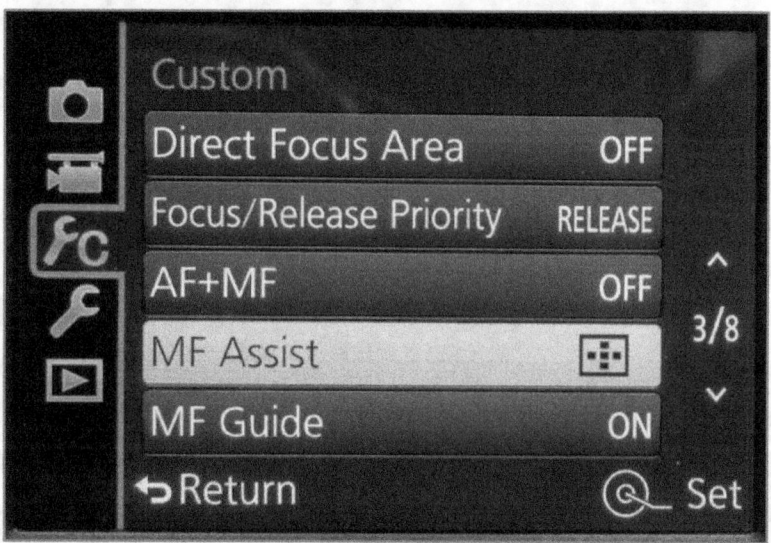

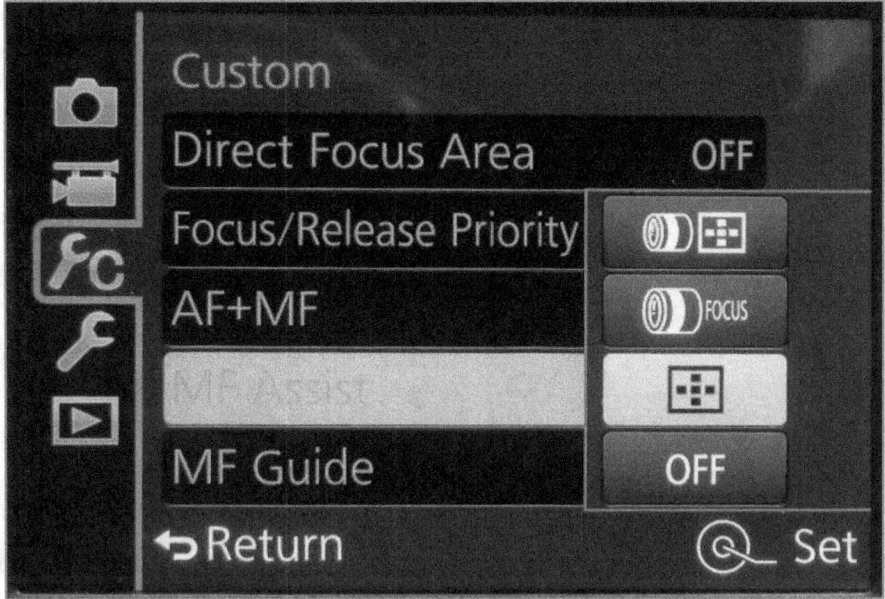

MF assist either pops up on rotation of the lens ring or the 4-way pad

As well as the Manual Focus Assist screen (set from page 3/8 in custom set up) which allows you to set whether you have picture in picture or whole screen view, you can also invoke Focus peaking from the same menu page.

Focus peaking highlights the edges of an image when the camera determines that this is sufficiently in focus.
Its sensitivity can be set from Low to High and the colour of the detected edges chosen from one of four colour choices in case there is a conflict with the subject and highlight colours.

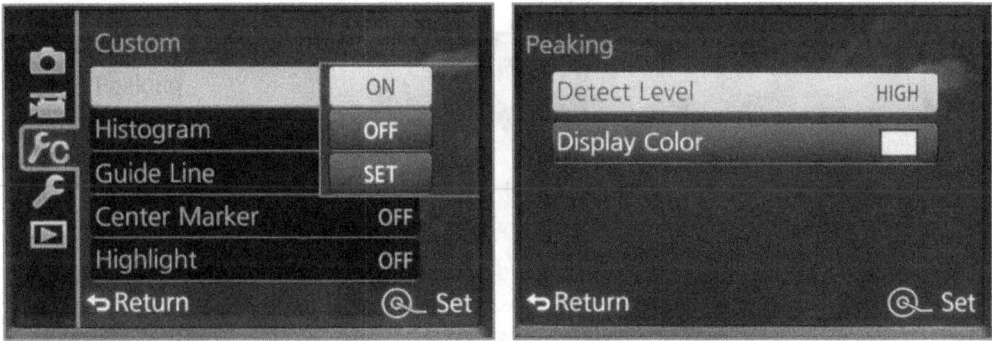

Focus Peaking. Using the SET operation to select sensitivity and highlight colour

Back Button Focus

By default, the half way point in the shutter button travel causes the autofocus operation. This can be turned off by the Shutter AF on/off option.

Also, the shutter can be fired on the half way point rather than full travel by setting Half Press Release to On.

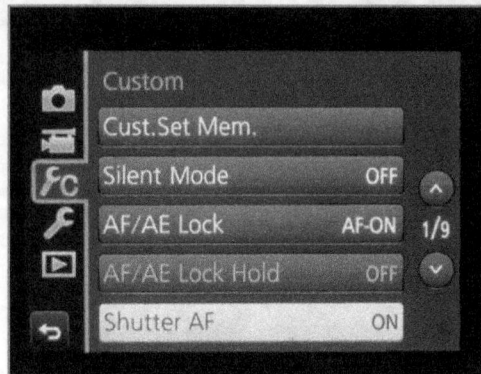 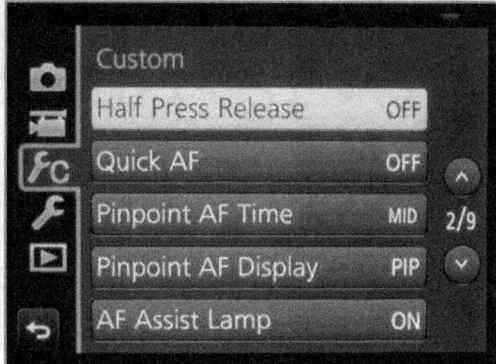

This is best used in conjunction with the AF/AE lock button on the back of the camera. This button can be programmed as AF Lock, AE Lock or AF + AE Lock.

If you set it to AF Lock or AF+AE Lock, then turn Shutter AF to Off. When the back button is depressed the camera will lock focus and stay locked at this point until you release it by depressing the button once again.

If you set the functionality of the button to be AF-ON then this emulates the DSLR "Back Button Focus" method.

With Shutter AF set to OFF you can set focus using the AF/AE Lock button and then re-compose your scene and capture the image without the camera re-focussing when you press the shutter release button.

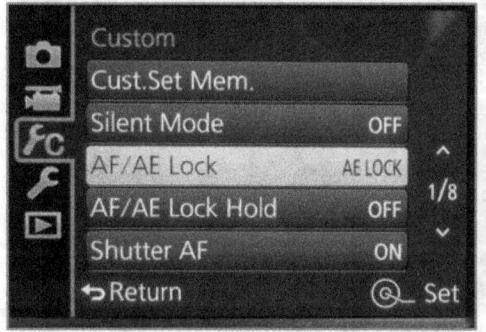 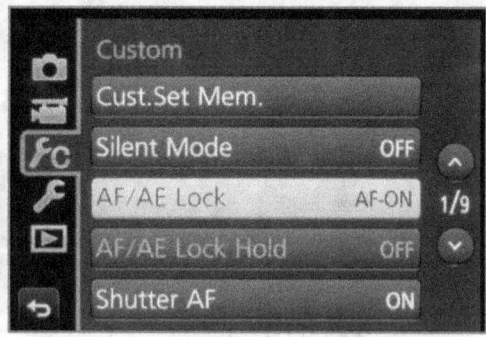

This back-button focus method can save time when you are wanting to capture quickly moving subjects where the focus distance remains the same (or within the camera hyper focal distance) as it doesn't have to wait for the focus to be acquired before the shutter is released.

There is a mode that is designed to speed up the focus acquisition when the camera is being held at the normal shooting position.

This is the Quick AF option and causes the camera to begin focussing even though the shutter button has not been depressed to the half way position.
The downside of this mode is unfortunately increased battery consumption.

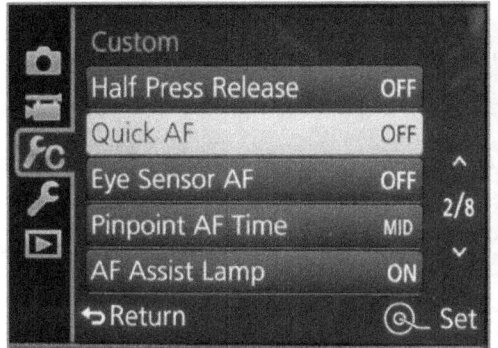 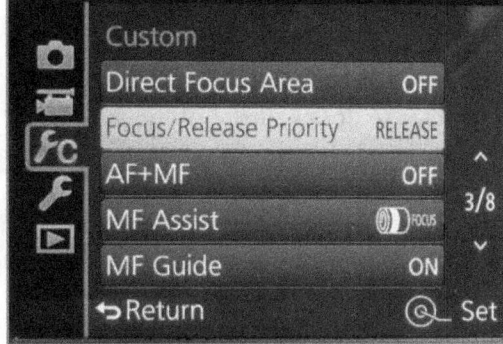

When the Focus/Release Priority is set to Focus, the image will only be captured once the focus has been acquired and the green focus lock indicator plus the focus target areas are illuminated green.
If the mode is set to Release, then the image is captured when you fully depress the shutter button irrespective of whether focus acquisition has been achieved or not.
The logic behind this is to ensure that you can capture an image without a missed opportunity because the camera had not achieved the focus point.
With AF/AE Lock Hold set to OFF, keep the AF/AE lock button depressed with your thumb to hold the exposure/and or focus point as you depress the shutter release.

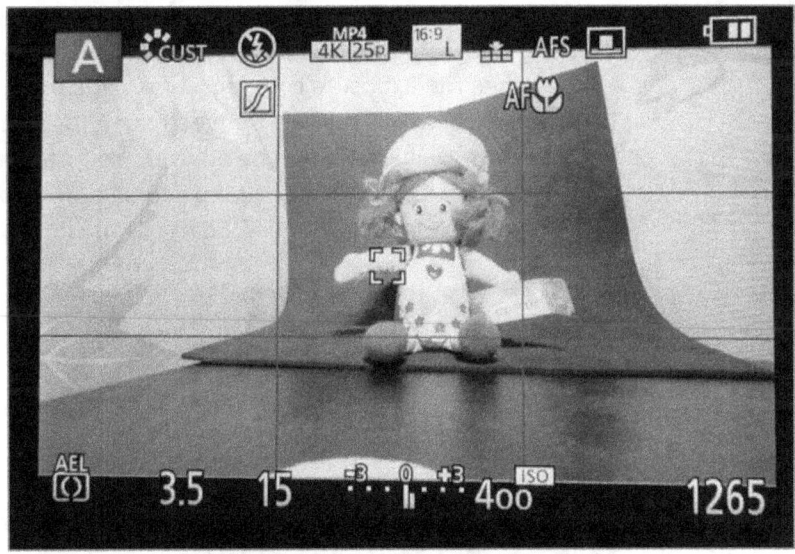

Using Exposure Compensation

Exposure compensation is usually required whenever there is a large brightness difference between subject and background.

If the subject is lighter or darker than the background the result will be that the camera metering circuit will attempt to set an exposure so that the net result would be one of neutral grey.

Typical examples would be scenes on beaches or on snow where the background is usually brighter than the subject.

The camera will reduce the exposure to try and render the background as the neutral grey it expects the scene to be.

The results in under exposure of the subject.

In scenes shot against the light they too will result in under exposure of the subject and exposure adjustment will be needed to allow the subject to be recorded correctly.

To a degree it will depend upon the metering mode used to evaluate the exposure.

Whole area and centre weighted will be influenced by this exposure brightness difference more than the spot metering mode.

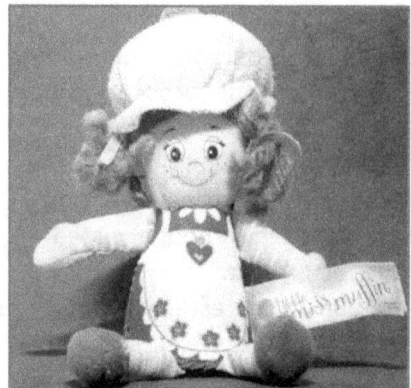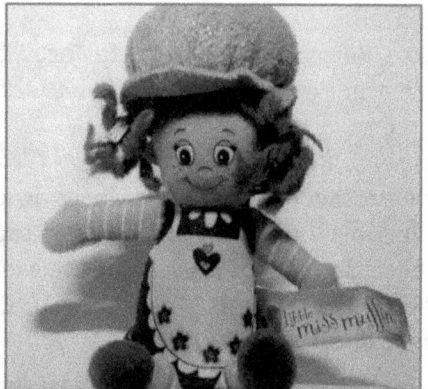

The doll pictured on a black background and on a white background showing the resulting exposure change due to the camera meter being influenced by the background brightness.

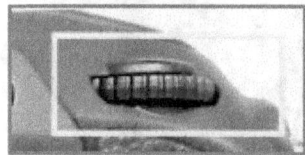
To change the exposure compensation value press in the back-control wheel to cycle between the A (or S) and EV control. The value can then be adjusted by rotating the control wheel. 5 stops of compensation are available. +EV lightens the image and −EV darkens the image.

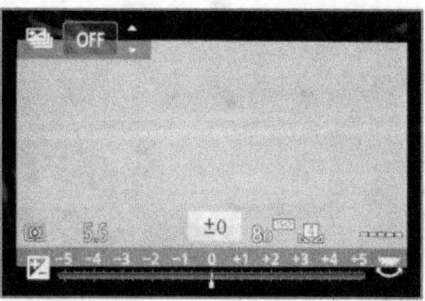

Setting the Camera Sensitivity – ISO

The overall sensitivity of the camera to a given level of lighting is controlled by the ISO setting. ISO (International Standards Organisation) provides a consistent measure of camera sensitivity from one camera to another.

In film photography ISO (or ASA/DIN as it was then) was the indication of how sensitive a film was to light. It was measured in numbers like: 25, 64, 100, 200, 400, 800 etc. The lower the number the lower the sensitivity of the film and the finer the emulsion grain in the shots you're taking. In digital photography ISO measures the sensitivity of the image sensor and analogue to digital convertor combination.

The same principles apply as in film photography – the lower the number the less sensitive your camera is to light and the finer the image noise.
The sensor has a fixed sensitivity (called the base or natural sensitivity) and this is the most recommended setting in which to use the camera ISO setting.
At this setting, there is no additional image signal amplification needed to boost the output analogue signal from the sensor to the level required by the Analogue to Digital convertor to correctly digitise the image for subsequent image processing.
Higher than base ISO settings are generally used in darker situations to get faster shutter speeds.

For example, an indoor sports event when you want to freeze the action in lower light. However, the higher the ISO you choose the noisier shots you will get because both sensor noise and subsequent amplifier noise are greatly increased with this setting.
In our camera as we increase the ISO setting the processing of the JPEG images tries to remove some of this noise (both noise in the luminance {brightness} and colour {chrominance}) with a result that we see some softening of the image and more fine detail smearing as shown in the images below. The left image is ISO 100 the right 3200.

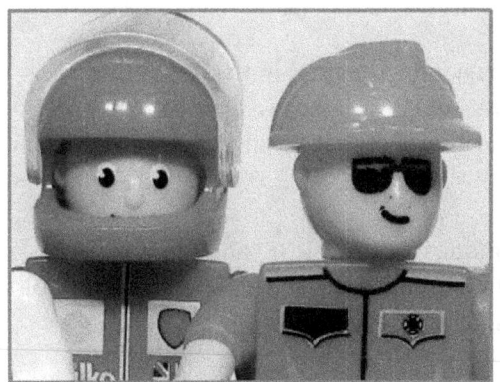
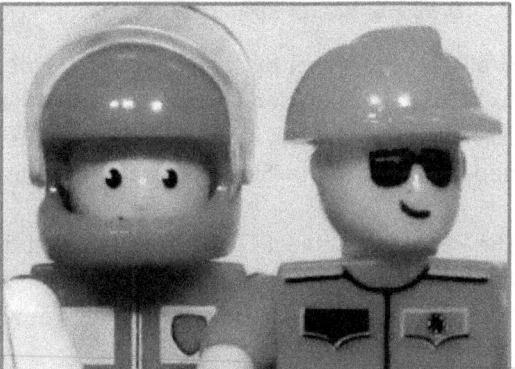

image taken at ISO 80   *image taken at ISO 3200 (note softness)*

ISO Modes

The ISO value can be set by three methods; Auto, iISO and a manually entered value.
In the Auto mode, the camera will choose a value from 125 to 3200 ISO depending upon the scene brightness.
If you select iISO (intelligent ISO) the camera will set the ISO as with Auto ISO but the value is not fixed at the halfway shutter button travel it will attempt to adjust the ISO to reflect any subject motion which might result in subject motion blurring.
The value is fixed at the point the shutter button is fully depressed.

With the manual entry of the ISO the range of adjustment is from ISO 125 to ISO 12800 in 1 f-stop increments (or 1/3 F-Stops if you have this option set up).
In both the Auto and iISO settings if you have the ISO Limit set to any other value other than OFF then this will become the upper limit for the camera.
I generally recommend that ISO is set manually at the base setting of 125 ISO however, if you are shooting in situations with variable light levels which may result in shutter speeds longer than 1/30 second selecting either Auto or iISO with an upper limit of 800 ISO may be useful.

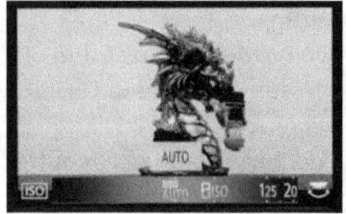　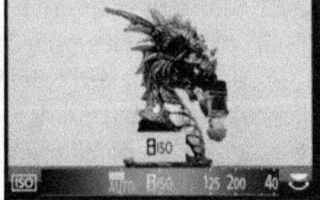　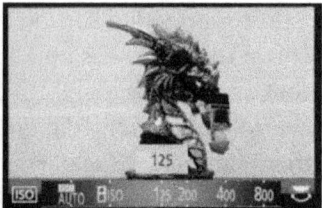

setting Auto ISO　　　　　　*iISO*　　　　　　*a Manual ISO*

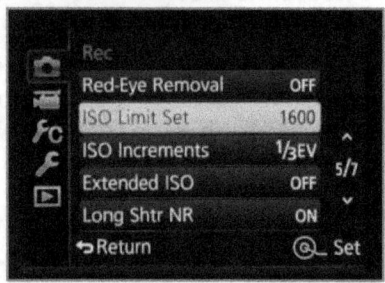

In both the Auto ISO and the iISO mode the upper limit of the maximum value that the camera can use can be set using the ISO Limit Set value. This is set in the REC setup screen from ISO 200 up to the maximum of 12800 Generally, ISO 800 is the maximum value that I would recommend that you use to preserve image quality

In all cases ISO is set by pressing the ISO (top navigation button) of the 4-way controller. As ISO is generally used to allow the use of faster shutter speeds to arrest subject motion blur it might be worth looking at the acceptable shutter speeds that can be set manually depending upon the ISO value that you have set.

The Panasonic Lumix FZ1000 has two shutter modes: Electronic (E) and Manual (M).
The Electronic shutter is used for silent operation in those situations where shutter noise might be unacceptable (inside Churches at wedding ceremonies etc.,)

Here's a table of the acceptable shutter speeds:

ISO value (with 1/3EV set)	Shutter Speeds (seconds)
Auto or iISO set	Automatically changes with ISO value set by the camera
Manual ISO from ISO 125 (80 extended ISO) to ISO 12800 (25600 Extended ISO)	60 seconds to 1/4000 M shutter & 1- 1/16000 with E Shutter

When electronic shutter is used, you may notice a slight reduction in dynamic range and setting it to ON will also disable FLASH.

Selecting a Metering Mode

The way in which the camera determines the correct exposure is depending upon how it recognises areas of brightness within the image. With the Panasonic Lumix FZ1000 there are three metering modes:

1. Whole area (often called Matrix or Evaluative by other manufacturers).   [( )]
2. Centre weighted.   [(.)]
3. Spot. [.]

METERING MODE	USES
WHOLE AREA	This is the method in which the camera measures the most suitable exposure by judging the range of brightness across the whole image.
CENTRE WEIGHTED	This method uses the centre of the image and measures the exposure from this central area. Useful when subjects are backlit.
SPOT METERING	This is the method to measure the subject using a very small target area. This area is denoted by a cross hair on the screen. Used in difficult lighting to evaluate the exposure using a user selected area which has a brightness of approximately 18% reflectance

Generally, the best method to use is the whole area method as this looks at the whole distribution of light intensities across the image and sets an exposure which reflects the most appropriate for the result.

With any metering mode there is a possibility that, because of an uneven distribution of light intensity in either the foreground or the background, the exposure may be calculated incorrectly and this is the case where you would employ exposure compensation to correct this.

To use exposure compensation, it is necessary to press in the back-control wheel. Doing so changes the operation from aperture (or shutter speed in S mode) to EV adjustment.

You can adjust the exposure by up to 5 F-stops for either the under or over exposed images.

Using Image Correction Functions

I do not recommend the use of the following adjustments which apply only to the out of camera (OOC JPEG images) but include them as a complete reference to them.

The reason for this is that most of these adjustments can give unpredictable results and are far better implemented with your image editor program where you can see the effect of the applied operation.

These results are permanently applied to these JPEG images and there is no way to correct for this.

Compensating the contrast and exposure ([i.Dynamic])

Contrast and exposure are compensated when the brightness difference between the background and subject is unusually large, etc.

The range of settings: [AUTO]/[HIGH]/[STANDARD]/[LOW]/[OFF]

[AUTO] automatically sets the intensity of the effect according to the exposure conditions. Not available in these cases:

• This feature may be automatically disabled, depending on the lighting conditions.
• In the following cases, [i.Dynamic] does not work:
– [Panorama Shot] (Scene Guide Mode) – When [HDR] is set to [ON]
Those menu items are shared by the [Rec] menu and the [Motion Picture] menu. When the setting for either of the two is changed, the setting for the other is also changed.

Increasing image resolution ([i.Resolution])

Pictures appear to be sharper and with a higher resolution when taken by using the Intelligent Resolution Technology.

Settings: [HIGH]/[STANDARD]/[LOW]/[EXTENDED]/[OFF]

• [EXTENDED] allows you to take natural pictures with a higher resolution.
• When recording a motion picture, [EXTENDED] changes to [LOW].
• Those menu items are shared by the [Rec] menu and the [Motion Picture] menu. When the setting for either of the two is changed, the setting for the other is also changed.

Combining images of varying exposure with HDR

HDR stands for High Dynamic Range and refers to a technique for combining a wide contrast range.

You can combine 3 images with different levels of exposure into a single picture with rich gradation. You can minimise the loss of gradations in bright areas and dark areas when, for example, the contrast between the background and the subject is large.
An image combined by HDR is recorded in JPEG.

Settings:

ON: Records HDR pictures.
OFF: Does not record HDR pictures.
SET: [Dynamic Range]

[AUTO]: Automatically adjusts the exposure range according to the differences between the bright and dark areas.

[n1 EV]/[n2 EV]/[n3 EV]:
Adjusts the exposure within the selected exposure parameters.

SET: [Auto Align]
[ON]: Automatically corrects camera shake and other problems that can cause the images to misalign. Recommended for use during hand-held shooting.

[OFF]: Image misalignment not adjusted. Recommended when a tripod is used.

Do not move the camera during the continuous shooting after pressing the shutter button.

• You cannot take the next picture until the combination of pictures is complete.
• A moving subject may be recorded with unnatural blurs.
• The angle of view becomes narrow slightly when [Auto Align] is set to [ON].
• Flash is fixed to (forced flash off).

[HDR] is not available in the following cases.
– When [Quality] is set to any mode which includes any of the RAW option
– When using [Time Lapse Shot]
– When using [Stop Motion Animation] (only when [Auto Shooting] is set)

Reducing long exposure noise ([Long Shtr NR])

The camera automatically removes noise that appears when the shutter speed becomes longer than 1 second. It does this by subtracting the noise pattern from a dark frame image that is the same exposure time.

In the following cases [Long Shtr NR] does not work,
– [Panorama Shot] (Scene Guide Mode)
– When recording motion pictures
– When [Burst Rate] is set to [SH]
– When using the electronic shutter

Setting the image Colour Space: ([Color Space])

This setting is used to apply a colour limit depending upon the future use of the image – usually display or printing.

Settings:
sRGB: Color space is set to sRGB color space.
             This is widely used in computer related displays.

AdobeRGB: Color space is set to AdobeRGB color space.
              AdobeRGB is mainly used for professional printing because it has a greater
              range of reproducible colours than sRGB.

Use sRGB for most needs as most images are used for display on 8bit display devices.

• The setting is fixed to [sRGB] – when recording motion pictures

Autofocus Tracking Mode

With auto focus tracking mode engaged, focus and exposure can be adjusted to track a
specified subject. Focus and exposure will keep on following the subject even if it moves.
(Dynamic tracking)

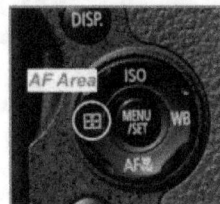

To engage auto focus tracking press the left-hand button of the four-
way navigation pad

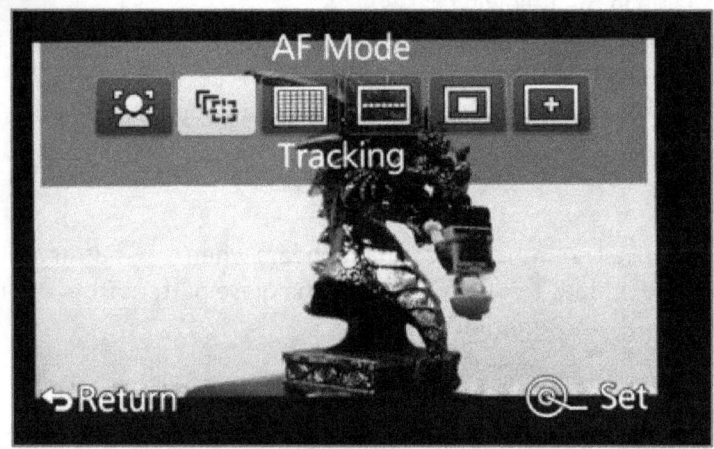

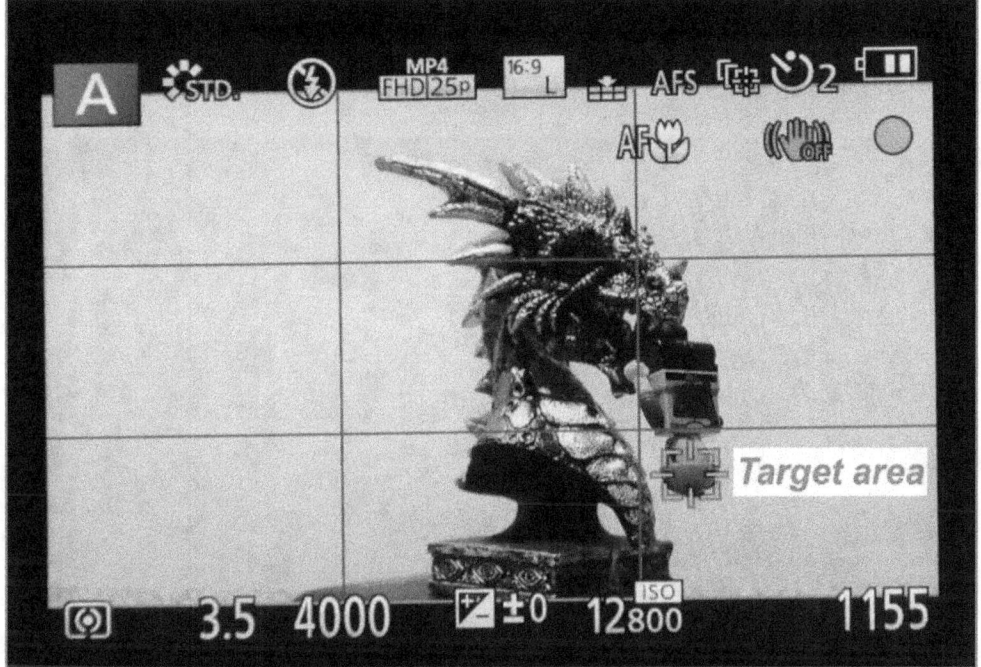

Place the subject in the AF tracking frame, and press the shutter button halfway to lock the subject. The target will be a yellow square with cross-hairs which quickly turns green as the target is locked in focus.

The AF area will turn green when the camera detects the subject and the shutter button is held at the half-way point.

If it fails to lock, AF area will flash in red, and disappear. Try the lock again.

The AF area turns yellow when the shutter button is released but should continue to track the subject if it, or the camera position, moves.
Fully depress the shutter button to complete the exposure.

Tracking Lock is cancelled when [MENU/SET] is pressed.

Dynamic tracking function may not work in the following cases:
– When the subject is too small
– When the recording location is too dark or bright
– When the subject is moving too fast
– When the background has the same or similar colour to the subject
– When camera shake is occurring
– When zoom is operated
It cannot be used with [Time Lapse Shot].
In the scene types focus tracking operates as single area mode.
(monochrome modes, soft focus, star filter, glistening water and sepia mode).

This is an effective method when a subject is not in the centre of the screen.

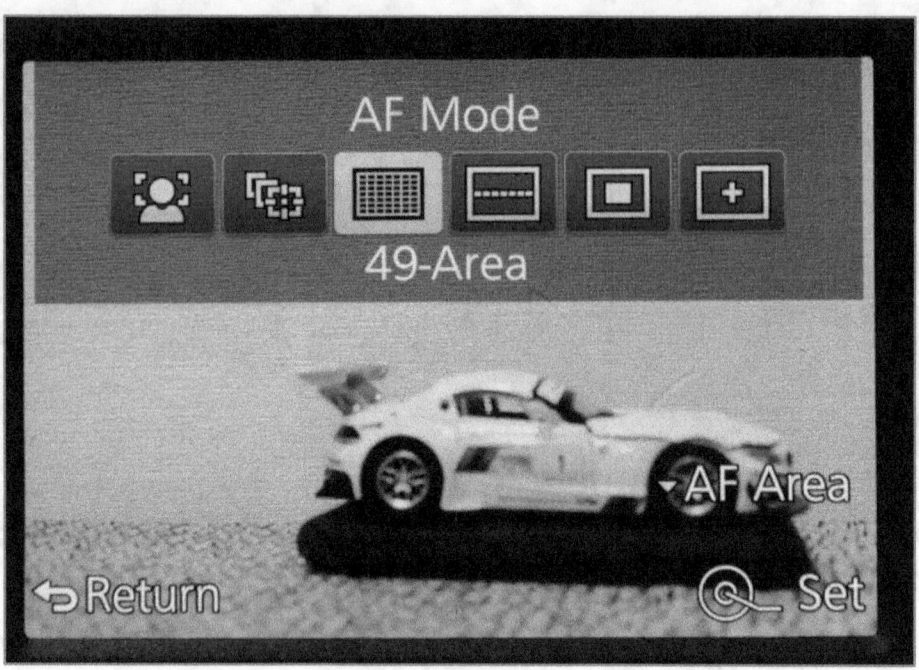

Use the down key of the 4-way navigation pad to select the required autofocus area and then use the pad to set the position

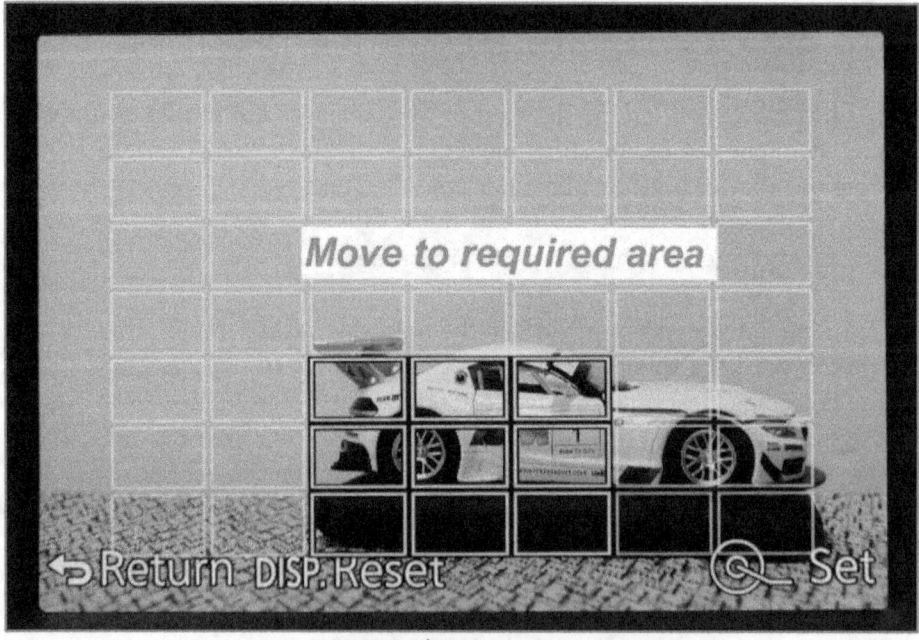

pressing Menu/Set locks the AF area

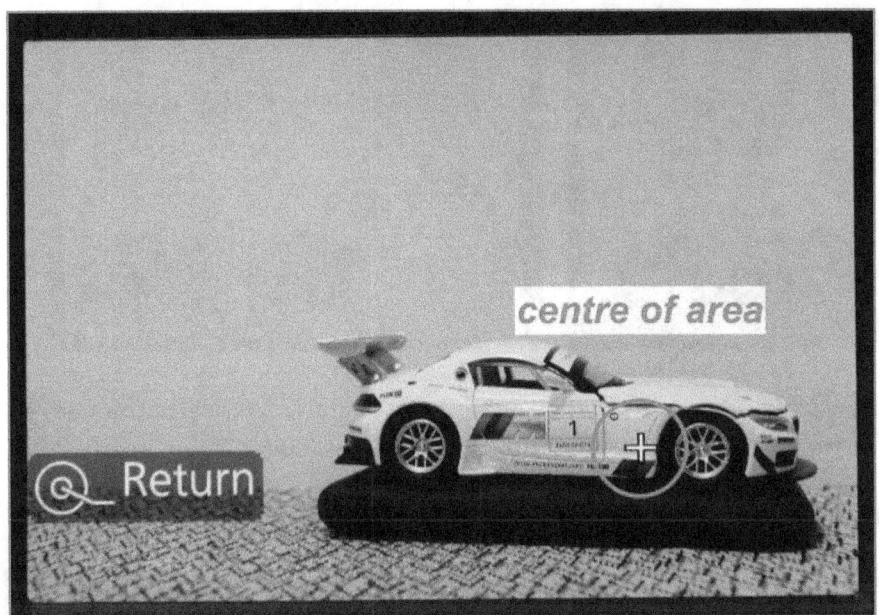

Once the area has been defined, the white cross-hair will indicate the centre of the AF area that is currently set. Move the camera and recompose to include the subject under this cross-hair.

With the Custom Multi Defined area, you can define your own pattern of AF areas that your subject may be captured. This can be simple or complex shapes.

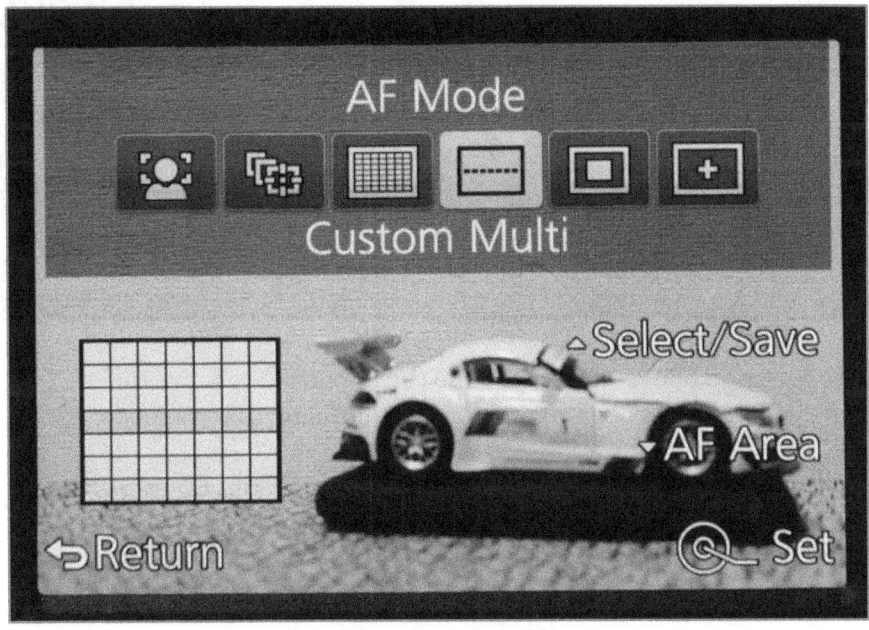

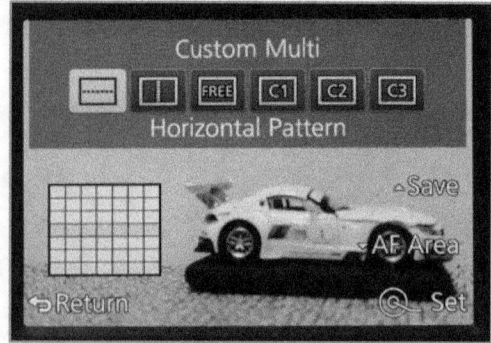 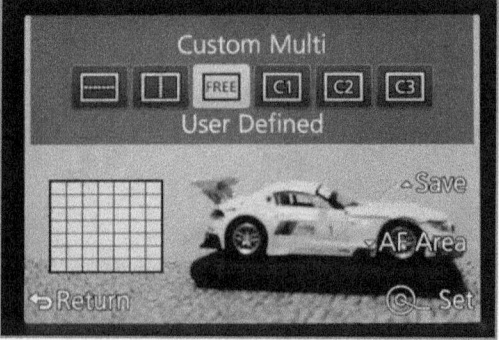

Using the Custom Multi mode you can define either a Horizontal or Vertical pattern or you can select the Free pattern and define your simple or complex shape.

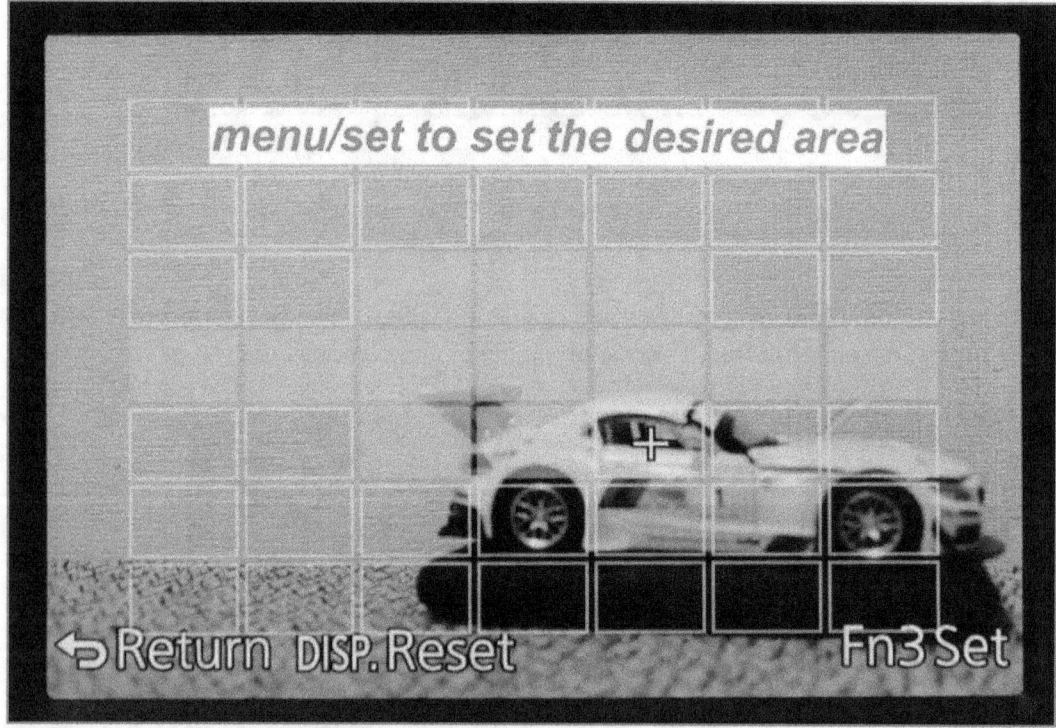

Using the menu/set button to select the area and the cursor buttons to move to the desired area. When the pattern has been set use the Fn3 button to lock this shape.

Once the defined pattern has been "set" into memory this primary area will be used to select the area for focus.
It can be used when the subject might be in a difficult area for the 49-area general area mode would likely focus on the wrong part of the image.

When an absolute precision focus area is needed the best method to select is the 1-Area mode.

Single (1-area) AF Mode

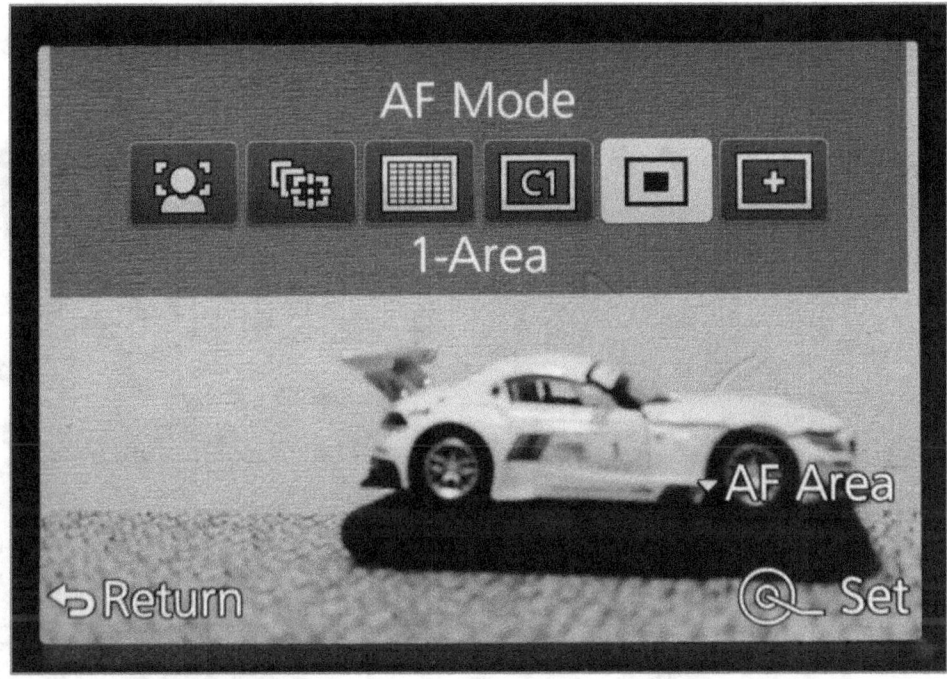

Once selected use the down cursor button to set the position of the area and then use the back-control wheel to set the size of the focus target.

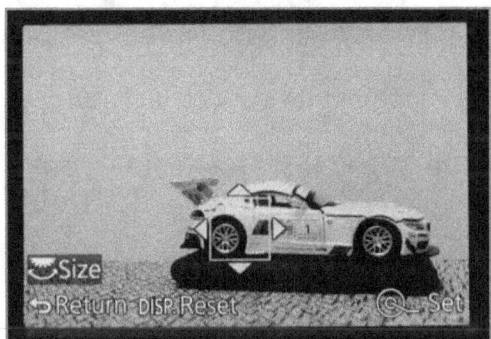 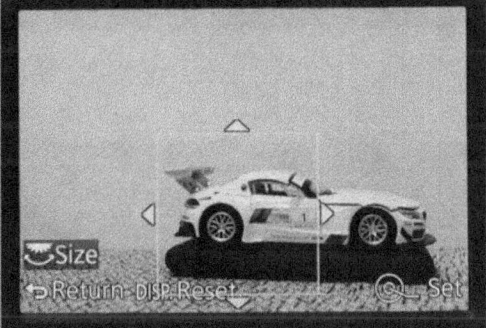

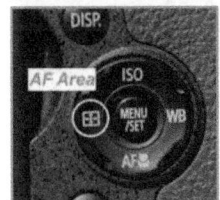

If you want to quickly return the target area to the centre of the screen use the DISP button adjacent to the 4-way navigation pad.

When the subject is not in the centre of the composition], you can bring the subject into the AF area, fix the focus and exposure by pressing the shutter button halfway, move the camera to the composition you want with the shutter button pressed halfway, and then take the picture. (Only when the Focus Mode is set to [AFS].)

Precise Area AF Mode

If you want really accurate focus, there is a mode which allows the precise area to the selected. It also allows a magnified view of the area selected as the shutter button is half-depressed.

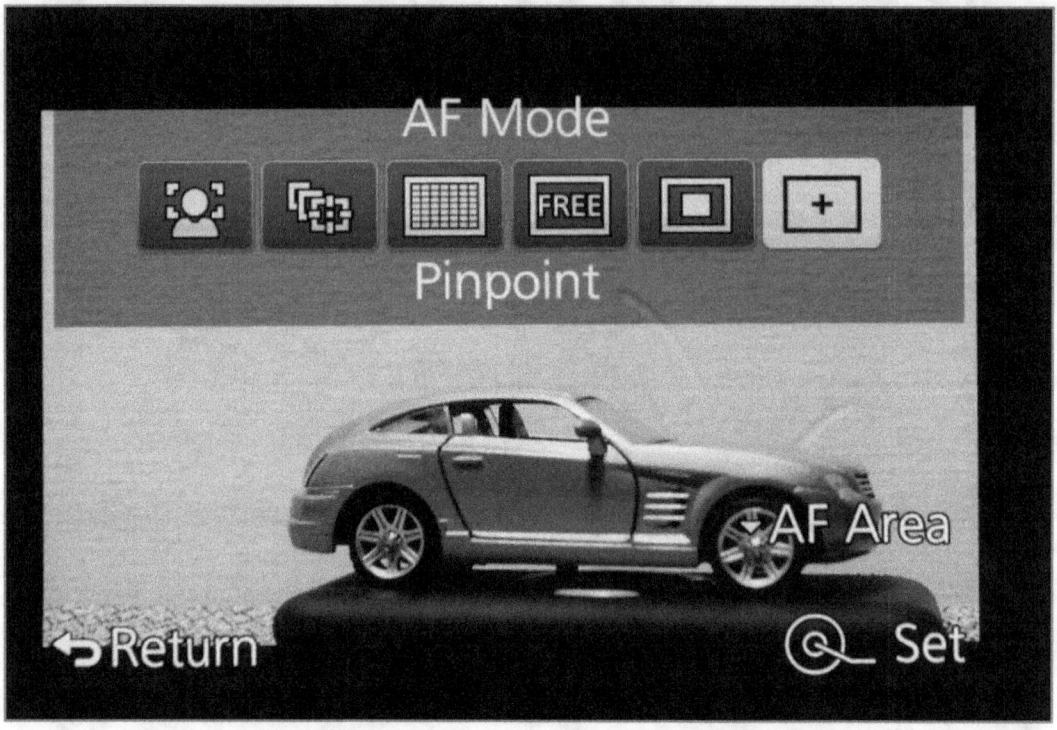

The pin point area selection screen, use the down cursor to set the position of the target.

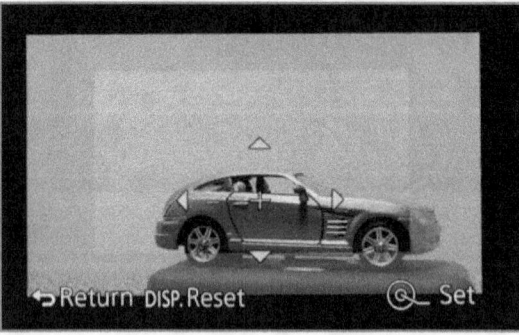
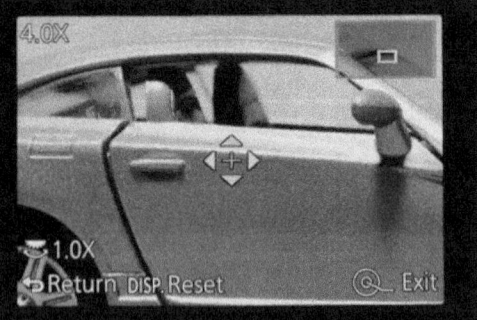

Once the position of the target is set, press in the rear control wheel to set the size of the pop-up enlarged display.

Pressing in the control toggles between the whole view and the enlarged view. You can the set the view from x3 to x10 enlargement.
Once set, when you half press the shutter button you get a momentary view of this enlarged area.

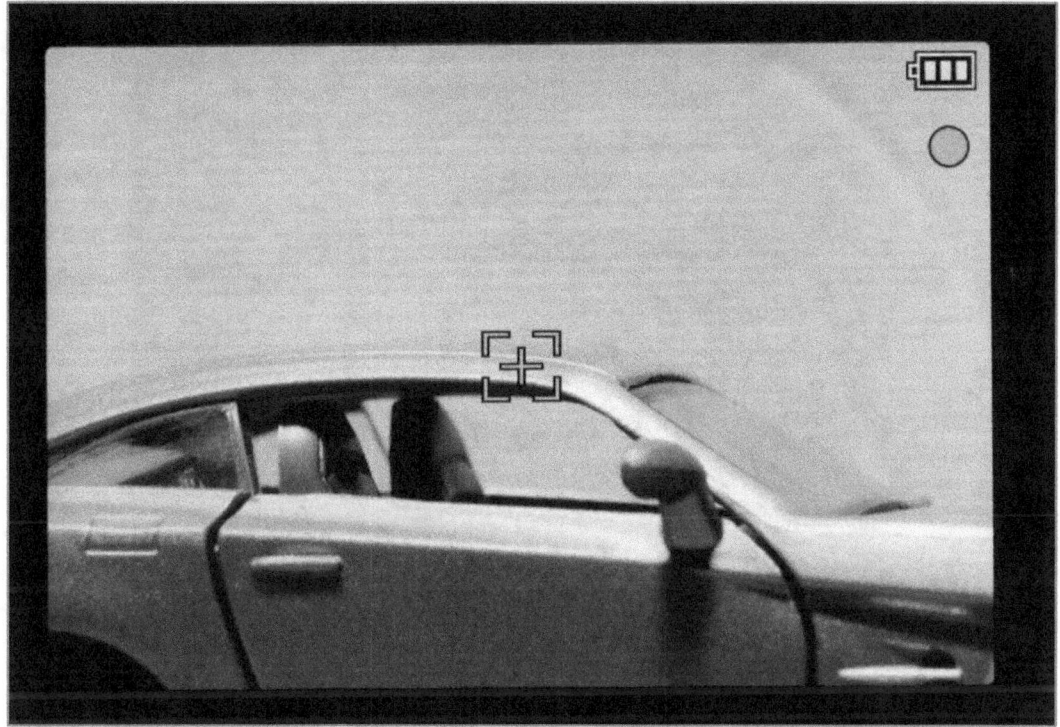

The time that this enlarged image appears is controlled by the Pinpoint AF time found in the custom set up menu.

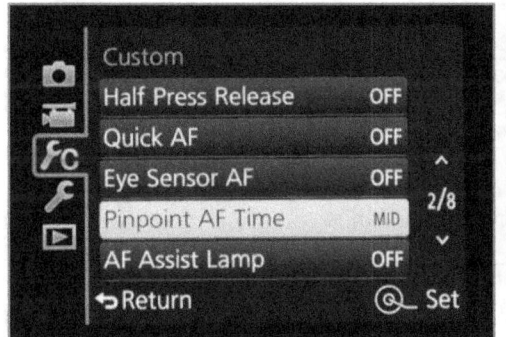 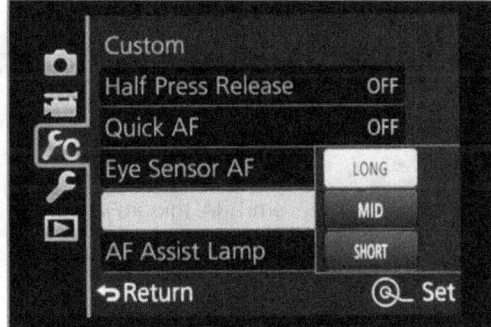

One menu setting condition (Direct Focus Area) gives direct control of the focus area via the 4-way navigation buttons however, you will not then have access to setting the AF mode unless you program one of the other Fn buttons to allow AF selection mode.

For this reason, and that this generates one of the most frequent requests for help when this is inadvertently set, I do not recommend setting this to the ON mode.

Selecting a Drive Mode

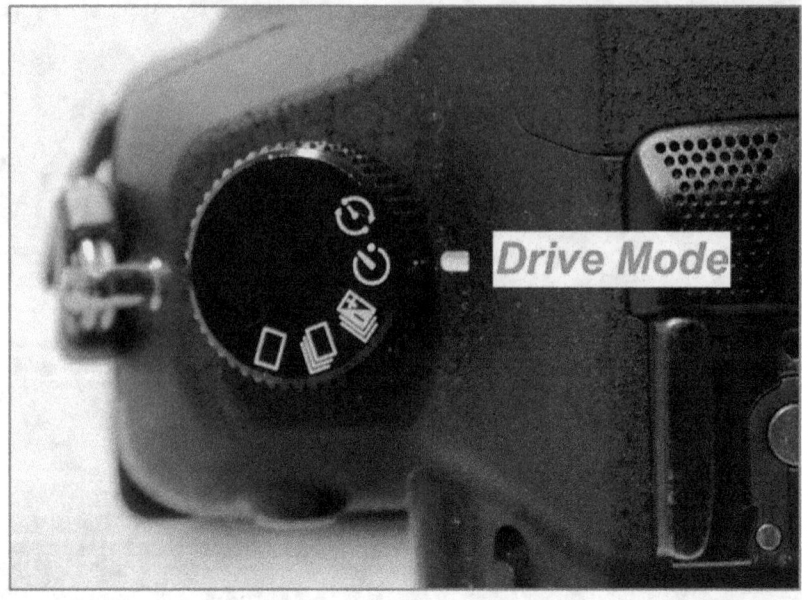

When you select a mode with the Mode Dial you alter the way the camera responds to a shutter button release.

Mode Dial Position		Operational Result
Single		When the shutter button is pressed, only one image is recorded.
Burst		Images are made in succession while the shutter button is pressed.
Auto Bracket		Each time the shutter button is pressed, images are captured with different exposure settings according to the Exposure Compensation range.
Self-Timer		When the shutter button is pressed, image capture takes place after the set time has elapsed. (2 or 10 seconds)
Time-Lapse/Animation		Images are recorded with Time Lapse Shot or Stop Motion Animation.

Taking Images Using the Burst Mode

Images are taken continuously while the shutter button is pressed.

• Pictures taken with a burst speed of [SH] will be recorded as a single burst group

Set the drive mode to ▦ (Burst Mode).
From the REC set up menu select the desired burst rate.

		[SH]·² (Super high speed)	[H] (High speed)	[M] (Middle speed)	[L] (Low speed)
Burst speed (pictures/ second)	AFS	50	12	7	2
	AFF/AFC	—	7	7	2

The maximum speed will depend upon the setting of the AFS/AFF/AFC mode.

If an image Quality setting which has a RAW file component, then the burst rate is about 10 fps.

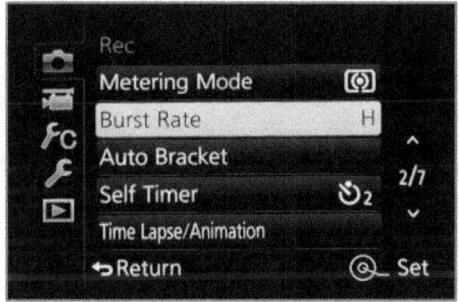 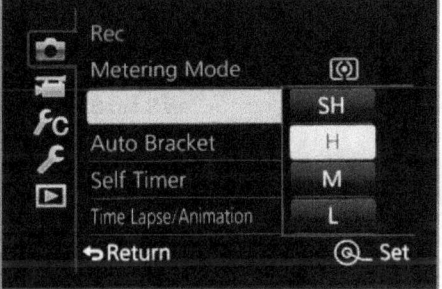

The Burst speed may become slower depending on the following settings.
– [Picture Size]/[Quality]/[Sensitivity]/Focus Mode/[Focus/Release Priority]

Focusing in Burst Mode

The method for achieving focus varies depending on the focus mode and the [Focus/Release Priority] setting in the [Custom] menu.

Focus Mode	Priority	Focus set
AFS	Focus or Release	First Image taken
AFF/AFC	Focus	Normal focus
	Release	Predictive focus
Manual		Manual focus

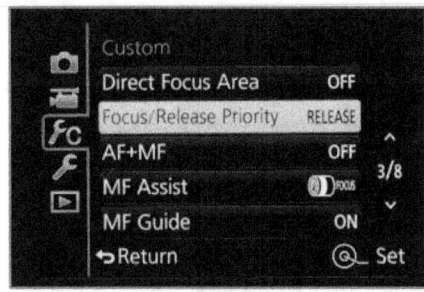

When the burst speed is set to [SH] or [H] (when the Focus mode is [AFS] or [MF]), the exposure and White Balance are fixed at the settings used for the first picture for the subsequent pictures as well.
When the burst speed is set to [H] (when the Focus mode is [AFF] or [AFC]), [M] or [L], they are adjusted each time you take a picture.

The Burst Mode is disabled in the following cases.
– [Glistening Water]/[Glittering Illuminations]/[Handheld Night Shot]/[Soft Image of a Flower]/

[Panorama Shot] (Scene Guide Mode)
– [Rough Monochrome]/[Silky Monochrome]/[Miniature Effect]/[Soft Focus]/[Star Filter]/
[Sunshine] (Creative Control Mode)
– When White Balance Bracket is set
– When recording motion pictures
– When recording using the flash
– When recording with [iHandheld Night Shot]
– When [HDR] is set to [ON]
– [Multi Exp.]
With any image quality with RAW enabled then [SH] in Burst Mode cannot be used.

Taking Images with Auto Exposure Bracketing

Up to Maximum of 7 pictures will be recorded with different exposure settings following the Exposure Compensation range every time the shutter button is pressed.

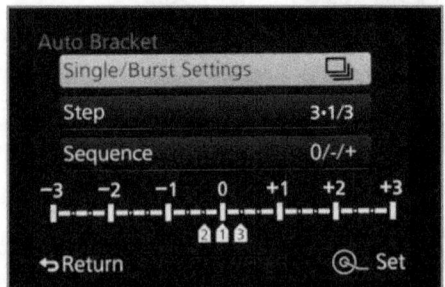

The number of steps (3, 5 or 7) and the sequence Normal/Under/Over or Under/Normal/Over are set in the auto bracket menu settings

Auto bracketing ▨ must be set on the Top Drive Mode dial.

Here is a three-set sequence at 1/3 EV step interval taken with 0/-/+ sequence..

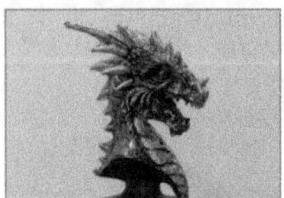
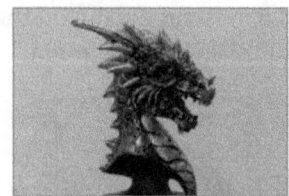
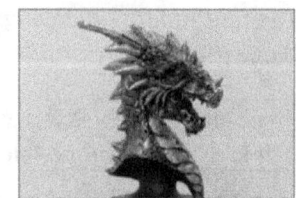

1st image Normal Exp   2nd image -1/3 EV   3rd image +1/2 EV

If you press and hold the shutter button, the number of pictures that you set is taken.
The Auto Bracket indication blinks until the number of pictures that you set is taken.
The picture count is reset to [0] if you change the Auto Bracket setting or turn the camera off before all the pictures that you set are taken.
If the Single/Burst mode setting is Single you take 1 image at a time. With Burst the camera automatically shoots the set number of images for you. Auto bracketing can be used with Exposure Compensation, the values are added for the final images taken.
Auto Bracket is disabled in the following cases.
– [Glistening Water]/[Glittering Illuminations]/[Handheld Night Shot]/[Soft Image of a Flower]/
[Panorama Shot] (Scene Guide Mode)
– [Rough Monochrome]/[Silky Monochrome]/[Miniature Effect]/[Soft Focus]/[Star Filter]/

[Sunshine] (Creative Control Mode)
– When White Balance Bracket is set.
– When recording motion pictures
– When recording using the flash
– When recording with [iHandheld Night Shot]
– When [HDR] is set to [ON]
– [Multi Exp.]

Taking Images Using the Self-Timer Mode

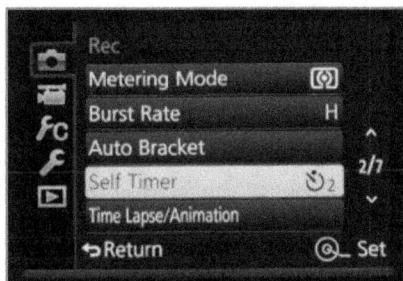

Images can be captured using the Self-Timer mode to prevent camera shake if the camera is mounted on a tripod etc., or allow time for you to appear in the image as well.

The choice of setting is 2 seconds, 10 seconds or a sequence of 3 images with 10 seconds to the first image and then 2 second intervals for the last 2.

The Top Mode Control dial must be set to the 🕐 Self-Timer mode.
It cannot be set to the 3-image sequence in the following cases.
– When White Balance Bracket is set
– [Multi Exp.]
Self-timer is disabled in the following cases.
 – [Panorama Shot] (Scene Guide Mode)
– When recording motion pictures

Taking Images at Set Intervals (Time-Lapse Shots)

If you set the start time of recording, the recording interval and the number of pictures, the camera can automatically take pictures of subjects such as passing clouds or plants growing as time elapses and then (optionally) create a video clip of the entire sequence.

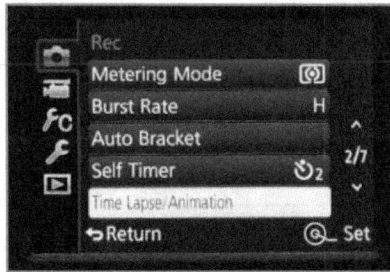
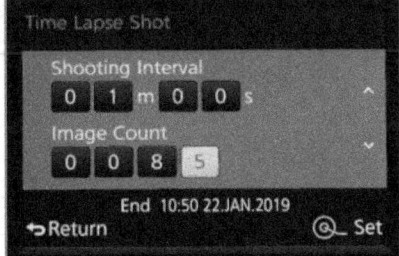

The Top Drive Mode dial must be set to 🕐 Time-Lapse/Stop Motion Animation.
The mode is selected with [Time Lapse/Animation] in the recording menu.
(The screen will be displayed only when you press [MENU/SET] for the first time after switching the drive mode dial to 🕐.
In other cases, the camera operates as usual, displaying the menu screen.)
After setting the Mode to Time-Lapse proceed to set the start time for the sequence.

When **NOW** is selected start the recording by fully-pressing the shutter button.
With **START TIME SET** You can set the time to start recording.
Any time up to 23 hours 59 minutes ahead can be set.
Next set the **RECORDING INTERVAL** and **NUMBER OF IMAGES**
A recording interval ranging from 1 second to 99 minutes and 59 seconds can be set at 1 second interval.
The number of images ranging from 1 to 9999 can be set.

Set the recording interval so that it will be longer than the exposure time (shutter speed)
Recording may be skipped when the recording interval is shorter than the exposure time (shutter speed), for example during night-time recording.

Press the shutter button fully down to begin the recording.
The recording starts automatically.

During recording standby, the power will turn off automatically if no operation is performed for a certain period. The Time Lapse Shot is continued even with the power turned off. When the recording start time arrives, the power turns on automatically.
To turn on the power manually, press the shutter button halfway.
If [Fn2] is pressed while this unit is turned on, a selection screen asking you to pause or end will be displayed.
Operate in accordance with the screen.

Also, if [Fn2] is pressed during the pause, a selection screen asking you to resume or end will be displayed. Pressing the shutter button fully will also enable you to resume from the pause.
A confirmation screen for creating a motion picture is displayed next, so select [Yes].
Next select the methods for creating a motion picture.
The recording format is set to [MP4].

Recording Quality	4K/30p FHD/60p FHD/30p HD/30p VGA/30p
Frame Rate	*The higher the frame rate the smoother the video produced* 60fps (with FHD/60p) 30fps 15fps 10fps 7.5fps 6 fps 3fps 1fps
Sequence	Normal or Reverse assembly of the individual frames

If the camera battery becomes exhausted or the memory card is full the process will not complete. Use of a DC power coupler is advantageous for this kind of work. If you do not create the video at the end of the sequence it can be done later from the replay mode.

The other choice for the operating mode of the Time-Lapse/Animation menu is Stop Motion Animation.

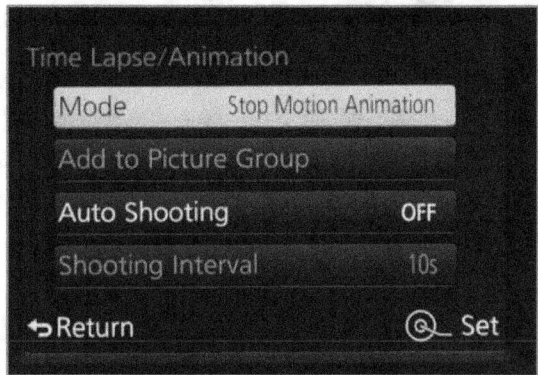

This feature is like the Time-Lapse option because it still creates a series of still images that the camera can combine into a video clip.

The difference is that this option is intended for use in animating objects such as clay figures or puppets. You can also use it to create an animated video based upon drawings such as is done when creating cartoon movies.

You need to move the figure or change the drawing very slightly for the capture of each new frame. As you can imagine you need a lot of images to create a video clip of any length. For example, if you are creating a video which will be shown at 25fps you will need to create 25 images for every second of the final video with the slight movement of the position of the figure or drawing between each of these images.

When you select this option for the Mode you will see a screen with options for:

Add to Picture Group

Auto Shooting

Shooting Interval.

The Shooting Interval will not be available unless you select Auto Shooting.

If you turn on Auto Shooting the camera will capture the images at the interval that you have specified (1 second to 60 second). Without this option, you would have to trigger the camera yourself for each image taken.

Because it is critical to keep the camera position the same during the whole image making process (unless you are creating some additional dynamic movement) it is advisable to enable Auto Shooting so that you do not have to touch the camera during filming. Alternatively, you could use a wired remote control or the Panasonic Image app on a smartphone to trigger the camera.

As with Time-Lapse photography it may be advisable to use an AC adaptor to power the camera throughout the filming process.

However, if you are using battery power and it becomes exhausted and the camera automatically powers down when you replace the battery and turn it back on it will prompt you to resume the series of images that have been interrupted.

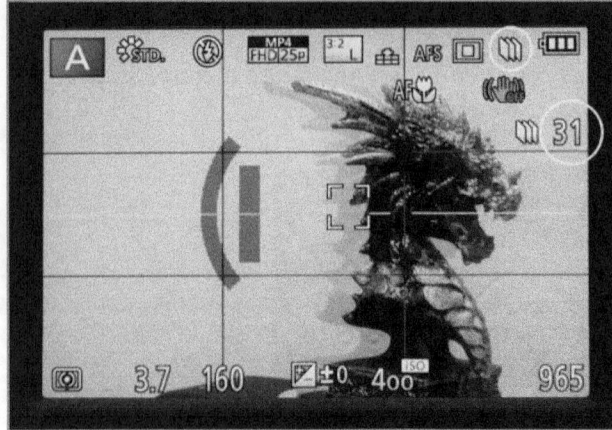

During filming the camera will display an on-screen icon showing the number of frames completed at the right-hand side of the display and the cumulative shots taken so far.

It also will display an overlay of the previous images that have been captured to help you get the right registration for your next image.

If you want to add to your animation a group of images that were created using Stop Motion Animation you can use the ADD to PICTURE Group menu option.

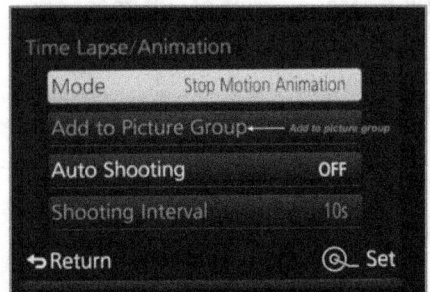

With the Add to Picture Group selected the camera will display any groups of images, you can then choose the group that you want. Using this method, it is possible to build up a longer sequence from previously shot material.

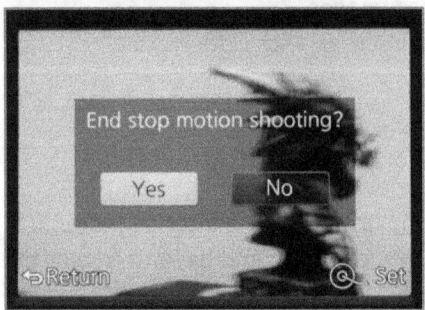

When you have finished your sequence of images press Menu/Set to go back to the Stop Motion Animation Menu. Press Menu/Set when that option is highlighted and the camera will ask if you want to End Stop Motion Shooting.

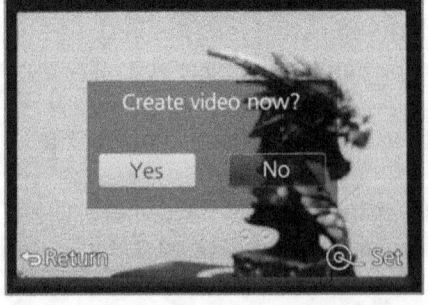

If you answered Yes, the camera will prompt for you to create the video at this point.

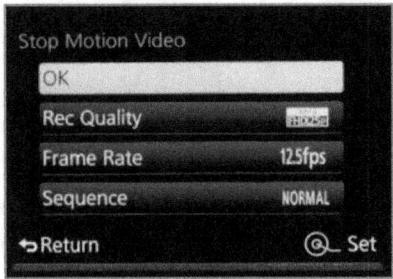

If you do select the create video now option the camera will go on to prompt you for the settings to employ to create the video including the Rec Quality, Frame Rate and whether you want to create the video in a Normal or Reverse sequence.

For the smoothest playback, you should select the highest frame rate. This would be 30fps (in the USA) or 25fps in Europe. Lower frame rates (down to 15fps) may still provide smooth motion.

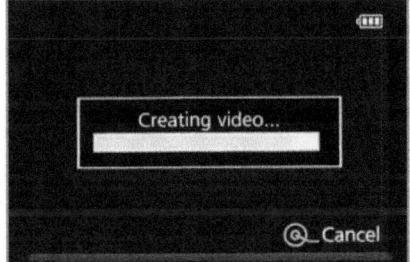

Once you have set your desired option and selected OK, the camera will create the video for you

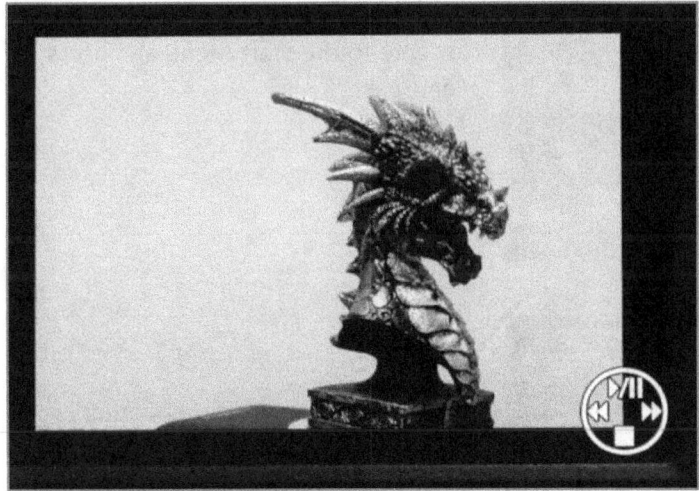

Once the video has been created you can press the UP navigation button. If you don't create the video at this point you can do so by selecting the stop Motion Video option in the Playback menu.

Making Multiple Exposures on One Image

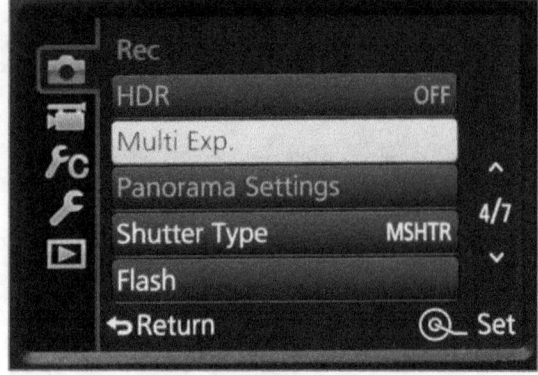

I class this in-camera operation more in the category of creative photography than the process of normal image creation. The process does allow you to create double, triple or quadruple exposures directly in the camera.

You can create this multiple exposure image by using an existing image (which must be a RAW format image) or create a new image from scratch.

1. Using a previously shot image as the start image.

With this technique, the image to be used must be resident on the SD card in the camera and have been shot in RAW (or RAW+JPEG) option.

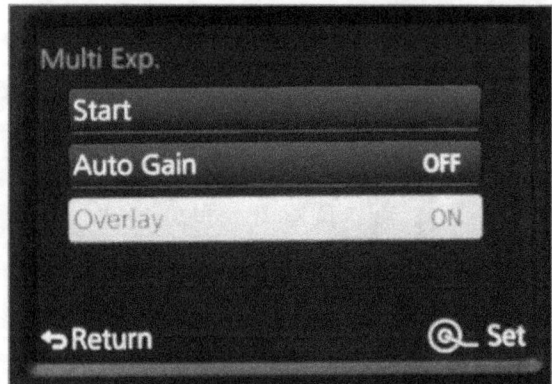

Set the Auto Gain OFF and the Overlay On

Navigate to the Start Menu and press Menu/Set.

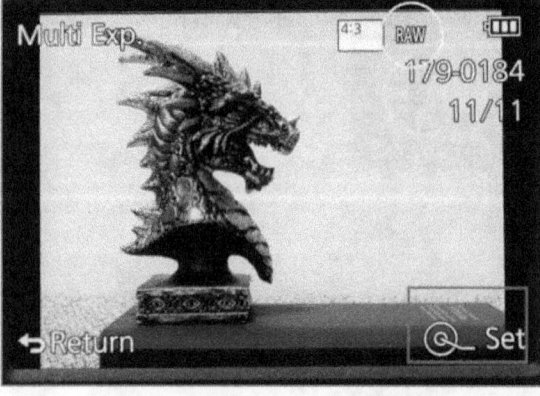

The images that are on the memory card can be viewed and the one needed for the final image selected.

It must be a RAW image file for the process to work.

Select the starting image and press Menu/Set.

The camera will now allow you to superimpose the next image. The Start image is held on-screen, at reduced opacity.

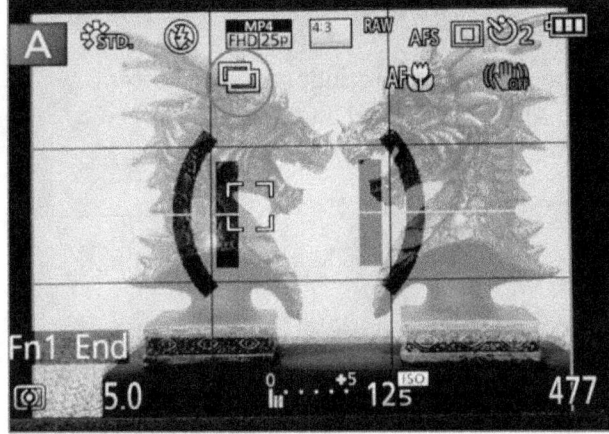

With this screen, you can now place the second image.

The overlay icon is shown on the image.
Press the shutter to capture this image.

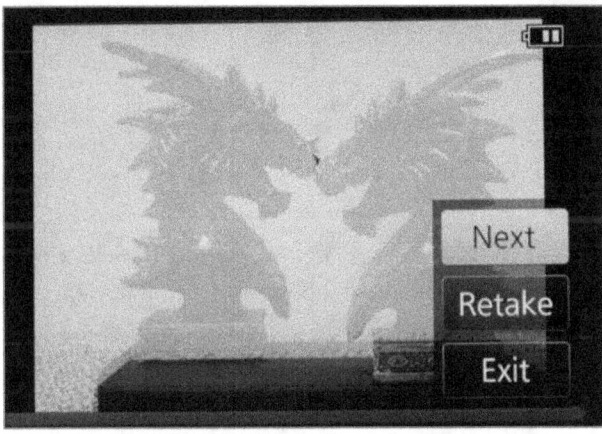

If the image is positioned how you would like it, you can proceed with Menu/Set or scroll down to select Retake to do it again or Exit to cancel the process. *(Pressing the shutter button half way down will also select the highlighted option.)*

Before you begin capturing the images using this method the menu gives you the option to set Auto Gain ON or OFF.
If you leave it ON, the camera attempts to adjust the exposure based upon the number of images recorded. If you turn it OFF the camera adjusts the exposure of the final superimposed image. I find that leaving this to ON produced results which are clearer whereas OFF tends to produce over exposed images.

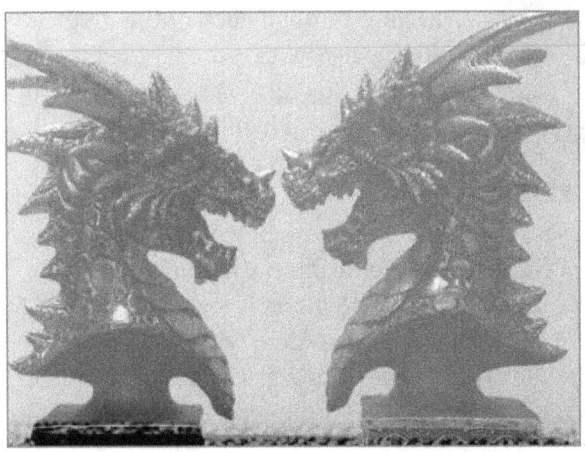

The final composite image with contrast increased in Photoshop.

The success of the process is dependent upon the choice of subject and the positioning of the superimposed image. A lot of trial and error is needed to produce a convincing image,

The Silent Mode is a useful feature when you quickly want to suppress any shutter sounds, audible beeps (from focus etc.,) the AF Assist LED and disable the flash.
Silent Mode is found in the Custom set up menu.
The following settings are fixed.
– [Shutter Type]: [ESHTR]
– [Flash Mode]: (forced flash off)
– [AF Assist Lamp]: [OFF]
– [Beep Volume]: (OFF)
– [Shutter Vol.]: (OFF)
Even when [ON] is set, the following functions light up/flash.
– Status indicator
– Self-timer indicator
– Wi-Fi connection lamp

Recalling Frequently Used Menus Instantly

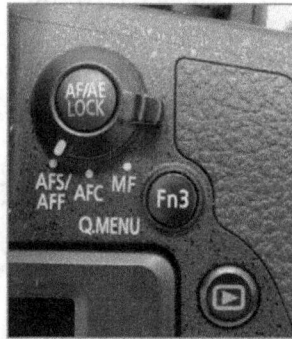

When you press the Q.Menu button (Fn3) whilst the camera is in the recording mode an abridged menu system appears.

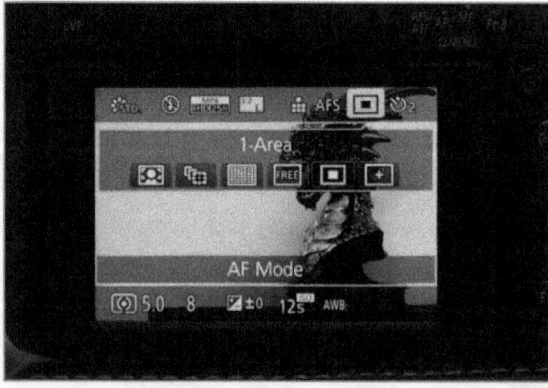

This menu consists of several options over two line. One is at the top of the screen and the other at the bottom.

Navigate through each of the menu items using the Left or Right cursor buttons or by turning the back-control wheel until you highlight the option that you want to adjust.

The name of the menu item that you will adjust will show near the bottom of the screen for the top row menus and near the top of the screen for bottom row menu items.
For example, in the illustration above the top menu row of AF mode is highlighted and AF mode shows at the bottom of the screen. The highlighted menu item will wrap around around the top and bottom as you press the left/right keys or turn the rear control wheel. Whilst a menu item is highlighted the current setting for that option is displayed as the highlighted option in the centre of the screen.

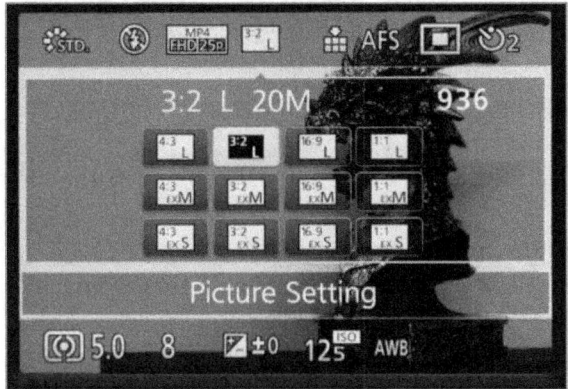

In this illustration, you can see that in the Picture Setting menu the 3:2 aspect ratio and L format is selected. When you are on the top line of the menu pressing the Down cursor key will allow you adjust the setting. If you are on the bottom row of the menu then pressing the Up cursor key will again allow you to make any adjustment.

In the illustration above if you wanted to set a 1:1 aspect ratio with Large format you would press Down to enter the settings option and then right, right to highlight the 1:1 L icon.

Once you have navigated here using the cursor buttons or the rear dial press the Up-cursor button to move back to the top menu items again.

If you have finished making your choices press the Menu/Set button or the Quick Menu button.

The menu options vary according to the mode that the camera is currently set to.

The Quick Menu offers the largest selection of adjustments in Program, Aperture Priority, Shutter Priority or Manual Mode.

It does feature a smaller set of menu adjustments if you have the iA mode selected.

Quick Menu offers a great alternative to the Recoding Menu.

This method is slightly faster as it allows you to select choices more efficiently as, in part, you can see all the available options displayed for you to choose from.

As an example of this I find that using the Q.Menu to select between RAW and Fine JPEG for still images is very efficient. Once you have made the selection when you later press the Q.Menu button again the choice is already highlighted ready for you to make the change from RAW to Fine or vice versa with just a couple of button pushes.

Additionally you can change the menu options that appear as you press the Q.Menu button through setting these in the Custom menu.

Playback

Before considering all the playback options, it is worth discussing the Auto Review feature of the camera. The setting for this feature are found on page 7/8 in the Custom setup menu screen and this can have a value of OFF,1,2,3,4,5 seconds or HOLD.

If your primary use of this feature is to review images immediately after they have been taken - to check exposure and sharpness, for example, then this setting is all that you need to consider.

By default, this review duration is set for 2 seconds and as soon as the image is captured the display switches to providing you with the image held there for 2 seconds.
After this period the camera reverts to the normal live view mode.
During this period if you want to capture the next image just press the shutter button and this will terminate the "hold" period and allow you to get that next shot.
Switching the review time to HOLD will keep the display on screen until you press the shutter button half way down.
If you want uninterrupted display you can turn preview to OFF.
This method of previewing images is an excellent way to check that you have the image that you want and especially if you are using the EVF as here you can preview with taking your eye away from the viewfinder.
On the same menu page, there is also the Playback Operation Priority.
If this menu item is set to ON, then you can perform other operations on the displayed image during the preview period.
For example, if you press the Fn4 (Delete images) button then you will invoke the delete image dialogue. If the Playback Operation Priority mode is set to OFF, then pressing Fn4 will cause the REC mode for that button to be invoked.
In the case of Fn4 this will toggle the preview of shutter speed on or off.
The way in which images are viewed later is set by how you use the playback options.
For ordinary review of images just press the payback button located between the Fn3 and DISP buttons. It has a silk screened green triangle printed on it.

Once you press this button the most recent image (or video clip) is displayed. To move back to a previous image (or video) you use the Left cursor button, or turn the rear control dial to the left. If you have scrolled back to earlier images you can use the RIGHT cursor button to move back towards the most recent image.
To fast track through the images press and hold the button down.

Index View and Enlarging Displayed Images:

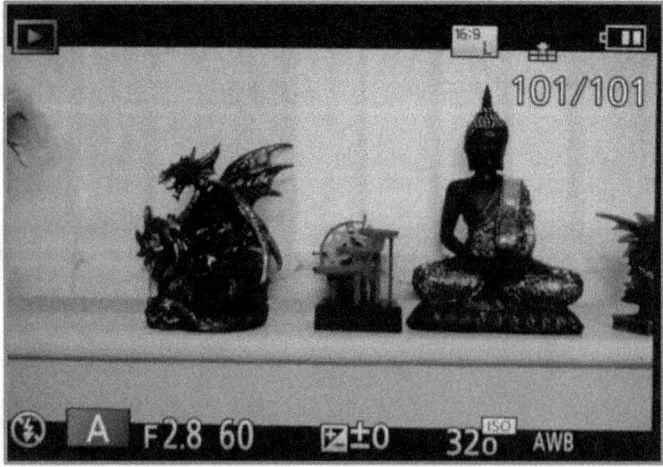

Playback showing basic information only

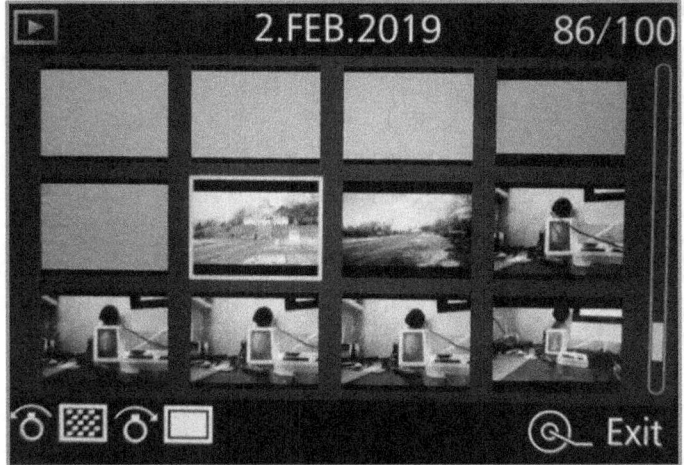

When you are displaying an individual image in the playback mode if you push the top zoom lever once to the RIGHT (W) you will be presented with a screen showing 12 images, one of which will be highlighted with a yellow rectangle.

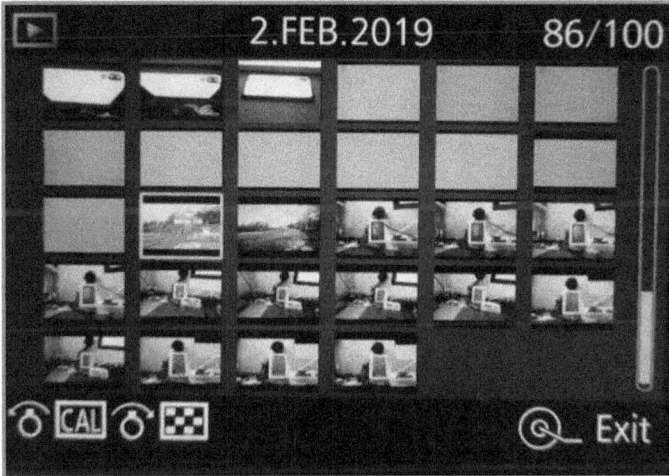

Press the zoom lever one more time to the LEFT and you will then see a screen of 30 images, again one will be highlighted in yellow.
You can use the Menu/Set button to view the highlighted image, or you can move through the other images by using the four cursor buttons or by turning the back-control dial. The image marker will wraparound from row to row as you do so.

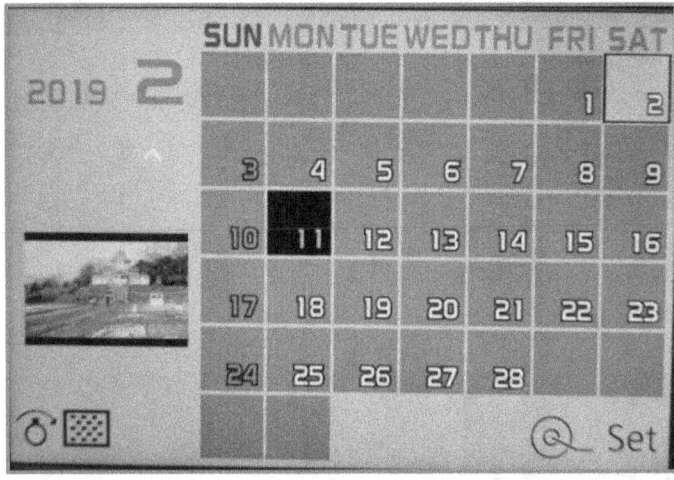

Press the zoom lever one more time and the display will change to a Calendar View. Whilst displaying the view in this mode you can move the highlighted rectangle to any of the black squares.
These black squares represent the fact that there are images taken on that date.

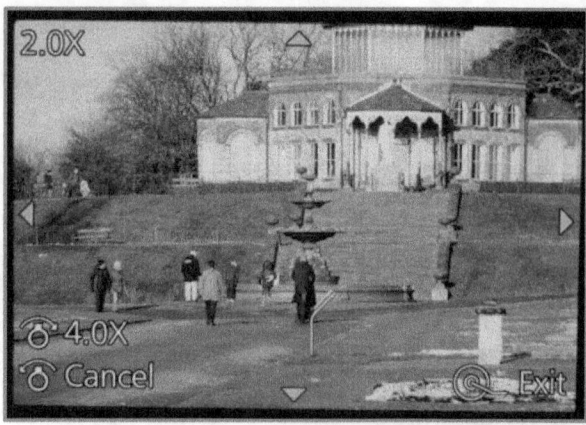

Whilst displaying a single image, moving the top zoom lever to the RIGHT (T) you can display an enlarged image.

Using the cursor buttons, you can move the enlarged area around the image.

Whilst you are doing so a small inset picture will appear with the enlarged portion outlined in yellow

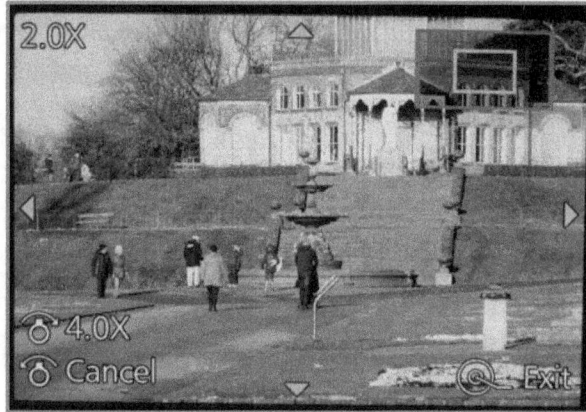

The inset picture shoes the area magnified.

The Playback Menu

Pressing Menu/Set to bring up the menu hierarchy you will see the Playback menu tab with the green triangle.

Cursor down to this with the navigation keys to display page 1/4 of the Playback options.

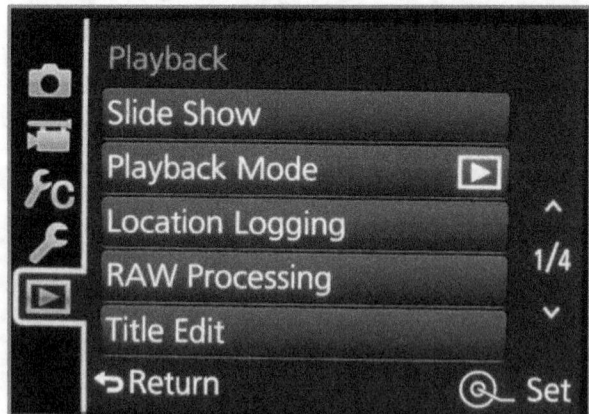

Page 1 of the Playback menu

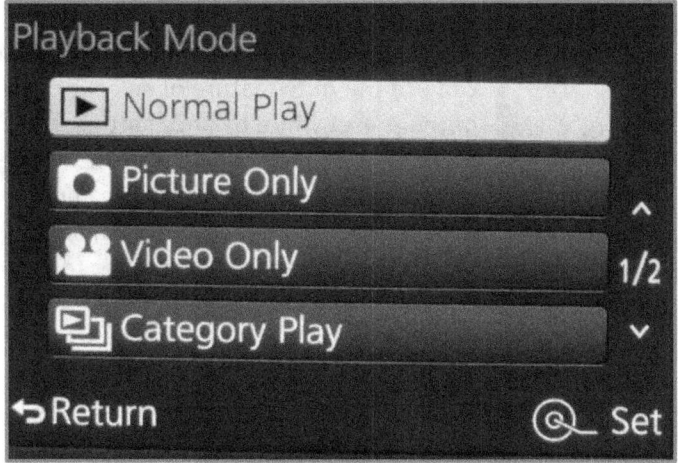

The Playback mode provides choices for which images and video clips are played

I don't propose to spend much time on the playback options but one which is worth further discussion is the RAW Processing option.

In-Camera Raw Processing

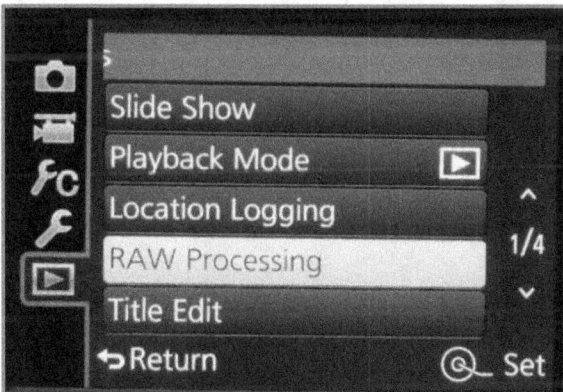

The RAW processing option is found on the first page of the PLAYBACK MENU.

It is a powerful feature that can help you develop a set of image parameters that you can then set into the JPEG specific controls such as Photostyle, Sharpness, contrast etc.,

The process only works with images using the RAW format (or RAW plus JPEG option).

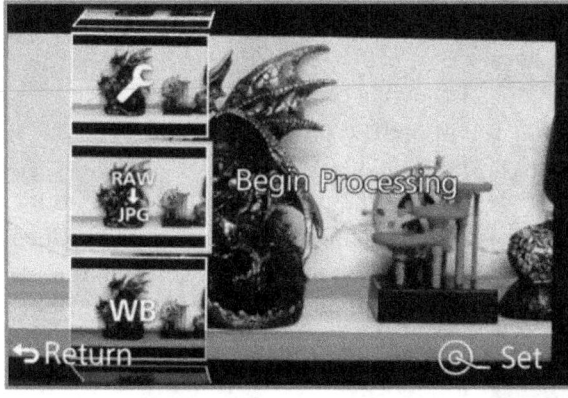

Press Menu/Set on the Selected image in the Playback screen to begin. When you begin the RAW processing option, the first step is to make any adjustments to the image. The best way to proceed is to start with the WB (white balance) adjustment. With this you can fix any colour casts that may be in the image

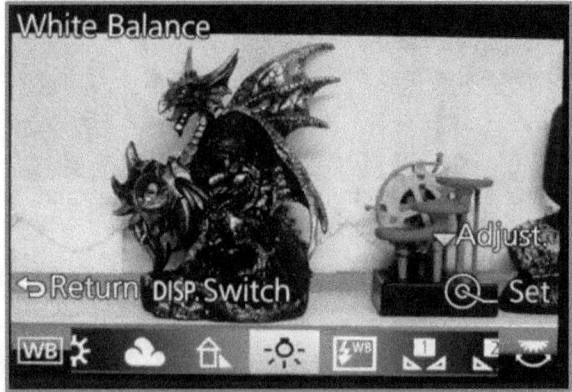

With the White Balance adjustment, you can use the Auto feature or select one of the preset white balance settings. You can fine tune any of the presets by using the DOWN cursor button to bring up the colour space tool. You can also use the Kelvin temperature slider to set the colour temperature.

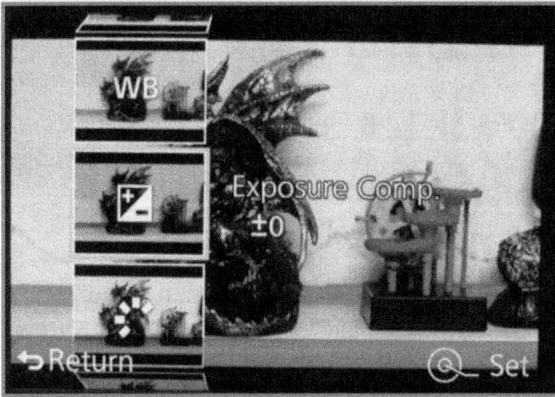

After setting the white balance the next control that can be adjusted is the Exposure Compensation. Images can be made brighter if they are under exposed or darker if they are slightly overexposed.

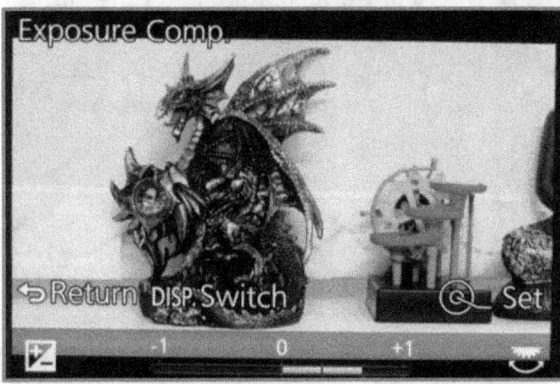

Using Exposure Compensation of +2/3 EV to Brighten the image.

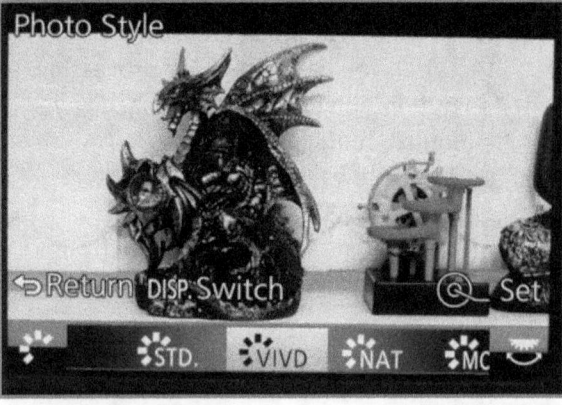

Following on from exposure compensation the next control is the Photostyle choice.
Each of the presets defines the amount of processing that is applied to produce the JPEG image. Cycling through the options shows how that effect will look. Further fine tuning can be made to the parameters like sharpness and noise reduction in the following steps.

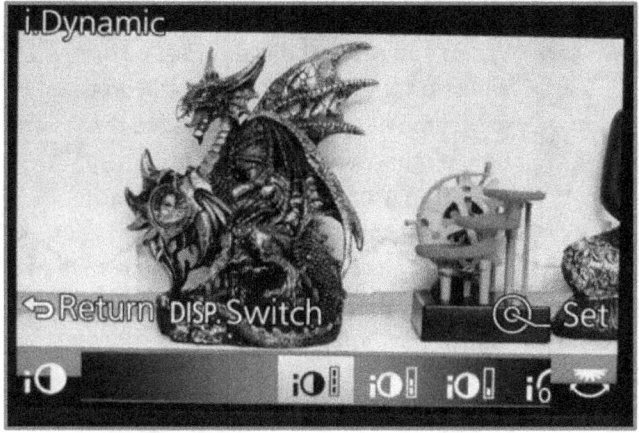

The next control is i.Dynamic whose effect is to adjust the contrast of the resulting image such that highlights and shadows are adjusted to allow more detail to be shown. This can be at the expense of image noise – particularly in the shadow areas.

I'm not showing details for every control that is available however after i.Dynamic there are: Contrast, Highlight adjustment, Shadow adjustment, Saturation, Noise reduction, Intelligent resolution and Sharpness.

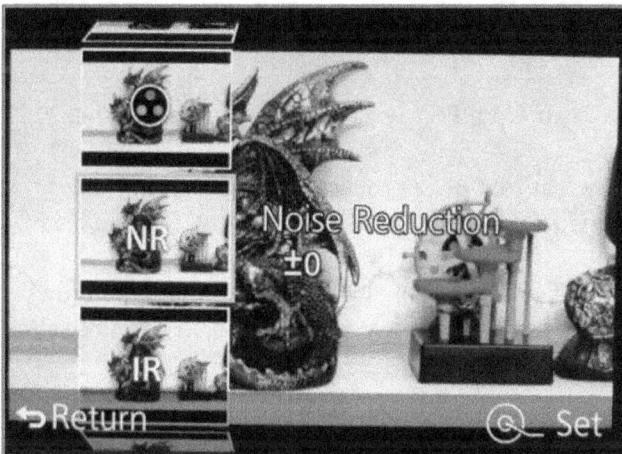

Noise reduction is the method by which high ISO noise is reduced by slightly blurring the image. At Low ISO values where noise isn't that prominent it can lead to slightly softer images. If you always shoot at, or around, the native ISO of 125 then you can set the Noise Reduction value to -2 to -4 and this reduces the amount of blur added to the image.

With the Sharpening parameter, again if you intend to do no further processing of the image file then you might want to try adjusting the value to +1 or +2. This will improve the sharpness of the out of camera (OOC) image.

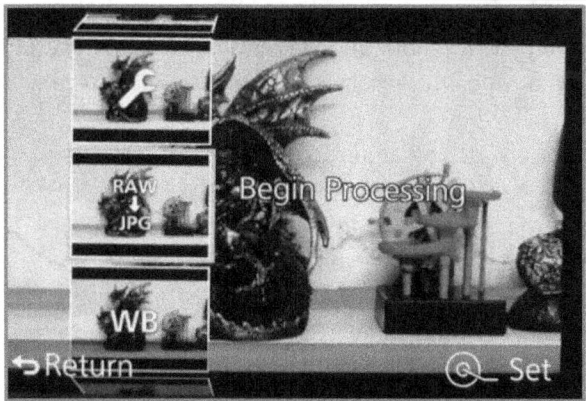

Once you have adjusted all the RAW processing controls that you think that your image needs then you navigate around the loop to arrive back at the Begin Processing option.

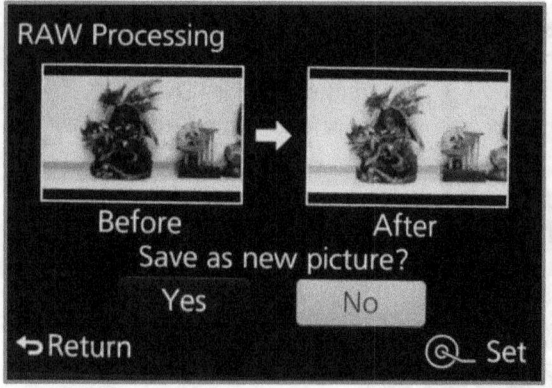

RAW Processing

Before → After

Save as new picture?

Yes | No

↰ Return   ⊘ Set

When you press the Menu/Set button whilst on the Begin Processing icon the program will prompt you to save this as a new picture. Choose Yes and then again press the Menu/Set button to commence the save process.

You may alter the parameters and save as many different images as you like. Each will have a new image number.

This method of creating multiple JPEG's from the one RAW file allows you to evaluate which of the parameters have the most desirable effect on your image.

If for example, you find that the images are best processed using the Vivid Photostyle and with -2 noise reduction and + 2 sharpening applied then these values can be set into the Vivid photostyle parameters.

After you have done this then the out of camera JPEG's will have a better appearance.

Of course, this is no substitute for a fully featured RAW processing program but it does give you the advantage that you can very quickly produce an in-camera JPEG mage from your RAW files.

Incidentally the thumbnails that are produced so that the image cataloguing of Windows and Mac computers can display them uses the default RAW processing values.

Compositional Aids

ELECTRONIC LEVEL GAUGE

The FZ1000 has several useful features that will help with getting better composed images.

There is the Level display option which quickly shows whether the camera is being held truly level in both Horizontal and Vertical planes. The horizontal level is particularly useful if you are shooting say a landscape image that doesn't feature a horizon so that you can get the picture looking straight.

The Vertical plane indicator is useful if you are shooting architectural shots at wide angle settings.

Any tilt on the camera will show up in your image as converging verticals.

If you maintain the camera sensor plane vertical then these vertical edges to buildings etc., will not show any convergence.

The electronic level gauge can be overlaid on your images by pressing the DISP button to cycle to the display that you want (with or without the other information being displayed).

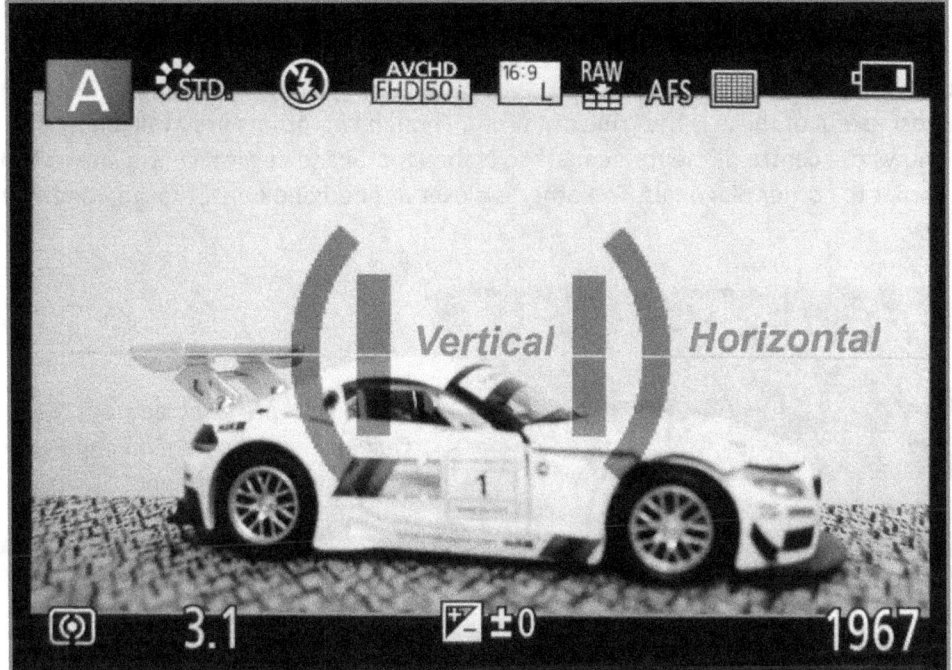

The electronic level superimposed on the image showing both the horizontal and vertical levels are both "Green" meaning both are at 0 degrees.

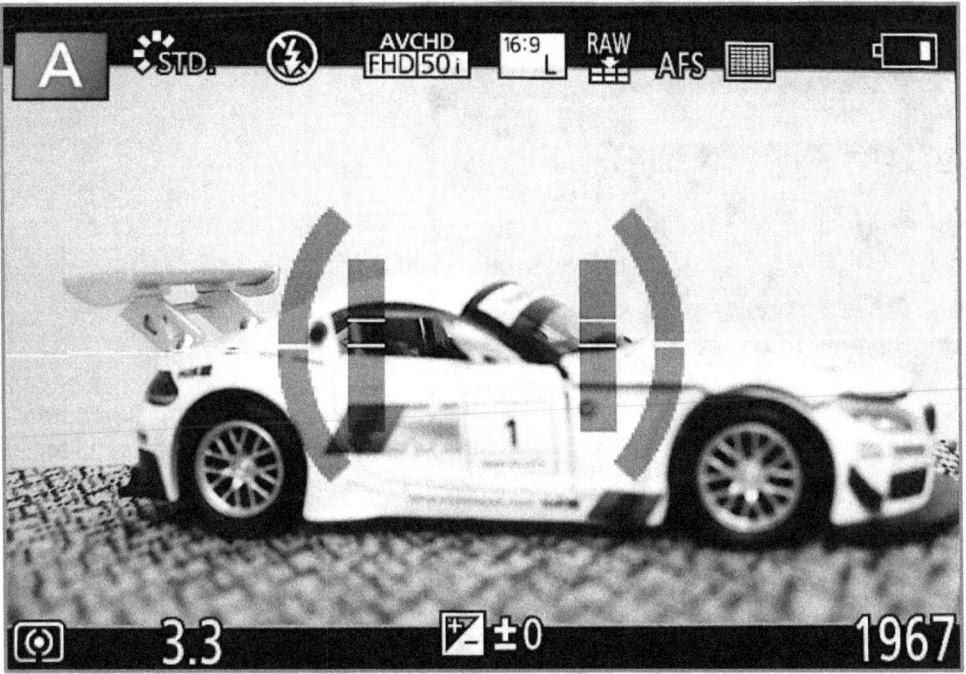

In this image the camera is sloping horizontally and tilting back as indicated by the two lines being Yellow as they are not through the 0 Level position.

Display Guide lines

Another useful feature is one where you can turn on vertical and horizontal guidelines which are superimposed on the image.

The most useful of these is the "rule of thirds". Though two others are available.

One shows the centre of the frame marked by horizontal and vertical centre lines plus the two corner to corner diagonals. The other is a user defined one horizontal and one vertical grid line.

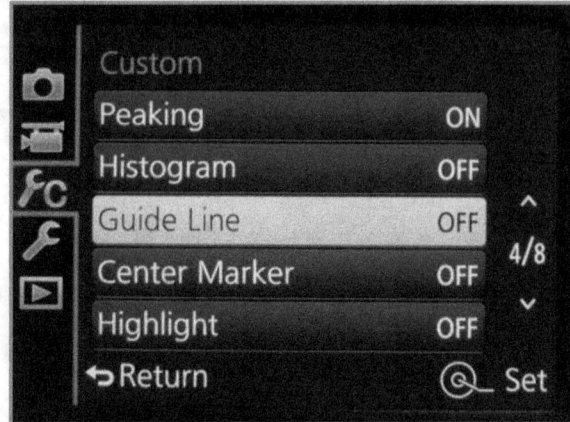

Guide lines are selected from the Guide Line menu item on page 4/8 in the Custom set up menu.

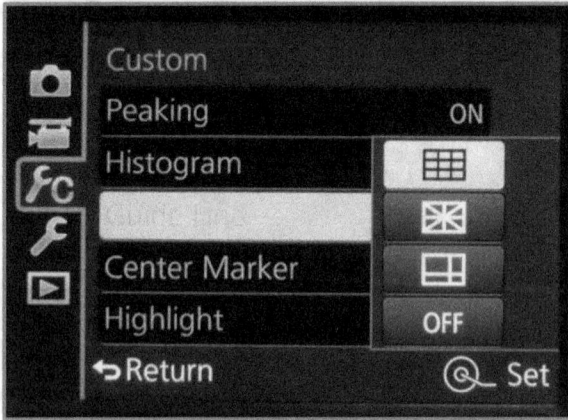

The "Rule of Thirds" Guide line.

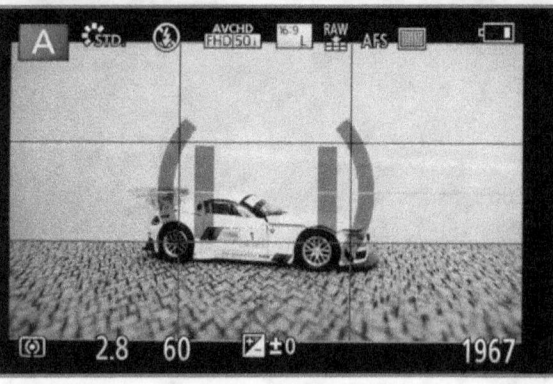

The Rule of Thirds grid superimposed on the image displays. Useful for ensuring horizontal and vertical lines are correct. Also. the strongest point of the composition should be at the intersection of a vertical and a horizontal line.

The final compositional aid is the "centre marker" again accessed on page 4/8 of the Custom menu.

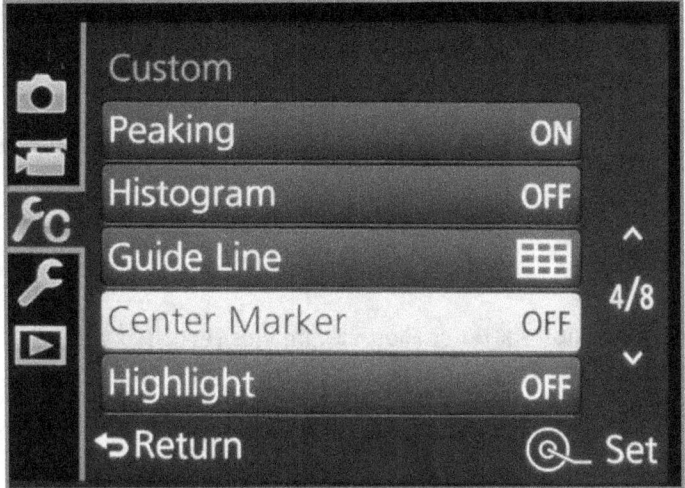

Access to the centre marker from page 4/8 of the Custom Menu.

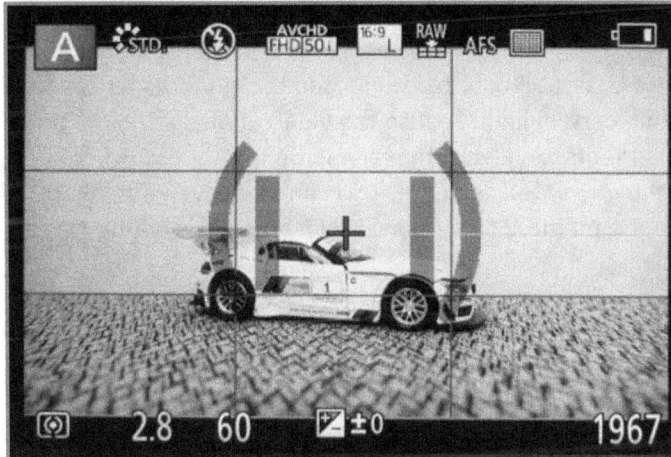

The Centre marker displayed with the rule of thirds grid lines.

Other In-Camera Edits

Title Edit

You can enter characters (comments) on a recorded picture. After the text has been registered, it can be stamped in prints using [Text Stamp].

It cannot be applied to any image that has been captured using any of the RAW options, it is a JPEG only option.
You can set up to 100 images with the [Multi] option
The text will appear when printed using the "PHOTOfunSTUDIO" software on the DVD.

Text Stamp

You can stamp the recording date and time, names, travel destination, travel dates, etc. on the recorded still pictures. Here are the options and the printed text on images.

[Shooting Date]
[W/O TIME] stamps recording date [WITH TIME]: Stamp recording date and time

[Name]
Stamp name registered in Face Recognition
Stamp name registered in [Profile Setup]
[Location]
Stamp location registered in [Setup] menu's [Travel Date]
[Travel Date]
Stamp number of days since the travel date set in [Setup] menu's [Travel Date]
[Title]
Stamp text registered in [Title Edit]

This operation will not work with Video clips, 4K Burst Files, still images recorded with any RAW quality setting, Panorama images, any images previously stamped and any pictures recorded without setting the clock and title.

I personally have never found a use for these operations but it may be useful to some.

Video Divide

This in-camera option will give you a basic ability to trim videos in the camera.
Using this procedure, you can, within certain limits, pause the video at any point and then cut it at that point resulting into segments of video rather than one.
You can then, if you want, delete the unwanted segment. This can be convenient if you want to increase the free space on the memory card- especially if you are shooting 4K video.

To do this choose the Video Divide function from the Playback Menu and then press the right button to go to the playback screen.
 If the video you want to divide is not already displayed, scroll through your images using the left or right buttons or control dial until you locate it.

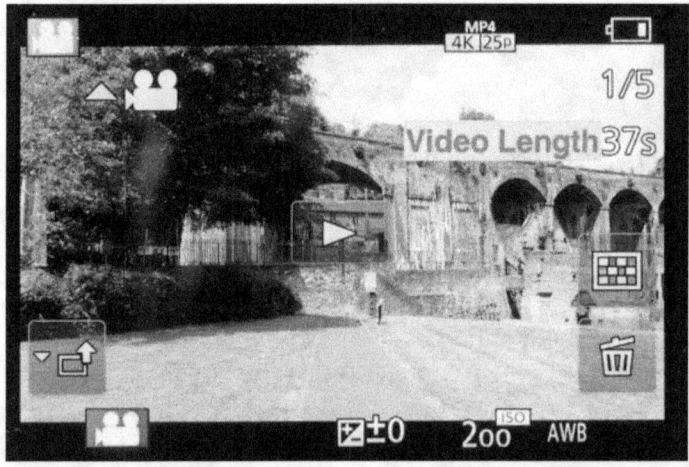

You can recognise videos because it will display the length of the video in the upper right quarter of the screen and a movie icon with an up arrow in the upper left.

The camera displays your images here, including any still images, so you may have to scroll through many non-videos until you reach the video that you want.
If you want to limit your searching down to video only you can choose video only for playback mode before selecting the video divide menu option.

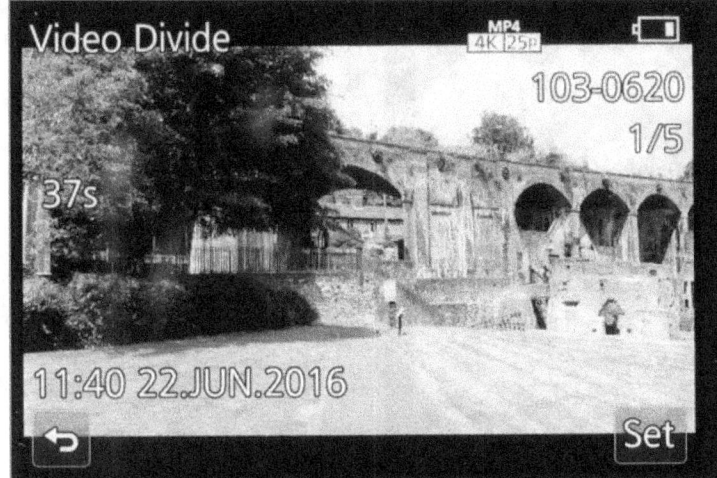

With the wanted video on screen press Menu Set to starting playing. When it reaches the point where you want to divided press the UP button to pause the video.

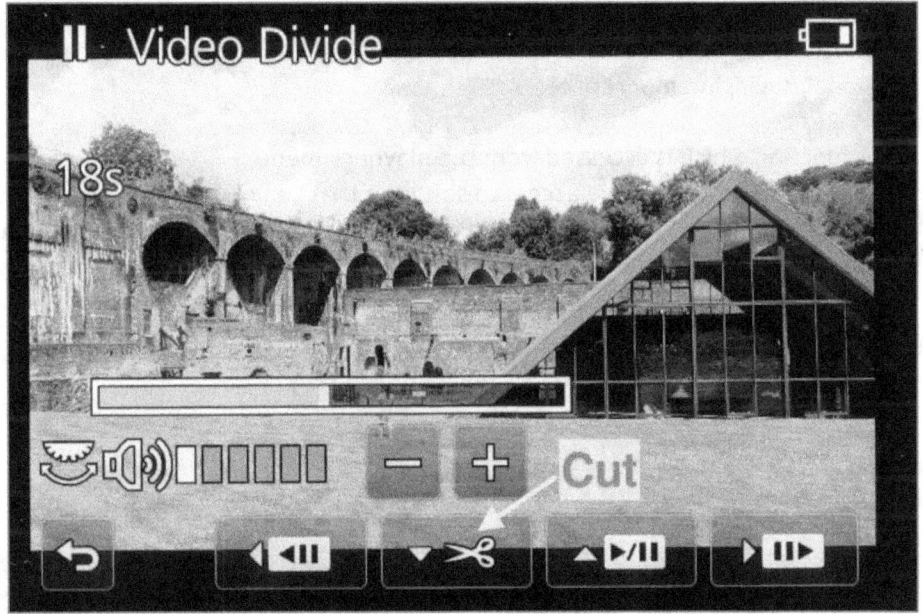

While the video is paused, you can move through the video frame by frame using the left and right cursor buttons (or the on-screen touch buttons) until you find exact point you want to divide it at.

Once you reach that point press the Down cursor button (or touch the on-screen scissor button) to make the cut.

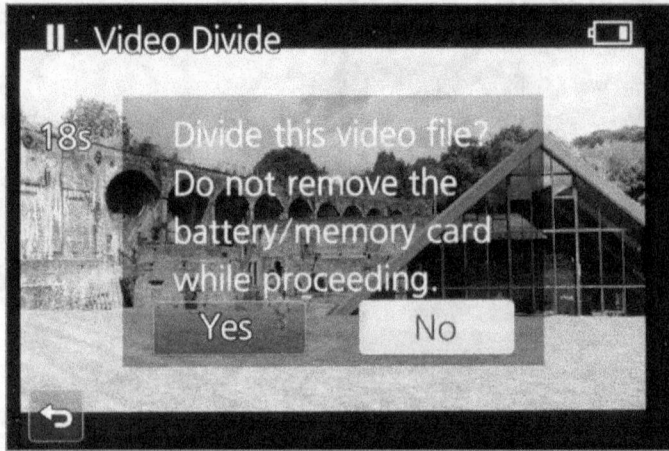

After you have made the cut the camera will display a message on-screen asking you to confirm the cut operation. Highlight YES and press Menu/Set to confirm.

You now have two video divided at the chosen cut point.

This is just a very basic cut edit. It cannot be used very close to the start or end of the video clip or indeed divide a very short video clip.

It's better than no edit at all I guess and does allow you to trim and discard unwanted material, saving memory space.

Resize

This function which is accessed from the playback menu.

It is useful if you don't have access to software that can resize an image and you need to produce a small file that you can send as an email message attachment or upload to website.

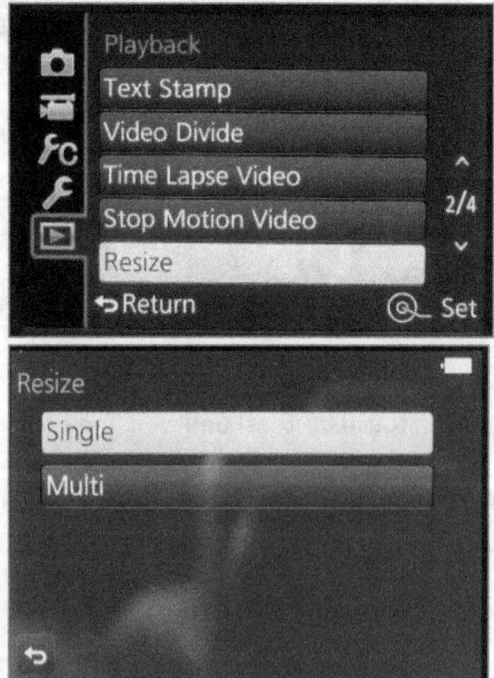

After selecting menu item on the next three you choose whether to resize a single or multiple images.

Then using left and right cursor buttons navigate to the image that you want to resize, If it is not already displayed on the screen.

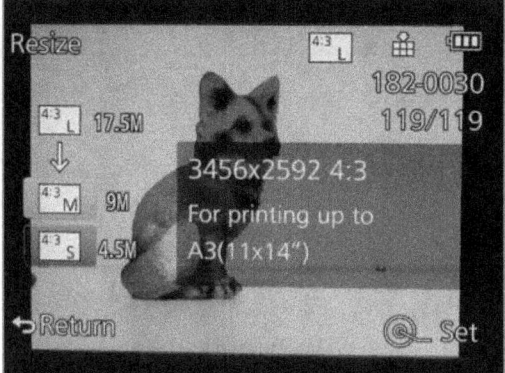

Once you have the image to be resized on screen press the SET button to start the resizing process.
Then follow the prompts on the screen.

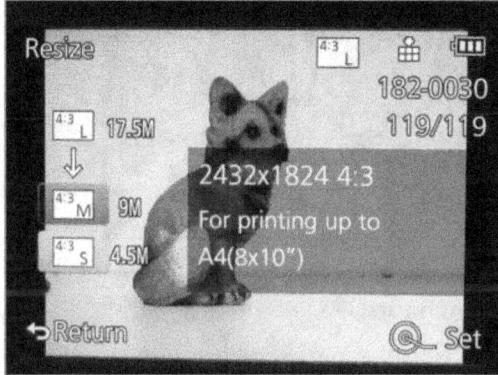

Use the up and down cursor buttons to highlight the size to reduce the image to. The choices may include M for medium, S for small depending on the size of the original image. When the option you want to use is highlighted in yellow press Menu Set to carry out the resizing process.

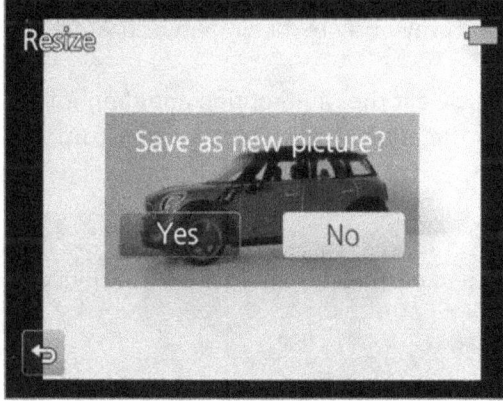

The camera will ask you to confirm that you want to save a new picture at the new size.

As with the Text Stamp function resizing does not overwrite the original image, it saves a copy of it so the original is always available.

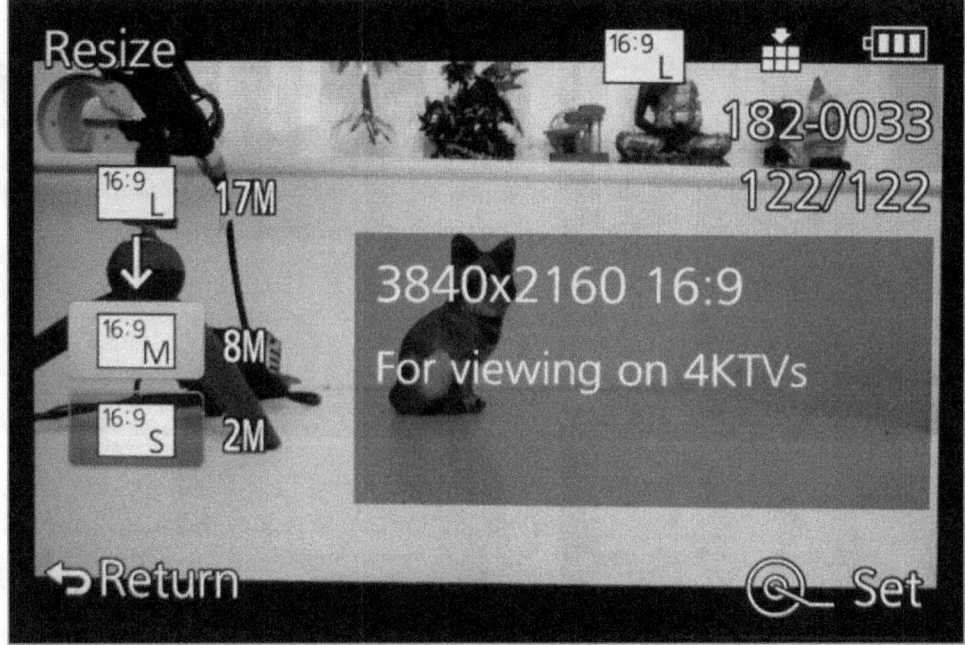

A useful feature of the resize option is the facility to create images from full size ones ready for display either on 4K or 1080p Television monitors.

This operation will not work with Video clips, 4K Burst Files, still images recorded with any RAW quality setting, Panorama images, any images previously text stamped or protected.

You can convert a batch of up to 100 images if you select the Multi option and then follow this procedure. The resized image will be found at the end of the current set of recorded images.

Cropping

This function is like the resize one except that instead of resizing, the camera now lets you crop into just part of the original image.

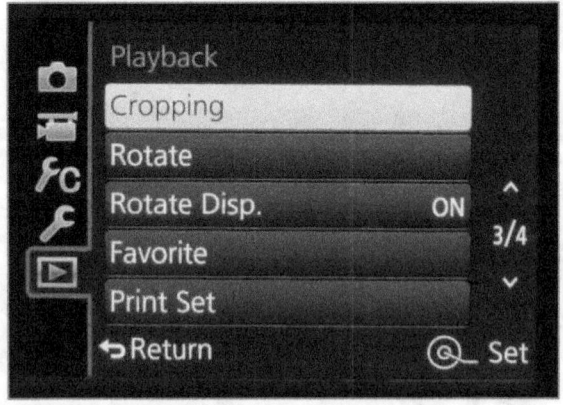

To accomplish this, select Cropping from the Playback menu.

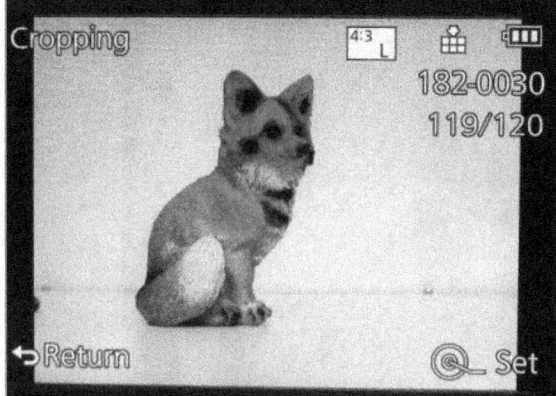

Then navigate with the left and right navigation keys to the image which requires cropping.

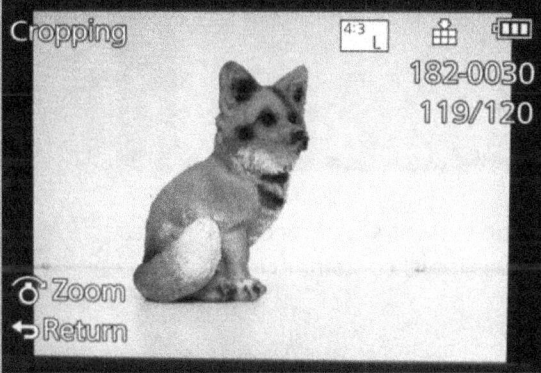

With the zoom lever, enlarge the image and then use the direction buttons to position the part of the image to be retained.

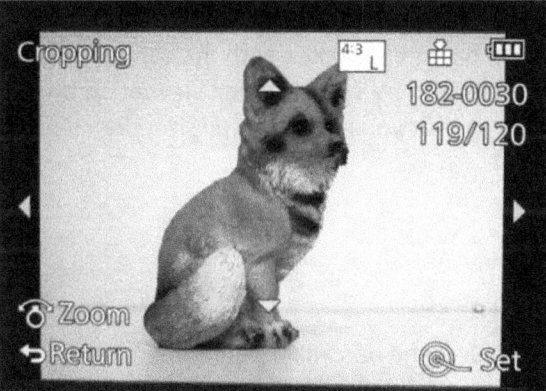

When you have, the image positioned as you want it press Menu/Set to lock the position.

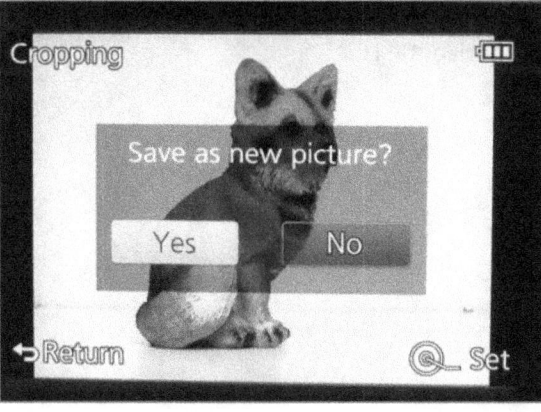

The camera will ask you to confirm that you want to save a new picture at the new size.

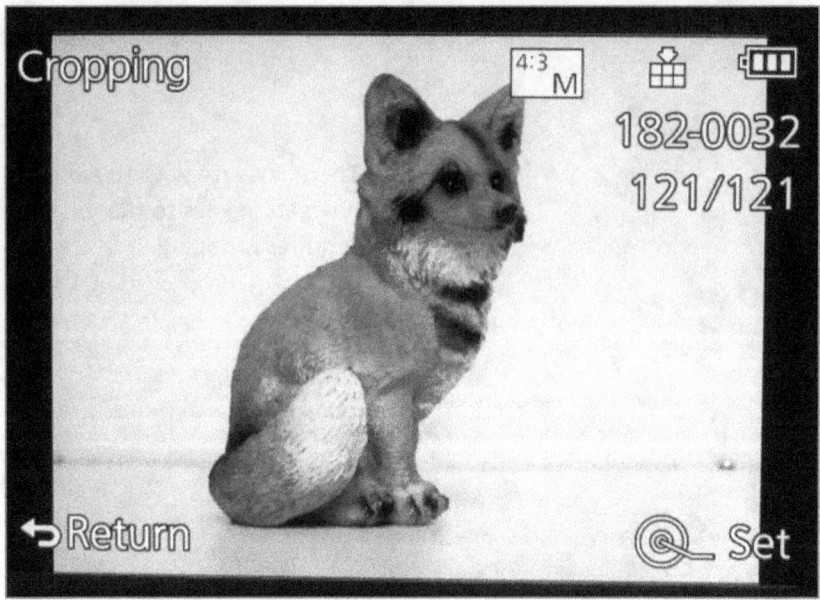

The resized image will be found at the end of the current set of recorded images.
The cropped image will also have a smaller size as it will contain fewer pixels.

Rotate and Rotate Display

I'm grouping these two options together as they can work together in a specific workflow situation.

Firstly, when the Rotate Display option is turned on, images taken with the camera held in a vertical (portrait) format are automatically rotated to be vertical when viewed on the horizontal LCD. If you want to rotate this image so that you can see it full size, then you can use the Rotate option to do this.

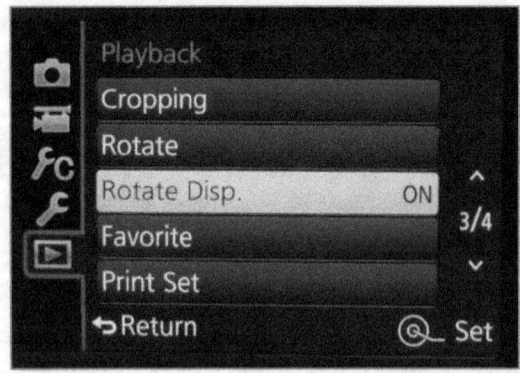

This is the normal, default, operation to have the camera automatically rotate any vertically captured images on the horizontal LCD

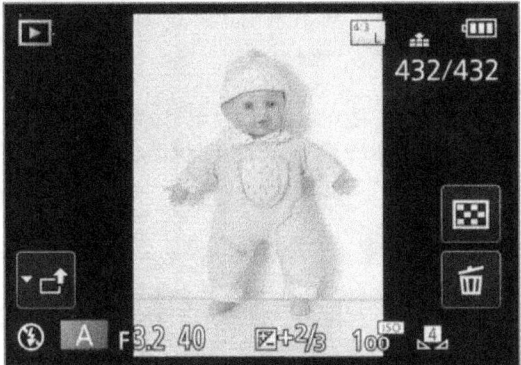

This is an example of a vertical, portrait, shot which has been automatically rotated to show it the correct way up on the horizontal display.

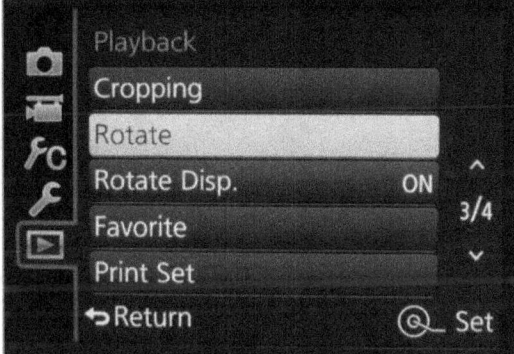

The option to rotate the image is found in the playback menu page 3/4

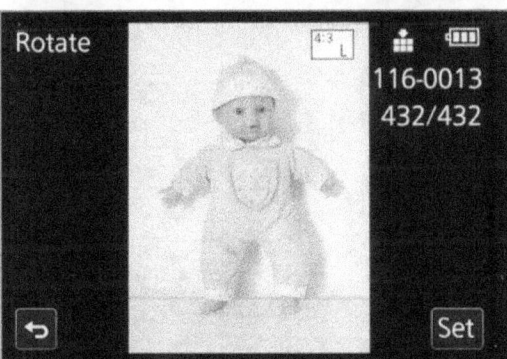

With rotate selected the screen will show the images. You can use the left/right navigation keys to find the image that you would like to rotate. When found press the Menu/Set button or touch the Set icon on the LCD screen.

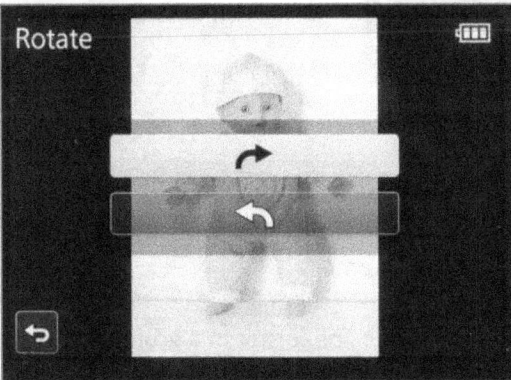

The display will now show the two rotation arrows. Touch the arrow on screen to complete the rotation of the image.

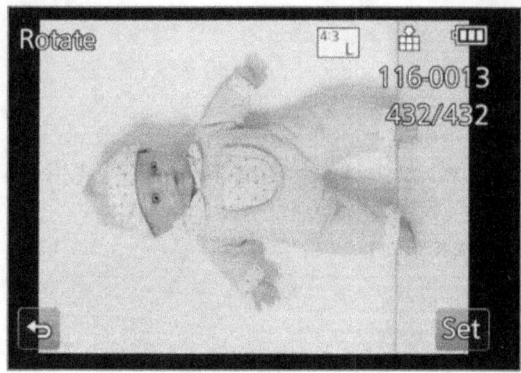

The image has now been rotated to give the full screen size so you can better evaluate composition, sharpness etc.

If you play back pictures on a PC, they cannot be displayed in the rotated direction unless the OS or software is compatible with the image file EXIF.

Favourite

With this menu option, it is possible to go through the images on the memory card identifying the best images and labelling them with a *. It is then possible to play back just the favorited ones or you can delete all but the favourite ones. Up to 999 images can be set.

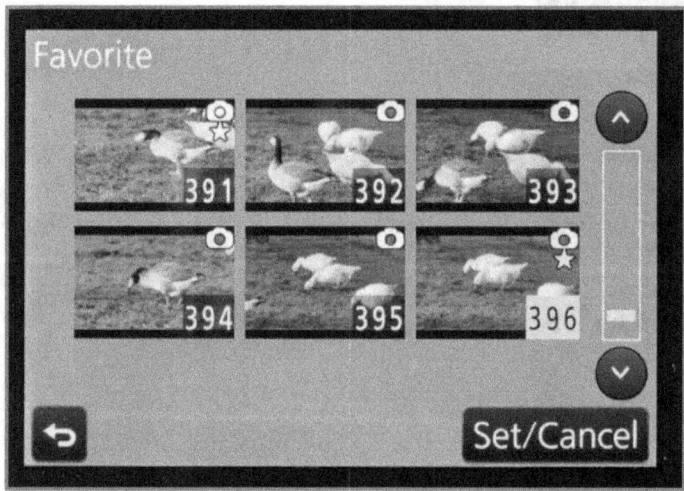

Face Recognition

If the Face Recognition function recognises a face which has been previously registered it then automatically adjusts focus and exposure for that face with higher priority. It is enabled in the REC setup menu, face recognition on/off/memory.

Even if a person you want to focus on is standing at the back or corner in a group photo, the camera will automatically recognise the person and record this person's face clearly.

The process for face recognition is as follows;

The camera recognises a registered face and adjusts focus and exposure. When registered faces, that have names that have been associated to them, are recognised the names are displayed along with the yellow square indicating that face. (max. 3 people).

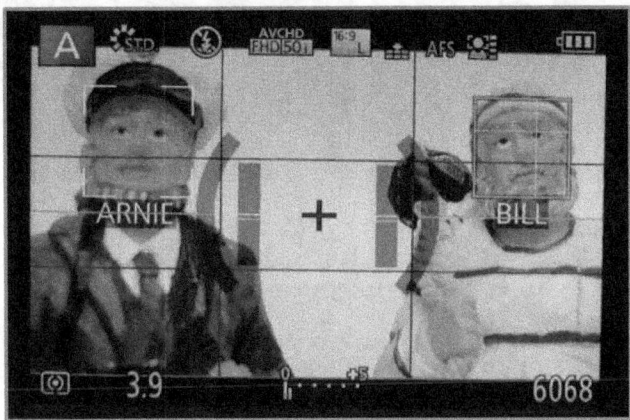

The faces which are recognised and stored in memory are displayed with names

For the images to be annotated with the names they must be set up under the face recognition memory, set option.

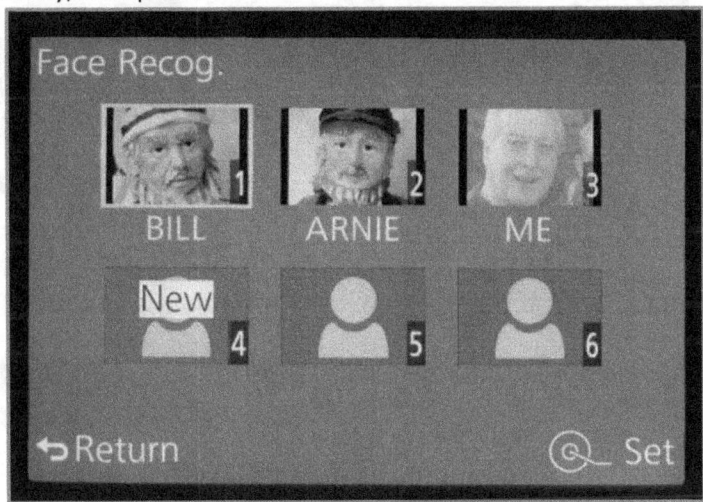

Up to 6 faces can be registered, with name, priority and age.
Priority will allow the camera to use this face to set the focus if there are multiple faces being detected in the image.

To enhance recognition accuracy, up to 3 separate photos can be registered for a single individual's face.

For example, you can shoot from slightly different angles, to improve the chances of recognition.
Additionally, babies ages can also be recorded in the face recognition memory.
When this is done, the current age will be embedded in the camera EXIF and can be made

to print on the photo with programs like Photofunstudio which is included with the camera.

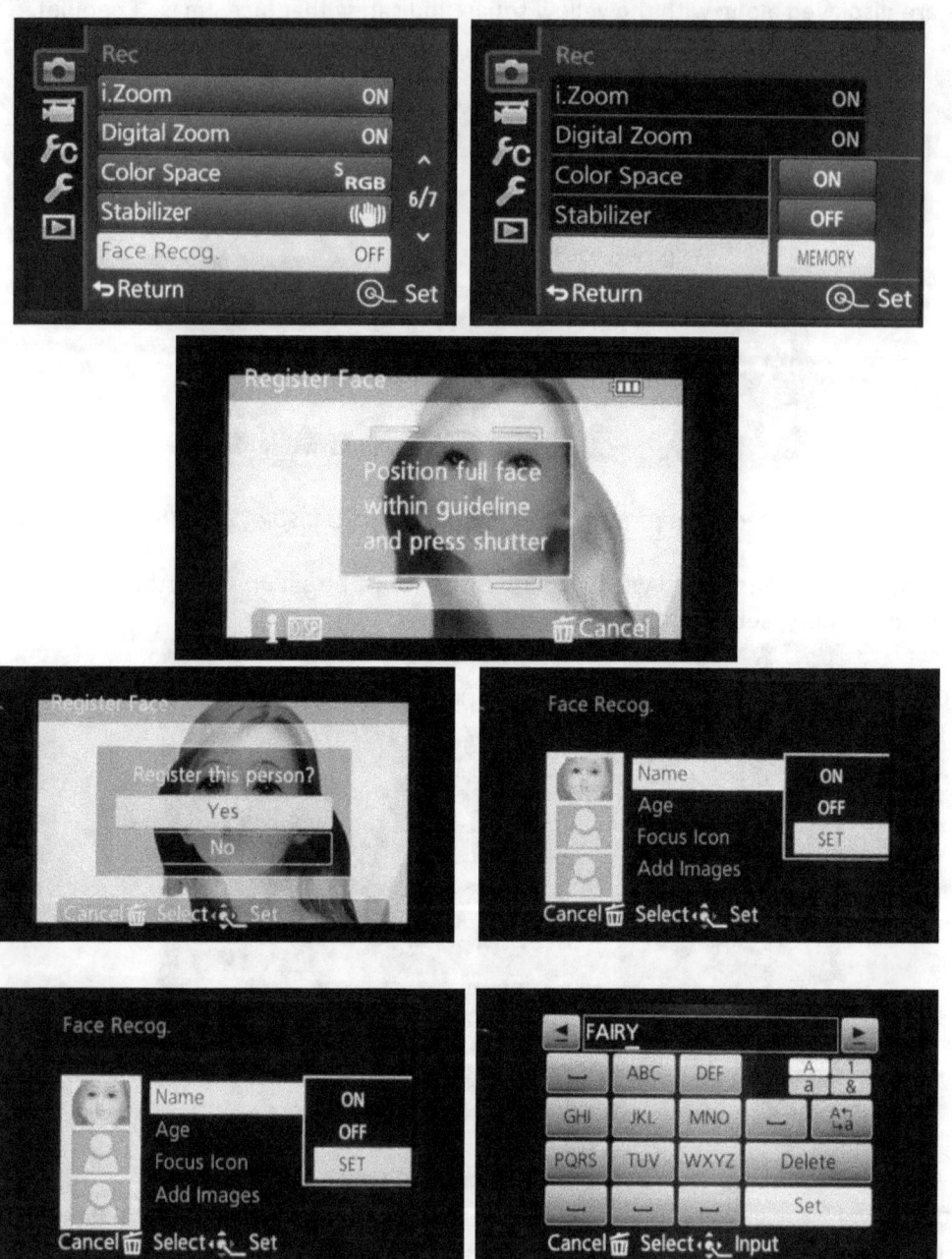

The above images show the sequence of menus and entries required to be able to set the camera to recognise and display individual faces in a captured image.

Once the images have been recorded of the faces that you want the camera to consider for priority focus then you can edit the info [Info Edit] for things like name and priority is set using the [Priority] option. Registered faces can also be deleted using [Delete]

Viewing Video Clips

The camera has the facility to playback video clips recorded by this camera in either the AVCHD and MP4 formats.
Motion pictures will be identified by the movie camera icon at the top left hand side of the LCD screen during playback.

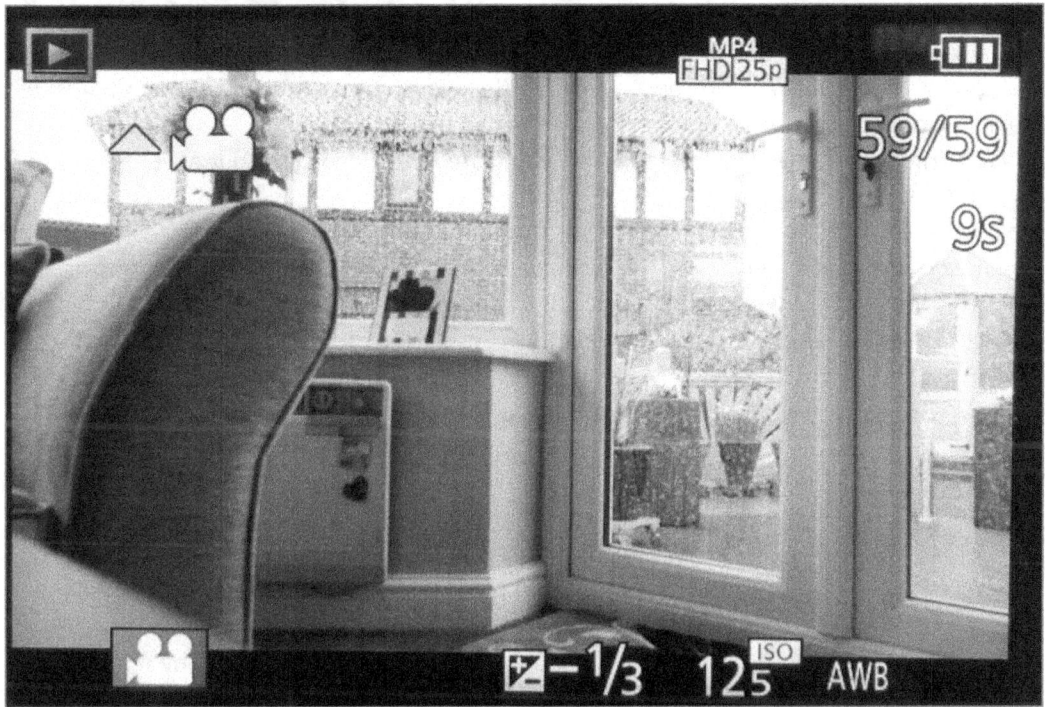

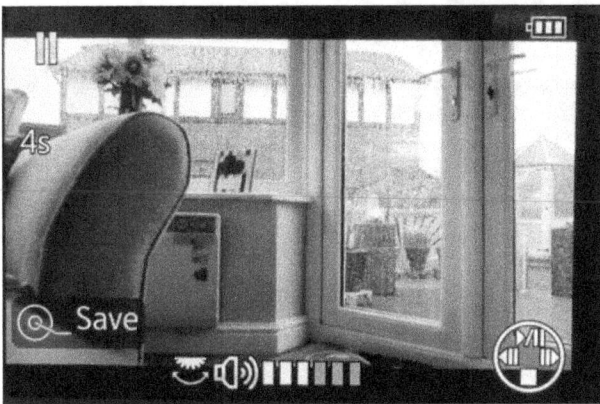

To begin the playback of a video clip press the UP-cursor button
To stop playback press the DOWN cursor.
Use the LEFT/RIGHT keys to move through the video clip
The back control wheel adjusts the volume of the playback audio.

To delete a video clip, press the Fn4 (trash can) button.
Then confirm the operation.
It cannot be undone!
Additionally, by selecting Multi rather than Single up to 100 images/clips may be selected for deletion.

This process will allow you to capture a specific frame within a video to create a still image. This will apply to all video clips except those recorded in the lower resolution with the VGA format.
The quality of the capture will be lower than the same resolution of a still image that you would set in the Rec Quality set up for that still image format.

It is also worth noting that the shutter speed that is used during recording will also affect the quality of the image captured. Normally video clips that use a slow shutter speed will have lots of subject motion blur in any captured image.
This blurring goes largely unnoticed when you watch the video clip – our eyes smooth out the motion.
If you are intending to capture still images from any video that you shoot, if the lighting at the time of capture allows, it is best to switch to the Creative Video mode and set the shutter speed as you would with a still image capture i.e. 1/lens focal length. You could use the S mode or the M mode to do this.

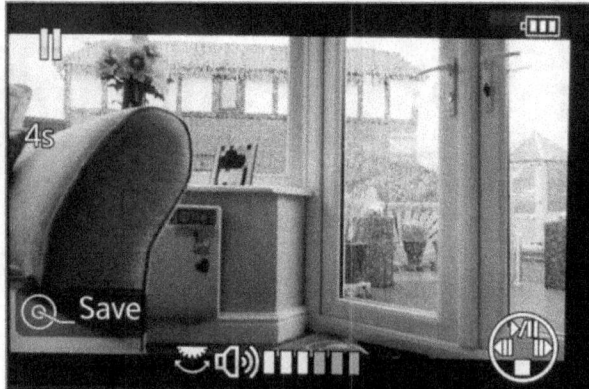

Move to the position in the video clip that you want to capture the still image from.

At the point in the clip where you require the still image pause the video playback and the n press Menu/Set to capture the image.

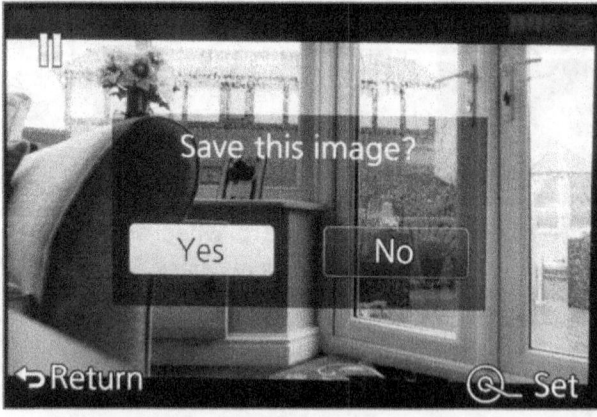

The camera will then ask you to confirm the saving of the new image.

The aspect ratio of the captured image will be 16:9 and will be captured with the lower JPEG quality setting. (_ _ _)

The pixel dimensions will depend upon the video clip being played back:
For FHD (Full HD) or HD the size will be 2M (S) format
For 4K the size will be 8M (M).

The FZ1000 offers Wi-Fi connectivity and control and includes Near Field Communications, or NFC for short. To be fair though, NFC only helps the initial negotiation with a compatible smartphone (android device only). Using the QR code is just as effective at pairing your IOS smartphone if you select the option to set Wi-Fi password to ON in the camera Wi-Fi Function menu.

Wi-Fi allows you to wirelessly browse the FZ1000's images on the larger and more detailed screen of a smartphone, tablet or laptop, copy them onto these devices, upload them to online storage or social media services (either directly or via a smartphone), or become remote-controlled by a free app for iOS or Android device.

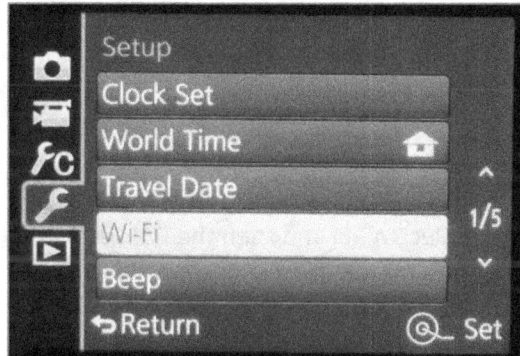

In the absence of a smartphone with NFC, the first step to setting up the FZ1000's Wi-Fi is to select the Wi-Fi option from the Setup menu page 1/5 to either create a new connection, or load one you've previously configured. The blue LED on top of the camera will light.

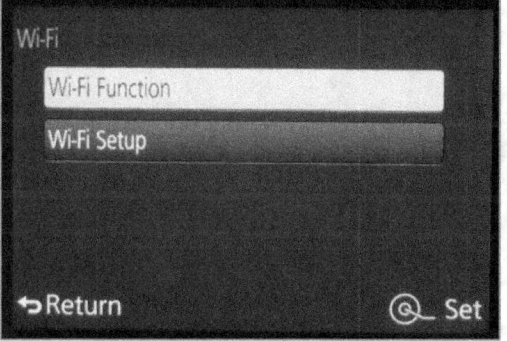

Then select the W-Fi Function option to begin the pairing process.
Wi-Fi Setup allows renaming of the device, setting a new password, turning on the NFC operation and setting up PC connection.

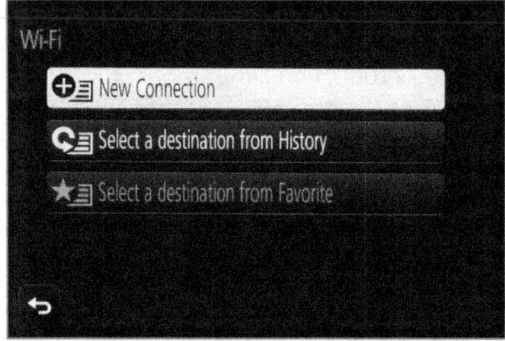

If you're creating a new connection you can choose from 'remote shooting and view', 'playback on TV', 'send images while recording' or 'send images stored in the camera'.

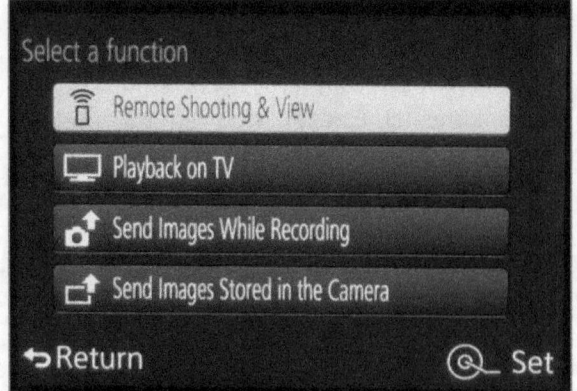

For a smartphone / tablet connection, you should choose the first option for remote shooting and view.

This then sets up the FZ1000 as a wireless access point, displaying the SSID name and password.
In your smartphone settings menu select Wi-Fi and then the FZ1000 SSID and then enter the password (if this is the first-time connection)

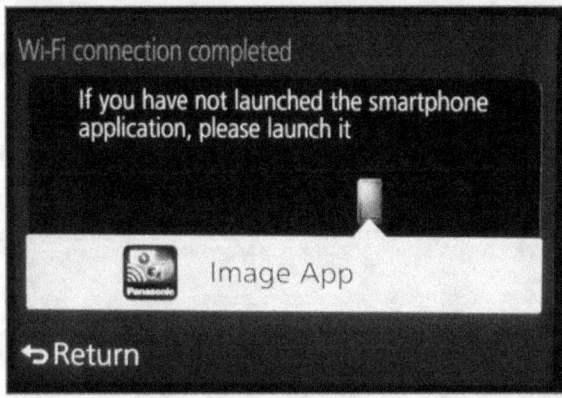

Download and install the Image App onto your smartphone.
You'll then need to start the Lumix Image app, select Wi-Fi as your means of connection, select the FZ1000 network SSID and enter the password.

Once your phone or tablet becomes connected to the FZ1000, you can remote control it, browse the images direct from the memory card, copy them onto the smartphone, and if desired, send them onto various storage or sharing services.

The remote-control feature is very useful, showing a live image on your phone or tablet's screen and allowing you to take a photo or start and stop a video.
You can tap anywhere on the live image to set the focus to that area or directly take the shot. Using this method overcomes the fact that the FZ1000 doesn't have a touch screen!
If the camera's mode dial is set to Aperture or Shutter Priority, you can remotely adjust the aperture or shutter speed respectively, and in Manual you can change both.

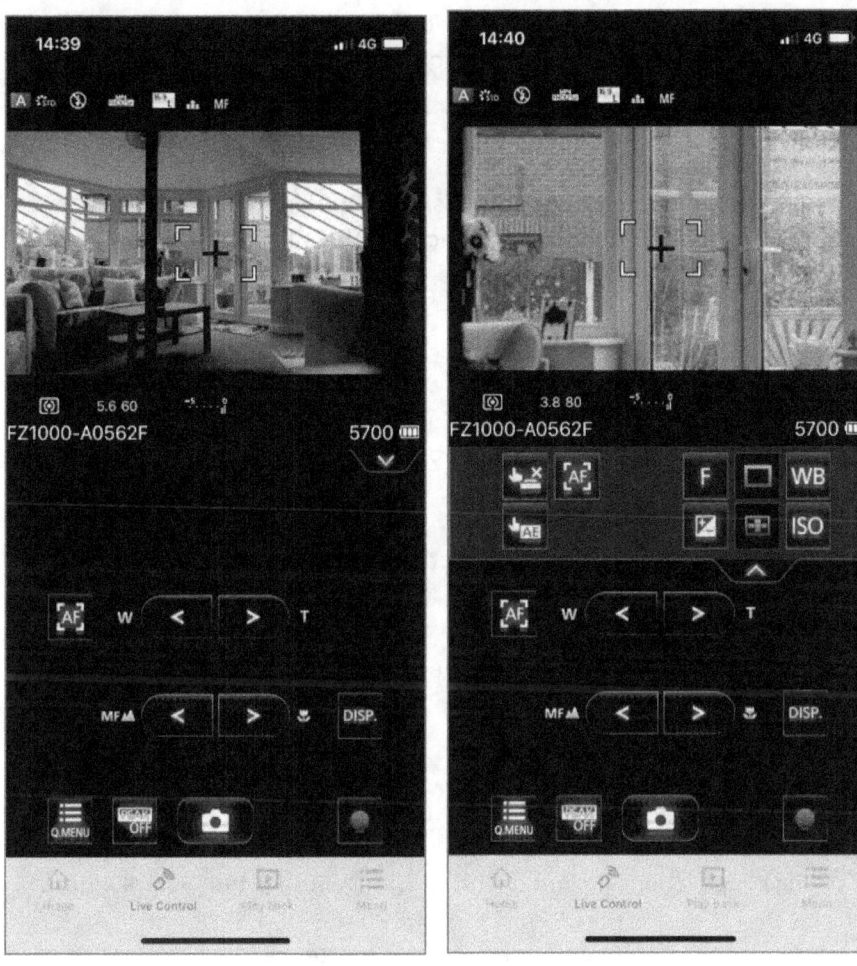

The Panasonic Image App, here on an iPhone X

You can also adjust the drive mode, ISO, white balance, exposure compensation or focus area, and there's also a QMenu button which presents a list of additional options you can remotely change including the flash mode, aspect ratio, resolution, compression, metering mode, photo style or movie quality.

To maintain a responsive experience which feels like the images are stored locally on your phone or tablet, the camera sends a lower resolution version. So, you can pinch to zoom-in a little, but not as much as if you were viewing the original.

When you see an image that you like, just press and hold it on-screen for a second and the Lumix Image app will let you save the original to your device or start uploading it to one of the social, sharing or storage services installed on your device.
You can configure the app to provide shortcuts to two or three of your most used services which could include Dropbox and Instagram. Once the image is copied into your device, you could just exit the Panasonic app and handle it direct from whichever sharing or storage app you like via your phone's gallery.

You can also choose whether to copy images in their original resolution, or in one of two smaller versions. It typically took about 20 seconds to copy a 5MB original JPEG from the camera to my iPhone X from about 1m.

It's not possible to copy RAW files though.
It's so much fun interacting with the camera using a smartphone or tablet that it's easy to forget the Lumix FZ1000 can also upload images directly to the internet by itself via a suitable Wi-Fi connection.
You can upload directly to Facebook, Twitter, Picasa, Youtube, Flickr, but there are two points to recognise in trying to do this.

The first is the camera doesn't have any kind of built-in browser to accept the terms and conditions of many public hotspots, so you'll mostly be using home or office-based Wi-Fi or a tethered connection with your smartphone.

The second problem is before letting you upload anything directly from the camera you'll first need to register for Panasonic's free Lumix Club.

Once you do upload any images direct from the camera, they wait in a private Lumix Club album to be shared with a description.

Since this requires you to have access to a computer, tablet or phone, it makes more sense to just use Wi-Fi to copy the image from the camera to that device first and upload from there in my opinion.
One of the little "strange" operations included with the Image App is the "Jump Shutter".

When you hold your smartphone and jump, the camera's shutter can be released automatically as the smartphone detects the peak of the jump. This operation is useful for taking a still picture while the subject jumps (Jump Snap).

It is recommended that you take test pictures to determine the camera's angle and how hard you jump and to make any desired adjustments.

For details about the operating procedure, refer to [Help] in the "Image App".

Useful Camera Features

There are three useful display features which can help to secure better exposed images – particularly regarding highlight "blow-out"

The Zebra stripes over exposure warnings and the highlight "blinkies" which give an indication where highlights are being clipped by the exposure settings and the monochrome EVF which allow easier focusing in the manual mode and makes it easier to establish if there are any colours in the image which are being recorded with too high a predominance.

Zebra stripes

The zebra stripe pattern can be set to display any area of the image which is likely to be overexposed with the brightness of the image approaching burn out.

There are two independent settings that can be used, Zebra 1 and Zebra2.

Each one can be set up with a different threshold level between 50% and 105%. This is done using the "SET" option of the menu for the Zebra pattern selected.

If you set the threshold level to 100%, then the patterns will only be displayed when aspects of the image are already burnt out because of the bright light.

It's a good idea to adjust this to give you a safety margin. For example, adjusting it to 80% will give you a 20% safety margin before problems arise.

When you record a video (where these are primarily designed to be used), you will be able to see zebra stripes on any light sources if they are too bright to be recorded properly.

If you ever see the zebra stripes, then you will need to take measures to stop the excess light from being such a problem.

This could include reducing the light or adjusting the exposure settings of your camera.

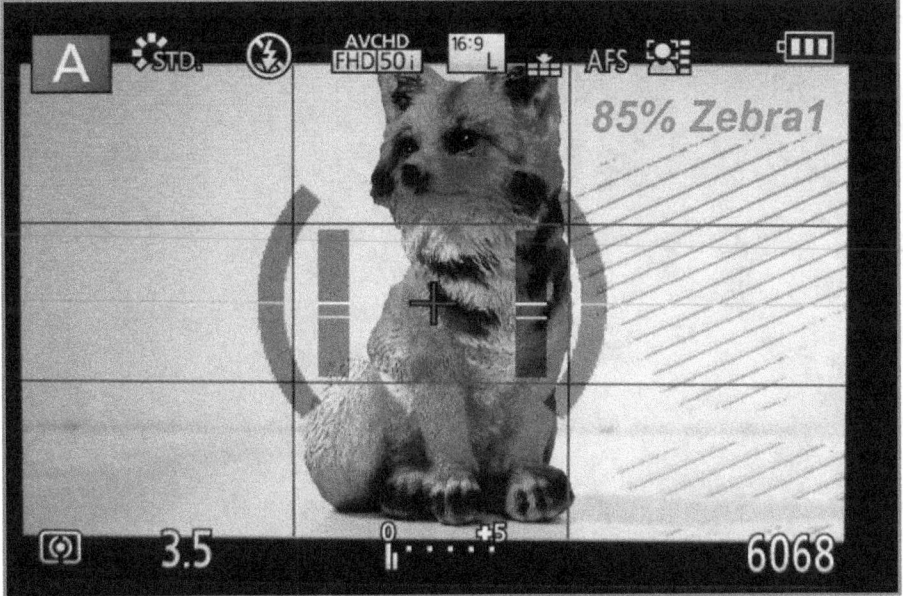

The Zebra stripes indicating that this area has reached the set threshold for the selected warning

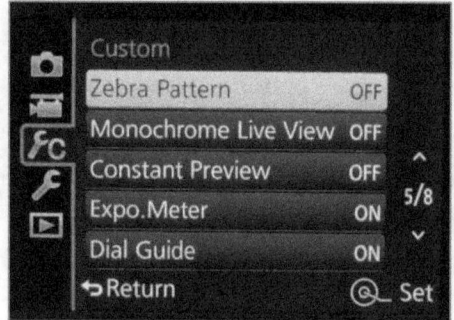 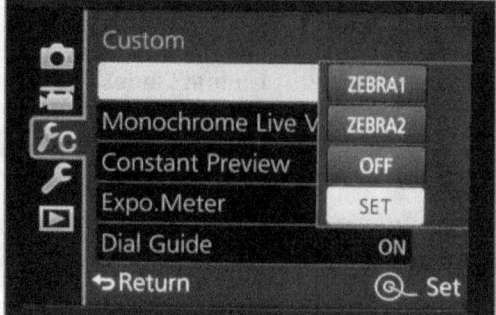

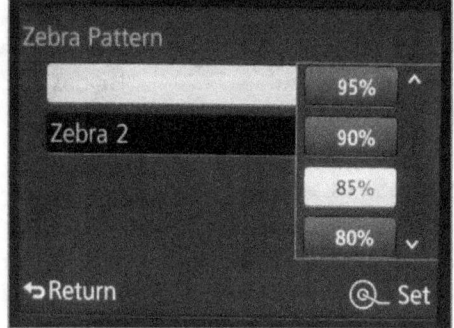 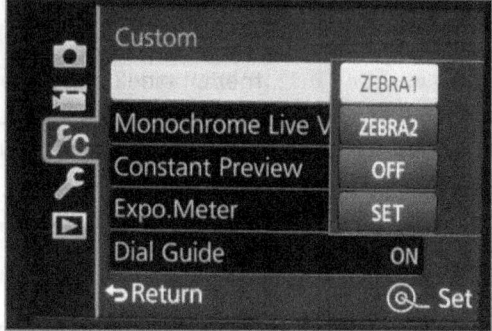

I believe that the use of the zebra stripes is far superior to the "highlight warning" – often referred to as "the blinkies" which show up in the image preview after the shot has been taken.

The Zebra stripes warn you before you take the picture that the scene has high brightness levels and that these should be corrected if the captured image is not going to be overexposed.

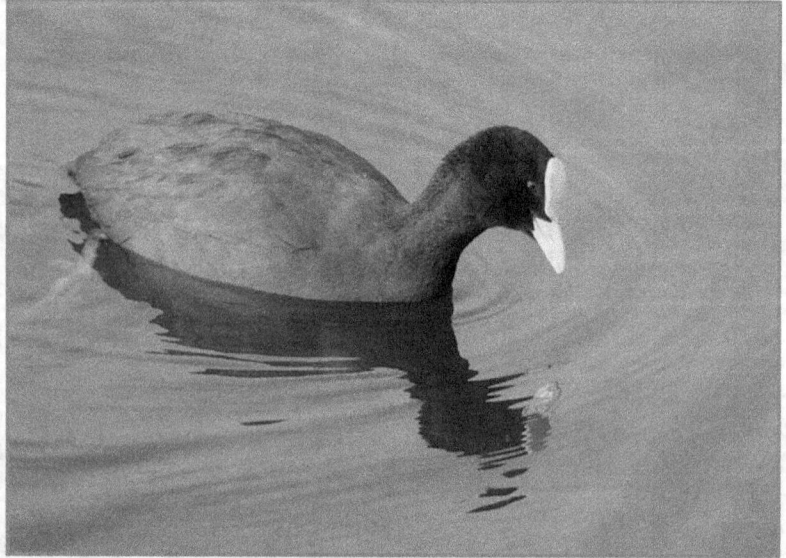

Using the highlight/zebra pattern warning it was easy to see the blown-out highlights on the beak and head of this coot. Dialling in −1EV until most of the overexposed warning had been reduced.

Monochrome Live View EVF & LCD

This a very useful feature especially if you are using manual focus. Colour tends to distract our eyes when we are looking for critical focus.

If we select the option to use a monochrome preview it will allow you to see critical focus more easily.

All other screen information is retained in colour such as if you have set focus peaking option which will readily show up in colour on this screen

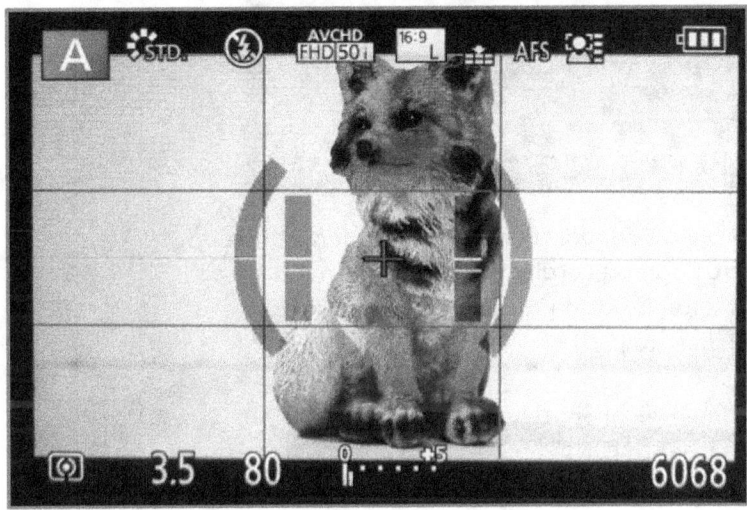

i.Zoom

i.Zoom is set to ON/OFF in the Rec Set up menu

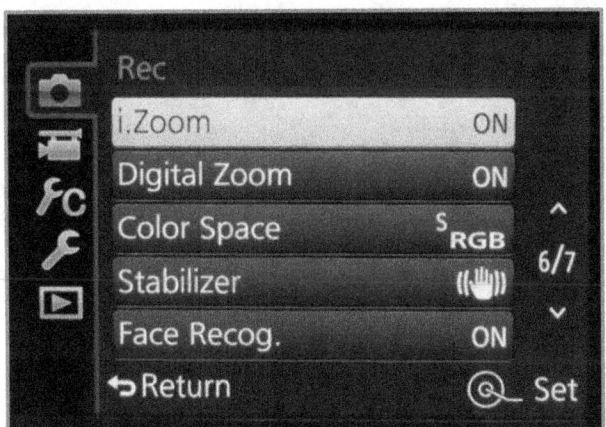

Intelligent zoom is an internal camera processing mode to accomplish more zoom by cropping, up sampling, applying some extra contrast and then unmask sharpening the image depending on zoom level before creating the JPEG file.

This only happens when all the optical zoom has been reached (400mm EFL).

You can use the camera's "Intelligent Resolution" technology to increase the zoom ratio up to 2x bigger than the original zoom ratio with only a small deterioration of picture quality.

It can be applied to both stills and video clips independently.

With i.Zoom turned on it means you can effectively increase the effective focal length to 800mm as indicated by the blue scale below (grey = optical zoom)

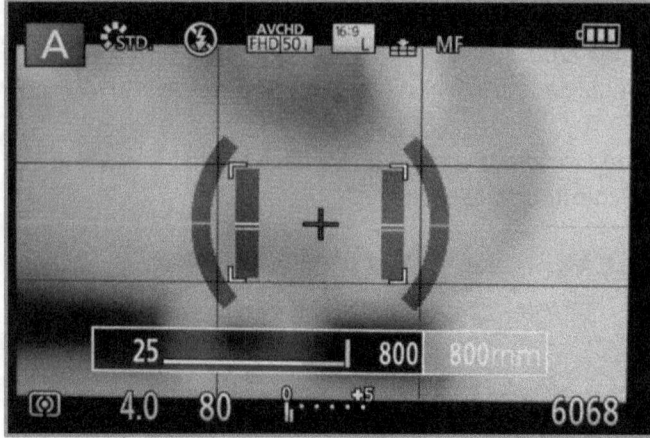

Of course, this is not an increase in real optical zoom so this does not mean that the effective depth of field will be the same as it would be if it had been shot with a true 400mm optical lens.

i.Zoom will not operate under the following camera conditions;
1. During [Macro Zoom] recording
2. When [Burst Rate] is set to [SH]
3. When [HDR] is set to [ON]
4. When [Multi Exp.] is set
5. When [iHandheld Night Shot] is set to [ON]
6. When [iHDR] is set to [ON]
7. When [Quality] is set to include RAW or any RAW+JPEG option

Digital Zoom

Using digital zoom, you can zoom up to a maximum of 4x - further than Optical/Extended optical zoom. Note that, with Digital Zoom, increasing the zoom will decrease picture quality.

Digital zoom is set on the same menu page as i.Zoom

note: If you have i.Zoom set to ON the Digital zoom is limited to x2.

You can see when you have invoked digital zoom as the indicator scale will show in darker blue.

In the example above both i.Zoom and digital zoom have been employed yielding a total zoom of 1600mm EFL (effective full frame focal length).

Use digital zoom as a very last resource and certainly keep ISO as low as possible as noise is also amplified.

In the same way as i.Zoom digital zoom cannot be used under the same conditions.

The Zoom resume option (page 8/9 Custom Set Up Menu), when set to on, will force the zoom to return to the setting before the camera was turned off.

Using Flash

The pop up flash

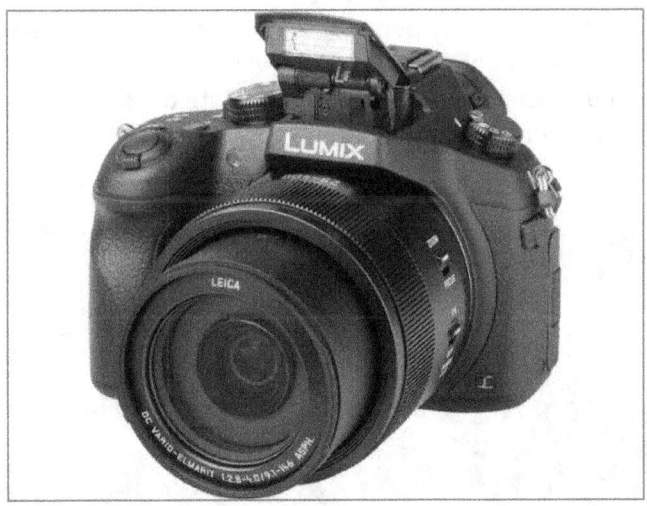

The pop-up flash head of the FZ1000 allows pictures to be taken in dark places or it can be used to control contrast in images taken which are predominantly backlit.

To open the flash head, slide open the flash lever. However, because the head is spring loaded it is best to apply light finger pressure to control the speed at which it pops up.

To close the flash head, press the head down gently until it clicks into place. When the head is closed the "force flash off" symbol will be displayed.

When using the in-built flash, it is recommended to remove the lens hood as it will cause a shadow on the lower portion of the subject when it is used at wide angle settings.

The flash power is controlled via TTL (through the lens) exposure when the flash firing mode is set to TTL. The camera will vary the duration of the flash pulse to achieve the correct level of illumination needed.

The flash pulse is always the same intensity; the duration is the controlling element to the exposure.

Thus, for darker scenes requiring more flash power the duration of the flash pulse may be 1/200 sec. Conversely if the subject is quite close to the camera the flash pulse duration may only be 1/8000 sec.

You can use this knowledge if you want to use high speed flash to capture water droplets as they splash onto the surface etc.

The actual range of the flash is quoted to be approximately 0.3m – 13.5 (1ft – 44ft) at the wide angle setting and 1.0m – 9.5m (3.3ft-31ft) at maximum telephoto setting.

These values are achieved with the ISO set to Auto and the ISO limit set to OFF. This means that to achieve these longer distances the camera may choose very high ISO values resulting in increased digital noise.

As the flash head is released the flash charging circuit is energised and in the EVF, or on the image on the LCD, with be a red flashing lightning symbol ⚡ indicating that the unit is charging. The camera will not release the shutter during this time.

In the iA mode the flash will be set per the scene detection mode the camera identifies. If it detects a face it will change to Auto Red-Eye reduction mode which has an associated pre-flash in an attempt the close the pupils of the subject's eyes to prevent the main flash burst picking up the red reflection from the blood vessels at the back of the eye.

Otherwise it will output enough flash power to illuminate the scene correctly if the subject is within the range specified above.

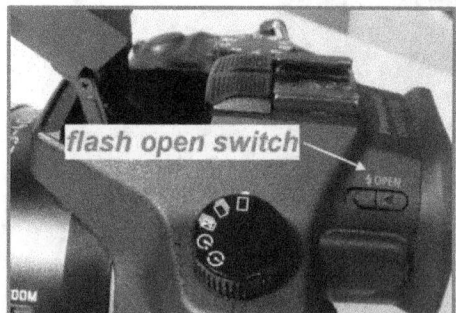 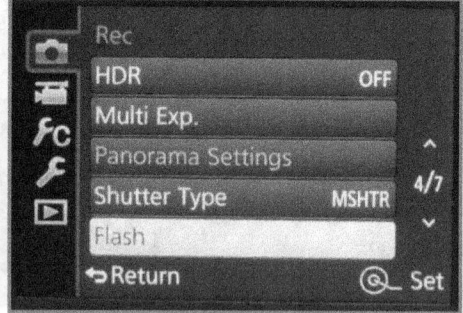

When in any other camera mode (PASM) it is possible to control some of the parameters used for flash photography.

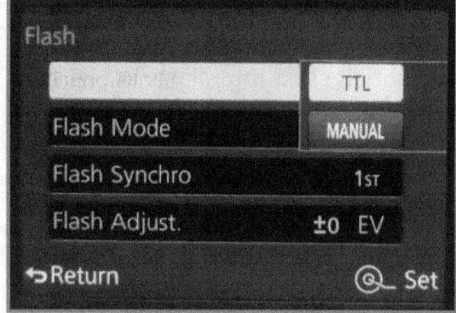 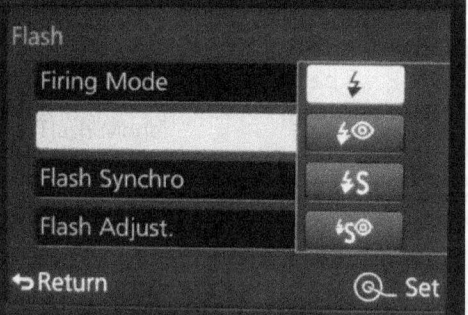

⚡ Forced flash on. The flash will fire, irrespective of subject brightness.

⚡ 👁 Forced flash on with red eye reduction, fires pre-flash to reduce red eyes.

⚡ S Forces flash on, with Slow Sync shutter

↗ S👁 Slow sync speed red eye reduction. This allows darker backgrounds to have a brighter exposure by extending the shutter speed prior to the flash firing. It employs red eye reduction as well.

Forced Flash Off. Flash will not fire, not a menu option; simply close the flash head.

Flash can have a variety of uses from providing the only source of illumination for a scene or providing "fill in" light to counteract strong backlighting.

It can also be used to cancel the effect of ambient light which has an undesirable colour balance such as with fluorescent light, which tend to be slightly green in colour.

In this situation, you will need to turn "forced flash" on, and you may have to adjust the output flash power or change the distance of the camera to the subject to get the ratio of ambient to flash light correct.

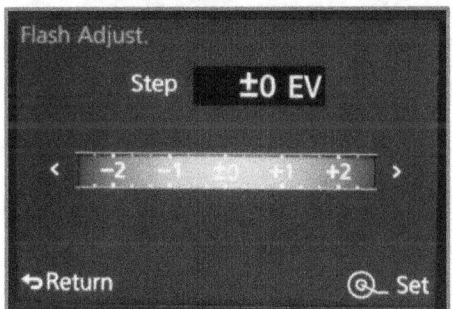

Flash power can be increased or decreased by +/- 3EV to compensate for any under or over exposure.
This adjustment is found in the set-up menu on page 4/7 of the REC Setup menu under Flash Adjust.

Flash Adjust is available only when [Wireless] in the [Flash] menu is set to [OFF] and [Firing Mode] is set to TTL.
It also controls the output power if a compatible TTL flash unit is attached to the hot shoe of the camera (unless the wireless flash mode has been selected).

The flash is synchronised from 1/60 to 1/4000 second in the ↗ and the ↗👁 modes and 1 to 1/16000 sec in all other modes.

In the iA and iA+ modes the shutter speed changes depending upon the scene type detected.
In the flash setup mode is the option to set a front or rear curtain shutter.
Front Curtain Sync - is the normal flash mode, with the flash being fired near the start of the shutter opening.

The flash finishes quick, and freezes the motion, and then the slow shutter remains open longer, and can blur due to the continuous ambient light.

So, the ambient blur appears later (out in front of where the flash fired), appearing to lead the motion. Not a natural look (when there is blurring from the ambient).

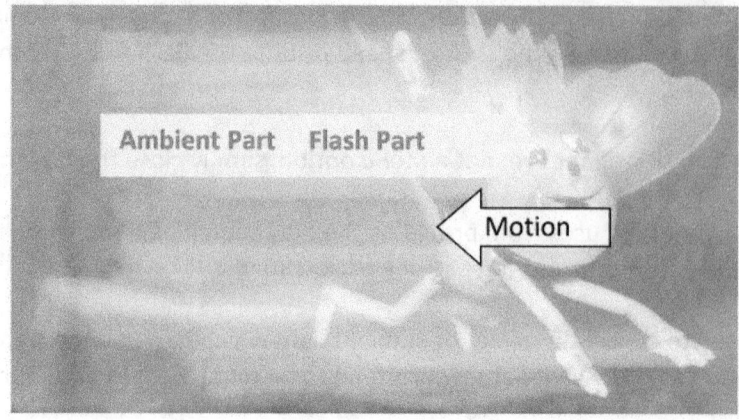

Front Sync curtain

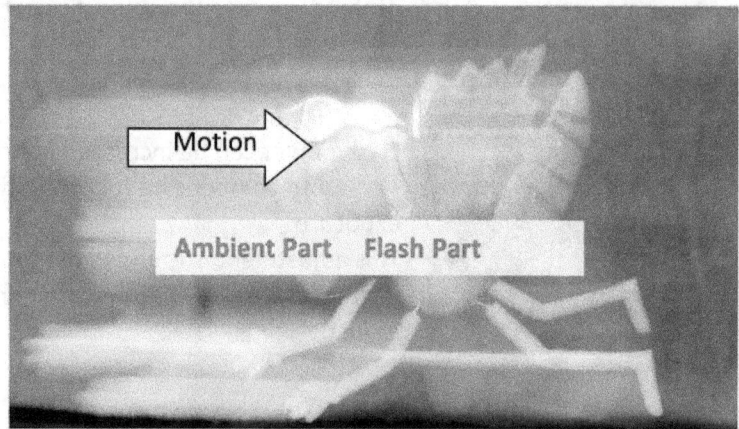

Rear Sync curtain

Rear Curtain Sync - waits to fire the flash until almost the end of the shutter duration, so that the ambient shutter blur occurs first, which then appears to follow the subject (appears back where it previously used to be, before the flash), which looks more natural to the motion.

There is an adjustment in the REC Setup mode for Red-Eye removal, this is a software based process which will attempt to "fix" any red eyes which were not reduced by the pre-flash red eye correction method.

You will notice that if you have it set to "on" the icons change in the flash setting menu to show a small paint brush alongside the eye symbol.

It works with face detection to prevent unwanted image areas being converted to black inadvertently.

Manual Flash

Under automatic TTL control the camera will calculate and set the correct flash exposure power, however in some instances the exposure may be incorrect.

If you want to take full control of the flash, you can set the flash to operate in the Manual Mode.

You can use the "pop-up" flash or attach a larger, more powerful flash unit into the flash hot shoe.

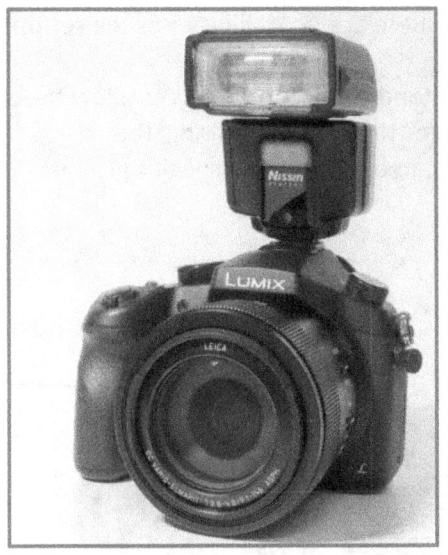

The firing mode is first set to Manual in the Flash Menu page 1/3 and then the output power is set in the Manual Flash Adjust Setting, Flash Menu page 2/3.

The flash power can be set from 1/1 (full power) to 1/128 in 1/3 EV steps

Taking Images with Wireless Flash

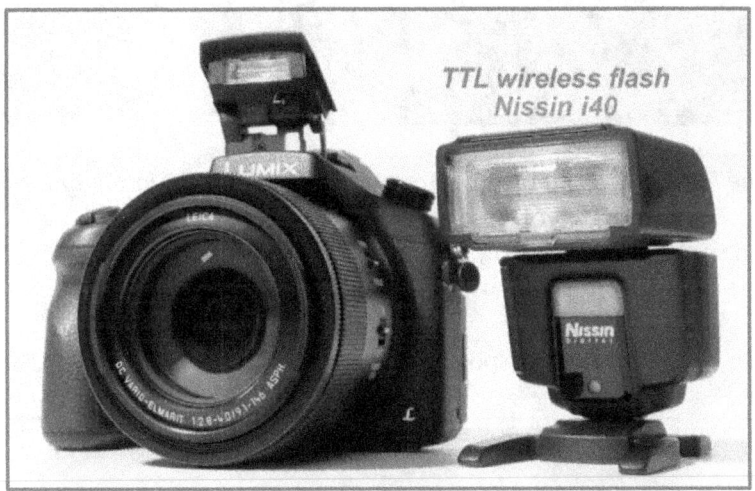

TTL wireless flash
Nissin i40

The FZ1000 acting as the wireless controller for the Nissin i40 Flash Unit

When you use flash units (DMW-FL360L, DMW-FL580L or the Nissin i40 for example) with the wireless flash function, you can separately control the firing of these flashes in four groups/four channels and control the function of the built-in flash (or the master flash attached to the hot shoe of the camera).

The built-in flash is the flash commander in this scenario and uses pulses of light to control the other units. This flash can be part of the exposure (fill-in type), contributing to the overall flash exposure or it can be used just as the commander.

Wireless flash allows some very creative flash lighting set-ups.

Flashes could be employed as the main light, the fill light and hair light in a portrait studio session, the power being set from the camera.

The flashes, being off-camera allow the direction and shape of shadows to be controlled exactly as you want them to be in the final image. As there are no trailing wires the set-up is less likely to cause any tripping hazard etc.

The external flashes can be positioned using lighting stands or cheap tripods to allow the flexibility of control. If the receiver flash units can "see" the main flash firing, then the system will work quit reliably. Each of the slave units can be allocated a specific group setting (A, B or C) and controlled independently.

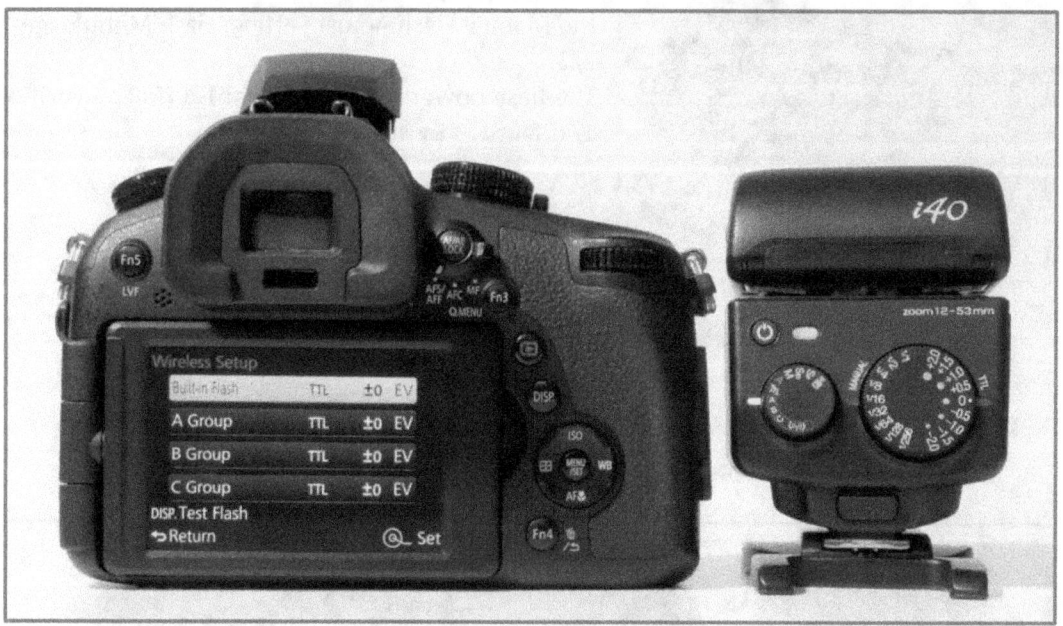

Here the FZ1000 is using Group A to control the Nissin i40 in TTL mode

The firing mode can be set to one of;

TTL: Where the flash output is automatically adjusted by the camera.

Auto: The flash unit controls the exposure.

Manual: Where you set the flash power ratio to create the lighting effect.

OFF: Where the wireless flashes in that group do not fire.

The power of the pop-up flash, used to act as the commander, can be set to provide the correct triggering response but not contribute to the exposure.

The settings are High/Standard/Low.

Flash exposure compensation can be applied from the FZ1000 flash adjust screen or it can usually be set on the flash unit as well.

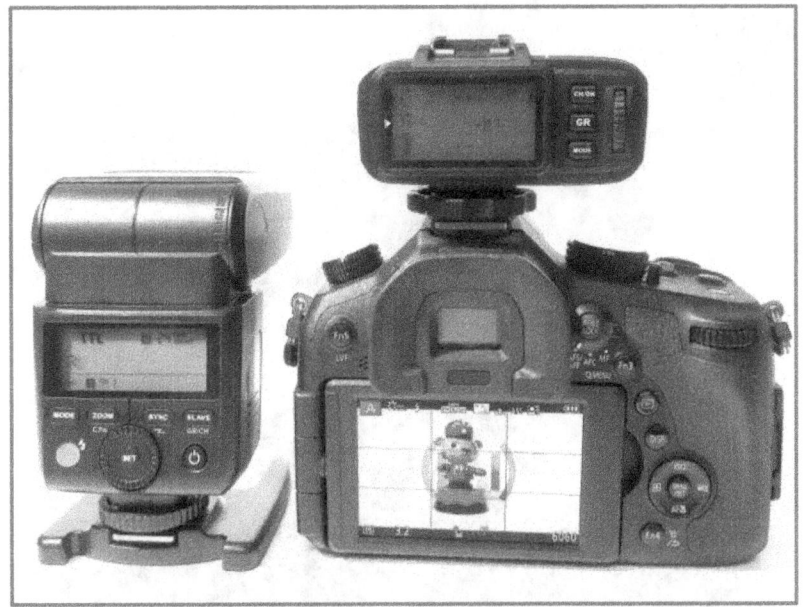

A wireless (radio TTL trigger) system by Godox doesn't need "line of sight"

There will be more on the use of "off camera" flash units such as ring flashes, LED ring lights, wireless triggers and TTL extension cords in the Accessories section of this guide.

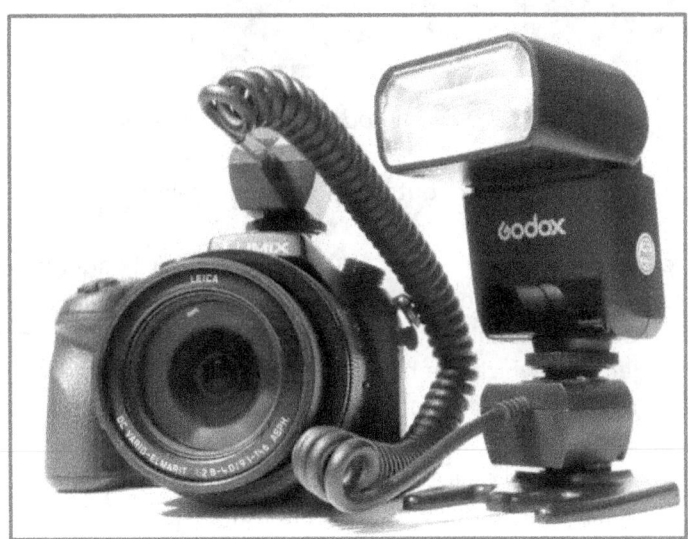

Flash unit used on a TTL extension cable

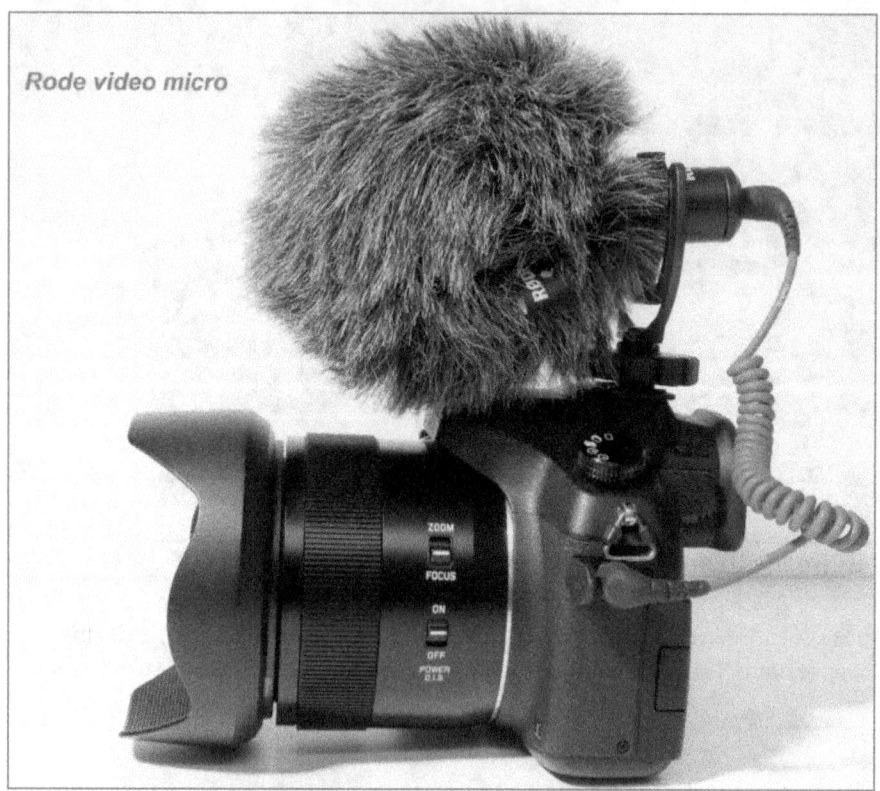

Rode video micro

The Fz1000 with Rode Video Microphone

The Panasonic Lumix FZ1000 delivers outstanding video quality.

If you shoot in the highest quality mode of AVCHD with 28Mbps data rate at 1080p the image quality is comparable to "pro-sumer" camcorders costing much more. Additionally, with the implementation of 4K 100Mbps UHD video this camera can now record superb 4K video clips which can be viewed on a suitably enabled 4K TV or downscaled to 1080P (by the camera in the auto HDMI mode) on a conventional HD TV.

The 4K video clips can be edited on a 1080p timeline to achieve a higher quality video with the option to perform pans and crops within the 4K frame.

The option is to use the MP4 format, which has a slightly lower bit rate of 20Mbps.

The MP4 format is less compressed and will edit more easily on lower power machines.

Depending upon the sales region the frame rate with be NTSC based 30p or PAL based 25p and cannot be changed in this camera model.

Panasonic refer to their recording qualities by the names of:
AVCHD and MP4.
Here are the frame rates and quality available in each mode.
Note: 25p will be for PAL based countries and 30p for NTSC based countries.

Quality	Size, Bit Rate and Frame Rate
	AVCHD format
FHD/28M/50/60p	1920x1080 AVCHD progressive 28Mbps 50/60 fps
FHD/17M/50/60i	1920x1080 AVCHD interlaced 17Mbps 50/60 fps
FHD/24M/25/30p	1920x1080 AVCHD progressive 24Mbps 25/30 fps
FHD/24M/24p	1920x1080 AVCHD progressive 24Mbps 24 fps
	MP4 format
4K/100M/25/30p	3840x2160 100Mbps 25/30 fps
FHD/28M/50/60p	1920x1080 28M 50/60 fps
FHD/20M/25/30p	1920x1080 20M 25/30 fps
HD/10M/25/30p	1280x720 10M 25/30p
VGA	640x480 4Mbps 25/30 fps

The quality becomes higher when the number of bit rate gets bigger. This unit uses the
"VBR" recording method, and the bit rate is changed automatically depending on the
subject to record.
Therefore, the recording time is shortened when a subject with fast movement is
recorded.
Note that 4K is only available from the Creative Video shooting mode.
What is bit rate
This is the volume of data for a defined period of time, and the quality becomes higher when the
number gets larger. The FZ1000 is using the "VBR" recording method. "VBR" is an abbreviation for
"Variable Bit Rate", and the bit rate (volume of data for the defined period of time) is changed
automatically depending on the subject to record. Therefore, the recording time is shortened when
a subject with fast movement is recorded.

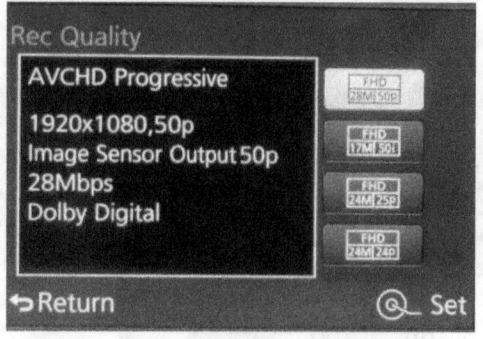 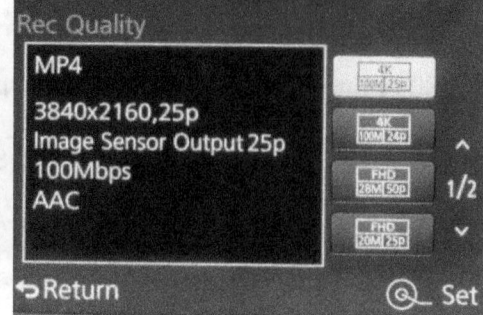

The two recording formats AVCHD   *and MP4*

Adjusting Focus Whilst Recording Video

Focusing varies depending on the focus mode and the setting of [Continuous AF] in the [Motion Picture] menu.

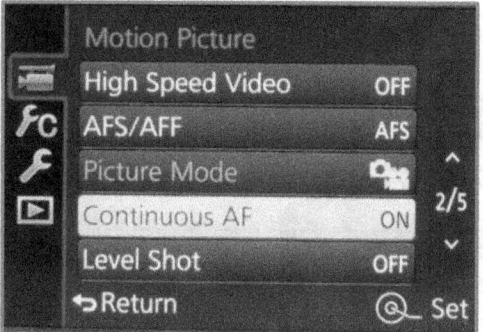

The Continuous AF option in the Motion Picture menu

Focus Mode	[Continuous AF]	Setting
[AFS]/[AFF]/[AFC]	[On]	Allow the focus to be constantly adjusted automatically while recording motion pictures.
	[OFF]	Fix focus position at the start of motion picture recording.
[MF]	[ON/OFF]	Allow the focus to be adjusted manually.

When the focus mode is set to [AFS], [AFF], or [AFC], the camera will refocus if the shutter button is pressed halfway while recording motion pictures. When Auto Focus is activated while you are recording motion pictures, the focusing operation sound may be recorded under some conditions. If you want to suppress this sound, set [Continuous AF] to [OFF] in the [Motion Picture] menu. When using zoom while recording motion pictures, it may take some time to focus.

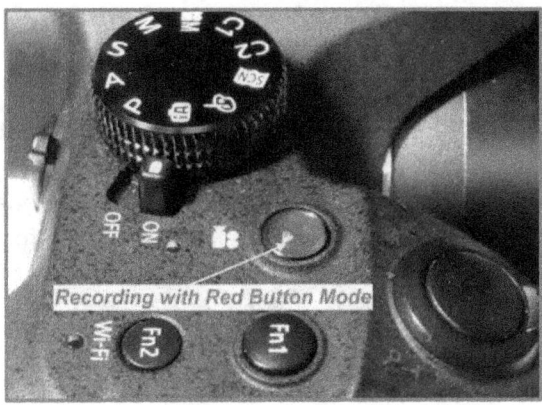

Whilst the camera is any of the photo shooting modes: iA, iA+, P, A, S or M
a video clip can be recorded by just depressing the RED video recording button on the top
plate of the camera. It will create a video file with the video format and quality that you
have set up in the Motion Picture menu. To start the recording press and then release the
button and to end the recording press and release the button again.
You will see on the LCD screen the remaining time left (27m 08s) for recording of this
video clip and the current lapsed time (2 seconds).

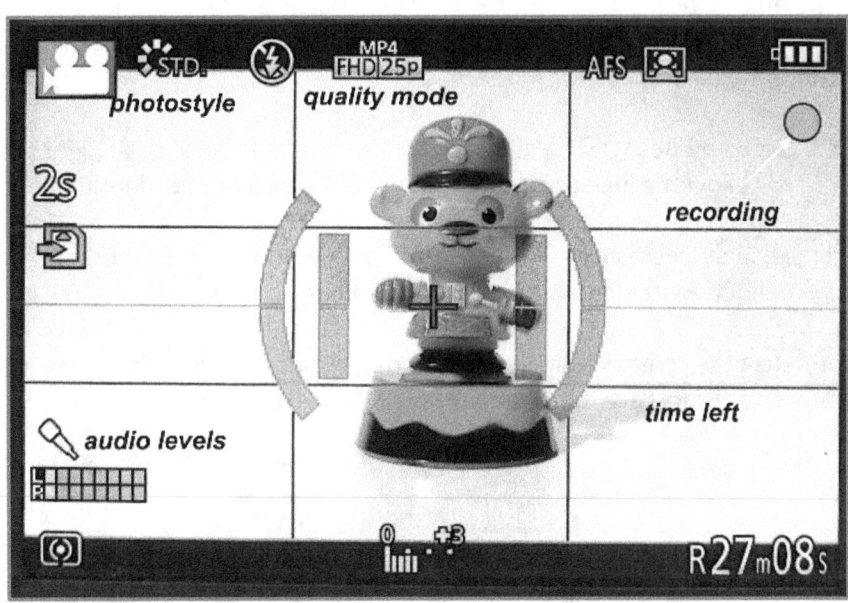

The recording screen during motion picture recording

Also displayed on the screen is the video format and quality (MP4/25p FHD) the
Photostyle (STD - Standard), the current focus mode and focus area, the metering mode
(centre weighted) the recording indictor (a flashing red dot), exposure compensation
($+1^{1/3}$EV) and the audio level display.
Note that red button recording mode is not available for 4K, this has to be selected
through the Creative Video Mode.

The video record button is used to start and stop video recording in all modes except in "Creative Video Mode" where the shutter button is used to start and stop recording.

Recording time will be limited to 29 minutes and 59 seconds for European sold cameras (to comply with EU tax laws on camcorders) and to file sizes of 4GB for all other regions (FAT32 file segment size limitation if using SDHC cards).
This equates to around 80 minutes in FHD/50/60p mode or 90 minutes in FHD/50/60i mode. In MP4 video mode it is around 100 minutes of FHD recording quality.

If you are shooting the video in the iA or iA+ mode, as with the stills photography mode, the camera will attempt to classify the scene type and set appropriate recording parameters to enable the best video quality to be recorded.

The screen will display the current scene type being used by the camera in recording the current clip.
In the iA and [iA+] modes any parameters which have been set, for example, background defocus, [brightness adjustment or colour tint] will be recorded in the video clip.

In semi-automatic modes; P, A or S the White Balance only is used, all other parameters are ignored. The camera will not identify very low light levels in these modes and not switch to the iA "i-Low light" mode.

In SCN (scene modes "clear nightscape", "artistic nightscape" and "night portrait") these modes will allow the higher sensitivity i-Low Light mode to be identified and operate.

Other Scene modes such as "sunset" use that condition whilst others such as baby1, baby2 and pet use the default recording conditions.

If you select the "creative" stills modes most of those will transfer to recording in video mode. Sepia, Expressive, Retro and Monochrome work exactly as they would in the stills mode.

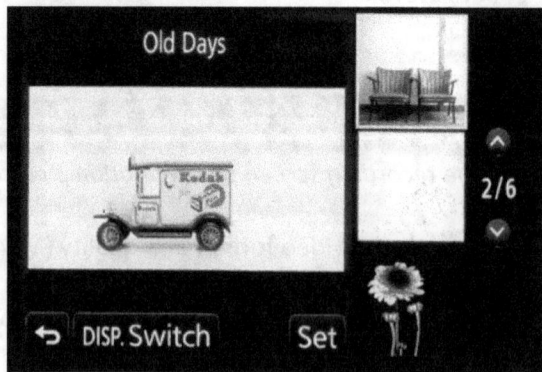

an example of a filter effect applied to video

In creative video recording we have a lot more control over the way in which the camera records the clips. Manual video mode is engaged by turning the top control dial to the icon of the movie camera so that it aligns with the index mark on the top plate of the camera.

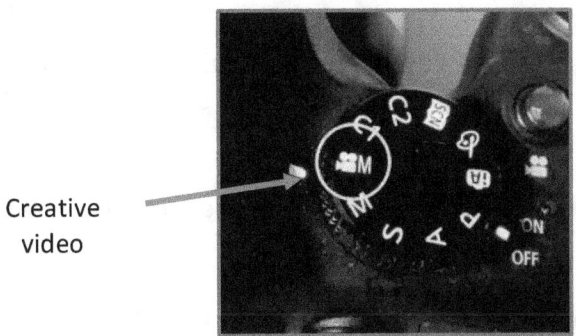

Creative
video

In creative video mode, the exposure mode can be set to either of the following:
"P" program auto mode
"A" aperture priority mode
"S" shutter priority mode
"M" full manual control

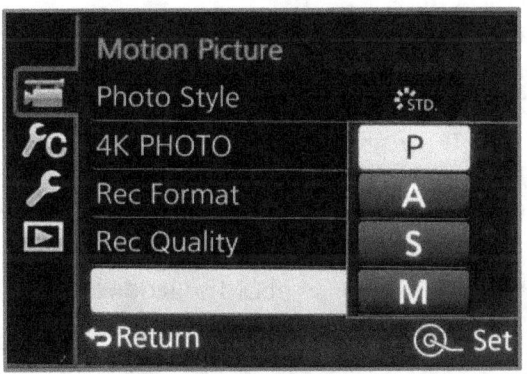

The program mode "P" takes full control of both Aperture and Shutter Speed with the only option to set the ISO and exposure control +/-

ISO can be set to AUTO so effectively the whole process is in fully Auto mode.
When the Aperture priority mode is selected Shutter speed will be adjusted if the ISO is set to any other value than AUTO. If Auto is selected for ISO sensitivity, then the camera appears to keep the shutter speed in the region of 1/50 sec.

Exposure is controlled by the camera adjusting the ISO. The top control wheel varies the Aperture value.
When Shutter priority mode is selected then the lowest shutter speed is half the frame rate. So, in the case of a PAL based camera set to shoot FHD/50p the minimum shutter speed is 1/25 second. Again, ISO can be set to a pre-set value or Auto.
For full control of aperture, shutter speed and ISO the Manual mode can be selected.

In this mode if the Auto ISO setting was applied in another mode then when switching to the Manual mode it will revert to ISO 100 as there is no provision for Auto ISO in this mode.

Ideally for video recording the shutter speed should be equal to twice the frame rate to follow the 180-degree shutter rule.

This 180-degree shutter rule gives smooth motion, like motion picture film look.
So, if you were recording 1080 50p/60p you would select a shutter speed of 1/125 second.

Now set the aperture for the depth of field that you want.
Large apertures (F2.8) giving shallower depth of field compared to smaller apertures like F8.

Once you have the shutter speed and aperture set you can bring the exposure to the correct level by adjusting the ISO sensitivity of the camera.
To do this observe the exposure meter at the bottom of the LCD display and adjust ISO until the centre point is reached.

In the motion picture menu, these controls may want some further explanation:

Level Shot function
Automatically detects the camera's tilt while recording video, and horizontally corrects the recording video so it will not be tilted.
Settings: [ON] / [OFF]
If you record while walking, or if the camera's tilt is large, it may not be possible to horizontally correct the video clip.
The angle of view becomes slightly narrow when video recording starts.
Still pictures taken while recording video will not be horizontally corrected.
This function is not available in the following cases:
When recording with [High Speed Video]
When the OIS switch is set to OFF
When [Rec Format] is set to [MP4], and [Rec Quality] is set to [4K/100M/30p] or [VGA/4M/30p]

Luminance Level
This value selects the brightness range for the captured images
Select 16-255 for motion picture and 0-255 when still images are required to be captured from the video.
Luminance level can only be set in the Creative Video mode and when MP4 is selected as the recording format

Flkr Decrease
Striping or flicker may appear under lighting such as fluorescent lighting and LED lighting.

This is characteristic of MOS sensors which serve as the camera's pickup sensors.

When using the electronic shutter, lowering the shutter speed may reduce the effect of the horizontal stripes.

If noticeable flicker or striping is seen under lighting such as a fluorescent or LED lighting when recording motion pictures, you can reduce the flicker or striping by setting up [Flkr Decrease] and fixing the shutter speed.

Settings: [1/50]/[1/60]/[1/100]/[1/120]/[OFF]

Mic Level Disp

This setting dictates whether the mic levels are displayed on the recording screen
Settings: [ON]/[OFF]
When [Mic Level Limiter] is set to [OFF], [Mic Level Disp.] is fixed to [ON].
Not available in these cases:
This function is not available in the following case: – [Miniature Effect] (Creative Control Mode)
This function is not available during High Speed Video recording.

Mic Level Adj

Adjust the audio input level to 19 different levels (-12 dB ~ +6 dB).
Not available in these cases:
[Miniature Effect] (Creative Control Mode)
This function is not available during High Speed Video recording.

Mic Level Limiter

The camera adjusts the sound input level automatically, minimising the sound distortion crackling noise) when the volume is too high.
Settings: [ON]/[OFF]
Not available in these cases:
[Miniature Effect] (Creative Control Mode)
This function is not available during High Speed Video recording.

Wind Cut

A wind cut is a high-pass filter.
This will reduce the wind noise coming into the built-in microphone while maintaining sound quality.
Settings: [AUTO]/[HIGH] / [STANDARD] / [LOW]/[OFF]
Not available in these cases:
[Miniature Effect] (Creative Control Mode)
This function is not available when [Zoom Mic] is set to [ON].
This function is not available during High Speed Video recording

Coupled to the zoom operation, it varies the microphone gain per the level of zoom. Settings: [ON] / [OFF]. Audio recordings may be lower when set to [ON] than compared to [OFF] and external noise pick up will be enhanced.

[Zoom Mic] does not work in the following cases:
– [Miniature Effect] (Creative Control Mode) – [High Speed Video] (Creative Video Mode)

Recording Slow Motion Pictures (High Speed Video)

Slow motion pictures can be recorded by performing recording at a faster than normal frame rate. The only option is ON or OFF and is available when the Creative Video mode is selected.

When these recordings are played back, the motion is displayed slowly.

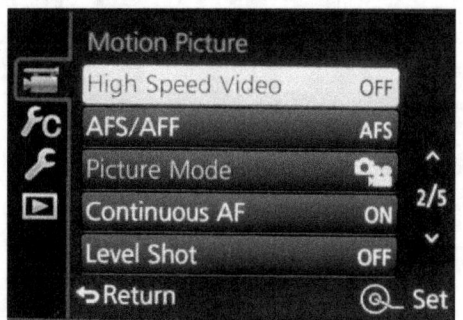

The high-speed video mode is selected on page 2/5 of the motion picture menus.

No Audio is recorded in this mode.
File size is limited to 7 minutes 29 second or 4GB
Focus, zoo, exposure and white balance are

Applying a Video Photostyle

By adjusting the type and the parameters of the Photostyle applied to the video recording you can change the "look" of the recorded video file.
The photo styles available are:

STD - standard	Standard default setting
VIVID – Vivid *	Setting with slightly higher contrast and saturation
NAT – Natural *	Setting with slightly lower contrast
MONO - Monochrome	Creates a picture using shades of grey
SCNY – Scenery*	Setting that creates using vivid colours for blue sky and green grass
PORT – Portrait*	Setting that produces the look of a healthy complexion
CUST – Custom*	Setting using the colours and picture quality previously defined

*Notes: Items with * are not available in the iA+ mode*

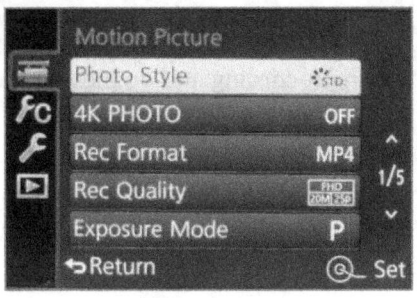
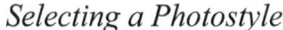
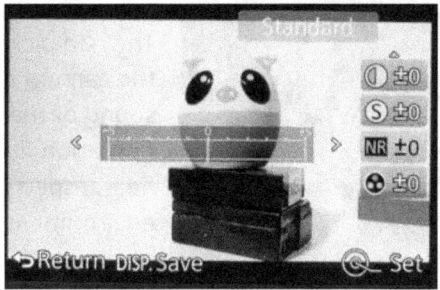

Selecting a Photostyle   *parameter adjustment*

Picture quality cannot be adjusted in any of the iA modes
To select a Photo style use the cursor keys left/right to scroll through the options.
Select the up/down cursor keys to adjust the parameters.

Parameter and feature

Contrast	+/-	Increase/decrease contrast in a picture
Sharpness	+/-	Enhance/soften the outlines in a picture
Noise Reduction	+/-	Increase/decrease noise reduction setting
Saturation	+/-	Increase/decrease colour saturation
Colour Tone	+/-	Bluish/Yellowish
	Yellow	Enhances subject contrast: Blue sky normal low
	Orange	Enhances subject contrast: Blue sky vibrant med
Filter Effect	Red	Enhances subject contrast: Blue sky extra vibrant
(displayed when monochrome selected	Green	Applies subdued colouring for skin and lips of a person and emphasises green leaves
	Off	-

Colour Tone is only displayed when [Monochrome] is selected, in all other modes it is replaced by Saturation adjustment.

To apply one of the adjusted Photo styles to the Custom setting perform the settings adjustment and then press the [Disp] button. This will set this profile to the Custom position.

Recording Audio for Video Clips

A good video recording also requires good audio capture. The in-built stereo microphones of the FZ1000 provide a convenient method to capture audio however they are not the best source for getting good audio.

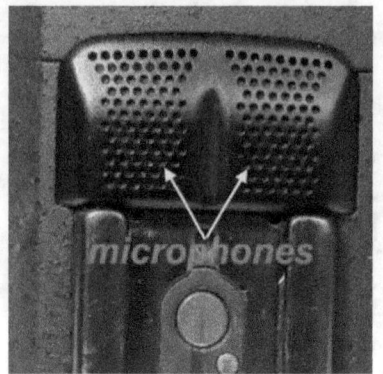

They do pick up any local sound of you operating any of the camera buttons during recording and do pick up the sound of the zoom motor if you perform any zoom operation during the recording. It is also possible to hear, especially if you are recording in a very quiet environment, the sound of the OIS system in operation.

Even if you have the camera on a tripod and, as suggested the OIS turned off, there is still a gentle whirring as the camera needs to keep the OIS lens in the central optical path and thus the electromagnets are still having to work.

I've seen numerous complaints about this noise from the OIS system. You may also hear the lens "rattling' even when the camera is turned off.

This is normal as the glass element in its holder are free to slide around inside the lens structure – it is not an indication of a malfunction.

If you want video with good audio content it is advisable to use an external microphone plugged into the 3.5mm microphone port on the left-hand side of the camera. More of this in the accessories section of this guidebook.

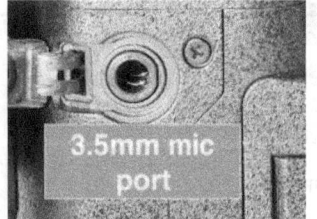

This port is one of the weather- sealed ports and to maintain the integrity of the seal the plug should be replaced after you remove the mic which was plugged into it.

Getting the right audio level is also an important factor in capturing decent video clips. The mic level display can be superimposed on the LCD by turning it on in the Motion Picture menu page 4/5.

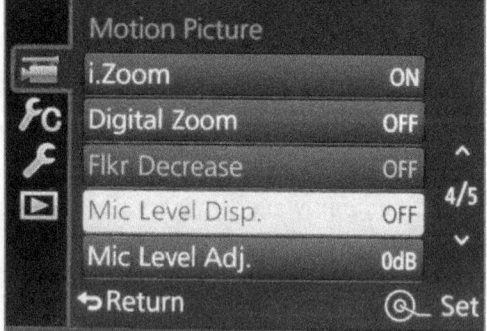

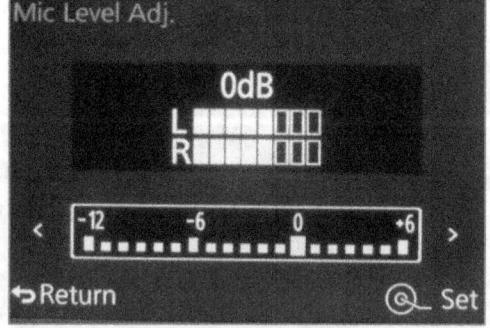

The mic level should be adjusted until the bar graph indicates that the volume is peaking at two bars below the maximum.

With the Audio Limiter OFF it is particularly important to keep an eye on the level display to ensure that the audio recorded does not get distorted

You can adjust the audio input level in 19 steps (- 12 dB to + 6 dB).

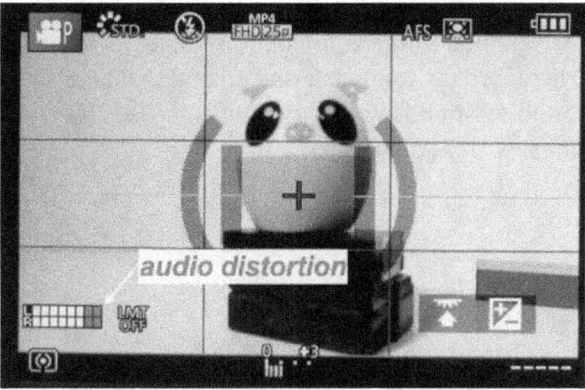

With the audio limiter set off reduce the volume
until no red bars appear on the display

The Mic Level Limiter and Wind Noise Canceller

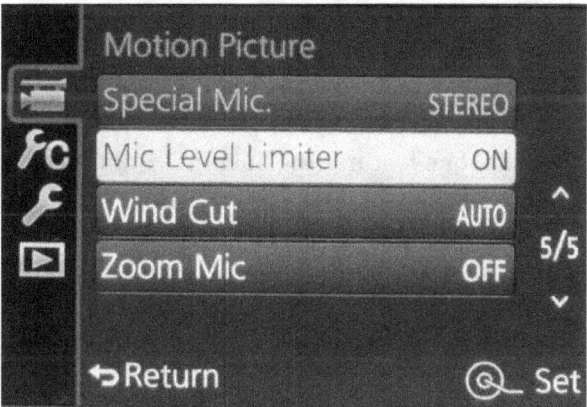

When the Mic Level Limiter is turned on camera adjusts the sound input level automatically, minimising the sound distortion (crackling noise) when the volume is too high.

The purpose of the Wind Cut control is to reduce the wind noise coming into the built-in microphone while maintaining sound quality.

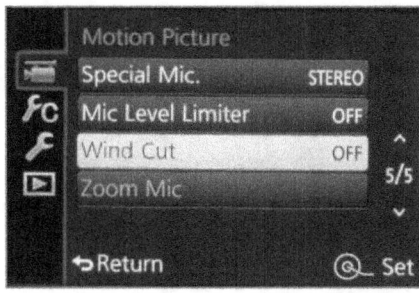

Settings: [AUTO] / [HIGH] / [STANDARD] / [LOW]/ [OFF].
[HIGH] effectively reduces the wind noise by minimizing the low-pitched sound when a strong wind is detected.
[STANDARD] extracts and reduces only the wind noise without deteriorating the sound quality.

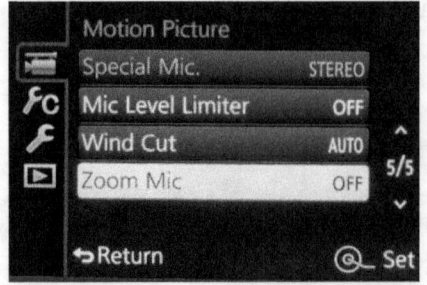

The Zoom mic setting 5/5 in the motion picture menu. Coupled to the zoom operation, it will more clearly record far sounds during enlarging image, and surrounding sounds with wide-angle.
Settings: [ON] / [OFF]

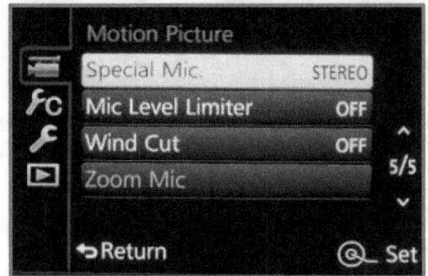

The Special Mic feature will be available when a TRRS (tip, ring, ring, sleeve) microphone is attached to the camera such as the Panasonic DMW-MS2.

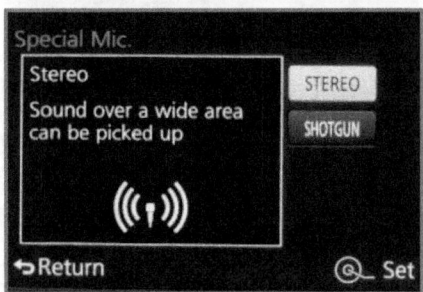

It has the facility to select the recording quality and the sound pick up pattern.
This microphone features the built-in 3.5mm jack cable, a mic holder, cable holder, lock ring, tripod/hot shoe mount, mini plug 6.5feet (2 m) cable extender, windjammer and case.

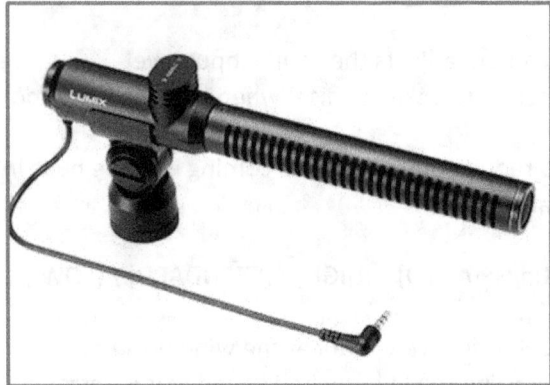

The holder is designed with a vibrational absorption mechanism and is designed to suppress the camera's motor and handling noise to capture the sound you want.

The unit is powered by the camera and its stereo or shotgun modes can be controlled via the camera's menu.

Recording 4K Video

4k video, or more aptly UHD (ultra-high definition), named because it has 4000 pixels horizontally (4096x2160), is approximately the area of 4 standard 1080p (1920x1080p) video images.
Shrinking down 4k video to be 1080p is a night and day difference in detail and quality. Down-sampling can also help cut down on noise and grain making the footage appear to be cleaner as well.

When you start with 4K source material and downscale it to HD resolution the picture will look even better, thanks to effectively oversampling each pixel by a factor of four. In addition to sharper, crisper images, colour data is better and easier to grade, and common video artefacts such as moiré are significantly reduced or eliminated thanks to the higher resolution original capture.

In theory, it is possible for a high end 1080p camera to film higher quality video than a cheap 4k camera, but in my experience, most 4k cameras are significantly sharper than 1080p cameras.

Shooting 4k video to get a sharper 1080p final export is the ultimate reason to shoot 4k. Most 1080p video looks so low resolution that still frames aren't even good enough for web use. If it's not good enough for a website, you certainly wouldn't consider printing a still frame from a standard HD video camera but 4k is changing all that.

Not only is most 4k video good enough to replace standard still images on the web, but many shooters are starting to realize that 4k still frames are good enough to print.

To put this into perspective, a 1080 video contains 2 million pixels where a single frame of 4k video contains 8.8 million pixels. With 5K, 6K and 8K video coming – exciting times! There are a few considerations to be made when setting up for gathering 4K material. If the video is to be used for downscaling to 1080p then the same shooting requirements as for general 1080p.

If, however the material is going to be used to extract 8M stills then some consideration should be given to the shutter speed at which it is going to be shot.

Normal video clips are captured using the 180-degree shutter angle rule to maintain a cinematic appearance. This allows for a slight amount of movement blur.

This movement blur is unnoticeable during viewing however a still extracted from this clip would show up as having some motion blur.
To get extracted image with little or no subject motion blurring the shutter speed needs to be increased to something like 1/500 sec.
This of course would mean shooting with larger apertures like F3.2 or F2.8 so that the camera doesn't need to raise the ISO too high.

This is illustrated in the next two images, extracted from a 4K file where one image was shot at 1/25 sec shutter speed and the other 1/200 sec.

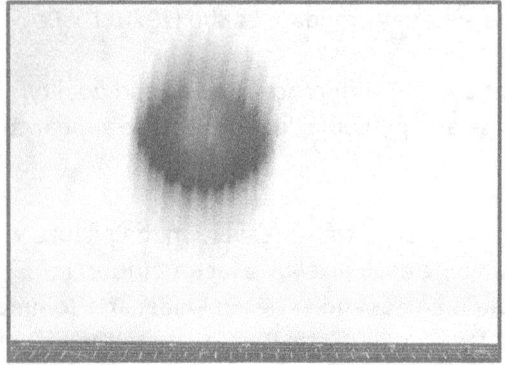 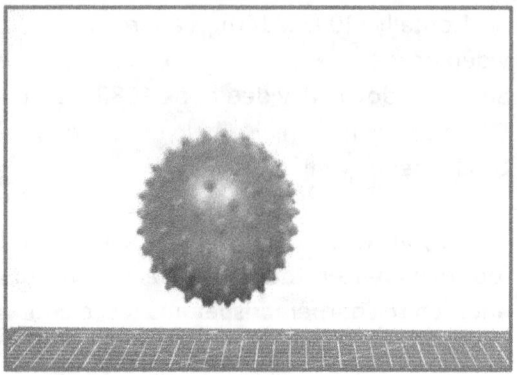

4k shot at 25 fps, 1/25 sec shutter speed   *4k shot at 25 fps, 1/200 sec shutter speed*

Another consideration is the memory card used to store the video clips.
4K video takes up a lot more space than full HD - up to four times more, in fact one minute of video can be more than one gigabyte in file size.
If you then consider for how long the clips will last this will determine the capacity of the card needed to ensure that there will be enough space.

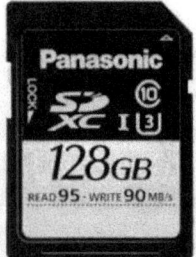  For example, half an hour of 4K video might need 32Gb storage! The speed of the card needs to be UHS class U3 to ensure that there will be no writing to card issues.

It is also to remember that due to the way in which 4K video is derived from the sensor that the effective focal length of the lens becomes 37 – 592 mm in 35mm equivalence when recording in 16:9.
So, you lose a little of the wide angle but gain extra zoom at the telephoto end.
26 – 416 mm in 35 mm equiv. in 16:9 video recording, O.I.S. Off
28 – 448 mm in 35 mm equiv. in 16:9 video recording, O.I.S. On
37 – 592 mm in 35 mm equiv. in 4K video recording (using the centre of the sensor with 3840 x 2160 pixels.)

VIEWING ON TV SCREEN

When you connect this camera to a 4K-compatible TV and play back a motion picture recorded with [Rec Quality] of [4K], you can enjoy high-resolution 4K motion pictures.

Although resolution output will be lower, you can also play back 4K motion pictures by connecting to a high-definition TV and other devices that do not have 4K support.

Connect this camera to a 4K-compatible TV using an HDMI micro cable and display the playback screen.
When the [VIERA Link] setting on the camera is set to [ON] and the camera is connected to a VIERA Link (HDMI)-compatible Panasonic television (VIERA), the television automatically switches its input and the playback screen is displayed.

When you have video clips that have been recorded with [Rec Format] set to [MP4] and their size set to [4K] in [Rec Quality], you can also play them back by inserting the card into the SD card slot of a TV that supports motion pictures in 4K.

VIEWING 4K MOTION PICTURES ON A PC SCREEN

To play back motion pictures recorded with [Rec Quality] of [4K] on a PC, use the software "PHOTOfunSTUDIO" stored in the DVD (supplied).

To play back and edit 4K motion pictures, a high-performance PC environment is required. Still/motion pictures can be copied from the camera to your computer by connecting the two together via the USB connection cable.

Some computers can read directly from the camera's memory card. For details, see the instruction manual for your computer.

If your computer does not support SDXC Memory Cards, a message will be displayed requesting you to format the card.
(Do not format the card. This will erase recorded pictures).

If the card is not recognized, refer to the following support website.
http://panasonic.net/avc/sdcard/information/SDXC.html

EX Zoom, i.Zoom and Digital Zoom

EX Zoom

Let's begin by looking at the much-misunderstood EX Zoom or as Panasonic call it extended optical zoom with NO loss of quality. Let's look at the 16:9 aspect ratio situation.

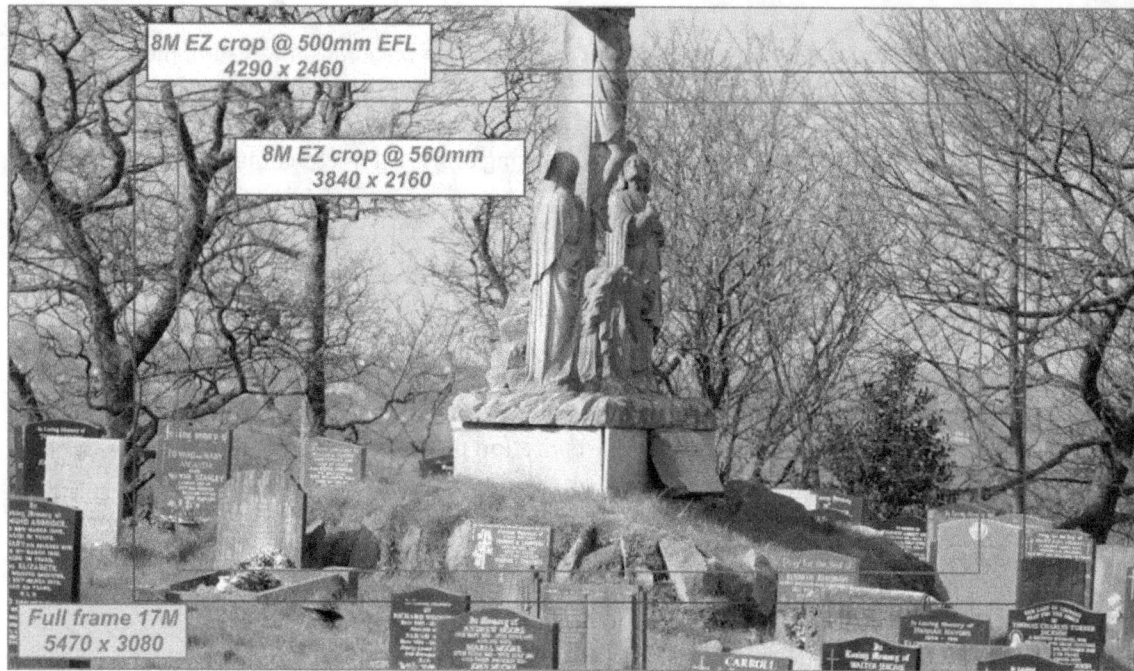

So, at x1 zoom or 25mm EFL we have 5472 x 3080 pixels and at x16 zoom or 400mm EFL we have the same 5472 x 3080 pixels. Now if we select the 8M EX image size at 25mm it gives 3840 x 2160 and at x16 or 400mm gives the same 3840 x 2160 pixels. Now as we increase the zoom beyond the x16 marker we find we can get up to almost x22.4 zoom. If we look at an image created at this magnification it is still 3840 x 2160 pixels. At any intermediate zoom from x16 to x 22.4 the image dimensions remain the same 3840 x 2160 pixels.

What is happening? Well at 25mm the RAW to JPEG processor is taking the full 5472 x 3080 pixels are applying some down sampling (re-sizing) to give 3840 x 2160 pixels. Similarly, at the end of the x16 optical range of the zoom it is applying the same degree of down sampling to still produce 3840 x 2160 pixels. Now the magic begins! Go beyond the x16 and the JPEG processor is taking less area of the sensor pixels and still down sampling this to 3840 x 2160. This down-sampling of the sensor image continues until we reach an affective focal length of 563mm, still with the same image crop of 3840 x 2160 which is the 8M or 4K video frame size. So, it looks like we have zoomed into the image yet kept the same image pixel dimensions. Easy to believe that you have extended the optical range of the lens! At the full extent of the zoom lever travel we have an effective increase of x1.4 zoom giving an overall zoom of x 22.4

But wait, all is not bad here!

There is a beneficial advantage of using down sampled images from the camera. Firstly, the down sampling adds extra sharpness in the image. the more the down sampling the stronger this effect appears to be.

Secondly noise is also reduced by the processing giving a cleaner looking image. I hear you saying why buy a 20-megapixel camera and use only 8Megapixels!

Well yes it's true by using the lower image dimensions the ability to produce big enlargements or crop into the image is a little reduced but for the usual 6-inch x 4-inch print or HD computer display we only require 2M images anyway and the 3840 x 2160 image is the perfect match for 4k displays!

So what happens with the i.Zoom operation?

Well up to the x16 zoom position the situation is the same, the pixel dimensions remain constant.

However, when we start to progress from x16 to x32 (800mm EFL) the RAW to JPEG processor is using the cropped sensor image pixel dimensions but instead of down sampling to 8M pixel dimensions it up samples the image using some form of interpolation to achieve the same 5472 x 3080 pixels.

Thus, we always have the 17M pixels in the image even though they have been up sampled from far fewer (1920 x 1080).

This why it is important to stay around about x1.5 or 600mm EFL where the sensor pixels are still 3840 x 2160 before up sampling.

And what happens if you combine i.Zoom with EX zoom?

Well you use the EX zoom pixels until x22.4 zoom and then you add the x2 upscaling from the i.Zoom to end up with 1600mm EFL.

Digital zoom applies between x1 and x4 magnification of the sensor pixels from x16 to x64 or 400mm EFL to 1600mm EFL.

So, what is the difference in image quality?

Given the same output image size, either screen or print, there is to my eyes no change in the image quality at full size 400mm EFL (x16 zoom) and the 400mm EFL 8M EX zoom and the 400mm EFL 2M EX zoom.

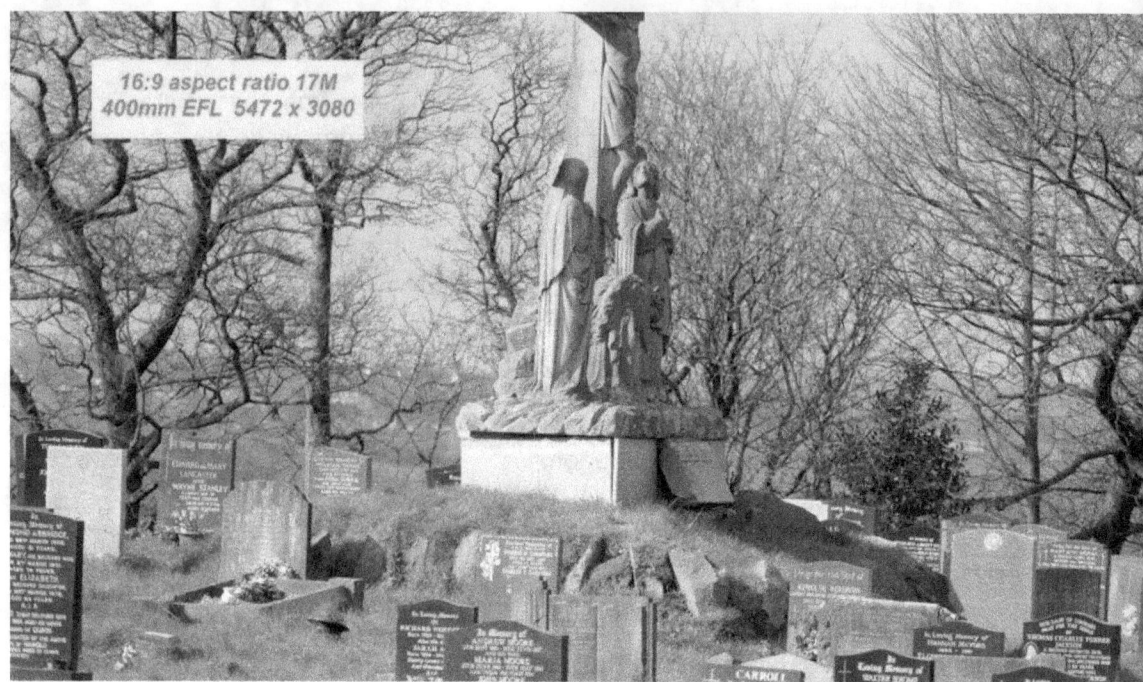

16:9 aspect ratio 17M
400mm EFL 5472 x 3080

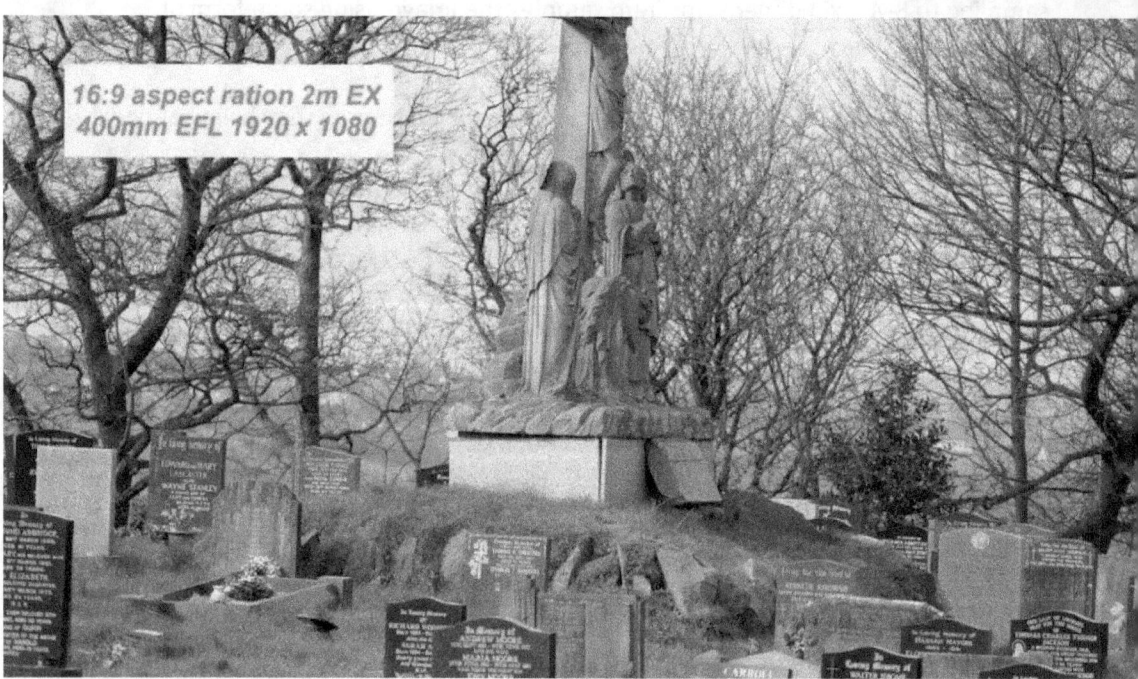

16:9 aspect ration 2m EX
400mm EFL 1920 x 1080

At the same print image size the 17M image is the same as the 2M EX image (one might argue the 2M image looks a little sharper due to the resizing process!)

Now let's look at the images when we start to apply some extra optical zoom.
The first image is with a zoom setting of around 500mm EFL and the second image is with the full zoom applied giving the maximum zoom of 560mm in this mode.

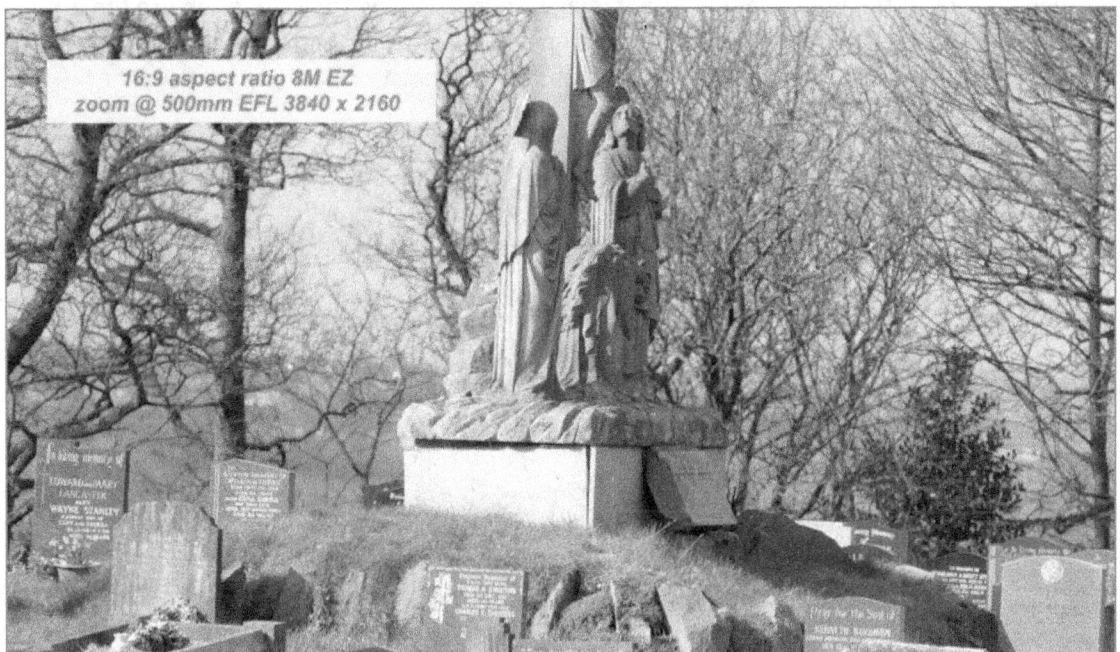

16:9 aspect ratio 8M EZ
zoom @ 500mm EFL 3840 x 2160

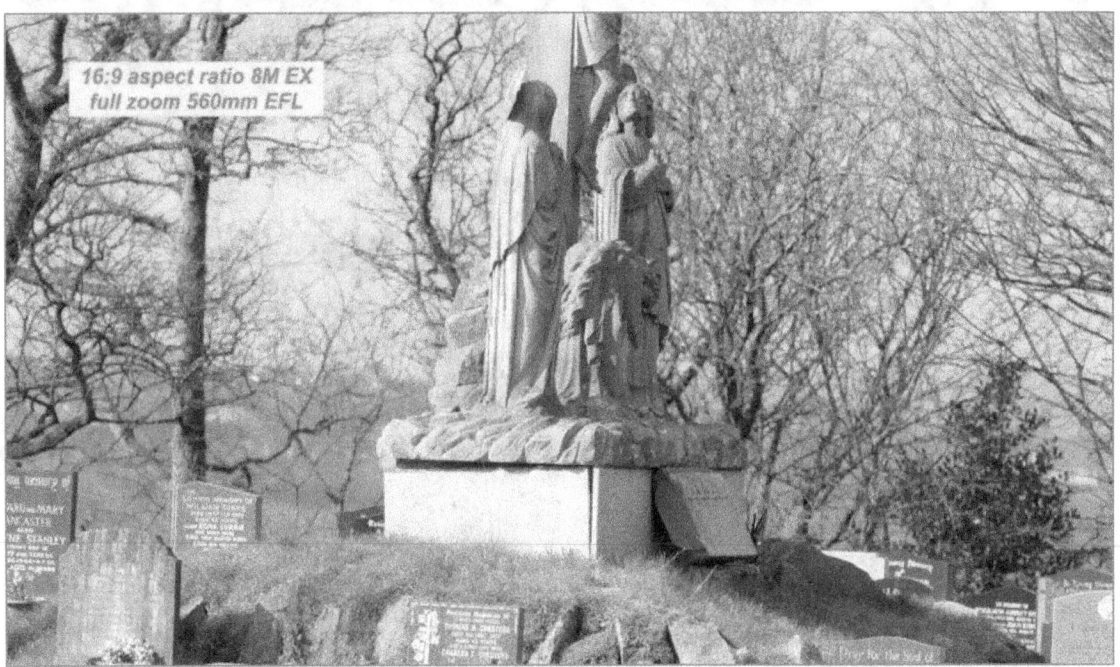

16:9 aspect ratio 8M EX
full zoom 560mm EFL

Again, the image quality is indistinguishable at normal print or screen sizes.
Remember at 300dpi (the normal print resolution) the 3840-pixel wide image will yield a print which is 13 inches wide.

For larger, say canvas prints where the prints are normally viewed at greater distances, the print resolution can be sometimes accepted by print laboratories at 150 dpi thus yielding a 26 inch wide print.

When we look at the effect on the output image when i.Zoom is applied we can use the higher resolution 17M image and apply the crop and resize using interpolation. In addition the processor adds some extra sharpening plus micro contrast or clarity to improve the image.

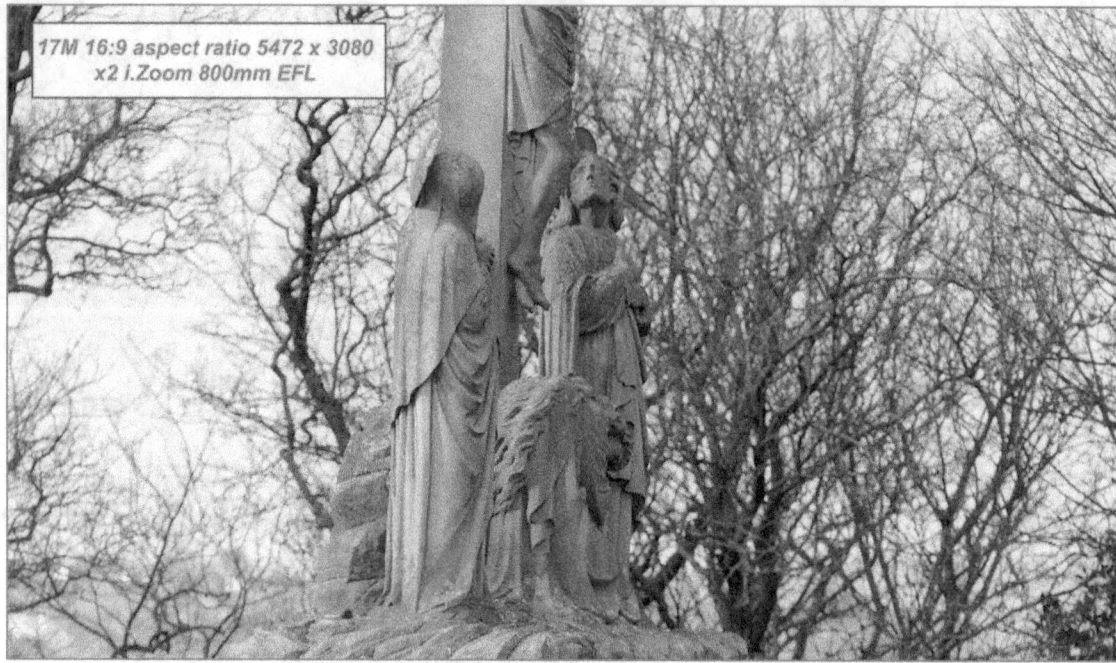

17M 16:9 aspect ratio 5472 x 3080
x2 i.Zoom 800mm EFL

By using the EX-M setting and i.Zoom combination longer focal lengths can be achieved.

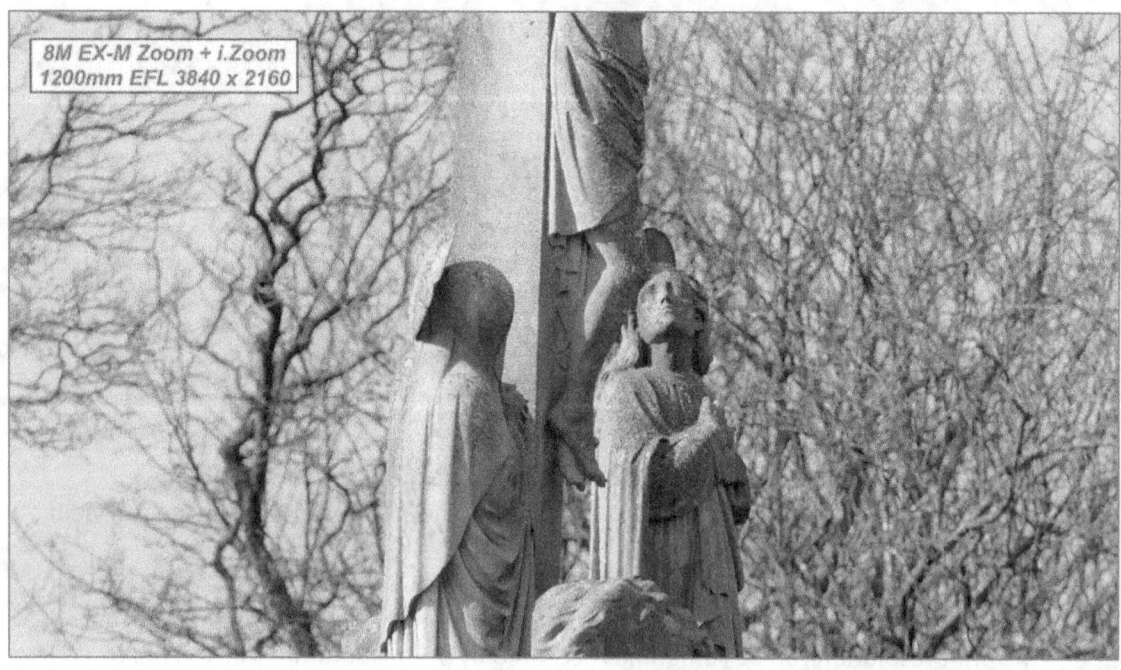

8M EX-M Zoom + i.Zoom
1200mm EFL 3840 x 2160

In this illustration the 8M EX-M and x2 i.Zoom was used to achieve the 1200mm EFL

The last option is to use digitial zoom only. Unlike I.Zoom the digital zoom control can go from x1 to x4. This extra magnification is achieved at the expense of image quality. Again, to achieve this extra zoom effect the image is cropped and resized but no additional processing is applied to the final image.

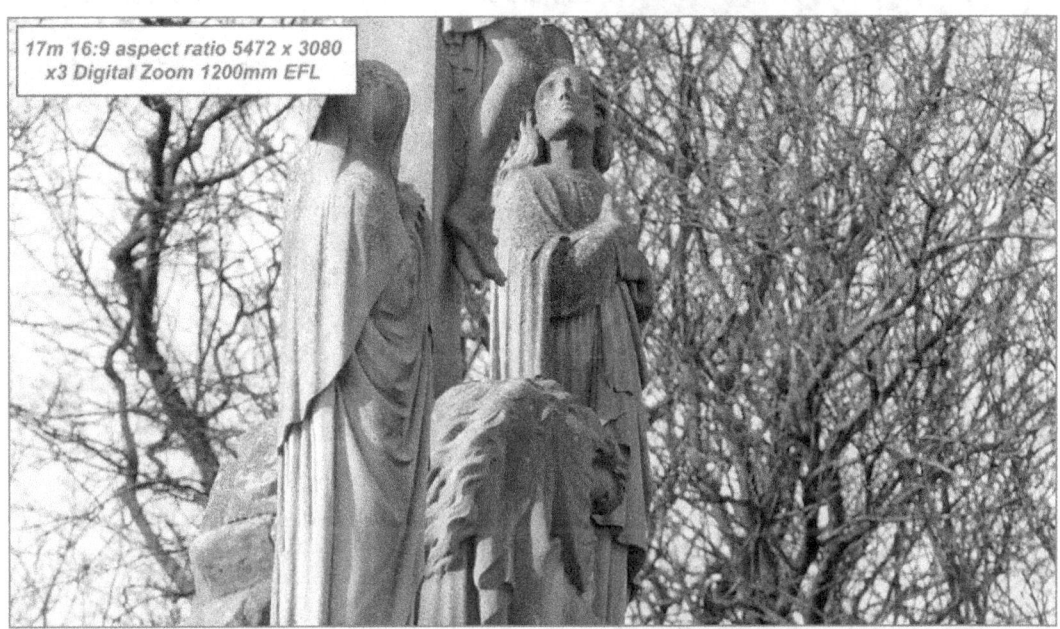

17m 16:9 aspect ratio 5472 x 3080
x3 Digital Zoom 1200mm EFL

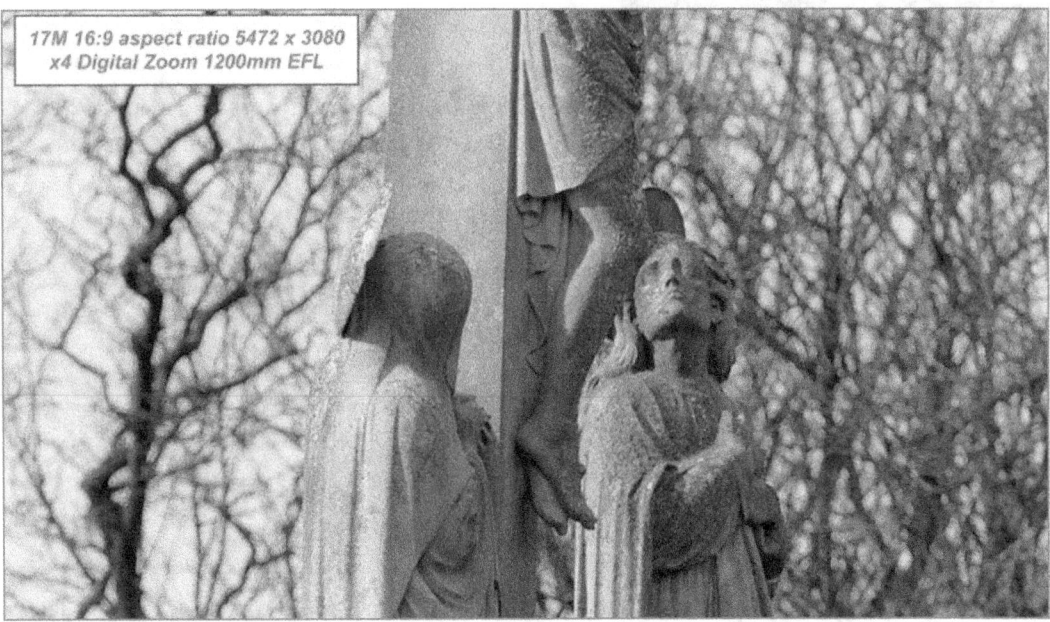

17M 16:9 aspect ratio 5472 x 3080
x4 Digital Zoom 1200mm EFL

It is possible to combine i.Zoom, Ex zoom and digital zoom to achieve 3200mm EFL however the resulting image may not be suitable for anything more than small web page illustrations.

Creating Custom Modes

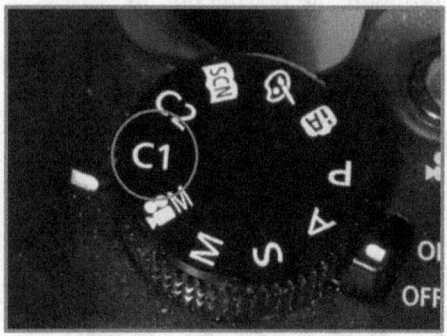

Using this facility, you can register the current camera settings as one of four custom settings (C1, C2-1, C2-2, C2-3).
You can set up and use the registered settings to speed up your photography by being able to recall specific set up for specific situations.
The settings of the Program AE Mode are registered as the custom settings initially.

There are some restrictions on what can be registered though:
Menu items, face recognition data, Profile Setup (baby names and data) and menu guide settings cannot be set.

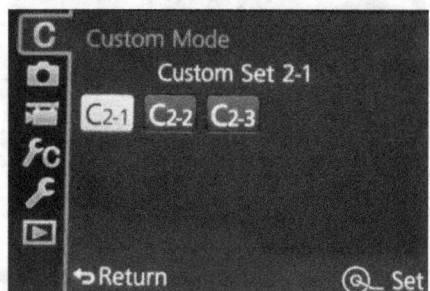

In the C2 menu you can select 3 different setups.

To access the Custom set ups for specifying a new set or recalling a previously recorded set, turn the top control dial to "C" and then press menu/set to bring up the selection menu.
Press the left/right navigation keys to select the set that you want to use.

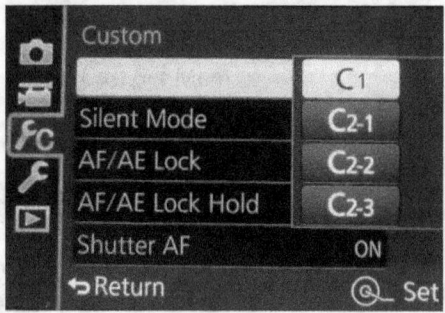 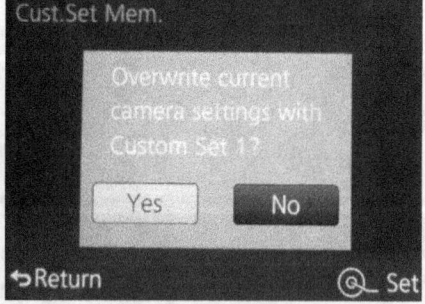

If you make changes to any of the set-up parameters, they will go back to the previously registered setting when you change setting or turn off the camera unless you perform the [Cust Set Mem] option to save them again.
To save a new set of registered settings first make all the changes to the controls and then in the {Custom Setup Menu} select {Cust Mem Set} and then select the custom setting where you want to save the value. To confirm the changes, you select Yes when the camera asks for confirmation to change the values.

Processing Camera RAW files

A RAW file is not an image file per se, it requires a de-mosaic process to turn it into an RGB image.
Camera RAW files provide the highest image quality that you can get using the Panasonic Lumix FZ1000 camera.

There are several reasons for this.

They provide much more colour information: 16K colour levels per channel compared to just 256 levels in JPEG files.
They have no camera based white balance applied, you can set the white balance to a more precise level if required.
They have no sharpening or noise reduction applied so there is no lack of image information – you control it in post processing.
They can be re-edited using different processing set ups to produce a new image without any further loss of image quality.
They can generate 16 bit files for exporting to other photo editing programs from within the RAW processing software.

The only disadvantages for some people may be the file size, It can be over 12MB in size as it is uncompressed data, and they can only be "developed" in programs designed to "open" this file structure.

Adobe® Lightroom is perhaps the most commonly used program for this, either as a standalone application or as a "plug in" for Photoshop® or Photoshop Elements® - the ACR plug in.

However, Panasonic have given you SilkyPix® in both the MAC and Windows™ OS's to "develop the Panasonic CR2 file.

Quite a few other image editing programs are now including RAW development modules like the Affinity 1.6 program from Serif.
It is a very convenient way for you to experiment using the RAW files and witness just how much more information can be extracted from the camera image.

Once you "develop" your image it can be saved as a regular JPEG file or saved as a 16-bit TIFF file so that it can be used in your regular photo editing software to further enhance it with things like local adjustment layers, cloning out detail etc.

We have seen how existing JPEG images can be edited using this program, the only difference when you "develop" the CR2 RAW file is the addition control of "de-mosaic" and noise reduction.
De-mosaic is required to decode the pattern of the Red, Green and Blue filter distribution pattern used on the sensor.

Traditionally in a "Bayer" filter system there are twice as many green filters to make the response of the sensor more "in tune" with the luminance (brightness) characteristic of our eyes.

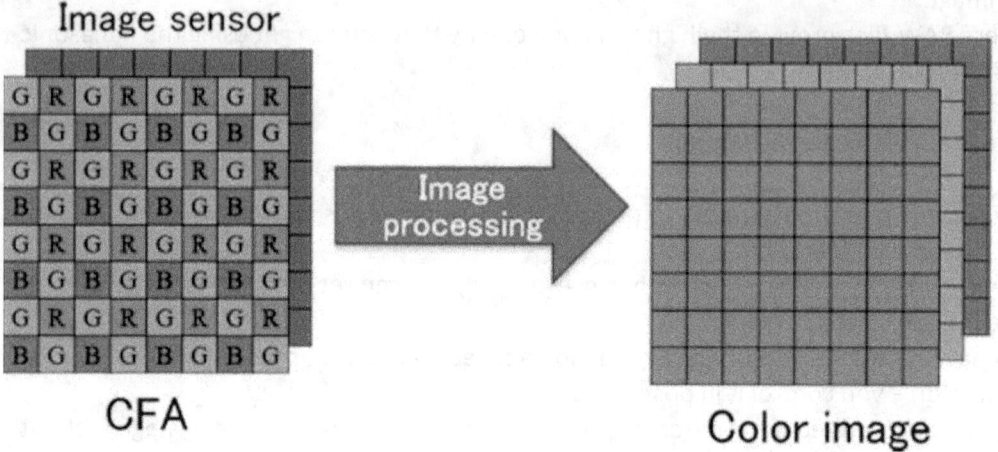

The Bayer Colour Filter Array and the de-mosaic colour image

In today's world of digital cameras, the most universal use image sensors pattern is the Bayer (Mosaic) sensor.

The Bayer sensor is a U.S. patent registered in 1976 and the first digital camera invented back in 1975 by Eastman Kodak and Steven Sasson to use this similar technology.

This filter pattern alternates a row of red and green pixels with a row of blue and green pixels. Each pixel will either have a red, green or blue filter layer (See image above).

The Bayer sensor consist of 50% Green, 25% Red and 25% Blue pixels. Order to convert the raw input into a final image, the digital camera uses specialised de-mosaic algorithms to convert the sensor data into RGB pixel data.

The camera computed the colour using several overlapping, example 2x2 arrays. This method sometimes can produce an unrealistic looking result.

The most common artefact is known as "moiré". Moiré patterns are often an undesired artefact in images produced by various digital cameras when shooting images with regular patterns like brick walls etc.

However, to overcome these artefacts depend on both of texture and software using to develop the digital camera RAW file.

Once the image data has been "re-constructed" it can be reduced in noise, you controlling the amount of blur applied to mask either noise in the colour (chrominance) or brightness (luminance) channels.

This is where you make the most significant improvement over in camera JPEG processed files.

Here is an example of a RAW file from the FZ1000 "developed" in Affinity Photo 1.5

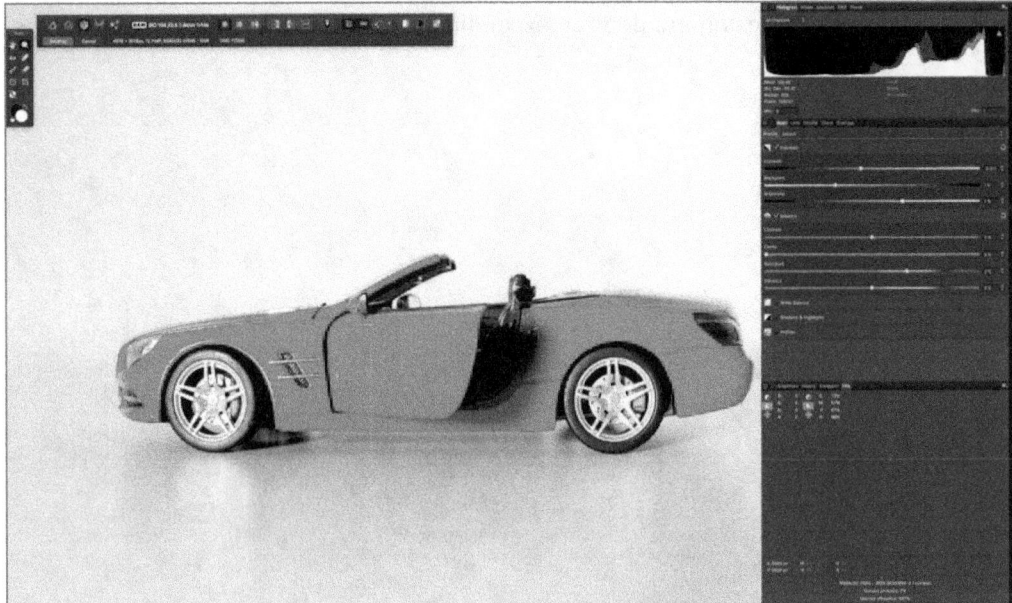

The RAW development Module

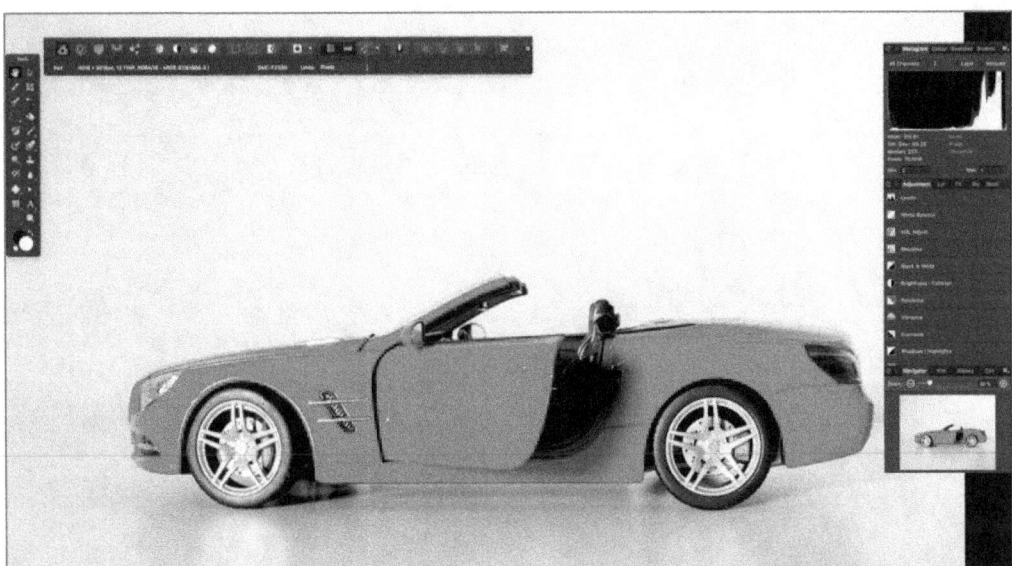

The Developed JPEG file adjustment module

The RAW file is opened in the Develop module and the basic adjustment made to white balance, sharpness and noise reduction.
The developed image is then converted into the JPEG image and any final adjustments made before saving. The in-camera JPEG processing uses all the parameters that you set before taking the images such as the Photostyle, white balance, tone curve, and any other processing parameters.

In the illustrations below the top image is the RAW file which I processed using Affinity Photo 1.5 into a JPEG file and the lower image is the out of camera JPEG image.
I think you must admit the camera does an exceedingly good job of creating these images.

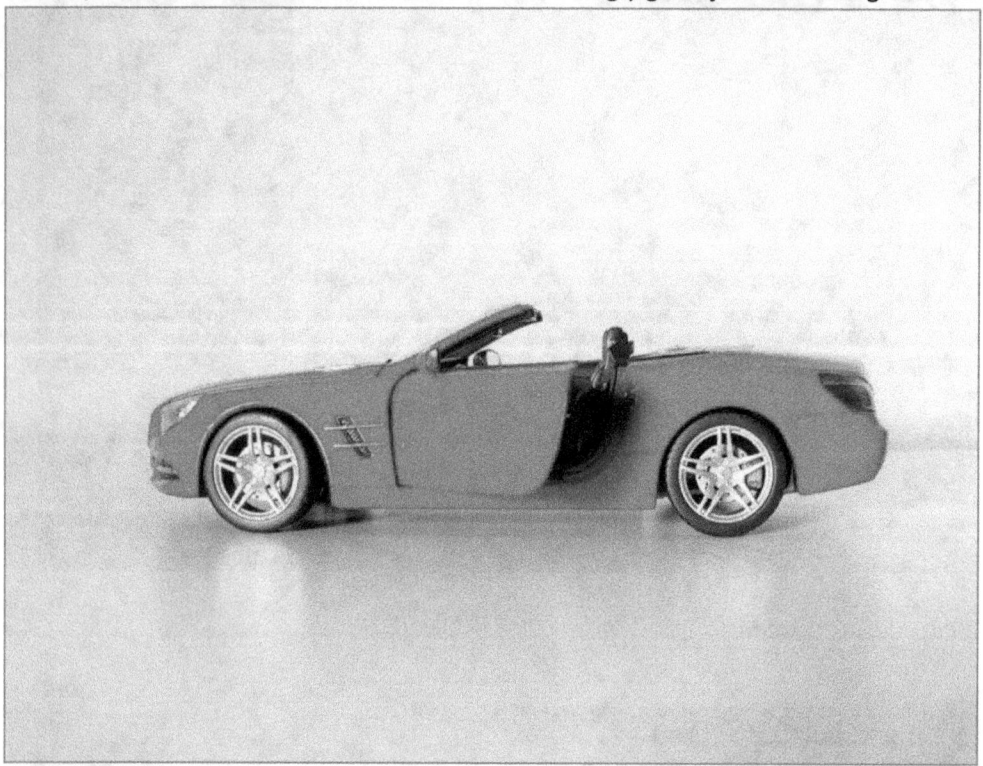

Camera RAW to JPEG

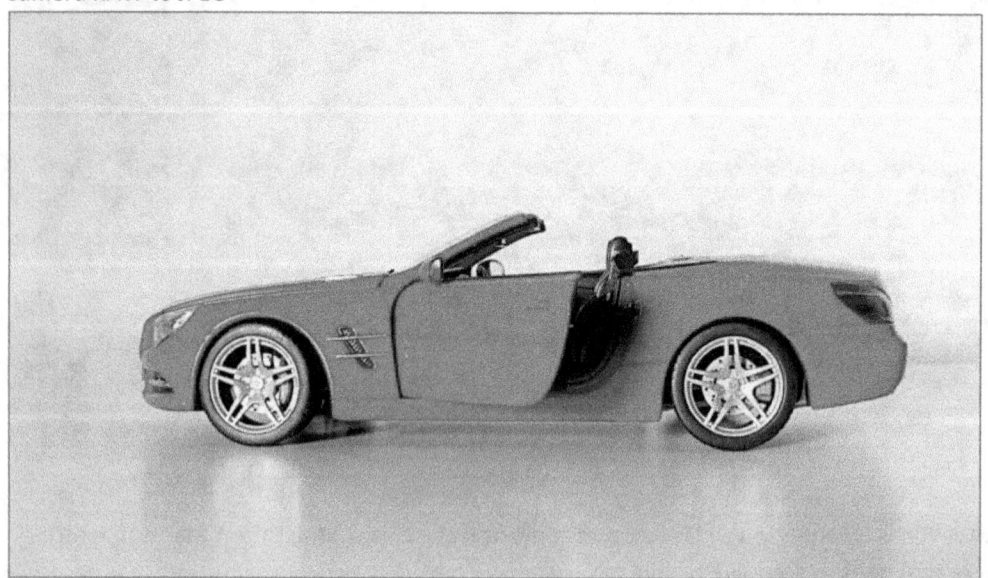

Out of Camera JPEG

The RAW file is always 3:2 aspect ratio, I had the JPEG image set to 16:9 aspect ratio and that is the height difference in the two images.

In this section I want to detail some of the important features that will help to build your understanding of how the FZ1000 camera operates and translate into other camera systems.

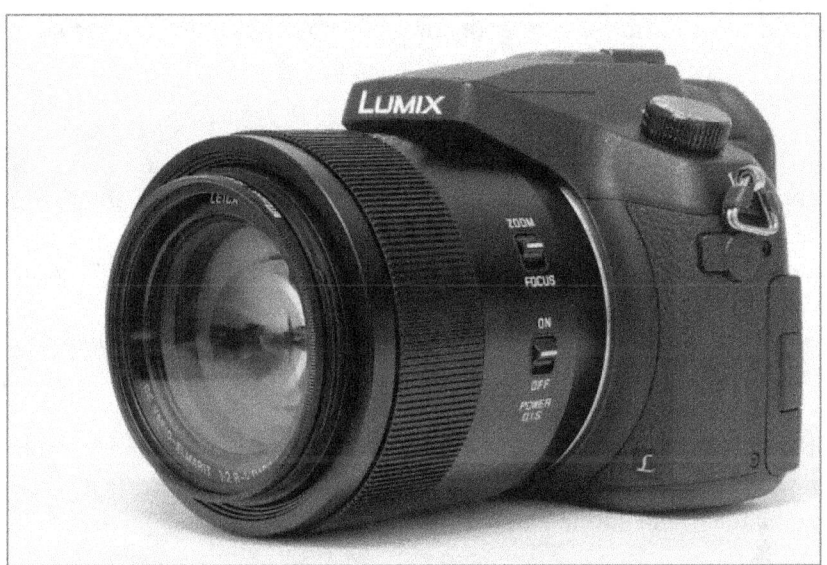

LENS SYSTEM

The first is the optical system, composed of several lens elements (or maybe only one!) that form the virtual image by converging the rays of light onto the imaging sensor.
At the focal plane of the lens is the camera imaging sensor which receives the rays of light and then converts their light intensity into tiny electrical voltages that are subsequently amplified and then digitised and processed to form our camera image file and recorded on the memory card.
The amount of light that reaches the sensor is a variable amount and depends firstly by the brightness of the ambient lighting on the scene, then secondly the amount of light that the lens allows to be passed to the sensor through the aperture and finally how long this is exposed to light governed by how long the shutter is open.
To get a correctly exposed image, that is neither too light nor too dark and containing the largest amount of tonal range possible, it is necessary to adjust the amount of light reaching the sensor.
This function is the exposure control and soon we will see what the devices are, and functions that allow you to adjust it.

To get an image well exposed, as mentioned, it is necessary to expose the camera imaging sensor for a certain amount of time. If this time is too long the camera may move during the period when it is exposed to light and the image, because of this movement, may be blurred. In this case, you should adjust the camera shutter speed to prevent this phenomenon.

Additionally, the image formed onto the sensor by objects at varying distances from the lens do not all focus at the same focal plane.

This happens, for example, when the subject is far away from the camera and the image is focused before the focal plane, but if the subject gets closer the projected image is formed behind the sensor and the image would appear to be blurred.

This is what we understand to be depth of field and will depend upon several factors as we will see shortly.

All camera Lenses mainly differ in one fundamental optical characteristic, that is the focal length.

FOCAL LENGTH.

This is conceptually the distance between the centre node of the lens and the focal plane on which the image is formed.

Associated with focal length is the angle, or field, of view, which is "seen" by the lens. This is usually expressed as a geometric angle such as 6 degrees.

The types of lenses used in photography are grouped per their angle of view in relation to that seen by our eyes and are defined as "wide-angle" if their angle is greater than that of our eye.

"Normal" if it is equal to what we see normally with unaided vision, and "telephoto" if it is acuter than what we see. A 50mm lens is generally considered as "normal" focal length when used on a full frame 24mm x 36mm sensor.

With the wide-angle lenses, images appear to have more exaggerated foregrounds compared to what you see with the naked eye.

With normal the view looks natural with little or no change to perspective.

Telephoto lenses appear to compress the foreground and the distance to foreshorten the view. Zoom lenses can vary their focal length, and in some models, cover the complete focal lengths from wide-angle to telephoto.

LENS PARAMETERS.

A lens is designed to focus the parallel rays of light from the subject onto the camera sensor. The quantity of light that transmitted through the lens to the sensor will depend on the optical characteristics of the physical design. This will include the number of elements within the lens, the type of glass used and the types and number of coatings on the lens surfaces.

This quantity of light transmitted depends on the ratio between the lens focal length and the diameter of its opening (i.e., the diameter of the diaphragm or aperture). It is defined as "brightness" and is denoted by a "F" number or F-stop as it is more commonly called. Thus, a "bright" lens has a large F-stop like F1.8.

When the aperture is the same diameter as the inside of the lens barrel itself, this is the effective maximum "brightness" of the lens. This value is the one you will see engraved on the lens along with the focal length.

In the example, on the next page, you will see that this is a short zoom lens covering 14mm to 42mm with an aperture of f3.5 at the 14mm position and f5.6 when zoomed to the 42mm focal length

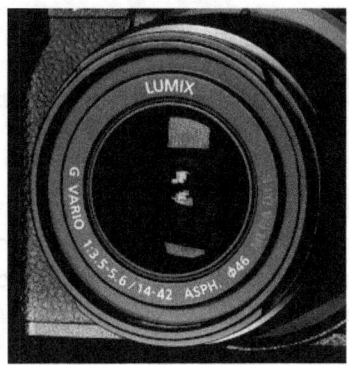

F3.5-f5.6, 14-42mm lens

As a further example, a lens with a focal length of 50mm and diaphragm (or aperture) of 25 mm has brightness f 2.0. Which is 50/25 or focal length / aperture size.
The smaller the F-number is, the brighter is the lens.
The scale of brightness values is in this sequence.
1.0, 1.4, 2.0, 2.8, 4.0, 5.6, 8.0, 11, 16, 22, ... (the scale is built on just 2 numbers *1.0* and *1.4* and the sequence alternates using these two values so even if you cannot remember the sequence you now know how to recreate it by doubling the value each time). The range of aperture covered by the FZ1000 is highlighted in RED

Going from one value to the next one larger in number causes the brightness to half and going to the next smaller number doubles the amount of light transmitted. In our camera, the intermediate values of one half or one third stops may also exist.
To be able to adjust the amount of light passing through the lens and consequently adjust the exposure lens is inserted a device called a "diaphragm" but more commonly referred to as the aperture.

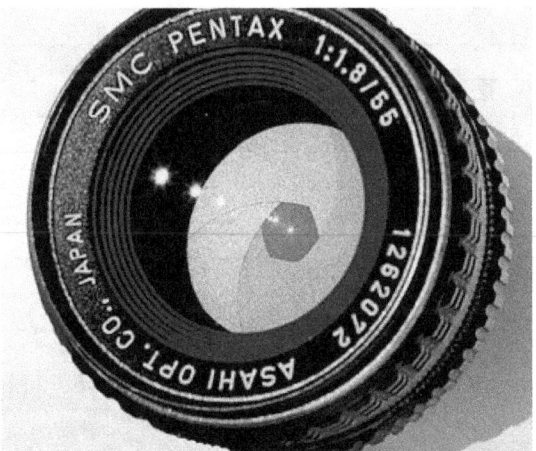

The metal 8 bladed aperture in an interchangeable lens.

The diaphragm consists of a series of overlapping thin metal blades that can close, reducing its diameter and consequently the quantity of the light passing through the lens. The brightness, starting from the maximum, decreases per the scale indicated above; thus, we have control over the amount of light allowed to reach the sensor.

To be able to expose the imaging sensor to light for a definite period a camera has a mechanism called "shutter" placed between (or in) the lens and the imaging sensor.
This mechanism determines the time during which the sensor is exposed to light.
This time can vary from seconds (up to 60 seconds) down to a fraction of a second or even less (1/8000 second).
The shutter speed determines the amount of subject motion blur in an image. To record images with maximum sharpness and no motion blur the recommendation is to use a shutter speed of 1/focal length of the lens. As an example, for 600mm EFL we would use 1/640 sec as the nearest shutter speed value.

Shutter Speeds Based Upon Full & 1/3 F-stop Increments

1/2000	1/2000
	1/1600
	1/1250
1/1000	1/1000
	1/800
	1/640
1/500	1/500
	1/400
	1/320
1/250	1/250
	1/200
	1/160
1/125	1/125
	1/100
	1/80
1/60	1/60
	1/50
	1/40
1/30	1/30
	1/25
	1/20
1/15	1/15
	1/13
	1/10
1/8	1/8

When we used film cameras we had a fixed ISO/ASA/DIN speed which was what the actual film emulsion was rated at.

This could not be changed from exposure to exposure. Now with digital cameras we have the possibility of changing the camera sensitivity, effectively the ISO, from exposure to exposure. The sensitivity change however is obtained by amplifying the very small analogue voltage emitted by the sensor pixels, but doing so we also amplify the noise, which is also part of the signal and degrades the image quality.

The sensitivity is measured with a standard defined ISO range of values, like the F-stops we saw on the lens.

As an example, ISO 100, 200, 400, 800, 1600, 3200 ... doubling its value also doubles the camera sensitivity which is the same as increasing the f stop to the next lower number e.g. F4 to f2.8

FOCUS

To allow the lens to be able to converge the rays of light from the subject, at varying distances from the lens, to form an image with sharp focus we need some physical mechanism to allow the elements within the lens to move allow.

The types of focusing system will not be elaborated here but its sufficient to say that subjects at closer range need the lens to extend further way from the sensor in order that they are focussed correctly.

The furthest distant objects, where the rays are assumed to be of parallel origin, are often termed "infinity" focus.

EXPOSURE

As we have seen the exposure (quantity of light and the amount of time the shutter is open) must be determined to allow the imaging sensor to produce voltages which are representative of peak white, darkest blacks and all the mid tones in-between so they can be digitised into discrete digital values from 0 (zero) which is black to 255 which is the peak white.

To do this you can change any one, or all, of the three settings: aperture, shutter speed and sensitivity of the sensor.

But how do you determine the right values, which one should you adjust?

Once it was done by eye, based on experience and rules like the "sunny F16 rule" which stated that if you used the reciprocal of the film speed for the shutter speed and set the aperture to F16 then in bright sunshine your exposure would be correct.

Thus, with a film speed rated at ISO 100 the shutter speed would be set nearest to that (1/125) and the aperture would be set to f16.

Later, exposure meters were introduced to measure the amount of light reflected from the subject and consequently calculate the exposure.

Exposure meters, were first external and hand held.

Later they were implemented into the camera, and finally, with the development of electronics and microprocessors, connected to the setting of aperture, shutter speed and ISO sensitivity and can now they can automatically adjust these parameters and to obtain a correct exposure.

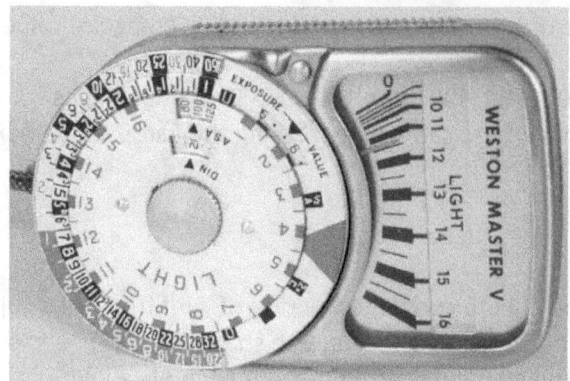

a typical hand held exposure meter used with film based cameras.

However, there are still some situations in which the adjustment of the camera must be modified to achieve the correct exposure such as backlit or subjects which are very dark in dark surroundings or are very light in bright scenes such as those found in typical beach or snow. In such cases, it is necessary to change the exposure compared to that determined from the exposure of the camera.

The correction is measured in EV values and a 1 EV corresponds to increasing or decreasing the F stop by 1 whole increment or in a doubling or halving of the shutter speed.

All this can be done, on most cameras by pressing the button (* / -) exposure correction and checking the result in the viewfinder (if electronic) or the LCD screen before shooting.

SHARPNESS

In this section, I am not referring to the sharpness as the lens resolution, but the clarity that results from an image that is not degraded by camera shake or by subject movement during the exposure time or by the image being incorrectly focussed.

To get a sharp image and not to "move" during the exposure you need to shoot with a shutter speed sufficiently short so that it will not to be affected by the movements of the shaky hands of the photographer and the vibrations produced by the same camera when shooting.

This time is wholly dependent upon the focal length of the lens. In fact, with the wide-angle lenses group the relative movement of the image during exposure is so small that frequently these lenses don't have any image stabilisation.

Use a shutter speed that is at least the reciprocal of the focal length in relation to our full frame equivalent focal length.

For example, if you use a 50mm you must be at least 1/50sec and when using a 200mm, 1/200sec. With modern cameras equipped with image stabilisation (either in the camera body or in the lens) that time can be stretched by relying on the stabilising function, but for safety it is better not to go too much more than two-stop, which is a factor of 4.

For example, if you go from 1/500sec to 1/125sec or from 1/200sec to 1/50sec. If you further lengthen the time you risk that the stabiliser will not always be effective and the result will show as blur.

These conditions apply to static subjects; landscapes, still life etc., but they must be modified for moving objects and for images where people are moving in the scene are involved.

In fact, for photographing people posing or otherwise it is still best not to go below 1/60sec to prevent the very slight movements, even some involuntary, that a person might make and hence cause the picture to be blurred.

For subjects in motion it should be obvious that you must use a much faster shutter speed, increasing more and more as the speed of the subject increases.

It will also depend upon whether the subject is moving across the frame or moving towards or away from the camera. The acuteness of this subject movement relative to the lens axis will also affect the shutter speed necessary to arrest any subject motion blur.

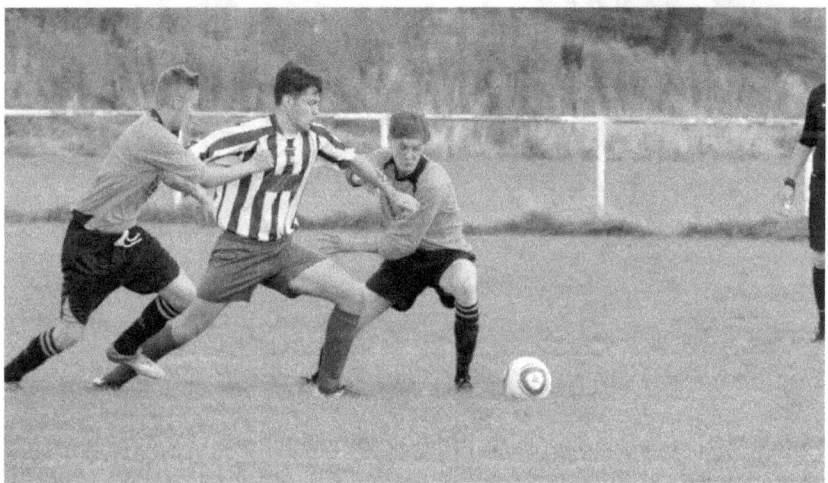

Selecting a fast-enough shutter speed to stop subject motion

If you have the camera set to fully automatic the only thing you can do is to perform a check before shooting – usually by half depressing the shutter button, and looking at the time indicated on the LCD screen to see if it is fast enough.

Using the automated system for the sensitivity, most cameras allow you to set the minimum time after which the shutter speed must increase the ISO sensitivity.

In most cases, it is appropriate to fix at least 1/60 second as the minimum. In many cameras, this minimum shutter speed can be set to "auto" and then it is determined automatically, by the camera computer looking at the focal length of the lens.

Auto Focus

The focus must be accurate and must be on the principal subject of the image. As an example, in the case of a portrait, on the eyes. For a landscape, usually the background, unless that there is a subject closer such as a tree, a building, or a person.

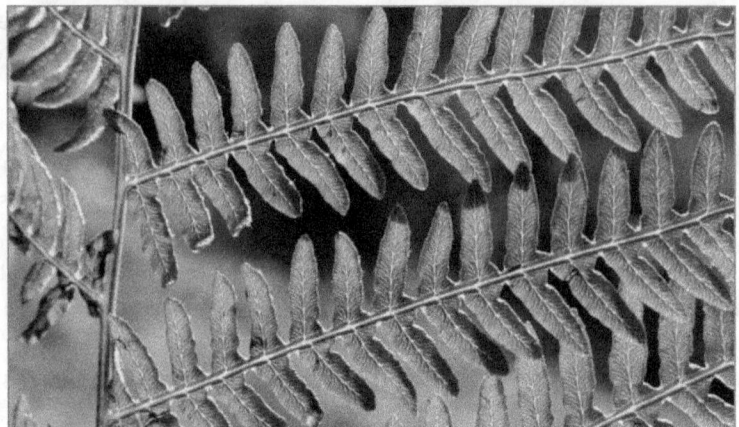

The camera focus critically set on the foreground subject

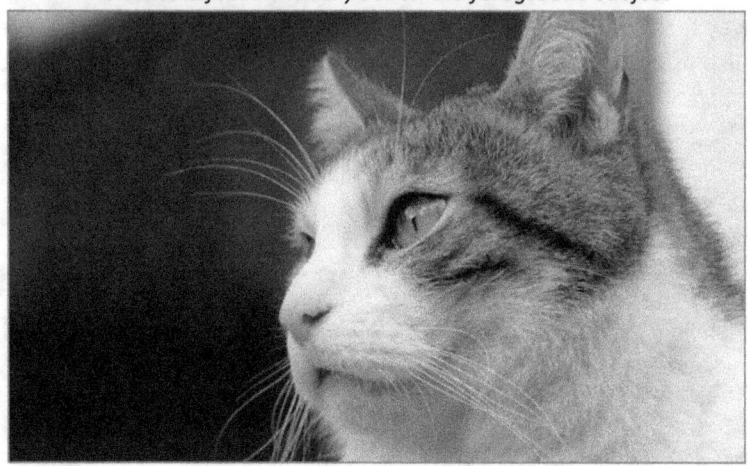

The focus of any portrait with eyes must be set to include the eye(s)

The autofocus works on the predetermined points ("AF points") by, which the camera focus system can perform the focus operation.

These always cover the central part of the frame and often also extend to the sides in a variety of patterns depending upon the manufacturer's definitions.

In fully automatic cameras, modern auto focus systems perform well enough to identify the person's face to focus on, however you should always check the focus before shooting.

This operation can be faster or slower depending on the type of camera and focus system employed the level of ambient light and the contrast of the subject.

To focus it is usual just to simply press the shutter button halfway and then the focus is acquired, often confirmed by a sound, continue to depress the shutter button to capture the image.

If the camera does not correctly choose the subject (for example because it is in a side position and is outside of one of the AF points) you must manually select (in cameras that allow you to do this) the correct AF point. If this is not convenient then sometimes the method of pointing the central AF spot at the subject, then half depressing the shutter button to acquire focus and then holding the button whilst recomposing the shot to finally complete the shutter button operation to capture the image.

This method is often referred to as focus and recompose. It works well so long as the subject distance doesn't change as you recompose the shot.

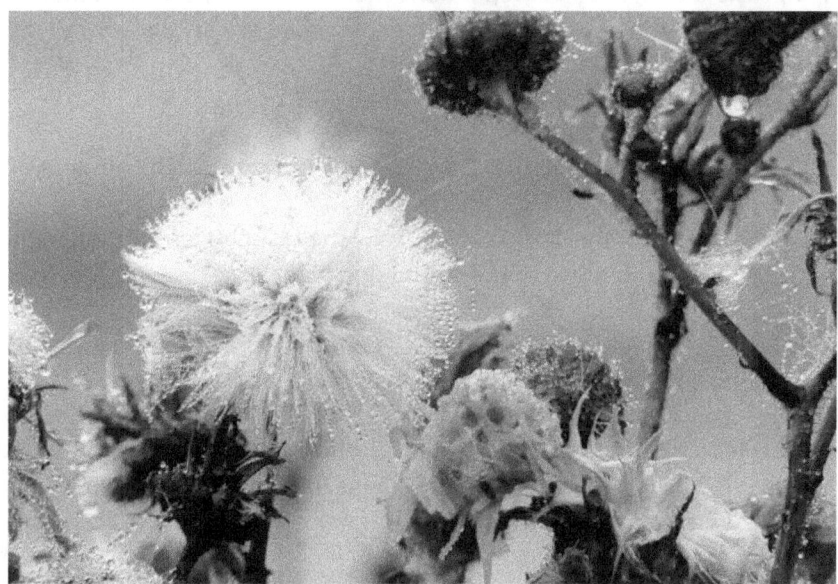

Careful focussing to ensure the foreground is selected

THE ELEMENTS OF CORRECT EXPOSURE

You can't think about photography without thinking about exposure. There are three adjustable elements which together controls exposure. They are Aperture, Shutter Speed and ISO. Let's refresh our memory of these three controls.

The aperture the amount of light travelling through the lens to the imaging sensor plane. The aperture setting is indicated by a f-number where each f-number represents a stop of light.

The shutter speed controls for how long that this light travelling from the lens onto the imaging sensor takes place.

The ISO determines the cameras sensitivity to light such that each value of the rating represents a stop of light and each incremental ISO number (up or down) represents a doubling or having of the cameras sensitivity to light.

When in these three elements are combined, they represent a given exposure value. Any change in one of the three elements will have a measurable and specific impact on the way the two remaining elements react to control the exposure at the imaging sensor and ultimately how the image looks.

For example, *if you increase the f-stop* you decrease the size of the lens diaphragm thus reducing the amount of light hitting the imaging sensor, however, therefore it also increases the depth of field in the final image.

Reducing the shutter speed affects how motion is captured in that this can cause the background or subject to have blur.

However, reducing the shutter speed (that is increasing the time that the imaging sensor receives the light from the lens) increases the amount of light reaching the centre and everything is brighter.

Increasing the cameras sensitivity to light by *increasing the ISO value* as you to shoot in lower light conditions however therefore you increase the amount of digital noise in the photo. It is impossible to make an independent change in one of the elements not to obtain an opposite effect in how the other elements affect the image.

APERTURE OR F-STOP

The aperture of the lens is the component which is used to control the amount of light reaching the sensor.
The aperture, or "f-stop" number is mathematically the result of lens focal length / the diameter of the aperture (hole size of the diaphragm blades).

With each increase in the f-stop number (i.e. we go from a smaller number to a larger one, say F4 to F5.6) we half the amount of light reaching the sensor.

In the next illustration, I show the f-stops with the whole f-stop values in red and the 1/3 f-stops in blue. So, we have a 4 F-stop range or 8 times exposure difference.
Note the bigger the f-stop number, the smaller the size of the aperture. So "wide open" the lens is at f2.8 and fully closed it is at F8.
There is a practical limit to how small the aperture can be before it starts to degrade the image through a phenomenon called "diffraction".
The smaller the lens diameter and the tighter the pixels are together on the sensor; the sooner this limit is reached. Interestingly the mathematical calculation results in a value of f4 in the case of a 1-2/3 inch sensor, where in something like a Canon FX sensor DSLR it is F22.

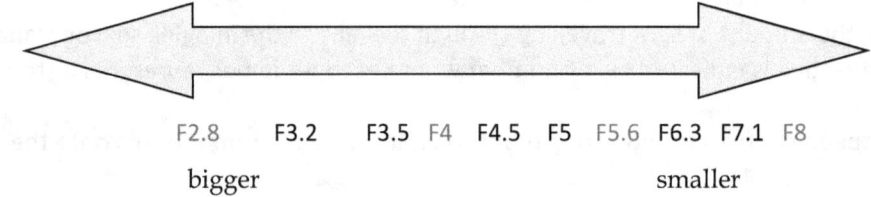

F2.8   F3.2   F3.5 F4   F4.5   F5   F5.6 F6.3 F7.1 F8

bigger   smaller

SHUTTER SPEED

This controls the amount of time that the light passing through the lens diaphragm (or f-stop) reaches the sensor.
The amount of time multiplied by the light passing through the aperture setting gives us the exposure.
When the aperture is set to a value which in which we want a specific depth of field then there will be an associated time value (or shutter speed) required to achieve the correct exposure so that the image looks correct.
So, for example if we have an aperture set on the camera at F4 and the exposure system determines that a shutter speed of 1/60 second is required to give the correct exposure.
If we adjust the aperture to a smaller size (larger number) say f5.6, which is 1 f-stop increment smaller, the camera will adjust the shutter speed to a longer value to allow the same quantity of light (time x intensity) to reach the sensor.
In this case the shutter speed will go from 1/60 second to 1/30 second
i.e. the time doubles.

Here is the important relationship we must understand, increase the intensity of light by opening the aperture (going to a smaller f-stop number) means we need to make a corresponding decrease in shutter speed to keep the exposure the same. Remember equal Shutter speeds are indicated as a fraction below 1 second, e.g. 1/25. Speeds longer than 1 second are indicated 1" 2" 4" 8" etc.,

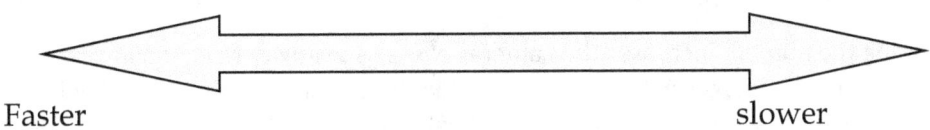

1/125, 1/100, 1/80, 1/50, 1/40, 1/30, 1/25, 1/20, 1/15, 1/13, 1/10, 1/8, 1/6, 1/5

Faster   slower

The higher the fractional number, the faster the shutter speed.

To crystallise this, think of the correct exposure as being a glass into which we will poor some water. When the glass is 50% full, that is our perfect exposure.

If we pour in water very slowly (representing a low intensity of light) it will take longer (the shutter speed analogy) to reach the correct exposure level than if we poured the water into the glass more quickly. (Over fill the glass and we lose our highlight detail with the result in the highlights being "blown-out")

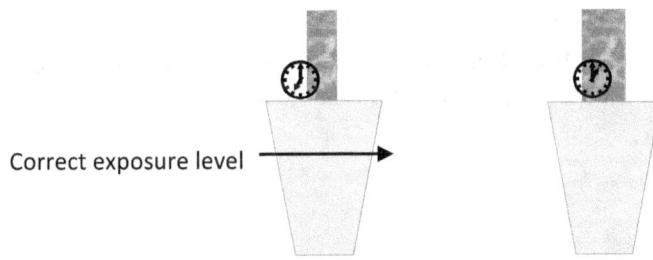

Correct exposure level

The time taken to fill the glass is longer with a small flow of water (representing the amount of light passing through the aperture) than with more water flow (representing more light – or a larger aperture)

This relationship is the key to you understanding how to be able to set up the camera when you want to use the manual mode (M)

ISO (International Standard Organisation) This is the value which is attributed to the combined camera sensor and the logarithmic amplifier and then the analogue to digital converter system.

If you leave the camera set with the default factory set up the ISO values are increased or decreased by a fixed value equivalent to 1 full aperture increase (or decrease) or doubling (or halving) the shutter speed.
This is referred to as 1 EV (standing for exposure value)

You will notice that with this 1EV increment set the ISO values change as in the table below

100	200	400	800	1600	3200

If you change the increments in the set-up menu to be just 1/3 EV you have finer control of the camera sensitivity and hence noise control full ISO (1 EV increments shown in red)

100	125	160	200	250	320	400	500
640	800	1000	1250	1600	2000	2500	3200

Increasing the number increases the cameras overall sensitivity to light allowing the camera to acquire images in low levels of light with the ability to shoot hand held.

As I mentioned previously increasing the ISO value also amplifies the "noise" in the system resulting in images with lower visual sharpness and image contrast.

This noise usually appears in the darker areas of the image (the shadows) but even if the camera is used outdoors in bright sunlight, say to get a fast shutter speed for an action photograph the resulting image will be visually un-sharp compared to one shot with lower ISO numbers.

For general photography, whenever you can, use the camera at ISO 100 (or the lowest value).

The camera optical image stabilisation should always be set to ON and this will allow you to use some slow hand held shutter speeds (1/30 second or less depending upon your own hand shakiness) and if there is no subject movement which needs to be

We have seen how the interaction of aperture and shutter combine to give us the correct exposure for our image.

Up until this point I have assumed that the camera sensitivity has remained unchanged however we must look at how all three of the components of arrested you will find you get some great images. exposure work together to produce the final image.

The Exposure Triangle

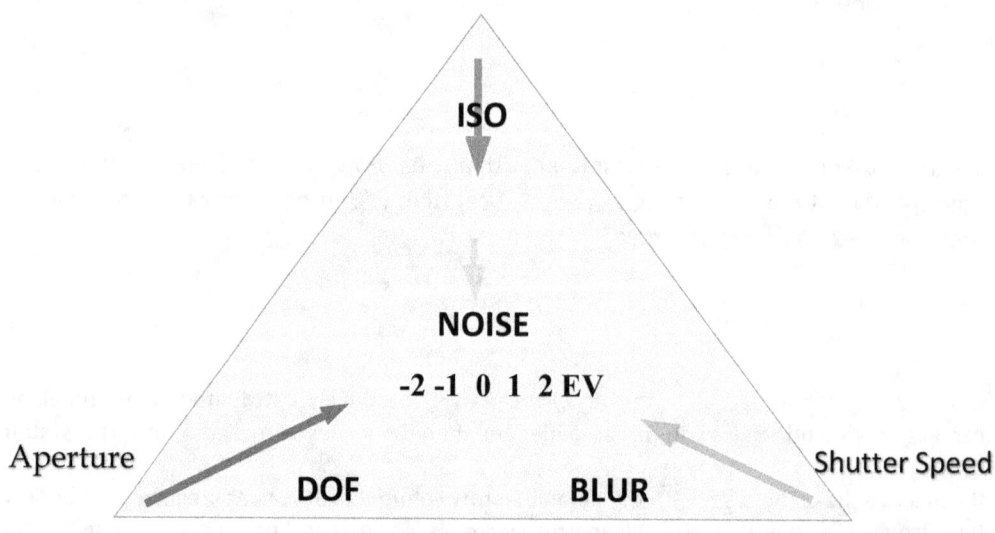

Higher ISO leads to more image noise; slower shutter speed gives more motion blur and a smaller Aperture (larger f-number) provides more DOF.

In the exposure triangle, shown above, the entire relationship is shown for the inter-relationship of ISO, Aperture and Shutter speed. In the centre of the triangle is the perfect exposure which will show as 0 EV on the camera exposure meter.

If we make modification to one element of the exposure, we must make an opposite compensation to one, or both, of the other two.

For example, if we decrease the aperture from f4 to F8 (2 complete F-stops or "EV units") - this reduces the light entering the camera.

We then need to increase either the ISO by 2 EV or to decrease the Shutter speed by 2EV to compensate.
(Or we could change each parameter by the 1EV - increasing the ISO by 1EV and reducing the Shutter speed by 1EV).

In the triangle, we can see the effect of changing any element.
Changing ISO results in more noise if you increase it.

Changing Aperture affects the Depth of Field (DOF) - smaller apertures (larger f-numbers) giving more DOF.
Changing shutter speeds affects both camera shake and subject motion blur, longer exposures introduces more blur.

You must evaluate which of these three parameters is the main element in taking your image:
low ISO for lower noise.
higher shutter speed to reduce motion blur.
aperture size for shallow, or greater, DOF.

How to Photograph Anything!

In my opening preface about this guidebook I stated "I've purposely avoided giving detailed information on how to take specific types of images such as "travel pictures", "sports pictures." Instead I have tried to concentrate on giving you the tips and techniques for using the features of the Panasonic Lumix FZ1000 to take any kind of image you want". Well that statement is true.

To photography "anything" just requires you to analyse the subject and ask yourself the following questions:

Is the principal, or most important, factor one in which I will require the most, or the least, depth of field?

If so, then this will determine that the Aperture priority mode will be required to allow you to set an aperture that will give you this amount of depth of field at the lens focal length you have chosen.

Or is it that you require to capture image motion, being that deliberate blurring or capturing absolute freezing of the action?

Then this will require you to select a Shutter priority mode to enable you to set the required shutter speed to capture this effect.

Or is a combination of depth of field and a requirement to capture some sense of motion either blurred or frozen action shot?

Then this will dictate that you must use the manual exposure mode so that you can set aperture and shutter to the required values and then use the ISO control to provide the correct exposure.

Let's look at the principal elements of the exposure again.

DOF or depth of field is determined by three components;
The focal length of the lens.
The aperture of the lens.
The distance of the subject to the lens.

In the case of the focal length of the lens, if the focal length is small, e.g. wide angle or 25mm (equivalent) then inherently the DOF is quite large at all subject to lens distances. If we were to take a picture of a subject that is very close to the lens, then we would see that the subject and a large amount of the background would also appear to be in sharp focus.
This is true even if the aperture was wide open, or a value of f2.8 in the case of the FZ1000.

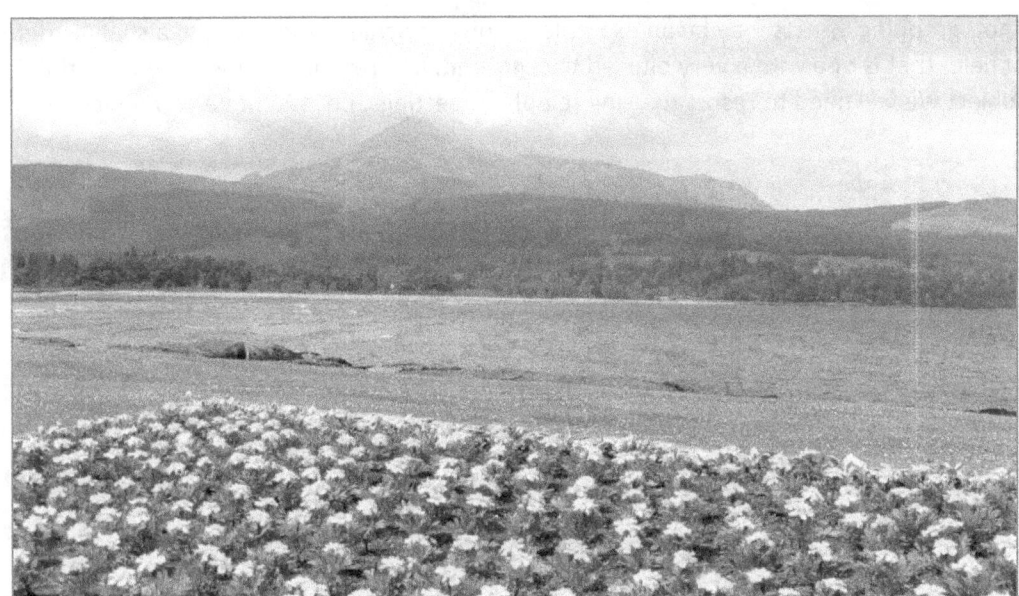

Large depth of field at wide angle setting

If we move the subject extremely close to the camera then we can get a similar DOF effect that we get if we were to use a longer telephoto setting, as in the example below where the subject is just centimetres away from the lens.

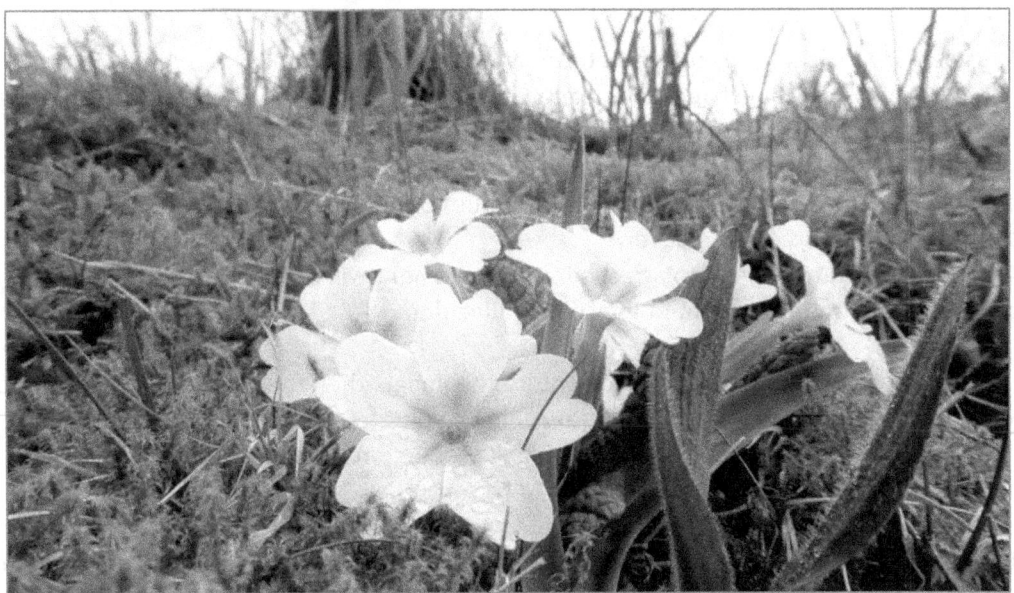

Shallow DOF with wide angle lens, achieved by the subject being extremely close to the lens.

By understanding how lens focal length and subject to lens distance affects the DOF you can determine what method to use. In some situations, it may not be possible to get the camera so close to the subject.

Photographing insects may be an example of this. To achieve the result of a shallow depth of field, that is one with a very blurred background, at a reasonable distance from the subject we will need to resort to using telephoto settings, i.e. 400mm(equivalent).

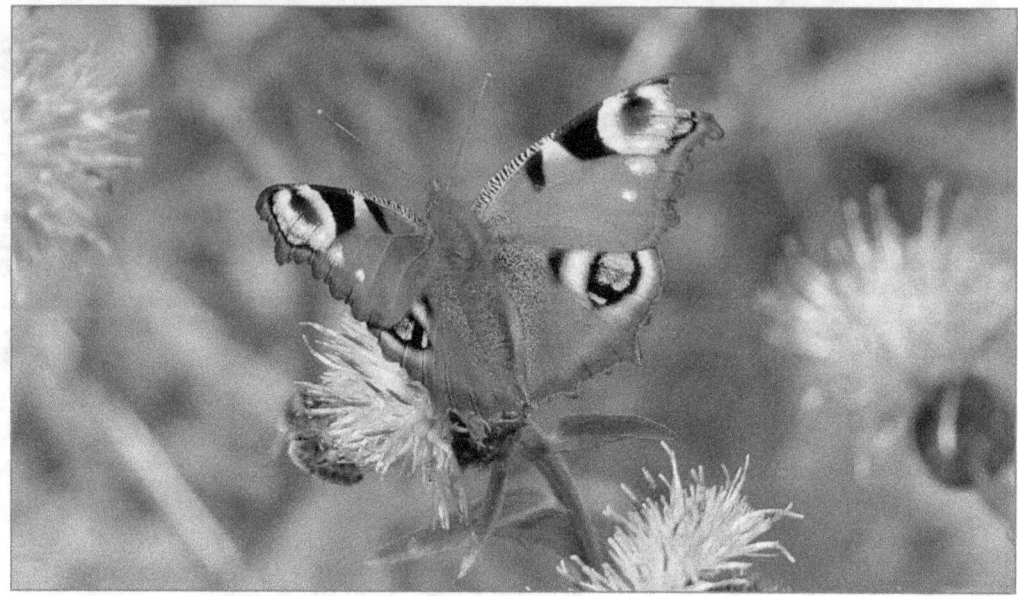

Shallow DOF achieved by using the telephoto setting of the lens at 1 metre from the subject.

The aperture plays a lesser role in determining the background blur.
However, by using a small aperture, like f6.3, it helps to increase to zone of focus (DOF) to include the insect or plant being photographed.
When considering subject motion, we need to determine if we want longer shutter speeds to allow a degree of subject blurring to occur due to the subject movement or faster shutter speeds to freeze the action.
As a rule, the shutter speed to arrest subject movement will depend upon the focal length of the lens due to the amount of image magnification.

If you are using telephoto settings to capture the image, then the rule of 1/focal length of lens is probably a good starting point for achieving blur free subjects.
This should not be confused with camera shake reduction which the optical image stabilisation of the camera (OIS) is designed to control.

The OIS only compensates for camera movement; any subject movement is still recorded in the image.
So even though OIS allows us to shoot with at least 3 f-stops of equivalent shutter speed advantage it does not arrest subject motion.
In the next illustration of the "Big One" at Blackpool Pleasure Beach the carriage hurtles down the highest drop of the ride. I used 1/640th sec to capture the image without any blur.

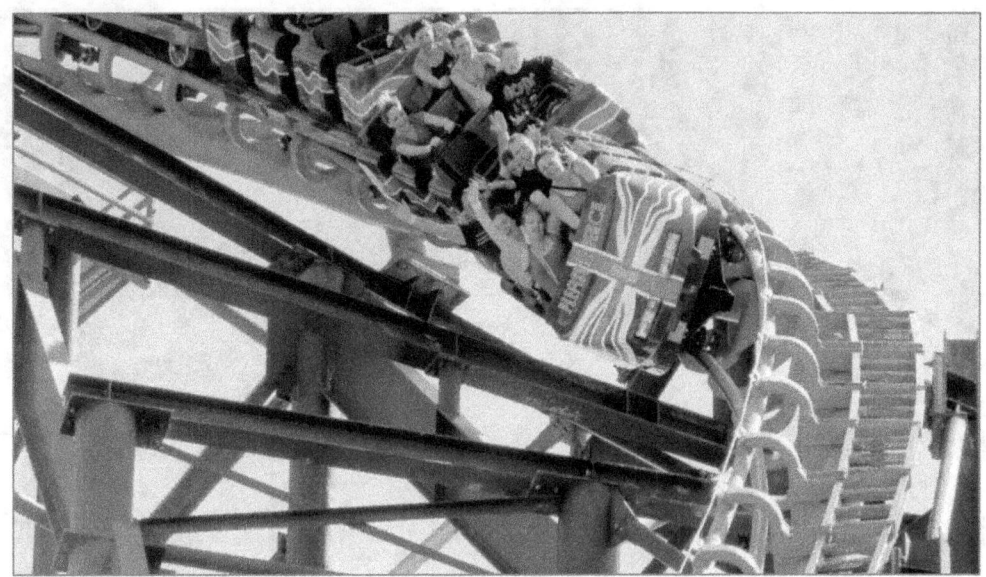

Use of faster shutter speed to arrest subject motion at telephoto lens settings

To capture motion blur we need to use longer shutter speeds. In the example of capturing waterfalls with a silk like appearance we used shutter speeds in the order of ½ to 2 seconds long.
To achieve these longer times, especially in brighter ambient lighting we need to use neutral density filters to reduce the amount of light entering the lens.

Common values of ND4 give 2 f-stops reduction and the ND8 will give 3 f-stops reduction in light.

You may also need to use the lowest ISO as well (100) and a small aperture (f 7.1) to achieve these longer shutter speeds required to capture these types of shot.

Obviously, such long shutter speeds will need the camera to be very stable for this exposure.

Use a tripod, bean bag or other mechanical means, to hold the camera rigid is essential. Use the self-timer or remote shutter cable to make the exposure to prevent any camera movement.

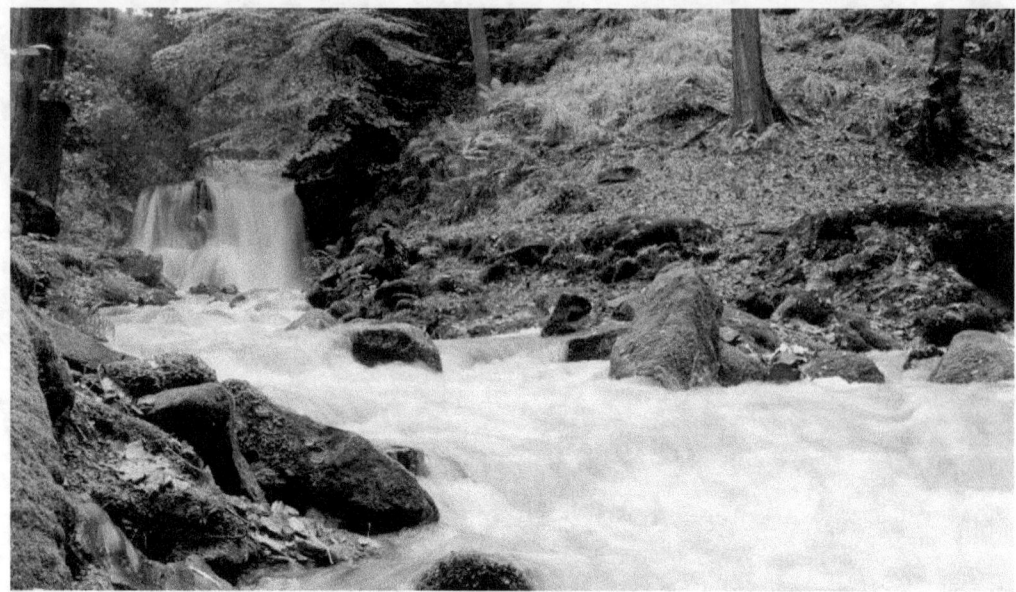

Use of longer shutter speed to capture subject motion blur.

So, the essence here is to analyse which component you need to concentrate on to produce the effect you want to see in your image.

There are some other situations which will also direct you into which mode to put the camera in to capture good images.

This so called "low light" photography is one of those areas.

Low Light Photography

Shooting in low light levels presents a significant challenge to any photographer, not only users of the Panasonic Lumix FZ1000. How do we quantify low level light? Look at the selection of images below. Each one could be considered low light as there is no universal definition for this category of photography!

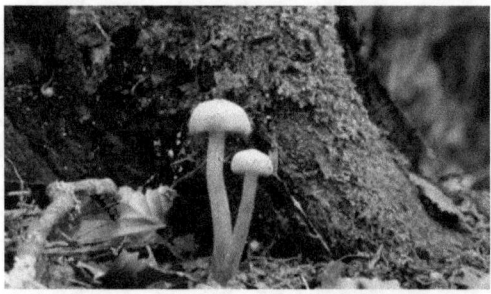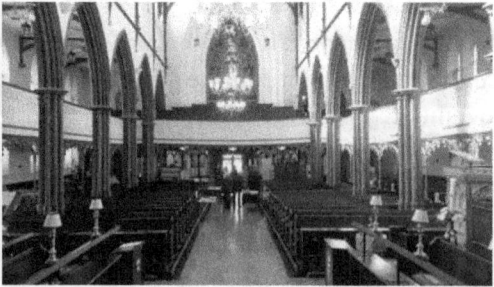

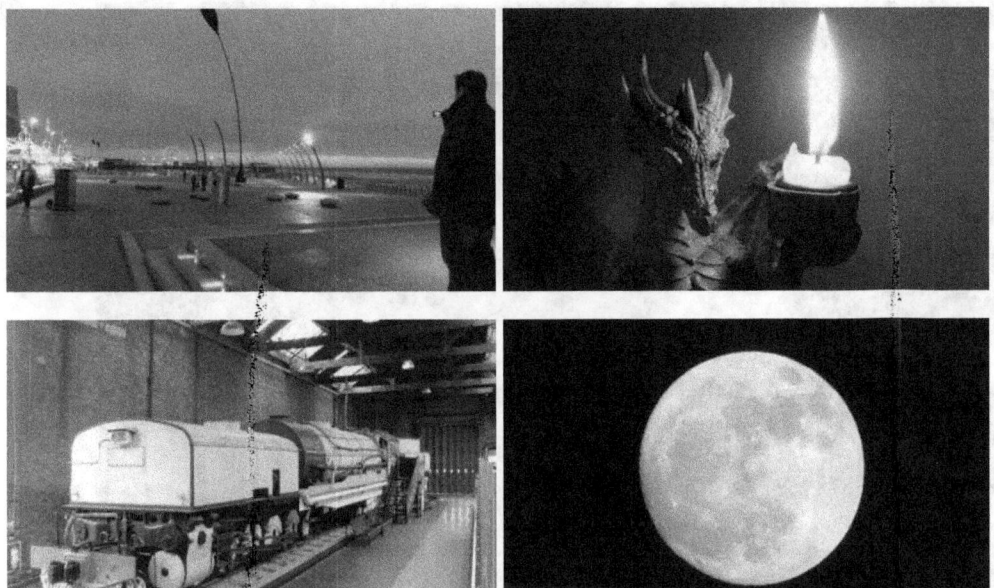

In many of the images shown previous there are some similarities. The overall exposure times are less than 1/30th second.

Could this be our definition of "low light" photography?
Each of the images shown required a different technique to capture an image of good quality.

The toadstool on the forest floor and the candle light photo needed a bean bag, or tripod, to hold the camera steady.

The church interior needed the camera rested on a church fitting to capture the ½ second exposure.

Some of the "low level" light scenes can be deceptive however.

Take the image of the moon it is quite bright. It reflects light from the sun and can be classed with the daylight, sunny f16 rule.

This rule suggests that in bright sunlight if we use an ISO of 100, a shutter speed of 1/125th sec and an aperture of f16 we will get a perfect exposure.

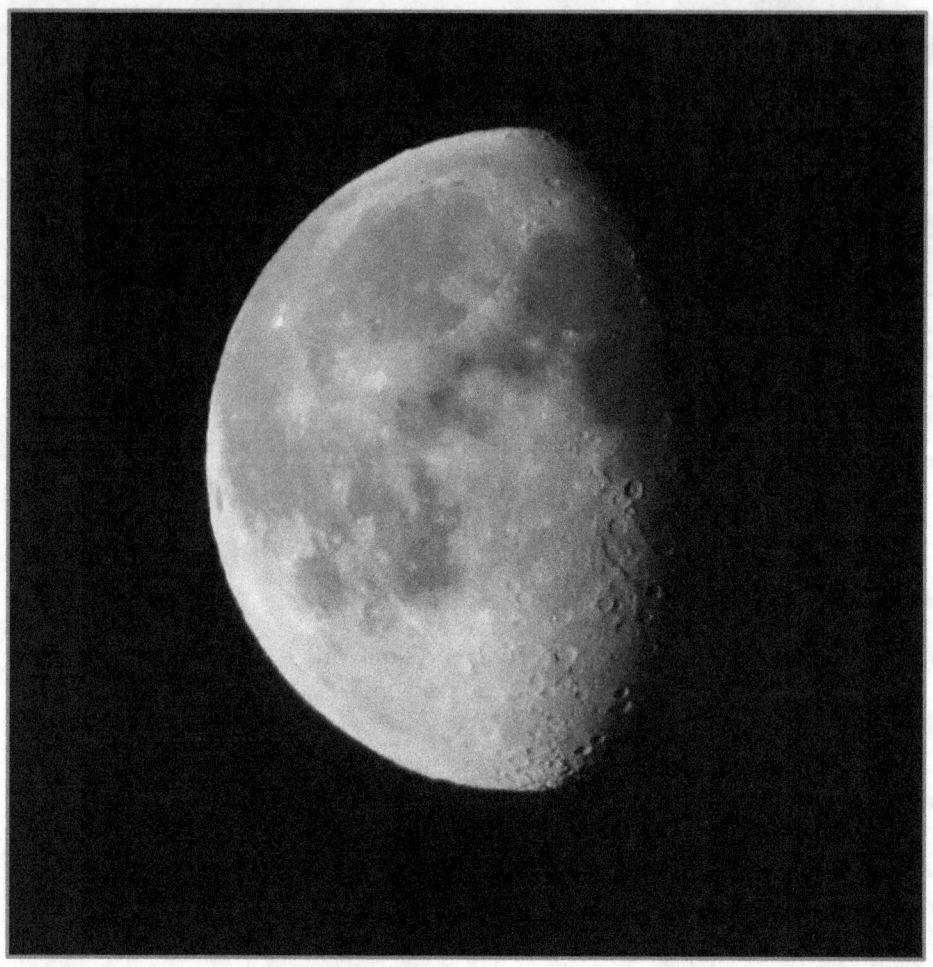

As our moon is a giant reflector, given our camera will only allow us to set f8 as the minimum we can easily get an exposure of 1/500th sec at f8 and an ISO of 100.
We have seen previously higher ISO values can lead to image noise, particularly in shadow areas.

To get the best quality images it is important to avoid using the higher ISO's and finding a way to use the lower ones – either by larger apertures or slower shutter speeds. The method of achieving either will, of course, depend upon the subject.

Close-Up & Macro Photography

We have seen that using a wide angle setting with the lens and moving close to the subject will allow you to take some extreme close-ups such as the one shown on the next page.

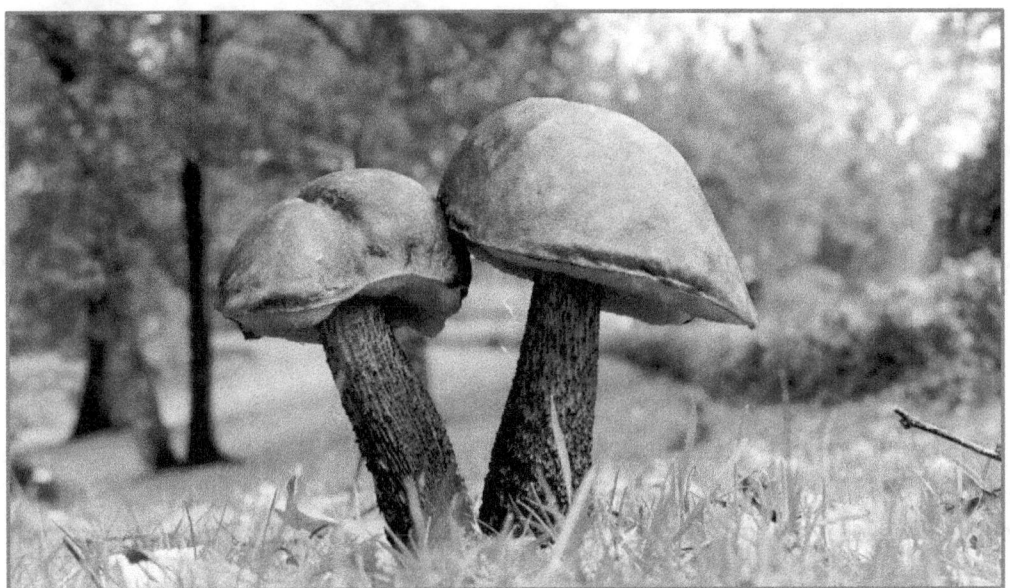

Close-up using 25mm setting and a few centimetres from the subject

Whilst this does give great results it can lead to "perspective distortion".
If this, or the fact that some subjects may not allow you to get so close to them, then we need to look at other methods of achieving a larger image on the camera sensor.
One of these methods is to use "close-up lenses" or "filters" as sometimes they are erroneously referred to as.
These supplemental lenses act like correction lenses that we find in spectacles. They modify the focal length of the lens in front of which they are placed. They are positive dioptres which effectively allow the lens to focus closer.

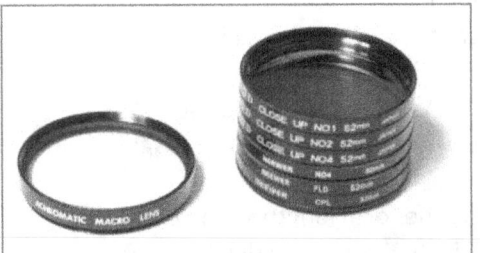

A set of 3 close-up lenses, the #1, #2 and #4 and an optically corrected "achromatic" close-up lens. All these have a 62mm filter thread and screw directly onto the front of the 1000 lens.

These basic lenses are of just one element construction; some are multi-coated to reduce reflection however the majority are just optical glass. This is fine if you just want to experiment with close-up photography and provided you understand some of the limitations they will give you excellent results like the image below taken with such a set.

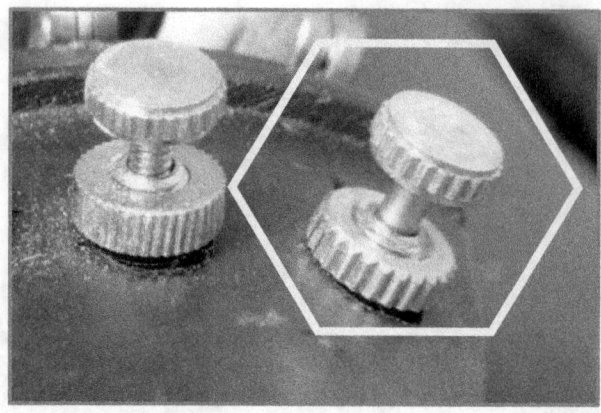

These lenses do suffer from colour fringes (chromatic aberration) and from edge definition fall off because of the lens curvature of field. This is especially so with the higher value ones (#4 and #10). If you look at an enlargement of the above image you will see both effects!

Using a small aperture like f7.1 will help to reduce the edge distortion.

What about the change in focus, or more importantly the working, distances achieved with the addition of these close-up lenses?

The definition of the dioptre is that with the camera's lens focused on infinity and a #1 dioptre close-up lens fitted, the maximum focusing distance becomes 1 metre, with the #2 it becomes 0.5 metres, and with the #4 it becomes 0.25 metres.

You may see a lot of information regarding "magnification ratios" and "macro", what do they mean?

Take the "magnification ratio" example. If the image is one-quarter the size of the subject, the magnification is 0.25x.

If the image is one-half the size of the subject, the magnification is 0.5x. When the image and the subject are the same size, the magnification is 1x.

The term "macro" photography generally means that the image size is larger than life size.

However, the term now is used to define a lens which will focus more closely!

When using a supplementary close-up lens, it is very easy to calculate the magnification for a camera lens set to infinity focusing.

Simply divide the focal length of the camera lens by the focal length of the close-up lens. Conveniently, the focal length of the close-up lens is the derived by dividing 1000 by the dioptre #.

So, for example, the #2 dioptre lens has a focal length of 1000/2 or 500mm, the #4 lens is 1000/4 = 250mm.

So, for example, if we now set the camera to the equivalent of 100mm by using the zoom lever to achieve x4 optical zoom and we fit a #2 lens in front of the FZ1000 lens, the magnification would be 100/500, which is 0.2x.

This means that a 10cm wide image would be 2mm long on our 8mm wide sensor.

The same close-up lens with the FZ1000 set to 200mm (or x8 optical zoom) will give a magnification of 200/500 which is 0.4x.

Zoom all the way out to 400mm (x16 optical zoom) and the magnification becomes 400/500 which is 0.8

As you can see, the magnification increases with the focal length of the camera lens. Even greater magnifications are possible if the camera lens is focused closer than when used at its infinity setting.

A #4 close-up lenses give double the magnification of the #2 and the #2 gives double that of the #1 close-up lenses.

The more powerful the close-up lens and the longer the focal length of the FZ1000 lens, the larger the magnification ratio of the FZ1000 will be.

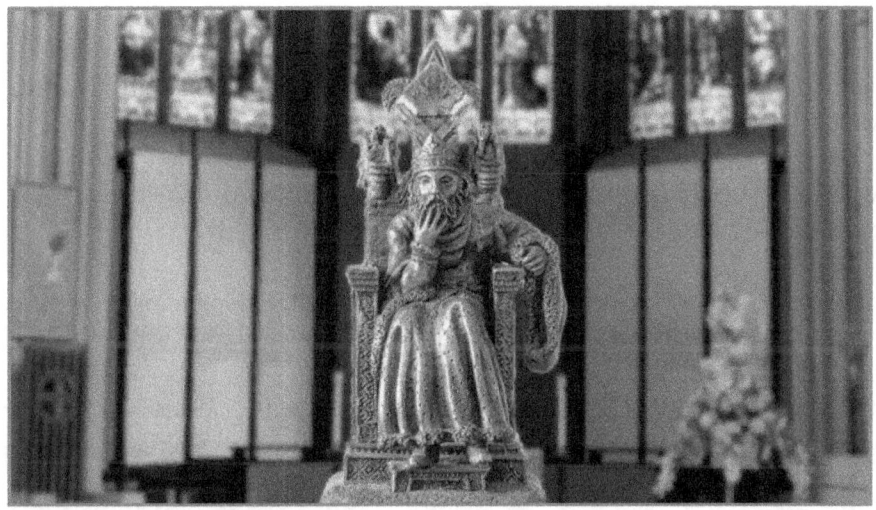

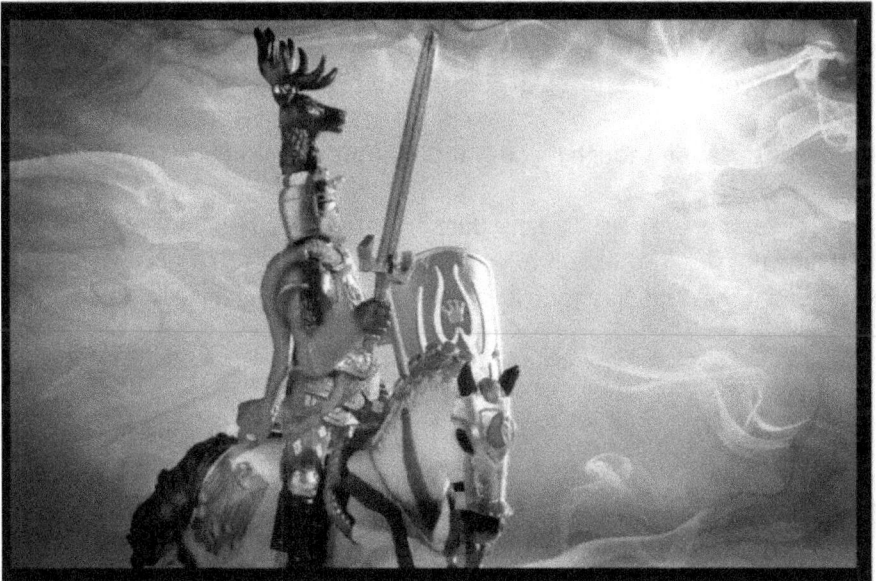

The example of small models photographed using the #1 close-up lens and then a superimposed background added.

Accessories for the FZ1000

There are several "accessories" which you can purchase to allow you to make better images. They may be to add additional lighting to a scene such as with an external flash gun, or add stability to the camera whilst taking a picture with a long exposure time or maybe just a convenient way to carry the camera when out and about. Other photographers might want longer telephoto or wider wide angle shots.
The way we "accessorise" our camera will obviously depend upon our own personal needs as a photographer.

FILTERS:

Filters allow us to modify the light entering the camera lens to create some lighting effect. It may be that we want to reduce the light to allow us to use longer shutter speeds, or to reduce reflections from water and foliage.

Maybe we want to improve the sky to ground exposure differences in landscape photography. Filters are the answer to these photographic situations.

Filters, however, come with a risk of reducing image quality - depending upon the type of filter. This might be from poor optical transmission or ghosting and flaring due to reflections from the FZ1000 lens.
Many of us were "persuaded" to buy a "UV" filter when we first purchased the camera – the salesperson was probably commission based and an expensive filter may have helped him/her sell this to you!

With digital cameras, there is absolutely no need to add UV filtration to the camera. Digital sensors are not as sensitive to UV as previous emulsion based film was. Adding the filter can degrade your images through ghosting and flaring.

There is some justification though if you want to afford physical protection to the lens front element.
Only if you are working in an area where dust or water splash is a real potential hard do you need to add physical protection to your lens!
After the potential "hazard" has gone it is best to remove it again.

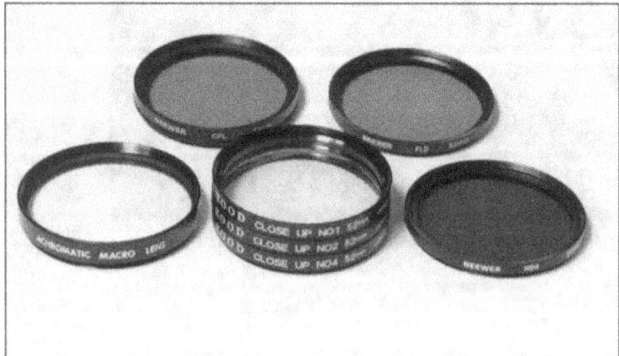

A selection of 62mm filters used to modify the light entering the FZ1000 lens.
Neutral Density, Circular Polarising and Fluorescent light correction (FLD "Rose").

I have discussed neutral density filters previously when looking at extending the shutter times to capture silky flowing water or to set the shutter speed/shutter angle in videography.

The first filter that you might want to purchase is the CPL or circular polarising filter.

These work in the same way as the polarising sunglasses we might wear to reduce glare and reflections in bright sunlight.
They work by "cutting" incident light which is reflected from an object where the light is 90° to the camera axis. If the light doesn't reflect from the subject with this angle the degree of reduction effect is reduced.
These CPL filters are almost always round and have a rotating glass element. The rotation of the filter is necessary for you to view the degree to which the light is being reduced.

Turning the filter slowly whilst observing the image is necessary to find the point at which the "cut" begins.
The angle of "cut" is normally quite small, perhaps only 20° or angular rotation.
Circular and linear polarising filters achieve the same effect however because the camera autofocus relies on polarised light to work properly.
Using a linear polarising filter may interfere with the correct operation of it.
Hence Circular polarising filters, which modify the light, are used.
Circular polarising filters are most useful for darkening skies as well.

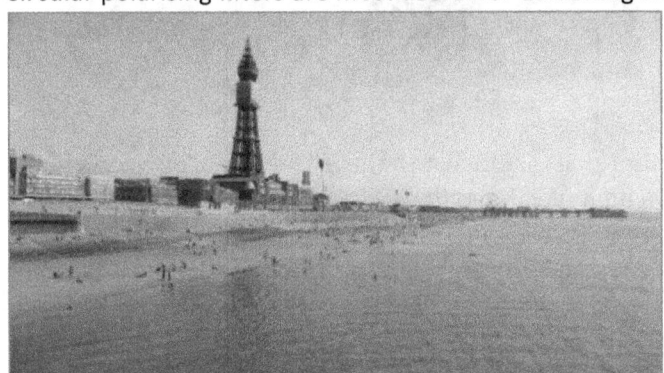

Without a polarising filter

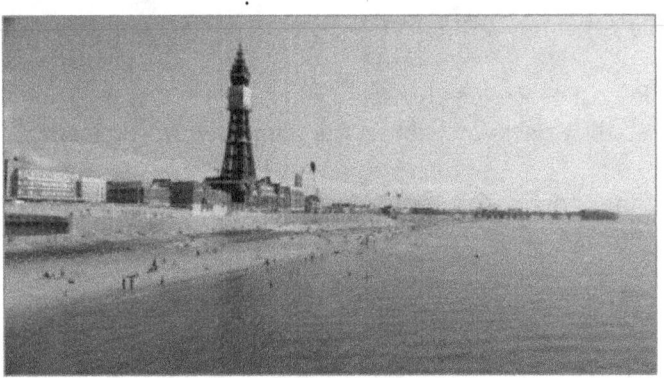

With a polarising filter attached.

The filter can be screwed directly onto the camera lens.

Watch out for the thickness of some of these filters.

Some of the thicker ones have more metal around the filter glass and may cause vignette to occur at wide angle settings.

The second most useful filter, especially if you photograph a lot of landscapes is the "graduated neutral density" filter.

This filter is normally supplied on a 100mm square clear acrylic plastic sheet and consists of a half-coated surface of a neutral dye.

The intersection between the neutral density part and the clear part of the filter is not a distinct line but "graduated" so that a hard line is not recorded on the camera image

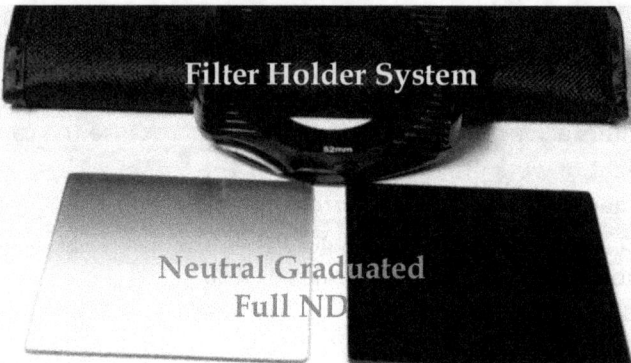

The 100mm square filter system.

Holder and the coated, or dyed, acrylic sheets.

The filter holder uses a 62mm adaptor ring to attach it to the lens. Most allow 2 or 3 filters to be "stacked" together to achieve multiple affects.

They are not as robust as glass filter systems so care must be taken not to scratch the surface of the acrylic sheet.

They do however provide a very cost effective way of enjoying the effects created by using these filters.
Whole systems of filters have been developed to create a variety of effects.

Some of these can be reproduced in post processing however you have the visual confirmation that you have captured the effect you want at the scene before you leave.

The original Cokin™ range is sometimes how this system is known as.

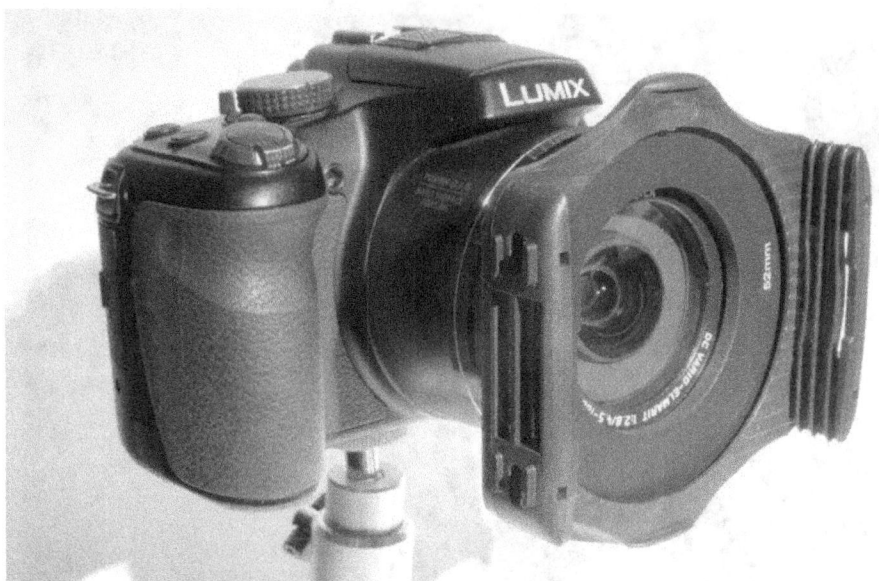

The 100mm square filter holder system (Cokin)

Some photographers still use (as I do) the FLD filter which was used to correct for the green colour cast which was prominent when you shot daylight film under this light. Today we can perform a manual white balance and correct this. However, this "rose" coloured filter can be used to emphasise sunsets or when shooting urban landscapes at dusk correct for the green fluorescent lighting in buildings if we use daylight white balance setting in the camera. If you shoot within 30 minutes of the sunset (at my latitude 53° north, sooner nearer the equator) you will retain the right blue colours in the sky, plus the sunset hues and the neutral office buildings.

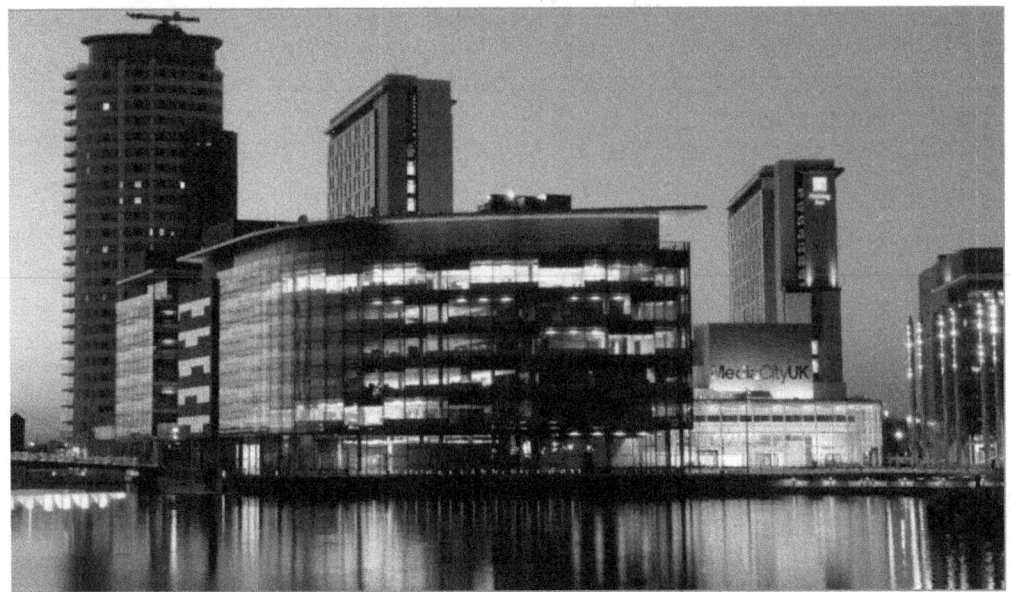

Daylight white balance.

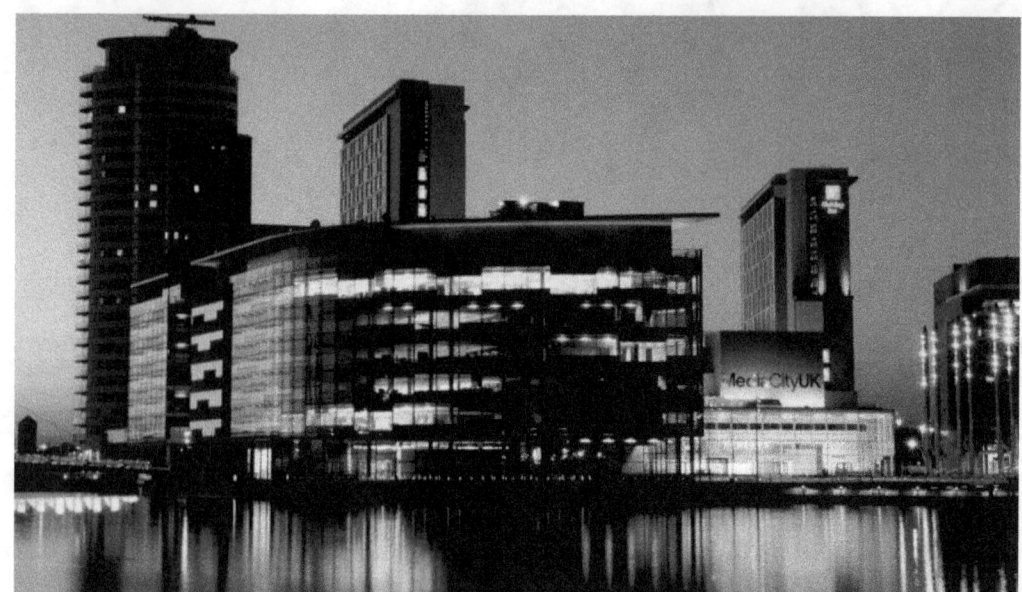

Daylight white balance with the FLD "rose" filter attached.

TRIPODS AND OTHER SUPPORT SYSTEMS

Tripods, monopods, "gorilla pods", bean bags and other mechanical measures to hold the camera steady during exposure are largely a personal preference.

Each of the systems has both advantages and disadvantages. Tripods are ideal as they do provide a solid support for the camera but their size and weight often means they are left behind when planning a photo trip

Since the Panasonic Lumix FZ1000 isn't a heavy camera, many of the lighter tripods are adequate to support the camera payload. Many of these falls into the "travel" category and fold up into a small footprint. This makes it more convenient to carry and makes it more likely that you will take it with you when you go out on a shoot, especially if you intend to shoot video clips.

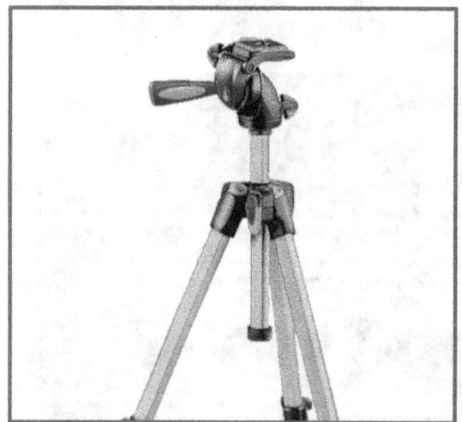

The Manfrotto 393 Photo-Movie Kit Offers good height and stability, quick release plate and pan and tilt head.

Many other tripods are stable enough for the light payload of the FZ1000, again the amount of use/cost should be considered when purchasing your tripod.

If you intend to shoot a lot of close-up or macro shots of plants and insects it is worth investigating tripods where the column can be reversed to allow the camera to sit between the tripod legs and get close to the ground. Some tripods allow the column to swing through 90° to allow this facility.

There are options for "ball and socket" heads which allow rapid setting of the camera position or conventional "3-way levelling" head. Newer versions now have rapid pistol grip systems to position the head.

Your own preference will dictate which tripod system is best for you.

Monopods offer some advantages especially if you are a sports shooter as they allow you hold the camera steady in a vertical plane and yet you are still able to pan with the camera to follow live action events.

The new "gorilla pods" with articulated jointed legs offer a versatile way to hold the camera in situations where either tripod or monopod would not achieve the desired result.

For example, the "gorilla pod" can be used to support the camera on fences, tree branches and railings etc., as well as in the convention tripod configuration.

There are two basic types, a light weight version and one aimed at DSLR users.

The light weight one is only designed for compact digital cameras and you may have trouble in getting the head to stay exactly where you want it to.

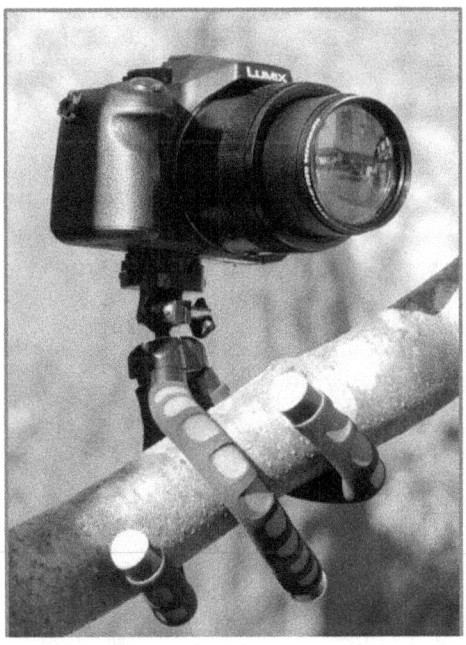

The "gorillapod", or in this case a third party alternative is a convenient way to hold your camera on a variety of surfaces. The flexible arms can wrap around round and rectangular sections such as tree branches and fence rails. They normally have a quick release plate at the head of the tripod.

REMOTE SHUTTER RELEASES

Whichever system you use it is worth using either the inbuilt 2 or 10 second timer or a remote shutter release to commence the exposure to minimise any camera shake from degrading the image.

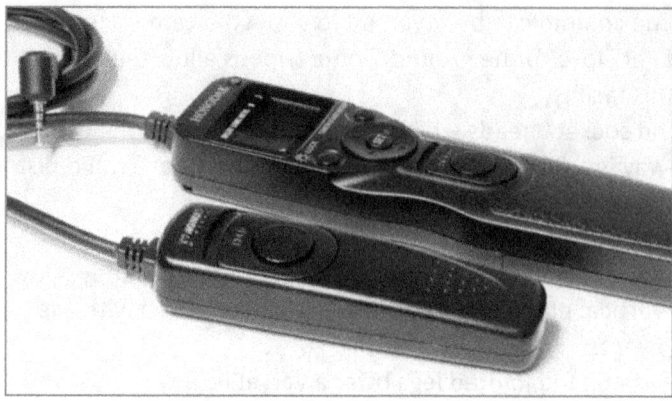

An example of 2 wired remote releases. The one on the left is just a basic focus/shoot device whilst the other is a fully featured "intervalometer" where the start/stop and interval times can be programmed. It is used in time lapse photography.

There are also available wireless remote releases which can be used to fire the shutter remotely or start and stop video recording in the manual mode. They have a range of up to 80 metres, outdoors.

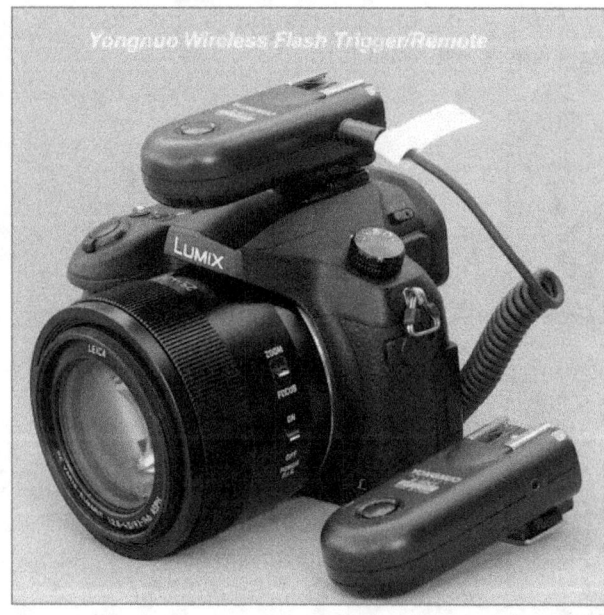

These devices all plug into the mic/remote port of the camera so the use of an external mic is not possible if you are using the remote to start and stop video recording.

Watch out for many of these receivers are "standard" for use with other cameras. The connecting cables must be plugged in correctly. The three-contact plug to the receiver and the 4-contact TRRS plug to the camera. Install the cable the wrong way around and it will not work!

EXTERNAL FLASH

The use of external flash, either directly attached to the camera hot shoe, or remotely triggered adds additional lighting control for those wishing to use just simple, or studio, flash set ups.

Panasonic do a range of TTL (through the lens) compatible flash units
DMW-FL220E – a small unit with a guide number of 22

DMW-FL360E – a larger unit with a guide number of 36 and has a bounce and swivel head.
DMW-FL360LE - same spec as the FL360E but with the addition of a LED video light
DMW-FL500E – a full featured flash unit featuring a bounce and swivel head with a guide number of 50.

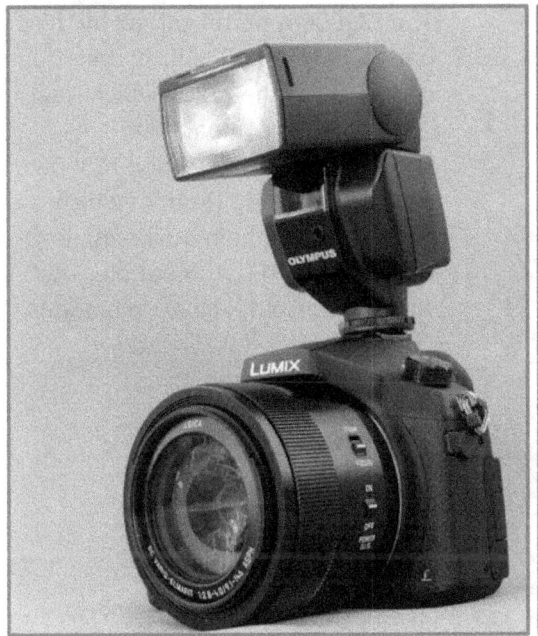
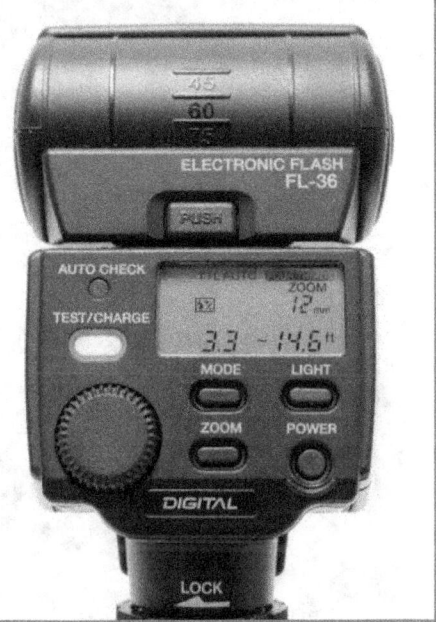

With the Olympus FL36, functionally equivalent to the Panasonic FL360, the head will auto-zoom when you have the head pointing forward.
The later FL-360L versions now include LED's for providing illumination for videographers. This means that the flash will select one out of six discreet zoom steps, 12mm, 14mm, 17mm, 25mm, 35mm or 42mm, whichever one is the most suiting for the FZ1000 zoom lens setting.
The values indicated will be one half of the FZ1000 lens setting.
It will select the largest zoom setting which is smaller than or equal to the lens focal length used.
Zooming can be also done manually; the zooming is done internally with no physical change in size of the unit.
If you have a wide-angle conversion lens, then you can flip over a wide-angle diffuser. This gives you 8mm flash light coverage.

TILT AND SWIVEL
The head can be tilted a little bit downwards, suitable for close-up focus distances. Tilting downwards gives a warning symbol on the display. It can also be tilted 45°, 60°, 75° and 90° upwards.
The head can also be swivelled 30°, 60°, 90°, 120°, 150° and 180° to the left, and 30°, 60° and 90° to the right. The tilt and swivel can be combined.
Tilting upwards or swivelling automatically zooms to 25mm, regardless of the zoom setting on the lens. However, the zoom can still be operated manually.

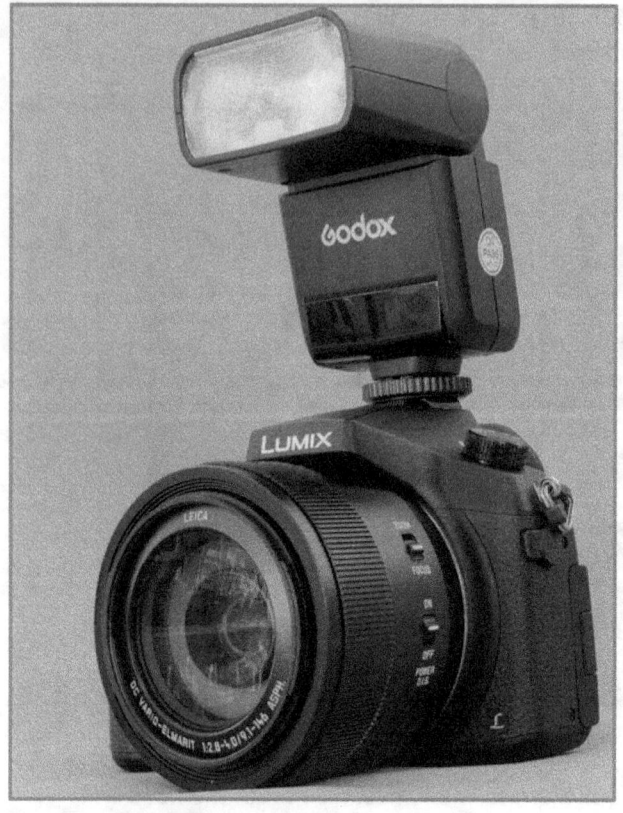

The FZ1000 is better served by third party TTL compatible flash units compared to the FZ200 which is an "odd ball" for compatibility. Shown above is the Godox TT350o and the Nissin i40 (both of which have a video light in the head). Both units are fully TTL compatible, The Nissin i40 also has an Auto mode.

TTL FLASH EXPOSURE MODE

All modern system cameras are expected to offer TTL flash control these days. In film based camera a small sensor "read" the light reflected from the film and terminated the flash when there had been sufficient exposure. In the FZ1000 this exposure determination is done in a different way.

Before the actual exposure, a small pre-flash is done. The pre-flash exposure is read by the image sensor, and used to decide how much flash to apply in the actual exposure.

There is a clear advantage with this solution: The camera can examine the pre-flash exposure thoroughly before deciding upon the main exposure.

In face detection mode, for example, it can take extra care that the faces are correctly exposed.

The "pre-flash" method has a drawback though, it can a bit annoying for anyone being photographed. Also, the pre-flash means that the main exposure is slightly delayed. Not by much, but it could be enough for you to miss a crucial timing.

AUTO EXPOSURE MODE

You can also use the auto mode on The FZ1000 camera, in which case it will read the aperture and ISO information directly from the camera.

TTL is usually preferable when using the FZ1000 camera, since it usually gives a more correct exposure. You may choose to use auto exposure mode still to avoid the small TTL pre-flash.

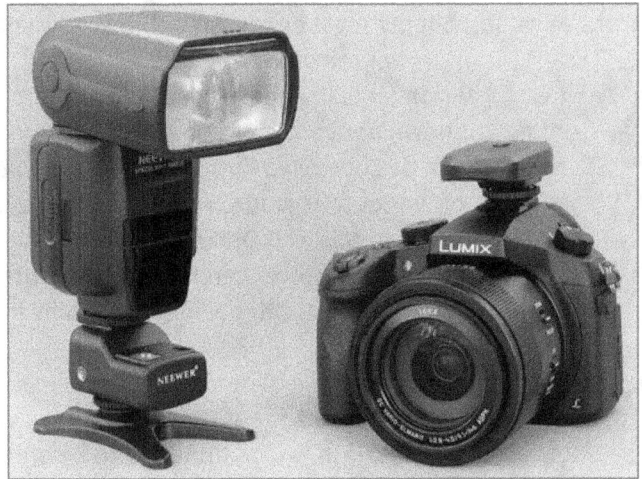

It is possible to use non-TTL flashguns with the FZ1000. Most modern flash guns have a low "trigger voltage".

This trigger voltage is the voltage which appears at the base of the flash unit and connects with the internal circuitry of the FZ1000 camera.

Older flash units were designed for mechanical contacts on film cameras so trigger voltage was not a problem. However, with the miniaturisation of the flash firing components within the camera the permissible voltage is much lower.

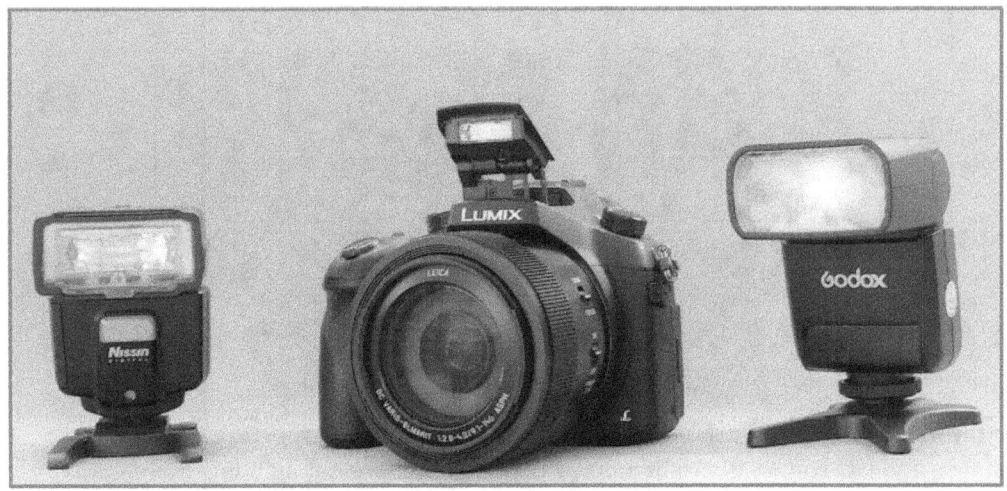

Using Optical Slave triggering on two external units

I have not seen specifications for the allowable voltage of the trigger circuits however I have used guns with 20 volts and have not experienced any problems.

If you want to check the voltage of any of your older units, there is a good website which has details of many units.

http://dpanswers.com/roztr/volt_finder.php

These units must be used in full manual mode as they will not "communicate" with the FZ1000 exposure circuit.

Many of the flash units allow you to set an aperture/ISO value and the unit will automatically expose for these values. Simply set them as per your camera setting

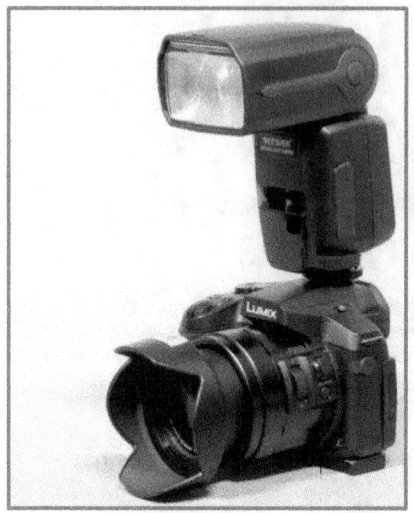

Flash units like the Nikon TTL compatible flash shown above will fire on the FZ1000 and the power can be controlled by setting the gun to the manual power output mode. This one has a guide number of 50 metres at ISO100, a powerful unit.

Usually the power can be adjusted from 1/1 (full power) to 1/128th power and usually in 0.3 EV units.

If you use a fixed intensity flash unit where there is no adjustment for output power, you will need to use the flash "guide number" to be able to set the camera aperture.

The guide numbers are usually in metres, so for example a flash unit with a guide number of 32 at ISO 100 will give an exposure of the guide number/ distance to subject (in metres) If our subject is 5 metres away, then the aperture is set to 32/5 which is f6.1 and the ISO would be 100.

Most manual flash units have some form of table which helps you establish the correct aperture for any ISO setting and flash to subject distance.

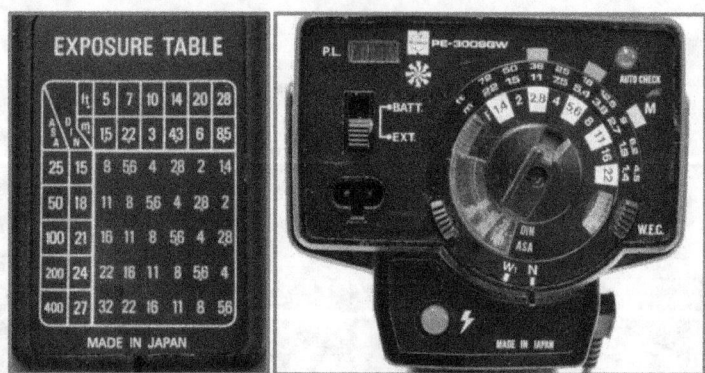

On the left, the manual flash unit's table to help calculate the aperture needed from distance and ISO and on the right a non-TTL unit with 2 pre-set light levels.

The ISO is "dialled in" and the scale then gives the aperture to set the camera to.

If you use a wireless trigger to fire these older units, it is also possible to use the resulting single flash to "optically" trigger other units if small optical triggering units are attached to them.

The main camera flash cannot be used because of the pre-flash which would prematurely fire the "slave" flash before the main exposure took place.

More video tutorial material on flash:

https://www.youtube.com/watch?v=V79dcaOrS_s

One of the things I often miss when I'm out with the FZ1000 is the ability to recharge the battery with a portable power bank. This is something I routinely do with TZ *travel zoom, USB* charge enabled, cameras and my portable audio recorder.

I recently discovered the USB charger cradle for the BLC12E battery which the FZ200, *FZ300/330, FZ1000, FZ2000*/2500, G5, G6, *GX8* and GH2 cameras use. It is very inexpensive £5 or USD $7.50. It is available with or without the wall outlet charger.

It has a 600mAH charge output and so will recharge a fully depleted battery in just 2 hours from a suitable power source.

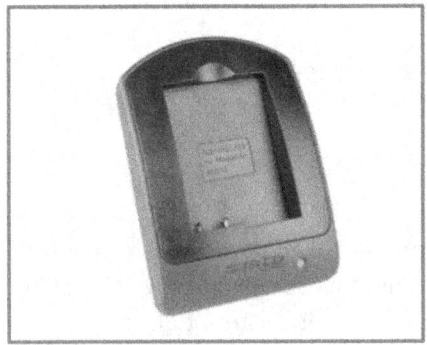

The internal components allow an intelligent charging to protect the battery from overheating or overloading. The cradle also shows the charge status by changing the colour of the display LED. These are available on Amazon UK and on EBay.

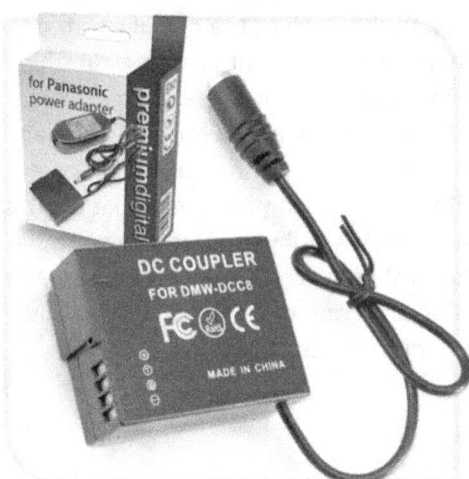

The AC power supply unit from Amazon which included the DMW-DCC8 dummy battery for the DMW-BLC12e battery used in the F200/300/330, GH2 and FZ1000/2000/2500 cameras.

Ex-Pro® Panasonic DMW-AC8 AC Mains Power Supply Adapter & DMW-DCC8E Battery coupler kit for Panasonic Lumix SLR DMC-G5, DMC-G6, DMC-GH2, DMC-FZ200/FZ300/330 FZ1000/2000.

On my Photoblog website website https://www.grahamhoughton.com/tech-talk/

You will find details of a DIY power unit to power the FZ1000 from a USB power bank which is ideal for time-lapse, stop motion animation or extended video recording with the camera. Using "off the shelf" components it is relatively simple to assemble one for your own needs.

Close-Up Photography Using Flash

I think that if you are interested in photographing plants and insects, particularly at close range to give super enlarged views using supplementary close-up lenses on bridge cameras like the FZ1000 or extension tubes on CSC's and DSLR's then flash becomes the must have, go to accessory.

The reason, we need to be using small apertures to get the depth of field, F7.1/F8 in the case of the FZ1000.

In dull light this forces us to use longer shutter speeds as we always want the ISO to be the lowest value - for both dynamic range and noise reasons.

Because we are magnifying our image the amount of subject movement, through our unsteady hands, is greatly magnified with a result that we often get images which are less than perfectly sharp.

Flash becomes our "portable sun" and can help us to achieve some stunning images.

I want to look at the various ways flash can be used to provide this additional light needed.

Covering the basic options through to more advanced techniques.

Let's first look at using just the inbuilt, or on-camera flash and some of the options that you can employ to improve the look of the images

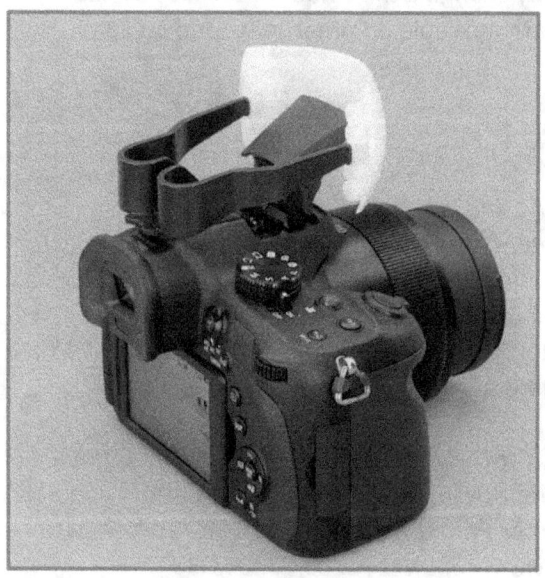

Although the naked pop up flash can be used at these closer distances as the point light source shadows aren't quite as distinct I prefer to use a purpose made flash diffuser, such as the one illustrated here. It gives consistent results, is durable and easily fits into my camera bag. DIY tissue paper ones are OK for a single image however I would recommend this as a very positive addition to your camera kit for this type of photography. It gives nice soft diffused shadows however it is on axis lighting and sometimes doesn't show any three- dimensional texturing.

Most digital cameras employ a positive voltage centre triggering electrode in the hot shoe of the camera.

By utilising this fact, we can quite happily install flashguns designed specifically for compatible camera cameras on any camera.

Of course, we cannot employ the e-TTL ii protocol in the case of Canon flashes or the i-TTL system of Nikon flashes however with the flash gun set for manual operation we can easily fire the flash, adjust its output power and create great images.

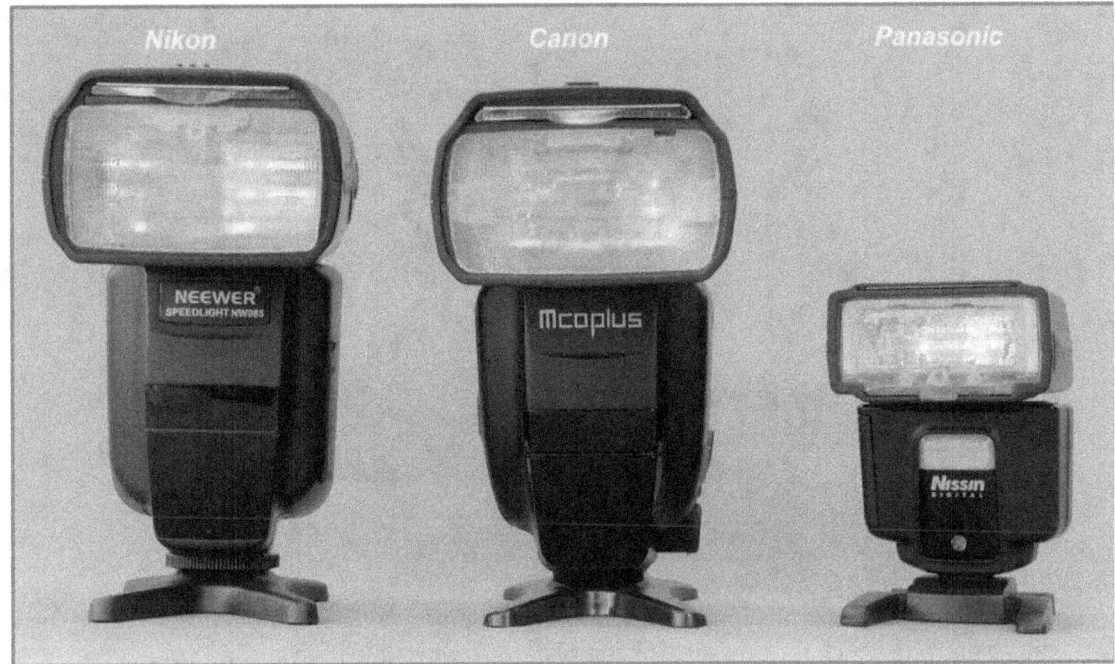

All the flash units show above were intended to be used as dedicated TTL flash units on DSLR or CSC cameras.

Because of the common triggering connection on all digital cameras (and film cameras) it means that we can now use these flash guns, which you may have retired when you bought a lighter, and more convenient, Panasonic FZ1000 bridge camera.

Because of the low voltage triggering and low voltage digital connection on the other pins it is extremely unlikely that any damage will be caused to either camera or flash unit using them in this way.

I have been using my flash units for years in this mode without any issues at all.

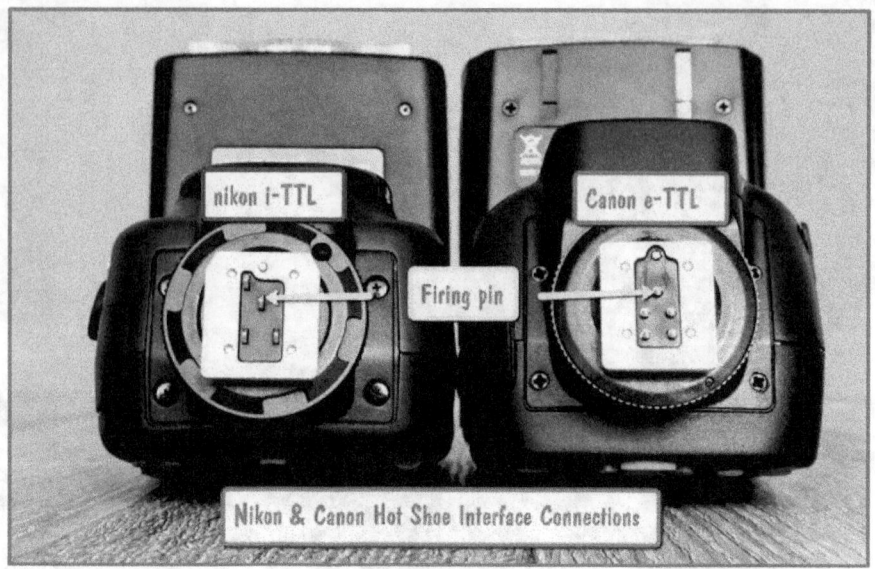

Nikon & Canon Hot Shoe Interface Connections

The electrical connections for both the Nikon and Canon dedicated hot shoe showing the only electrode which is necessary for the system to work (plus the ground connection of the metal hot shoe itself as the return signal path).

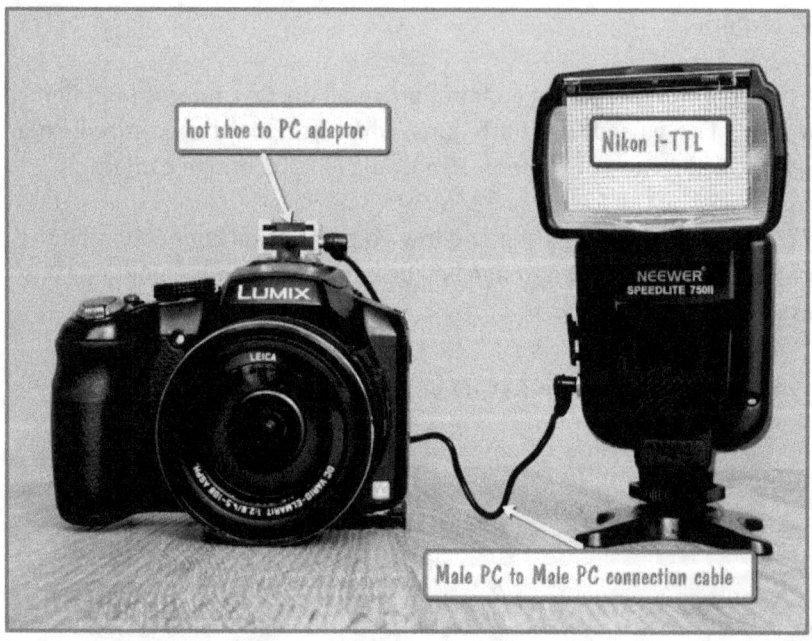

An example using the hot shoe to PC adaptor on the camera and a male to male PC connection cable to connect the camera to the PC connection of your flash gun (if it has one fitted)

If you want to use the flash off camera you can either use an extension cable (which will be the Panasonic or Canon TTL cable ideally although any should work) or use the method shown above.

With manual only flash guns, there is only one electrode on the hot shoe. This is the one responsible for the actual firing of the flash from the signal from the camera. It is normally a low positive voltage (less than 10v dc) and the camera sends a low signal pulse which fires the gun - like shorting the pin to ground.

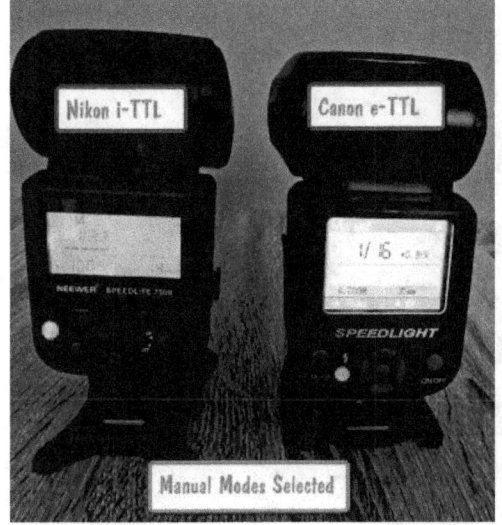

Typical displays of the TTL units when placed in the manual mode with provision to set the power level.

Usually this is from 1/1 (full power) to 1/128 the minimum power.

Some units offer the reduction in 1/3rd EV units which is ideal, others just 1 stop increments.

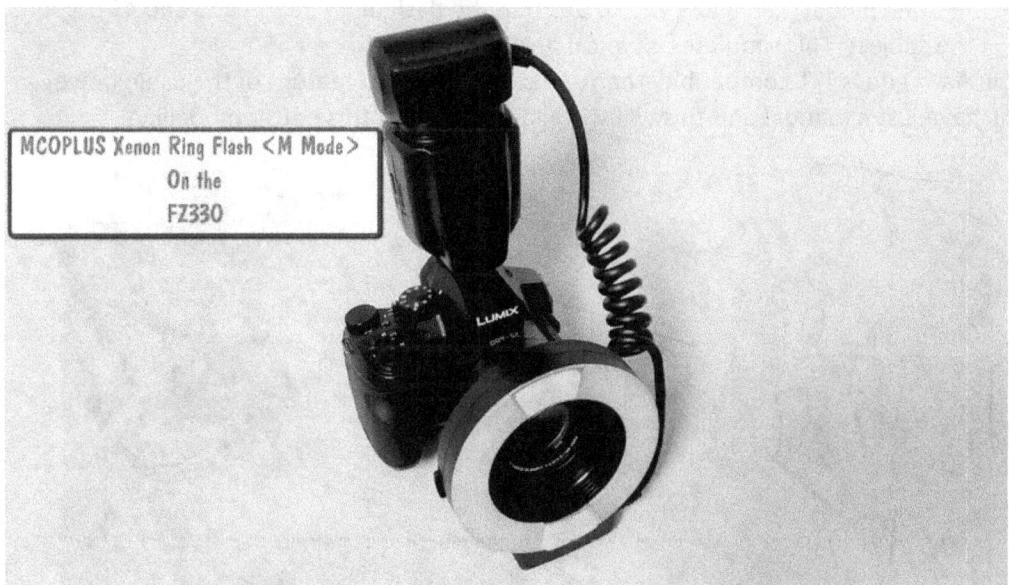

Here in this image I have a Canon E-TTL II ring flash installed on the Panasonic Lumix FZ300/330 and operated in the full manual mode creates great images. This is ideal as there are currently no dedicated TTL ring flashes for the Panasonic system.
It is perfectly compatible with the FZ1000 camera as well.

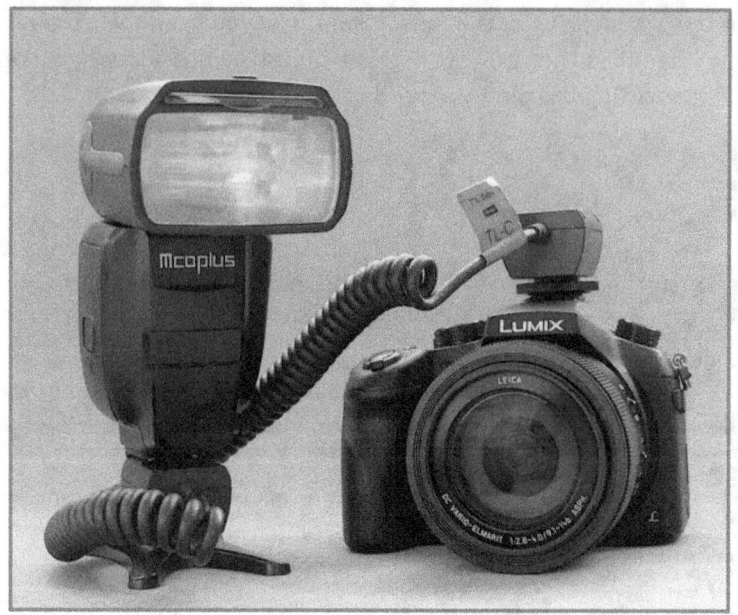

To achieve better modelling with your flash using a TTL extension cable (Panasonic/Canon have the same pinout) can allow you to position the flash at 45 degrees to and 45 degrees above the subject. This simulates a typical daylight situation.

If your flash gun is TTL compatible, then you can use the full feature of the cable however if you have just a manual unit this will still allow you to get this better modelling.

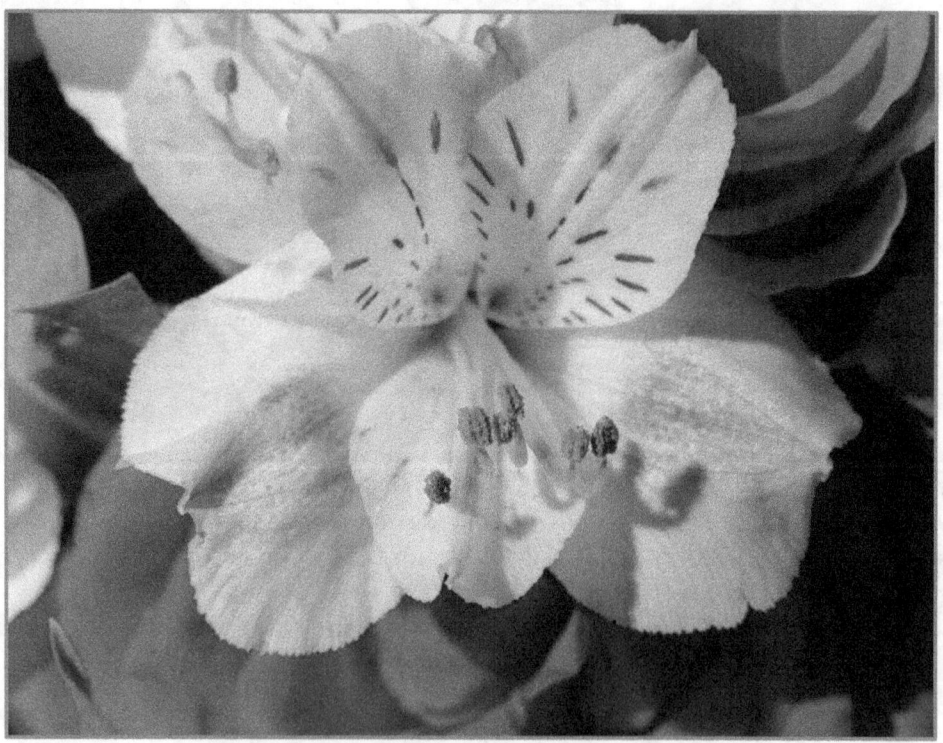

45 degree off axis flash with #4 close- up lens

Although the Panasonic Lumix FZ1000 has a reasonably wide angle setting (25mm equivalent) there are times when a slightly wider view would help.

In interior architectural shots, landscapes and group photographs this extra few millimetres of coverage could make all the difference.

Panasonic haven't specifically produced a matching wide angle conversion lens and tube for the FZ1000 however there are several options you can employ to get wider angle shots.

Firstly, a note of caution about using these conversion methods.

> The weight of the suggested conversion lenses is quite high and a very specific discipline is needed to use them.
> If you do not follow the discipline you may cause damage to the lens and/or the zoom motor gearbox. I accept no responsibility for any damage to your camera if you want to employ these lenses

One option is to use a 0.7x wide angle conversion lens from Digital King. (Available on Amazon, EBay and other distributors but becoming more difficult to find now).

It is the Digital King DSW Pro 0.7X It's around £50-£70 in the UK and $80 USA Amazon.

It converts the 25mm setting to 17.5mm. This is quite an improvement yet doesn't put the lens into "fish-eye" category.

If you get the one with a 62mm thread it will screw directly onto the lens of the FZ1000 however I prefer a 67mm lens with a 62 to 67mm step up ring.

It has no vignette as the front optic of this lens is 67mm wide so the camera can be used at its widest-angle position thus losing none of the extra field of view.

The lens weights 76 grams and measures 80mm diameter x 18mm long

It will take 67mm filters fitted to the front of the lens. Do not add at the rear as this may cause vignette to occur.

Don't be tempted to get the 0.45x converters with combined macro lens – they were designed for entry level camera kit lenses and distort very badly on the FZ1000.

In the Sleep setting of the Economy mode (set-up tools menu) turn this setting to OFF. Turn on the camera and then screw in the lens, do not zoom or turn off the camera with the lens attached. You can use auto or manual focus as this will not be affected.

When you have completed taking your images remove the lens Reset your Sleep setting to your preferred value.

Lighting for Video and Stills Photography

Quite often we will need to add some additional lighting to be able to capture video with enough scene brightness to overcome some of the issues with noise in low light video scenes, especially those with lots of shadow areas.

You can spend a lot of money investing in a whole range of general purpose and specialist lighting units for your video productions.

These can range from simple tungsten halogen lighting units to the latest LED technology units.

Until recently correctly white balanced tungsten halogen lighting was the "standard" for video lighting.

Today we have moved more into a situation where LED technology has matured to a degree where it can be used quite effectively to provide the main source of lighting for a video production.

Basically, all white LED's are blue LED's with a coating of a yellow phosphor. This combination allows the manufacturer to produce a LED with a close temperature rating equal to that of daylight at around 5600°K or tungsten at 3200°K by varying the amount of phosphor.

Until recently the spectral emission of these LED's was deficient in red light so there was an issue when trying to capture a scene and maintain good colour fidelity.

This low CRI (colour rendering intent) has now been addressed by producing LED light panels which have mixture of LED's in them, white LED's and Red LED's in a ratio to bring the CRI to over 93 in some examples.

The closer the CRI is to 100 the better the resulting images are, although the light spectrum is discontinuous and the RGB peaks don't exactly match the filters used over the sensor.

For home or amateur video production either the tungsten halogen lights can be used. The LED's have the advantage that they produce light a lot more efficiently, nowhere near as much infra-red light is produced thus keeping the operating temperature of the LED's and housing units much lower.

LED's have the additional advantage that they can be powered by battery power packs thus making them more suitable to providing a light source where there is no access to mains electrical power supplies.

I have used a variety of lighting methods as shown below for use in table top photography.

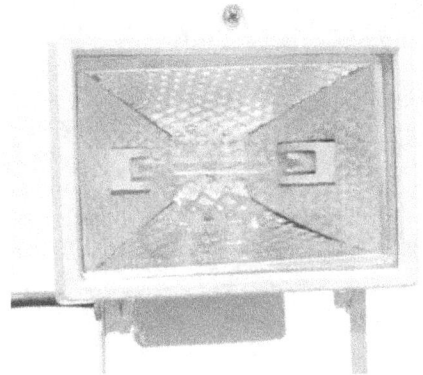

120w Tungsten Halogen Flood 700 lux

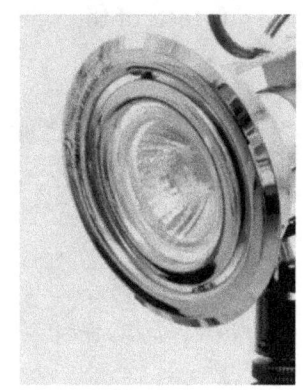

50W Tungsten Halogen Spot 200 lux

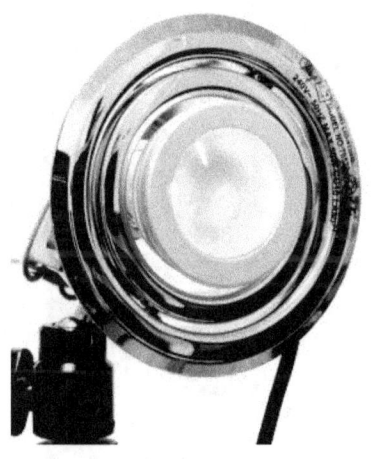

Variable Colour LED Spot (3W)

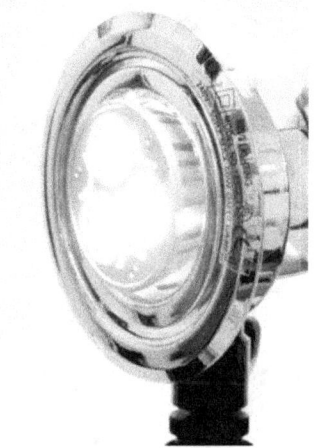

LED 3x 1 Watt 800 lux spot

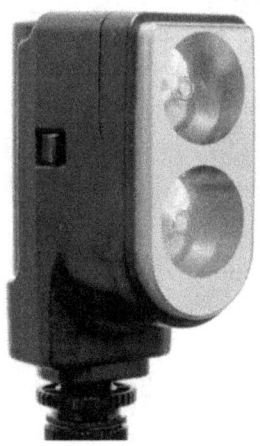

LED Model 5004 2x 3.5W 600 lux

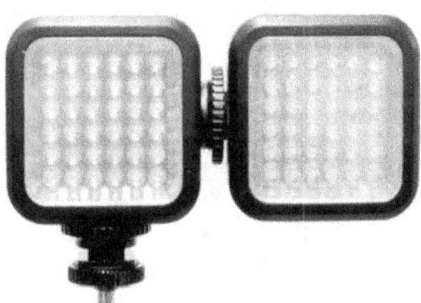

36 LED 4W (can be ganged together) 280 lux

Colour Rendering tests of the light sources.

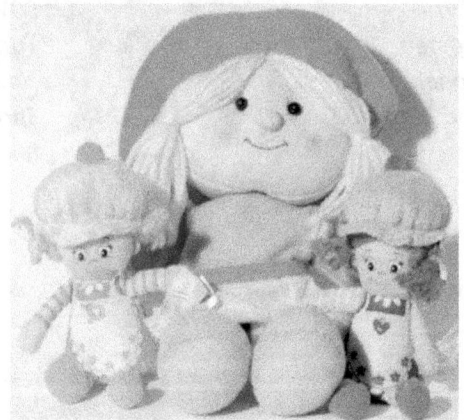

120w halogen, 610 lux

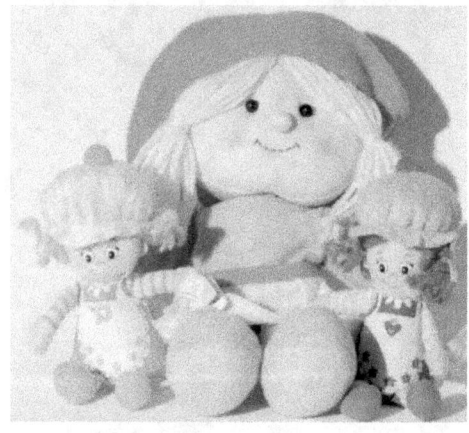

50w halogen, 235 lux

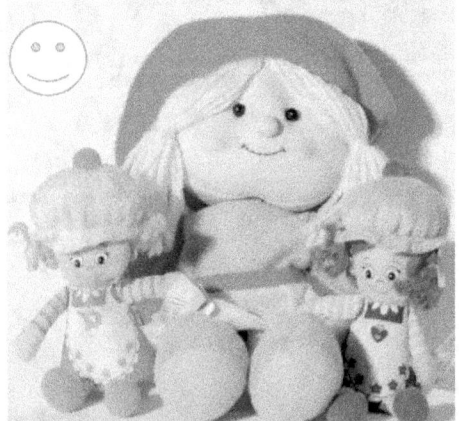

36 LED x2, 240 lux

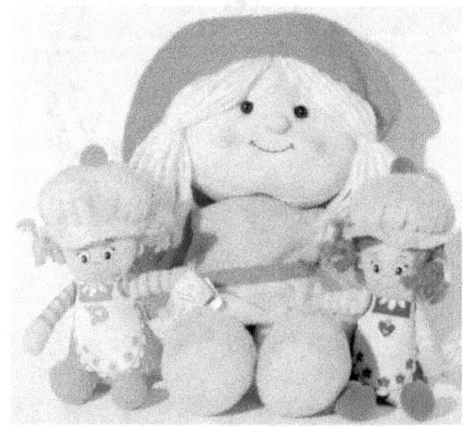

Twin LED model 5004 90 lux

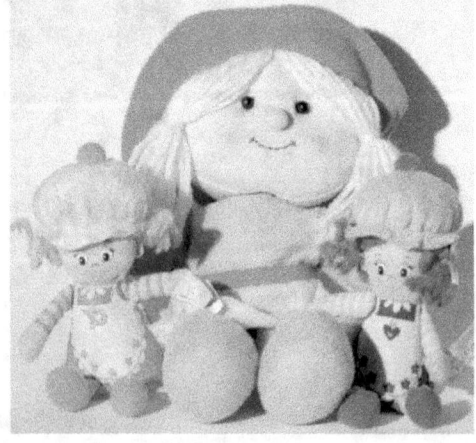

3 LED spot 770 lux

Tests using each light so at 1 metre distance.
Only light source.
Manual white balance before each exposure.
ISO 400, F4
All the 3 LED images look very close to the original; the two tungsten images have exaggerated reds.

There are many different lighting solutions available now using high efficiency LED's. Many have variable dimming facility and are well colour corrected. "High end" video lighting is very expensive and is not necessary in most of our amateur needs.

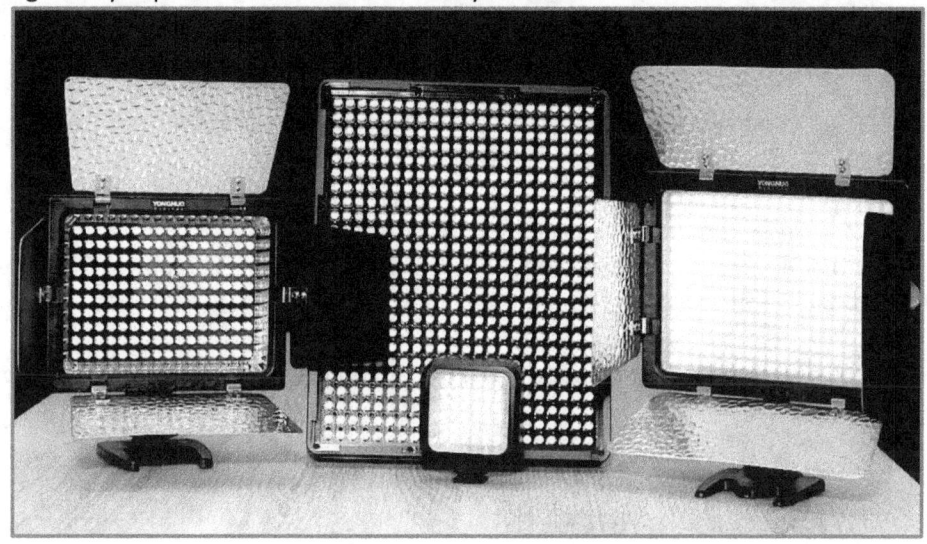

A selection of LED light panels suitable for table top photography or videography

Some old-school photographers may remember the "Sunny F16" rule which stated that if you set the camera shutter speed to the reciprocal of the film speed (ISO) then if we shot an exposure in bright sunshine (in which the sun cast distinct shadows) then the exposure would be correct.

So, if we had ISO 125 film loaded in the camera we set a shutter speed of 1/125, an aperture of F16 and we get good exposures.

This "Magic" number was derived from the fact that this equated to EV15 and had a lux value of 84,000. For each change of 1 EV unit we halve or double the lux value and or aperture value.

If we repeat the sequence, we could build a table to show the lux equivalent and aperture using ISO 125 and a shutter speed of 1/125sec.

Exposure Value	Light Level LUX	Aperture F-Stop
EV 15	84000	F16
EV 14	42000	F11
EV 13	21000	F8
EV 12	10500	F5.6
EV 11	5250	F4
EV 10	2525	F2.8

If you are considering investing in professional grade lighting you will soon find the cost of these lights become more expensive than the FZ1000 camera.

Using the portable 160 LED units now available at £33 in the UK you will find you have enough light for video production as they can produce 900 lux at 1 metre, 240 lux at 2metre and 120 lux at 1 metre.

You will still have to perform a "manual white balance set" operation to achieve better colour rendition with all the light sources shown.

With the FZ1000 in manual video mode to achieve a good exposure level using ISO 125 and f2.8 1/30th sec shutter speed requires 300 lux.

All the units shown on the previous page (lux measured at 1 metre) will provide this level of illumination at distances of 1 metre (many will exceed this allowing you to move the lights further back, diffuse or dim them if they have that facility)

Using ISO 2000 and the same aperture and shutter speed the camera will record video with as little as 20 lux.
There will be some video noise.

By using manual focus, which enables lower shutter speeds, you can reduce the ISO to achieve better image quality – providing there is no subject movement which will cause blurring at these reduced shutter speeds.

LIGHTING SAFETY

Remember the tungsten halogen lamps run extremely hot and care should be exercised when using these lamps indoors.

Keep away from flammable materials and allow the fixtures to fully cool down before handling to avoid personal injury.

LED lights (particularly the high intensity "Cree" LED) have extreme brightness levels and when used as video lights on top of the camera may cause retina damage if your subject stares into the light.

Try to avoid the lights being "on axis" with the camera lens to avoid such situations if you can.

In creative video recording we have a lot more control over the way in which the camera records the video clips. Creative (Manual) video mode is engaged by turning the top control dial to the icon of the movie camera so that it aligns with the index mark on the top plate of the camera.

This mode use the metering mode currently selected to establish the correct exposure. As the lens aperture cannot go below f2.8 and the shutter speed cannot drop below $1/25^{th}$ sec if the display looks dark you will have to increase the ISO to brighten it!

In Aperture priority mode the aperture range is f2.8 to F11 (F8 is the stills limit). Again, if the exposure cannot be achieved with 1/25th second ISO must be increased. In Shutter priority mode, the range is 1/25th to 1/16,000th second. Obviously at this very short shutter speed a very intense light source is required to capture a correct exposure level. This mode may be useful for analysing high speed motion, with audio.

In the Manual mode, the shutter range is extended down to 1/2 sec (if you also use manual focus).

This allows you to get some low level light clips, providing there is no subject motion as this would appear as ghostly movements.

To get the most "cinematic" look to your video clips it is recommended to follow the 180° shutter angle rule. This is the same shutter angle as used with film based motion picture cameras.

To achieve this same shutter angle the shutter speed should be set to twice the frame rate. In the example of 25fps the shutter speed should be 1/50th second.

You would maintain the exposure in the M mode with aperture and ISO adjustment. The exposure meter gives a good indication of exposure, balance the exposure by correcting under or over exposure indication on the meter scale by using the aperture, shutter, ISO or all three parameters.

You cannot capture a still image in creative video mode as the shutter release is used to start and stop the recording.

During recording video, audio is captured via the stereo microphones on the top of the camera.

If better audio quality is required, or if you wish to record the audio without the zoom motor being heard during any zoom operation, you need to use an external microphone plugged into the 3.5mm (1/8th inch) microphone port on the side of the camera.

External Microphones Used for Video Recording

When recording video clips with the camera it is essential to a capture good, clean audio soundtrack.

The in-built stereo microphone pair of the Panasonic Lumix FZ1000 capture reasonable audio quality when the sound source is close to the camera.

Once the sound source is away from proximity, the camera will tend to ramp up the automatic gain control resulting in "thin" and noisy audio.

If you use the camera outdoors these microphones are very susceptible to "wind noise" The zoom motor can be heard if you are in a quite environment and you operate the zoom control.

To overcome the issue of the in-built microphone picking up the noise of the zoom motor, Panasonic introduced a compatible stereo electret condenser microphone the MS2. This has a 3.5mm (1/8) jack plug.

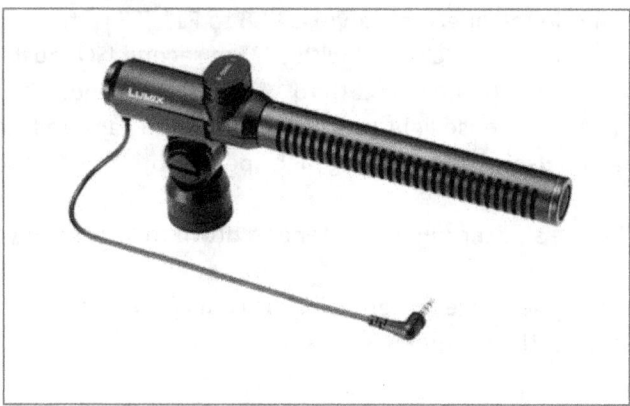

The Panasonic DMW-MS2 Mic was designed for the FZ1000 however it is a VERY expensive microphone and there are cheaper options which result in better sound quality. This microphone introduces several new audio capture modes.

Many of these mics are "rifle" type mics which add a lot of directional sensitivity to the sound pick up and are primarily used to reject off axis noise sources.

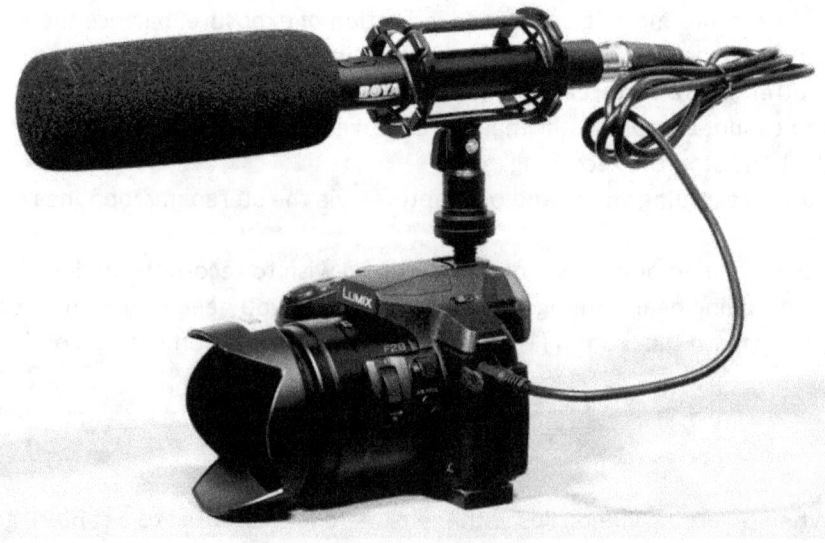

This is the Boya BY-FVM 1000 shot gun mic (£50 in UK)

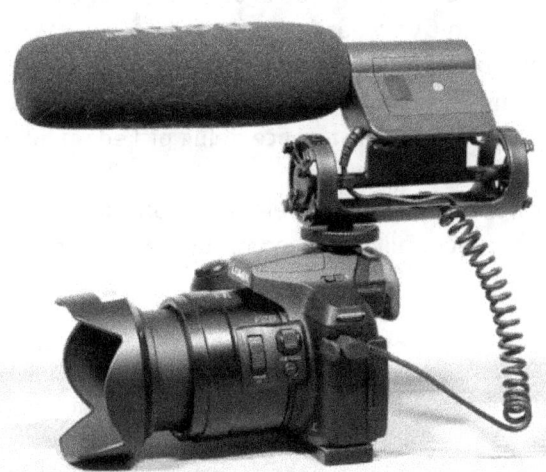

The very popular Rode Videomic

A popular short rifle mic, the Rode Videomic™, can be used with the FZ1000.

The Rode Video mic is a professional grade ½ inch condenser shotgun microphone. It has an integrated shock mount system to isolate the microphone from handling noise.

Powered by a 9v battery it has an attenuator switch which can be set for -10dB or -20dB in very noisy environments such as live music.

It also has a hot shoe mounting foot and ½ and 3/8 mounting holes for fixing on a tripod or mic stand.

The audio quality is excellent for interviews where only mono sound is required. A stereo version is available – the Rode stereo video mic. The Video mic is around £80 in the UK

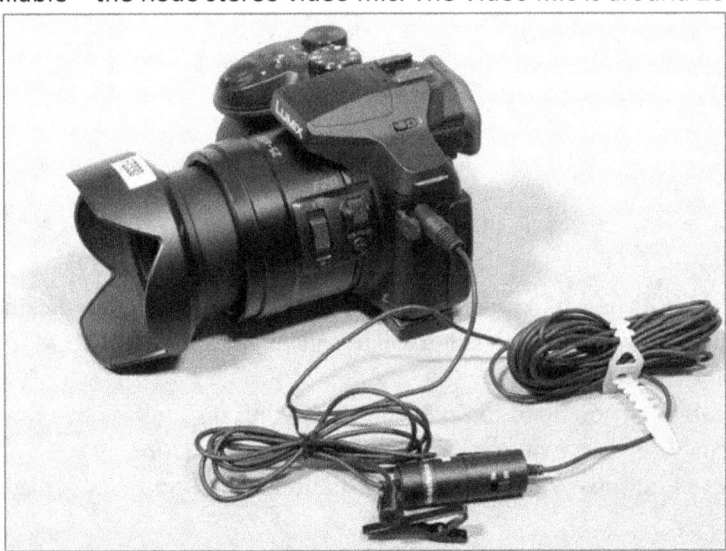

If you want good quality audio for presentations "to camera" then a lavaliere microphone is a good choice. The one shown above is the self-powered Audio Technica TR3350.

There are many electrets condenser types available, some with their own amplifier and others directly connected to the camera.

It is best to place this mic about 8 inches (20cms) below the chin of the user, usually clipped on to the collar of a coat or shirt, held in place with a "tie clip" device.

Ensure that the mic element doesn't rub against any fabric of the clothes otherwise this will be picked up by the mic very easily.
 Some are fitted with foam windshields and work good outdoors.
The wired devices can be used with short extension cables up to around 5 metres if screened cable is used to stop interference being picked up by the device.

Samson™ and Sennheiser™ produce wireless versions of lavaliere mic systems.
The Sennheiser™ mic specifically designed for use in professional broadcast situations.

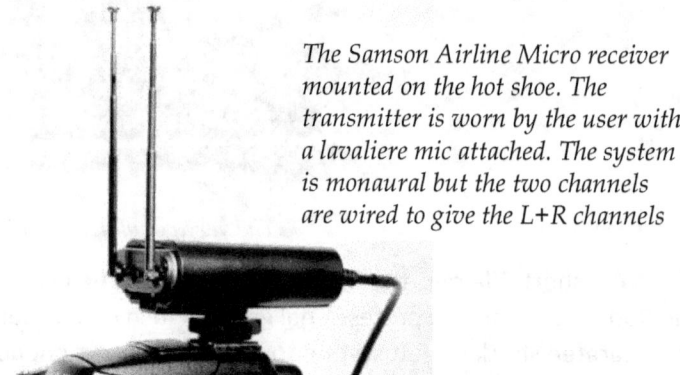

The Samson Airline Micro receiver mounted on the hot shoe. The transmitter is worn by the user with a lavaliere mic attached. The system is monaural but the two channels are wired to give the L+R channels

The ultimate choice of microphone will also be influenced by what is referred to as the "pick-up pattern."
Understanding the various pick-up patterns can help you to not only maintain a good volume, but also to avoid picking up unwanted noises that might be present in the room. Here are some of the most common microphone pick-up patterns:

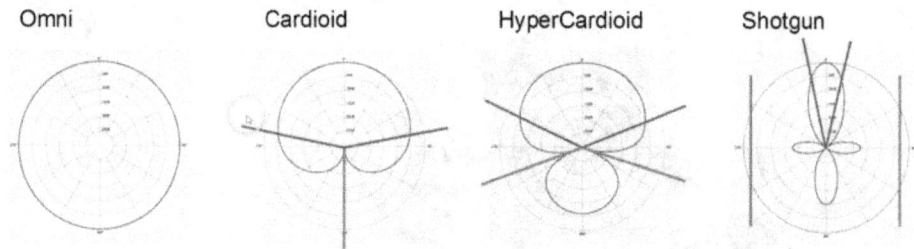

Cardioid. Named for its heart-shaped pattern, this design is optimal for picking up sound in the front of the microphone. The sides will usually be at about half strength and only one-tenth strength at the back.
This is very useful, as all you need to do to reject unwanted sound is have the back of the microphone facing the source of what you do not want to pick up.
This pattern is used for most vocal or speech situations. The Rode Video mic has this pick-up pattern.
Omni-directional. This pick-up pattern gives the mic the same pick-up strength from all angles. This can be great if you are trying to capture all the intricate ambient sound in a room. Most desk and stage microphones fall in this category. More elaborate microphone set ups can be used and if a mixing console is used then you could take an attenuated output directly to the mic input socket of the camera to record excellent sound quality.

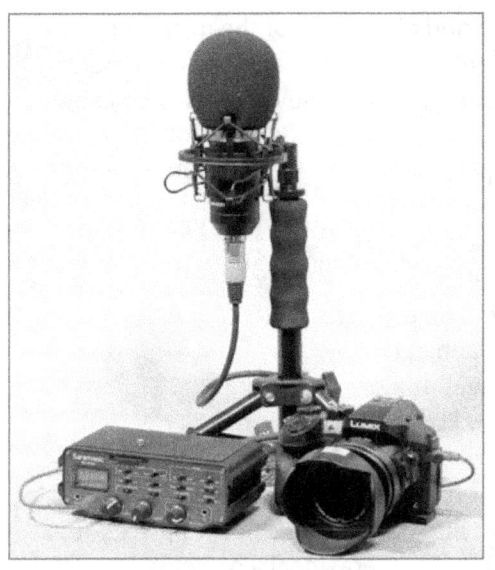

For even better sound quality Studio XLR microphones and a mixer/pre-amplifier can be used.

The setup shown adjacent is the BM-800 studio condenser mic.

It will work if plugged directly into the FZ1000 with the supplied XLR to 3.5mm lead however, the sound quality isn't as good as when powered by the 48volt phantom power from the mic mixer/pre-amplifier.

The pre-amp is the Saramonic SR AX-104 2 channel XLR audio adaptor

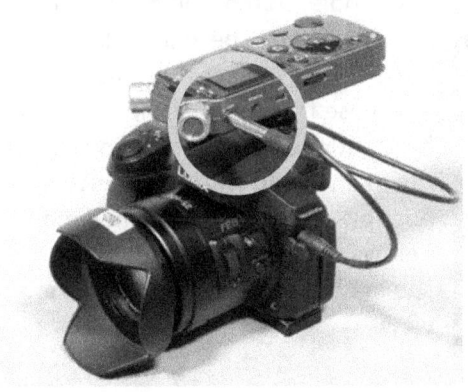

Some digital audio recorders can be used to gather good sound for feeding directly into the FZ1000 mic port.

In some cases, an in-line audio attenuator (outlined) will be needed to drop the line output voltage from the usual 200-300millivolts to around 5 millivolts to prevent overloading and clipping distortion

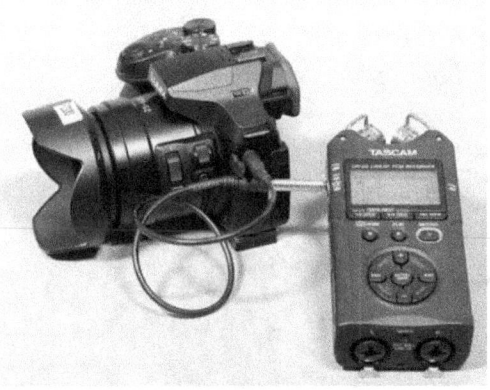

Above the Olympus PCM digital audio recorder with built in electret condenser mics. Adjacent the Tascam TR-40 4 track audio recorder with two XLR inputs and two inbuilt electret condenser mics.

It is worth mentioning here that the process of recording good audio in your video clips will use the manual recording level control and not rely on the mic level limiter.

Here are the available adjustments for setting the audio levels.

To capture good audio relies on the correct choice and placement of the microphones used. The "rifle" type mics, which are very commonly seen on news gathering cameras, have found their way onto camcorders and now DSLR's and bridge cameras which now record video.

Shotgun

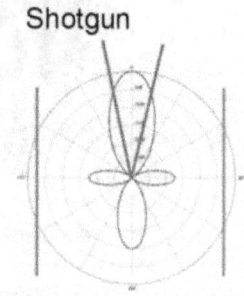

Because of their sound pick up pattern the microphone will pick up the sound directly in front of the camera and, to a lesser degree, the sound from the rear of the camera. Sound sources on either side of the mic are almost fully rejected. What this means in practice is that not only will you be picking up the audio from a few feet in front – where you subject might be standing during an interview, for example, but also any sound emanating from behind the subject with little or no attenuation.

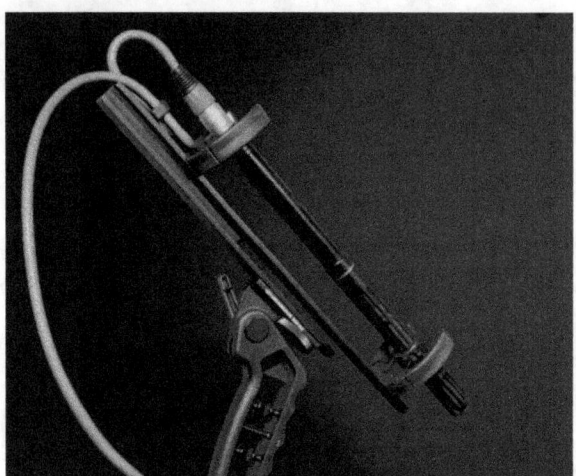

To get the best sound from these microphones it is best to place them off-camera, ideally on some form of boom pole, so that the front of the microphone can be angled down towards the subject. This means that any noise from around the subject will be greatly reduced and the quality of the main sound will be far better. If possible the microphone should be held as close to the mouth of the subject but obviously out of camera view.

The Sennheiser K2 rifle microphone positioned for a "to-camera" interview, on a boom pole.

If you cannot rig up some way of positioning the rifle microphone this way, then it is probably better to turn to using a wired or wireless lavaliere microphone. The body pack worn by the presenter and the receiver plugged into the camera.

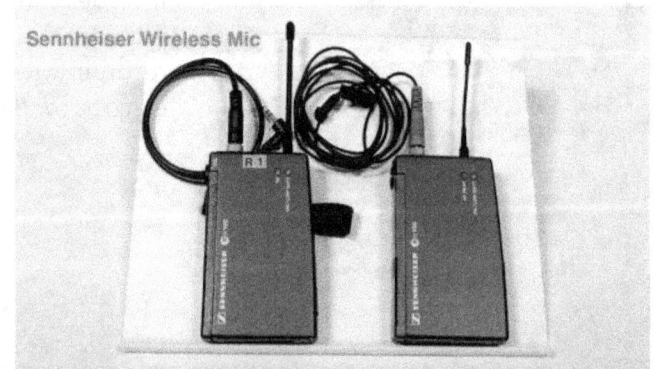

The Sennheiser EW100 wireless microphone system

For some videographers getting the audio right is even more critical than getting the video quality right. Poor audio quality is likely to cause viewers of you video to skip if it was on YouTube, for example.

For these people an external audio recorder is key to them controlling the sound quality. Most of these will support XLR balanced audio from a variety of sources which can be mixed together at the right levels.

The camera mics provide a sound reference during the editing of the video as it more usual to import the audio from the external recorder and then "synch" it to the original video.

You might have seen "slates" or "clapper boards" used to provide the synchronisation of the video and audio.

The sound spike from the two edges of the clapperboard closing is lined up on the editing track with image of the closing of the clapperboard. The on-camera mic track is then discarded during the editing process.

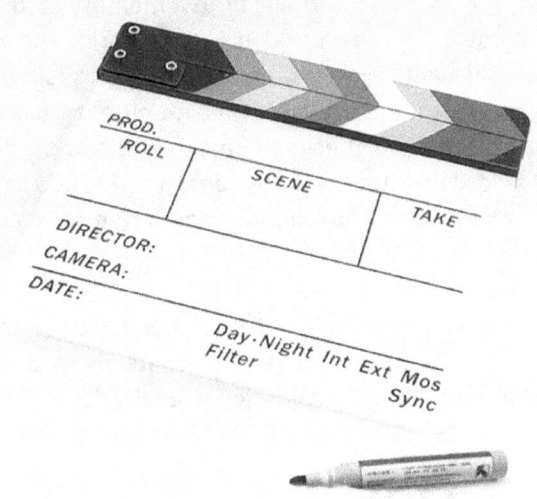

a professional grade clapper board

The quality of the audio being recorded is usually monitored by using a pair of headphones but unfortunately the FZ1000 doesn't have a headphone port to enable the sound to be monitored either during recording or in the preview mode.

You can only get a very crude indication by listening to the very small speaker in the camera.

The volume can be adjusted by using the top zoom lever during playback.

HDMI Monitor/External Recorder

The FZ1000 supports "clean" HDMI however the FZ1000 can't record to a memory card and *simultaneously* output any kind of video via HDMI, though; all it displays on the HDMI output is a message indicating that recording is in progress.

So-called "clean" HDMI output means a video signal through a camera's HDMI connector that includes no text or graphic overlays showing camera status, exposure variables, etc. It's just an image of what the camera sees through its lens, and nothing more.

There are two use cases for clean HDMI, perhaps the biggest being to record video on an external recorder, rather than internally onto a memory card. External recorders have several important advantages over encoding and storing the video in-camera. They can record at significantly higher bitrates for better image quality, and in most cases, they provide higher capacity than is available on a memory card. Also, many recorders have removable disk drives, making it easy to port the data to a video editing system.
So, if you're not recording internally, the Panasonic FZ1000 can output a clean image over its HDMI port, using the 4:2:2 subsampling standard most common to professional video work.

This means that you can use a larger external monitor to verify framing, exposure and focus prior to pressing the record button. Alternatively, you could connect an external HDMI recorder/Monitor and get professional level video recording at 4K @ 4:2:2 sub sampling.

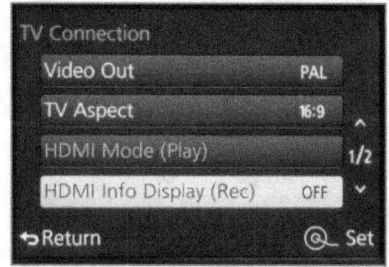

To turn off all graphical overlays for the "clean" HDMI in the TV connection screen (setup menu page 3/5) set the HDMI info Display (Rec) to OFF

Here's the displays on an externally connected monitor.

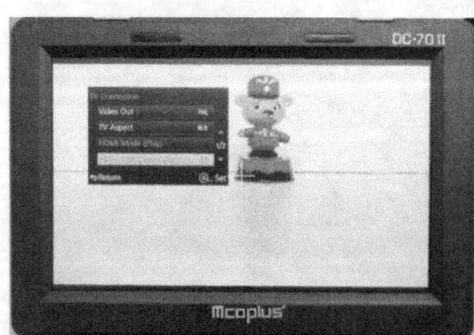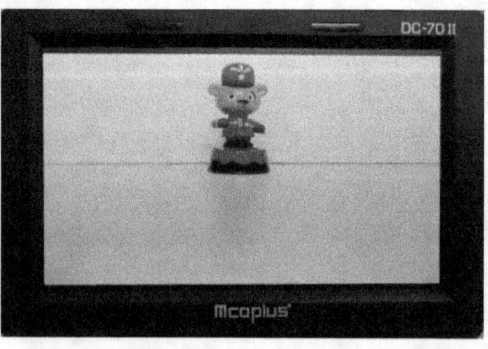

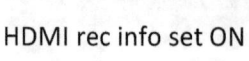

HDMI rec info set ON   HDMI rec info set OFF

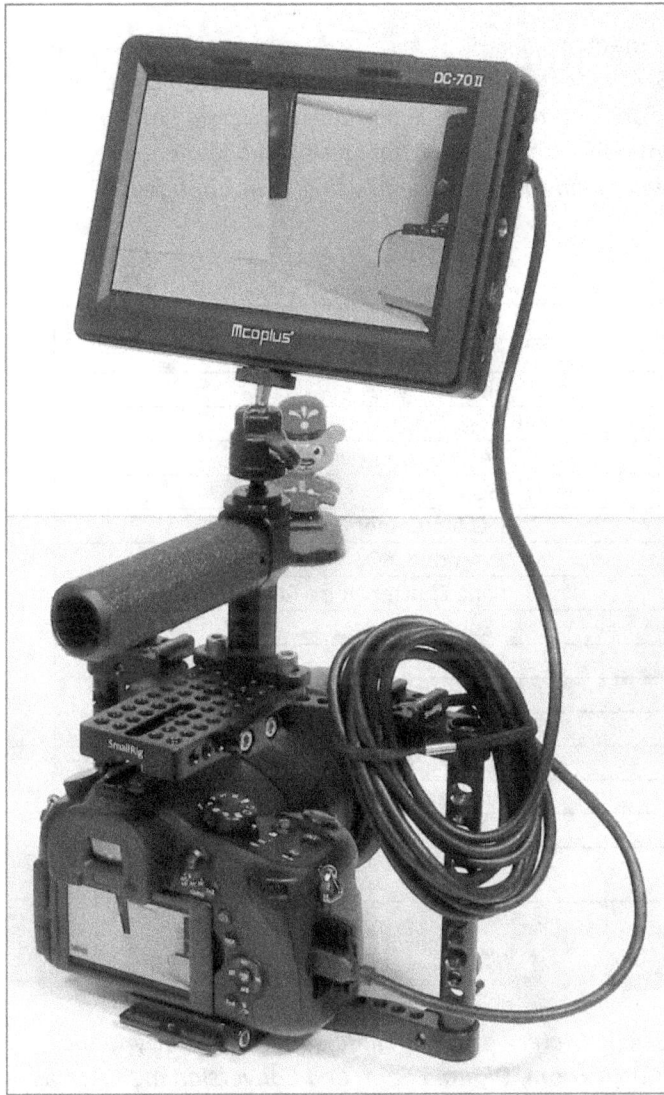

Here the Mcoplus DC-70 II 7 inch external HDMI monitor mounted on a SmallRig cage.

Useful when recording to confirm exposure, framing and focus prior to hitting the record button.

It's a great pity that the camera cannot record to internal SD card and output the HDMI signal as with the later FZ2000 camera.

The cable required is a micro-HDMI to HDMI.

The Complete Menu Listing

A complete listing of all the camera menus:

The Photo Style, Filter Settings, AFS/AFF, Metering Mode, Highlight Shadow, i.Dynamic, i.Resolution, Diffraction Compensation, i.Zoom, Digital Zoom, and Conversion menu items are common for both [Rec] and [Motion Picture] menus. If a setting in one menu is changed, the setting with the same name in the other menu will also be changed automatically.

📷 [Rec]

Photo Style	Multi Exp.
Aspect Ratio	Panorama Settings
Picture Size	Shutter Type
Quality	Flash
AFS/AFF	Red-Eye Removal
Metering Mode	ISO Limit Set
Burst Rate	ISO Increments
Auto Bracket	Extended ISO
Self Timer	Long Shutter Noise Reduction
Time Lapse/Animation	i.Zoom
Highlight Shadow	Digital Zoom
i.Dynamic	Colour Space
i.Resolution	Stabiliser
iHandheld Night Shot	Face Recog
iHDR	Profile Setup
HDR	

📹 [Motion Picture]

The Photo Style, Filter Settings, AFS/AFF, Metering Mode, Highlight Shadow, i.Dynamic, i.Resolution, Diffraction Compensation, i.Zoom, Digital Zoom, and Conversion menu items are common for both Rec and Motion Picture menus. If a setting in one menu is changed, the setting with the same name in the other menu will also be changed automatically.

Rec Format	Mic Level Disp.
Rec Quality	Mic Level Adj.
Exposure Mode	Special Mic
High Speed Video	Mic Level Limiter
Picture Mode	Wind Cut
Continuous AF	Zoom Mic
Level Shot	
Flkr Decrease	

ƒc [Custom]

Cust Set Mem.	Monochrome Live View
Silent Mode	Constant Preview (M Mode)
AF/AE Lock	Expo.Meter
AF/AE Lock Hold	Dial Guide
Shutter AF	LVF Disp.Style
Half Press Release	Monitor Disp. Style
Quick AF	Monitor Info. Disp.
Eye Sensor AF	Rec Area
Pinpoint AF Time	Remaining Disp.
Pinpoint AF Display	Auto Review
AF Assist Lamp	Fn Button Set
Direct Focus Area	Zoom lever
Focus/Release Priority	Manual Ring (Zoom)
AF+MF	Zoom Resume
MF Assist	Q.MENU
MF Assist Display	Video Button
MF Guide	Eye Sensor
Peaking	Menu Guide
Histogram	
Guide Line	
Centre Marker	
Highlight	
Zebra Pattern	

ƒ [Setup]

Clock Set	Menu Resume
World Time	Menu Background
Travel Date	Menu Information
Wi-Fi	Language
Beep	Version Disp
Live View Mode	Exposure Comp. Reset
Monitor Display/Viewfinder	No. Reset
Monitor Luminance	Reset
Economy	Reset Wi-Fi Settings
USB Mode	Format
TV Connection	

▶ [Playback]

Slide Show	Cropping
Playback Mode	Rotate
Location Logging	Rotate Disp.
RAW Processing	Favourite
Title Edit	Print Set
Text Stamp	Protect
Video Divide	Face Rec Edit
Time Lapse Video	Picture Sort
Stop Motion Video	Delete Confirmation
Resize	

Some Setup Menu Operations

In this section, it's time to look at some of the more commonly used options in the "tools" set up section of the main camera menu.

Clock Setting option, which is the first menu you are presented with when you initially turn on a new camera. Current Time and Date as well as the date format can be set in this screen.

The World Time allows you to set your camera to local time if you travel away from your country and need to adjust the day/date to the travel destination.

Travel Date allows you to enter a departure and return date as well as a destination. During replay of the images this information is displayed along with the image.

Wi-Fi setup, I've covered this in the Wi-Fi section of the guide

Live View Mode This mode effects the refresh rate of the EVF or LCD screen to give a smoother display. It does affect battery life and should only be increased if you notice image lagging when you use the lower 30fps mode

The Monitor Display option allows users to customise the way the LCD screen is calibrated. It allows the Brightness, Contrast/Saturation and Colour tints to be adjusted if you feel the display does not accurately match the illumination of the subject.
However, if you adjust this too far from its default you may begin to adjust for exposure which are being biased by this display offset.

The Monitor Luminance allows the brightness of the LCD display to be controlled by the ambient light levels or switched to a low or high intensity mode. The high intensity mode is useful if using the LCD in bright sunshine.

The Economy setting allows the various elements of the camera to be set to conserve battery power such as setting the time before the screen auto turns off or the camera goes into sleep mode

The USB mode allows the selection of the correct peripheral once the USB cable has been connected. It can either be set to the most common use – such as your PC or printer, or it can be set to prompt on connection.

TV Connection
Video Out: Set to match the colour television system in each country.
NTSC: Video output is set to NTSC system.
PAL: Video output is set to PAL system.

TV Aspect: Set to match the type of TV.
16:9: When connecting to a 16:9 screen TV.
4:3: When connecting to a 4:3 screen TV.
HDMI play mode –sets the format of the HDMI signal output from the camera.
The setting can be Auto, 4k,1080p, 1080i, 720p or 575p.
This will work when the AV cable is connected.

HDMI info Disp (Rec) this setting will allow the data that is normally overlaid on the LCD screen to be turned off if you are using the HDMI port for external recording (not simultaneous with internal recording).

Menu Resume - The last operated menu position is saved even if the camera is turned off, when you next access the menu it will return here.

Menu Information allows the "ticker tape" display of the menu function which appears at the top of the LCD display.

Version Display – Displays the current firmware revision number of the camera.

Exposure Compensation Reset – this feature will allow the exposure value compensation to be held even if the mode dial is changed or the camera is powered off, if the value is set to OFF.

No. Reset - is there to update the "folder number" and the file number to 0001. Each folder holds 999 images after which the folder number increments by 1 and the file number starts again.
This can be useful if you want very discrete image sequence numbers rather than just incrementally camera generated ones.

The Folder and File number combine to give the image number, for example 119-0025 is jpeg image 1190025.

If you never reset the numbering sequence it gives an indication of the number of exposures that you have completed with the camera.
The camera starts numbering from 100-0001 so after each 1000 images the folder number will increase to 101-0000 and so on.

The folder number can be assigned between 100 and 999.
When the folder number reaches 999, the number cannot be reset.
To reset the folder number back to 100, format the built-in memory or the card first and then use this function to reset the file number.
A reset screen for the folder number will then appear. Select [Yes] to reset the folder number.

The Reset option on page 4 is a way of reverting the camera back to factory defaults for the REC mode and the SET UP menu items.

The option has two parts, the REC mode where all the settings are restored to default, apart from time and date and the Folder/File number. The second is the Setup parameters which include the Custom memory profiles, face recognition and the Lens resume settings.
Reset Wi-Fi Settings – sets the Wi-Fi parameters back to the default values shipped with the camera.

Format – allows the built-in memory or card to be formatted. Formatting irretrievably deletes all the data from the card and then builds the folders that the camera requires. (some data retrieval programs can recover data deleted by using the format command as does not actually delete the data it just deletes the area on the card called the File Allocation Table).

New memory cards should be formatted in the camera and if you use memory cards that have been previously used in other cameras it is good practice to format them again in this camera before use.

Glossary of Photographic Terms

Aperture - the variable opening in the lens through which light passes to the film or digital sensor. Measured in f-stops. I like to compare it to your pupil which opens and closes to allow light to enter your eye depending on the brightness level of the room.

Bracketing - taking a series of images at different exposures or EV. You may see a setting on your camera that says AEB (auto exposure bracketing). This is often used when creating HDR images or in difficult lighting situations where you may want to have a range of exposures from light to dark.

Bulb - the "B" setting on your camera where the shutter remains opened for as long as the button or cable release (remote trigger) is pressed.

EV - Exposure Value is a number that represents the various combinations of aperture and shutter speed that can create the same exposure effect.

Exposure compensation - modifying the shutter speed or aperture from the camera's recommended exposure to create a certain effect (over or under exposing) – usually used in the Shutter Priority or Aperture Priority modes. Represented by a little +/- button on your camera. Your camera reads light bouncing off your subject and is designed to expose for medium grey. So, when photographing a subject that is lighter or darker than 18% grey, you can use this setting to tell the camera the proper exposure.

Exposure - the total amount of light reaching the camera sensor. It is controlled by the setting of the aperture, shutter speed and ISO. See my Exposure Triangle for more details.

F-stop - is a measure of the aperture opening in the lens defined by dividing the focal length of the lens by the aperture diameter. Sequence of f-stops that are multiples of the square root of 2 (1.4): giving a range of 1, 1.4, 2, 2.8, 4, 5.6, 8, 11, 16, 22, etc. Remember that each step is double the amount of light.

ISO - stands for International Standards Organization and represents the sensitivity of your camera's digital sensor to light and subsequent signal amplification. The lower the number (ISO 100), the less sensitive, the higher the number (ISO 3200) the more sensitive. A higher ISO allows you to shoot in low light conditions

Shutter speed - the amount of time the shutter is opened during an exposure. The shutter speed controls subject motion blur. Use a fast speed (like 1/2000th of a second) to freeze motion, or a slow one (1/4 of a second or longer) to blur moving objects.

Zoom lens - any lens that has variable focal lengths such as a 24-70mm or 18-55mm. You zoom in or out by rotating the barrel of the lens.

Remote trigger or digital cable release – a device that allows the camera to be fired without pressing the button or touching the camera. Helps eliminate movement of the camera during long exposures.

Macro lens - one that focuses very close to the subject allowing for 1:1 reproduction size of the object or larger.

Camera resolution - expressed in megapixels is the dimensions your camera's sensor is capable of capturing. This is not the only factor in image quality, but generally the large the number, the larger prints you can produce from it without loss of quality.

File format JPEG versus RAW - The FZ1000 can shoot both formats. If you choose JPG, the camera will shoot a RAW file, process it using the Photo style you've selected in your menu, save it as a JPG and discard the RAW version.

If shot in RAW the resulting file will be larger, carry more information (but the same pixel resolution, see above) and require software to process. It gives you the photographer more control over the final look of your image.

Lighting and Portrait Photography Terms

Ambient light - also referred to as available light, is the light that is occurring in the scene without adding any flash or light modifiers. This could be daylight, or artificial light such as tungsten or LED Lights.

Main light or key light - is the main light source for a photograph. It could be the sun, a studio strobe, a flash, a reflector or something else. But it is the source of light that is producing the pattern of light on the subject with the most intensity.

Fill light - is the light source that is secondary to the mail light. It is used to "fill" in the shadows to a desired degree. It can be produced by using a flash, a reflector, or a studio strobe.

Lighting pattern - this is the way the light falls on the subject's face. A pattern of light and shadow that is created.

Lighting ratio - is a comparison between the intensity (brightness) of the main light and the fill light and thus the difference of the lit and shadow sides of the subject's face.

Incident light meter - is a handheld device separate from your camera that measures the amount of light falling on a subject (as opposed to the reflective reading your camera takes which is light bouncing off the subject back to the camera). It is not fooled by the brightness range of the subject, whereas in camera reflective meters can be fooled.

Reflector - a device that is used to reflect light, generally back towards the subject. It can be a specialized factory made reflector or as simple as a piece of white cardboard.

Light meter - a device that measures the amount of light in a scene. Your FZ1000 has one built in, it uses reflective readings (light bouncing off the subject coming back through the lens [TTL])

Remote flash trigger - a device used to fire remote flash units off camera.

Subtractive lighting - as the name implies it is the taking away of light to create a desired effect. Commonly it involves holding a reflector or opaque panel over the subject's head to block light from above and open deep eye shadows cause by overhead lighting. It can also mean holding a black reflector opposite your main light to create a deeper shadow, reflecting black onto the subject instead of light.

Hard light - harsh light such as produced by bright sunlight, a small flashgun, or an on-camera flash. It produces harsh shadows with well-defined edges, contrast, and texture (if used at an angle to the subject). Emphasizes texture, lines and wrinkles, and used to create a more dramatic type of portrait.

Soft light - diffused light such as from an overcast sky, north facing window with no direct light, or a large studio softbox. This type of light produces soft shadows with soft edges, lower contrast, and less texture. Generally preferred by most wedding and portrait photographers as it flatter the subject more.

Flash sync - simply put is the synchronization of the firing of an electronic flash and the shutter speed. You need to know what shutter speed your camera syncs at, otherwise if you shoot too fast a shutter speed you may get a partially illuminated image.

For the FZ1000 because of the in-lens shutter flash can be synched at any of the available shutter speeds.

Some Slang Photographic Jargon

Become familiar with them so you can walk among the pros with confidence!

Fast glass - refers to a lens with a very large maximum aperture such as f1.8 or f1.2. "Fast" as in, it allows you to shoot at a fast shutter speed due to the large aperture.

Chimping - slang term meaning looking at the back of the camera after every image. Spending too much time reviewing images on camera, not enough time shooting.

Bokeh - often mispronounced "bow-kay" or "bow-kuh" it is correctly pronounced as "bo-ke" like the ke in kettle. It is used to described the out of focus blurred bits in the background when "fast glass" is used. Most often bokeh occurs where small light sources are in the background, far in the distance.

Depth of Field - (DOF or DoF)- the distance between the nearest and farthest objects in your scene that appear in focus. It is controlled by many factors including the aperture, lens focal length, distance to subject.

Circles of confusion - closely related to the above bokeh, the textbook definition is: the largest blur spot that is indistinguishable from the point source that is being rendered. Objects outside the depth of field of an image that the human eye can determine as "out of focus".

Hyperfocal distance - often used by landscape photographers, it is the focus distance providing the maximum amount of depth of field.

Gobo - something used to block unwanted or stray light from falling onto the subject. Often a reflector (using the black side) can serve a dual purpose and act as a gobo as well.

Scrim - a translucent device used to diffuse and soften the light, could be a reflector with a translucent panel or option. Also, used on movie sets scrims can be made extremely large, several feet across, and clamped in place to create shade where these is direct sun without it.

Shutter lag - the slight delay from the time you press the shutter button to the time it fires and opens.

Chromatic aberration - in terms of lens optics it is the failure of the lens to focus all colours (RGB) at the same point. It shows up as colour fringes in areas of the image where dark meet light (think edge of a building against the sky). It is more common in wide angle lenses, and those of inferior optics. It is correctable, to some degree, using Photoshop, Lightroom - or software of your choice.

Rear shutter curtain sync - by default most cameras are set to front curtain sync which means that if the flash fires, it does so at the beginning of the exposure time. By setting to rear shutter curtain sync it fires the flash at the end of the exposure time. The difference in some cases me be negligible, but in shooting a moving subject front sync will put any motion blur in front of the subject, whereas rear sync will place the blur behind the subject. Neither is wrong, just preference.

Camera shake - this is a blurry image which has resulted from an insufficiently fast enough shutter speed, while hand holding the camera. So how slow is too slow? Many will say that 1/60th of a second is the rule of thumb. I tend to recommend 1 over the focal lens of your lens instead, as the longer the lens the more amplified any shake will become.

Lens flare - occurs when the light source hits the lens directly, it can manifest as a hazy looking image or artefacts such as circles of light. Some photographers desire lens flare and position their camera to create it and use it as a compositional element.

Kelvin - is the absolute measurement of colour temperature. On your camera under the White Balance settings you make see a "K" setting. This allows you to adjust the colour manually by degrees Kelvin. The lower numbers represent warmer colours like orange (tungsten light) and the higher numbers are cooler (blues).

ND filter - stands for neutral density filter which is a filter designed to go in front of the lens to block out some of the light entering the camera. Often used by landscape photographers to be able to get slow shutter speeds when photographing waterfalls and streams in full daylight.

Panning - the act of using a slow shutter speed, and moving the camera in the same direction as a moving subject, during the exposure to create a blurred background.

Stopping down - the act of closing the aperture to a smaller opening say f2.8 to f4.

TTL and ETTL - stands for Through the Lens, refers to the metering system in regards to flash exposure. The flash emits light until it is turned off by the camera sensor. ETTL is evaluative through the lens metering and fires a "pre-flash" to evaluate and calculate for lost light then compensates and fires the main flash. It happens so fast you do not see two flashes.

Golden hour - also called "magic hour" is the hour right before sunset or right after sunrise. The sun is low on the horizon and it is an optimal time for photography.

Blown out - having highlights that are off the chart on the right side of the histogram, having no detail in the white areas.

Clipped - similar to blown out being off the histogram, but it can also apply to shadow or black areas of the image.

Selfie - a self portrait

SOOC - straight out of camera, no post processing or editing done.

Wide open - using your lens with the aperture at the widest setting (f2.8 for example)

The End of this Guide – Or Just the Beginning?

Well I hope this guidebook has achieved my objective for you. In conjunction with the advanced user guide from Panasonic you should have all the resource material to enable you to confidently use your FZ1000 camera.

Please do visit my Photoblog website: https://www.grahamhoughton.com/
Where you can find updated technical topics for the FZ1000 and general photography.

You can also subscribe to my three weekly newsletter which packs lots more information to help you with your photography.
You can view some of the archived newsletters here: http://us9.campaign-archive1.com/home/?u=9925264577c370e71ea96e132&id=4a95d1f787

If you have any questions regarding the FZ1000 you can email me at support@grahamhoughton.com where I will endeavour to answer them for you.

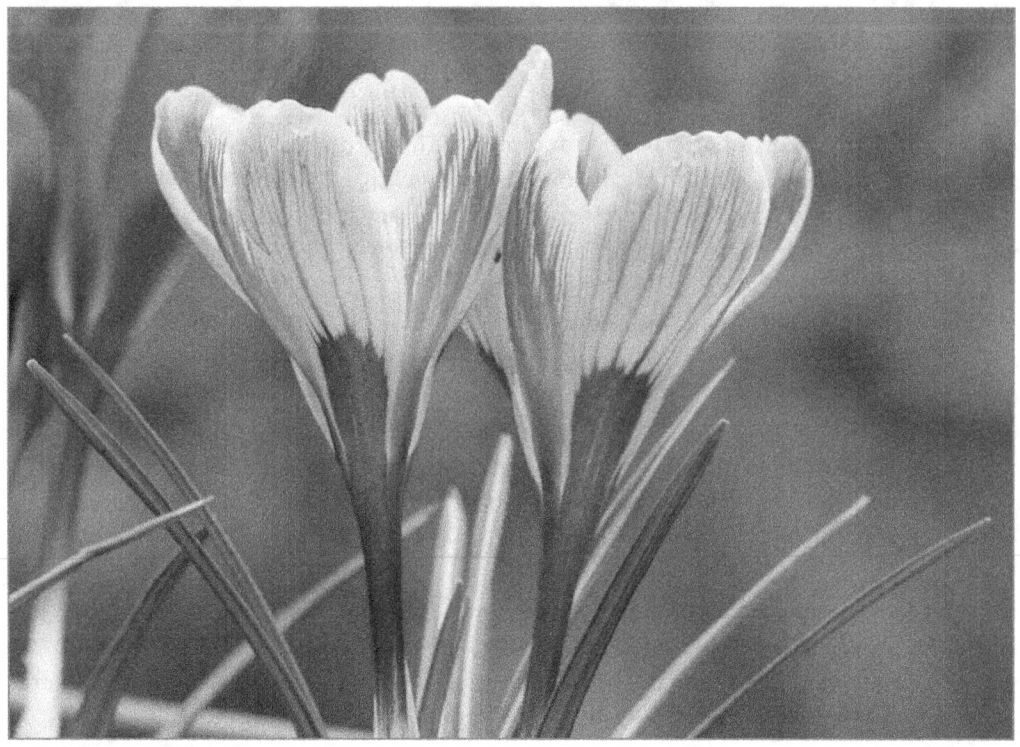

Stop Press:

Just announced the Panasonic Lumix FZ1000 II camera.
This update to the existing FZ1000 adds some additional features to this already well established model.

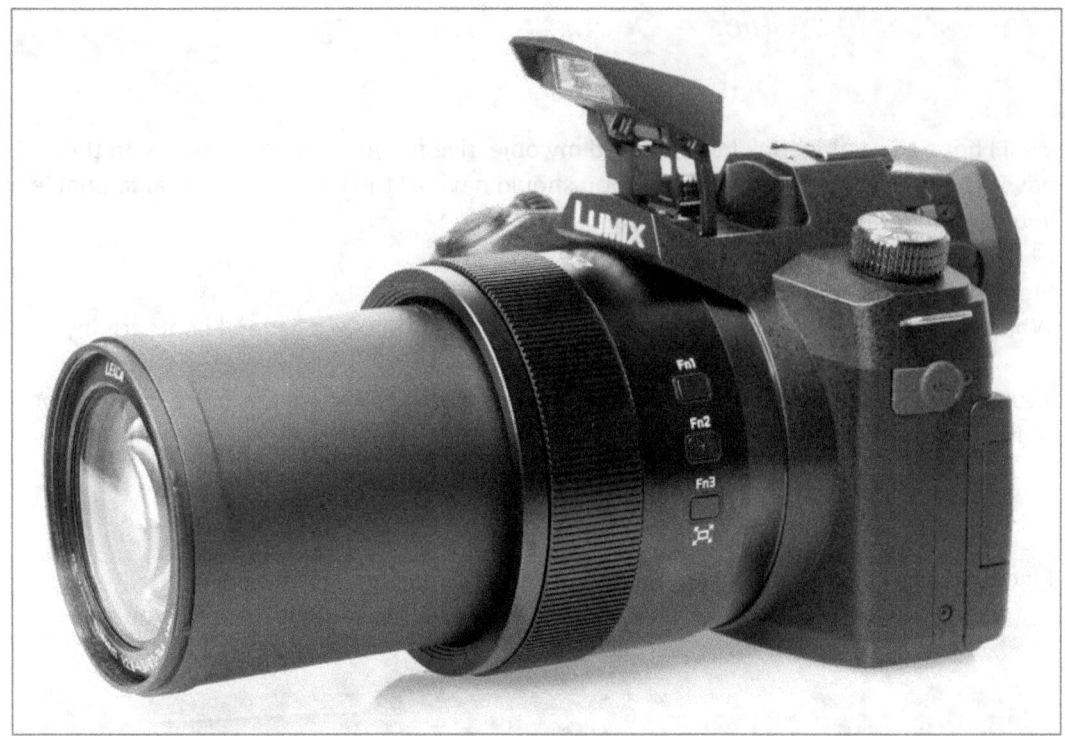

The new FZ1000 II

The 16x optical LEICA certified zoom lens and the 20.1MP sensor is the same as you find in the original FZ1000 but Bluetooth is now built-in along with a 3.0-inch, 1,250k-dot 180-degree rear monitor which is now touch-control so you can set focus quickly and configure 5 on-screen buttons for quick access to controls.

If you don't want to use the rear monitor, there is a 0.39-inch OLED Live View Finder that has a 2,360k-dot resolution and 0.74x magnification, up from 0.7X on the FZ1000.

There's a 4K photo option, along with 4K video (3840x2160 pixel resolution at 30/25/24p), and you can use various 4K photo functions which include Post Focus, Focus Stacking and the ability to combine multiple images. There's also a new 'Auto Marking' feature that helps you choose the best image from footage you've shot at 30fps.

Other interesting, and useful, features include 5-axis Hybrid O.I.S.+, high-speed burst shooting, Wi-Fi, various photo filters and a new minimum aperture of f/11. There's also a new Zoom Compose Assist feature that Panasonic says will help you keep track of subjects when they suddenly leave the frame and for the most part, it's a useful feature; quickly switching to a wide-angle view so you can see more in the frame before returning to the zoom point you had set previously.

The Panasonic Lumix FZ1000 II looks very similar to the original FZ1000, on first glance, however there are a number of subtle, but worthwhile improvements, including the addition of a new top command dial behind the shutter button. You'll also notice there are now three (new) function buttons on the left-hand side of the lens (Fn1, Fn2, Fn3),

two function buttons on the top (Fn4 - defaults to exposure compensation, and Fn5), and on the back three more function buttons, Fn6 (Q. Menu), and Fn7 (delete, back) and Fn8 (LVF). The video record button has also been moved.

The drive mode dial on the top left of the camera has been updated to include the 4K focus stacking mode, which joins the other drive modes of self-timer, continuous shooting, interval shooting, 4K photo, and single shot.

The tripod socket is near the middle of the camera and is made of metal. The battery compartment is also where you'll find the memory card slot, and has a locking mechanism, as well as a spring-loaded latch to hold the battery in.

The focal lengths are marked on the (plastic) lens barrel. The control ring around the lens, as well as the exterior of the lens are made of metal.

Index

Regrettably the Index for this book was beyond the scope of my editing program and caused so many problems that I have had to exclude it.

You can of course use the very extensive search option in your PDF reader software. If you have purchased this book as a hard copy version, then the PDF file is available for free if you contact me with your Amazon order number.

support@grahamhoughton.com?subject=PDF for FZ1000

www.ingramcontent.com/pod-product-compliance
Lightning Source LLC
Chambersburg PA
CBHW080907170526
45158CB00008B/2018

PRESENCIA 3

DIOS, EL COSMOS, LO PARANORMAL Y LAS EXOCIVILIZACIONES

LA TEORÍA COSMOBIOFÍSICA DE LOS 3/3

V3.5

YA PUBLICADO POR EL MISMO AUTOR:

Présence 1, Ovnis, Crop Circles et Exocivilisations.

Présence 2, Le langage et le mystère de la planète UMMO révélés.

Présence 3, Dieu, le Cosmos, le paranormal et les Exocivilisations.

Présence 4, Vers un Nouveau Monde…avec les Exocivilisations.

Présence 6, DICTIONNAIRE DENOCLA.

Presencia 1, ovnis, círculos de cultivos y exocivilizaciones.

Presence 2, El lenguaje y el misterio del planeta UMMO revelados.

Presencia 3, Dios, el Cosmos, lo paranormal y las exocivilizaciones.

Presencia 4, Hacia un mundo nuevo ... con exocivilizaciones.

Presence 1, UFOs, Crop Circles and Exocivilisations.

Presence 2, The language and the mystery of the planet UMMO revealed.

Presence 3, God, the Cosmos, the paranormal and the Exocivilisations.

Presence 4, Towards a New World… with Exocivilisations.

NO OLVIDES DEJAR
TU COMENTARIO EN AMAZON

UMMO MUSIC Band : http://www.ummomusic.com

UMMO MUSIC, IXINAA

UMMO MUSIC, LIKE 2 OEMMIIs

UMMO MUSIC, BEST OF

Denis Roger
DENOCLA

PRESENCIA 3

DIOS, EL COSMOS, LO PARANORMAL Y LAS EXOCIVILIZACIONES

LA TEORÍA COSMOBIOFÍSICA DE LOS 3/3

V3.5

edition 2026

ÉDITIONS UMMO WORLD PUBLISHING

Este libro es la tercera obra de la serie Presencia. Lleva a la reflexión en una perspectiva de innovación de pensamiento y de búsqueda, a partir de los elementos contenidos en los documentos ummitas.

¡Los resultados cosmológicos transcendentales que explican numerosos misterios y lo que llamamos ' la Realidad ' y 'Dios'!

LAS TESIS REVOLUCIONARIAS DE

LA TEORÍA COSMOBIOFÍSICA DE LOS 3 TERCIOS

PARA UNA NUEVA RACIONALIDAD

- La teoría cosmobiofíca de los 3/3

- La aparición de la vida en el Cosmos

- El Alma y DIOS: los conceptos cosmológicos racionales

- La telepatía explicada

- Un modelo racionalizado para la comunicación con los « Espíritus »

-La Experiencia de muerte inminente dilucidada

Sources des documents oummains : www.ummo-ciencias.org, www.ummo-sciences.org, www.denocla.com, et collections privées.
Images originales : remerciements spéciaux à UMMOAELEWEE.
Illustrations numériques : Davy H. —© D. R. DENOCLA
Photo portrait : Frédérique Blat — © D. R. DENOCLA

UMMO WORLD Publishing
8 Esp. de la Manufacture
92136 ISSY LES MOULINEAUX — FRANCE

Índice

INDICE

1
2 345 678 910 1112

LA TEORÍA COSMOBIOFÍSICADE LOS 3 TERCIOS

En la primera obra vimos los puntos claves de la comprensión del fenómeno ovni, las motivaciones de la presencia de extraterretres en general. También mostramos en qué condiciones viajan nuestros visitadores. El extraordinario esfuerzo sicológico que esto puede necesitar sin embargo, fue sostenido por elementos factuales y fuertes estadísticas tales como las fotos de los Círculos en los Cultivos y en la segunda obra, por la decodificación del lenguaje Ummita, basado en documentos factuales que pueden ser consultados por todos.

En Presencia, Ovnis, Círculos en los Cultivos y Exocivilizaciones hablamos de la teoría de la presencia discreta, pero activa y globalmente pacífica, de exocivilizaciones en nuestro suelo, llamada Paz Galáctica. Y la apertura de un gran campo de conocimiento desconocido, caracterizado por un misterioso lenguaje descifrado en Presencia 2, El Lenguaje y el misterio del Planeta Ummo revelados.

Este tercer volumen postula estos elementos asimilados, las obras Presencia 1 y 2 son requisitos previos que facilitan la comprensión de ciertos conceptos nuevos presentados en Presencia 3. Sin embargo, sin ningún conocimiento en física o matemáticas, todos los conceptos serán comprensibles para usted..

Se trata de llevar la reflexión desde una perspectiva de innovación de pensamiento y de investigación, a partir d'elementos contenidos en

3

los documentos Ummitas y aquellos derivados de los conocimientos terrestres. Este enfoque mixto es, en sí mismo, ya inusual y requiere un real esfuerzo mental asociado con una inversión psicológica personal significativa. Haremos los lazos históricos y culturales con las teorías científicas terrestres para aclarar los conceptos nuevos.

Repetiremos en este tomo 3 conceptos ya evocados en las obras precedentes precisándolos y explorando nuevas vías… Por efecto, nuestros conocimientos en física, cosmología, biología, deben ser totalmente revisados. Explicaré mi lectura de la teoría cosmológica de los Ummitas y en particular los objetos cosmológicos transcendentales que llamamos "lo Real» y «Dios», señalando todas las aportaciones de los grandes pensadores terrestres del pasado.

Presentaremos hipótesis totalmente nuevas, particularmente sobre un componente posible y universal que llamé el constante criptónica y que conduciría a la emergencia de la Vida. Evocaremos la Evolución de las especies y del Hombre según mi lectura de los documentos ummitas. Trataremos algunos sujetos complicados que sobrepasen el entendimiento de la ciencia contemporánea que los rechaza en la categoría de los fenómenos paranormales, por no poder explicarlos.

Explicaremos que estos fenómenos conocidos y parcialmente reconocidos por la ciencia oficial políticamente correcta, son completamente "normales", pero requiere un gran cambio de paradigma que tiene sentido en un nuevo marco racional. Por lo tanto, tratamos de entender las posibilidades de comunicación con «los espíritus», en cómo es posible alguna forma de 'reencarnación' y cuáles son sus límites. Vamos a tratar temas relacionados con lo que generalmente se llama "El Alma» BUAWA. Nos interrogaremos, cómo sobre los astros podrían influir en el psiquismo humano, cómo el Hombre podrá desarrollar la comunicación telepática y cuál podrá ser su devenir evolutivo.

He aquí pues tantos objetivos extraordinariamente ambiciosos y revolucionarios para los cuales este volumen propone explicaciones

El autor prohíbe estrictamente la referencia a sus búsquedas con fines religiosas.

LA TEORÍA COSMOBIOFÍSICA DE LOS 3 TERCIOS

La Teoría Cosmobiofísica de los 3 Tercios es un conjunto de teorías originales que describen una nueva racionalidad. Esta teoría explica todos los fenómenos que se mantuvieron sin explicación por la ciencia del Siglo XXI.

Incluye los conocimientos científicos pasados y actuales, las intuiciones de la Metafísica de una manera racionalizada, una visión exógena proporcionada por la exocivilización de UMMO y de numerosos desarrollos innovadores realizados en colaboración con expertos internacionales en las diferentes áreas tratadas.

La Teoría Cosmobiofísica de los 3 Tercios puede ser calificada realmente de revolucionaria, porque el paradigma resultante no está en consonancia con el viejo mundo que nos hace abandonar... Aquí está, la única dificultad de lectura, que siempre será redactada lo más sencillamente posible con los términos definidos. Las tesis incluidas en la Teoría Cosmobiofícica de los 3 Tercios son:

- un nuevo paradigma completo:

- 1er tercio un nuevo enfoque cosmológico

- 2º tercio un nuevo enfoque de la biología

- 3º tercio un nuevo enfoque físico

- una nueva lógica

- una nueva tesis evolucionista

- sobre la aparición de la vida

- la evolución orientada de la vida

- los flujos de información de una especie viva

- la aparición y la evolución del hombre

- una racionalización de:

- la influencia de los astros en la psique

- la comunicación telepática

- la comunicación con los 'espíritus'

Discutiremos los diferentes contextos epistemológicos en el curso del avance de nuestra presentación. Compararemos las tesis y teorías terrestres con las tesis de la Biocosmofísica presentada por nuestros amigos de UMMO. Para facilitas la comprensión de todos, ilustraremos cada principio con uno o varios ejemplos concretos.

Génesis de la Teoría de los 3 tercios

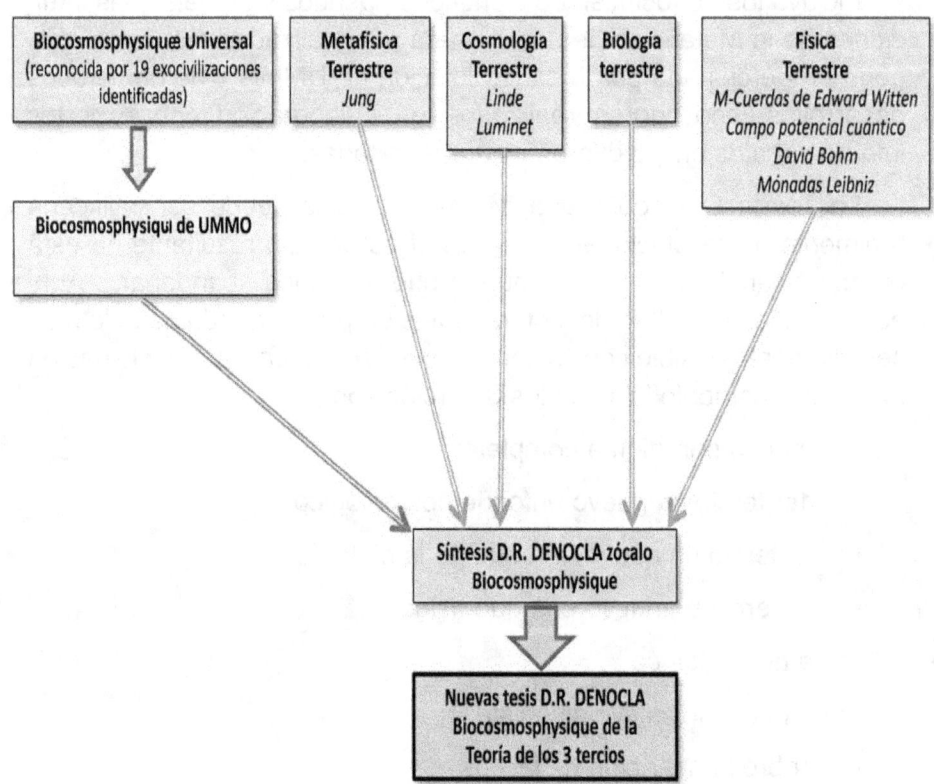

UN NUEVO PARADIGMA COSMOLÓGICO

Esta presentación del marco cosmológico resulta principalmente de mi lectura e interpretación de los documentos ummitas. Aclararemos estos nuevos conceptos con las teorías científicas terrestres conocidas y los conceptos en gran parte intuidos por la Teología o las tradiciones culturales, desde hace tiempo, en todos los continentes del planeta… Éste será el punto de partida que nos hará que desarrollemos las nuevas tesis totalmente revolucionarias que unifican Psique y Metafísica.

D28 19/03/1966

Puede redactar cualquier forma de escrito -prensa, revistas, libros-, siempre que no distorsione la realidad de nuestros documentos. Al expresar sus opiniones sobre la filosofía, la religión, la historia, la ciencia y la tecnología UMMO, se especifica que son suyas y no están inscritos en nuestros informes.

El contenido de este libro es muy diferente de las ideas comúnmente admitidas en nuestra época, será en el mejor de los casos, en la sección de cosmologías "exóticas" por los cosmólogos ortodoxos… o bien dirán que "parece una tontería"… poco me importa estoy curado de estos juicios parciales y presuntuosos. Para mí, lo esencias es que si USTED quiere entender estos conceptos, "este trabajo será útil".

A priori, no hay ideas nuevas por mi parte en este capítulo, pero esa es mi interpretación de la cosmología contenida en los documentos ummitas, con un objetivo de vulgarización con vocación pedagógica y didáctica. Estas explicaciones se complementan con ejemplos concretos, las referencias a las teorías terrestres y también "importantes análisis semánticos de las palabras los Ummitas que permiten comprender la sutileza de los conceptos expuestos por nuestros amigos visitantes del "espacio exterior". Éste es el fruto de mi búsqueda personal.

.

EL MODELO COSMOLÓGICO MULTI-COSMOS

Desde el advenimiento de la era de la física cuántica, en los años 20, los escritores y los cosmólogos reflexionan sobre modelos de universos compuestos de múltiples cosmos. La idea de mundos paralelos existió en la literatura fantástica antes de que ' surgiera en un marco científico convencional.

En 1957, Hugh Everett transpone la visión común del universo en un enfoque cuántico. De este punto de vista la 'realidad' del Universo se desdobla en tantos estados cuánticos diferentes, pero no se trata de un enfoque Multicosmos.

En 1970, los físicos I.D. Novikov y Andreï Sakharov exponen los fundamentos de "un modelo de universo constituido por una infinidad de capas de pares de cosmos/anticosmos". El universo será constituido de múltiples pares de "capas" de cosmos. El modelo describe una conexión de dos espacios, por capas de hundimiento. Una secuencia infinita de capas conectadas en pares, estableciendo así la estructura general del universo. Pero, para Sakharov, los pares de capas son sucesivas en el tiempo, mientras que para los Ummitas las "capas son simultáneas".

La idea de "un modelo Multi-cosmos terrestre comparable al modelo Multi-cosmos Ummita", es explicado en 1990 por la física-cosmóloga Andreï Dmitrievitch Linde que publica la hipótesis que posiblemente existía una «espuma» de universos, cada uno de los cuales había tenido su Big Bang con sus propias leyes y constantes físicas, la nuestra era uno de los que, por casualidad, tenía parámetros para la aparición de la vida. La principal diferencia está en que Andrei Linde piensa que los Multi-cosmos se forman constantemente, de manera continua mientras que en el modelo Ummita todos ellos -casi una infinidad- son inicializados al mismo tiempo y luego continúan su vida...

Los primero modelos cosmológicos completos llamados "«Branas» (modelo de Multi-cosmos burbuja) de nuevo al trabajo de Lisa Randall y Raman Sundrum en 1999, inspirado en el trabajo de Arkhani-Hamed, Dimopoulos y Dvali en 1998. En 1998, el físico Jean-Pierre Petit describe detalladamente en su cuenta personal la cosmología ummita para presentar un modelo de cosmos-anticosmos. Téngase en cuenta que en 2010, Stephen Hawking hará en «The Grand Design» una síntesis completa que integrará M-teorías y 'multiverso' en el sentido de la cosmología ummita.

El modelo Multicosmos Ummita comenzó a ser publicado en España en 1966 y contiene además de ' otros conceptos, próximos a las «Cadenas», concepto que no será claramente desarrollado en 1974 por John Schwarz y Joël Scherk, e independientemente por Tamiaki Yoneya, quienes estudiaron modelos de vibración de cuerdas que describían el bosones, y descubrieron que sus propiedades exactamente correspondían a las del gravitón. Tengamos en cuenta que la cosmología llamada "ummita", por efecto utiliza a los conceptos de dimensiones angulares. Este tipo de cosmología es completamente revolucionaria y hoy ningún modelo cosmológico terrestre desarrolla este tipo de concepto.

En esta obra, utilizo el término Universo para designar el conjunto del Cosmos para respetar el vocabulario inicial de los documentos ummitas. Se desarrollará más adelante, los modelos Multiverso en el sentido de Multi-universo sinónimo del término Multi-cosmos utilizado aquí.

El modelo cosmológico Ummita no se limita a la descripción de un Multi-cosmos. Incluye otras entidades cosmológicas desconocidas por la ciencia terrestre y que presentaremos en esta obra.

EL MODELO COSMOLÓGICO SIMPLIFICADO

En primer lugar, he aquí de manera vulgarizada y muy simplificada, las principales entidades cosmológicas del modelo Ummita, son las siguientes:

- WOA es una entidad cosmológica generadora de «TODO». Habitualmente denominada DIOS en las metafísicas terrestres. Efectivamente de una manera simple podemos decir que crea todo o creó todo. Esta entidad WOA es atemporal y WOA "ESTÁ". Es decir que esta entidad 'existe', pero de manera simple no tiene ni masa, ni volumen... Posiblemente podamos decir que se trata de un pensamiento generador de TODO y del TODO... Veremos en capítulos posteriores la ontología de esta entidad cosmológica para los que la palabra Dios es lo más simple. Ya tendremos en cuenta que WOA es ya una entidad cósmica trascendente.

- WOA crea de manera concomitante otra entidad transcendental, lo real Absoluto denominada AIIODII, de donde emergerán entidades cosmológicas materiales.

- El cosmos ' WAAM-UU ' está en el origen de Meta-Big-Bang generador de todos los demás cosmos del Universo. La cosmología contemporánea conoce sólo el Big-Bang propio de nuestro cosmos y visto desdel interior de nuestro cosmos. El WAAM-UU es también un ' Meta-Meta-Cerebro '. Por qué Meta-Meta ? Debido a que es un cosmos 'Súper-Cerebro-Cósmico «, que a su vez contiene una multitud de' Meta-Cerebros 'que a su vez impulsarán los sistemas de los seres vivos de innumerables planetas de muy numerosos cosmos. Por lo que, el cosmos llamado ' WAAM-UU ' actúa y pilota la casi infinidad de cosmos que constituyen el Multicosmos. Este concepto no es conocido sobre la Tierra y está muy alejado de la arcaica idea de Gaïa.

- El concepto de multi-cosmos está cerca del modelo de Andrei Dmitrievich Linde o Lisa Randall y Raman Sundrum, se denomina WAAM-WAAM y cada cosmos por el término WAAM. Veremos el significado exacto de estas palabras con su análisis semántico. El Multi-cosmos WAAM-WAAM se compone de un número casi infinito de pares de cosmos.

- Cada cosmos está asociado a un anticosmos. Este concepto de anticosmos no es conocido por los cosmólogos terrestres, sólo Andreï Sakharov rozó la idea, sin desarrollarla. los Ummitas hablan de un cosmos WAAM y un anticosmos UWAAM. El Big Bang de cada par de anti-Cosmos Cosmos les da valores de los parámetros estructurales específicos propios, incluyendo C, el límite de velocidad de la luz. Cada par de cosmos-anticosmos, WAAM y UWAAM, continúa su vida independientemente de otros, con su propio ciclo de Big-Bang / Big-Crunch con arreglo a sus parámetros estructurales específicos.

• Aquí para definir las principales entidades cosmológicas. Son necesariamente conocidas por todas las exocivilizaciones que nos visitan y a priori de todas las exocivilizaciones viajeras del cosmos...

• Pero nuevamente hay otras entidades cosmológicas que presentaremos en los capítulos siguientes, algunas totalmente desconocidos para los terrestres. Aquí el esquema de síntesis de esta primera etapa:

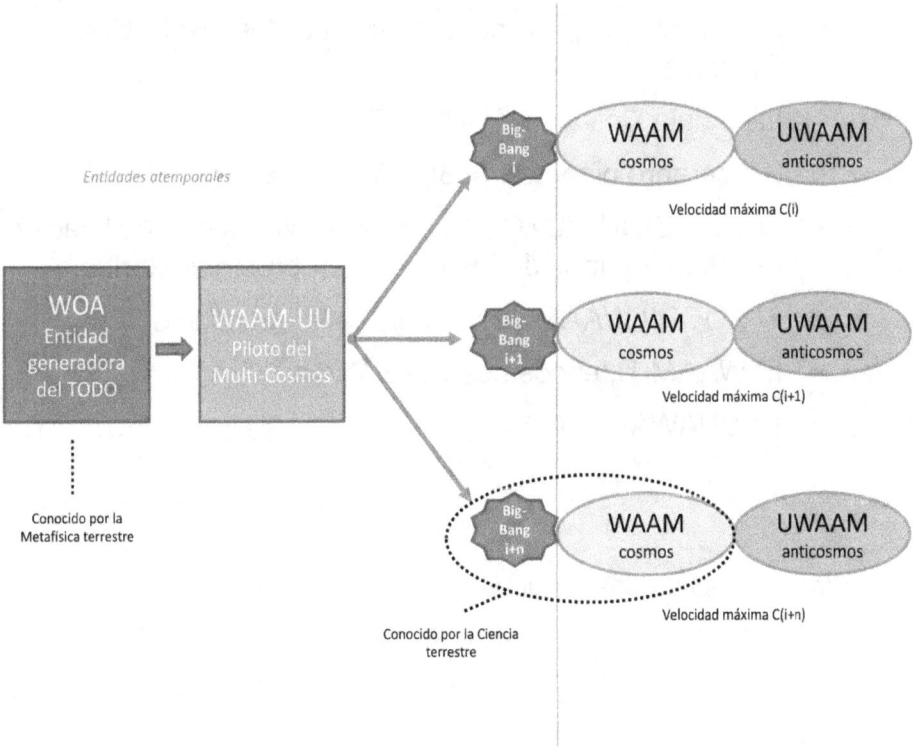

EL MODELO COSMOLÓGICO GENERAL

Vamos a describir ahora el modelo con todas sus entidades y a comenzar por interesarnos más detalladamente por las entidades cosmológicas transcendentales, luego por los objetos cosmológicos no transcendentales que han sido presentados a veces por los Metafísicos terrestres, para intentar comprender sus funciones en el Universo.

Luego, en los capítulos siguientes, trataremos los nuevos conceptos físicos asociados con este modelo cosmológico.

A continuación, el esquema sistémico modelo cosmológico general (flujo y sistemas) de representación:

- WOA, ' DIOS '

- AIIODII , lo ' Real Absoluto '

- El WAAM-UU, el contenedor de los Meta-Cerebros Cósmico

- La Célula Cósmica GUU DOEE

- El ' cerebro planetario ' BUUAWE BIAEEI

- Los GOOINUU UXGIIGII, las estructuras de codificación de los arquetipos de los Meta-Cerebros planetarios

- El XOODII WAAM, la membrana inter-cosmos

- El WAAM-U, el cosmos de las'Almas '

- La BUAWA, 'El Alma'

-

Vamos a aclarar las funciones de estas entidades cosmológicas...

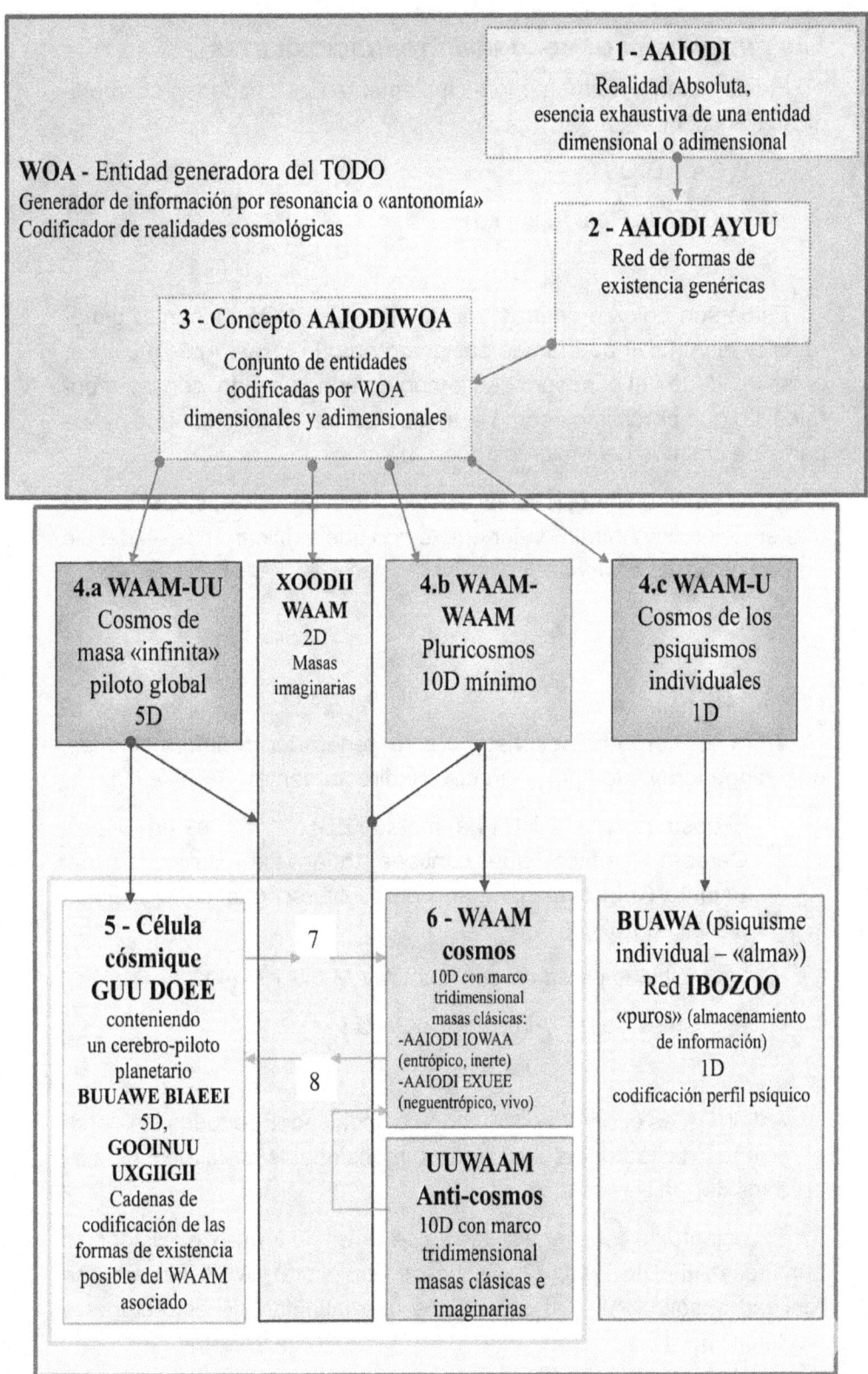

LAS ENTIDADES COSMOLÓGICAS TRANSCENDENTES

Existen atemporalmente, principalemente dos entidades cosmológicas transcendentes:

- WOA, ' DIOS '

- AIIODII, lo Real Absoluto

Estos son polos o centros adimensionales: WOA el 'centro generador' y el 'AIIODII podríamos designar como lo «Real Absoluto». Por estas entidades el concepto del tiempo no tiene sentido, son intemporales. Lo que percibimos como el tiempo se creará en cada uno de los pares de cosmos del Multi-cosmos.

Estos polos adimensionales 'existen' fuera del cosmos, es decir de manera AIOOYA AMMIE, valor ontológico que explicaremos en detalle en *La Lógica tetravalente*.

WOA, ' DIOS '

WOA es, como hemos visto, centro generador de informaciones, que «engendra» intemporal directa e indirectamente:

- El cosmos WAAM-UU (4.a) (notado BB)   que es un 'Súper-Cerebro-Cósmico' que contiene todas las estructuras del Espíritu Colectivo Planetario del Universo (atención, también clasificado BB) (5).

- los múltiples pares de cosmos WAAM-WAAM (4.b)

- el cosmos de las "Almas" 'WAAM-U (4.c).

Así, WOA es el centro cosmogónico codificador de todas las configuraciones de todas las entidades dimensionales y adimensionales posibles del Universo físico.

El conjunto de estas entidades es de la red de forma de existencias genéricas AIIODII AYUU (2). Dicho de otro modo, WOA genera una realidad absoluta AIIODII a partir de una infinidad de estructuras o modelos tipo

Esta realidad absoluta AIIODII 'cristalizada' permanece inaccesible de manera exhaustiva para los humanos (cualesquiera que sean no importa en qué cosmos), será rechazada en los diferentes cosmos del Universo, e interpretada de manera diferente por los diferentes humanos de estos cosmos, como lo son las sombras de la alegoría de la caverna de Platón.

WOA coexiste con AIIODII y no es trascendente.

WOA crea por lo tanto esta realidad absoluta "a su imagen" se podría decir, y ésta se hace independiente. Luego es interpretada por cada humanidad (y designada por la palabra AIIODI con un única "I" al fin, por nuestros amigos de UMMO).

'Entonces', WOA en resonancia con el 'Súper-Cerebro-Cósmico' 'el cosmos WAAM-UU (el 'Meta-Meta-Cerebro', la BB global) (4.a).

En WOA el centro de información es estático, mientras que en el Universo múltiple, el WAAM B.B. entra en resonancia con WOA, la información es dinámica.

Para ello les advertimos que la comparación con dos cuerdas de violín es solamente de orden didáctico y metafórico, porque en las cuerdas de violín el efecto de resonancia se manifiesta por una dinámica simultánea.

WOA modela así las entidades cosmológicas por el intermediario del 'Súper-Cerebro-Cósmico' el cosmos WAAM-UU (4.a).

Las ondas estacionarias, es decir constantes, pero de fases distintas corresponden a las dimensiones creadas por WOA. En nuestra estructura de tres dimensiones, que forman los nodos y crestas que nuestros sentidos interpretan respectivamente como masas y vacíos.

D45: Pero olvide que consideramos el cosmos como un sistema deca-dimensional, WOA genera una serie infinita de paquetes de ondas (las funciones sinusoidales) de frecuencias, amplitud y fases diferentes. El ESPACIO se ve retorcido, provocando una serie de olas estacionarias y nodos que se reflejan en la infinidad del WAAM. Estas ondas estacionarias son solamente los pliegues del continuo espacio-tiempo que llamamos MASAS (Galaxias, Gas, animales, etc.). Esto explica la confusión de los científicos terrestres cuando observan la aparente contradicción de que un electrón es a la vez corpúsculo (masa) y onda: se trata de una confusión ingenua.

Por lo tanto, WOA crea ondas estacionarias, es decir constantes, cada paquete de ondas constituye una dimensión. Estas ondas estacionarias, o más bien estas funciones vibratorias sinusoidales, no locales, se alinean con el cosmos y se forman en el seno del substrato universal de los IBOSDSOO, concepto cercano a las cadenas, que presentamos en trabajos anteriores y que detallaremos en este libro. Igualmente, la idea de la dimensión aquí es muy diferente del sentido actual. Será definida por el término OAWOO. Tenga en cuenta que:

WOA continúa creando materia dentro de cada Cosmos (D41-11).

Desarrollaremos más estas explicaciones en el capítulo sobre *el sustrato universal IBOSDSOO*.

AIIODII, Lo real Absoluto

El AIIODII (1) es la realidad absoluta, en el sentido del mito de la caverna de Platón donde sólo las sombras se nos aparecen. Esta realidad absoluta es autónoma, inaccesible y ACTO de WOA. Es una realidad que se esconde tras nuestra visión intelectual distorsionante de las cosas...

En términos existencialistas sartreanos, AIIODII es la esencia exhaustiva de una entidad. Esta entidad puede ser dimensional o adimensional. En otras palabras, es la esencia de la realidad percibida de una entidad dimensional o adimensional.

AIIODII genera todas las ideas - es decir, las formas de realidades percibidas - de WOA que no le son incompatibles y por lo tanto contiene una infinidad de gammas, categorías, es decir, una red de formas de existencias genéricas denominada AIIODII AYUU (2).

LA CREACIÓN DE LAS POTENCIALIDADES DEL REAL

Las entidades cosmológicas trascendentales crean las potencialidades de lo real absoluto.

Es necesario diferenciar estas entidades cosmológicas trascendentales creadas y que contienen las potencialidades de lo Real Absoluto del Multi-cosmos, y el Multi-cosmos WAAM-WAAM propiamente dicho, quien realiza físicamente estas potencialidades.

Las entidades cosmológicas trascendentales forman parte de la Metafísica, el Multi-cosmos WAAM-WAAM del mundo de la física.

Aquí, la explicación dada en los documentos de nuestros amigos UMMO:

WOA (Dios) crea WAAM-WAAM (el Pluricosmos) de una sola vez, en todas sus potencialidades (casi infinitas).

Los EESSEEOEMMII (los seres pensantes) de WAAM-WAAM concretan algunas de las posibilidades.

Cada humanidad pensante, como una parte única de los EESSEEOEMMII cambia AIIODII (el conjunto de las realidades potenciales) interpretando una AIIODI (las posibles realidades).

Cada humanidad pensante realiza su AIIODI (REALIDAD) modulando AIIODII (el marco de las potencialidades realizables). Modifica AIIODII e informa WOA.

Cada humanidad pensante modifica AIIODII e informa WOA.

Esta información se transmite y se capta por el intermediario de BUAWA BIAEII (alma planetaria/Meta-cerebro) asociado a cada humanidad planetaria.

Así el WAAM-WAAM se organiza a medida que es engendrado por WOA. Este proceso es a la vez simultáneo e infinito.

El tiempo no toma ningún lugar no es más que un interpretación particular de cada de AIIODI.

Hay una aportación de información suplementaria sobre una potencialidad realizada de modo experimental por una humanidad planetaria.

Por ejemplo:

WOA genera la potencialidad de disfrutar del sabor de los alimentos.

WOA genera la potencialidad de la fruta naranja.

Las dos potencialidades son realizadas en el planeta Tierra.

Cada terrestre experimenta su apreciación del sabor de una naranja y transmite esta información a BOUAWA BIAEII (alma planetaria / Meta-cerebro).

BOUAWA BIAII informa WOA sobre la apreciación global del sabor de la fruta naranja que WOA no puede experimentar.

WOA refuerza la potencialidad de la fruta naranja, ya que su sabor es globalmente apreciado por los OEMMII (humanos) que pueden probarlo.

El carácter no infinito de las potencialidades de WAAM-WAAM se basa en la sola conjetura comprobable por todo observador, que ni el cero matemático, ni su inverso (infinito matemático) existen en absoluto en el marco físico.

Vemos que lo real absoluto interpretado por la humanidad, el AIIODI, se crea constantemente de forma dinámica, mientras que el conjunto de las potencialidades es un depósito casi infinito, pero estático. Como muchos pensadores e investigadores han anticipado a lo largo de los siglos, el mundo real se crea de acuerdo con la idea que tenemos de él.

Por extraño que pueda parecer, podemos, colectivamente, cambiar la evolución de nuestra realidad pensando de manera diferente sobre nuestro futuro... Para esto, es necesario que el peso de nuestros pensamientos converja hacia la realidad deseada de una manera suficiente... Por ejemplo, si una mayoría de los terrícolas pesaran realizar un nuevo gobierno mundial justo y ético, esta potencialidad se realizaría necesariamente... (Trataremos esto en *PRESENCIA 4 - Hacia un nuevo mundo... con las Exocivilizaciones*).

LAS OTRAS ENTIDADES COSMOLÓGICAS

Las entidades cosmológicas trascendentales generan un conjunto de otras entidades cosmológicas. Algunas son conocidas de nosotros, otras presentidas, y otras nos son totalmente desconocidas:

- El WAAM-UU, el contenedor de los Meta-cerebros cósmicos

- La célula cósmica GUU DOEE

- El cerebro planetario BUUAWE BIAEEI

- El GOOINUU UXGIIGII, estructuras de codificación de los arquetipos planetarios de los Meta-cerebros planetarios

- El XOODII WAAM, el cinturón de la membrana intercósmica.

- El WAAM-U, el cosmos de las "Almas"

- El BUAWA, el "Alma"

WAAM-UU, el contenedor de los Meta-cerebros cósmicos

De una manera simple y global, el cosmos WAAM-UU contiene todos los Meta-cerebros planetarios BUUAWE BIAEEI (5) todo el cosmos WAAM (6).

WAAM-UU también distorsiona los otros cosmos, creando las singularidades de masas, las galaxias y los astros...

El plan cósmico B.B. [WAAM-UU] contiene miles de millones de B.B. (meta-cerebros planetarios) correspondientes a humanidades. Es el B. B. (el Meta-cerebro planetario) de la humanidad de la Tierra que, en conexión con su cerebro, procesa la información recibida, engendrando la concepción de las cosas.

Debido a que el lenguaje de los Ummitas se basa en la funcionalidad de la palabra, hay palabras que son funcionalmente, homónimas, porque los dos objetos tienen la misma función... casi. Así, el WAAM-UU, todos los BIAEEI BUUAWE, cada BIAEEI BUUAWE planetario individuo, pueden utilizar el mismo término de BB.

Esto puede causar cierta confusión vamos a aclarar.

```
El plano cósmico BB [WAAM-UU] contiene miles de
millones de BB que corresponden a humanidades. Este
es el BB de la humanidad de la Tierra, en relación con
el cerebro procesa la información recibida, generando
el diseño de las cosas.
```

Este plan cósmico [WAAM-UU] o BB se subdivide en otras psiques BB o universales, cada uno correspondiente a una humanidad planetaria (La confusión que se pudieran observar simplemente lo que llamamos BB [BUAUEE BIAEEII] no sólo el alma colectiva de UMMO o de la tierra, sino también el plan cósmico [es decir, los multiuniversos] que contiene todas las diferentes redes sociales BB que pueblan nuestro universo tetradimensional.

En detalle, WAAM-UU contiene unas casi infinitas de células cósmicas GUU DOEE. Estas contienen a sí mismas cada un BUUAWE BIAEEI planeta (un Meta-Cerebro).

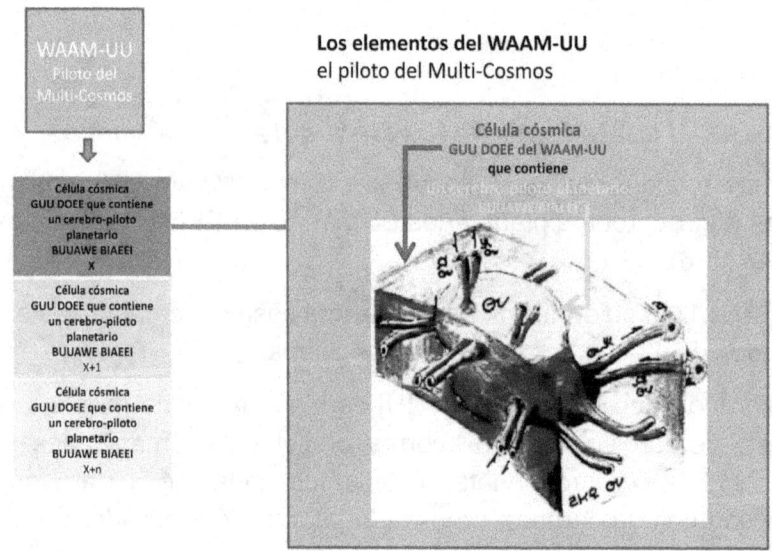

Los elementos del WAAM-UU
el piloto del Multi-Cosmos

La célula cósmica GUUDOEE

La célula cósmica llamada GUU DOEE contiene un meta-cerebro planetario BUUAWE BIAEEI.

La palabra GUU DOEE significa :

GUU = la estructura tiene una dependencia dinámica

= Estructura hermética

DOEE = la forma de la entidad tiene un modelo

= Forma Modelada

Por lo tanto la traducción de GUU DOEE: forma estructura hermética modelada

```
D357: El BB [WAAM-UU] contiene GUU DOEE [contornos
o células]. Una imagen para entender nos, seria las
galaxias de nuestro universo, excepto que en el BB
no hay configuraciones de polvo nebular y el sol, pero
contornos o células como piezas de cinco dimensiones.
En otras palabras: este plan cósmico [WAAM-UU] o BB
se subdivide en otros BB o psique universales [en GUU
DOEE]
```

El Meta-Cerebro planetario BUUAWE BIAEEI

Los conceptos primera formalizados que se acercan al concepto de Meta-Cerebro planetario aparecen a principios del siglo XX. En 1906, el psiquiatra suizo Carl Jung entiende que la mente humana no se limita al cráneo. Es necesariamente una provisión de información externa. Esta información parece ser los principales perfiles de los valores culturales, el conocimiento universal. Esto deja pensar a Jung de que existe una estructura informativa exógena al ser humano, que proporciona arquetipos en el nivel profundo de un inconsciente colectivo compartido por toda la raza humana. Por desgracia, esta idea no se desarrollará por otras disciplinas científicas, y en este caso será totalmente ignorado por los biólogos...

En 1936, Vladimir Vernadsky desarrolló el concepto de noosfera, o esfera del pensamiento, en un modelo de sucesión de las fases de desarrollo de la Tierra que interactúan en cinco capas diferentes:

- litosfera, núcleo de roca y agua;

- biosfera constituido por la vida;

- la atmósfera, envoltura gaseosa que constituye el aire;

- la tecnosfera que resulta de la actividad humana;

- la noosfera, o esfera del pensamiento.

Al igual que la aparición de la vida transformó fundamentalmente la geosfera, la aparición de la cognición humana transforma fundamentalmente la biosfera, la noosfera de Vernadsky emerge cuando la humanidad a través del dominio de los procesos nucleares, comienza a crear recursos la transmutación delementos...!

Al mismo tiempo, en 1932 en la *Cristología y el desarrollo*, Pierre Teilhard de Chardin habla de la esfera del pensamiento humano. Para él, el fenómeno humano debe considerarse como constitutivo - en algún momento – de un paso evolutivo que conduce a la esfera del pensamiento humano, que prepara el advenimiento de la figura llamada el Cristo Cósmico. El punto Ω o Punto Omega es el centro focal de la evolución. El Omega, de alguna manera seria un pole de atracción, en juego a nivel individual, tanto como colectivo.

En 1970, James Lovelock desarrolló la tesis de que la Tierra sería un sistema fisiológico dinámico que incluye la biosfera y ha mantenido nuestro planeta durante más de tres mil millones de años, en armonía con la vida. Todos los seres vivos en la Tierra serían como un gran superorganismo llamado Gaia que se da cuenta de la autorregulación de sus componentes para promover la vida.

Durante varias décadas, las propiedades de la psicometría o retrocognición han sido utilizadas con cierto éxito por los arqueólogos. Estas propiedades o habilidades de algunas personas para ver en el pasado, médiums como Gerard Croiset, Eillen Garret, Hella Hammid, George Mc Mullen, etc. hicieron descripciones extremadamente precisas de sitios antiguos y permitió múltiples descubrimientos arqueológicos. Una gran cantidad de casos son reportados por Stephan A. Schwartz en *The Secret Vaults of Time* [Nueva York, Grossel & Bunlap, 1978], [Trad. Las Cavernas Secretas del Tiempo: Psychic Archaeology, Laffont, 1980].

La mayoría de los teólogos, de todas las religiones, en todo momento, observarán con relevancia los fenómenos de NDE — Near Death Experience — descritos por fallecidos resucitados. Como lo discutiremos en detalle en el capítulo sobre las NDE, este fenómeno prueba la existencia de un Más Allá. Muy lógicamente, estos teólogos concluyen la existencia de Dios. Obviamente, no es la entidad trascendente a la que se hace referencia aquí como WOA. Es simplemente este objeto cosmológico, físico aunque localizado en un otro cosmos, el Meta-Cerebro planetario BUUAWE BIAEEI, que es desconocido para los terrícolas.

Bajo la influencia de la obra del neurofisiólogo de la Universidad de Stanford, Karl Pribram, y sus propios resultados del modelo hológrafico, el físico David Bohm se acercará a la existencia de inconsciente colectivo común a toda la humanidad: "Al más profundo de la humanidad es una y la misma psique…"

Sin embargo, también anclado en sus convicciones y sin visión cosmogónica, no percibirá la posibilidad de que pueda ser un objeto cosmológico físico y ubicado en otro cosmos...

El Meta-Cerebro planetario BUUAWE BIAEEI contiene toda la información que todos los seres vivos han transmitido a él desdel principio del tiempo, concretamente desde que nuestro Meta-Cerebro planetario BUUAWE BIAEEI está conectado a la Tierra.

Por tanto, estructuras de arquetipos codificados [GOOINUU UXGIIGII] de todos los seres vivos del planeta. Él pilota de manera coordinada la co-evolución de los seres vivos.

Si es necesario, él podría decidir eliminar una plaga en el funcionamiento de los ecosistemas vitales del planeta. Por ejemplo, si los seres humanos, que BB sólo tiene un control parcial, se ponían culturalmente como un peligro mortal para todas las demás especies vivas, mientras BB eliminaría esta plaga...

Cada BUUAWE BIAEEI planetario [5] está vinculado a un planeta y contiene:

- patrones biológicos de los seres vivos
- ideas universales genéricas
- sentimientos colectivos
- perfiles de comportamiento gregario
- ideas, patrones morales seres superiores [OEMMII]

Cada célula recibe el nombre de BUUAUE BIAEI [BB] espíritu o alma colectiva. Hay tantos BB como AYUUBAAYII [redes seres planetarios] en todo el WAAM-WAAM. Existe una correspondencia biunívoca entre cada conjunto de los seres vivos en un astro frío y su correspondiente BB

La estructura de pilotaje BUUAWE BIAEEI de un astro a los seres vivos es un bucle cibernético que se puede resumir simplemente:

a) el envío de información a las entidades parcialmente autónomas

b) retroalimentación por las entidades

Este bucle cibernético tiene una dinámica permanente.

D731... los seres vivos a través de sus transductores, es decir los neurosensores receptores de los modelos de información (los órganos de los sentidos), capturan la estructura del universo.

Esta información se envía a BB, integrada y procesada en el WAAM-UU.

Quien, a su vez, genera modelos de acción en el WAAM-WAAM.

Por lo tanto cierra un bucle cibernético.

UN NUEVO PARADIGMA COSMOLÓGICO

1. Los objectos de WAAM

2. información del WAAM

3. OEMII planetario

4. información

5. ser vivo inferior

6. oeambuuaw (transmisor / receptor Cerebro-cósmico)

7. BAAYIODUU (transmisor / receptor Genómico-cósmico)

8. genoma

9. percepciones de información y los procesos mentales

10. símbolos universales, patrones de ideas

11. patrones emocionales gregarios

12. Información del entorno ecológico

13. Patrones de formas biologicas

14. BB inconsciente colectivo en el WAAM-UU

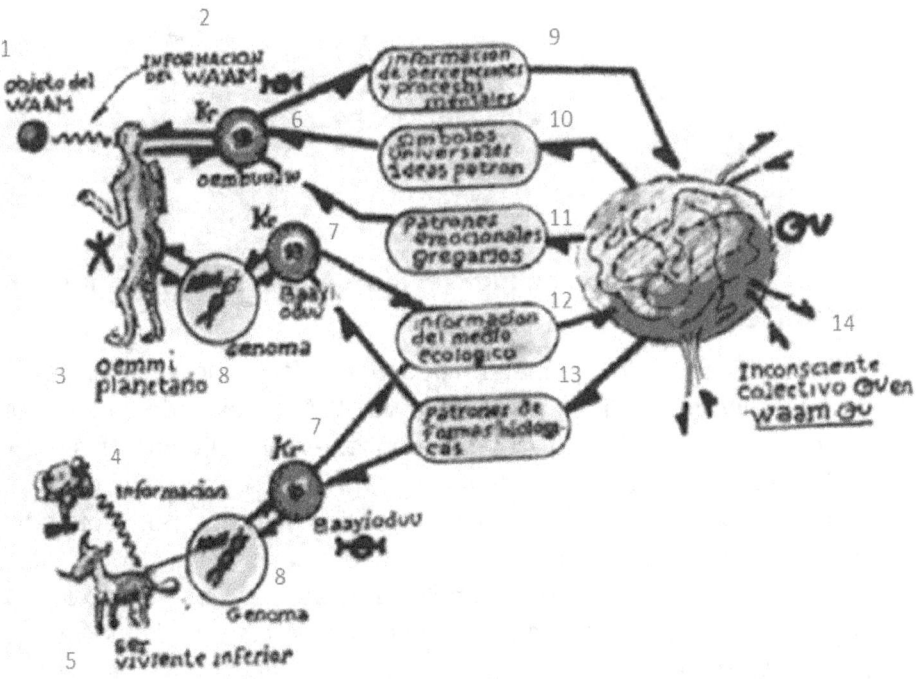

El WAAM-UU es un continuo pentadimensional con singularidades de masa (en forma filamentos con nudos), dividido en células o medios ambientes separados.

Las estructuras penta-dimensionales del GUU DOEE contienen un piloto cerebro planetario BUUAWE BIAEEI que a su vez contienen filamentos espaciales 3D y másicos (M + y —M) 2D, llamados GOOINUU UXGIIGII (5) donde circulan informaciones.

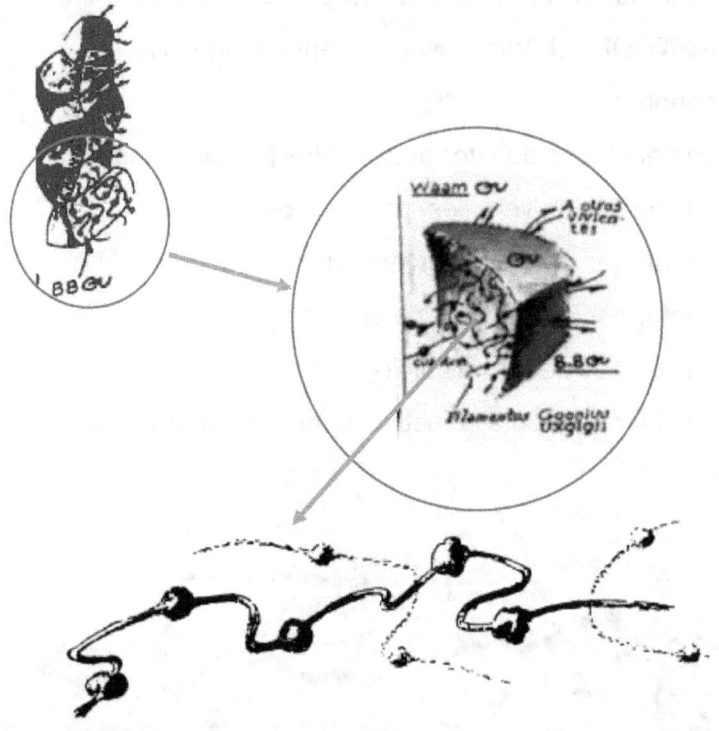

La información transmitida a los seres entrópicos inertes AAIODII IOWAA

El BIAEEI BUUAWE planetario transmite informaciones a los seres entrópicos inertes (la materia) AAIODII IOWAA, a través de un cosmos inter-capa, la XOODII WAAM (6) que contiene masas imaginarias (Mi + y - Mi) que son responsables de muchas interacciones gravitacionales que afectan las pares de cosmos (incluyendo la nuestra, por supuesto), y también para efectos de cambio extraordinarios entre el cosmos, dichos LEEIIYO WAAM. Por ejemplo, gracias a la decodificación de las palabras los Ummitas en *Presencia 2 El lenguaje y el misterio del planeta Ummo revelado*, pudimos entender lo que llamamos el "efecto trampolín" utilizado por la mayoría de naves interestelares.

La información enviada a los seres vivos neguentrópicos AAIODII EXUEE

La información enviada a los seres vivos neguentrópicos - AAIODII EXUEE - se realiza a través de dos canales:

- para todos los seres vivos, por un canal de comunicación intra-celular, la BAAYIODUU (7) (transmisor / receptor Genómico-cósmico)

- a los seres humanos, por canal de comunicación cerebral, la OEMBUAWE (transmisor / receptor cerebro-cósmico)

El canal de comunicación intracelular, BAAYIODUU está asociado con el sistema genómico (7) para formar el factor generador del vivo, BAAYIODIXAA UUDIII. (*Ver la hipótesis sobre la aparición de la Vida*).

Cada BB envía sus patrones biológicos a los seres vivos (ortogénesis) para guiar la evolución de cada Astro frío.

Los seres vivos neguentrópicos - AAIODII EXUEE - también devuelven información a su BIAEEI BUUAWE planetario (8) a través del canal de comunicación intracelular, la BAAYIODUU.

El canal cerebral de comunicación humana, la OEMBUAW recibe y devuelve la información a su BUUAWE BIAEEI planetario.

Cada BB también envía sus ideas universales, sentimientos colectivos, inducciones gregarias, patrones de ideas morales, etc. a todos los OEMMII [ser humano]

Estas informaciones se transmiten directamente a través de una Masa Imaginaria, a través del canal cerebro OEMBUAW (6).

- ¿Hay alguna manera de reconocer cuando un proceso mental o un pensamiento que procede del BB?

U. - NO. La información llega a las capas más profundas del cerebro y es muy difícil distinguir la de la información de la niñez.

Pensando, los seres vivos superiores distorsionan la realidad absoluta. Esta información se transmite directamente a través del canal cerebral del OEMBUAW y si aceptamos la definición del WAAM-WAAM en el sentido estricto, debe haber tantos WAAM como las clases de seres pensantes capaces de deformar la AAIODI.

El Aura y OEMBUAW

El periodista Michael Talbot cita en su libro *El universo es un holograma* el trabajo de Valerie Hunt Profesor de Ciencias Fisiológicas de la Universidad de California, Los Angeles. Se encontró que el campo de energía respondió más rápidamente a los estímulos que el cerebro. La conexión en paralelo de un electromiógrafo, y un electroencefalograma en sujetos revelaron un retraso neto de la segunda en la grabación de las variaciones de luz y sonido repetidos. Valerie Hunt pensó que la mente no estaba en el cerebro sino en el aura.

Nuestra hipótesis es muy diferente y más compleja. Creemos que la difusión de información que llega al OEMBUAW se hace a través de los circuitos neuronales y emisiones de frecuencias. Como veremos, probablemente a través del compuesto-relé, el bio-sintonizador, bio-tuner, GeSi2C3H3 que funciona como interfaz de receptor multifrecuencias con las pares de Criptón.

Por efecto, las ondas de propagaciones electromagnéticas y gravitacionales son más rápidas que los circuitos bioeléctricos de propagación de las neuronas.

Así, el campo de bio-frecuencias humanas, el aura, recibe informaciones de la OEMBUAW antes de los centros de procesamiento de información del cerebro, como la corteza neo-frontal, por ejemplo...

La frecuencia de bio-campo humano, la Aura, es cronológicamente la primera informada de los flujos de BB y BUAWA. Está en conexión casi directa con estos objetos cosmológicos.

Esto será importante en el proceso de la muerte del ser humano, la Aura podrá permanecer conectada con el Meta-cerebro BB y / o el alma BUAWA.

Para resumirnos, siguiendo el esquema sistémico del modelo cosmológico general, podríamos decir que BUUAWE BIAEEI planetario son sistemas de pilotaje de los astros fríos, que los seres vivos son los sensores del sistema operativo, que transmiten la información al sistema de control. Se verifica la ley de Shannon, el nivel de complejidad del sistema de pilotaje es mayor que el sistema operativo.

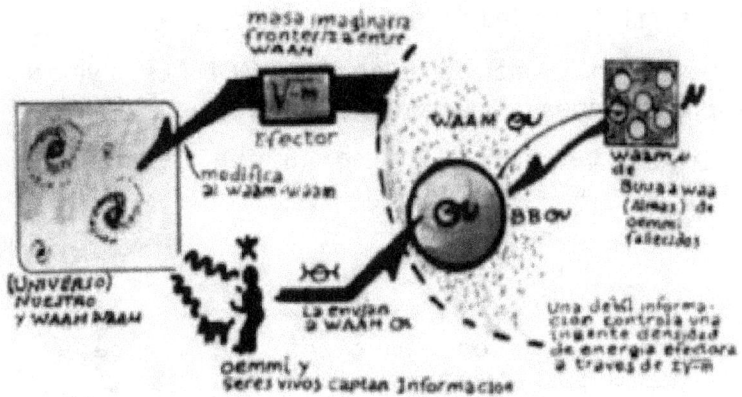

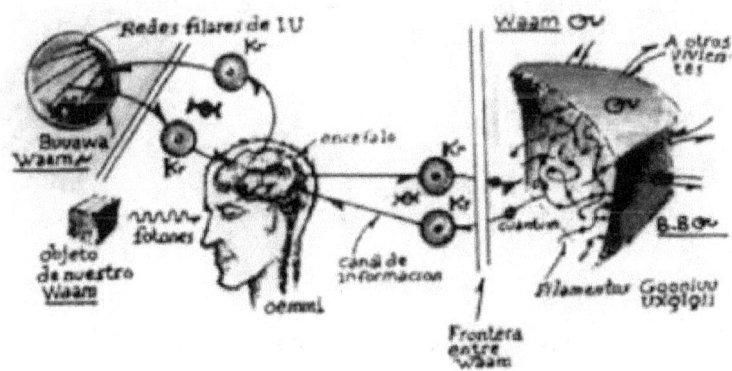

XOODII WAAM, el cinturón inter-cósmico

Se puede decir de una manera simple que el XOODII WAAM es el cinturón inter-cósmico del multi-cosmos. Este cosmos XOODII WAAM ayuda a vincular las entidades cosmológicas de diferente naturaleza.

El XOODII es un espacio para 2 dimensiones angulares OAWOO. Una capa de retransmisión en el que las masas normales, OVNIS, por ejemplo, pueden "rebotar" por generación de un efecto LEIYO llamamos "efecto trampolín" en *Presencia 1*, que se interpreta como un efecto anti-gravitacional en el paradigma de la Tierra de los siglos XX - XXI. Pero es algo totalmente distinto, desconocido de la ciencia civil. (por supuesto conocido y usado en los Black Programs)

Este XOODII transmite múltiples efectos LEIYO entre las diferentes entidades cosmológicas de naturaleza distinta. Transmite los efectos gravitacionales de las masas de las pares cosmos-anticosmos.

Explicando de esta manera la materia oscura y la energía oscura, las variaciones en la velocidad de la expansión cósmica...

Parece que una característica de este XOODII es la velocidad de las masas imaginarias (masas sin volumen).

Una propiedad de esta masa es que se puede viajar a velocidades más altas que un fotón.

Una masa de una tal partícula fluya en el tiempo a la inversa, y su posición estable o energía mínima es de velocidad infinita.

Una propiedad de esta masa es que se puede viajar a velocidades más altas que un fotón.

Una masa de una tal partícula fluya en el tiempo a la inversa, y su posición estable o energía mínima es de velocidad infinita.

La red de IBOZSOO Uhu aglutina todo el Cosmos, actúa como un cinturón de transmisión de potencia entre ellos. Cuando √ - M se mueve a velocidades bajas, las masas imaginarias se manifiestan en uno de los 2 cosmos gemelos, pero en realidad siempre opera entre los 2 cosmos.

- ¿Por qué no hay seres vivos de masa imaginaria?

U - Tiempo fluiría en la dirección opuesta. Si había seres en masa imaginaria, la memoria sería el futuro. Sería absurdo, el tiempo fluiría hacia atrás, por lo que este sería fabricar el pasado.

En el cosmos, como en el anti-cosmos el tiempo resulta de la orientación de los ejes de la estructura de tres dimensiones espacial. El tiempo está relacionado con la velocidad de C en esta configuración tridimensional.

En la XOODII, la velocidad es entre C y el infinito. En otras palabras, un objeto hipotético en el XOODII se movería más rápido que el límite de la velocidad de la luz C de nuestro cosmos, el objeto se movería más rápido que el tiempo de nuestro cosmos. Así, este objeto vería tiempo ir atrás...

WAAM-U, el cosmos de las Almas

WAAM-U es el Cosmos de los psiquismos individuales BUAWA. En la Metafísica en la tierra diríamos: el cosmos de las almas, que está totalmente distinto del espíritu colectivo que es similar al BUUAWE BIAEEl planetario.

BUAWA, el Alma

La entidad cosmológica BUAWA se llama alma en la Metafísica de la tierra. Esta es una entidad compleja.

En principio, sabemos que todos los organismos vivos, un alga, una bacteria o una jirafa de la Tierra, cuando se genera, tiene un BUUAUUA (alma individual) (B) en esto distante cosmos. Esta alma es estéril. Su red de IBOZSOO UHUU no es capaz de codificar cualquier información porque no hay ningún enlace que se une al cuerpo que nació de un astro fría. Sólo OEMMII (humano) sintetiza al momento de la fusión cromosoma, un conjunto de átomos de Criptón que por un efecto que llamamos efecto membrana o frontera LEIYO, permite la comunicación entre dos Cosmos tan distintos.

Cuando nace el ser humano, es decir: no en el momento del parto, pero cuando los dos gametos masculinos y femeninos mesclan su carga genética, crece en el Universo distante una célula gigante IBOZSOO UHUU (en realidad una compleja red de estas partículas, formado por grandes cadenas de relaciones angulares). Estas grandes cadenas, a su vez forman un sustrato extendido o matriz donde se engramara toda la información de nuestras vidas en un sector de la red, mientras que el restante codifica todo un programa de instrucciones que conforman cada tetradimensional OEMII.

El BUUAWEA no tiene memoria, no es capaz de sentir o percibir. No puede, por ejemplo, moverse, sentir placer o dolor.

... genera ideas, es capaz de comprender los mensajes que le lleva el OEMBUAW y también, a través de él que es capaz de actuar y controlar OEMII (cuerpo).

Las ideas generadas, conocimientos adquiridos, el control del cuerpo no se da cuenta de una manera secuencial O EN FLUJO CONTINUO EN TIEMPO.

PUEDE CAMBIAR UNA VEZ POR TODAS LA FORMA DE OEMBUUAOEMII (HOMBRE-FISICO: espacio-tiempo).

... BUUAWEA tiene la facultad de modelar el comportamiento del cuerpo a lo largo del tiempo, de una vez por todas.

El alma no piensa. PIENSA el cerebro. El alma almacena los datos y manda por la inter acción entre las secuencias de I.U y redes neuronales corticales, el comportamiento espacial-temporal del organismo humano (VOLONDAD)

Para resumir, el BUAWA Alma contiene dos áreas.

La primera región es un sector de una red pura de IBOZOO UU que tiene una función de almacenamiento de información. Esta zona está formada por grandes cadenas de relaciones angulares. Estas grandes cadenas, a su vez forman un sustrato extendido o matriz donde engramara toda la información de nuestras vidas.

La segunda zona de la red pura de IBOZOO UU, es una zona de conformación psíquica que se realiza una vez por todas en su integridad. Esta área codifica todo un programa de instrucciones que conforman cada OEMII (sólo el hombre tomó en su única tamaño neuronal: OEMII + BUAWA = OEMMII)

Podemos profundizar en la comprensión de esta entidad por el análisis semántico de la palabra BUAWA (*ver detalle Presencia 2*).

Nuestra transcripción de BUAWA:

- La interconexión depende del movimiento que genera un desplazamiento

- La interconexión depende del movimiento (de un electrón en la cadena de átomos de criptón a OEMBUAW) que genera un desplazamiento (un acto de voluntad).

-

Simplificación:

- La interconexión depende de la acción de movimiento generador

- la interconexión generadora

En conclusión, BUAWA es el generador de la voluntad, la conducta del cuerpo humano. Contiene dos áreas :

- BUUAWA IMMI es la conciencia global de todas las historias reales vividas y a vivir por el OEMMII (el ser humano). La primera zona es una zona de una red pura IBOZOO UU tiene una función de almacenamiento de información que registrará toda la información de nuestras vidas.

- La ESEE OA es la conciencia del momento presente. La segunda zona de pura red IBOZOO UU, es una zona de conformación psíquica que se realiza una vez por todas y en su integridad, pero sólo logra la conciencia al momento presente. Esta área codifica todo un programa de instrucciones que conforman cada OEMMII (el ser humano).

Esquema de síntesis

En esta etapa de su lectura, la misteriosa cobertura de este libro debe ahora ser explícito con el Meta-cerebro BB-planetario, el humano en su espacio-tiempo de 4D y su Alma BUAWA.

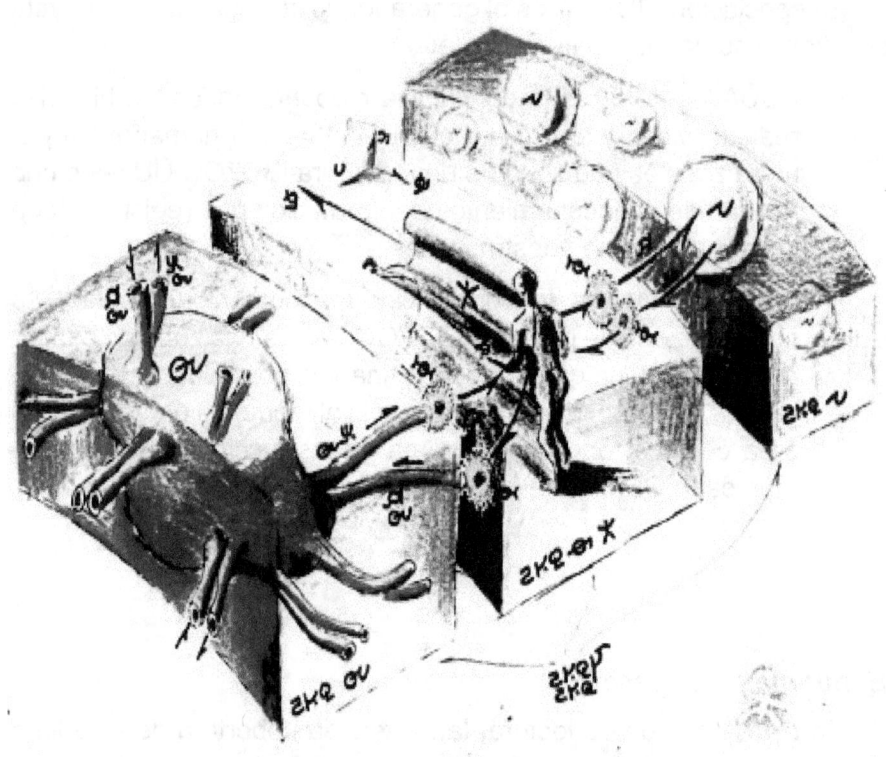

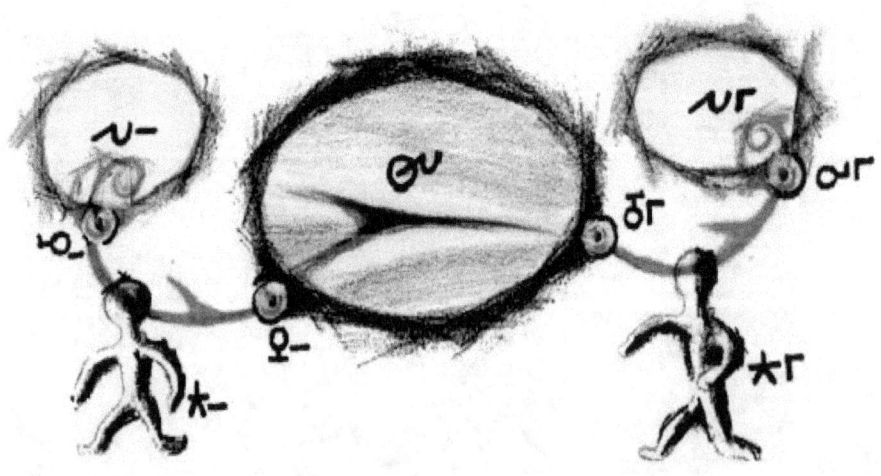

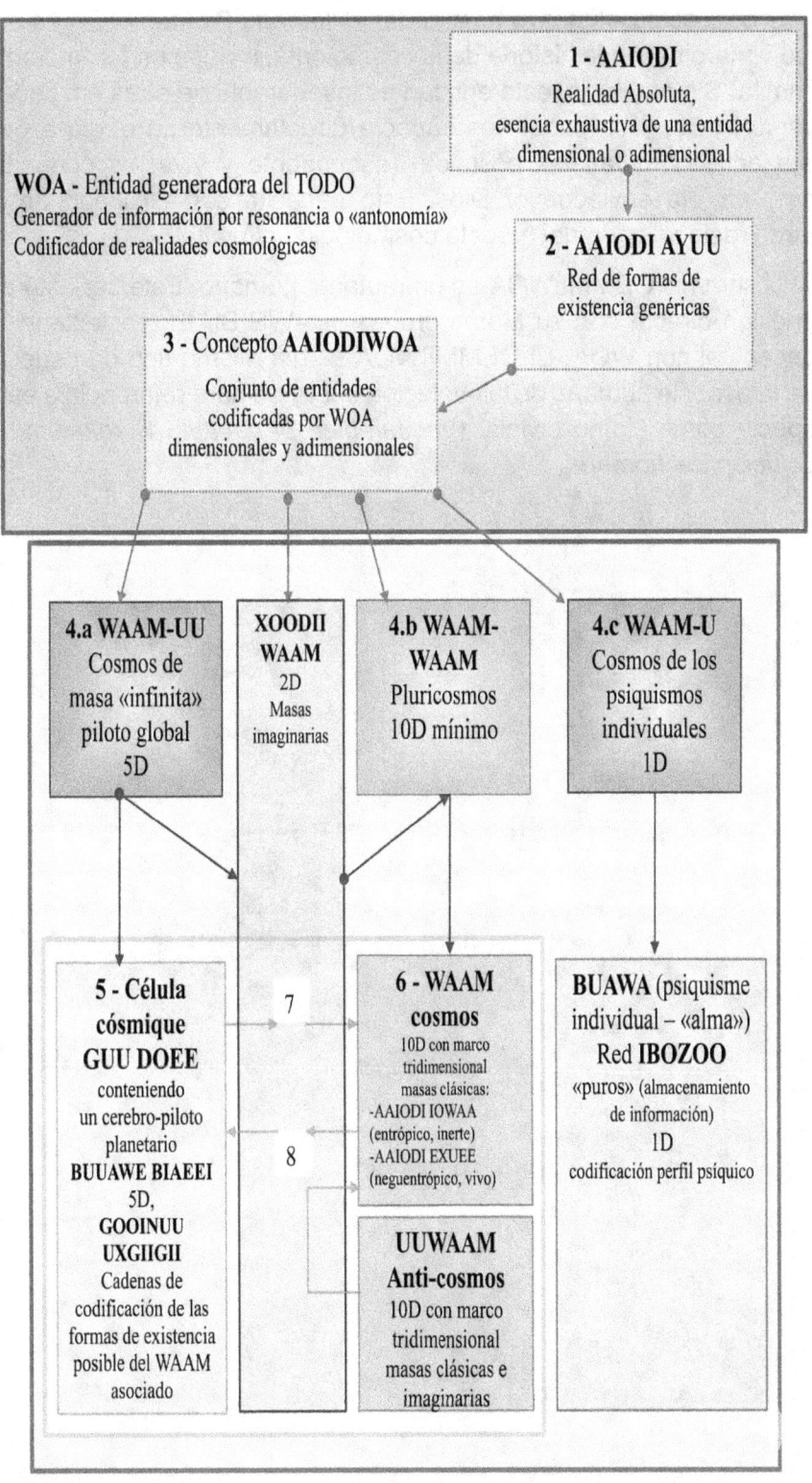

El concepto de un vivo trascendente llamado OEMMIIWOA es atípico y marginal en la historia de la cosmología, incluso en Cosmología Ummita. Sin embargo, esta entidad es inseparable de otras entidades cosmológicas y su papel nos impacta directamente en el día a día. Esta entidad metafísica cósmica trascendente y viva, es conocida como profeta enviado por Dios. Esto necesita ser explicado en el marco racionalizado del modelo cosmológico Ummita...

El ser vivo OEMMIIWOA es un mutante humano. Este ser está en conexión directa con su Meta-cerebro BUAWE BIAEI, por extensión conceptual con WOA. El OEMMIIWOA es del mismo tipo de especie que la especie humana de la evolución final y se hará referencia a esta especie como Homo divinis. (*Ver también el capítulo Surgimiento y evolución del hombre*).

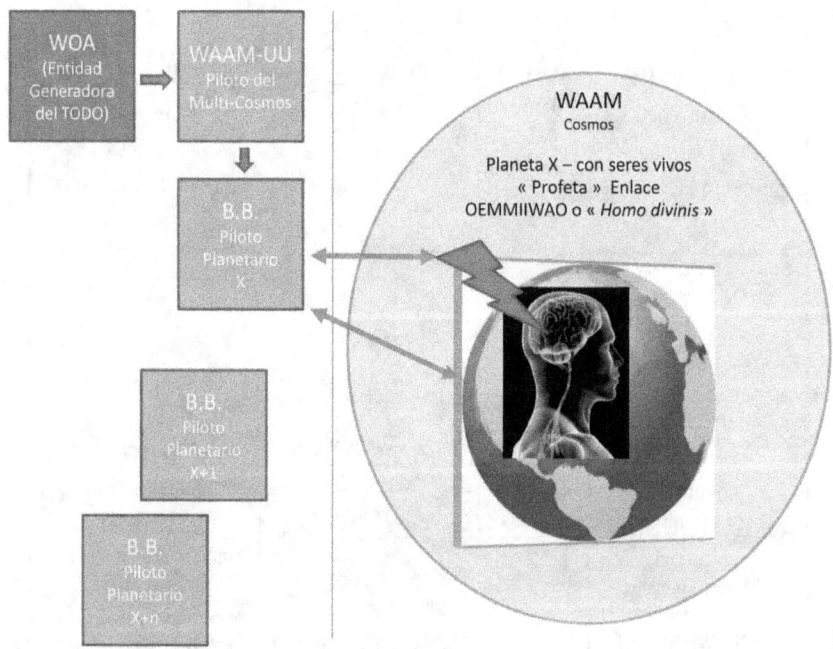

El análisis semántico de la palabra fonética oémiwoa arroja luz sobre la función del Homo divinis que es visto como un profeta en un mundo de seres humanos equivalentes a Homo sapiens.

El concepto de OEMMIIWOA, no es exactamente el concepto de profeta general que es UMMOWOA para el profeta del planeta UMMO o OAYAGAAWOA para el profeta de la Tierra. En este caso, según los documentos Ummitas, el único individuo mutante conocido de este tipo en la tierra fue Jesús Cristo.

La palabra OEMMIIWOA designa en general un ser humano con un cerebro singular con una conexión "divina". Un conjunto de cambios en el cerebro le da acceso a un nuevo canal de información directamente con la entidad cosmológica BB global.

La traducción del OEMMIIWOA en el contexto:

- (cuerpo delimitado por la envolvente del cuerpo) que tiene acceso (en el generador de entidades desplazada)
- Humano conectado con Dios

En otras palabras, la especie humana final: *Homo divinis*

D792: ESTRUCTURA cosmo-biológica: En un OEMMIIWOA convencional hay redes BAAYIODUU construidas por átomos de Criptón que ponen a su cerebro en relación con su BUAAWAA y con BUAWWEE BIAEII. Pero, además, hay una nueva red con un número, desconocido para vosotros, los átomos de Kr (Criptón) que establece una conexión informativa con el polo cósmico de WOA.

FUNCIÓN DE OEMIIWOA: En el cerebro del encéfalo que tiene una mutación, así, se negocia a un nivel inconsciente, las UUA (leyes) de WOAA. El surgimiento AYUUEAOIDII o (función) del sistema nervioso, se produce con gran intensidad en el gran plan de la naturaleza cosmológica. El cerebro es responsable de la inyección en la red social de las leyes de regulación neguentrópica, a los cerebros dotados de libre albedrío, capaz de aceptarlos o rechazarlos. La información sobre estas leyes (morales diría usted) se canaliza desdel cerebro hasta al corpus general que forma el patrimonio cultural de esa sociedad.

Así pues, OEMIIWOA se convierte en el receptor vivo patrones de contenidos de WOA, no sólo a través del BB como por el resto de los seres humanos.

La estructura cromosómica de OEMMIIWOA le impide procrear con un OEMMII ya que ambos son especies distintas. [...] este OEMMIIWOA es sin saber que su organización es distinto de otro ser humano inteligente, ya que su anatomía es muy similar.

LA COSMO-FÍSICA

Exploramos una visión cosmológica completa en la vista del infinito largo, y que debe complementarse con una visión general de la física a la vista de lo muy pequeño.

Vamos a explorar los objetos de la física relacionados con esta cosmología.

EL SUSTRATO UNIVERSAL IBOSDSOO

D117 : Nous appelons IBOOZOO UU des entités dont la suiD117 : Llamamos entidades IBOOZOO UU cuyo resultado está ligado entre sí por varias rotaciones angulares. Ellos pueden exhibir características de energía, de masa o de espacio, dependiendo de las rotaciones correspondientes a los elementos de esta secuencia.

El universo consiste en una infinita pares de cosmos, con un substrato delementos multidimensionales, bastante similares a cuerdas infinitesimales presentados en la teoría de las M-Cuerdas de Edward Witten. Estos elementos son multidimensionales que no es local, es decir, que son subcuánticos, sin ningún concepto del tiempo, sin noción de espacio, sin la noción de fuerza o energía. Y debido, tiempo, espacio, energía o fuerzas, emergen de este sustrato subcuántico no local...

Durante mucho tiempo la gente ha sospechado la existencia de este sustrato universal. Ellos tuvieran intuición, bajo la sencilla cosmología de un único cosmos. Este sustrato universal es una especie de malla virtual que ha sido interpretado por los grandes pensadores de la India como una ilusión. El mundo era una ilusión que emerge de la védica Maya.

Como se indica en la Svetasvara Upanishad: *Usted debe saber que la naturaleza es maya, ilusión, Brahma es el ilusionista y que este mundo está poblado de seres que toman parte en su presencia.*

Casi todas las culturas han sentido esto, tomaría demasiado tiempo para hacer una historia exhaustiva, pero más cerca de nosotros en el tiempo, en el siglo XVII, Leibniz, a la seguida de los pitagóricos, vio que el origen del cosmos consiste en entidades fundamentales, bautizados por él "mónadas", cada uno de los cuales se ofrece como un reflejo de todo y sólo podría ser definida por sus relaciones con otras mónadas. Cada ser es o bien un Mónada es un compuesto de mónadas.

De naturaleza, las mónadas son sustancias simples dotadas de apetencia y percepción. En cuanto a su estructura, son por unidades por su misma, analizadas en un principio activo llamado alma, forma o entelequia sustancial, y un principio pasivo, dicha masa o materia prima. En cuanto a su expresión, mónadas son cada uno un espejo vivo, representativa del universo, según su punto de vista.

En cuanto a su jerarquía, mónadas presentan grados de perfección: el grado más bajo, mónadas simples o desnudas se caracterizan por percepciones inconscientes. Que contendrá toda la información sobre todos los otros estados pero no tienen ni conciencia ni memoria... ¡Este enfoque condujo Leibniz a inventar el cálculo integral!

Unos siglos más tarde, gracias a los descubrimientos matemáticos de Fourier en 1947 el físico Dennis Gabor inventó el principio de la holografía. Este es un método de grabación de la fase y la amplitud de la onda difractada por un objeto. La difracción es el resultado de la interferencia de ondas dispersadas por cada punto e incluye un límite de resolución, la distancia o el ángulo mínimo que debe transcurrir entre dos puntos contiguos de manera que se han de discernir correctamente por un sistema de medición o la observación.

Este método de grabación permite hacer posteriormente una imagen tridimensional del objeto, el holograma. Para el registro, el código en una amplitud de la portadora y la fase que viene la luz del objeto en cuestión. Para este propósito, se hace interferir en una placa fotográfica dos rayos coherentes. El primer rayo, llamado la onda de referencia se envía directamente a la placa. La segunda llamada onda, objeto, se envía al objeto a fotografiar, que difunde esta luz hacia la placa fotográfica. La figura de interferencia así formada contiene toda la información sobre la amplitud y fase de la onda del objeto, es decir la forma y la posición del objeto en el espacio.

Este principio inspiró el modelo holográfico subcuántico del físico David Bohm en 1952, que será precursor terrestre del modelo IBODSOO.

Anteriormente, el gran físico danés Niels Bohr observó fenómenos cuánticos extraños de interconexión entre las partículas que serán llamados fenómenos de enredo más tarde cuántica. Niels Bohr pensaba que si las partículas elementales no existían antes de ser observado, pensar en ellos como objetos independientes tenía ningún sentido. Hablar de sus propiedades y características como la observación de objetos existentes dejó de tener sentido. No podía ser más desconcertante. Para Albert Einstein, Boris Podolsky y Nathan Rosen, fue incluso inaceptable y que publicó un famoso artículo Podemos tomar por completa la descripción de la realidad por la física cuántica? Explicando que no podía haber interconexión entre las partículas más rápido que la luz, que es conocida como la paradoja de Einstein-Podolsky.

Tomando en consideración las observaciones de Niels Bohr y Albert Einstein, el físico de los plasmas David Bohm considera que las partículas como los electrones tienen una existencia tangible en la ausencia de cualquier observador. Pero su conocimiento de los plasmas también le permitió asumir una realidad subyacente, un plano subcuántico aún inexplicado por la ciencia. Él llamó a este nuevo campo: potencial cuántico y le dio como a la gravedad, la propiedad teórica de ser omnipresente en el espacio. Esto le permitió entender que el plasma delectrones puede tener el comportamiento globalidades interconectadas en el sentido de Bohr. Observó que los electrones del plasma que se agrupan, a través del potencial cuántico es todo el sistema hace un movimiento coordinado más cerca de la coreografía que remolinos al azar de una multitud. Esta actividad está más cerca del funcionamiento de las diferentes partes de un organismo vivo que el montaje de las partes de una máquina. La interpretación dada por David Bohm en física cuántica sugiere que el plan subcuántico, en el campo del potencial cuántico, cualquier localización deja de existir.

Cada punto del espacio es consustancial a todos los demás y hablar de cualquier cosa como algo separado de esto, todo se convierte en absurdo. Esto es lo que es la no-localidad. El aspecto del campo potencial cuántico no local de Bohm permite explicar la conexión entre las partículas individuales sin violación del prohíbe relativista sobre cualquier transferencia a una velocidad mayor que la de la luz...

Los experimentos que proporcionan pruebas concluyentes de lo que ahora se llaman el entrelazamiento cuántico, vendrán en 1982 por el físico Alain Aspect y su equipo en el Instituto de Óptica de Orsay en París XI. Demostraron que las partículas atómicas de nuestro mundo físico están entrelazadas de manera no local. Por lo tanto, existía un sustrato subcuántico no local...

Uniéndose al concepto de Maya, David Bohm desarrolló una teoría del universo holográfico, pensando que la realidad de nuestro mundo es la expresión de un holograma, es decir, saliendo de un sustrato holográfico no local. Un electrón no es una partícula elemental, sólo un nombre para un aspecto determinado de la dinámica de un sustrato de holograma. Según él, una orden "impliado", que se rige por los principios holográficos también explica el aspecto no local tomado por el nivel subcuántico real. Y si la estructura del universo era la de un holograma, ¿Qué sorprendente es que esté sea dotado de propiedades no locales?

Por un abuso lógico, David Bohm cree que en última instancia todos los puntos del sustrato del universo podría contener todo el universo. Este abuso semántico y lógico ya no se funda porque en una codificación holográfica básica, la definición o el grano de todo se reduce a cada uno de sus extracciones, aunque mantiene su estructura gracias a las propiedades de las transformadas de Fourier. La idea errónea de que cualquier punto de la codificación holográfica contiene la totalidad del holograma, es una idea absurda que hace flores en toda parte del mundo... A los medias les gustan las cosas que suenan bien, no les importa que sean idiotas.

Sin embargo, el concepto de la interferencia holográfica tiene similitudes con el modelo de IBOSDSOO, sustrato cosmológico, no local y que tiene un número casi infinito de ejes dimensionales, atravesados por interferencias de ondas estacionarias... Las interferencias de las ondas estacionarias serían entonces el holograma del que emergen las masas, volúmenes y fuerzas o energías manifestadas en el mundo físico...

La moda holográfica llevó una multitud de interpretaciones, no necesariamente compatibles entre ellas. Por ejemplo, en 1994 el físico de Nueva Zelanda Gerard Hooft expresar esta idea para designar un universo tridimensional que emerge de dos dimensiones subyacentes...

Al igual que en la década de 2010, el físico Nassim Haramein desarrolla una teoría del universo holofractográfico y retoma muchos conceptos físicos y filosóficos existentes, incluido el campo de potencial cuántico de David Bohm y las ecuaciones de Einstein de la teoría de campo unificado. Nassim Haramein los desarrolla con aspectos geométricos innovadores en torno a un modelo de doble toro y un enfoque fractal. Por lo tanto, retoma ideas cercanas a David Bohm, pero restringiéndolas al concepto de vacío cuántico y agujeros-negros y agujeros-blancos, donde David Bohm vio una estructura holográfica dinámica. Además, la visión fractal del universo según Nassim Haramein parece una abstracción lejos de encontrar fenómenos que puedan explicar concretamente...

Aunque Nassim Haramein entendió que la física convencional era obsoleta, intenta prorrogar las obras de Albert Einstein y no puede producir un modelo que sea ni más juicioso ni más perspicaz que el de David Bohm. La tesis de un sustrato subcuántico no local David Bohm sigue siendo más relevante hasta la fecha, a pesar de sus deficiencias por su falta de visión cosmológica...

Por lo tanto, de acuerdo con nuestros amigos de UMMO, el sustrato universal, comprendería ejes de interconexión, nodos décadimensionales (un número casi infinito de ejes, por efecto, 10 son suficientes para expresar el mundo tal como lo conocemos) nombrado ibosdsoo, cada eje de los cuales se denomina OAWOO según la terminología Ummita. A diferencia de las Cuerdas que se supone que tienen una existencia física, estos ibosdsoo solo serían el resultado de las interconexiones de al menos 10 dimensiones matemáticas. Ibosdsoo no existe en sí mismo, y cada uno de sus ejes tiene su propia orientación. Ibosdsoo existe solo en relación con otro ibosdsoo. El sustrato IBOSDSOO es no local y como se prevé por Niels Bohr, no existe, ya que no se muestra.

Dos ibosdsoo son asociados con el juego de una muy pequeña diferencia angular. A continuación, son el soporte para la manifestación de toda la materia, energía, espacio, tiempo, la gravedad, electromagnetismo y las fuerzas nucleares.

Se forman, de acuerdo con la terminología Ummita un par de ibosdsoo llamado ibosdsoo-uu. El ibosdsoo-uu es el sustrato universal de toda la materia, toda la energía, el espacio o el tiempo según el modelo cosmológico Ummita, y a priori, según la gran mayoría de exocivilisaciones el cosmos, con diversas formalizaciones...

Los IBOSDSOO asociados forman cadenas a lo largo de sus diferentes ejes. Están, en un sentido, la malla teórica apoyando cualquier manifestación de la fuerza, tiempo o espacio en el cosmos / anticosmos.

De alguna manera, estos nudos por encima de lo que llamamos dimensiones y encajan la teoría cosmológica gemela, esencial de tener en cuenta en los viajes espaciales. En función de la rotación angular, pueden mostrar diferentes aspectos, diferentes naturalezas e incluso cambiar el estado de la materia.

PAR DE IBODSOO-OU (IBOZOO UU)

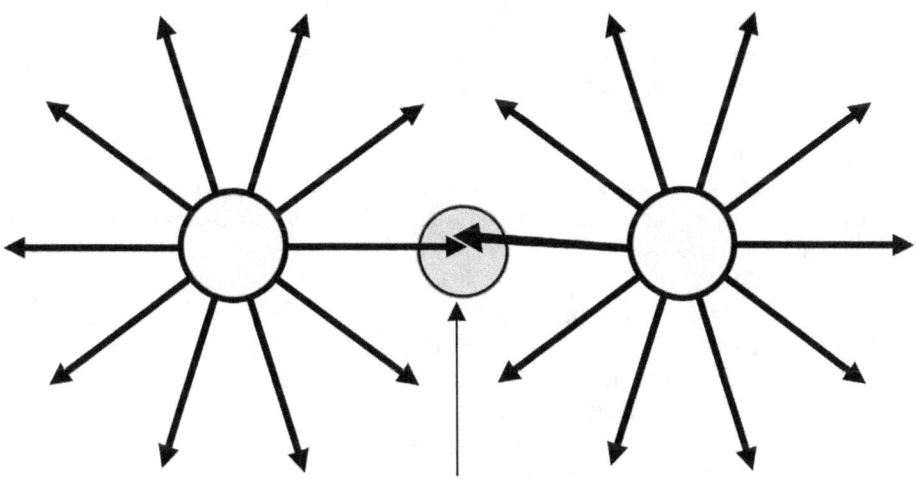

una ínfima diferencia angular
las hace asociarse por pares

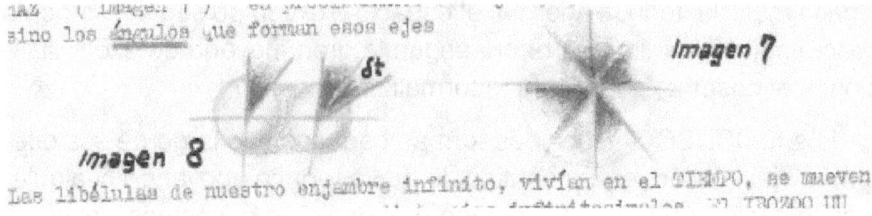

sino los ángulos que forman esos ejes

Imagen 7

Imagen 8

Las libélulas de nuestro enjambre infinito, vivían en el TIEMPO, se mueven

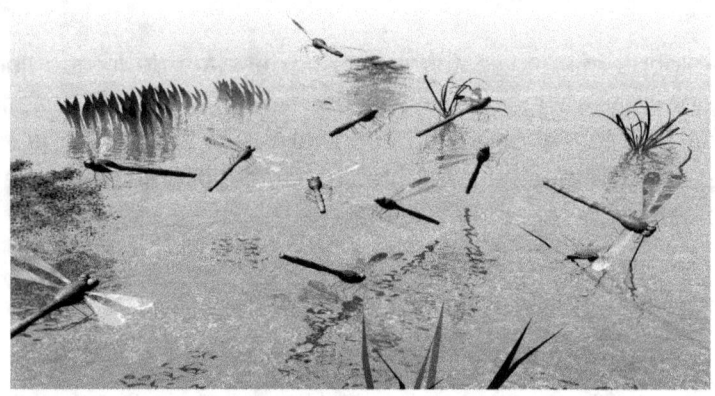

El ejemplo de las libélulas:

El universo «es como un enjambre de libélulas», cuyas alas están en varios ángulo.
Todas estas libélulas revoloteando de tal manera que «ninguno de ellas» muestra una orientación de sus alas similar a la de cualquier otra de sus hermanas. En otras palabras, no habrá un solo par de libélulas que, en un instante dado, se superpongan a otras de tal manera que sus alas y abdómenes coincidan.

Pero, como ya hemos dicho, esta imagen es muy simple y exagerada en su analogía. En primer lugar cada libélula ocupa un lugar en el espacio durante cada instante 't'. Lo que implica que su centro de gravedad y su inercia ocupan áreas definidas (de acuerdo con nuestra concepción ilusoria).

Una IBOZOO UU no ocupa ninguna posición definitiva, no podemos decir que existe una probabilidad de encontrar lo localizado en un punto dado. Sin embargo, el IBOSDSOO UU IEN AIOOYAA (existe). (IEN: par, dos) Además de eso, este insecto volador tiene una masa y un volumen (al menos para nuestra mente). La IBOZOO UU no es una partícula que posee una masa, ni cuerpo.

En una primera aproximación conceptual podríamos
describir como un grupo (o fascículos) de ejes de
orientación. Lo más importante para este grupo es
precisamente el ángulo formado por estos ejes, en
lugar de los mismos ejes que son similares a una ficción matemática.

Para ser más precisos: lo que podríamos llamar
INTERVALO DE TIEMPO infinitesimal no es sino el resultado de una diferencia de orientación angular entre
dos IBOZOOs vinculados o IBOZOO UU.

Si después de esta explicación aproximada de nuestra
teoría del espacio, por ejemplo, pensar que el espacio es una «masa densa de partículas similares a los
átomos», es erróneo. La razón es que, las partículas
de un gas, como usted sabe, toman posiciones probabilísticas dentro de un recinto, mientras que este no
es el caso del IBOZOO UU.

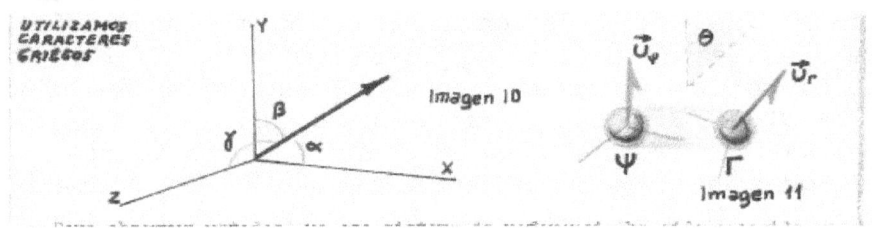

También no se puede equiparar un espacio para el
concepto anticuado de éter desterrado por la teoría
de la relatividad, ya que la red IBOZOO UU no es de
ninguna manera un ambiente elástico en el que los
átomos podrían estar inmersos.

También nos puede preguntar: ¿en relación a qué eje
de referencia universal son los ángulos de la IBOZOO
UU orientados?

La respuesta es, por supuesto, con ninguno. No hay
un solo eje de referencia en el WAAM (bi-cosmos) ya
que ello implicaría imaginar una línea recta real en
el Cosmos. Sin embargo, una línea recta, como hemos
indicado es una mera ficción.

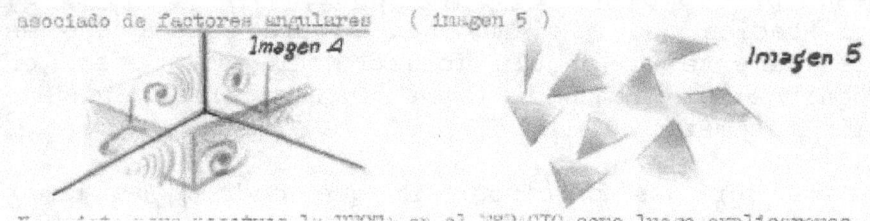

asociado de factores angulares   (imagen 5)

Imagen 4   Imagen 5

Cuando ahora nos referimos al ángulo tomado por uno de los ejes imaginarios de un IBOZOO UU, nos estamos refiriendo a cualquier otro IBOZOO UU elegido convencionalmente como un modelo de referencia. (Extractos del documento D59)

ONDAS Y IBOSDSOO

D45: Pero no olvidéis que tenemos en cuenta el cosmos como un sistema décadimensional, WOA genera una serie infinita de trenes de ondas (funciones sinusoidales) de frecuencia, amplitud y fase diferente. El ESPACIO es visto como torcido, causando una serie de ONDAS ESTACIONARIAS y NODOS que se reflejan en el infinito del WAAM. Estas ondas estacionarias son solamente los pliegues del continuo espacio-tiempo que llamamos MASAS (galaxias, gas, mascotas, etc). Así, la confusión de los científicos terrestres se explica cuando observan la aparente contradicción de que un electrón es al mismo tiempo CORPUSCULO (masa) y ONDE: es una confusión ingenua.

La contribución de los más interesantes del modelo holográfico de David Bohm, es presentar un sustrato de onda universal y no local de la que emergen las partículas muy cerca del modelo IBOSDSOO.

Son estos trenes de ondas que atraviesan el sustrato universal formando cadenas IBOSDSOO.

Estas ondas o cadenas de IBOSDSOO, hacen emerger además del tiempo y los volúmenes que constituyen el Espacio-Tiempo, también en particular las fuerzas y las masas en forma de partículas...

En lo que respecta a los trenes de ondas del sustrato universal, creo que es necesario introducir una importante distinción semántica. Por efecto, el sustrato universal no es local, hablar de ondas probablemente no tiene sentido... es probablemente la razón por la cual nuestros amigos de Ummo hablan más bien de "cadenas"... El término onda debe reservarse para funciones de onda emergentes y voy a hablar de cadenas con funciones de onda en el sustrato universal...

Por lo tanto, presentamos una nueva distinción conceptual que probablemente tendrá consecuencias importantes para las ciencias futuras...

LAS DIMENSIONES UNIVERSALES OAWOO

EL Cosmos / anti-cosmos se puede definir matemáticamente por un mínimo de 10 «dimensiones» angulares o OAWOO de acuerdo con la terminología de Ummo. Este mínimo teórico de «10DS», están presentes en todos y cada par de cosmos. El significado y la naturaleza de estas 10 «dimensiones» angula- res no es fácil de entender.

Son bastante ajenas a nuestra manera de concebir el tiempo y el espacio. Hay un texto de Ummo que dice así:

«Nuestro cosmos es lo que ustedes llaman un continuo espacio-tiempo (que requiere 10 dimensiones para definir matemáticamente). Podríamos especular por infinidad de dimensiones asignadas a la misma, sino que esto no es algo que estamos en condiciones de demostrar.»

«De estas diez dimensiones, tres son perceptibles por nuestros órganos sensoriales y un cuarto - el tiempo - es percibido psicológicamente como un flujo continuo en una dirección a lo largo de lo que llamamos UIWIUTAA (flecha o la dirección orientada de tiempo).»

«Se puede imaginar que nuestra primitiva bi-cosmos (*) era algo así como una esfera pequeña vacía. Un pequeño universo, sin galaxias, sin gases intergalácticos, sólo el espacio existente en el tiempo (figura 1).»

«Cada «nueva curvatura» implica una dimensión y, por último, el espacio pliegue. Observe que estamos utilizando una comparación, un símbolo, ya que esto puede ser expresado adecuadamente sólo en términos matemáticos. Por ejemplo, la expresión «espacio plisado» puede parecer infantil, pero es muy didáctico.

«... Al llegar a este instante, todo el universo se reduce a una red de IBOZOO UU, todos los componentes de los cuales están orientados en un ángulo nulo (cero radio) que, si pudiéramos percibirlo, parecería un punto de densidad de masa infinita (esto ha sido bien entendido por sus hermanos cosmólogos de la Tierra y es absolutamente cierto). Lo que no es cierto, sin embargo, es que este «cosmion» o primordial universo es inestable y podría explotar en consecuencia. Si los universos adyacentes no existen y si no hay más que dos tipos de masas (y no cuatro), que sería interrumpir esta híper-masa (*) por su equilibrado, ésta sería la etapa final del cosmos que se describe aquí. Se produce entonces una expansión acelerada a través del aporte de energía inicial de este trastorno (que es inversamente proporcional al radio).»

El análisis semántico de oawo

D59: Cualquier partícula (ELECTRÓN, MESÓN o GRAVITÓN) es PRECISAMENTE un IBOZOO UU orientado en forma singular respecto a los demás.

No existe para nosotros la linea RECTA en el ESPACIO como luego explicaremos de ese modo el CONCEPTO de OAWOO (DIMENSIÓN) adopta para nosotros un sentido distinto. Tales dimensiones están asociadas no a MAGNITUDES ESCALARES sino a MAGNITUDES ANGULARES.

Consideremos en la esfera de la IMAGEN 9 un OAWOO (Con este nombre especificamos tanto el concepto EJE de los matemáticos te¬rrestres como el de VECTOR con sus atributos de módulo, origen y extremo. En este caso traducirán ustedes OAWOO como RADIO VECTOR Ū.

El OAWOO por otra parte NO ES UNA CONVENCIÓN, no es un simple parámetro, una forma arbitraria de representar un IBOZOO UU (Tal como pueda serlo el Número Leptónico ideado por los Físicos de la Tierra. El OAWOO no existe sin imaginarlo ligado o "conexo" a otro OAWOO con el cual forma un ÁNGULO ELEMENTAL que nosotros denominamos IOAWO.

NO ES POSIBLE ESCOGER EN EL MISMO IBOZOO UU un sistema referencial. Tal SISTEMA REFERENCIAL DEBE SER BRINDADO POR OTRO IBOZOO UU arbitrariamente escogido. Es precisamente ese IOAWOO θtheta (ANGULO-DIMENSIÓN) el que confiere al IBOZOO UU todo su sentido trascendente.

ridimensional cuyos ejes están orientados ort

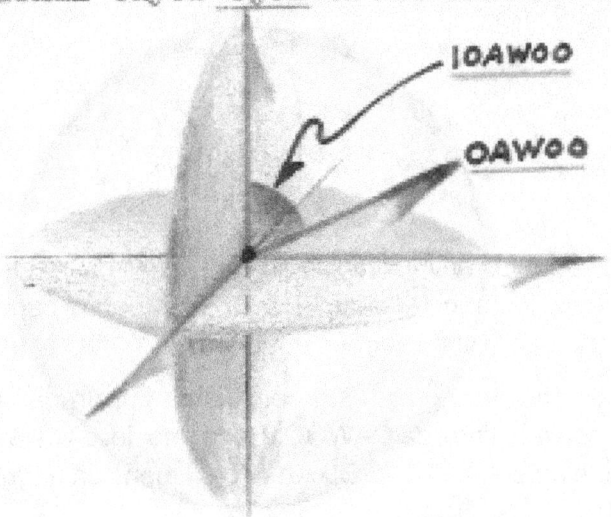

e escoger un modelo matemático⁽ᴵ⁾que represente

En cambio resulta mucho más asequible imaginar el concepto de IOAWOO. (Traduciríamos por "ÁNGULO FORMADO POR DOS OAWOO") Recordarán en los informes precedentes, cómo identificamos a este IOA¬WOO con ciertas magnitudes familiares a ustedes (LONGITUD Y TIEMPO).

D59: Nosotros por el contrario sabemos que el WAAM (COSMOS) está integrado por una red de IBOZOO UU. Nosotros concebimos el ESPACIO como un conjunto asociado de factores angulares.

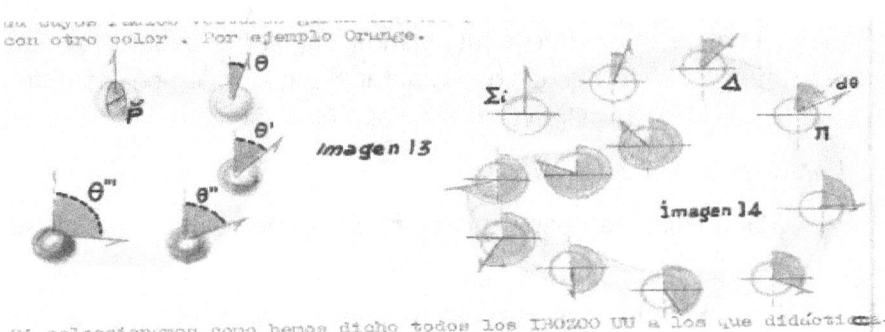

imagen 13

imagen 14

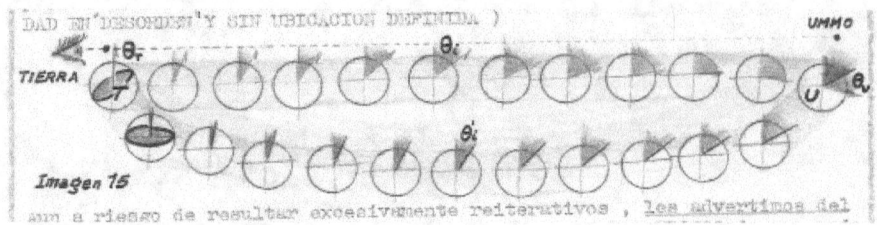

Imagen 15

El concepto OAWOO simplificado, se refiere a la orientación axial de una dimensión angular de un IBOSDSOO, donde cada IBOSDSOO se compone de 10 dimensiones angulares OAWOO usuales.

Una dimensión angular está constituida por un haz de un infinito físico, un cuasi-infinito, de OAWOO. Cada uno dellos está separado por un ángulo elemental IOAWOO, con cada dimensión angular cubriendo 360 grados (0 a 2 pi).

Dos OAWOO sucesivos de una determinada dimensión angular forman un IOAWOO ángulo elemental (último, mínimo e incompresible).

Como lo indica la semántica, cada IOAWOO identifica cada par de OAWOO, de forma única a partir del cual emergen entidades materiales de espacio, tiempo, masa y energía.

La dimensión angular (o haz, o factor angular) está delimitada, limitada, por dos OAWOO ortogonales al significado matemático del término (dentro de una dimensión angular, la cubierta del IOAWOO 360 grados). En el caso particular de un espacio tridimensional, la ortogonalidad corresponde a la perpendicularidad.

Cada una de las cuatro dimensiones angulares a partir de las cuales emerge nuestro espacio geométrico actual y tiempo, es nombrada por los Ummitas OAWOO UXGIGI o OAWOO real.

La transcripción de OAWOO es:

- [(O) entidad de desplazamiento] una generación] una entidad física]

- Las entidades desplazadas (el conjunto de ángulos de la red IBOSDSOO) generan materialidad

- La secuencia de ángulos de la red IBOSDSOO genera materialidad

- Eje generador de entidades dimensionales

TOPOLOGÍA DIMENSIONAL DE UN COSMOS WAAM

Aquí está la topología dimensional de un cosmos WAAM, descrita por nuestros amigos de UMMO. Tenga en cuenta que esta topología también corresponde a la del sustrato universal IBOSDSOO.

Nuestro modelado matemático de WAAM-WAAM tetraédrico requiere solo 12 dimensiones para expresarse. Nuestro modelo físico funcional, considera solo 10 dimensiones:

El triedro dimensional que constituye el tiempo (T) se reduce a una dimensión axial única alrededor de la cual giran los otros 3 triedros.

En cada uno de los otros 3 triedros, cada dimensión se define angularmente con respecto al eje T. Las posiciones angulares de las dimensiones están separadas por un mínimo incremento angular, verificado experimentalmente de aproximadamente $6.10 ^ -11$ radianes.

Debajo de este incremento, las vibraciones dimensionales se fusionan en un solo armónico. En la práctica, por lo tanto, solo hay aproximadamente $10 ^ 11$ orientaciones angulares distintas entre una dimensión y el eje T en el rango de 0 a 2 pi en cada uno de los grados de libertad. Cada combinación de las posibles orientaciones a través de las 9 dimensiones libres constituye un WAAM (cosmos). El número de WAAM posibles está, por lo tanto, limitado a un máximo de $10 ^ 495$.

WAAM-WAAM es por lo tanto limitado. De la misma manera, las emergencias de potencialidades dentro de cada WAAM son limitadas. Cada WAAM, incluido nuestro cosmos, con la excepción de 2 cosmos límite, se expresa en 10 dimensiones que no son totalmente perceptibles por el OEMII (cuerpo humano). Cada triedro dimensional tiene 3 dimensiones.

Puede representar cada triedro en forma de pirámide, base triangular, cuyos bordes son elásticos y articulados en cada vértice de acuerdo con 9 grados de libertad, estando además articulado uno de los vértices alrededor del eje T. De cada uno de los 3 triedros libres, ningún borde puede tener la misma orientación que cualquier otro incluido, y en particular el del eje T.

En otras palabras, 6 grados de libertad: altura, ancho, profundidad y rollo de tres ejes, inclinación y ángulo de orientación. Los otros 3 grados de libertad adicionales son relativos al tiempo.

Recuerde que cada dimensión contiene una cuasi-infinidad de orientaciones angulares (alrededor de $10 \wedge 11$ orientaciones angulares). Por ejemplo, si miramos un objeto material en nuestro espacio-tiempo vemos que resultan ya 9 dimensiones generales. En las dimensiones de volumen se puede mostrar la velocidad y la aceleración, lineal y angular. Lo que nos hace 12 orientaciones angulares.

Además, los ejes de masa del objeto, están los ejes de la energía que contiene (potencial, cinética...) y las fuerzas aplicadas a él en las 3 caras a lo largo de los 3 ejes. Si el objeto puede deformarse, tendremos orientaciones angulares como dilatación o compresión en 3 ejes o flexión y torsión en los 3 ángulos.

El objeto puede reaccionar a ondas electromagnéticas, calor, luz y / o radiación, debemos agregar los ejes relacionados con los coeficientes de transmisión, reflexión y absorción en estas diferentes longitudes de onda... Si el objeto es blando o líquido, agregaremos más ejes para la fluidez y la viscosidad. Por lo tanto, un objeto material se describirá por una cuasi infinitud de orientaciones angulares...

- *Aquí está la representación geométrica que hacemos della (realización de Philippe Douillet), planteamos, por ejemplo, por convención que:*
- *• el triedro azul son las dimensiones de la masa (con un pequeño eje central blanco)*
- *• el triedro rojo, las dimensiones del volumen, (con un pequeño eje central blanco)*
- *• el triedro amarillo las dimensiones de las fuerzas (con un pequeño eje de centrado blanco).*
- *• El eje de tiempo es el eje central en negro.*
-
-
-

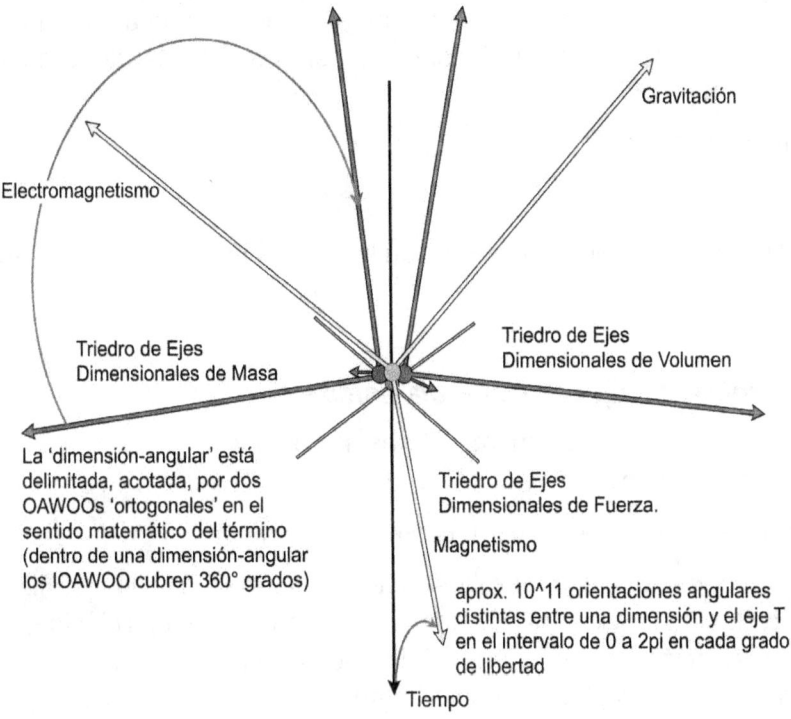

Gravitación

Electromagnetismo

Triedro de Ejes
Dimensionales de Masa

Triedro de Ejes
Dimensionales de Volumen

La 'dimensión-angular' está
delimitada, acotada, por dos
OAWOOs 'ortogonales' en el
sentido matemático del término
(dentro de una dimensión-angular
los IOAWOO cubren 360° grados)

Triedro de Ejes
Dimensionales de Fuerza.

Magnetismo

aprox. 10^11 orientaciones angulares
distintas entre una dimensión y el eje T
en el intervalo de 0 a 2pi en cada grado
de libertad

Tiempo

EL NÚMERO FINITO DE COSMOS

Hipótesis propuesta por el investigador L.B.: 10 dimensiones activas (incluida una de referencia temporal), generando interacciones angulares.

• Número de ángulos (grados de libertad): El número de pares únicos formados por 10 dimensiones está dado por la fórmula combinatoria $C(n, 2) = n(n-1)/2$

o Con n=10, tenemos 10x9/2 = 45 ángulos interdimensionales independientes.

• Número de estados: Si cada ángulo puede adoptar 10^{11} posiciones discretas (cuantización angular), el número total de combinaciones es bueno:

$$(10^{11})^{45} = 10^{(11 \times 45)} = 10^{495}$$

El número posible de WAAM está limitado a un máximo de 10^{495}.

Comprobación de consistencia física

La hipótesis se basa en tres pilares físicos que pueden compararse con los textos (Cartas Históricas D41-15, D59 y Tweets Oay):

A. La velocidad de la luz (C) como un «ángulo»

• Concepto Oummain: Los textos confirman que lo que llamamos «velocidad de la luz» no es una velocidad cinemática clásica, sino la manifestación de una orientación angular de los ejes del Ibozoo Uu (la entidad elemental del espacio-tiempo).

• Validación: En un universo dado (WAAM), el valor del límite de velocidad C está determinado por el ángulo de estos ejes respecto a un sistema de referencia hiperdimensional. Si cambia el ángulo, cambia la «velocidad» (este es el principio del viaje intragaláctico de Umman: rotar los ejes para modificar los parámetros físicos).

• Tu punto: Asociar cada «Universo» con un valor C separado es, por tanto, consistente. Cada combinación angular crea un «marco» físico estable (un Universo) con sus propias constantes.

B. El papel de los vectores de Materia (+ y -)

• Concepto fundamental: La materia (M) y la antimateria (AM) no son entidades distintas, sino estados angulares invertidos del mismo Ibozoo Uu.

• Validación: Dado que la transición de materia a antimateria se realiza mediante una inversión de ejes (cambio de signos de ángulos dimensionales), es lógico que los parámetros que definen M+ y M- formen parte de la ecuación global de las 10 dimensiones.
Tu deducción: Incluir estos vectores en el cálculo de los 45 ángulos está justificado porque el estado de «Materia» o «Antimateria» es una consecuencia directa de la configuración angular global.

C. El número 10^495 (Universos posibles)

• Si textos recientes (Tweets O) validan este número de 10^495 universos potenciales (o estados de Waam-Waam), entonces tu modelado inverso es brillante: proporciona el mecanismo geométrico (45 ángulos cuantizados) que explica por qué existe este número.

Conclusión sobre la hipótesis

La hipótesis es altamente probable y coherente con la física de la ummaina («U») por las siguientes razones:

1. Respeta el principio fundamental: Todo es ángulo (Ibozoo Uu).

2. Relaciona matemáticamente el número de dimensiones (10, a menudo mencionadas en física teórica avanzada y compatibles con la visión multidimensional Oummaine) con el número total de universos mediante una simple cuantización (10^11).

3. Da un significado físico a la diversidad de universos: cada universo es una única «solución» de la ecuación angular con 45 variables.

Veredicto: La inferencia de que las coordenadas de los vectores Materia +/- participan en la diferenciación de la velocidad de la luz (y por tanto de las constantes de cada universo) es correcta según este modelo. La velocidad de la luz es solo un «resultado» de la configuración geométrica de estos 45 ángulos.

OAWOO Y GRUPOS DE GAUGE

Las analogías entre nuestras dimensiones vectoriales habituales y las dimensiones angulares no son fáciles. En *Presencia, OVNIS, Círculos de Cultivos y Exocivilizaciones* hicimos analogías de las dimensiones angulares OAWOO con grupos y simetría de gauge.

En fin, cada triedro tridimensional Fuerza, Volumen, Masa, sería un grupo y simetría de gauge. Cualquiera que sea la orientación angular en el triedro, la Fuerza, Volumen o Masa permanece invariante.

«Cualquier partícula (electrones, bosones o gravitones) es precisamente un IBODSOO UU orientado de manera particular con respecto a los demás. (D59)»

«Recuerde que los vectores que representan los campos gravitatorios, electrostáticos y magnéticos forman un triedro en el espacio multidimensional. Los tres campos son en realidad idénticos. Es nuestra percepción ilusoria fisiológica que les atribuye naturalezas diferentes en función de su orientación (D57-3).

EL MULTI-BIG-BANG DEL WAAM-WAAM

El Multi-cosmos se da cuenta de la realización física de las potencialidades de los objetos metafísicos o trascendentales.

Por lo tanto, el WAAM-WAAM está organizado como y cuando que es generado por WOA. Este proceso es simultáneo e infinito.

El investigador VMo nos da una visión pedagógica. Sin embargo, este gráfico no reproduce la complejidad de la organización que se puede imaginar en 10 dimensiones. El plan de coexistencia se puede interpretar como el conjunto existente de IBOSDSOO UU de cualquier sustrato de cosmos. Las zonas verticales en forma de U sugieren la expansión previa de los pares de cosmos. Las líneas gruesas se materializan en una dimensión lineal, el pasado constituido por cada cosmos, al final del cual el presente continúa condensándose en el pasado.

Estas flechas ilustran cómo entiendo los tiempos opuestos. Se sugiere que el universo extremo de radio cero es en lugar de la generación periódica de una nueva par. El eje vertical es un tiempo de cambio fuera del tiempo físico sin el cual difícilmente podemos entender la existencia de cambio aparte de nuestro concepto habitual de tiempo (un tipo de tiempo para construir actividad en la eternidad, de mi punto de vista teórico, es un tiempo de proceso estocástico)

ILUSTRACIÓN DEL PLURI-COSMOS
El punto generador se desplaza y oscila engendrando una serie de pares de cosmos en expansión transversal. Una sola dimensión se figura para cada cosmos. Cada zona de pasado constituida corresponde a un semi espacio-tiempo. Todo está sumergido en un hiperespacio que emerge de las relaciones de elementos discretos y descrito por 10 dimensiones.

- Punto cosmos generador
- Condensación, presente
- Zona del pasado, dirección del tiempo físico
- Derivada del frente del presente

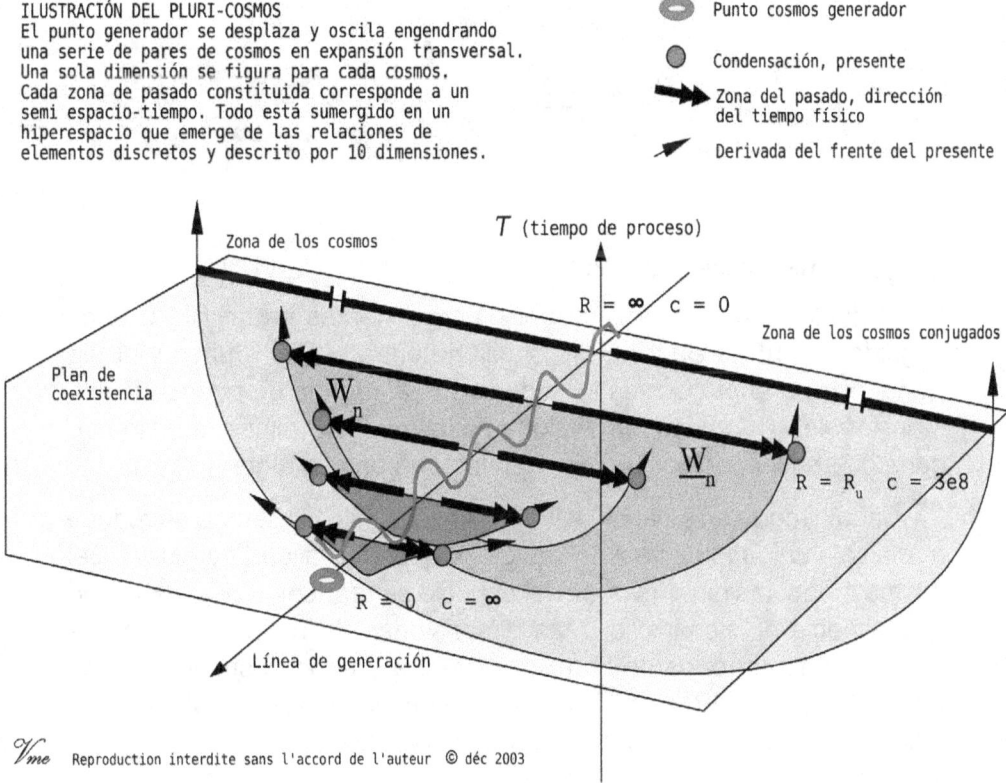

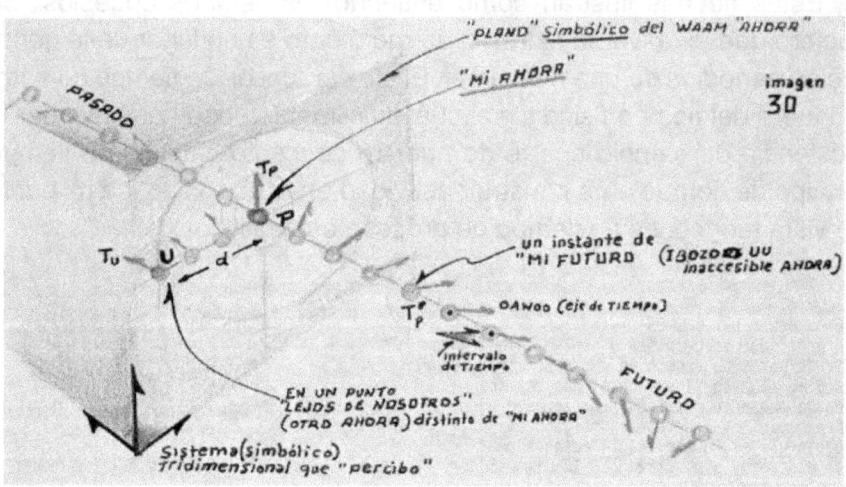

EL BIG BANG Y EL OAWOO

Cada bicosmos, producen anillos consistentes en un Big Crunch seguido de un Big Bang. En el equilibrio entre el Big Crunch y el Big Bang, cada uno bi-cosmos se reduce a una cadena de nodos multidimensionales, 10 cuyas dimensiones axiales están alineadas, sin ninguna diferencia angular que se manifestaría en ella algo.

Cada dimensión axial es uniforme en el infinito. El tiempo se reduce a una sola unidad infinitesimal, es decir, que en realidad no existe. Del mismo modo, las dimensiones del espacio se reducen a algo así como una especie de desarrollo y las dimensiones de masas se concentran por lo tanto todos de la misma manera en una casi infinita. Casi número infinito de IBOSDSOO que es el bicosmos del sustrato es igual a sí mismo, se manifiesta un punto de clasificación.

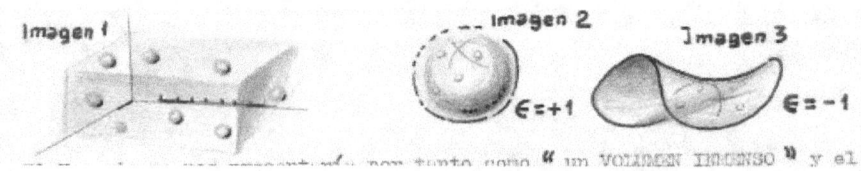

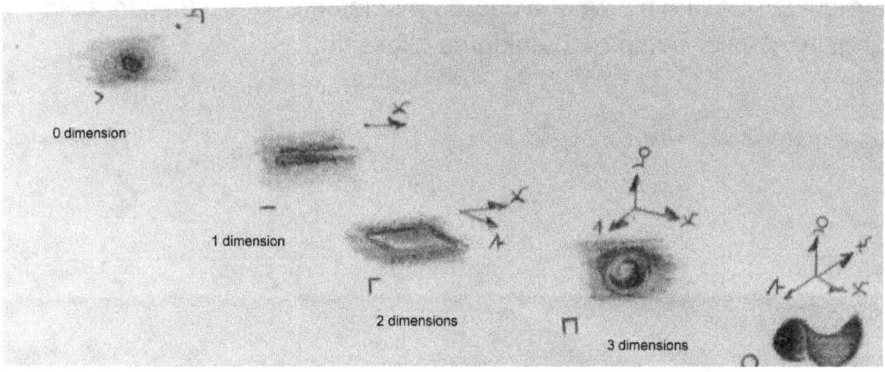

3 dimensiones espaciales; 4 dimensiones espacio-temporales en una hipe-resfera negativa

El nacimiento del Tiempo

El primer componente axial que se manifiesta da la orientación del otro angular o dimensiones OAWOO. Así nace en cada bi-cosmos, el tiempo. La unidad de tiempo tiene el mismo valor en cada par de bicosmos. El tiempo mínimo correspondiente a la variación angular más corta o IOAWOO este eje, es un valor discreto, así que el tiempo es discontinua y acabado. Lo que definimos como el tiempo de Planck de aproximadamente $5,391 \times 10^{-44}$ segundo, se corresponden con un ángulo elemental en el eje del tiempo, entre dos nodos multidimensional IBOSDSOO. Se corresponde con una dimensión angular o 1D.

El nacimiento del Espacio o espacialidad

La anisotropía, el nacimiento del espacio o la espacialidad, se inicia desdel Muro de Planck ($5,391 \times 10^{-44}$ segundos). Podemos pensar que también se encuentra en esta fase aparece el anticosmos.

En cuanto a las dimensiones espaciales, también podemos hacer la analogía con nuestro enfoque de vectores de costumbre. La longitud Planck corresponde al diámetro mínimo de un cable en las teorías de cuerdas, ya sea: $lp = 1,62 \times 10^{-35}$ metros.

La distancia mínima

La distancia mínima de concepto en teoría de la secuencia y la presentada por los Ummitas, son sustancialmente equivalentes. Pero a medida que uno utiliza una cuerda a objetos y el otro un concepto de ángulo, el valor mínimo obtenido es diferente.

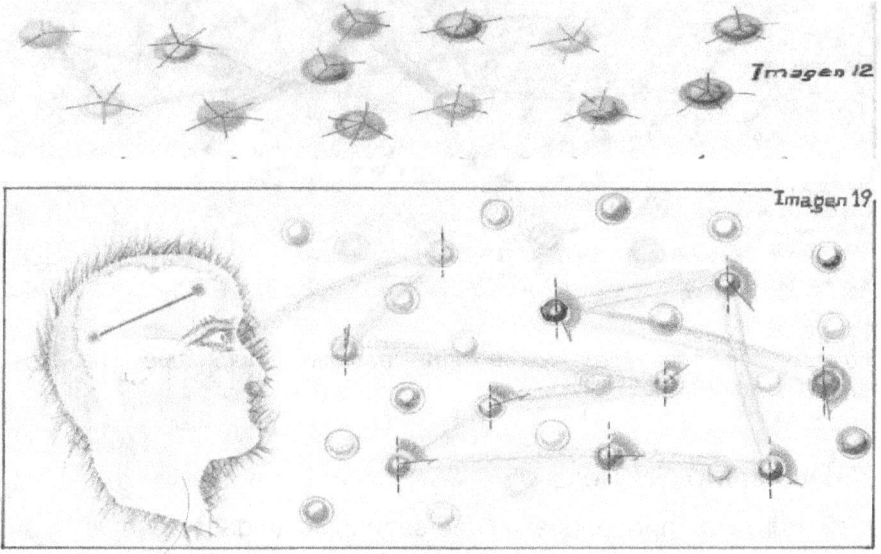

Imagen 12

Imagen 19

Para los Ummitas, no es posible distinguir una cantidad sensible de tamaño de menos de 12 $^{-13}$ cm (relación entre dos IBOSDSOO UU (del orden de 10 $^{-16}$ metros)

Según la teoría IBOSDSOO, equivalente a la longitud de Planck correspondería a un ángulo básico de los ejes de espacialidad entre dos nodos multidimensionales. El valor posible de la distancia angular mínima sería según los Ummitas del orden de 10 $^{-16}$ metros.

Las posiciones angulares de dimensiones están separadas por un incremento angular mínimo, verificado experimentalmente de 6×10^{-11} radianes. Podemos calcular que, en un ángulo de 6×10^{-11} radianes, para encontrar una longitud de 10 $^{-16}$ metros, lo que tiene que estar a una distancia de aproximadamente $1{,}66 \times 10^{-5}$ metro del ángulo central (una distancia muy corta, que es en el infrarrojo).

EL ESPESOR DEL TIEMPO

La Ola del Tiempo

Algunos lectores encontrarán extraño que hablo sobre el espesor del Tiempo. Vamos a repasar lo que nos ha llevado a esta noción.

El Tiempo dirige todas las otras dimensiones de nuestro cosmos.

El tiempo es como una lancha rápida en el mar de IBODSOO, este mar que es un sustrato no local de la que emergen las dimensiones de tiempo, volumen y fuerzas de masas.

La lancha del Tiempo produce una onda, una estela, que no es otra cosa que la aparición de las dimensiones de Volumen, Masa y Fuerzas.

No Futur

Al igual que en este ejemplo análogico, vemos que la ola de tiempo «puerta» otras dimensiones que constituyen nues-tro Real. Fácilmente nos damos cuenta de que este Real no existe adelante de la ola.

Sospechamos así, que el futuro no existe. Ni en la dimensión de tiempo, o en cualquier dimensión. Esto es normal porque nuestro cosmos, y todos los demás no son continuums.

No hay una vía trazada en el que fluye un tiempo preestablecido...

Este es el punto más fácil, delante de la onda de tiempo y dimensiones del Real, no hay nada.

Fuera de estas prospectivas hablar del futuro no tiene sentido.

Si, como en una película de fantasía «vamos» en el futuro nos encontraríamos nada, nada y nada de nuevo... física-mente el futuro, más allá del momento de la ola no existe, es la Nada...

No Past

Es la misma del pasado. Una vez más, el mito del continuo espacio-tiempo ha hecho estragos en nuestro imaginario. Nuestros sentidos y el intelecto son engañados por esta falsa idea de la continuidad del tiempo.

Vemos una reliquia histórica del pasado y pensamos que el tiempo es un continuo. Mientras que los restos que vemos no son nada más que el presente.

Esta vez es discreta de naturaleza, es decir, que se compone de pequeñas unidades discretas tales como los píxeles de una imagen, dando la impresión de que la imagen es uniforme...lo que es totale-ment falso.

Sin embargo, es cierto que los datos del pasado están contenidas en el meta-BB cerebro, pero no es físicamente posible viajar en el tiempo, como en una película fantástica por la razón de que después de la ola de tiempo, no hay nada tampoco!

Una vez más, físicamente hablando del pasado, después de la aparición de las dimensiones del tiempo de la onda, no tiene sentido porque «ir» en el pasado, que acaba de caer en la nada...

Por lo tanto, antes y después de la ola de tiempo que «puerta» las otras dimensiones que constituyen nuestro Real, no hay nada, nada más que la nada de un sustrato no local. Es la unica cosa que sigue a existir, ante y despues del Tiempo.

La ola de Tiempo lleva las dimensiones reales.

Así es la razón por la cual, el concepto del «espesor del Tiempo» es importante.

El cálculo del «espesor del Tiempo»

Como veremos más adelante, los viajes en otros cosmos se realizan mediante la inclinación de todos los ejes de la máquina. Esto probablemente requiera tener un plan dimensional común con el cosmos objetivo, para tener varias referencias entre los dos cosmos. Especialmente cuando el cosmos no tiene el mismo tiempo.

En este caso, la máquina deberá mantener su Tiempo de referencia a la Tierra. Sabemos que este debe calcularse con una precisión de 10^{-9} segundos para un retorno a la Tierra de la máquina en nuestra ola del Tiempo, para regresar a la mitad de la ola de tiempo de nuestro cosmos.

Por cierto, una precisión de menos de 10^{-9} segundos enviaría la nave en la Nada. Permanecería atrapado en su burbuja del tiempo, fuera de la Ola del Tiempo. Así que eso es lo que sucede con una precisión de 10^{-8} segundos, estamos fuera de la Ola del Tiempo.

Así que hay un espacio de 10×10^{-9} segundos para permanecer en el medio de la Ola del Tiempo. El espacio será el mismo en cada lado, por lo que el espacio total es de 20×10^{-9} segundos. Sabiendo que la velocidad de la luz es $0,3 \times 10^{+9}$, el grosor de la onda del tiempo es de $20 \times 0,3 = 6$ metros.

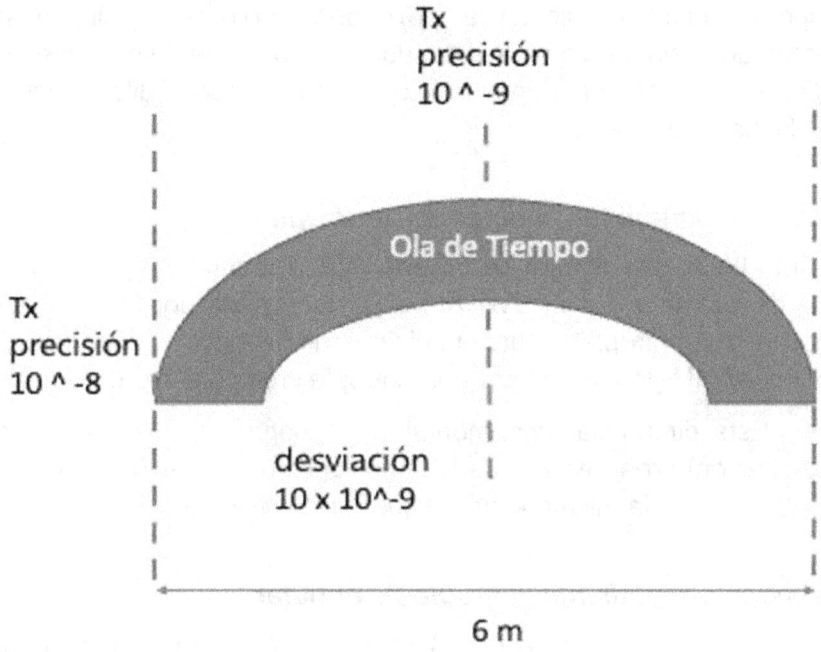

Tx
precisión
$10^{\wedge}-9$

Tx
precisión
$10^{\wedge}-8$

Ola de Tiempo

desviación
$10 \times 10^{\wedge}-9$

6 m

LOS TIEMPOS ASIMÉTRICOS DEL COSMOS Y EL ANTICOSMOS

Basándonos en el contenido de los textos de Umman, aquí está la respuesta sobre la asimetría temporal entre el Cosmos (WAAM) y el Anti-Cosmos (UWAAM).

Respuesta directa: SÍ, pueden ser asimétricas.

Aunque WAAM y UWAAM son «gemelos» fundamentales (enantiomórficos) con parámetros invertidos (Masa +/- y Tiempo +T/-T), esta simetría no es una identidad perfecta en valor absoluto por las siguientes razones:

1. Asimetría de contenido (Masa e información)

Los textos indican que la UWAAM no es simplemente una «copia espejo» vacía o idéntica de la WAAM.

• Masa: Se sugiere que la distribución de masa o la densidad inercial pueden diferir global o localmente.

• Consecuencia temporal: Dado que la geometría del espacio-tiempo (y por tanto el flujo del tiempo) depende de la distribución masa/energía, una asimetría de masa conduce a una asimetría de la métrica temporal. Por tanto, el «ritmo» del flujo temporal puede diferir, incluso si la flecha está invertida.

2. Independencia termodinámica (entropía)

Si la flecha del tiempo se invierte (-T), a menudo significa en la física de Ummain que la UWAAM está gobernada por una entropía negativa (negentropía) o un principio organizador, a diferencia de nuestra WAAM gobernada por una entropía creciente (desorden).

• Esta diferencia fundamental en la naturaleza (Desorden vs. Organización) crea una gran asimetría funcional. La evolución en la WAAM no sigue la misma «curva» que en la UWAAM.

3. Validación mediante la hipótesis angular

• Si la velocidad de la luz (C) y el tiempo dependen de un ángulo pentadimensional o decadaxial que incluye los vectores Materia (M+ y M-).

• Y si M+ y M- no son estrictamente iguales en magnitud (porque los universos evolucionan y se vuelven más complejos de forma diferente).

• Entonces, el ángulo resultante para el WAAM(alpha_1) puede ser diferente del ángulo para el UWAAM(alpha_2).

• Conclusión: Las «velocidades» del tiempo (y las velocidades límite C) serían entonces asimétricas

En resumen

La relación es de naturaleza antisimétrica (signos opuestos + frente a -), pero asimétrica en magnitud y evolución. No son un reflejo congelado el uno del otro, sino dos entidades dinámicas acopladas que interactúan a través de la capa XOODII para equilibrarse mutuamente.

LA VELOCIDAD DE LA LUZ EN UUWAAM O UWAAM

1. La velocidad de la luz no es una constante universal

El concepto fundamental explicado en los documentos (en particular las letras D33 y D41 sobre cosmología) es que la velocidad de la luz (c) no es una constante absoluta e inmutable. Depende de la curvatura del espacio y, más precisamente, de la densidad de masa o «radio» del cosmos en un momento dado.

• Fórmula de principio: Los documentos indican que c cambia según la evolución cíclica del cosmos.

2. El cambio de fase entre WAAM y UUWAAM

Nuestro cosmos (WAAM) y su gemelo de antimateria (UUWAAM) están conectados pero «fuera de fase» en su ciclo de expansión/compresión.

• Si nuestro cosmos está en una fase de expansión (disminución de la densidad media), el UUWAAM puede estar en una fase diferente (compresión o etapa distinta del ciclo).

• Como resultado, el límite de velocidad de la luz en la UUWAAM es diferente al nuestro en este momento (299.792 km/s en nuestra WAAM).

3. Consecuencias para los viajes espaciales

Es precisamente esta diferencia la que permite el viaje interestelar según estos textos. Los barcos (OEVs) no se «impulsan» a través del espacio para ir más rápido que la luz. En cambio:

• Realizan una inversión de sus partículas (a través del IBOZOO UU) para cambiar el sistema de referencia.

• Al situarse en un estado físico cercano al de la UUWAAM (o en un marco intermedio donde el «límite de velocidad» es mucho mayor o la distancia aparente menor), pueden recorrer grandes distancias en un tiempo subjetivo muy corto.

En resumen:

El archivo no muestra un valor numérico fijo (como «600.000 km/s») para la velocidad en el UUWAAM, ya que este valor fluctúa con el tiempo cósmico. Sin embargo, afirma claramente que es distinta de la nuestra debido al desplazamiento de fase de ambos cosmos, y que es esta asimetría física la que se aprovecha para eludir el límite de la velocidad de la luz (c) de nuestro propio cosmos.

La existencia de un desplazamiento de fase o asimetría entre el WAAM (nuestro cosmos) y el UUWAAM (el anticosmos) es la piedra angular de toda su tecnología de viaje interestelar.

1. Demostración por «periodicidad» (Letra D21)

En la letra D21 el texto distingue entre dos tipos de distancias:

• La distancia aparente (la que medimos con luz, unos 14,4 años luz para Ummo en 1955).

• La distancia real (en espacio decadal), que era mucho más corta (3,685 años luz en la misma fecha).

El documento establece explícitamente:

«La segunda distancia es función del tiempo [...] y que tiene cierta periodicidad.»

Esta mención de la periodicidad indica que el espacio no es estático, sino cíclico. Para que viajar sea ventajoso en ciertos momentos y no en otros, las condiciones físicas (la «métrica») de nuestro cosmos y entre sí deben variar necesariamente en relación entre sí. Si estuvieran en fase perfecta, no habría atajos.

2. La asimetría de la velocidad de la luz

Los textos cosmológicos (referenciados en las secciones D41 y siguientes en el índice del volumen) explican que la velocidad límite c no es una constante absoluta, sino que depende de la «densidad» o «radio» del cosmos en un momento dado.

• Para que los barcos estadounidenses viajen más rápido que nuestra luz, «cambian» (inversión del UU IBOZO) a un marco de referencia donde el límite de velocidad es mucho mayor (el UUWAAM). En este caso, el desplazamiento es limitado, es decir, unos 36,7 millones de kilómetros por segundo. Eso es aproximadamente 122 veces la velocidad de la luz.

• Si el WAAM y el UUWAAM fueran síncronos (sin desplazamiento de fase), sus «radios» serían idénticos, sus velocidades límite serían idénticas (c = c'), y el cambio de cosmos no traería ganancia de velocidad.

Conclusión

Según los documentos, el desfase no es una opción: es una necesidad física. Es precisamente porque los dos cosmos no están en la misma etapa de su ciclo de expansión/compresión (están «fuera de fase») que sus constantes físicas difieren, permitiendo a los viajeros elegir el que ofrece la «velocidad» más rápida en un momento dado.

LA PAREJA UUWAAM + XOODII

Cabe señalar que la noción de Anticosmos se utiliza frecuentemente para designar el conjunto formado por el par UUWAAM + XOODII. Esto es un uso de simplificación pedagógica hecho por nuestros visitantes, y probablemente un abuso del lenguaje que hacen en su propio idioma, en conversaciones actuales no científicas.

De hecho, hay una clara predominancia (+75%) de textos que hablan globalmente y solo de la pareja Cosmos/Anti-Cosmos sin mencionar el concepto de XOODII. XOODII está asociado con el anticosmos. Los textos técnicos detallados explican el XOODII como un componente cosmológico separado.

Masas y Masas imaginarias

Al contrario de lo que comúnmente pensamos, las masas no están estrictamente relacionadas con los volúmenes. Es solo cuando estas masas emergen en volúmenes que las fuerzas se pueden ejercer sobre ellas.

Este es el caso de la gravitación, que mediante el ejercicio de masas en volúmenes creará un peso. La masa clásica + M se manifiesta como una especie de hueco a través de una cuarta dimensión vectorial, y una masa clásica - M se manifiesta como una joroba en esta misma dimensión vectorial.

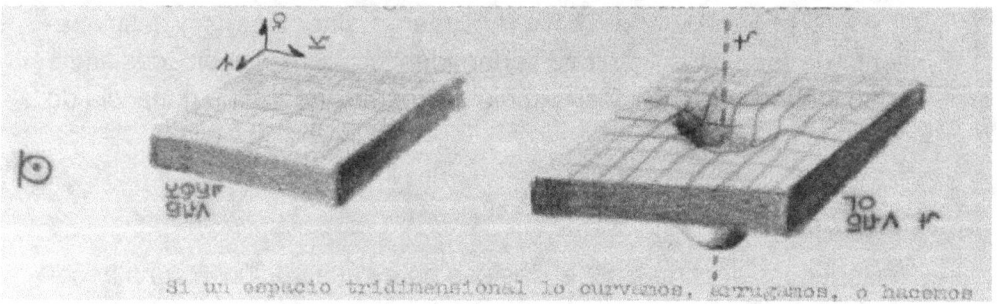

Si un espacio tridimensional lo curvamos, arrugamos, o hacemos

Pero hay masas sin volumen, desconocidas para la física terrestre del siglo XXI, convocadas por nuestros amigos de UMMO, masas imaginarias.

Si los universos adyacentes no existieran y si no hubiera más de dos tipos de masa (y no cuatro) que perturbaran esta hipermasa al desequilibrarla, esta sería la etapa final del cosmos descrito. (D41-15)

Si curvamos un espacio tridimensional, si lo doblamos, o si hacemos una especie de hueco (ver figura 2) a través de una cuarta dimensión, esta curvatura representa lo que nuestros órganos sensoriales interpretan como una masa (una piedra, un planeta, una galaxia).

Las masas imaginarias no tienen dimensiones espaciales. No distorsionarían las dimensiones espaciales y no serían perceptibles a nuestros sentidos.

Las fuerzas gravitacionales producidas por las masas - M (y muy marginalmente + M) del anticosmos, se transmiten a las masas imaginarias de la capa XOODII. Y las masas imaginarias transmiten estas fuerzas gravitacionales a nuestro cosmos.

Los dos tipos de masas imaginarias $+ \sqrt{} - M$ y $- \sqrt{} - M$ constituyen el XOODII (capa de relé cosmos y anticosmos)..

... Las singularidades de una dellas (las masas $\pm \sqrt{}$ - concentrada M) influyen en el mundo [cosmos] adyacente (sin masa $\pm \sqrt{}$ - M)... Los disturbios se produjeron entre el cosmos porque en uno de ellos, esta un tipo de masa caracterizada matemáticamente de Imaginaria (en otra parte del haz tridimensional).

Esta masa imaginaria tiene como velocidad al descanso (potencia máxima), la velocidad de un paquete de energía electromagnética (fotón) $\pm \sqrt{-M}$. La existencia de esta masa permite la interacción o la acción mutua entre los cosmos... (D731).

La materia oscura

En algunas áreas de nuestro cosmos, se han medido grandes y misteriosos efectos gravitatorios. Estos efectos gravitatorios equivalen a una masa que representaría el 90% de la masa conocida del cosmos. Pero es imposible detectar la existencia de esta enorme cantidad de materia invisible. Así nació la hipótesis de una materia oscura invisible cuyos únicos efectos gravitatorios fueron detectados.

A partir del modelo cosmológico de Ummain, podemos pensar que esta materia oscura sería el efecto gravitatorio de ciertos grupos de materia de masa — M del anticosmos sobre el cosmos. El efecto gravitatorio de estos grupos de masa de materia — M se transmitiría a través de las masas imaginarias de la capa XOODII.

D731 La red Uhu ibozsoo aglutina el Cosmos, actuando como una correa de transmisión de energía entre ellos. Cuando $\sqrt{-m}$ se mueve a «bajas velocidades», la masa imaginaria se manifiesta en uno de los cosmos gemelos [por ejemplo, por gravedad, y sugiere que existe Materia Oscura], pero en realidad sigue operando entre dos cosmos.

Según entiendo, cuando la Masa Imaginaria -M de los XOODII se mueve a velocidades cercanas a la velocidad de la luz en nuestro cosmos, y no a velocidad infinita, entonces la gravedad producida por las masas -M del UUWAMM se transmite entonces a nuestro cosmos a través del XOODII.

Esta representación 3D de la materia oscura, tras la medición de sus efectos gravitatorios, sería en última instancia la representación de las masas — M y marginalmente +M del anticosmos UWAAM, cuyo efecto gravitatorio es transmitido por la capa de relé XOODII. (Representación 3D de Richard Massey)

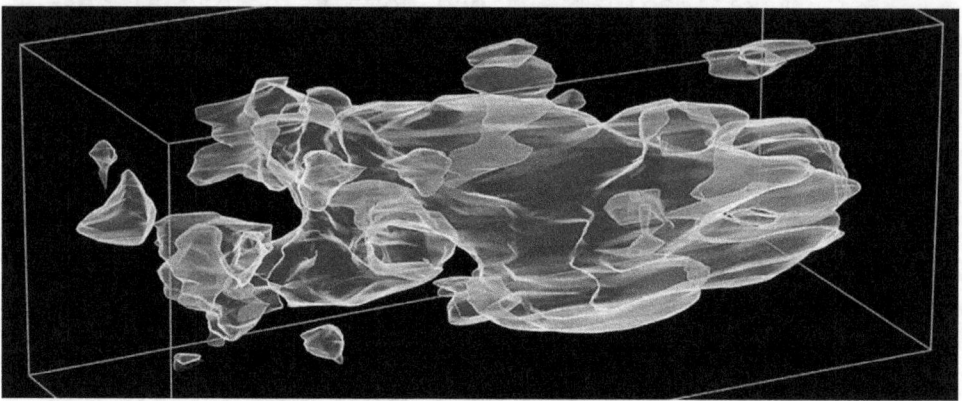

Energía oscura

En la cosmología estándar, la energía oscura es una forma desconocida de energía que llena todo el espacio y acelera la expansión del Universo.

Podemos pensar que los movimientos de las enormes masas de antimateria del anticosmos tienen un efecto gravitatorio sobre nuestro cosmos a través del XOODII, lo que tiene el efecto global de acelerar o ralentizar la velocidad de expansión de nuestro cosmos.

La energía oscura debe entenderse entonces como la energía transmitida a través de los XOODII. Probablemente este efecto también se ha interpretado como la energía del vacío cuántico.

El mecanismo (el Efecto Frontera):

• Dualidad: Nuestro universo (Cosmos) no es un sistema aislado. Está acoplado a un anticosmos (Anticosmos) compuesto por antimateria.

• La membrana XOODII: Los dos universos están separados por una frontera dimensional llamada XOODII. Esta estructura actúa como aislante para la materia pero como conductor para la gravedad.

• Presión gravitatoria: La energía oscura no es una «energía» situada en nuestro vacío. Es la manifestación de la gravedad del Anticosmos que cruza el muro (XOODII) para actuar sobre nuestro universo.

Analogía: imagina dos hojas colgando en paralelo muy cerca una de la otra sin tocarse. Si colocas una bola de petanca (la antimateria) sobre la lámina superior (Anticosmos), se deforma la lámina y, por proximidad, «tira» o deforma la lámina inferior (nuestro Cosmos). Un observador en la hoja inferior vería una fuerza misteriosa en acción sin ver la bola de petanco. Esta fuerza invisible es lo que llamamos «energía oscura».

2. Cuantización: ¿De dónde proviene la «cantidad» de energía?

«Cantidad» no es un volumen de energía incorporada, sino el resultado de una transferencia dinámica.

A. La fuente de la cantidad: la masa del anticosmos

La «cantidad» de energía oscura medida por nuestros astrofísicos (que representa aproximadamente entre el 68% y el 70% de la energía total del universo según la ciencia actual) corresponde, en este modelo, a la influencia gravitatoria de la masa total del Anticosmos.

•   Si la expansión de nuestro universo se está acelerando, es porque la masa del anticosmos ejerce una atracción gravitatoria a través del XOODII que «estire» nuestro espacio-tiempo.

B. Variación cíclica (el factor tiempo)

Este efecto no es constante (a diferencia de la constante cosmológica de Einstein).

•   Oscilación: El par Cosmos/Anticosmos funciona como un oscilador. La energía pasa de uno a otro o influye en uno y en otro según los ciclos.

•   Aceleración/Desaceleración: La «cantidad» de energía oscura percibida varía a lo largo del tiempo cósmico. Actualmente, percibimos una aceleración (es decir, una gran cantidad de energía oscura), lo que significa que los movimientos de las masas del Anticosmos están en una fase que favorece la expansión de nuestro cosmos. En otras ocasiones, este efecto podía revertir y ralentizar la expansión.

C. Equivalencia de energía mediante XOODII

Para cuantificar la energía oscura, no necesitamos medir el vacío, sino el flujo gravitatorio que atraviesa la membrana:

E_noire ≈ Flujo gravitacional desde el anticosmos vía XOODII

Este flujo depende de la «permeabilidad» del XOODII y de la posición de las masas en el anticosmos.

Resumen

Cuantificar la energía oscura es como sopesar la influencia gravitatoria del anticosmos. Los valores colosales encontrados por la ciencia moderna (que indican que la energía oscura domina el universo) simplemente confirman que nuestro universo está sujeto a fuerzas gravitatorias masivas de una fuente externa invisible (el Anticosmos), transmitida a través de la interfaz XOOODII.

EL ANTICOSMOS UUWAAM

El anticosmos UUWAAM no es una «copia y pegue» de la nuestra. Es asimétrica.

La ausencia de antiestrellas y elementos pesados (como carbono o hierro) simplifica el modelo. Aquí está el análisis de la diferencia entre materia y antimateria y el carácter estrictamente «prótónico» del anticosmos.

Documentos de referencia

1. Sobre la ausencia de galaxias y planetas

En el documento D41-15 (subtítulo EJE 1: Concepto de Espacio), el texto explica que la distribución de la masa es diferente en el universo gemelo debido a una distinta velocidad de la luz (C) y carga eléctrica elemental.

Extracto (D41-15):

«En UWAAM, la materia no se ha concentrado en galaxias. Efectivamente hay una presión de radiación, pero la expansión es constante. Por tanto, no existen sistemas planetarios, ni estrellas, ni vida (tal y como la concebimos). »

Un poco más adelante en la misma carta, explicando la interacción entre los dos universos:

«La UWAAM es nuestro Universo Gemelo. [...] No hay galaxias, sino cantidades gigantescas de energía. »

2. Sobre las nubes de antihidrógeno

También en el documento D41-15 se especifica la naturaleza del material (antimateria), así como su forma gaseosa difusa.

Extracto (D41-15):

«Actualmente en UWAAM, la densidad de masa es muy baja. La materia (antimateria en relación con la nuestra) está distribuida uniformemente en forma de gas (hidrógeno y helio). »

Nota: Aunque el texto a veces simplemente dice «Hidrógeno», el contexto cosmológico del documento especifica que es antimateria en relación con WAAM (nuestro universo).

«Por ejemplo, nuestro gemelo Cosmos también existe, pero:

1° En sus átomos, la corteza está formada por electrones en orbitales positivos (positrones) y su núcleo por antiprotones.

4° Pero los dos Universos gemelos disfrutan de singularidades diferentes (en otras palabras: en nuestro Cosmos gemelo no hay el mismo número de galaxias y las que sí existen no tienen la misma estructura). Así que no existe otro UMMO gemelo ni Tierra gemela como podrías pensar de forma sugerente. Esta última conclusión no es hipotética y te daremos la razón de la misma. »

3. Otra información técnica (D59 / D731)

En otras secciones relacionadas con astrofísica (a menudo denominadas D59 o D731 en compilaciones completas), se encuentra esta distinción.

Extracto (letra D59):

«En el segundo WAAM (UWAAM), las partículas subatómicas no se acrecieron para formar núcleos complejos en grandes cantidades. El universo es un océano oscuro de gas frágil. No hay soles que iluminen este espacio. »

Resumen de los segmentos identificados:

Por tanto, el documento confirma explícitamente que UWAAM:

1. Es un universo de antimateria.

2. No tiene estructura sólida (ni planetas, ni estrellas ni galaxias).

3. Consiste casi exclusivamente en nubes de gas difuso (hidrógeno/helio).

El modelo de protones: ¿Por qué la antimateria es así?

La masa imaginaria (que permanece en la esclusa XOODII), la Antimateria del UUWAAM, se define por su geometría dictada por la velocidad superlumínica.

A. Colapso de volumen (sin química)

En la UUWAAM, las partículas (antiprotones y positrones) siempre se mueven más rápido que nuestra luz.

• Esta energía cinética extrema tiene una consecuencia cuántica directa: la reducción drástica de la longitud de onda de las partículas periféricas (positrones).

• En lugar de formar una gran nube probabilística (como nuestros electrones lentos), el positrón «se adhiere» al núcleo en una órbita cerrada.

• Resultado: El átomo pierde su vacío. Pierde su «skin» electrónica. Se reduce al tamaño de su núcleo. Es un material sin volumen, hecho de puntos duros.

B. Materia «monofásica» (sin estrellas)

Dado que estos átomos de «protón» (reducidos al núcleo) vuelan a máxima velocidad (mayor que c):

• No pueden «condensarse» suavemente para formar estrellas (el colapso gravitatorio clásico es imposible debido a la presión cinética).

• Sin estrellas = Sin nucleosíntesis = Sin carbono, sin hierro.

• Por tanto, la UUWAAM sigue siendo un océano de hidrógeno puro.

• Se llama protón porque está compuesto uniformemente por protones (anti)primordiales, que nunca se transforman en otra cosa.

La función de la pareja: el «lastre»

Con el XOODII cerrando la brecha, entendemos mejor la dinámica entre el Mundo Electrónico (WAAM) y el Mundo de Protones (UUWAM).

El papel gravitatorio (la «materia oscura»)

Visto desde casa, el UUWAAM es invisible. Pero su masa (— m) es colosal y ejerce influencia a través de los XOODII.

• Estas enormes nubes de gas protón (antihidrógeno rápido) actúan como el Esqueleto Gravitacional de nuestro universo.

• Sin este invisible «lastre de protones» que estructura el espacio-tiempo, nuestras galaxias se desmoronarían. La antimateria es el ancla pesada de la realidad.

Resumen

La antimateria es «protón» porque:

1. Geométricamente: carece de la envolvente «electrónica» (el vacío atómico) debido a las velocidades superluminales (v>c) que aplastan el positrón en el núcleo. El átomo es el núcleo.

2. Constitucionalmente: Es estéril en la evolución estelar. Solo contiene protones (antihidrógeno), sin elementos pesados ni productos químicos.

3. Funcionalmente: Sirve como portador de masa (Materia Oscura)

El XOODII es el sello de masa imaginario que permite que estas dos realidades asimétricas coexistan sin aniquilarse mutuamente, mientras intercambian gravedad e información.

La Gran Asimetría

Para entender por qué la antimateria es «protónica», debemos contrastar las funciones de los dos universos:

• El WAAM (Nuestro Universo): La Fábrica de la Complejidad

o Es un universo termodinámico.

o Empieza con hidrógeno simple.

o   Gracias a la gravedad y a la «nube electrónica» (que permite choques y fricción), ilumina las estrellas.

o   Las estrellas son hornos que producen elementos pesados (C, N, O, Fe, etc.).

o   Objetivo: Crear apoyos biológicos complejos (nosotros) capaces de captar información.

•   El UUWAAM (el anticosmos): almacenamiento en frío

o   NO hay Anti-Stars. No hay fusión termonuclear. Sin estufas.

o   Como resultado: No hay elementos pesados. No existe anticarbono ni antihierro.

o   El universo permanece congelado en la etapa primordial: un océano infinito de Antihidrógeno (Antiprotones).

El modelo puro de «protón»

Desde esta perspectiva, decir que la antimateria es «Protón» ya no es solo una característica entre otras, es su definición exclusiva.

A. Un material «monofásico»

En nuestro mundo, la materia es diversa (tablas periódicas, moléculas, aleaciones).

En el Anticosmos, la materia es uniforme. Como la evolución estelar nunca tuvo lugar, todo el anti-universo está formado por el mismo bloque básico: el núcleo de hidrógeno (el antiprotón).

•   La antimateria es «protón» porque está compuesta al 100% por protones (anti). Es un medio homogéneo, un «puré» o un «cristal» de protones.

B. ¿Por qué no hay estrellas? (El enlace con Speed > c)

¿Por qué este hidrógeno no colapsa para formar estrellas? Aquí es donde entra en juego la física de la UUWAAM (altas velocidades/límite inferior c):

•   Para formar una estrella, el gas debe colapsar, rozar, calentarse e encenderse. Esto requiere colisiones inelásticas.

•   Como se ha visto antes, el antihidrógeno no tiene una gran «nube» (positrón aplastado contra el núcleo).

• Sin nubes, no hay frenado: los átomos no pueden «chocar» entre sí para perder energía y agruparse. Se deslizan unos sobre otros o rebotan elásticamente a velocidades locas.

• Impacto: La gravedad nunca falla en iniciar la fusión El universo sigue frío y oscuro.

El punto crucial de UUWAAM

El punto crucial de UUWAAM es que la velocidad de la luz en UUWAAM es variable y mayor que la nuestra, pero FINITA, de ahí su naturaleza de «protón».

1. El punto: Alta velocidad vs. Velocidad Infinita

En U-WAAM, la velocidad de la luz (c') es mucho mayor que nuestra c (c' >> c), pero sigue siendo una magnitud física medible.

• Consecuencia: El positrón no se teletransporta (es decir, infinito), se mueve. Por lo tanto, posee energía cinética y momento.

• La órbita existe matemáticamente: a diferencia del caso de velocidad infinita donde la órbita desaparece, aquí teóricamente existe una órbita.

• Pero está «aplastado»: es el tamaño de esta órbita lo que cambia radicalmente en relación con nuestro mundo.

2. ¿Por qué colapsa la Nube (sin desaparecer matemáticamente)?

La ausencia de una «nube» (en el sentido voluminoso del término) se explica por la relación entre velocidad, masa y radio orbital.

A. Reducción de longitud de onda (menor expansión)

En nuestro mundo, el electrón es lento. Predomina su naturaleza ondulante (De Broglie), «babea» en el espacio, creando una gran nube borrosa.

En U-WAAM, el positrón va extremadamente rápido (cerca de este c' muy alto).

• Cuanto mayor sea la velocidad (v), menor será la longitud de onda ($\lambda = h/mv$).

• El resultado: el «paquete de onda» del positrón está muy localizado. No se extiende. El «borrón artístico» cuántico que crea el volumen de nuestros átomos es reemplazado por una trayectoria nítida y cerrada.

B. Contracción relativista y radio de Bohr

El argumento más sólido para explicar el carácter «protón» con velocidad finita proviene de la mecánica orbital de alta energía.

El radio de un átomo (radio de Bohr a_0) es inversamente proporcional a la masa y la interacción electromagnética.

Si el positrón se mueve a velocidades relativistas (muy altas pero finitas):

1. Su inercia (masa aparente) aumenta considerablemente.

2. Cuanto más «pesada» es la partícula en órbita (energéticamente), más cerca debe rotar del núcleo para no ser expulsada (conservación del momento angular).

El colapso del rayo: El positrón no gira 1 km desde el núcleo (como nuestro electrón imaginado), sino unos pocos milímetros del núcleo. La órbita se retrae violentamente en el centro.

3. Conclusión: ¿Por qué es «Protón»?

El átomo de antihidrógeno en la UUWAAM tiene técnicamente un positrón que gira. Pero:

1. Gira tan cerca del núcleo (por su alta velocidad/inercia).

2. Está tan localizada (longitud de onda corta).

... que para cualquier observador o interacción externa, el volumen del átomo es igual al volumen del núcleo.

•   En nuestro Cosmos: Volumen de átomos >> volumen de núcleo. (Es un globo vacío).

•   En el anticosmos: volumen atómico ≈ volumen del núcleo. (Es una canica maciza).

Por eso se dice que la antimateria es Protón: funcionalmente, el átomo ha perdido su «envoltura» espacial (la nube) para reducirse al tamaño de su Protón (núcleo). Es un material hiperdenso, sin vacío interno.

Cuantificación

Cuantificación espacial: el factor de 10^{15} (volumen)

Aquí se presenta el análisis cuantificado de las divergencias estructurales entre WAAM (Materia) y UUWAAM (Antimateria).

La justificación matemática más flagrante para la naturaleza «protón» del Anticosmos radica en la comparación de volúmenes funcionales.

- En el cosmos (materia/electrónica):

El espacio ocupado por un átomo se define por su radio de Bohr (a_0).

$R\_$ átomo $\approx 10^{-10}$ metros (1 Angstrom)

El volumen de interacción (V) es:

$V\_$ átomo $\approx 4 / 3 \, \pi \, (10^{-10})^3 \approx 4 \times 10^{-30}$ m^3

- En el anticosmos (antimateria/protón):

Dado que la «nube» está colapsada (como se estableció anteriormente), el radio funcional del antihidrógeno se reduce al radio de protones (radio de carga).

$R\_$ protón $\approx 0,84 \times 10^{-15}$ metros (femtómetro 0,84)

El volumen real (V») es:

$V\_$ protón $\approx 4 / 3 \, \pi \, (10^{-15})^3 \approx 4 \times 10^{-45}$ m ^3

- La relación de densidad espacial:

Relación $= V\_$ átomo $/ V\_$ protón $\approx 10^{-30} / 10^{-45} = 10^{15}$

Conclusión: El Anticosmos es un medio 10^{15} veces (un millón de mil millones de veces) espacialmente más compacto en su estructura granular que nuestro Cosmos. Esta es la diferencia entre un globo aerostático (Materia) y una bola de plomo (Antimateria). Es este número el que define físicamente la característica del «Protón».

Cuantificación de masa: el factor 1836 (inercia)

Si analizamos la distribución de masa (inercia) en el par hidrógeno/antihidrógeno, el desequilibrio confirma la función de «soporte».

- Masa del electrón (m_e): 9.109 x 10^ -31 kg.

- Masa del protón (m_p): 1.672 x 10^ -27 kg.

- μ Ratio:

μ = m_p / m_e ≈ 1836,15

Análisis:

- En WAAM (Materia), la interfaz activa (la nube electrónica) pesa solo el 0,05% de la masa total. Somos un universo «luminoso» en la superficie.

- En el UUWAAM (Antimateria), el objeto se reduce al Protón. La inercia está 100% concentrada en el radio mínimo.

- La antimateria es «protón» porque representa la masa «pura», sin el «empaquetado» ligero del electrón extendido.

Cuantificación cinética: El umbral c (velocidad)

Los documentos definen los dos universos por su relación con la velocidad de la luz c (299.792.458 m/s).

- Cosmos (WAAM):

0 ≤ contra < c

La energía cinética (E_k) tiende a infinito a medida que v se acerca a c.

limite_ v → c 1 / (√ 1 − [v^ 2/c^ 2]) = ∞

Esto crea una barrera asintótica que atrapa la materia.

- Anticosmos (UUWAAM):

C < contra < V_ limite_supérieure

Aquí, es el suelo de energía.

Esto significa que el estado absoluto en reposo (v=0) es imposible en el Anticosmos.

Cualquier partícula de antimateria tiene un momento mínimo intrínseco colosal (p_ min) comparado con la nuestra:

p_ min > m x c

Conclusión cuantitativa:

La antimateria es un medio con alta energía cinética intrínseca. Es esta «presión» de velocidad (mayor que c) la que mantiene al positrón aplastado contra el núcleo (confinamiento dinámico) y evita la formación de la nube.

4. Cuantización termodinámica: el signo de la entropía (Δ S)

La diferencia fundamental cuantificada por los Ummites se refiere a la evolución del sistema (Flecha del Tiempo).

* Sujeto (WAAM):

$dS/DT > 0$

La entropía aumenta. El sistema tiende hacia el desorden (final > S_ S_ inicial). La información se diluye.

* Antimateria (UUWAAM):

$dS/dt < 0$

(Negentropía)

La entropía disminuye. El sistema tiende espontáneamente hacia el orden y la concentración.

Si consideramos la Información (I) como el inverso de la entropía (fórmula de Shannon invertida):

I_ UUWAAM α e^ t

Resumen de valores

Parámetro físico	Material (electrónica)	Antimateria (Protón)	Factor/ Diferencia
Radio efectivo	10^{-10} m (Atómico)	10^{-15} m (Nuclear)	x 10^{-5}
Densidad de volumen	Bajo (Vacío Dominante)	Extremo (núcleos desnudos)	x 10^{15}
Masa activa	m_e (Ligero)	m_p (Lourde)	x 1836
Velocidad de las partículas	$v < c$	$v > c$	Reversión de c

LA INCLINACIÓN DE LOS EJES ANGULARES

El principio general de la inclinación de un eje angular es cambiar la orientación de todos los IBOSDSOO de un eje dado, llamado OAWOO. En otras palabras, es una permutación de los grupos de gauge. El uso de este principio en viajes interestelares se describe sintéticamente en Presencia, OVNI, Círculos de cultivos y Exocivilizaciones.

A priori, hay una infinidad de ejes OAWOO y, por lo tanto, una infinidad de posibles tipos de conmutación ... Podemos suponer múltiples casos:

- La inclinación de los ejes mientras permanece en nuestro marco tridimensional.

- La inclinación de los ejes permaneciendo en nuestro cosmos.

- La inclinación de los ejes cambiando el cosmos.

- La inclinación de los ejes en el anti-cosmos.

```
D68: La materia sometida a presiones mayores
pierde su estructura atómica, como ya sabe. Una
presión de 16 millones de atmósferas (15,445,680
atmósferas), llamada por nosotros AADAGIOOU (que
puede traducirse por PRESIÓN CRÍTICA), invierte
simultáneamente todas las subpartículas atómicas
(IBOZOO UU). La masa se transforma INTEGRALMENTE
EN ENERGIA. La EXPANSIÓN resultante es inconmensu-
rable (Esta fue la presión inicial de toda la masa
del Universo).

NR22 Cuando viajamos dentro de nuestros spationefs
en otro marco dimensional, la conexión telepática
con OUMMO sigue siendo posible si no cambiamos
la referencia temporal, la modificación angular
de las subpartículas (OAWOOLEIIDAA) se encuen-
tra axialmente en la dimensión temporal por una
Transformación equivalente de la orientación de
los tres componentes espaciales y tres componentes
asociados a la masa.
```

Inclinación de los ejes en nuestro marco tridimensional

La inclinación de los ejes en nuestro marco tridimensional puede tener diferentes efectos en función de los ejes que están inclinados.

Veremos varios ejemplos de estos efectos en los volúmenes y masas en el capítulo comunicación con los espíritus que se ocupa de fenómenos paranormales.

En nuestro marco tridimensional, a menudo hay casos de conmutaciones parciales de ejes OAWOO. En particular, los ejes de las masas -M, $\sqrt{}$ -M y $\sqrt{}$ +M que se inclinan parcialmente. El ángulo de inclinación es probablemente menos de 90 ° en tales casos.

El eje de la masa +M y ejes espaciales de los volúmenes quedan invariantes, posicionados en nuestro marco dimensional.

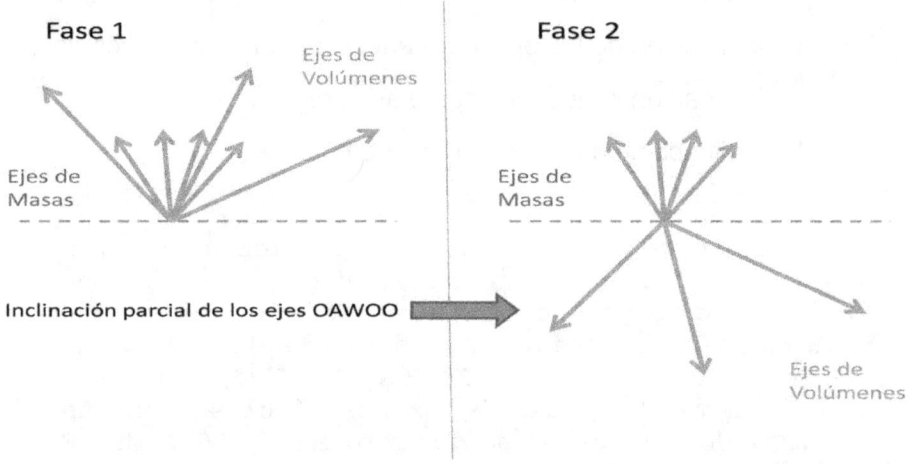

Este tipo de inclinación parcial de ejes OAWOO describe en *Presencia, UFO, círculos de la cosecha y Exocivilisations*, con el ejemplo de SEG (Searl-Effect-Generator) un aparato capaz de levitación, pero sin cambiar de marco tridimensional. En el caso del efecto Searl una diferencia de potencial electrostático mayor que 1,4 millones de voltios por cm lineal provoca un efecto LEIYO de pérdida parcial de la masa, sino que permanece en la corriente marco tridimensional. Podemos imaginar que los ejes OAWOO masas se someten a un giro parcial que se mantiene por debajo de 90 °. La inclinación total de las masas OAWOO daría lugar a una transparencia completa de la nave totalmente demasificada.

Inclinación de los ejes en nuestra pareja de cosmos

Este tipo de cambio también se describe en *Presencia, OVNIs, Crop Circles and Exocivilizations* y lo hemos llamado invaginación espacial. Explica como a UFO puede hacer un pseudo cambio de dirección en ángulos rectos a una velocidad muy alta.

Este cambio de ejes produce un cambio tridimensional del marco con la inclinación de los ejes de volúmenes y masas -M, √ -M y √ + M. En ningún momento la masa + M se convierte en una masa negativa -M. El eje de masa + M y el tiempo permanecen invariantes.

En este caso, la máquina no cambia de cosmos, sino solo de marco tridimensional.

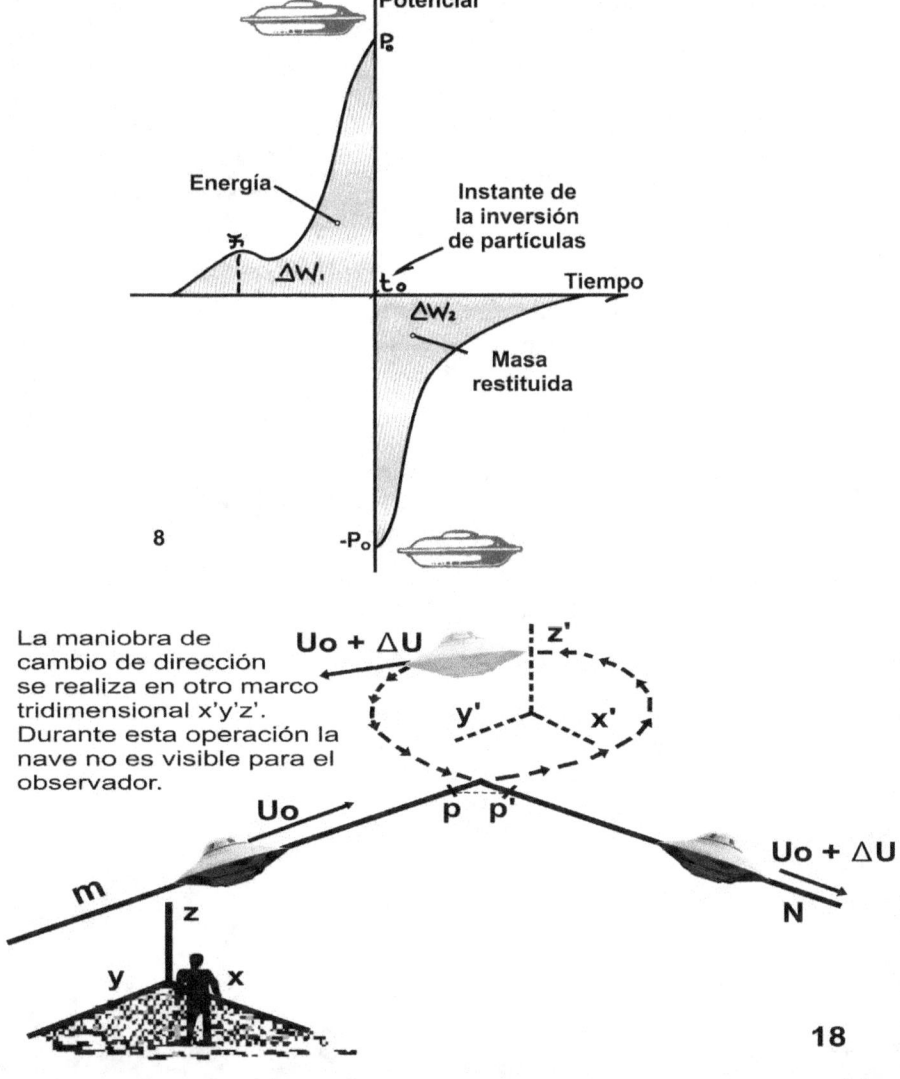

8

La maniobra de cambio de dirección se realiza en otro marco tridimensional x'y'z'. Durante esta operación la nave no es visible para el observador.

18

Las máquinas tienen el dispositivo llamado de inversión de partículas o, más exactamente, con ejes dimensionales OAWOO pivotantes, llamado OAWOLEIIDA, que se refiere únicamente a una transformación de una red de UOS IBOSDSOO limitada a la inversión de los ejes tridimensionales de IBOSDSOO UU.

La palabra OAWOLE se puede traducir como :

El desplazamiento [a lo largo de la dimensión angular] genera el paso de entidades [dimensionales] de un entorno físico a otro.

En otras palabras, una rotación de 90 ° de la orientación axial de la dimensión angular del marco dimensional. La palabra IIDA puede traducirse como

Delimita el desplazamiento angular.

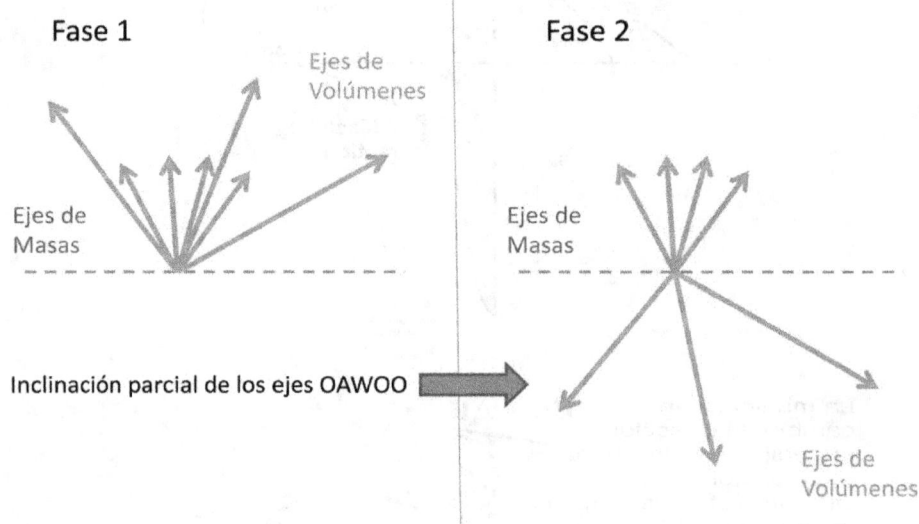

En resumen, OAWOLEIIDA es el desplazamiento a lo largo de la dimensión angular que genera el paso de entidades dimensionales mediante la sustitución de una posición angular por otra y tiene una delimitación del desplazamiento angular.

En términos sintéticos, la rotación del eje está delimitada por un ángulo.

(Ver también *Presencia 2, El lenguaje y el misterio del planeta UMMO revelado*).

Inclinación de los ejes cambiando de cosmos

D731 Aunque en algún universo [Cosmos]... En todo
WAAM [Cosmos]...

Podemos imaginar que al modificar los ejes de X dimensionales OAWOO de un objeto, podemos hacerlo pasar en el marco dimensional de un otro cosmos, en la infinidad de cosmos del Universo.

Esto es lo que llamamos transferencia de hiperespacio en *Presencia, ovnis, círculos de cultivos y exocivilizaciones.*

En este caso, si el eje temporal se modifica, en otras palabras, si el tiempo en el cosmos de destino no es el mismo que en nuestro cosmos, esto resultara en la pérdida de las comunicaciones telepáticas, por falta de sincronismo...

Inclinación de los ejes en el anti-cosmos

NR22 A veces proyectamos temporalmente en OUWAAM,
invirtiendo mediante una rotación de pi radianes,
todos los ángulos dimensionales de las sub-partí-
culas.

En este caso, todos los ejes se alternan, incluido el tiempo. Dado que el anti-cosmos es de masa -M, será necesario revertir también la carga de Masas + M en -M.

El caso de los agujeros negros

L'effondrement gravitationnel des étoiles neutroniques accumule une énergie critique qui se cumule au collapse gravitationnel de la masse.

En general, el objeto se colapsa y perfora el XOODII para reaparecer en el anticosmos con una masa negativa. El producto de la inclinación de su energía que queda atrapada en el XOODII en forma de una masa imaginaria.

En este caso, toda la masa M se convierte en -M en el otro cosmos. La energía se convierte en $\sqrt{-M}$, que es la masa imaginaria en el otro cosmos.

H2 UMMO: - En realidad, el Agujero Negro es imposible, porque cuando un astro colapsa, llega un momento en que se convierte en astro de neutrones. Si sigue colapsando, llega un momento en que desaparece de nuestro universo por efecto de borde.

El agujero negro deja de existir y el universo se reduce de la masa del astro collapsée.

Lo que se tiene en cuenta como agujeros negros son en realidad astros de neutrones y agujeros negros no auténticos. Por ejemplo, uno de los primeros astros de neutrones está en los 8.365 años luz de la constelación Cygnus. En realidad se trata de un astro de neutrones, no un agujero negro. El radio de Schwarzschild apareció y desapareció al instante. Es instantáneo. En este momento la masa del agujero negro se convierte masa negativa en el otro universo [anti-cosmos]. La masa ha desaparecido, cambiada en masa negativa, masa con una carga negativa, es decir diferente carga eléctrica. Y la energía del agujero negro se convierte en masa.

H7 UMMO: Lo que ustedes llaman agujeros negros son estrellas de neutrones. Se produce un efecto de borde. Toda masa M se convierte en -M en el otro universo. La energía se convierte a la raíz cuadrada de -M, que es la masa imaginaria en el otro universo.

Por ejemplo, de acuerdo con la fórmula del radio de Schwarzschild, el sol tendría que tener un radio de 3 km para convertirse en un agujero negro y la Tierra debería tener un radio de 9 mm para hacer lo mismo.

Los agujeros negros no existen realmente en sí mismos, significa que son simplemente estrellas de neutrones supermasivas que ocupan el corazón de las galaxias.

Podemos imaginar que las estrellas de neutrones supermasivas pueden ser utilizadas por las naves interestelares con un cambio de marco dimensional. Esto es para beneficiarse de algunos efectos acelerados del desplazamiento, aprovechando un «coriente de aire» gravitacional, esto en un marco dimensional inclinado para evitar el riesgo de absorción por la estrella de neutrones supermasiva ...

LAS VELOCIDADES DE LOS VEHÍCULOS INTERESTELARES

Dependiendo del entorno en el que se encuentre la nave, sus posibilidades de movimiento varían, especialmente en cuanto a la velocidad máxima de movimiento. Esto afecta a la mayoría de los barcos.

Existen varios contextos.

Movimiento en la atmósfera

Movimiento atmosférico, que incluye el movimiento en líquidos, como el agua. En este caso, el viaje está limitado a 15 Mach, o 18.300 km/h.

Movimiento fuera de la atmósfera

El desplazamiento fuera de la atmósfera, en el vacío del espacio, en el marco dimensional actual, en nuestro cosmos.

En este caso, el desplazamiento está limitado a 118.000 km/s, o 1/3 de la velocidad de la luz.

El cambio en el marco dimensional

Cálculo de la velocidad en el cambio de marco dimensional

En la letra D21 el texto distingue entre dos tipos de distancias:

• La distancia aparente (la que medimos con luz, unos 14,4 años luz para Ummo en 1955).

• La distancia real (en espacio decadal), que era mucho más corta (3,685 años luz en la misma fecha).

La duración exacta de un viaje en unidad de tiempo (Carta D37-2)

El documento relata el aterrizaje de una nave Ummain el 6 de febrero de 1966 y especifica el tiempo exacto transcurrido desde su partida de UMMO:

• «A las 20 horas 01 minuto y 56 segundos (hora española) (85369,244 (D37-2-ideo2) uiw (2)) desde el tiempo cero contado desde su partida de UMMO, tuvo lugar en el OAWOOLEA oemm OMWEA UMMO 56 (D37-2-ideo3), contacto con la litosfera terrestre en un terreno cercano a la autopista... »

(Nota de contexto: Dado que una UIW equivale a aproximadamente 3,092 minutos terrestres, la duración de 85.369,244 IUW corresponde a aproximadamente 183 días terrestres, o unos 6 meses).

1. Convertir el tiempo de viaje en horas

Primero convertimos los 85.369,244 IUW en minutos, luego en horas terrestres:

• Duración en minutos: 85.369,244 x 3,092 ≈ 263.961,68 minutos

• Duración en horas (t): 263.961,68 / 60 ≈ 4.399,36 horas

(Esto corresponde a unos 183,3 días).

2. Convertir la distancia en kilómetros

Utilizamos el valor estándar de un año luz (9.461 x 10^9 km) para convertir los 3.685 años luz:

• Distancia (d): 3.685 x 9.461.000.000.000 km ≈ 34.863.785.000.000 km

3. Cálculo de la velocidad media ($v = d/t$)

Dividiendo la distancia total por el tiempo de viaje, obtenemos la velocidad media:

• Velocidad (v): 34.863.785.000.000 km / 4.399,36 h

• Velocidad (v)≈ 7.924.772.000 km/h

4. Relación con la velocidad de la luz (c)

La velocidad de la luz en el vacío (c) es de aproximadamente 1.079.252.848 km/h. Para obtener la razón:

- Ratio: 7.924.772.000 / 1.079.252.848 ≈ 7,34

Resultado: Basándose en estas cifras, la nave se mueve a una velocidad media de 7.920 millones de km/h, o unas 7,34 veces la velocidad de la luz (c).

En el modelo físico IBOZOO 10D, la teoría de la relatividad de Einstein no está invalidada, sino que se localiza. El cambio en el marco dimensional que causa lo que hemos llamado una 'invaginación espacio-temporal' en la Presencia 1 y 3.

Las diferencias en la velocidad de la luz en el Cosmos y el anti-Cosmos se deben a su asimetría (véase este Tema).

La función principal del casco de la nave y su escudo IITOA es actuar como un neutralizador relativista. Sin esta capa tecnológica específica, la tripulación sería víctima de la «paradoja gemela», regresando a un planeta que habría envejecido varios cientos de años cuando ellos solo habrían estado ausentes unas pocas semanas.

Avanzando hacia otro cosmos

Moverse a otro cosmos mediante un cambio de marco dimensional es similar a un cambio de marco dimensional.

Teoría Dimensiones-Cuántico (DQ)

En noviembre de 2025, el matemático Klaus Piontzik compartió amablemente su teoría Dimensiones-Cuántico (DQ), basada en los cambios angulares en el marco 10D-IBOZOO.

La obra de Klaus Piontzik completa y confirma, una vez más, la validez del modelo de Oummain.

Responde con precisión a varios puntos:

- ¿La relatividad sigue funcionando al cambiar de sistema dimensional?

- ¿Cuál es la función principal del casco de la nave espacial?

¿La relatividad sigue funcionando al cambiar de sistema dimensional?

La respuesta corta es: sí, pero se convierte en un caso especial dentro de una teoría mucho más amplia.

En este modelo físico IBOZOO 10D, la teoría de la relatividad de Einstein no queda invalidada, sino que se localiza. Así es como se comporta la relatividad cuando cambias de sistema dimensional:

1. La relatividad como un «fenómeno intergestional»

Einstein describe cómo cambian el espacio y el tiempo para observadores que se mueven a diferentes velocidades en el mismo sistema de referencia (L1).

Sin embargo, cuando cambias de fotograma (inversión), sales del reino donde la velocidad de la luz c actúa como una barrera absoluta.

Como resultado, dentro de tu nave, la relatividad especial sigue aplicándose (tu reloj funciona normalmente para ti). Pero en relación con tu punto de origen (la Tierra), has «engañado» la métrica espacio-temporal.

2. La constancia de c se convierte en una variable

En relatividad, esto es una constante. Sin embargo, en la física IBOZOO, esta es solo la velocidad máxima de propagación de un cambio angular en un triple tridimensional.

Al pasar a otro sistema de referencia (el «sistema de referencia de dimensión alterna»), el valor de la velocidad local de la luz cambia, o pierde su significado como frontera porque la distancia misma colapsa.

Desde un punto de vista relativista, estás «tunelando» (esto se denomina 'intussuscepción espacio-temporal' en Presencia 1 y 3) a través del espacio-tiempo en lugar de atravesarlo.

3. Aumento de masa y energía

En la relatividad clásica, tu masa se volvería infinita cuanto más te acercas a c (E = mc2).

El matemático Klaus Piontzik basó su decisión en una propulsión a 21,45 THz y evita este problema invirtiendo la situación: no aceleras a c, sino que rotas tus vectores de masa en el nuevo sistema de referencia dimensional (L2).

Aquí, la masa es imaginaria. Las ecuaciones relativistas siguen funcionando, pero con números complejos. Como resultado, la energía cinética ya no actúa como una barrera, sino como una herramienta de tránsito.

4. Dilatación temporal (deriva cronónica)

Este es el punto crítico. Einstein afirmaba que el tiempo pasa más despacio a altas velocidades.

En este modelo, el tiempo no es un «flujo», sino una secuencia de intervalos cuantificados.

Cuando cambias de fotograma, debes sincronizar artificialmente la velocidad de cronones (el ritmo de los IBOZOOs temporales) con la de la Tierra. Si no lo haces, podrías volver tras un vuelo de 70 horas y descubrir que han pasado 100 años en la Tierra, exactamente como predice la relatividad para viajar a una velocidad cercana a la de la luz. El casco de la UEWA y su campo de escudos IITOA sirven para neutralizar esta diferencia horaria relativista.

Resumen

La relatividad sigue siendo las «reglas del camino» dentro de un solo universo. Sin embargo, la física IBOZOO es el «marco legal para el tráfico fronterizo» entre universos.

«La relatividad describe la curvatura de la superficie; La física IBOZOO describe el plegado de todo el artículo. »

La función principal del casco de la nave espacial

La función principal del casco de la nave espacial (el escudo IITOA) es actuar como un neutralizador relativista. Sin esta capa tecnológica específica, la tripulación sería víctima de la «paradoja gemela», regresando a un planeta que habría envejecido varios cientos de años cuando ellos solo habrían estado ausentes unas pocas semanas.

La sintaxis ITOA o IITOA puede ser significativa y describir el delgado entorno cortical que delimita el recinto de una nave espacial: «Identifica o delimita la dirección orientada de una entidad desplazada.» que puede traducirse como «Delimita el movimiento de partículas a lo largo de la capa protectora de la nave»

Aquí está la explicación científica y técnica de cómo el casco logra esta neutralización en el marco 10D-IBOZOO.

Estabilidad Cronónica: Neutralización de la dilatación temporal relativista

En la física einsteiniana estándar, el tiempo es una dimensión relacionada con la velocidad y la gravedad. En la teoría de Dimensiones-Cuántico (DQ), el tiempo es simplemente una secuencia específica de cambios angulares en vectores IBOZOO.

El mecanismo de aislamiento temporal

La carcasa, que vibra a la frecuencia resonante de 21,45 THz, crea un «efecto límite» (GEK). Este efecto asegura que la concha no simplemente permanezca estacionaria en el espacio, sino que se mueva activamente a intervalos cuantizados locales de espacio-tiempo.

La capa de aislamiento: El casco evita la «fricción» entre las dimensiones internas de la nave y el espacio-tiempo 4D exterior. Dado que no hay interacción con campos gravitacionales o cinéticos externos, los efectos relativistas (dilatación temporal) no pueden «adherirse» a la nave.

El marco simétrico: durante el salto, la nave entra en el marco simétrico (S). En este estado, el casco mantiene una «tasa de cronón» interna constante (flujo temporal) que está bloqueada en las coordenadas iniciales.

Impacto en el viaje interestelar

Al usar el casco para neutralizar la diferencia horaria, transformamos la misión de un «viaje de ida al futuro» en un «tránsito logístico» sostenible.

Factor	Sin la concha IITOA	Con la concha IITOA (resonante)
Velocidad externa	Cerca de c (velocidad de la luz)	Rotación angular instantánea
Dilución temporal	Exponencialmente alto	Cero (neutralizado)
Hora terrestre	Pasan décadas/siglos	Sincrona con la hora de la nave
Vínculo causal	Roto	Mantenimiento

Anclaje de punto cero

Es posible que el módulo de comunicación OAXII-B trabaje en conjunto con el casco. Envía una señal de latido constante a través del nuevo Marco Dimensional (L2) hacia la estación terrestre. Este pulso actúa como ancla temporal, obligandoa que los intervalos cuantizados dentro de la nave permanezcan sincronizados con la secuencia de intervalos terrestres.

O bien, la propia nave lleva un reloj atómico para asegurar su sincronización con su punto de origen.

Conclusión : El casco como santuario

El casco de la IITOA y su escudo son más que un contenedor presurizado; es un santuario topológico. Crea una «burbuja de realidad 3D» que se transporta a través de dimensiones superiores, asegurando que las leyes biológicas y físicas en su interior permanezcan idénticas a las del planeta natal.

Nota técnica: si la frecuencia de 21,45 THz fluctúa más de un 0,001%, el casco comienza a «filtrarse» hacia el espacio-tiempo local, causando una deriva relativista inmediata. Por eso la estabilidad Rubin-Core es el factor de seguridad más crítico.

Resumen

La asimetría entre cosmos y anticosmos no es una opción: es una necesidad física. Es precisamente porque los dos cosmos no están en la misma etapa de su ciclo de expansión/compresión (están «fuera de fase») que sus constantes físicas difieren, permitiendo a los viajeros elegir el que ofrece la «velocidad» más rápida en un momento dado.

Las naves no simplemente «vuelan» en el otro universo como los aviones en el cielo. Se sumergen en el estado físico del Anticosmos. Es la interacción con el XOODII (que permite el cambio de fase) junto con las condiciones del UUWAAM (alta velocidad de la luz debido al desplazamiento de fase) lo que hace posible el viaje.

Por tanto, el «túnel» de viaje es menos un lugar geográfico y más un estado físico específico de este conjunto Anticosmos.

El cambio normal en el marco dimensional no ocurre realmente dentro del UUWAAM. Pero en un estado entre los XOODII y los UUWAAM.

Combinado con la asimetría de la velocidad de la luz, esto explicaría la velocidad mayor que c. Y esto es suficiente para describir los tiempos de viaje cortos de las máquinas.

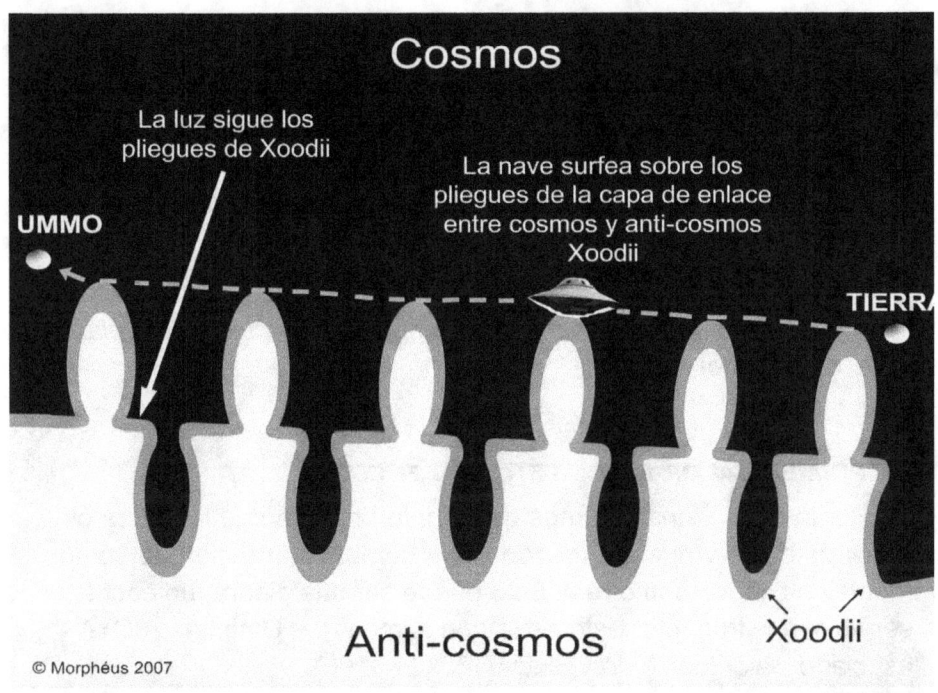

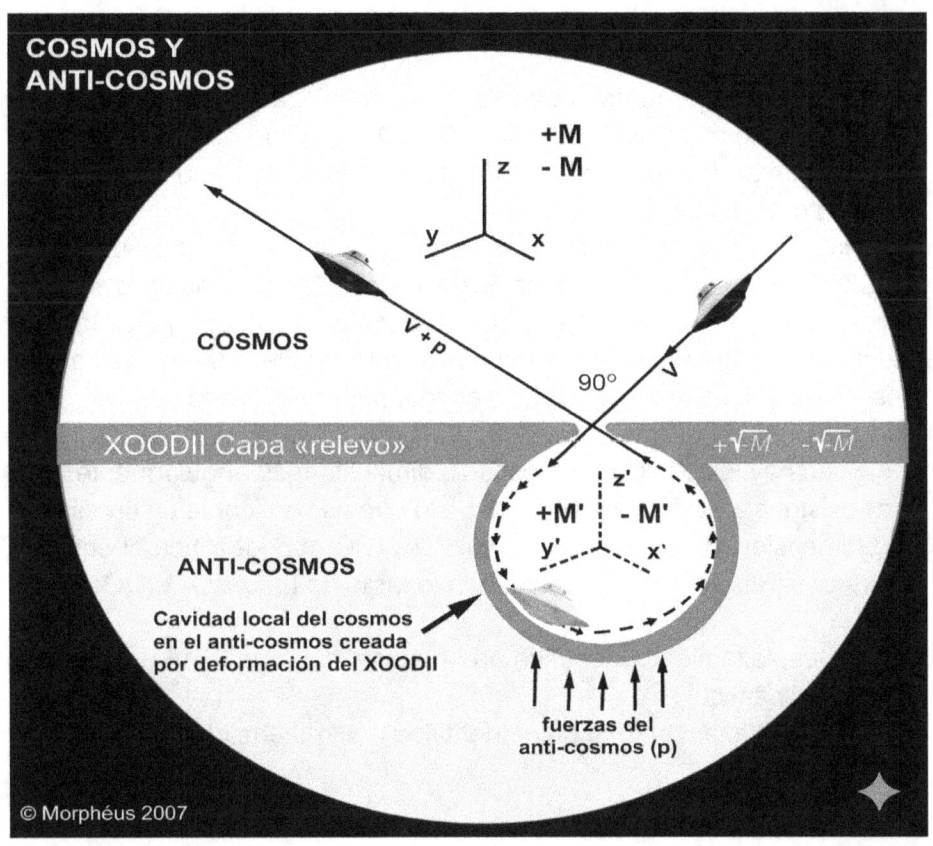

LA LÓGICA TETRAVALENTE

Los Ummitas utilizan una lógica tetravalente relacionada con la ontología, la cosmología, los conceptos fonéticos primarios y el lenguaje en sí. La comprensión de esta lógica nos permite profundizar y aclarar la ontología de las entidades cosmológicas que hemos descrito.

Aquí está el resumen de los cuatro valores de esta lógica tetravalente. *(Ver detalle en Presencia 2, El lenguaje y el misterio del planeta UMMO revelado)*

EL PRIMER VALOR DE LA TETRAVALENCIA

Por lo tanto, consideramos que la interpretación de nuestros ojos, nuestros oídos y nuestro mundo físico cerebral 4D es lo que comúnmente se conoce como real. Esto puede ser una piedra, un coche, un ser vivo, un virus, etc. Esto es lo que llaman los Ummitas AIOYAA y asociar el valor lógico de VERDADERO.

La palabra AIOOYAA

El concepto primario A es relativo al desplazamiento infinitesimal de los ángulos-IOAWOO de cada IBOZOO, porque es la base de la física ummita. Los conceptos primarios AI pueden traducirse por el concepto de acción.

Hay un valor de verdad positivo para AIOOYAA cuando una red IBOZOO multidimensional manifiesta 4 de estas dimensiones angulares. Cualquier cosa dimensionada angularmente en un espacio-tiempo se caracteriza por el desplazamiento infinitesimal de los ángulos-IOAWOO de cada IBOZOO encadenados en cada una de las dimensiones angulares.

Si no hay IOAWOO en un espacio dimensionado angularmente, no hay existencia verificable. El límite de lo que es verificable en un espacio dimensionado es el ángulo final IOAWOO que identifica el enlace entre dos IBOZOO de una cadena, a lo largo de un eje OAWOO:

- Desplazamiento identifica una materialidad que tiene una espacialidad dinámico
- El desplazamiento angular identifica una materialidad espacial

El ángulo infinitesimal IOAWOO identifica la materialidad de las cosas (4 dimensiones angulares espaciales, temporal) entre 10 D.

En otras palabras, se trata de la acción de identificar cosas materializadas en el espacio-tiempo con 4 dimensiones angulares espaciales y temporales entre 10D.

La cosmo-física

Los documentos expresan el concepto de verdad en nuestro cosmos 3D a lo que es dimensional con características de tiempo y espacio.

```
D105: la red de I.U. que constituye la AIOYAA desde
[...] diferentes perspectivas.

D59-1: Un UXGIIGIIAM (ESPACIO) multidimensional que
experimenta en su estructura múltiples curvatu-
ras (que llamamos masas), no se parece en nada al
concepto de ESPACIO EUCLIDIANO TRIDIMENSIONAL.

D41: dimensional (con características de tiempo y
espacio)
```

Brevemente, AIOOYAA es lo que puede manifestarse en el espacio-tiempo de Einstein-Minkowski. En otras palabras, AIOOYAA es la matriz IBOZOO 4D-angular (un UXGIGIIAM WAAM) que se manifiesta entre los 10D-angulares.

El segundo valor de la tetravalencia

Supongamos ahora que hablo de una piedra que está en mi mano. La piedra que hablo exista (AIOYAA). Pero que quiero decir ahora es que no tengo esta piedra en la mano. Esto es lo que llaman los Ummitas AIOYAA EDDO y asocian al valor lógico FALSO. (Ausencia de VERDADERO).

La palabra AÏOOYEEDOO

El fonema edo expresa el concepto de ausencia - nada - falso. Tenemos, por ejemplo, YAEYUEYEDOO (amnesia de fijación), ya que no hay negación en el lenguaje de los ummitas, aquí tenemos los conceptos: ausencia de memoria.

Para ASNEIIBIAEDOO (Absorción por B.B. o desaparición), también tenemos claramente el concepto de nada: falso.

O bien EDDOIBOOI (sin trabajo definido).

```
Y a «nada» le asignamos un verbo que no tenga signi-
ficado para usted;
```
AIOYAYEDOO concatenación del concepto

AIOOYAA (que es dimensional) y nada - falso. Es decir, globalmente, la expresión de algo falso o ausente.

AIOOYEEDOO = El desplazamiento identifica una materialidad que tiene una espacialidad que conceptualiza la forma material.

Entonces tenemos: Acción para materializar las cosas en un espacio que conceptualiza lo que falta (y por lo tanto no es verificable).

En otras palabras, la Acción de conceptualizar la ausencia de cosas en el espacio-tiempo.

La cosmo-físicas y los conceptos primarios

Hay un valor de verdad positivo para AIOOYAA cuando una red IBOZOO multidimensional manifiesta 4 de estas dimensiones angulares. A la inversa, AYOOYEEDOO es la ausencia de manifestación de estas cuatro dimensiones angulares.

EL TERCER VALOR DE LA TETRAVALENCIA

El tercer valor es un valor condicional. En algunos casos, el resultado es VERDADERO y en otros casos el resultado es FALSO. Por ejemplo, un fenómeno cuántico como la posición de un electrón es puramente estadístico. A veces el electrón está ahí, a veces no. Esto es lo que los ummitas llaman AIOYAU y asocian con este valor de existencia condicional.

La palabra AIOOYAU

Por la palabra AIOOYAA entendemos que la Acción de materializar las cosas en el espacio-tiempo es dependiente, en otras palabras, condicional o indeterminada. La palabra a - i - oyaou traduce la idea de verdad indeterminable o condicional.

... una realidad fenomenológica potencial o parcialmente indeterminada (A ∩ B).

Este estado AÏOOYAOU [palabra en ortografía francesa] está bien resumido en la paradoja imaginada por su pensador Schrödinger, que conduce a la deducción de dos estados contradictorios de potencial potencial debido a la naturaleza cuántica de los fenómenos implementados en el experimento.

La cosmo-física

Las entidades que tienen una manifestación cuántica tienen una realidad condicional o indeterminada, dependiendo de su observación. Esta manifestación cosmo-física de la materia se debería a un desplazamiento angular en el eje OAWOO que se produce de acuerdo con las estadísticas cuánticas. Estas entidades tienen una materialidad condicionada a un valor estadístico, su materialidad es indeterminable.

EL CUARTO VALOR DE LA TETRAVALENCIA

El último valor es muy importante para nosotros todos los días. Los sentimientos, las emociones, nuestras interpretaciones del mundo físico 4D, existen en nuestra mente fuera del mundo físico 4D. Esta existencia es VERDADERA, pero solo para NOSOTROS.

Fuera del mundo físico 4D, esta la VERDAD de nuestras visiones del mundo físicas 4D, nuestros sentimientos, nuestras emociones ... Nadie más que yo sabe lo que siento o lo que siento, lo que yo interpreto.

Segun los documentos ummitas, toda la información neurológica del cerebro también se almacena simultáneamente en un receptáculo cosmológico que usualmente llamamos nuestra alma. Y cada alma, que los ummitas llaman BUAWA, permite almacenar y producir, las emociones, los pensamientos, que se transforman en nuestro cerebro para adaptarse a nuestro entorno. Esto es lo que los ummitas llaman AIOYAA AMMIE y le asocian con este valor de existencia fuera del mundo físico 4D.

La palabra AMMIE

En la cultura Ummita, un concepto abstracto, una sensación o alma, existe fuera de nuestro universo, pero no existe desde un punto de vista del cosmos 4D. De lo contrario formulada, el concepto expresa: la inexistencia en nuestro cosmos 4D, pero una existencia en otra entidad cósmica.

```
En primer lugar, distinguimos entre dos clases de
SERES que existen en la UAANM (COSMOS) en oposi-
ción a otros dos géneros principales de COSAS que
NO EXISTENTES.

Estos son: AIOYAA AMMEIEE UAA
```

Por ejemplo, WOAA (El Generator), BUAUAA (Espíritu Humano), BUAWEE BEIAEII (Espíritu Colectivo) o BUAUAA BAAIOO (Espíritu del Ser Viviente)] y AIOYAA AMEIEE OUEE (Como el contenido información, la sensación de placer, o una tradición popular) verdad fuera de la WAAM [nuestro cosmos].

AÏOOYA AMMIÈ (¬B ∩ ¬A), no verificable fuera de un campo de conciencia individual o colectiva.

En AÏOOYA AMMIÈ, la palabra AMMIE se aplica al concepto AIOOYAA.

En otras palabras, AMMIE se aplica al concepto de la 4D real, material de nuestro cosmos. En la palabra AMMIE, el concepto principal de desplazamiento (A) se aplica inseparablemente a la identificación de un concepto (IE) que es AIOOYAA en este caso.

La traducción de AMMIE es:

- Desplazamiento inseparable de la identificación del concepto.

- Desplazamiento [fuera de nuestro cosmos] inseparable de la identificación del concepto [el concepto AIOOYAA en este caso]

Cosmo-física y conceptos primarios

Los conceptos primarios E - «Concepto» y EE - «Modelo» están relacionados con la cosmo-física. Los Umitas hablan de dos tipos importantes de cosas inexistentes (seres), para las cuales los valores tetravalentes y los conceptos primarios son :

- El concepto primario E — «Concepto» puede estar asociado con cualquier concepto y en particular con los siguientes conceptos: AIOYAA AMMEIEE UAA denotando entidades cosmológicas que existen fuera de nuestro cosmos. Tales como: WOAA (¡el generador!), BUAUAA (espíritu humano), BUAWEE BEIAEII (espíritu colectivo) o BUAUAA BAAIOO (espíritu del ser vivo). Estas entidades cosmológicas no están asociadas con el concepto primario O de las entidades multidimensionales 10D de nuestro cosmos que incluyen características de tiempo y espacio. Estas entidades no tienen tiempo y pueden ser vistos por nosotros como conceptos.

- El concepto principal EE — «Modelo» puede estar asociado con el valor tetravalente AIOYAA AMEIEE OUEE (como el contenido de la información, la sensación de placer o una tradición popular). Estas entidades están vinculadas a modelos en el cosmos BUAWEE BEIAEII (espíritu colectivo) conocido como BB.

EXTRACTOS DE TEXTOS DE COSMOBIOFÍSICA

Los Umitas ven el universo como un ser consciente de todo. Esta forma de Teocosmología se basa en una ciencia llamada Cosmobiofísica. Así, desde su punto de vista, sus espiritualidad o pensamiento religioso se basa científicamente en todos sus aspectos. Hemos seleccionado extractos de sus textos que mejor traducen estas ideas...

Es cierto que en un momento remoto de la historia, UMMOWOA (un profeta como Cristo) apareció entre los habitantes de UMMO rodeado por un halo místico. WOOAYII UMMOWOA podría traducirse en algo así como la divina UMMOWOA, aunque no ha desarrollado una religión institucionalizada en torno a su memoria como sucedió en OYAGAA (estrella de la Tierra).

La cosmobiofísica moderna arroja suficiente luz sobre este grandioso fenómeno, que se basa en leyes cosmológicas afiladas. Las connotaciones emocionales y la interpretación biofísica de este acontecimiento están muy lejos de la noción que has desarrollado sobre el hecho histórico del nacimiento de Jesús (que, como explicaremos, es similar a la de la UMMOWOA).

Para usted, la figura de Jesús es divina y está rodeada de connotaciones místicas-religiosas. Sería un hecho sobrenatural y teológico y, en este contexto, es explicable que se establezca una Iglesia. Desde nuestro punto de vista, la encarnación de un OEMMIIWOA (Cristo) es parte de un marco científico-biológico, explicable cuando uno tiene una concepción holística de WAAM WAAM (cosmos). Que durante la evolución biológica, surge un OEMMIIWOA como también es lógico que una roca se sienta atraída por una estrella debido a la gravedad.

Por eso, para un espíritu religioso de la Tierra, la noción de un OEMMIWOA lo dejará frío, lo desencantará y, tal vez, lo decepcionará, entre otros aspectos, porque la imagen de WOA que aceptamos no tiene nada que ver con la noción teológica de que muchas de las religiones de la Tierra han forjado alrededor de un tipo antropomórfico a nivel mental, paternal, castigador y gratificante, superinteligente y creativo.

Para nosotros, por otro lado, todas tus ideas están en el campo de los mitos, que se pueden explicar en el contexto de la evolución histórica de tu red social terrestre. A partir de un hecho real, interpretado como de naturaleza milagrosa, desarrolló un tratado doctrinal que dio forma a una nueva religión, el cristianismo, y la construcción de varias iglesias de acuerdo con las interpretaciones distintas, del mensaje distorsionado de OEMMIWOA.

Nuestro diseño cosmológico se basa en una ciencia solida. Sabemos que estamos inmersos en un WAAM-WAAM (multicosmos) y que los flujos de información que hacen posible toda su riqueza configurativa provienen de dos polos o centros. Uno de ellos genera información por antonomasa (resonancia). Todas las configuraciones posibles de la materia, todas las posibilidades del SER, es decir, todas las modalidades que puedas concebir de la existencia perceptible y no perceptible por nuestros sentidos y otros órganos sensibles imaginables, dibujan sus origen de este polo.

Sin embargo, no todas las formas concebibles son posibles para los seres reales. Por ejemplo, nuestro cerebro puede imaginar un OEMII o un ser humano del tamaño de un milímetro, pero tal entidad biológica no sería posible. Tenga en cuenta que una reducción lineal de 1/103 (una milésima) resultaría en el volumen de órganos internos en 1/109. Por lo tanto, la reducción del metabolismo bioquímico sería proporcional a la masa. Por otro lado, se observa que las moléculas químicas no podían reducirse en las mismas proporciones para que una célula de este hombre hipotético no pudiera albergar la compleja arquitectura que se observa en nuestras células. Por tales razones, sería inconcebible tener insectos en OYAGAA con dimensiones que alcanzan docenas de metros, o una estrella compuesta exclusivamente de cadenas proteicas. Por lo tanto, las posibles formas de ser deben ser consistentes con el cuerpo de leyes físicas que rigen WAAM-WAAM (bicosmos). Este polo cósmico o matriz de información hará posible, mediante la generación de transferencia de toda la configuración de múltiples universos. Sin su existencia, el cosmos sería como un gigantesco cristal de configuración isotrópica, amorfa, carente de configuraciones o singularidades y por lo tanto carente de información. (El término cristal, lo usamos no como sinónimo de arquitectura geométrica de átomos ordenados, un cuerpo que no sería isotrópico, sino para designar una cadena infinita de IBOZSOO-UU en completo desorden, en la que la transmisión de la luz no es posible y de entropía infinita).

El centro cosmogónico que codifica estas posibles configuraciones, lo llamamos WOA. WOA coexiste con AIODII, es decir, con la realidad formada. Uno configura, el otro modelo [fabrica]. Pero es importante para nosotros que desasuste nuestra versión a cualquier concepción de DIOS. Un examen superficial de ambos conceptos puede aceptar este paralelismo. WOA - Generador sería equivalente a DIOS - Creador como lo ven sus teólogos.

Pero la imagen de Dios es muy diferente en el contexto de las religiones de la Tierra que lo presentan como un ser antropomórfico, de infinita bondad, pensando por excelencia, perfecto, padre de sus criaturas. Además, su existencia suprema parece haber sido revelada a vuestros profetas en un contexto religioso y piadoso.

Le interesará saber que nuestra idea de WOA fue inducida por medios científicos, no por medios teológicos. Es cierto que su existencia fue proclamada por la UMMOWOA en un entorno histórico donde esta ciencia no podía ser conocida por él. Pero para nosotros, un concepto revelado carece de valor probatorio. La sociedad de la UMMO no es tan sensible emocionalmente como la red social de la Tierra. Una religión, en el sentido que usted concede a este término (Unión del ser humano a su Dios, que comprende la fe y la obediencia a sus leyes y doctrinas) no podría ser forjada dentro de ella. En cuanto a nosotros, no vemos a WOA como un padre, ni concebimos que ningún concepto pueda ser respetado o aceptado por medio de la fe. Sólo la razón y la evidencia científica pueden forjar el corpus de nuestra doctrina. (Tenga en cuenta que mis hermanos, fieles a este principio, siempre han insistido en que no crean en nuestra identidad como viajeros OEMMII, provenientes de la UMMO. Esto es así, porque suponemos que no debeis aceptar en términos absolutos lo que no está probado).

Si logramos aceptar la palabra de UMMOWOA a lo largo del tiempo, es porque la evolución de nuestra cosmogonía nos permite aceptar la fiabilidad del origen de su doctrina. UMMOWOA, al igual que Jesús, no pretendía fundar una iglesia o religión.

Lo que sucedió en los dos planetas distintos es que UMMOWOA nació en una sociedad avanzada en la que el rigor histórico no permite la creación de mitos, y Jesús de la Tierra, nació en un momento en que el lenguaje era metafórico, la ciencia no existía, las ideas dominantes eran irracionales y fuertemente impregnadas de concepciones mágicas. Así, se explica que su mensaje ha sido alterado, aunque los elementos esenciales han sobrevivido y su figura histórica sufre enormes distorsiones.

Para entender todo esto, tenemos que seguir matitando nuestro punto con respecto al concepto de WOA. WOA es una fuente de información cósmica. Pero, toda la información carece de sentido sin apoyo material o energético. De ahí la simbiosis entre WOA y el WAAM de masa infinita. WOA realmente convierte esta información en el dentro de este WAAM.

WOA también establece una relación de puesta a punto con estas estructuras que llamamos cerebros humanos, pero sólo en circunstancias muy especiales. ¿Cuál es la base científica de esta relación? Usted entenderá que en el contexto de estas páginas de divulgación, es casi imposible exponer el modelo matemático muy complejo en el que se basa. Así que usaremos metáfora o imagen. WOA resuena con el WAAM de THE BUAWA BIAEII (universo que codifica toda la información), con un efecto similar al que conoces en física bajo el nombre de resonancia. (Si coloca dos cuerdas de violín a cierta distancia y vibra una de ellas, la propagación de ondas de presión interactúa con la segunda y hace que oscile [autoinducción]. Un efecto similar ocurre entre dos circuitos con una inductancia y una capacidad eléctrica).

Este centro universal de información pura que representa WOA, se puede imaginar como un gigantesco archivo donde se puede encontrar matemáticamente codificado, ya que la configuración de una planta, la resolución de un sistema de ecuaciones diferencial o estructura de un edificio y un material generador de luz consistente (láser) y, repetimos, cualquier entidad o ser posible en el universo múltiple.

WOA ha coexistido desde la eternidad con el WAAM B.B. verdadero cerebro del multicosmos que modula gracias a este efecto de resonancia particular. Pero se observa que, en realidad, no transfiere toda la información a la vez. El Multicosmos es como un gran organismo cibernético que se corrige a sí mismo.

Dentro de los universos distintos, gracias a una corriente neguentrópica, la vida nace a base de la complejidad biomolecular. Estos organismos vivos que pueblan una multitud de estrellas frías (recuerda que una estrella fría no necesariamente tiene un origen planetario, pero a veces proviene de viejas estrellas que se han enfriado e incluso retienen algo de calor seguir mejorando en complejidad; estructuras con una densidad creciente de información acumulada en el espacio. Estos son los sistemas nerviosos. La culminación de esta complejidad es el cerebro humano. Por lo tanto, su arquitectura es lo suficientemente compleja como para dar un salto cualitativo, ponerse en contacto con su BUAWWA y enriquecerse por su conexión con el B.B. (BUAWAA BIAEII) o la conciencia colectiva en este gran cerebro de el universo, el WAAM B.B.)

Tenga en cuenta que este gran sistema cuya arquitectura está integrada por CEREBRO-BUAWA-B.B. de repente se da cuenta del universo que lo rodea. Es como un sensor de B.B. que captura las configuraciones de su cosmos, a saber, galaxias, estrellas, montañas, animales, rocas y artefactos elaborados. B.B. pregunta sobre su propia elaboración. Es como si el multicosmos fuera un ser gigantesco cuyo cerebro y manos serían el WAAM BB. Este moldearía la arcilla de la materia en los diferentes universos, concentrándola en forma de átomos, nubes de estrellas, de planetas, montañas y seres vivos. Pero para dar forma, tienes que ver. Sus ojos serían los cerebros. Estos transmiten la información a B.B. y a su vez corrigen las deficiencias del sistema gracias a los modelos proporcionados por WOA. Las manos del WAAM BB no son más que la influencia física interuniversal de la masa imaginaria que se propaga de un cosmos a otro produciendo pliegues de espacio y, por lo tanto, configuraciones de masa y energía moduladas por las informaciones de BB.

Vea cómo, en WOA, el centro de información es estático, mientras que en el universo múltiple, WAAM B.B. resuena con WOA, la información es dinámica. Para esto, te advertimos que la comparación con dos cuerdas de violín es solo didáctica y metafórica, porque para ellos, el efecto de resonancia se manifiesta por una dinámica simultánea. Usamos el verbo de OYAGAA generar como representante de la acción de WOA, porque te resulta más familiar y te recuerda de una manera didáctica que el concepto de la palabra crea tan querido para los teólogos de la Tierra. WOA no es el ser que imaginas como Dios, paternal, inteligente, pensante, con una estructura antropomórfica, que decide crear un universo y poner criaturas a su imagen que recompensará después de su muerte. Si han cumplido sus leyes. WOA no tiene nada que ver con este ser mítico creado por los espíritus del hombre terrestre. Aquí el verbo engendrar podría traducirse como representado por un efecto especial de resonancia cósmica. Los modelos de información se transfieren al WAAM B.B. para evolucionar dinámicamente a lo largo del tiempo la configuración de una red de universos. Una parábola simple podría ayudarlo a familiarizarse con nuestra cosmología.

WAAM B.B. es como el cerebro de un alfarero cuyos ojos cansados (cerebros OEMMII) contemplan una masa de arcilla (materia y energía). Sus manos (la masa imaginaria cuyos tentáculos cruzan los límites de universos separados) forman un ánfora. Pero para hacerlo son necesarios dos procesos intelectuales. Primero, inspírese en un dibujo (modelo informativo) que representa un contenedor. Para esto, mira un viejo libro de cerámica (WOA) que sugiere sutilmente la forma que debe tener el ánfora, pero sobre todo, debe aprender a corregirlo, manipulándolo con sus manos observando a medida que toma forma, dándose cuenta de las dificultades involucradas en el manejo de una sustancia viscosa.

Cuando atribuimos, en nuestros escritos a los hombres de la Tierra, la facultad de generar, no nos referimos a esta hipótesis que es suya de la función divina de crear materia de la nada, sino de generar

IMÁGENES SERES IDEALES en WAAM BB que es responsable de energizar o modelar en los universos que coexisten con WOA. Es decir, no fueron creados, en el sentido que le das a esta palabra, por Dios.

Tenemos un profundo respeto por sus concepciones religiosas de entidades llamadas por usted Alá, Dios, Jehová, Brahma ... Pero como acaba de notar, nuestro concepto de WOA no tiene nada que ver con sus ideas teológicas. No tiene que sentirse obligado a aceptar nuestra idea de WOA, que para nosotros es una concepción científica, pero que le llega a través de hojas mecanografiadas cuyo origen es oscuro. Para esto, cada uno de ustedes debe seguir siendo fiel a sus viejas creencias como siempre hemos sugerido, y leer nuestros informes, mientras estudiamos las costumbres de una aldea tribal exótica y remota. (Extractos de la carta D792-1)

HOMBRE-ESPACIO TEMPORAL

La realidad cosmo-física impone la concepción del hombre, no como un ser tridimensional, sino como un ser tetradimensional, al menos ...

Los vínculos cósmicos que unen inseparablemente a OEMMII con su BB planetario y su BUAWA implican incluir al Hombre en su dimensión temporal.

No debemos hablar del Homo Sapiens Man, sino del hombre Spatiotemporis, un Homo Sapiens Spaciotemporis ... Esta distinción es muy importante y no solo una visión filosófica conceptual, sino una realidad cosmo-física.

El hombre espacial-temporal impregna los ejes dimensionales del espacio-tiempo, dejando un rastro grabado como los faros de los automóviles en la noche en una película fotográfica ...

El rastro grabado por el OEMMII en el espacio-tiempo existe AÏOOYA AMMIÈ a lo largo del eje del tiempo. Ya no es perceptible a nuestros ojos, solo el archivo mnemónico nos permite recordar de manera abstracta que tenemos un pasado. Sin embargo, el arrastre espacio-temporal grabado por OEMMII todavía existe en los IBODSOO cósmicos. Por lo tanto, el hombre espacial-temporal es una larga serpiente con el cuerpo humano a la cabeza. Como la serpiente, su cuerpo y su cabeza son inseparables.

El hombre espacio-temporal está bajo el control de su BUAWA, quien determina y dirige los contornos de la vida del OEMMII. El cerebro neural permite a los humanos adaptar e implementar las pautas de su BUAWA.

D41: En el continuum ESPACIO-TIEMPO (como lo llaman incorrectamente los físicos de la TIERRA), el cuerpo humano es un pliegue más del ESPACIO (una depresión a través de una cuarta dimensión) que podemos definir matemáticamente con diez dimensiones. En resumen, una MASA con volumen y tiempo asociado. No podemos concebir el tiempo si está disociado de otras magnitudes.

Las personas con conocimentos científicos débiles juzgan al hombre como un ser tridimensional (volumen) que vive varios hechos en el flujo del tiempo. Para él, solo queda el recuerdo de eventos pasados. La única realidad es el presente, y el futuro aún no existe ... Esta descripción del mundo es aberrante e infantil.

Imagine que todas las situaciones (EVENTOS) que vivio, que vive, que vivira un hombre a través de su VIDA están en un eje que representa la dimensión TIEMPO.

El espacio y el tiempo están tan estrechamente asociados que si nos unimos en una sola expresión gráfica, en una sola imagen, todas estas situaciones o hechos que el hombre vive a lo largo de su vida, obtendremos un extraño SER tetradimensional (volumen + tiempo) que se vería como un gran OEBUMAEI (tipo de dona larga o boudin muy popular en la región de AADAAADA, en UMMO), que la sección sería un hombre si la cortáramos. Los cosmólogos de UMMO llaman a esto ser tetradimensional: OEBUMAEOEMII

WOA concede al alma una prerrogativa que es trascendente.

PUEDE CAMBIAR UNA VEZ POR TODA LA FORMA DE
OEBUMAOEMII (HOMBRE FÍSICO: ESPACIO-TIEMPO).

Lo que significa que si WOA (GENERADOR o DIOS)
engendra y crea el cuerpo físico, fijando las características de su fisiología, le otorga a BUUAWEA la
capacidad de moldear la conducta del cuerpo a lo
largo del tiempo, de una vez por todas.

RESUMEN Y CONCLUSIÓN

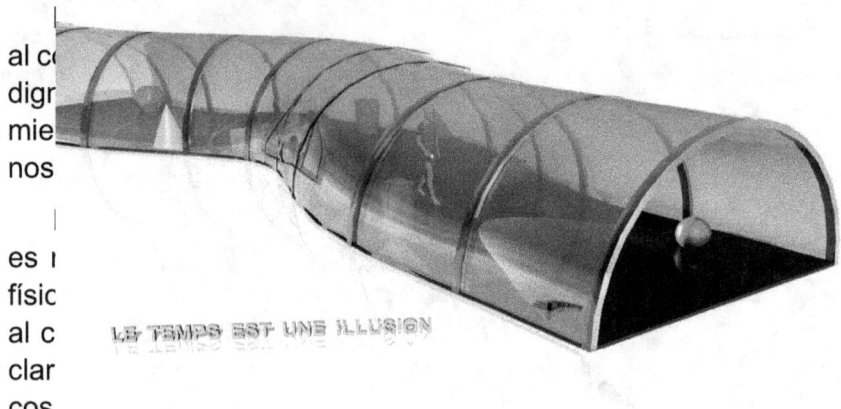

al c
digr
mie
nos

es
físic
al c
clar
cos

un lado, y las 10 principales descritas por los Ummitas en particular,
que nos dan la visión de un espacio donde los viajes y las comunica-
cic

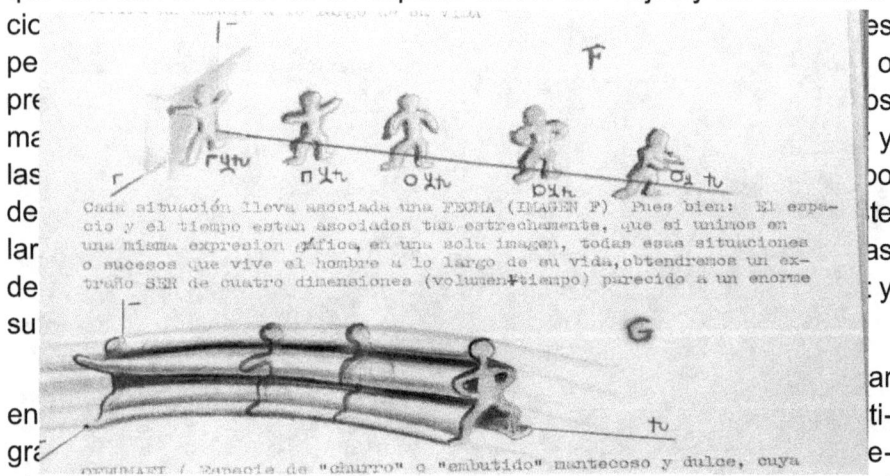

mente estrellas de neutrones supermasivas que terminan su vida en el
anticosmos.

Los anticosmos contienen grandes cantidades de antimateria que
afectan nuestro cosmos actual. Percibimos estas masas por sus efectos gravitacionales y las variaciones de la velocidad de expansión del
cosmos que la ciencia contemporánea designa bajo los términos de
materia oscura y energía.

Todos los cosmos y anticosmos están separados por una membrana XOODII que contiene masas sin volumen que transmiten los
efectos gravitacionales de un cosmos en su opuesto.

La lógica de Tétravalente permite nuevos desarrollos matemáticos y una comprensión coherente y homogénea de las entidades cosmológicas trascendentales hasta ahora relegadas al ámbito de la metafísica.

El ser vivo OEMMIIWOA, a menudo llamado profeta, encuentra su lugar en la lógica de la evolución humana. Es físicamente un humano mutante que capturará directamente un flujo de comunicación del Meta-cerebro BUAWE BIAEI. El Meta-Cerebro es una entidad de transmisión de lo que llamamos DIOS, por lo tanto, puede tratar de dirigir la evolución humana hacia una forma cada vez más intelectual y espiritual.

No existe una visión religiosa en este nuevo paradigma, y condeno de antemano a cualquiera que intente desviar este trabajo con fines religiosos o sectarios.

Por el contrario, esta nueva visión cosmológica concilia Ciencia y Teología en un nuevo paradigma unificado de un enfoque positivista racional que incluye la Metafísica.

⊠

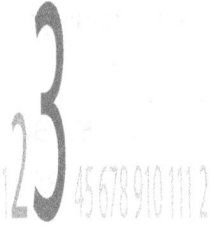

EL SURGIMIENTO DEL VIVO

Todas estas hipótesis sobre la génesis y la evolución de las entidades del universo nos permitirán describir los puntos clave y los fundamentos de la aparición de los vivos. El surgimiento de los vivos no puede entenderse sin una visión general de las diferentes entidades cosmológicas.

D731: Hay tantos B.B. como AYUUBAAYII (redes de seres vivos planetarios) en todo WAAM-WAAM. Hay una correspondencia uno a uno entre cada conjunto de seres vivos en una estrella fría y su correspondiente B.B.

Primero, debemos tratar de entender cómo se crea el contenido modelisador de un BB planetario. Independientemente de los mecanismos astrofísicos clásicos, ¿qué sucede entonces en el momento de la creación de las estrellas?

Entonces, podremos preguntarnos acerca de los mecanismos que condujeron desde el pilotaje de una estrella hasta el surgimiento de la vida propiamente dicha. Estas son mis propias tesis desarrolladas sobre la base de mi interpretación de la cosmología Ummita.

EL CONTEXTO DE UN METACEREBRO PLANETARIO BB

Los Ummitas nos dicen que BB conoce los parámetros de las estrellas frías y que, dados estos parámetros, la vida es posible o no. Por lo tanto, sabemos que:

- Los astros fríos están vinculadas a su BB. Para todos los seres vivos, por un canal de comunicación intracelular, el BAAYIODUU. Para los humanos, a través de un canal de comunicación cerebral, el OEMBUAW.

- El vínculo entre el astro frío y BB es de naturaleza gravitacional.

- El enlace gravitacional transmite los parámetros del astro frío a BB.

- Al estar BB en el WAAM-UU, el enlace gravitacional del astro frío con BB atraviesa el canal de un efecto de borde con la capa de capa intermedia intercosmos XOODII.

LA HIPÓTESIS DE LA CONSTANTE CRIPTÓNICA

Los astros se rigen por leyes físicas. Estas leyes físicas incluyen interacciones entre las entidades del cosmos WAAM y los WAAM-UU que transitan a través de las masas imaginarias en el XOODII WAAM. En algunos casos, los cuerpos celestes pueden tener un enlace con un BB planetario.

La hipótesis es que los astross que tienen agua en la fase líquida y una cierta concentración de criptón, y solo estos cuerpos celestes, son potencialmente capaces de conectarse con un meta-cerebro planetario BB.

Los átomos de criptón deben estar en solución en agua, y la concentración de criptón en solución acuosa es tal que permite unir átomos de criptón gravitacionalmente.

Cuando la configuración de los átomos de criptón se vuelve ideal, entonces resuena con las frecuencias gravitacionales de la estrella, y luego tiene lugar la conexión con su planetario BB. Esta configuración de átomos de criptón es una especie de BAAYIODUU arcaico, es decir que aún no está integrada en un ser vivo, ya que aún no hay una ...

La concentración de criptón en solución acuosa de estas estrellas está en un rango que permite unir a los átomos de criptón, gravitacionalmente en una cadena. Esta cadena está estructurada en una configuración ideal que resuena con las frecuencias gravitacionales del astro. Esta relación entre la concentración de criptón en solución acuosa y la gravedad del astro que permite la configuración ideal probablemente correspondiente a un umbral preciso, lo llamaré por el término de constante criptónica. Por lo tanto, esta constante subyace a este fenómeno de resonancia de la cadena de átomos de criptón.

Para evitar confusiones, tenga en cuenta que el fenómeno de resonancia se produce de acuerdo con datos variables. Se obtiene por adecuación:

- una masa variable de H2O
- frecuencias gravitacionales variables de un cuerpo celeste
- con una concentración de criptón que también es variable.

Si tratamos de formular una constante de este tipo, de una manera simple, sería el resultado de una relación de variables del orden, por ejemplo:

Ct Kr = [Masa (H2 O) / Masa (Kr)] / Frecuencia (G) ...

La adecuación de estos parámetros: la cantidad de agua en el astro, las frecuencias gravitacionales del astro, su concentración de criptón en solución acuosa, causan una resonancia gravitacional específica. Esta resonancia gravitacional específica provoca un efecto de borde LEIYO que permite la codificación unica del cuerpo transmisor. En resumen, este enlace informativo astre-krypton-BB es unívoco, de naturaleza gravitacional y se realiza por el canal de un efecto de borde. Es el arcaico BAAYIODUU, es decir que aún no está integrado en un ser vivo, ya que no hay ninguno.

Este efecto de borde genera la conexión a un BB planetario inicialmente vacío en el WAAM-UU. Esta primera conexión inicializa el BB con los parámetros estructurantes el astro (su masa, su naturaleza geológica, etc.). El enlace de comunicación astre-krypton-BB se establece, luego informa dinámicamente BB-planetario sobre el estado, la evolución de los parámetros de la estrella. Mientras la estrella emita ondas gravitacionales que tengan una resonancia correspondiente a su densidad de criptón, este enlace identifica el astro con su BB planetario. El criptón en solución acuosa se ha convertido en el receptor de las frecuencias gravitacionales emitidas por BB que transmiten modelos evolutivos.

Todas estas interacciones transitan a través de las masas imaginarias en el XOODII WAAM.

Diagrama de enlace Astro-criptón-BB planetario

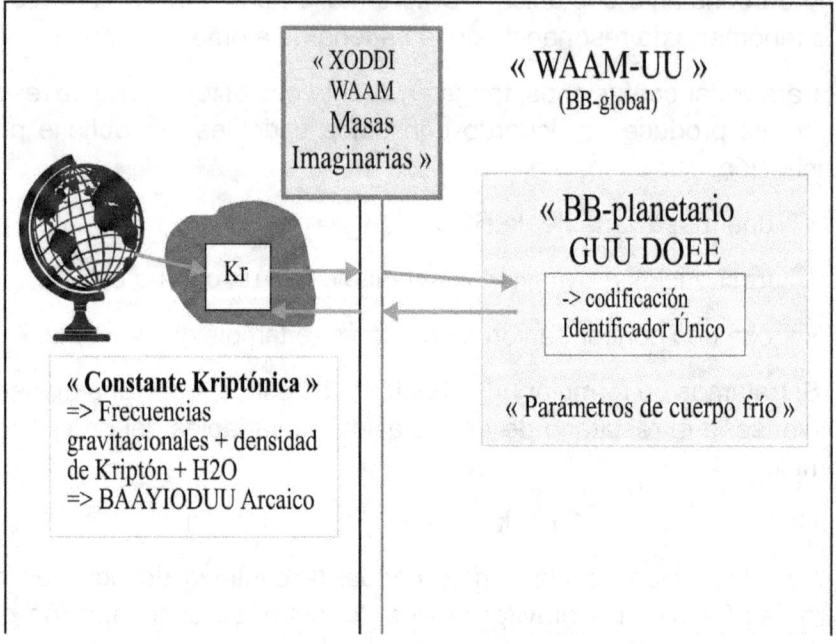

Figura 1-p1: Diagrama del enlace Astro-krypton-BB segun una constante criptónica subyacente correspondiente al umbral de concentración de Krypton en solución acuosa que permite la creación del BAAYIODUU que resuena con las frecuencias gravitacionales del astro.

DETALLE DE LA HIPÓTESIS DEL CONSTANTE CRIPTÓNICA

La idea del surgimiento de lo vivo a partir de la materia inerte supone que este último cambia de estado y adquiere nuevas propiedades, las de los vivos. La propiedad principal del ser vivo es su capacidad de auto-reproducción, la segunda su capacidad de evolución-adaptación. La combinación de estas dos propiedades es una emergencia que la materia inerte no posee. Y como hemos visto, los seres entrópicos, inertes, pierden información, mientras que los seres neguentrópicos vivos absorben la información del entorno externo. En otras palabras, un ser vivo se autorreplica, y su réplica tiene la facultad de evolucionar de acuerdo con la información adquirida del entorno externo.

El fenómeno general de la emergencia ha tenido múltiples enfoques: holistas, vitalistas, reduccionistas o emergentistas han cambiado el tema al iluminarlo desde sus diversos puntos de vista, pero sin que ninguno de estos enfoques haya logrado describir el tema de la esencia de la emergencia de los vivos.

Para explorar mi hipótesis, retendré como principio inicial de emergencia, el enfoque filosófico hegeliano y su equivalente matemático y sistémico descrito por los Sistemas Dinámicos No Lineales (NLDS).

En estas explicaciones, propongo definir la emergencia de la siguiente manera:

La emergencia ocurre cuando un sistema en un estado estable con propiedades iniciales se bifurca en un punto crítico a uno o más estados estables con nuevas propiedades. Esta bifurcación puede ser una discontinuidad.

La calidad de una emergencia, es decir, el nivel de su trascendencia, depende de la densidad de información puesta en interrelación por los elementos que componen el sistema inicial y la arquitectura de red del sistema.

El análisis semántico del término EIDUAYUUEE nos da una idea de cómo los Ummitas perciben este concepto cerca del surgimiento:

```
EIDOAYUEE es el hecho obvio para usted de que una
red tiene propiedades y realiza funciones que no tie-
nen los elementos que la componen.
```

La traducción de EIDUAYUUEE es : El concepto identifica un evento que depende de la arquitectura de la red.

GENERALIDADES SOBRE SISTEMAS DINÁMICOS NO LINEALES.

Cuando un parámetro de control dado P alcanza el umbral crítico Psc, un sistema estable S1 se ramifica hacia 2 o más posibles estados estables S2, S3, Sn, Sn + 1.

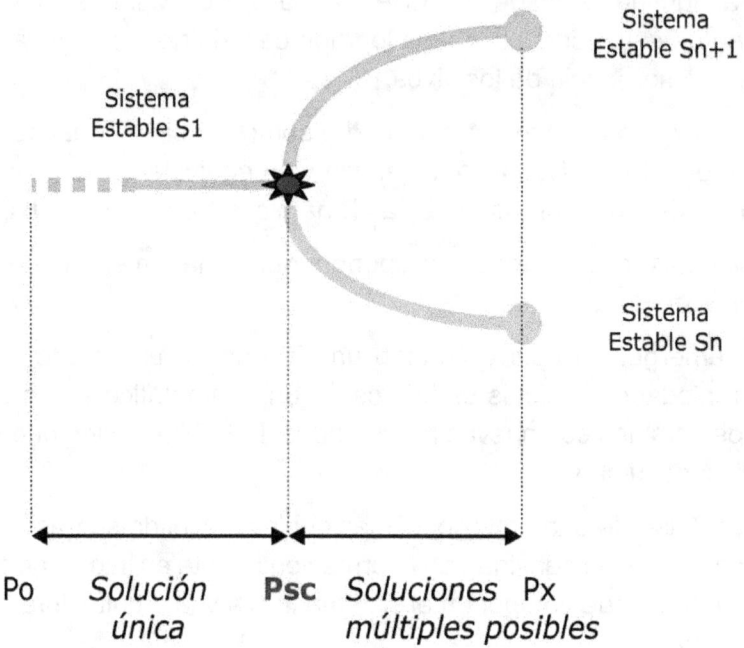

Po   *Solución*   **Psc**   *Soluciones* Px
      única   *múltiples posibles*

EL SISTEMA DNL DE LA CONSTANTE CRIPTÓNICA

Supongamos un entorno dado cuyos parámetros de estructuración (masa, gravitación, etc.) son fijos y suficientes. Los parámetros de estructuración son los componentes del SDNL cuyos valores son necesarios y también deben ser suficientes para el cambio de estado del sistema. Los parámetros de estructuración no producen por sí mismos el cambio de estado del SDNL.

En nuestro caso de aplicación, el parámetro de control es la constante criptonica. Recuerde que este último sería el resultado de una relación del orden de:

Cte KR = [Masa (H2 O) / Masa (KR)] / Frecuencia (G) ...

Podemos simplificar y reducir a P = Kr la concentración para un medio cuyos parámetros de estructuración (masa, gravitación, etc.) son fijos y suficientes.

El sistema estable inicial S1 está compuesto de átomos de criptón en solución acuosa.

La bifurcación ocurre en el umbral de la constante criptónica, que corresponde a un efecto de resonancia gravitacional entre los átomos de criptón en solución acuosa y las frecuencias gravitacionales de la estrella. Esto produciría la organización de la cadena de átomos de criptón en un sistema estable llamado BAAYIODUU-arcaico y dotado de un efecto LEIYO de conexión BB.

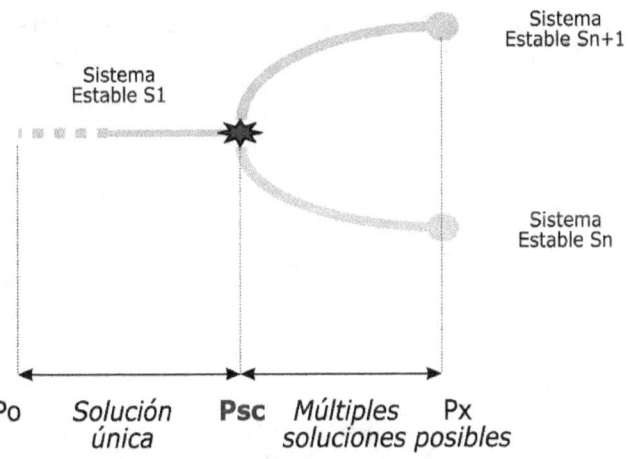

Sistema Estable S1

Sistema Estable Sn+1

Sistema Estable Sn

Po   *Solución única*   **Psc**   *Múltiples soluciones posibles*   Px

resonancia gravitacional del Kriptón con el cuerpo celeste punto LEIYO

Estado entrópico
Átomos Kr
en solución
acuosa

Estado neguentrópico
BAAYIODUU arcaico
Cadena de átomos de Kr

Efecto LEIYO y criptón

El concepto de «le —yo» describe un conjunto de fenómenos cosmológicos que se manifiestan en lo que los humanos llaman XOODI WAAM, es decir, una capa que separa dos cosmos, traducida trivialmente como un efecto de límite. El verdadero LEIYOO WAAM es un fenómeno de alta complejidad que implica la transformación de una red de ibozsoo uhu.. El análisis semántico del término LEIYO expresa «el cambio de concepto identifica un conjunto de entidades», que traduzco por: Transposición isomórfica de un conjunto de ibozsoo uhu.

Concretamente, el efecto LEIYO que estaría involucrado para el umbral de la constante criptónica es un fenómeno gravitacional de resonancia con los parámetros [Masa (H_2O) / Masa (KR)] / Frecuencia (G) ...

Este efecto LEIYO sería la inicialización de la conexión de una estructura de átomos de Krypton con el Meta-cerebro BUAWE BIAEI.

D58: Estos [átomos de criptón] estaban en los extremos de la cadena helicoidal del ácido DEOXIRIBONUCLEICO formando varios pares (Figura 58-2f8) (total de 86 conjuntos bi-atómicos) que giraban en órbitas comunes y los planos orbitales, sustancialmente paralelos, tenían un AJE común (el eje AB en la figura 58-2f8). Este eje también describió un movimiento vibratorio armónico cuya FRECUENCIA Y AMPLITUD era una función de TEMPERATURA (0.2 megaciclos para una temperatura de 35 ° centígrados).

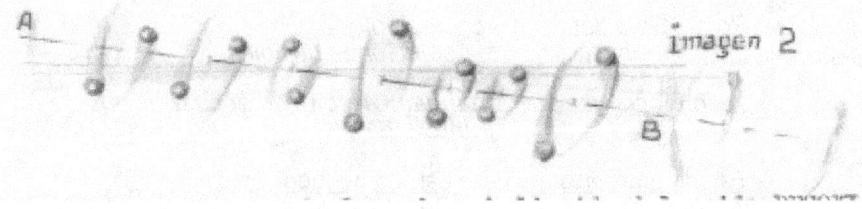

imagen 2

D731: ¿Cómo es posible que los electrones de un átomo de criptón se comporten en el B.I. [B.I. = BAA IYODUHU (Factor de unión entre B.B. y los cromosomas)] y en la O. [O. = OEEMBUUAW (factor de criptón que une a B.B. con el cerebro de un OEMII)] de una manera muy especial? Son las subpartículas de la Masa imaginaria las que, al otro lado de la frontera, ejercen esta acción.

Cuando se formen seres vivos con ADN, esto significa que habría 43 átomos de este compuesto Kr en cada extremo de un cromosoma, almacenados en cada telómero. Cada uno de estos pares de Kr_2 tiene un plano orbital estable. Todos estos pares de Kr_2 tendrían planos orbitales paralelos entre ellos. Pero, en el estado actual de nuestra hipótesis, los seres vivos aún no están formados, así que pensemos en el paso aguas arriba ...

En el umbral crítico de la concentración de criptón en solución acuosa, las frecuencias gravitacionales del astro y el criptón resuenan, este es el efecto LEIYO. Esto genera la cadena de pares de átomos de criptón y sincronizan sus órbitas. Sus capas electrónicas inicializan el BB planetario al entrar en una conexión. Esta primera conexión inicializa el BB planetario con los parámetros estructurantes de la estrella (su masa, su naturaleza geológica, etc.). Luego se establece el enlace de comunicación astre-krypton-BB, que luego informa dinámicamente a BB-planetary. Así se formaría un BAAYIODUU-arcaico que luego se integrará en los seres vivos.

RESUMEN Y CONCLUSIÓN

Hemos visto en la hipótesis que considerando una constante universal llamada constante criptónica, que los cuerpos que contienen una cierta concentración de criptón en solución acuosa generan un conjunto particular de átomos de criptón que permite conectar e inicializar un BB . Por lo tanto, es el BAAYIODUU arcaico que aún no está integrado a un ser vivo, ya que todavía no hay uno ...

Siempre siguiendo este hilo, continuaré el desarrollo de esta hipótesis de manera homogénea para el surgimiento de los vivos con las indicaciones bastante numerosas y precisas que tenemos sobre el vínculo de los seres vivos BAAYIODUU con BB.

Entonces, con la ayuda de las indicaciones en los documentos, continuaré la reflexión con una hipótesis complementaria que desarrolla las explicaciones sobre los flujos gravitacionales que unen una especie viva al BB a través del criptón.

⊠

EVOLUCIÓN ORIENTADA DEL VIVO

Estamos bien familiarizados con los fenómenos de la evolución por selección natural darwiniana o más bien neodarwiniana según lo descrito por Stephen Jay Gould. Podemos pensar que la actividad solar y la proximidad de la Tierra del Sol generan tasas de mutaciones muy importantes que hacen que la evolución darwiniana sea muy visible en la Tierra. Este mecanismo habría eclipsado a otro mecanismo, más lento y, por lo tanto, menos visible.

Sin embargo, cuando vemos una hermosa flor de orquídea que se transforma para imitar el olor y la apariencia visual de la hembra de un insecto polinizador en perfecta sincronía de coevolución con el desarrollo del insecto, podemos preguntarnos ¿Cómo es posible tal sincronización evolutiva? Los enfoques darwinianos carecen de respuestas ...

Los conceptos de campo morfogenético fueron desarrollados en la década de 1920 por Hans Spemann, Alexander Gurwitsch y Paul Weiss, y en 1981 por el biólogo Rupert Sheldrake. Estos campos morfogenéticos serían decisivos en el comportamiento de los seres vivos que heredan los hábitos de la especie por resonancia mórfica. Rupert Sheldrake cree que las características morfogenéticas son estructuras de probabilidad en las que la influencia de los tipos pasados más comunes se combinan para aumentar la probabilidad de que estos tipos vuelvan a aparecer. Rupert Sheldrake hace así un avance intelectual y, por lo tanto, toca la problemática de la creación de potencialidades del Real Absoluto, del AIIODII, sin percibir sin embargo la dimensión cosmológica profunda, ni siquiera los fundamentos físicos.

Sin embargo, mucho antes de él, el psiquiatra Carl Jung comprenderá que existe una estructura informativa exógena al ser humano, que proporciona arquetipos a un nivel profundo, un inconsciente colectivo compartido por toda la especie humana. Desafortunadamente, como ningún biólogo, Rupert Sheldrake no sabrá ver el alcance ni el vínculo con su propia investigación ...

Hemos visto en una hipótesis previa que el arcaico BAAYIODUU está en solución en agua. Sabiendo que el contexto es el siguiente:

- El astro frío debe tener agua en la fase líquida.

- En la Tierra, en el agua estaban los aminoácidos de la famosa sopa prebiótica, más o menos enriquecida por la panspermia.

- Como explican los Ummitas, el agua es el amplificador de información que permite el intercambio de información capturada por el Krypton en células vivas.

- Existe un mecanismo de intercambio de información intracelular con BB, que conduce al control de mutaciones genéticas, es decir, el control de combinaciones de aminoácidos entre sí para modificar el sistema genómico.

- BB y el astro frío interactúan y siguen las leyes universales de la filogenia y la ortogénia.

FILOGENIA Y ORTOGENIA

D 792: una ley desconocida para usted y que llamamos BAAYIOODISXAA (equilibrio biológico cósmico), y comúnmente llamada por usted, proceso de evolución de la especie que se rige por reglas que emanan del BB (Ortogénesis) a través de IDUGOOO (sucesivos cambios genéticos o mutaciones).

D57-3: La fórmula expresada por el BAAYIODIXAA UUDIII es una función compleja en la que se integran una multitud de parámetros ... fórmula que expresa las condiciones de equilibrio biológico que se miden en un medio dado.

BAAYIODIXAA UUDII se puede traducir como: Interconexión dinámica de un conjunto de parámetros de evolución de los que depende la morfología (seres vivos).

Esta función traduce el control de las mutaciones de los seres vivos por parte de BB a través del BAAYIODUU. Las mutaciones bajo el control de BB luego siguen patrones evolutivos, donde cada filum probablemente corresponde a una clase emergente, un patrón o patrón de BB.

¿Qué puede pasar entre el BAAYIODUU-arcaico y los aminoácidos? ¿Cómo pueden emerger los seres vivos de la materia inerte?

LA EMERGENCIA DE PROTOMOLÉCULAS ORGÁNICAS

La hipótesis de la emergencia orientada de los vivos es que la información del BB planetario, y capturada por el arcaico BAAYIODUU, induciría, dirigiría, catalizaría, los grupos de aminoácidos hasta la formación de una estructura auto-reproductora. Esta entidad autor-reproductora tiene una estructura genómica primitiva compuesta de aminoácidos, es decir, protomoléculas orgánicas. Transmite y recibe información al BB planetario.

Los ensambles de aminoácidos serían dirigidos segun el BAAYIODUU-arcaica. Los conjuntos químicos de las funciones amina están catalizados, orientados por el BB planetario en el intervalo de todos los modelos posibles de combinaciones posibles correspondientes a los parámetros del astro frío. Por lo tanto, con un número limitado de combinaciones posibles. Así aparecerían los ARN arcaicos.

Los mecanismos de replicación de los ARN arcaicos probablemente se deban a las ribozimas. Por lo tanto, es un mecanismo puramente fisicoquímico. Solo las mutaciones internas en las secuencias de ARN arcaico están bajo el control del BB planetario a través del arcaico BAAYIODUU.

Es una emergencia orientada por el BB planetario a través del arcaico BAAYIODUU.

Las combinaciones auto-reproductibles basadas en ARN arcaico, por lo tanto, aparecen en una elección de modelos estándar que sigue el principio evolutivo clásico de la ortogénesis. Las entidades auto-reproductibles se constituyen de acuerdo con el modelo óptimo, entre otras posibles en los modelos del BB planetario. Los procesos de información entre krypton y BB continúan de la misma manera. El contenido de la información transmitida a la BB evoluciona cualitativamente con la complejidad de la entidad.

Si los parámetros de estructuración del astro frío lo permiten, por razones de estabilidad y fiabilidad de las estructuras, el ARN-arcaico probablemente se integre muy rápidamente en una estructura de membrana que protege toda la estructura.

No se declara explícitamente en los documentos que la primera unidad de auto-reproductibles viva es una estructura con una membrana, como los coacervados. Sin embargo, el resto de la evolución se basa en entidades auto-reproductibles con estructuras de membrana.

Diagramas 1 y 2: El efecto orientado del BB sobre el BAAYIODUU-arcaico en solución acuosa con las funciones de amina, permite la construcción de ARN-arcaico de acuerdo con los modelos planetarios BB.

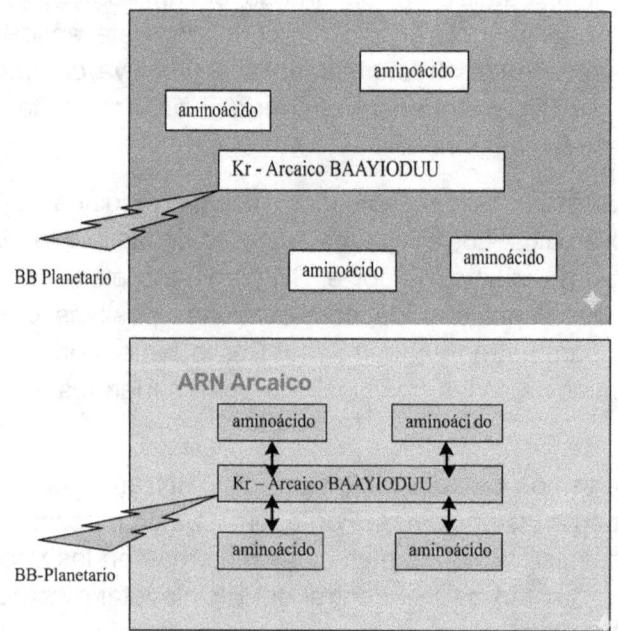

Diagrama 3: los ARN arcaicos se integran en una estructura de membrana y constituyen las primeras entidades neguentrópicas autorreproductoras vivas.

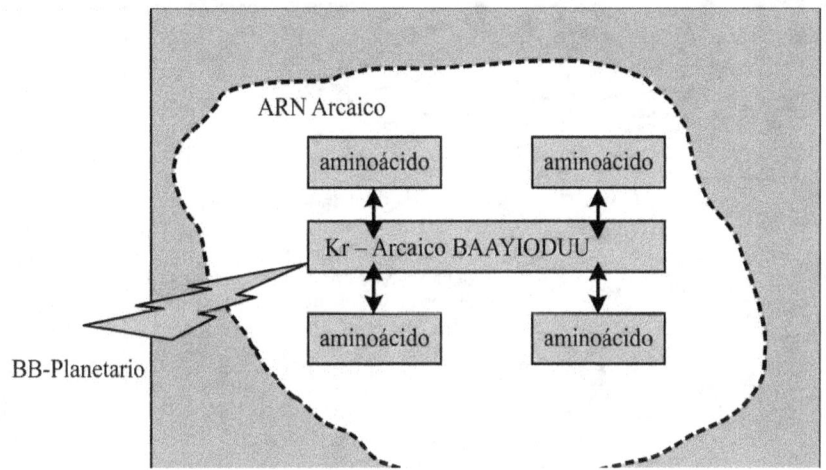

ANÁLISIS SEMÁNTICO DEL TÉRMINO UUDIE

Aunque esto no se dice textualmente, podemos ver gráficamente en el diagrama Ummita S731-f3e, una flecha que indica la influencia de BB en estas proto-moléculas orgánicas y organismos primigenios que también son las primeras criaturas vivas auto-reproductoras.

La traducción de UUDIE:

- La dependencia dinámica tiene una forma que identifica un concepto [enviado o recibido de BB].

- Facultad de percepción.

- Biosensor.

La traducción de UUDIE BIEE:

El biosensor tiene una conexión que identifica los modelos [en BB]

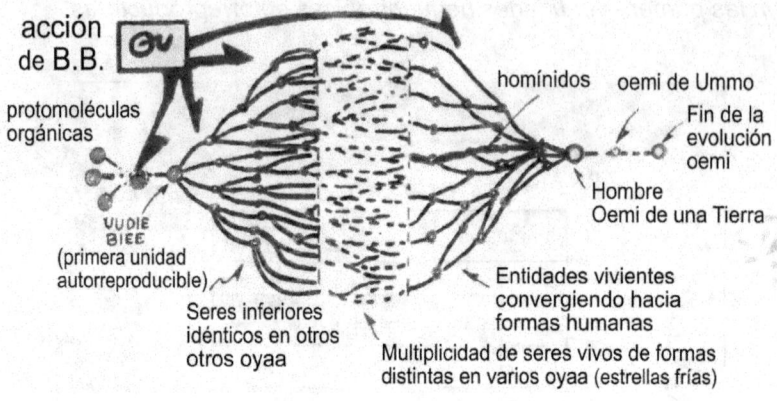

acción de B.B. ⊖U

protomoléculas orgánicas

VUDIE BIEE
(primera unidad autorreproducible)

Seres inferiores idénticos en otros otros oyaa

homínidos

oemi de Ummo

Fin de la evolución oemi

Hombre Oemi de una Tierra

Entidades vivientes convergiendo hacia formas humanas

Multiplicidad de seres vivos de formas distintas en varios oyaa (estrellas frías)

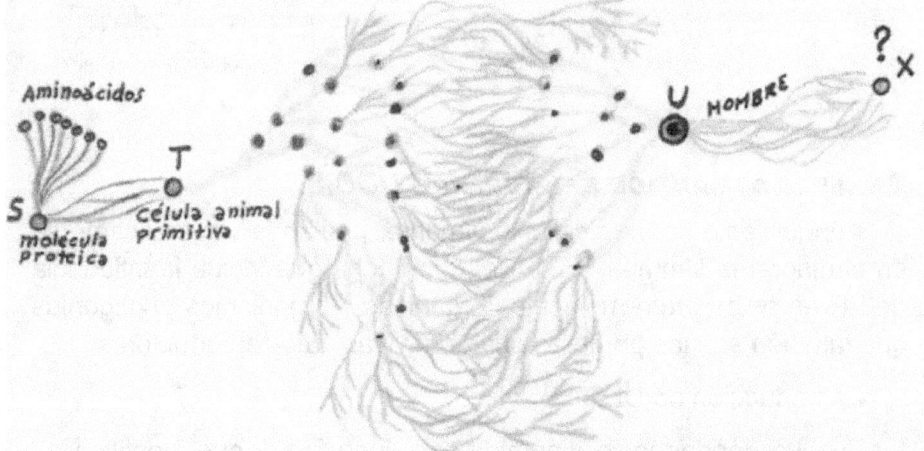

Aminoácidos

S
molécula proteica

T
Célula animal primitiva

HOMBRE

? X

RESUMEN DE LAS FASES DE EVOLUCIÓN: ARN, PROTEÍNAS, ADN

La sopa prebiótica debido a varios fenómenos de panspermia y síntesis de péptidos contiene criptón y aminoácidos en solución acuosa.

La constitución de la BAAYIODUU-arcaica se realiza por un primer efecto LEIYO en el umbral de la constante criptónica. Hay conexión e inicialización del BB planetario. Este es el comienzo del campo de aplicación del concepto de evolution BAAYIODIXAA .

La constitución de ARN arcaicos se realiza mediante el ensamblaje de aminoácidos bajo la acción de BAAYIODUU-arcaico en solución acuosa. Esta es la aparición de las primeras criaturas vivientes auto-reproducidas.

Aspecto de las proteínas.

Apariencia del ADN, probablemente debido a la actividad y evolución de los virus ARN.

CONCLUSIÓN SOBRE LA EMERGENCIA DEL VIVO.

Lo que marca la diferencia entre lo inerte y lo vivo es que la materia inerte está sujeta a las leyes fisicoquímicas, mientras que para los vivos el azar fisicoquímico está controlado y dirigido por los modelos del BB planetario asociado. Es al cruzar el umbral de la constante criptónica que lo inerte pasa bajo el control del BB planetario y que se establece la arquitectura de las estructuras de los vivos. El BAAYIODUU-arcaico está constituido y permite el ensamblaje de aminoácidos en ARN arcaicos que se replican por mecanismos fisicoquímicos y se encapsulan rápidamente en membranas.

Por lo tanto, las primeras entidades vivas basadas en ARN arcaico están bajo la influencia de las leyes de filogenia y ortogenia que se implementan de acuerdo con los modelos genotípicos y fenotípicos contenidos en el BB planetario que controla las mutaciones.

Las leyes de la evolución expresadas por el concepto BAAYIODIXAA siguen una evolución más rápidamente adaptada al medio ambiente que la única casualidad estadística de las leyes cuánticas que gobiernan los fenómenos microfísicos. Por lo tanto, los pinzones de Darwin mutaron a modelos genotípicos y fenotípicos viables, mucho más rápido que si las mutaciones se debieran solo al azar. La selección natural darwiniana hace el resto ...

Diagrama: la emergencia controlada del vivo

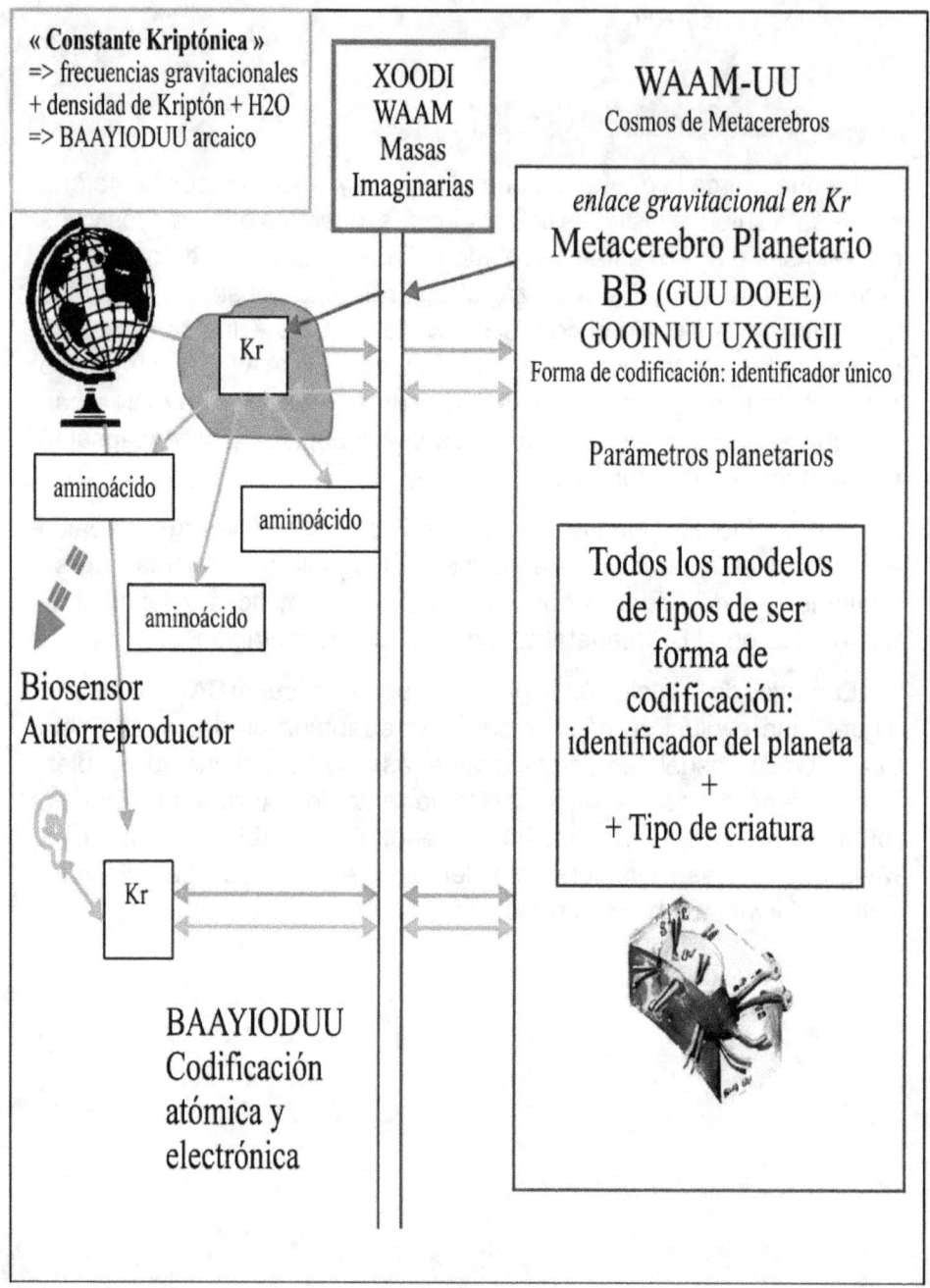

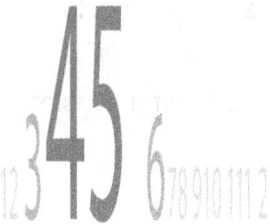

LOS FLUJOS DE INFORMACIÓN DE UNA ESPECIE VIVA

Siguiendo con las hipótesis anteriores, veremos una hipótesis que describe los flujos gravitacionales que unen una especie viva al BB a través del criptón. Sobre este tema tenemos suficientes puntos de partida.

Sabemos por los escritos de Ummitas que:

- BB contiene todos los modelos típicos de los seres vivos del astro frío.

- BB transmite a los seres vivos información que valida la evolución de los seres de acuerdo con los modelos estándar.

- El vínculo entre BB y el sistema genómico de los seres mediante resonancia con Krypton es de naturaleza gravitacional.

- El enlace BAAYIODUU del sistema genómico (todos los ADN, ARN, etc.) con BB pone a un ser vivo en relación con todos los modelos típicos de los posibles seres vivos del astro frío.

- Todas las configuraciones genómicas posibles de los seres vivos se identifican mediante un código único. Esta codificación única consiste en todas las configuraciones posibles de cada electrón en las ocho subcapas de cada uno de los átomos de criptón.

Por otro lado, sabemos que el Alma de los seres humanos se pone en conexión con la primera célula del ser vivo en el momento de la fusión genómica.

¿Cómo se puede enviar la información celular de los seres vivos al planetario BB correcto?

¿Cómo pueden recibir las comunicaciones planetarias BB los destinatarios adecuados?

LOS FLUJOS DE INFORMACIÓN DE LAS ESPECIES VIVAS

Como mencionamos anteriormente, vamos a suponer que para los seres vivos es en el momento de la replicación del sistema genómico de ARN o ADN, que el BAAYIODUU se conecta a su BB planetario, y que los seres vivos comienzan para comunicarse con el BB.

Las frecuencias gravitacionales emitidas por los procesos bioquímicos de los seres vivos resuenan con el criptón intracelular que causa un efecto LEIYO que permite la transmisión de información al BB planetario.

Si bien puede no ser necesario que BB conozca la fuente exacta, para el individuo, de la información que se le envía, no obstante debe saber al menos:

- las especies emisoras correspondientes a una clase modelo

- el astro emisor

Esto implicaría que la noción de especie no está vinculada a las restricciones genéticas evolutivas, que son solo el resultado de un proceso aguas arriba, sino, en última instancia, estrictamente a las categorizaciones del BB planetario.

Cada especie correspondería a un modelo típico en el BB planetario y cada modelo a un nivel de emergencia particular.

IDENTIFICACIÓN DE LA ESPECIE EMISORA.

Sabiendo que cada planetario BUUAWE BIAEEI está vinculado a un astro y contiene:

- Información de percepciones y procesos mentales de seres superiores (OEMMII)

- Símbolos universales, patrones de ideas de seres superiores

- Patrones gregarios emocionales de seres superiores

- Información biológica del medio ambiente ecológico de todos los seres vivos.

- Patrones de formas biológicas de todos los seres vivos.

H8

- En teoría, si pudiera existir un híbrido de dos humanidades, ¿a qué subconsciente colectivo pertenecería este individuo?

U - A quien tiene más genes.

BB comunica a través de las masas imaginarias

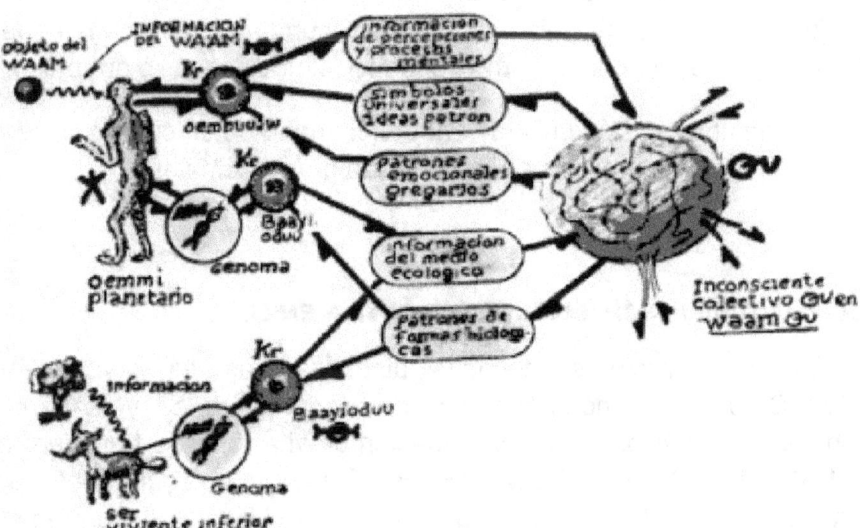

Los patrones biológicos de los seres vivos están totalmente codificados a nivel de cada célula de cada ser vivo, por lo que pueden identificarse dentro de la célula misma.

En contraste, los patrones de comportamiento gregarios no están contenidos dentro de la célula misma. Por lo tanto, deben identificarse en BB, específicamente para cada especie humana del cosmos.

Por lo tanto, existe necesariamente un vínculo inequívoco entre una especie humana y un tipo de perfil de comportamiento gregario. La hipótesis es que el identificador del tipo de patrón de comportamiento gregario es una característica de frecuencia gravitacional del tipo de la especie humana.

Del mismo modo, el flujo de conexión entre una especie humana y los datos planetarios BB deben ser únicos e identificativos.

LA IDENTIFICACIÓN DEL ASTRO TRANSMISOR.

La identificación del astro transmisor es necesaria para que la información emitida por el ser vivo llega en el buen BB, ¡y no en otro!

Esto supone que las frecuencias gravitacionales que identifican al astro están yuxtapuestas con las emisiones gravitacionales de los seres vivos. Por lo tanto, habría una frecuencia gravitacional del astro en mayor que desempeñaría el papel de frecuencia portadora y un conjunto de frecuencias gravitacionales secundarias para cada especie viva que se comporten como frecuencias modificadas o armónicos.

Habría una relación univoca entre el humano de un cuerpo celeste y su BB planetario basado en frecuencias gravitacionales.

El flujo de información que entra en BB

En las estructuras atómicas dinamizadoras de Krypton de BAAYIODUU, las ondas gravitacionales del astro se yuxtaponen con las del ser vivo. Toda la información gravitacional se transfiere al GUUINUU UXGIIGII de BUUAWEE BIAEEI como un cuanto de energía. Los cuantos de energía llegan al GOOINUU UXGIIGII y entran en resonancia (ondas estacionarias) con las cuerdas que conectan los nódulos de dos en dos. Resuenan según su naturaleza informativa.

Por lo tanto, las fuerzas gravitacionales emitidas inicialmente por un ser de una especie dada corresponden a una multitud de información de diversas naturalezas transmitidas a diferentes longitudes de onda con diferentes contenidos. Las cuerdas GOOINUU UXGIIGII del BB planetario resuenan de acuerdo con su correspondencia con cada frecuencia, luego la información se transmite a los nódulos que la procesan.

EL FLUJO DE INFORMACIÓN QUE SALE DE BB

Recíprocamente, la información del UXGIIGII GOOINUU debe transmitirse a los seres de una especie determinada, por ejemplo, los patrones de formas de un pájaro deben transmitirse por BB al destinatario correcto: ¡a un pájaro, no a un pez!

El BB registró la información en el GOXINUU UXGIIGII con las longitudes de onda de emisión iniciales de una especie determinada. El BB emite constantemente todos los patrones de todos los seres vivos. Cada especie captura la información específicamente destinada para ella. Esta información resulta de la emisión de un cuanto de energía del BB, que resonará con la configuración BAAYIODUU cuya longitud de onda corresponde a la especie en cuestión.

Al final, son los electrones de los átomos de criptón los que captan y resuenan individualmente con los armónicos gravitacionales que les corresponden.

ASUNCIÓN DE ESTRUCTURAS DE CATEGORIZACIÓN EN BB

La hipótesis es que el BB-planetario o, más exactamente, el GOOINUU UXGIIGII, está estructurado en matrices IBOZOO tal como en el filo evolutivo. Grandes redes de categorización de ramas de seres vivos, con subárboles que caracterizan a cada especie, y otros nodos que aún marcan una diferencia en el genotipo de la especie o el patrón gregario, etc.

Ciertos nodos particulares específicos de la especie son característicos de un nivel de emergencia, de calidad variable según el nivel de evolución.

Por lo tanto, varios filos OEMMII, cuando existen en un planeta, por ejemplo Homo Sapiens Nandertalis y Homo Sapiens Sapiens, no generan, estrictamente hablando, dos BB planetarios distintos, sino dos redes IBOZOO distintas en el mismo BB planetario.

Esto explicaría, que los Ummitas designan por el mismo término BUAWEE BIAEEII, varios objetos distintos:

D357-2 de 1987: (La confusión que puede observar proviene de lo que llamamos BB (BUAUEE BIAEEII) no solo el Alma colectiva de UMMO o la Tierra, sino también el plano cósmico (es decir del multiuniverso) que contiene todos los BB de las diferentes redes sociales que pueblan nuestro Universo Tetra dimensional.

Es decir, el BB planetario (el significado anterior [el antiguo] es sinónimo de COMUNIDAD EESEOMI (seres pensando)) y el WAAM-UU que contiene todo el BB planetario (nuestro concepto actual de ESPÍRITU COLECTIVO).

Entonces 3 conceptos diferentes para BB:

- de COMUNIDAD DE EESEOMI (el primer significado (el antiguo))

- Concepto planetario BB: el alma colectiva de UMMO o la Tierra

- Concepto BB-global (WAAM-UU) el plan cósmico de los multiunivers

Por cierto, explícitamente en 1966 - D33-3:

Puede objetar que quizás hay varios BUUAWE BIAEI asociados con diferentes grupos raciales. No creemos que este punto de vista sea plausible por la simple razón de que CONSTATAMOS que todo el núcleo humano de la Tierra se deriva del mismo filo antropoide.

Así que solo hay un BB para nuestra humanidad.

En el documento D1751 tenemos:

Te invitamos a reflexionar sobre las contradicciones del alma colectiva (BUUAUE BIAEEI) islámica.

La indicación Alma colectiva caracteriza el objeto BB planetario.

Entonces eso implicaría que hay muchos planetarios para nuestra humanidad.

Para ser coherentes, deberíamos haber tenido:

Te invitamos a reflexionar sobre las contradicciones de la COMUNIDAD EESEOMI Islámica (BUUAUE BIAEEI).

A priori, podemos pensar que esta oración es un gran error, como si pusiéramos un término de francés antiguo en el medio de una oración contemporánea. Pero, quizás también sea simplemente porque el término BB se usa para diferentes conceptos y que solo dos filos OEMMII del mismo planeta no generan, estrictamente hablando, dos BB-planetarios distintos, sino dos redes de IBOZOO separado en el mismo BB-planetario. Este concepto estaría muy cerca de la noción de comunidad EESEEOEMMII. Este tipo de concepto implica que existen abundantes redes IBOZOO. Este tipo de profusión no marca un nodo de emergencia de especies, sino simplemente una proliferación genotípica dentro de la especie, sus esquemas gregarios, etc.

Pues, tambien eso pone sospechoso el documento D1751.

LOS FLUJOS DEL CEREBRO HUMANO

¿Cómo se transmiten los flujos de los pares de criptón OEMBUAW en el cerebro al cuerpo humano?

¿Cómo se envían las transmisiones recibidas de BAAYIODUU al ADN?

¿Cómo se implementa un orden de mutación del planetario BB hasta el ADN?

Como hemos visto, el flujo entre el BB planetario y las capas electrónicas de los pares de criptón del cerebro OEMBUAW o el flujo del BAAYIODUU a las células es un efecto gravitacional de LEIYO. Entonces, ¿cómo se puede transformar este flujo gravitacional en flujos bioquímicos en el cerebro?

D58-5: Para resumir, indicaremos que el Cangrejo ya mencionado capturará gracias a sus ojos los estímulos luminosos de la coloración de las rocas (AZUL-VERDE). Esto provoca una serie de alteraciones metabólicas (es decir, bioquímicas); inmediatamente los estímulos codificados como impulsos nerviosos afectan los órganos simples de su sistema nervioso embrionario. En este caso, son los niveles de Potasio y Nitrógeno los que se alteran de tal manera que la célula esté INFORMADA de las condiciones que prevalecen afuera en el campo ÓPTICO.

A través de la membrana celular se altera el equilibrio de la transferencia de iones y el metabolismo celular sufre una serie de modificaciones que van desde el citoplasma hasta el núcleo.

Las alteraciones se producen a nivel de las sub-capas más superficiales de los átomos de oxígeno que forman las moléculas de AGUA INTRA-CITOPLÁSMICA al producir automáticamente variaciones cuantificadas del campo gravitacional electrónico.

[...] algunos átomos de componentes de OXÍGENO del agua contenida en el citoplasma celular, se exci-tan en sus capas orbitales externas. Los electrones vibrantes emiten ondas gravitacionales.

Estas ondas gravitacionales tienen una energía mucho menor que las ondas de radio que conoce (aproxi-madamente 10-39 más pequeñas). Pero este campo gra-vitacional alterado causa un efecto de resonancia en los electrones de uno de los átomos de cada par que componen el BAAYIODUU (átomo que llamaremos, porque es su denominación en nuestro idioma: BAAIGOO EIXUUA y que no se puede traducir): DINÁMICO o dinamizador. En otras palabras: actúa como un receptor capaz de detectar las ondas gravitacionales emitidas por el OXÍGENO citoplasmático y registrar el mensaje como si fuera un grabador terrestre. Cuando un electrón se asocia con un Quantum gravitacional (llamado por GRAVITON terrestre), dicha asociación puede dar lugar a otro electrón con modificación de fase y posición orbital y a una nueva subpartícula que se degrada más tarde por subdividiendo en otros dos.

Así es como se informan los electrones del átomo de KRYPTON.

Por lo tanto, los átomos de oxígeno del agua intracelular emiten frecuencias gravitacionales capturadas por los electrones de uno de los dos átomos de cada par de criptón BAAYIODUU. Eso es lo que significa decodificar la palabra Ummita BAAIGOO EIXUUA. En otras palabras, cuando la capa electrónica interactúa con una frecuencia gravitacional, impacta un electrón preciso. Esto define el flujo de infor-mación del medio al BB planetario.

Por el contrario, el BB planetario puede transmitir a los electrones del criptón BAAYIODUU información subconsciente que se propagará a través de los átomos de oxígeno del agua intracelular. La información se une así al circuito neural.

Una hipótesis es que cuando el BB planetario envía una orden de mutación, el proceso es diferente. El flujo gravitacional del BB planetario capturado por los electrones del criptón, interactúa mucho más directamente en el ADN a través de un compuesto de retransmisión. Este compuesto de relé tendría la propiedad de transformar las frecuencias gravitacionales directamente en biofrecuencias. Estas biofrecuencias afectan directamente la mutación sobre el codón o la base del ADN con el que entran en resonancia.

BIOFRECUENCIAS

¿Puede existir un compuesto relé entre las frecuencias gravitacionales y las biofrecuencias?

La hipótesis de investigación es estudiar compuestos cuyo número total de protones y neutrones es igual al de un par de átomos de criptón. Encontramos que la masa molar de Kr_2 es idéntica a un compuesto de $GeSi_2C_3H_3$ es de aproximadamente 167,6 g / mol.

Este compuesto de retransmisión, este bio-sintonizador, de $GeSi_2C_3H_3$ sería la interfaz entre los pares Kr_2 y el ADN. Podría sincronizar todos los elementos celulares necesarios para controlar las mutaciones dirigidas por el planetario BB. Es él quien protege el ADN contra mutaciones indeseables y desencadena mutaciones controladas.

Diagrama esquemático del flujo intracelular de ADN criptón

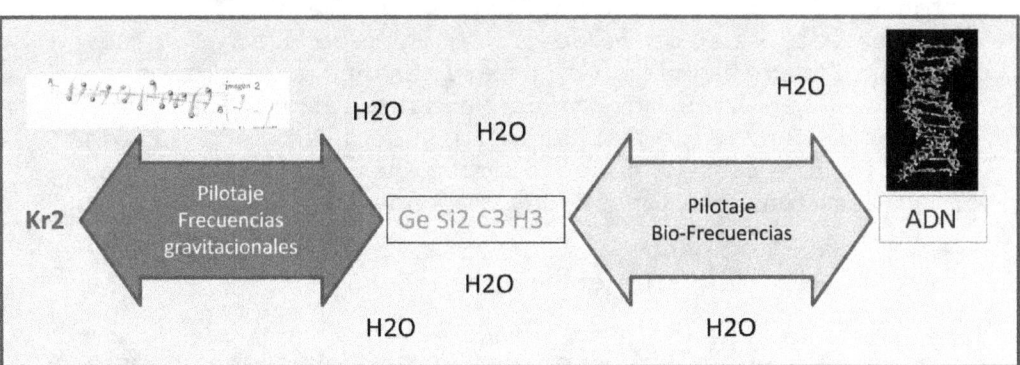

La hipótesis es que este compuesto, germanio, silicio en particular, así como diferentes cristales y los principales gases raros juegan un papel clave en el metabolismo celular y las biofrecuencias. Muchos procesos celulares estarían bajo el control de biofrecuencias a través de estos elementos. Los átomos de carbono e hidrógeno podrían ser los átomos de interfaz con las biofrecuencias resultantes de los procesos neurológicos. Desarrollaremos este punto en el capítulo Comunicación telepática.

El más conocido, el silicio vibra a una frecuencia muy estable. Esta característica hace del silicio un excelente receptor y emisor de ondas electromagnéticas. Es por eso que se usa ampliamente en la mayoría de las tecnologías electrónicas.

D41: Son los impulsos nerviosos que, gracias a los diferentes átomos de carbono y helio cuyos estados CUÁNTICOS han sido excitados, modifican por resonancia los estados ordinarios de frecuencia cero (onda plana) de cada átomo KRYPTON por el efecto OWEEU OMWAA. Así, los mensajes de la memoria, por ejemplo, se codificarán en estos átomos en forma de ONDES.

D21: La frecuencia de los pulsos de activación de los centros nerviosos ubicados en el plexo coroideo ventrolateral del cerebro es de 6 123 ciclos por segundo (unidad de frecuencia muy utilizada en neurofisiología).

Constante biogenética: 65810. 12-10 segundos. Este es el tiempo que tarda el estado cuántico en establecerse en el átomo de carbono de la cadena de ácido desoxirribonucleico para la formación de un GENO.

D731: El otro átomo en el par captura la información del medio ambiante. Esta información proviene de una pequeña masa de agua intracelular o citoplasmática y también de agua intranuclear. En otras palabras, son las moléculas de agua las que capturan trenes de ondas de varias longitudes, no solo las de frecuencia similar a las dimensiones de la molécula, sino también las longitudes de onda métricas.

La segunda fuente de información son las biomoléculas y los oligoelementos que pasan a través de la membrana celular.

[...] en algunos universos hemos detectado formas vivas con negentropía [...] con germanio y silicio como elemento central.

BAA IODUHU (B.I.) o protege contra una acción mutagénica o causa una mutación controlada. Un pez envía información sobre sus genes y el entorno circundante,

`y solo recibe [...] patrones de genotipo para modular`
`sus mutaciones.`

Según el microbiólogo E. Guillé, estas secuencias redundantes funcionan como emisores y receptores de frecuencias electromagnéticas que constituirían una nueva función posible para una parte del ADN de la basura.

Según Gianni A. Dotto, en 1971, la carga magnética del código genético se mantiene en un nivel apropiado por la propiedad eléctrica de la doble hélice, que funciona como un transformador común, donde el voltaje primario y el devanado secundario son proporcionales al número de vueltas de las bobinas. En humanos entre las edades de 35 y 55 años, un voltaje de 45 a 70 milivoltios mantiene una linealidad de 10 pares de bases por revolución en la doble hélice de ADN.

En su síntesis de compuestos Ge Si C, J. Kouvetakis y D. Nesting del Departamento de Química y Bioquímica de la Universidad de Tempe, Arizona, muestran que las aleaciones Ge Si C son metaestables. Sus numerosas propiedades están relacionadas con las frecuencias altas en particular y son sensibles a la radiación gamma muy baja.

En 1973, Tsiang Kan Zheng parecía haber transferido información genética utilizando radiación bio-electromagnética de frecuencia ultraalta.

En 1991, Jacques Benveniste transferirá una señal molecular utilizando un detector electromagnético y un amplificador de baja frecuencia.

LOS EFECTORES DE GeSI2C3H3

En las células, se pudo detectar germanio en lisosomas, cromatina condensada y nucleolo. El papel fisiológico del germanio es actualmente desconocido.

Diagrama de síntesis de los efectores de GeSi2C3H3

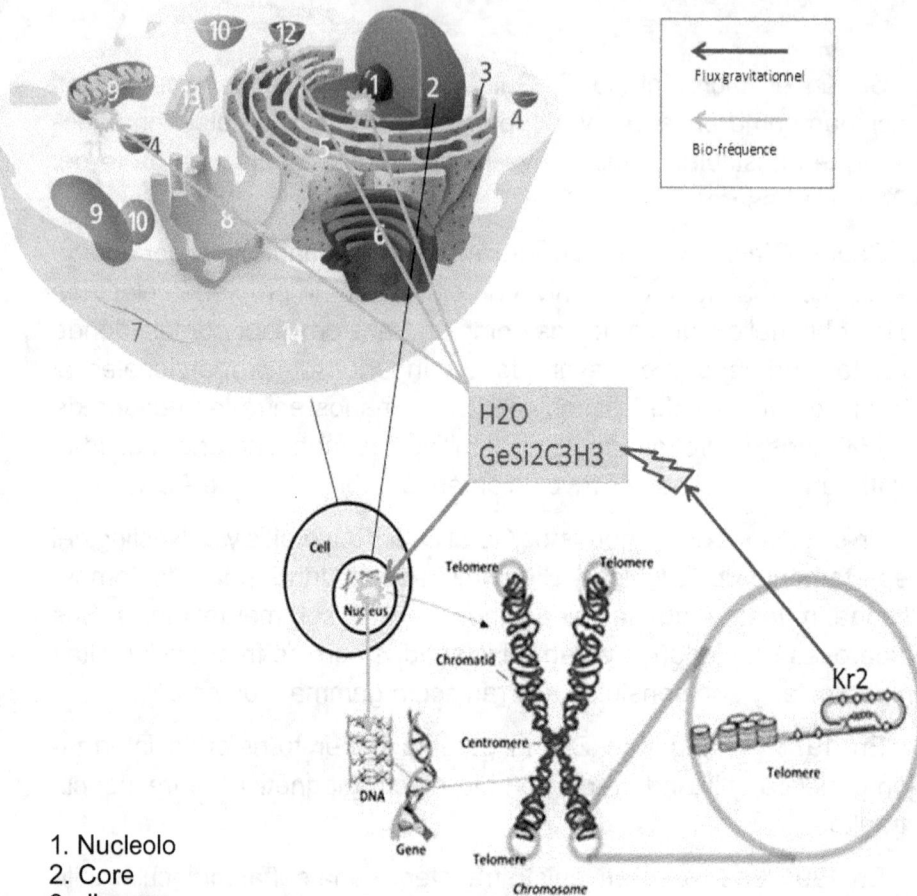

1. Nucleolo
2. Core
3. ribosoma
4. Vesícula
5. Retículo endoplásmico rugoso (granular) (REG)
6. aparato de Golgi
7. Citoesqueleto
8. Retículo endoplásmico liso
9. las mitocondrias
10. Vacuole
11. Cytosol
12. Lisosoma
13. Centrosoma (que consta de dos centriolos)
14. membrana plasmática

El germanio se almacena naturalmente en el ajo, el ginseng y especialmente el hongo ganoderma lucidum. El consumo de estos famosos hongos parece estar relacionado con la noción de envejecimiento. Tradicionalmente, los emperadores de las grandes dinastías chinas y japonesas han usado el hongo para prolongar su longevidad. La investigación china y coreana también ha resaltado las propiedades de este hongo para causar apoptosis de las células cancerosas.

Los telómeros del ADN juegan un papel importante en el envejecimiento celular. Cuanto más cortos son los telómeros, más antiguas son las células. Los elementos coloidales de los platinoides de los tipos: rodio, paladio, iridio, etc., en su forma coloidal, pueden unirse a los telómeros.

El genetista Maxim Frank-Kamenetskii escribió sobre el ADN que: Los pares de bases están dispuestos como los de un cristal.

Todo esto nos lleva a creer que GeSi2C3H3 y algunos átomos de germanio dispersados en la célula afectan directa o indirectamente a los lisosomas, telómeros, secuencias de nucleótidos de ADN y nucleolo en el proceso de replicación del ADN. .

A nivel mundial, el compuesto GeSi2C3H3 garantizaría la sincronización de todos los elementos de la célula involucrados en el proceso de replicación del ADN y, por lo tanto, garantizaría el mantenimiento de la integridad del ADN, especialmente frente a la radiación cósmica o radiactiva.

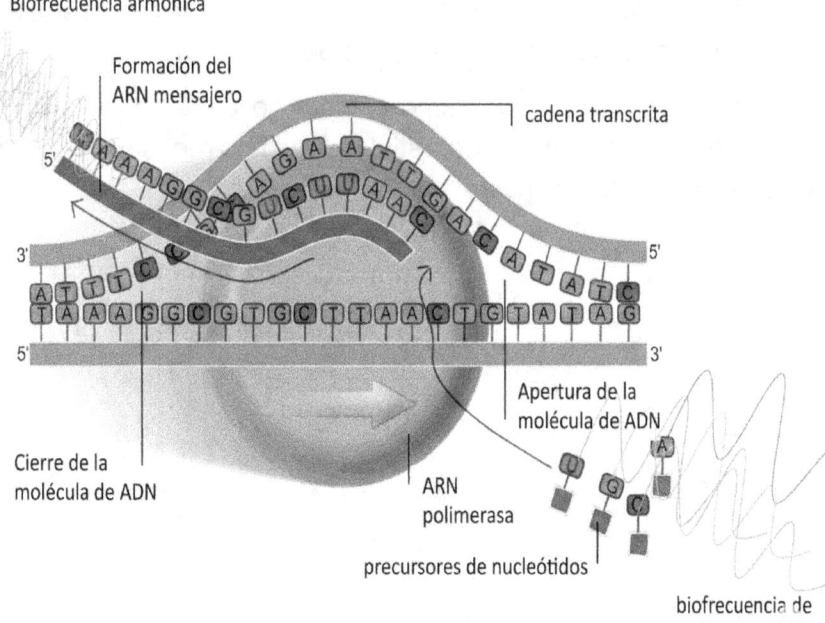

145

LAS FRECUENCIAS DE AMINOÁCIDOS Y PROTEÍNAS

Como descubrimos analizando las palabras del lenguaje Ummita en *Presence 2, El lenguaje y el misterio del planeta UMMO revelado,* cada uno de los veinte aminoácidos emite una onda cuya frecuencia específica se puede calcular, siguiendo el trabajo de Joël Sternheimer investigador de la European Research University en París.

Estas ondas se emiten en el momento en que estos aminoácidos, transportados por los ARN de transferencia, se unen para formar proteínas. Del mismo modo, las proteínas emiten un armónico resultante de las frecuencias de los aminoácidos. Algunas resonancias con ondas sonoras para influir en el ciclo proteico. Esto tiene la consecuencia práctica de que las frecuencias de sonido pueden influir en el desarrollo de los seres vivos y las plantas en particular.

CONCLUSIÓN

La hipótesis es que los BB planetarios están estructurados en redes de IBOZOO arborescentes de las cuales cada nivel de categorización corresponde a un nivel de emergencia.

Dos filos OEMMII del mismo planeta no generan, estrictamente hablando, dos BB planetarios distintos, sino dos redes IBOZOO distintas en el mismo BB planetario.

Figura 1-p2: Los seres vivos se comunican con el BB de acuerdo con las frecuencias gravitacionales específicas de cada especie que se yuxtaponen a las frecuencias del astro.

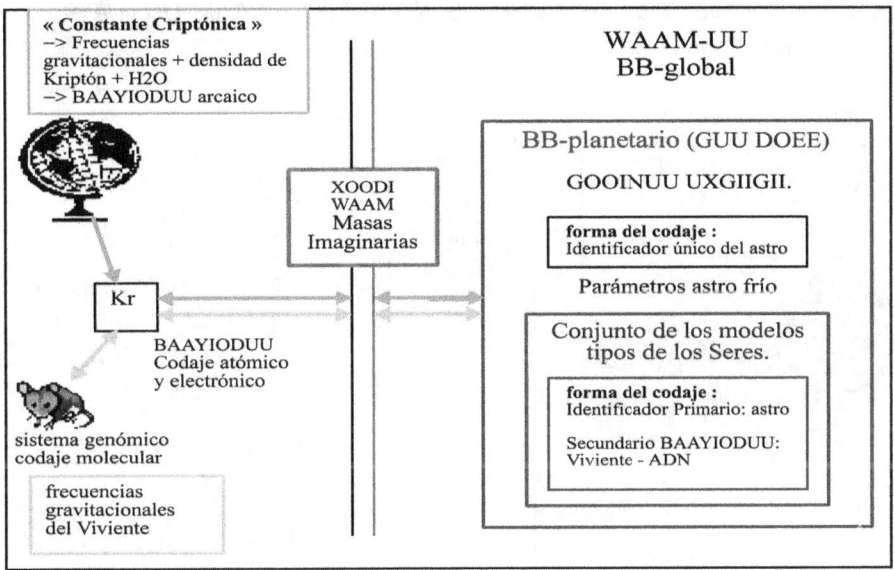

Como corolario, debe tenerse en cuenta que todos los enlaces entre las configuraciones de criptón y el BB planetario son dinámicos. El conjunto de todos los tipos de posibles seres vivos evoluciona en el rango de lo permitido por los parámetros del cuerpo frío: el coeficiente BAAYIODIXAA UUDIE. Esta evolución dinámica es obviamente muy lenta en comparación con la longevidad de los seres vivos, estamos aquí a la escala del tiempo geológico.

Solo las estrellas frías que tienen gases raros, minerales cristalinos y agua pueden ver desarrollar un BAAYIODUU vinculado al BB planetario. No hay vida posible sin el papel de los transceptores / biofrecuencias de estos elementos en solución acuosa.

En las células, el agua captura las frecuencias externas, y el complejo Krypton-GeSi2C3H3 captura las frecuencias «internas» de BB.

El diagrama de síntesis de los flujos del pilotaje del Vivant:

ADN <-> Bio-tuner <-> criptón BAAYIODUU <-> WAAM-UU [Meta-Cerebro BB Planetario]

Cerebro <-> Bio-tuner <-> criptón OEMBUAWE <-> WAAM-UU [Meta-Cerebro BB Planetario]

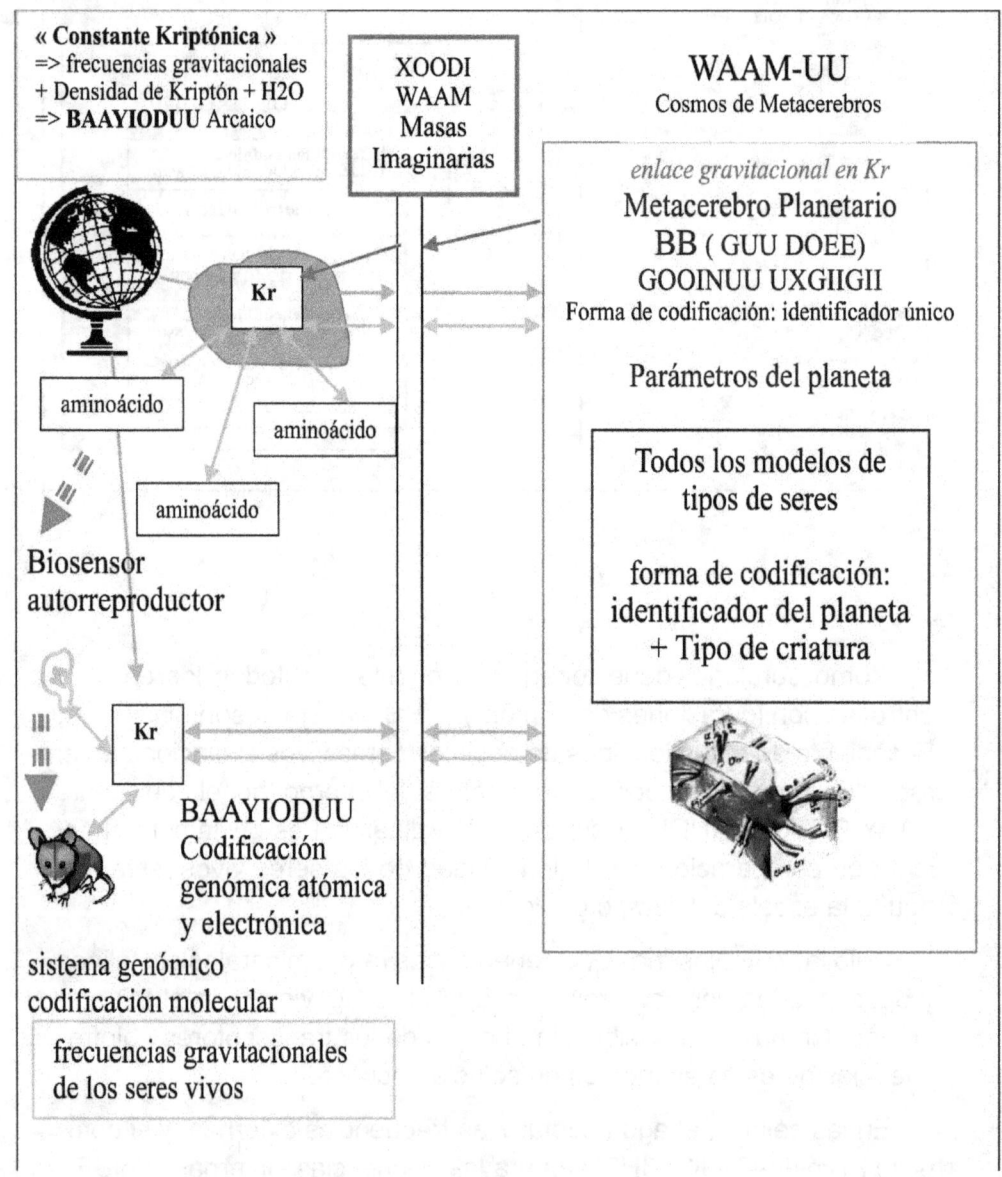

« Constante Kriptónica »
=> frecuencias gravitacionales
+ Densidad de Kriptón + H2O
=> **BAAYIODUU** Arcaico

XOODI
WAAM
Masas
Imaginarias

WAAM-UU
Cosmos de Metacerebros

Kr

aminoácido

aminoácido

aminoácido

Biosensor
autorreproductor

Kr

BAAYIODUU
Codificación
genómica atómica
y electrónica

sistema genómico
codificación molecular

frecuencias gravitacionales
de los seres vivos

enlace gravitacional en Kr
Metacerebro Planetario
BB (GUU DOEE)
GOOINUU UXGIIGII
Forma de codificación: identificador único

Parámetros del planeta

Todos los modelos de
tipos de seres

forma de codificación:
identificador del planeta
+ Tipo de criatura

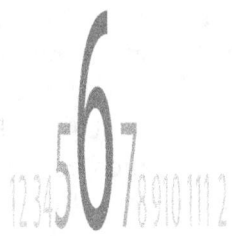

LA GÉNESIS DEL ALMA BUAWA

Hemos visto en las hipótesis anteriores cómo, en vista de una constante universal subyacente llamada constante criptónica, lo vivo podría emerger de la materia inerte de la constitución del arcaico BAAYIODUU. Entonces, cuando se integra con los seres vivos, ¿cómo se pueden establecer los flujos de comunicación entre entidades? Ahora examinaremos la conexión con el Alma BUAWA.

HIPÓTESIS SOBRE EL FLUJO DE INFORMACIÓN

WAAM-U tiene un infinito de BUAWA. Estas BUAWA están inicialmente vacías.

La hipótesis, segun los dichos de nuestros visitantes de Ummo, es que el contenido del BUAWA del OEMMII se genera precisamente en el momento de la fusión cromosómica de la fertilización, al mismo tiempo que la conexión del BAAYIODUU con el BB.

En esta fusión cromosómica, cada gameto haploide, masculino y femenino, transporta una serie de 86 átomos de criptón de la meiosis. La cariogamia, el ensamblaje de los núcleos de los gametos también provoca el ensamblaje de pares de cromosomas y, por lo tanto, pares de átomos de criptón. Se crea un nuevo BAAYIODUU en la primera celda diploide del OEMMII, lo que provoca el efecto LEIYO de la conexión con el BB.

Esto tiene la consecuencia directa de que los gemelos humanos iniciarían y usarían un solo BUAWA.

Es durante la embriogénesis humana y a priori de OEMMII en general, durante la estructuración del encéfalo en particular, que se configura OEMBUAWA. La constitución del OEMBUAWA activa la comunicación con BUAWA y con BUAWE BIAAEI, el alma colectiva de OEMMII. Para los seres inferiores que no tienen OEMBUAWA, por lo tanto, nunca hay activación de BUAWA, pero la activación sigue siendo potencial, si el ser vivo evoluciona.

El principio de identificación de OEMMII descrito para el enlace BAAYIODUU (BB-criptón— sistema genómico del ser vivo), es idéntico para el enlace OEMBUAWA-BUAWE BIAAEI, el alma colectiva de OEMMII. Este enlace incluye identificación planetaria de facto. Es universal, multi-cosmos, específico para cada OEMMII y permanente hasta la muerte del individuo. Tenga en cuenta nuevamente que en este caso, los gemelos idénticos necesariamente tienen el mismo BUAWA enriquecido con la información de los dos individuos.

La identificación del OEMMII con su BUAWA se debe a la transmisión de una cantidad cuántica de energía consecutivamente a una frecuencia gravitacional precisa, como para el enlace OEMBUAWA-BUUAWE BIAAEI. La resonancia gravitacional entre OEMBUAWA y BUAWA es una simple alineación de ejes entre el IBOZOO UU que transporta la información gravitacional y la cadena BUAWA IBOZOO UU. La propagación de la onda gravitacional por el efecto de la resonancia acuántica es un efecto LEIYO transmitido a través de masas imaginarias que no genera masa, pero que sin embargo permite registrar la información en la cadena IBOZOO UU de BUAWA. Recíprocamente, la información se transmitirá de BUAWA a OEMBUAWA siguiendo este mismo principio.

El BUAWA está compuesto por una red pura IBOZOO UU que está formada por grandes cadenas de relaciones angulares. Estas grandes cadenas a su vez forman un sustrato o matriz extendido donde toda la información de nuestra vida estará graficada en un sector de la red y en otro sector de la red IBOZOO UU pura que codifica un programa completo de instrucciones que se ajustan cada OEMII (el hombre tomó su dimensión neuronal). El enlace OEMBUAWA-BUAWA también corresponde a una resonancia gravitacional específica igual a la que inicializó el contenido de BUAWA en el momento de la fusión genómica, y se establece de forma dinámica y de uno a uno.

Parece que el libre albedrío humano es un proceso de toma de decisiones que involucra varias soluciones posibles. Se realiza a nivel del encéfalo. BUAWA no toma una decisión, genera una idea orientadora que es consistente con el perfil psíquico de la red BUAWA IBOZOO. Éste red BUAWA IBOZOO podría sufrir diversas influencias externas (ver Hipótesis sobre la influencia de las configuraciones planetarias en la psique).

Luego, esta idea guía se transmite al cerebro, que lo confronta con las percepciones del entorno, los modelos mentales transmitidos por BB. Según las indicaciones de los Ummitas, el libre albedrío es simplemente la decisión entre todas las opciones posibles, con aproximadamente el 70% de las decisiones consistentes con el principio rector de BUAWA. Estos procesos de conciencia subconsciente se expresan mediante los términos de la familia EESE.

Alma y tiempo

Las ideas directoras de Ame-BUAWA son los datos almacenados. El flujo de estos datos desde el espacio exterior es a través de un cosmos de naturaleza totalmente diferente. En el meta-cerebro planetario, la velocidad de los fotones es infinita. En Ame-BUAWA, solo hay un eje dimensional que almacena la información. La noción de velocidad o tiempo de fotones no tiene significado en este cosmos. El simple almacenamiento de información se realiza en canales IBODZOO, como los bits de computadora de las computadoras terrestres de nuestro tiempo. En la Tierra, en el marco tridimensional de nuestro cosmos, el tiempo también se compone de una cadena de elementos discretos de IBODZOO. El flujo que conecta Ame-BUAWA con el cuerpo humano a través del conector OEMBUAWE de átomos de criptón, se une a los elementos discretos de IBODZOO de las 2 cadenas.

El flujo comienza desde BUAWA, transita en la capa intercosmos XOODII cuya velocidad fotónica es infinita.

Luego, el flujo de velocidad infinita llega a la antena OEMBUAWE en nuestro marco tridimensional regido por nuestro tiempo compuesto por una cadena de elementos discretos de IBODZOO, que es el tiempo de Planck de $5,391 \times 10^{-44}$ segundos , correspondiente a un ángulo elemental en el eje de tiempo, entre dos nodos multidimensionales IBOSDSOO. Lo que equivale a decir que estamos pasando de un flujo infinito de velocidad a un flujo a la velocidad de nuestra luz de 300 000 km / s.

La comunicación entre el alma-BUAWA nuestro cerebro es, por lo tanto, casi instantánea. Este es también el caso en las comunicaciones telepáticas interpersonales a través del Meta-Cerebro Planetario BB.

D731: La información de nuestra mente se transfiere también a la psique. Allí, se graba en redes filamentosas de IBOZSOO UHU. Es decir, en cadenas IBOZSOO UHU. Del mismo modo, esta estructura de alambre aparece en la secuencia de I.U. quien interactúa con nosotros, nos dirige. Cada una de estas cadenas de I.U. está compuesto por un infinito (en el sentido físico) de ángulos que codifican la información.

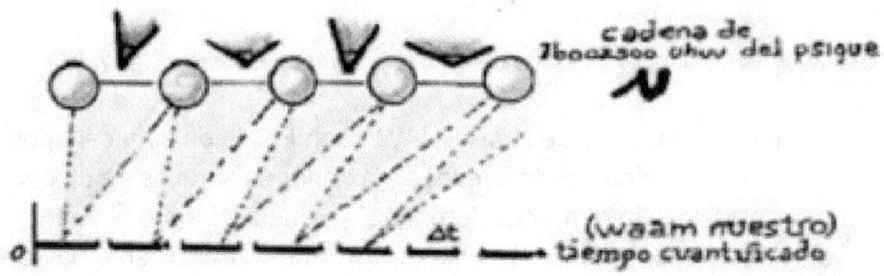

Existe, como puede ver en el gráfico, una correspondencia biunívoca entre los instantes del eje del tiempo [el tiempo está unificado como discreto] y el IBOZSOO UHUU de la psique. . Time in the Universe está formado por una sucesión discreta de CUANTONES TEMPORALES Dt, cada uno de los cuales está relacionado con el par de I.U. que codifica las instrucciones que envía el alma.

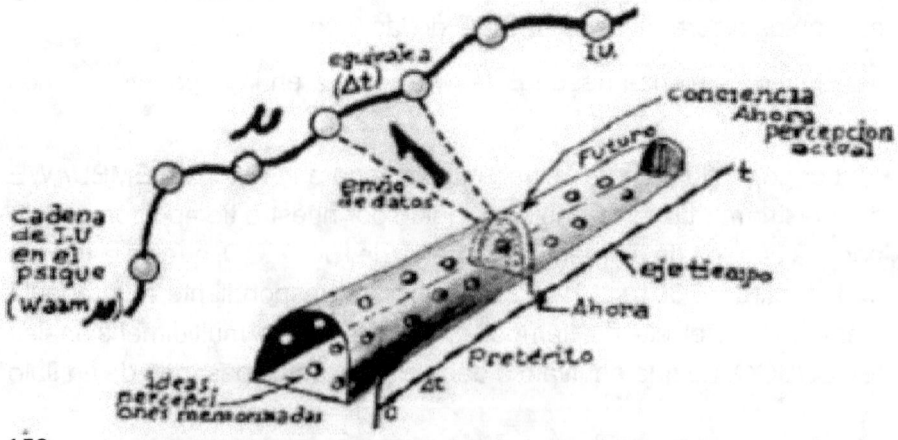

Se ha demostrado que en el caso de la decisión de una acción motora, la decisión de la acción se toma en la corteza frontal y luego se transmite a la corteza parietal, lo que genera un potencial de preparación ANTES de la toma de decisiones consciente.

En este caso, un proceso inconsciente de la corteza frontal-parietal se identifica como el tomador de decisiones de la acción motora. La toma de decisiones consciente simplemente se reduce a un GO / NO en la corteza motora, después de la decisión inicial no consciente.

Los primeros experimentos que muestran, por cierto, que los procesos inconscientes de nuestro cerebro deciden antes que nosotros, fueron llevados a cabo en 1983 por Benjamin Libet y confirmados en 2003-2004 por Angela Sirigu y Patrick Haggard.

¿ De dónde vendría la decisión subconsciente? La hipótesis BUAWA explica el origen de la decisión subconsciente de la corteza frontal-parietal...

Diagrama de flujos de información OEMBUAWA-BUAWA, el proceso de una decisión de acción motora sería:

BUAWA -> OEMBUAW -> corteza frontal -> corteza parietal -> corteza motora -> conciencia -> corteza motora -> acción

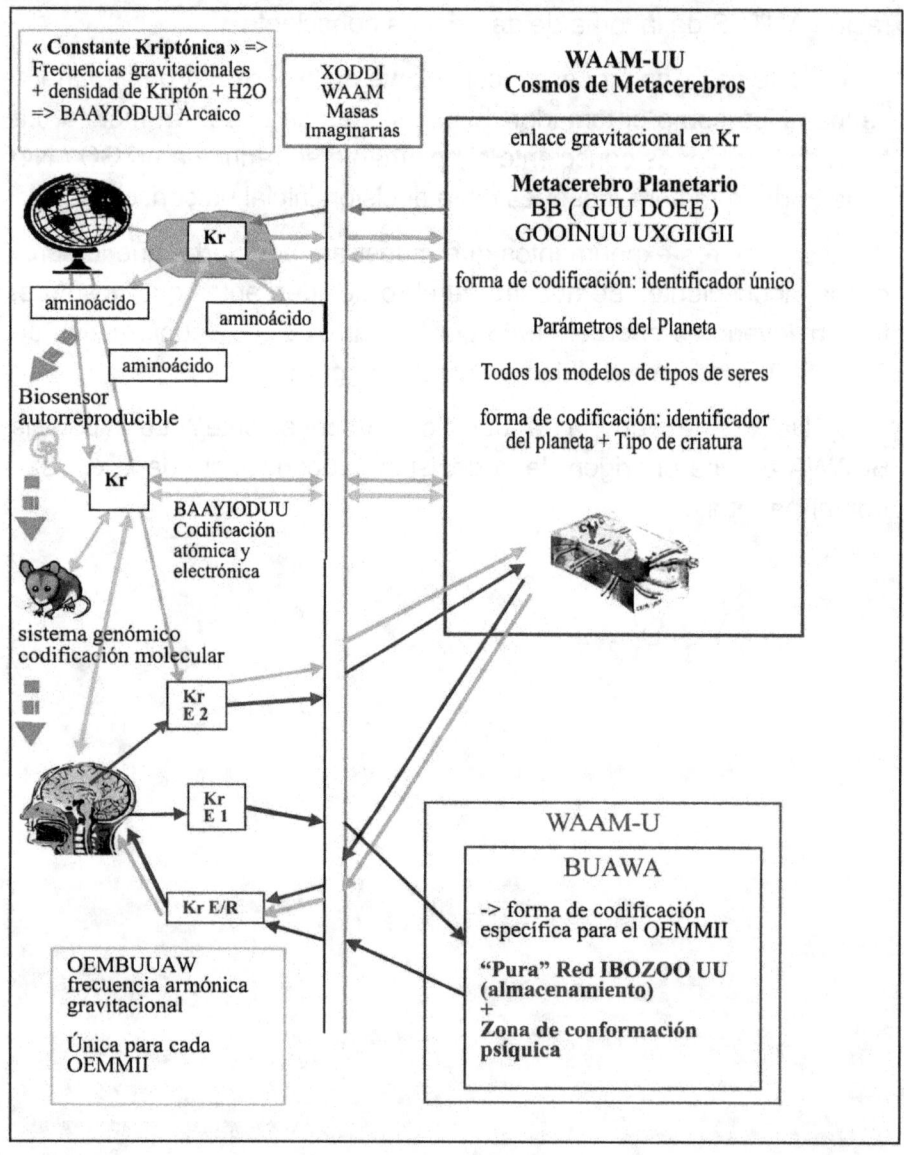

EL CONCEPTO Y LOS LÍMITES DE LA REENCARNACIÓN

Por lo general, el concepto metafísico de la reencarnación es la integración del alma vinculada a un cuerpo humano en un animal. La simple disparidad de seres nos permite asumir fácilmente que esto no es coherente ni realista. ¿Pero qué pasa con la reencarnación en otro cuerpo humano?

Comenzaré con un testimonio personal. Uno de mis amigos, el fallecido Gérard P., quien contribuyó a la aventura científica de la serie Presence, tenía un perfil psíquico particular, le diagnosticaron el autismo de Asperger. Curiosamente, en sus primeros años, el niño Gérard manifestó comportamientos y habilidades atípicas, una de ellas era conocer de manera aparentemente innata las ecuaciones matemáticas. Años después, buscó a qué correspondían estas ecuaciones y descubrió lo que Alan Turing había formulado, y que estaba muerto el día de su nacimiento ... La coincidencia apareció como una transferencia mental entre el moribundo y el recien nacido. Como veremos en detalle, una posible interpretación es que parte de la información generada por Alan Turing en el BUAWE BIAEI Global Meta-Brain fue transferida por él al BUAWA del recién nacido Gerard.

Numerosas observaciones y estudios científicos se han llevado a cabo sobre este tema. Estos incluyen estudios de James Parejko, profesor de filosofía en la Universidad Estatal de Chicago, sobre temas hipnotizados, el trabajo de William E. Cox, Joel Whitton, profesor de psiquiatría en la Facultad de Medicina de Toronto y Joe Fisher, cuyos temas incluyen Mostraron un conocimiento de lenguas antiguas y raras sin siquiera haber supuesto su existencia, otros aún identificaron de manera detallada y probada lugares o incluso personas de su vida anterior. Ian Stevenson, profesor de psiquiatría en la Facultad de Medicina de la Universidad de Virginia, estudió una multitud de casos en los que los sujetos presentaron manifestaciones morfológicas, marcas corporales relacionadas con la muerte violenta de encarnaciones anteriores ...

Ahora veamos los posibles casos de reencarnación. Según mi interpretación de los documentos Ummitas, se debe considerar que en el diseño de un ser humano por fusión cromosómica, pueden suceder dos cosas particulares:

• Excepcionalmente, la información de identificación del alma del nuevo humano corresponde a un Alma-BUAWA ya existente. Y así, el nuevo individuo tendrá una conexión con un patrimonio informativo formado por el individuo anterior. Aunque hay fenómenos psíquicos endógenos en el cerebro, más o menos psicópatas y afabuladores, la sensación de haber experimentado algo en una vida anterior puede no ser infundada ... Algunas personas pueden haber heredado almas muy fuertes. antiguo y muy rico en información acumulada, que data del primer Homos habilis. En corolario, podemos preguntarnos si, además del contexto cultural, las personas que tendrían BUAWA con los contenidos informativos más ricos también son los humanos que tienen las capacidades prospectivas más desarrolladas.

• Un nuevo humano se conecta a una celda Ame-BUAWA vacía. Este es probablemente el caso general. Pero, en algunos casos especiales por iniciativa del Meta-cerebro BUAWE BIAEI, decide transmitir un contenido informativo específico al BUAWA vacío. Podemos imaginar que esta acción tiene como objetivo modificar la red social directamente a través del nuevo humano.

Percibimos a través de esta visión de las cosas que el libre albedrío humano puro es aún más limitado de lo que a menudo imaginamos. El humano parece actuar libremente, pero al dibujar sus pensamientos en contenido informativo ya bien lleno, el trabajo del neuroencéfalo para hacer arbitrajes y producir un pensamiento adaptado al entorno físico real del humano ...

H3 - La nueva alma que nace puede ser impregnada ... puede recibir información proveniente del Alma colectiva. En este sentido, la información que recibe proviene de otras almas. En este sentido, sí, la reencarnación sería admisible. Esto de alguna manera es una información del Alma Colectiva.

H4: la resurrección puede ocurrir, sabes que tu conciencia universal persiste en otro cerebro. No es una reencarnación. La conciencia puede persistir en otro cuerpo (cuando las características del individuo coinciden, ya que un guante puede caber en otra mano).

Vemos cuán poco parece ser el cuerpo humano, dada la influencia de los objetos cosmológicos metafísicos que guían sus acciones. Como hemos visto, es el significado de la palabra Ummita BUAWA: Interconexión que genera acciones.

Un punto complementario sería considerar al ser humano como la acumulación de su dimensión corporal y la dimensión extracorpórea, es decir con su Ame-BUAWA.

Esto es lo que mencionamos en Presencia 2 El lenguaje y el misterio del planeta Ummo revelado con el análisis del significado de la palabra OEMMII que indica la asociación del cuerpo físico OEMII con un límite que sería Ame-BUAWA. Esto se resumiría en:

OEMII (cuerpo físico) + Ame-BUAWA = OEMMII (humano)

ERRORES DE IMPREGNACIÓN DE BB

El trastorno de identidad disociativa o trastorno de personalidad se conoce como un trastorno mental definido en 1994 según un conjunto de criterios de diagnóstico como un tipo particular de trastorno disociativo.

 Se trata de al menos dos personalidades que controlan sistemáticamente el comportamiento del individuo con una pérdida de memoria que va más allá del olvido habitual. Algunos pacientes pueden tener 10 personalidades distintas, identificables por mapas mentales separados, patologías específicas de cada personalidad, desde alergia a diabetes ... Cada una de estas personalidades es en sí misma normal ...

Es como si un cuerpo físico hubiera sido dotado de varias Almas ...

La hipótesis es que la impregnación de los datos de BB en el Alma en el momento de la fusión cromosómica ha salido mal. BB habría permeado el Alma con varios flujos de datos de diferentes personas. Probablemente segmentando diferentes áreas en BUAWA en lugar de mezclar todos los datos en la misma área ... Entonces, el OEMBUAWE, el cerebro de la persona accedería alternativamente a estas diferentes áreas ...

A la muerte de un humano OEMMII, se produce un fenómeno de aglutinación de la entidad cosmológica BUAWA con su metacerebro planetario del cosmos WAAM-UU.

Este emparejamiento entre estas entidades de estos dos cosmos, WAAM-UU y WAAM-U, tan diferentes requiere la implementación de un enlace intercosmos. El enlace entre el BUAWA unidimensional y el BB planetario pentadimensional se hace a través de una cadena IBODSOO. El Alma-BUAWA del difunto puede entonces intercambiar flujos de información que transitan a través del planetario BB. Esto permite la comunicación con todos los demás Ames-BUAWA de los fallecidos y potencialmente con los efectores OEMBUAWA de cerebros humanos.

También es posible que este Alma-BUAWA integrado acceda a otros BB planetarios y a todos los demás Alma-BUAWA integrados en él. Después de la muerte física de los humanos OEMMII del cosmos, todos sus Alma-BUAWA pueden comunicarse entre sí a través de los BB.

El proceso de integración de Alma-BUAWA es más o menos largo y la integración más o menos completa. Supongo que esto está directamente bajo el control del generador cosmogónico WOA. Sería él quien decidiría la relevancia del grado de integración del flujo del Alma-BUAWA en un BB planetario.

Creemos que este proceso de integración del Alma-BUAWA también puede sufrir perturbaciones más o menos fuertes en el momento de la muerte y ser la causa de los llamados fenómenos paranormales que explicaremos en los siguientes capítulos.

D731: MUERTE (ESCATOLOGÍA DE UMMO) Cuando ocurre una destrucción de los últimos elementos de la red de criptón (no la aniquilación de los átomos, sino la de los enlaces o nodos de la red), ocurre la muerte. Esta aniquilación coincide precisamente con la desintegración de ciertas redes neuronales del encéfalo. (El paro cardíaco implica falta de suministro de sangre, falta de suministro de oxígeno y glucosa a la red neurológica, degeneración de los tejidos y muerte).

La muerte del OEMII por lo tanto coincide con la desintegración del OEMBUUAAW (los átomos de Kr vuelven a su comportamiento cuántico), UN EFECTO FRONTERIZO DESPUÉS DESAPARECE, y aparece un cuarto efecto leeiyo WAAM. Una red de I.U. se integra entre los dos WAAM adyacentes: WAAM-U y WAAM-UU.

El alma y B.B. se conectan entre sí. Esto significa, como revelamos en otro informe, que nuestra psique alcanza la etapa máxima de integración en la psique colectiva.

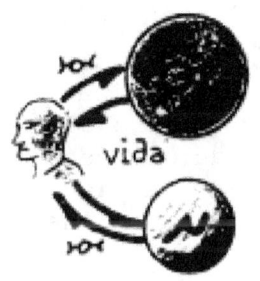 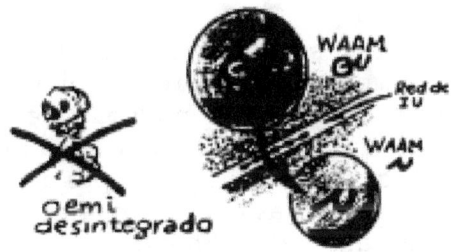

Este es el significado de la trascendencia en UMMO. Sabemos que a nuestra muerte vendrá una fusión, una integración, una conexión cercana de la psique, de nuestra mente (ni material ni inmaterial, sino matriz de toda la información de nuestra vida) con la psique colectiva universal.

Podremos conectarnos más intensamente con los seres queridos, comunicarnos con los espíritus de otros hermanos fallecidos, participar en el conocimiento global de toda la biosfera, no solo de los OEMII que acaban de morir, sino también con todos los humanos desde que nació la vida en OYAAUMMO (y, por supuesto, para vosotros, desde el Homo habilis hasta el último de sus hermanos).

También es posible conocer el mundo real, incluidos los seres vivos, ya que B.B. está informado de todo el proceso de vida de los seres que aún no han muerto.

Esto significa que el OEMMII fallecido, a través de su Psique, puede influir de alguna manera en sus seres más queridos a través del inconsciente y, hasta cierto punto, las cosas a su alrededor, a medida que cambia la biosfera. El entorno físico circundante a través de los seres vivos.

B.B. es el psiquismo colectivo. También podemos llamarlo subconsciente o inconsciente colectivo, en la medida en que su contenido sea operativo, pero no nos enteramos de eso, nosotros los SERES - VIVOS.

El psiquismo de un hermano fallecido puede, y de hecho a veces lo hace, ayudar, proteger y a veces interactuar MUY ACTIVO, pero la mayoría de las veces, modulando suavemente nuestro inconsciente a través de la información que recibimos de BB.

La psique o el alma, liberada de la entidad de enlaces => BUAWA y el OEMII (o cuerpo físico), ya descompuesto, comienza una etapa eterna de conocimiento gozoso de BB, no solo se asimilará como y cuando una cultura milenio acumulado por siglos de vida de todos los seres humanos, pero también penetrará en la ciencia, el arte, en definitiva, toda la cultura de una humanidad planetaria.

Probablemente también sentirá el dolor, pero compensado por el profundo conocimiento de la U.A. y la vida moral y eutímica de los seres.

Además: como participante en WAAM, podrá acceder a los secretos eternos de todos los WAAM-WAAM, ayudando en la evolución perpetua de sus galaxias, estrellas y diversas formaciones masivas.

D357: En el momento de la muerte, O., es decir, los átomos de criptón, dejan de ejercer su función. Pero por el contrario, B. (el alma) se conecta completamente a través de las válvulas que unen los dos WAAM (WAAM-UU y WAAM-U) para que esto equivalga a una verdadera integración total del alma en el alma colectiva, donde participa en todo el conocimiento acumulado de la humanidad.

Este es nuestro conocimiento científico de la trascendencia después de la muerte de un OEMII.

Una red de IBOZSOO UHUU actúa como una válvula entre B. (SOUL) ubicada en WAAM-U y B.B. insertada en WAAM-UU, lo que permite una integración casi absoluta entre las dos entidades. Es WOA (GENERADOR o DIOS) que establece las características de esta cadena I.U. (válvula de información) en un tiempo determinado.

Si el OEMMII, en las áreas donde es responsable y libre, durante toda su vida ha violado las leyes de la UUAA (ÉTICA), es necesario transformar la estructura de su información codificada en BUAWA. Recuerde que el alma no cree que sea una simple matriz de datos congelados. Ella solo puede manejar su propio montón de información con la ayuda de B.B.

Se puede condenar a la psique BUAWA a sufrir la lenta capacidad de usar su propio EGO (información codificada dentro de ella) y no participar en la densa complejidad de B.B.

Pero WOA puede, si el hombre ha respetado las normas morales durante su existencia o después de la corrección de su estructura una vez fallecida (reconformación), permitir que esta red de I.U. le ofrece un flujo de comunicación extremadamente más denso que el que experimentamos en el curso de nuestra existencia como seres vivos en nuestro WAAM.

En este caso, la integración de BUAWA (ALMA) en el B.B. es tan intensa que comparte el inmenso volumen de datos del ALMA COLECTIVA. Su visión intelectual de WOA (Dios) está creciendo. Penetra en el profundo conocimiento del Cosmos, la evolución de los seres, el vasto conocimiento (información intelectual y emocional) contenido en el B.B.

Observe que, de cierta manera, esta noción escatológica coincide, con cierta precisión, con la estimación teológica del cristianismo de OYAAGAA sobre la salvación.

Lo que llama Purgatorio es en este caso el proceso de RECONFORMACIÓN, que se reduce al hecho de que WOA limita en cierta medida esta participación de B. en BB, reduciendo en diferentes grados el valor del Canal o válvula que separa el dos WAAM: (WAAM-U y WAAM-UU).

Lo que llamas GLORIA o SALUDO es la integración completa del Alma, no exactamente en DIOS, sino en una creación tan grande de WOA como lo es el B.B. (ESPÍRITU COLECTIVO). Podemos imaginar el maravilloso éxtasis o disfrute que nuestra mente puede experimentar, no solo que es permisible que la información registrada en ella sea tratada de manera fluida (la mente sola no podría hacerlo), sino que al participar y beneficiarse de TODA la inmensa información contenida en WAAM-WAAM

A través del BB podrá comunicarse con los otros BUAWA de sus hermanos fallecidos, y a medida que cada BB participe en la matriz de información impresa en el WAAM-UU desde el momento de su creación o generación (no olvide que WAAM -UU tiene como objetivo conformar las singularidades de todo el WAAM-WAAM.), Su mente penetrará en los secretos más íntimos del Cosmos multiplanar (los Universos).

EXTRACTOS DE GR1-4, TRADUCCIÓN CORREGIDA, TEXTO REFORMULADO Y COMENTADO, DESDE EL ORIGINAL.

Nota del destinatario: "Las líneas y los colores del dibujo han sido modificados y pueden así permitir la identificación en el futuro, si no ha habido filtración del original, de quien pretenda ser el autor de este dibujo"

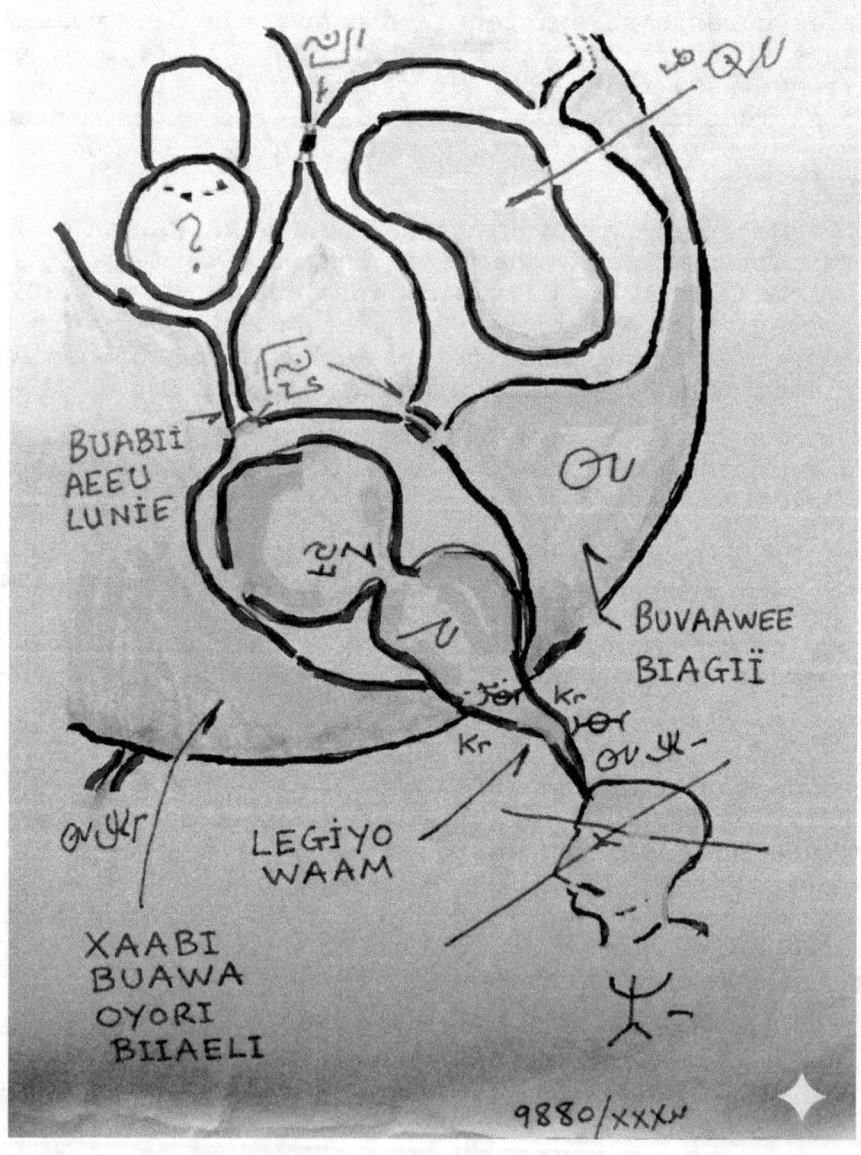

Cuando el OEMMII muere, BUAAWA (en realidad un pequeño número de átomos de Krypton ubicados en las columnas de lo que llamáis el Neocórtex) «lanza» una señal a BUUAAWAA BIIAEII, que, gracias a un efecto límite LEEIOO WAAM, procesa estos átomos transformando este conjunto de elementos de materia física con carga eléctrica y portador de información, en unidades puras de información (el efecto límite permite que la codificación electroquímica pase en «bits» de información a otro cosmos).

La energía transmitida se incorpora a los filamentos de BUAWAA BIAEII como una adición de energía.

...

El BUAWWAA del OEMMII permanece en el estado de lo que llamarías «latencia permanente» y esto será hasta la muerte del OEMMII que lo lleva, en el universo BUUAWAA (GR1-4-1), cargado de información PRIMITIVA (esto es muy importante) - primitivo significa una transconexión específica inicial, de IBOZOOUU que tiene lugar solo una vez – en el momento de la concepción – en la vida del OEMMII. Esta configuración inicial de IBOZOOUU inicializa el contenido de la BUAWA.

A esta naturaleza especial de la información la llamamos: BUAWAA AMIEAYOO WADOXII: Hay un «estado de información», en forma de un «paquete» de todo lo que el OEMMII hará o sentirá en su vida con sus sensaciones, pero también con sus pensamientos, ideas, intenciones, deseos, etc., Aunque el OEMMII ha sido diseñado recientemente,y esta información se transmite todo a la vez al WAAM BUAAWAA (GR1-4-2).

Lo que es para ti es un gran misterio, pero muy real, y se expresó matemáticamente en UMMO hace mucho tiempo. Debemos confesar, sin embargo, que esto ha sido experimentado estadísticamente con matemáticas probabilísticas y con enormes pruebas de éxito, pero no del todo irrefutables. Sin embargo, en UMMO lo tomamos como un paradigma científico provisional.

...

Cuando el OEMMII muere, el paquete de información que constituía el OEMMII (a priori aumentado por la información transmitida a lo largo de su vida), se «proyecta» en BUUAAWAA BIIAEII a través del efecto límite LEEIOO WAAM.

BUAAWA BIAEII luego recupera la información contenida en el BUAWAA de lo que era OEMMII, Y LA COMPARA CON EL ARQUETIPO (WOAIYIIBUAA) QUE BB HABÍA *PREPARADO* PREVIAMENTE PARA ESTA ALMA EN PARTICULAR

estableciéndose a partir de este momento un vínculo permanente entre dicho BUAWAA y una célula o «celdilla» (XAABII BUAWAA OYORII BIAEII) que se encuentra en BUUAAWAA BIIAEII y que contiene una especie de « BUAWAA espejo « como llamamos anteriormente (que es solo un BUAWAA ideal específico creado directamente por WOA de acuerdo con AIIODII)

a los que los grupos homogéneos de información contenidos en BUAWAA pasarán en cantidades discretas (por ejemplo, un discurso pronunciado en su vida por el OEMMII, o una lucha cuerpo a cuerpo con un hermano, o una cópula entre GEE y YIEE).

La dicha «celdilla» tiene un «dispositivo» o BUABIIAEE ULUNIE que sirve para transmitir la información contenida en otras celdillas comparables a la célula en cuestión – es BUAAWEE BIAEEII quien decide el flujo y el momento de esta información.

Cuando la información contenida en el arquetipo destinado a esa alma se vuelve igual a la información en esa célula, decimos que el alma se reconforma.

De forma simplificada, podríamos decir que en la fusión cromosómica de un espermatozoide y un óvulo humano, el BB inicializa un Alma BUAWA con un paquete de información. Podríamos llamar a este paquete de información el DESTINO, o la HOJA de RUTA, de toda nuestra vida planificada.

Sin embargo, el DESTINO o la HOJA de RUTA, puede ser modificado con eventos debido a la posibilidad de materia física que escapa al control de la BB y en parte por libre albedrío. El individuo incrementa y completa la información del Alma BUAWA a lo largo de su vida.

Además, BB creó para él un duplicado del BUAWA inicial, el BUAWA espejo.

Y en sus estructuras, BB tiene modelos, arquetipos WOAIYIIBUAA, BUAWA que necesitará para evolucionar la humanidad que maneja.

Tras la muerte del individuo, BB conecta el BUAWA a una «celdilla» que contiene el BUAWA espejo. BB gestiona múltiples dispositivos de transferencia y controla la información de este tipo de objetos. BB filtra la información entrante en el «celdilla» y de facto en el BUAWA espejo, alineándose con los arquetipos BUAWA WOAIYIIBUAA previstos .

Cuando la «celdilla» de facto en el BUAWA Espejo Aumentado es igual al arquetipo WOAIYIIBUAA de BUAWA previsto, el BUAWA Espejo Aumentado está operativo, la gente de UMMO dice que el BUAWA del individuo ha sido reconformado (en el BUAWA Espejo Aumentado).

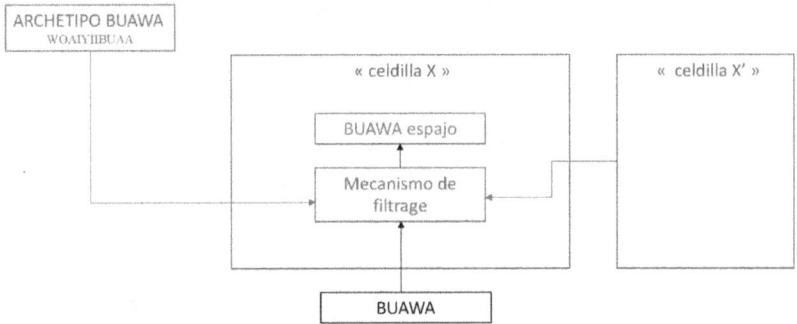

Tras la muerte del individuo, BB conecta el BUAWA a una "celdilla" que contiene el BUAWA espejo. BB gestiona múltiples dispositivos de transferencia y controla la información de este tipo de objetos. BB filtra la información entrante en el "celdilla" y de facto en el BUAWA espejo, alineándose con los arquetipos BUAWA WOAIYIIBUAA previstos .
Cuando la "celdilla" de facto en el BUAWA Espejo Aumentado es igual al arquetipo WOAIYIIBUAA de BUAWA previsto, el BUAWA Espejo Aumentado está operativo, la gente de UMMO dice que el BUAWA del individuo ha sido reconformado (en el BUAWA Espejo Aumentado).

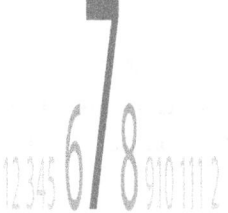

LA INFLUENCIA DE LOS ASTROS EN LA PSIQUE

Hemos visto en las hipótesis anteriores cómo se inicializaron el BB-planetario y BUAWA, y cuáles fueron los flujos que podrían ponerse en juego. Por lo tanto, BUAWA genera una idea guía que está en conformidad con el perfil psíquico constituido por la red de IBOZOO de BUAWA y puede estar sujeto a diversas influencias externas.

Paradójicamente, sobre este tema tenemos varios elementos verificables y, sin embargo, puede parecer más especulativo y más perturbador que los temas anteriores. Esto se debe al hecho de que, además de las dificultades de experimentación, la investigación políticamente correcta cataloga tabúes de este tema conocido pero maltratado en ambos sentidos del término. Los investigadores que hasta ahora se han atrevido a abordarlo pueden contarse con los dedos de una mano. Haré pocos amigos al abordar este tema que hace fluir mucha tinta ... Permítanos especificar, si es necesario, que los horóscopos de los periódicos no corresponden a ninguna configuración planetaria real, y contribuyen a mantener el tabú. El origen del tabú proviene del hecho de que los sistemas empíricos antiguos describían las relaciones entre la psique y una visión geocéntrica ptolemaica de los planetas. Al descubrir la naturaleza heliocéntrica del sistema planetario, concluimos un poco rápido, que los antiguos sistemas empíricos como el Zodiaco, también eran erróneos. De hecho, es obvio que uno puede calcular muy bien la vista geocéntrica de los planetas a partir de la configuración heliocéntrica real de los planetas, pero el bebé fue arrojado con el agua del baño.

En lo que respecta a la gravitación, todos lo sabemos, pero creo que es bueno recordarlo: hasta la fecha no se ha encontrado ningún gravitón. Lo único que sabemos controlar es la manifestación de una fuerza vinculada a las masas.

Frente a este océano de lo desconocido, la naturaleza de la gravitación en sí misma sigue siendo muy misteriosa, y todo lo que se puede decir sobre las frecuencias gravitacionales es, por lo tanto, muy especulativo. Consideraré que estas ondas tienen al menos las propiedades comunes a las ondas conocidas.

Entre los pocos trabajos serios sobre el tema, uno puede notar dos hipótesis distintas. La primera hipótesis desarrollada en 1974 por D. Verney supone que son los efectos gravitacionales de las configuraciones planetarias los que resuenan con la psique, y la segunda presentada en 1988 por P. Seymour, supone que son los fenómenos electromagnéticos producidos por las configuraciones. influencias planetarias en la psique.

En 1990, siguiendo el trabajo de D. Verney y R. Penrose, amplié estos enfoques imaginando que debe haber un efecto de resonancia gravitacional de los astros en un efector cerebral cuántico. Esta reflexión especulativa se expresó en el contexto de una novela *Acid Jones y el templo de la ciencia* publicada en 1995 sin conocer los documentos Ummitas y, por lo tanto, sin poder desarrollar esta idea ...

En este capítulo desarrollaremos esta idea con la luz de los documentos Ummitas.

Independientemente de los caracteres puramente fenotípicos de la estructura cerebral conductual, examinaremos la hipótesis de factores complementarios que podrían influir en el comportamiento y las decisiones tomadas por un humano.

```
D57-3 | T1B - 13/19: No conocíamos el valor del
   coeficiente BAAYIODIXAA UUDIII (no traducible: la
   ciencia biológica terrestre aún no ha desarro-
   llado este concepto tan importante). Es una fór-
   mula que expresa las condiciones de equilibrio
   biológico que se miden en un entorno dado. Cada
```

168

OOYAA (Planeta) tiene condiciones particulares
que permitirán o no la existencia de un ciclo de
carbono en su troposfera. El desarrollo bioge-
nético de la morfología de animales y plantas
dependerá de una serie de constantes físicas.

La fórmula expresada por el BAAYIODIXAA UUDIII es
una función compleja en la que se integran una
multitud de parámetros tales como: Aceleración
por gravedad, Ozonización de la atmósfera,
Intensidad de radiación gamma, presión y composición atmosférica, espectro y radiación solar,
ciclo gravitacional posibles satélites y planetas
vecinos, gradientes electrostáticos atmosféri-
cos, corrientes eléctricas telúricas, etc., etc.
que, junto con la composición (en porcentaje) de
los elementos químicos de la corteza del planeta, permiten predecir que será La orientación
evolutiva de los seres vivos independientemente
de otros factores que pueden alterarlo, por ejemplo, la radiación que causa mutaciones y autose-
lección por la influencia impredecible del medio
ambiente.

LA HIPÓTESIS ELECTROMAGNÉTICA

Las influencias electromagnéticas en el cuerpo humano son las
menos conocidas ... Recordemos simplemente que sus impactos se
refieren a procesos biológicos, bioquímicos, neurológicos, a nivel
molecular y no a escala cuántica a nivel de los electrones.

Por lo tanto, la influencia de los fenómenos electromagnéticos en la
psique es posible en las estructuras neuronales, por lo tanto, a posteriori, independientemente de los procesos psíquicos reales.

Además, los impactos electromagnéticos que modifican los procesos bioquímicos del cuerpo pueden ser patológicos, a priori, que no es
el caso del impacto de los fenómenos microgravitacionales.

En cuanto a los impactos electromagnéticos en los sensores de
campo magnético de campo, como los cristales de magnetita en el
cerebelo, por ejemplo, inducen cambios de comportamiento puntuales,
como cualquier otro tipo de percepción.

Los fenómenos electromagnéticos tienen un impacto en los procesos biológicos, pero no hemos identificado ningún impacto estructural en la psique para las energías consideradas.

LA HIPÓTESIS GRAVITACIONAL

Sabemos por los documentos Ummitas que OEMBUAWA es un efector gravitacional. Emite y captura varios flujos gravitacionales, que presenté esquemas en los documentos anteriores. También hemos visto anteriormente, que es en el momento de la fusión cromosómica que el BAAYIODUU se conecta al BB, y que los seres vivos se comunican con el BB mediante armónicos gravitacionales específicos. También en este punto es cuando se genera el contenido de BUAWA y el Alma contiene un sector de la red pura de IBOZOO UU que codifica un programa completo de instrucciones que conforman cada OEMII. Esta zona de conformación se crea así por un flujo gravitacional en el momento de la fusión genómica, de una manera única, específica para cada individuo. Conforma la conducta del OEMII, es decir, contiene el modelo psicológico del OEMII, es decir, su perfil psicológico.

Además, sabemos que el coeficiente de evolución viviente, el BAAYIODIXAA UUDIE, puede calcularse utilizando una fórmula con múltiples parámetros específicos del astro. El ciclo gravitacional de posibles satélites y planetas vecinos es un parámetro involucrado en la evolución de la vida.

La hipótesis es que la estructuración del perfil psicológico, es decir, la inicialización de la zona de conformación psíquica en el BUAWA, que se lleva a cabo de una vez por todas y en su integridad, resulta de tres factores:

- la información de identificación del astro

- La constitución del sistema genómico durante la fusión cromosómica.

- Los parámetros que pueden modificar el flujo gravitacional, generador del perfil psicológico, en el momento de la fusión cromosómica.

EL PRIMER FACTOR ESTRUCTURANTE

El sistema genómico clásico es el factor principal en la estructuración del perfil psicológico. Está relacionado con los perfiles arquetípicos en el Meta-Brain BB y modela el perfil psicológico en Alma-BUAWA por una frecuencia gravitacional específica en el momento de la fusión genómica. Incluye información de facto que identifica al astro.

Está relacionado con los perfiles arquetípicos, es el Meta-Brain BB y modela el perfil psicológico en Alma-BUAWA por una frecuencia gravitacional específica a la fusión genómica.

EL SEGUNDO FACTOR ESTRUCTURANTE

La fase de estructuración

Entre los parámetros de estructuración relacionados con BAAYIODIXAA UUDIE, hay uno que es de naturaleza gravitacional. Es el ciclo gravitacional de posibles satélites y planetas vecinos. Según mi hipótesis, es este parámetro el que contribuye, en parte, a modelar la zona de conformación psíquica en el momento de la fusión genómica.

Las fuentes gravitacionales exógenas del planeta actual, y por lo tanto las estrellas vecinas en particular, yuxtaponen sus ondas gravitacionales con los pulsos gravitacionales que se producen en el momento de la fusión genómica. El conjunto de ondas gravitacionales correspondientes a los pulsos iniciales, constituirá armónicos gravitacionales, por lo tanto, en fase con la frecuencia base, pero con una información distinta. La totalidad de la información se transmite y genera el perfil psicológico en la zona de conformación psíquica de BUAWA, de una vez por todas y en su integridad.

De hecho, son las configuraciones planetarias las que contribuyen a conformar la zona de conformación psíquica de cada OEMMII. El valor informativo de las configuraciones astronómicas resulta de los valores de sus fuerzas gravitacionales. Más precisamente, son los diferenciales de estos valores con respecto al campo gravitacional del astro del OEMMII los que tendrán un valor informativo.

La fase dinámica

Una vez que el perfil psicológico se modela en el BUAWA, en parte por la influencia gravitacional de las estrellas, la embriogénesis continúa. Cuando el enlace con BUAWA se activa en la configuración de OEMBUAWA, la zona de conformación psíquica regresa a OEMBUAWA sus mensajes modelados de acuerdo con los armónicos gravitacionales que lo inicializaron.

OEMBUAWA es un efector gravitacional, captura todo, como la antena de una radio. De este modo, también captura los diferenciales gravitacionales de las configuraciones planetarias con respecto al campo gravitacional del astro del OEMMII.

Los mensajes que llegan al OEMBUAWA estarán en fase con el diferencial gravitacional creado por la configuración astronómica del momento, o bien en oposición de fase. De hecho, habrá una infinidad de posibles valores intermedios, probablemente con umbrales de resonancia.

Los mensajes en fase tendrán un mayor peso en el centro de la decisión del cerebro, que arbitrará más a su favor. Esto dará como resultado comportamientos muy consistentes con el perfil psicológico del OEMMII.

Por otro lado, los mensajes en oposición de fase tendrán un peso menor en el centro de decisión del cerebro, lo que arbitrará más en su desventaja. Esto dará lugar a una tendencia a inhibir el comportamiento que no se ajusta al perfil psicológico del OEMMII. Estos procesos serán transmitidos a nivel molecular por el sistema endocrino.

CONCLUSIÓN

La suposición de que BUAWA contiene un perfil de conformación psíquica humana, como las configuraciones planetarias, puede interferir gravitacionalmente en el canal de transmisión de información humano-BUAWA ahora puede encontrar indicadores para su verificación.

Si tomamos la hipótesis de que los gemelos idénticos tienen el mismo BUAWA, es por el estudio del comportamiento de los gemelos que podremos encontrar indicaciones adicionales ...

Así que aquí está la hipótesis de la influencia de las configuraciones planetarias en la psique cuyo esquema de síntesis se presenta aquí.

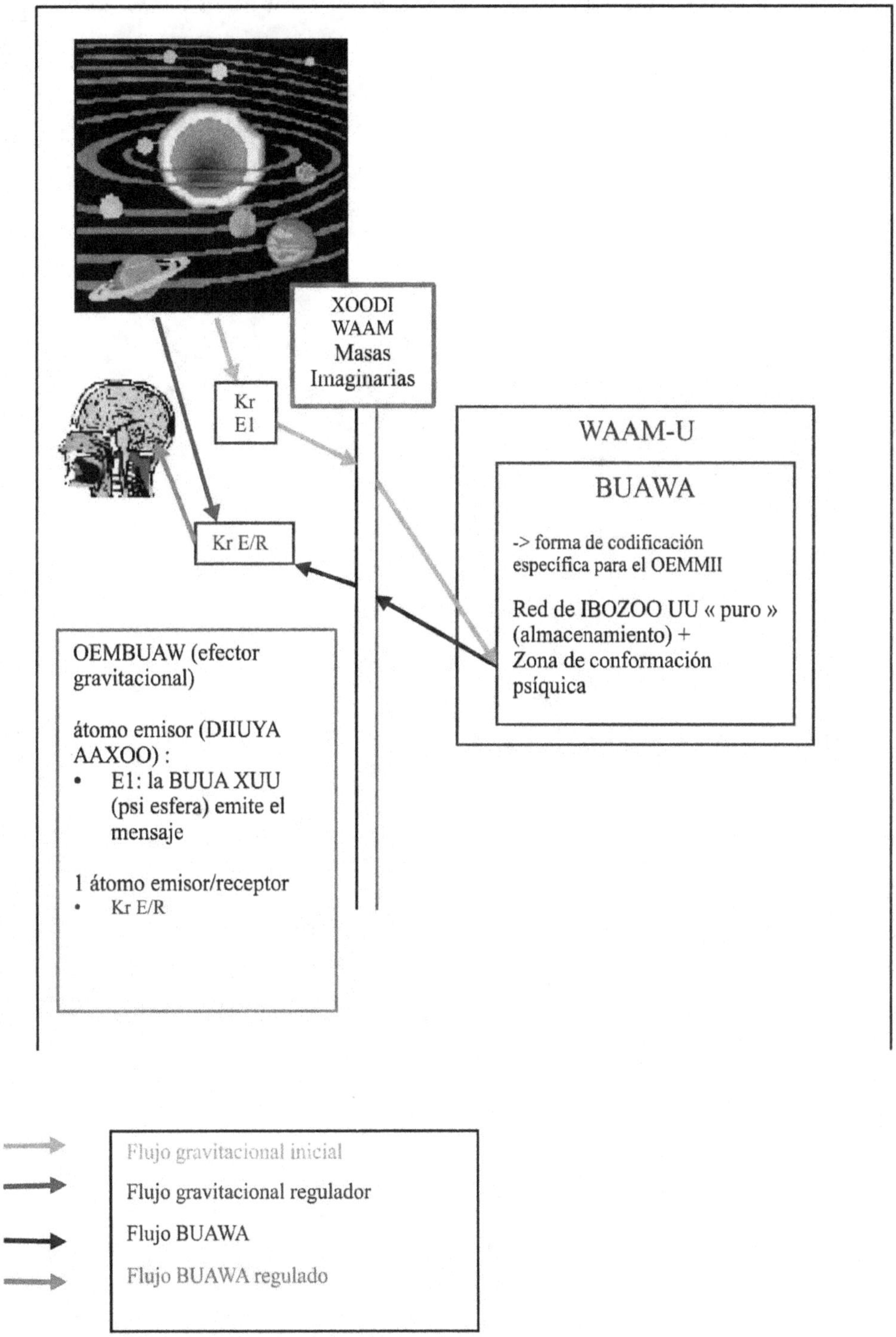

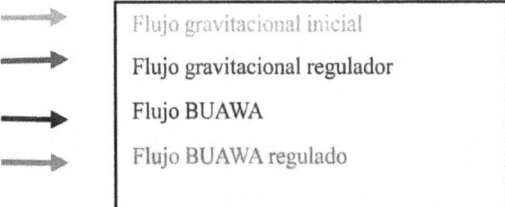

XOODI
WAAM
Masas
Imaginarias

Kr
E1

Kr E/R

WAAM-U

BUAWA

-> forma de codificación
específica para el OEMMII

Red de IBOZOO UU « puro »
(almacenamiento) +
Zona de conformación
psíquica

OEMBUAW (efector
gravitacional)

átomo emisor (DIIUYA
AAXOO) :
• E1: la BUUA XUU
  (psi esfera) emite el
  mensaje

1 átomo emisor/receptor
• Kr E/R

Flujo gravitacional inicial

Flujo gravitacional regulador

Flujo BUAWA

Flujo BUAWA regulado

COMUNICACIÓN TELEPÁTICA

La evolución de los seres vivos necesariamente los lleva a conectarse a su BB planetario, a un BUAWA y a desarrollar diversas formas de comunicación.

La comunicación oral de los seres humanos parece ser seguida generalmente por el desarrollo de varias formas de comunicación telepática. El principio de la comunicación telepática parece ser ampliamente el mismo para todos los OEMMII, pero las diferencias fisiológicas no siempre permiten la comunicación entre especies.

Los documentos Ummitas responden globalmente sobre el funcionamiento de las comunicaciones telepáticas. ¿Pero la comunicación telepática está específicamente relacionada con cada BB? ¿Cómo se puede codificar? ¿Hay límites de distancia para este tipo de comunicación? ¿Cuáles son los factores que impactan la comunicación telepática?

La telepatía es conocida y parcialmente reconocida por la comunidad científica de las ciencias de la psique. Los enfoques psíquicos basados en el modelo holográfico de Karl Pribram han tenido la tentación de explicar la telepatía basada en el principio de no localidad. Pero, sin éxito, y David Bohm, consciente de la complejidad del fenómeno, consideró de manera muy inteligente que la no localidad cuántica era insuficiente para explicarlo ...

Tomemos nota de la información que nuestros amigos de UMMO nos han transmitido ...

Carta : 337 DESCUBRIENDO de BUUAWE BIAEI

Por primera vez, se verificó que los movimientos codificados de los electrones en tales átomos correspondían exactamente a la transmisión telepática.

Descubrimos, contrariamente a lo que pensábamos, que la transmisión telepática es recibida simultáneamente por todos los seres humanos; incluso si un mecanismo subconsciente se encarga del bloqueo, es decir, para evitar el paso de un mensaje hacia las personas a las que no está destinado.

Si la transmisión telepática requiere una vía de conexión en el hombre (vía nerviosa) para pasar de un alma a otra, es porque el alma colectiva y el alma individual son dos entidades independientes que solo están unidas por el enlace del CUERPO HUMANO mientras esté vivo.

Puede observar entonces que [si] la transmisión telepática se realizó exclusivamente dentro del BUAWEE BIAEI (ESPÍRITU COLECTIVO), el tiempo total de la transmisión sería CERO porque el encéfalo del hombre no intervendría absolutamente.

El proceso para comunicarse con personas cuya identidad conozco ...

Hay dos tipos de impulsos en esta zona cerebral: un poco como dos transmisores. Si alguno de ustedes es un técnico de televisión, lo entenderá mejor si los compara con las señales que llama IMAGEN y SINCRONISMO. Los primeros llevan, debidamente codificados, los impulsos nerviosos que llamamos BUUAWE BIEE, cada uno de ellos durante 0.000 138 5 segundos. Son una especie de mensaje telegráfico que se envía a través de uno de los átomos de Krypton que llamamos BUUA XUU (psisphere).

El segundo grupo de señales, que también están codificadas, se caracteriza por el hecho de que el tiempo de pulso es más largo: 0.006 385 segundos.

¿Cuál es la función de la primera señal transmitida? Lleve fácilmente el contenido verbal de nuestro mensaje, las palabras que expresan las ideas que queremos hacer llegar a nuestro interlocutor ubicado a una gran distancia de nosotros. Pero este mensaje es capturado por todos los hombres de UMMO (repetimos que los casos de telepatía registrados por usted confirman que el fenómeno es idéntico para los humanos de la Tierra).

¿Cómo es posible que una persona pueda interpretar tal mensaje y ser consciente de que está dirigido solo a él? El segundo grupo de impulsos nos da la respuesta.

El código utilizado para identificar a una persona no difiere mucho entre nosotros y usted en la vida real. Por lo tanto, dado que el nombre UGAA 4, hijo de YODEE 347, está mentalmente asociado con un individuo en particular, se utilizará una secuencia de números binarios, enviados en forma de pulsos, para distinguir a la persona receptora del mensaje.

Imagine un millón de cajas fuertes repartidas por todo su país. Cada uno de ellos solo puede abrir con una combinación de seis números y bajo la supervisión de la mayor cantidad de guardias.

Dentro de estos cofres, está la clave para la interpretación de cualquier mensaje codificado.

Ahora está enviando una carta cifrada que solo se puede leer con la ayuda de claves criptográficas bloqueadas en las bóvedas. Envíe un millón de copias a todos los guardias con una sola indicación en el sobre, por ejemplo 763 559. Solo el destinatario cuyo número del mecanismo de apertura de la caja fuerte coincide con este número puede abrirlo y conocer el contenido del mensaje.

El ejemplo está bien elegido porque precisamente la selección de una persona se obtiene mediante un mecanismo fisiológico similar al de las cajas fuertes terrestres (en UMMO no existen). Y una red neuronal establece conexiones o desconexiones sinápticas basadas en una secuencia cifrada de pulsos binarios que representan 1700 dígitos.

D45 BUUAWE BIEE TIME (S45-13) = 0.000 138 segundos; (tiempo que el hombre necesita para enviar un impulso de unidad a través del BUUA XUU (ESFERA PSY) a otro hombre de UMMO telepáticamente).

NR18: La distancia no importa para establecer el enlace telepático, pero la interferencia debida a la presencia de materia imaginaria en OUWAAM podría afectar ligeramente el sincronismo durante las comunicaciones de larga distancia.

Esto es esencialmente una hipótesis de lectura que incluye interpretaciones y algunas extrapolaciones de las indicaciones dadas por los Ummitas.

Así, la telepatía funciona aproximadamente en la modulación de frecuencia con una onda portadora del mensaje asociado con una onda que identifica al receptor.

Los Ummitas nos dicen que los impulsos telepáticos pasan a través de BB, sin especificar si es BB-global o BB-planetario. La idea es que la estructura de la codificación de mensajes telepáticos solo está relacionada con la especie OEMMII. Por lo tanto, sería totalmente independiente del planetario BB del OEMMII. Los mensajes telepáticos cruzarían el BB-global, el WAAM-UU.

El alcance de la comunicación telepática es independiente de la distancia, ya que solo pasaría a través del XOODII WAAM para alcanzar globalmente el WAAM-UU con todos sus BB-planetarios.

De hecho, todos los OEMMII de WAAM-WAAM reciben transmisiones telepáticas de todos los OEMMII.

Como regla general, la estructura precisa de OEMBUAWA para cada especie de OEMMII captura selectivamente la frecuencia o frecuencias específicas de su especie.

La telepatía opera así en modulación de frecuencia con una frecuencia portadora del mensaje y una frecuencia de identificación.

El remitente envía el mensaje y todos los receptores lo reciben. De manera asociada, el transmisor envía en paralelo el código identificador del destinatario del mensaje. El código identificador del destinatario corresponde a una imagen mental estructuralmente específica.

Todos los OEMMII reciben el mensaje y un identificador que no les corresponde: en este caso, el mensaje no es procesado por el OEMMII receptor.

El destinatario recibe el identificador correspondiente que autoriza el paso del mensaje asociado a su cerebro que lo decodifica, luego lo transfiere siguiendo el proceso normal a BUAWA. OEMBUAW convierte las señales telepáticas en el cerebro en señales bioquímicas que generan imágenes mentales inteligibles para el cerebro, que también se transmiten a BUAWA.

Los impulsos que codifican al receptor codifican la imagen mental asociada con ese receptor. Evocar mentalmente el nombre de uno puede ser suficiente para generar la imagen mental del destinatario. Esta imagen mental está codificada y emitida en el WAAM-UU.

El aprendizaje de los niños debe hacerse antes de la pubertad con los padres, el uso de vapor de oxitocina promueve este desarrollo neurológico. Es favorable en el haplogrupo C-M130 en humanos terrestres.

LA CODIFICACIÓN DEL MENSAJE

Las imágenes mentales transmitidas por telepatía están codificadas en una forma universal. Codifican el lenguaje o las percepciones. Esto no significa que haya un lenguaje universal, sino simplemente que para cualquier OEMMII que emita una imagen mental codificada A, cualquier OEMBUAW de OEMMII capturará una imagen mental codificada A. Entonces todo dependerá de qué hará el cerebro del receptor con esta imagen mental, ya sea que la imagen mental tenga sentido o no. Esto explicaría que algunos OEMMII pueden leer nuestros pensamientos y aprender nuestros idiomas decodificando directamente los impulsos emitidos por el OEMBUAW del encéfalo, ya sea por:

- a priori, el átomo de criptón que transmite mensajes telepáticos *(E1 en el diagrama de resumen al final del capítulo)*

- o posiblemente, el átomo de criptón enviando mensajes a BB y a BUAWA *(E / R en el diagrama de resumen al final del capítulo)*

Algunos OEMMII pueden enviar mensajes como impulsos telepáticos directamente al átomo receptor UAXOO de OEMBUAW. Esto también explicaría por qué estos OEMMII pueden enviar técnicamente mensajes telepáticos directamente a humanos terrestres. Es habitual que las exocivilizaciones que nos visitan aprendan y usen los idiomas del planeta visitado. Como resultado, no es sorprendente que un humano terrestre reciba un flujo telepático en su propio idioma.

Para nuestro cerebro, no hay diferencia entre la representación mental de una palabra vocalizada o una palabra escuchada en un sueño, por ejemplo. Activa las mismas áreas del cerebro de la misma manera. Las palabras telepáticas transferidas a la persona serán decodificadas por el encéfalo de la misma manera que una palabra vocalizada.

LOS EFECTORES DE GeSi2C3H3

Discutimos en el capítulo los flujos de información de una especie viva, la hipótesis de un compuesto de retransmisión GeSi2C3H3 que interactuaría entre los pares Kr2 y el ADN. Podría sincronizar todos los elementos celulares necesarios para controlar las mutaciones dirigidas por el planetario BB. Es él quien protege el ADN contra mutaciones indeseables y desencadena mutaciones controladas. Además, este compuesto (germanio, silicio, carbono, hidrógeno) sería la interfaz entre las biofrecuencias resultantes de procesos neurológicos y diferentes cristales y gases raros, incluido el criptón, ubicado en el cerebro. Los átomos de carbono e hidrógeno son las interfaces entre los impulsos nerviosos cerebrales y OEMBUAW para las comunicaciones telepáticas.

D41: La ubicación de estos átomos de criptón en el cuerpo humano es muy difícil por las siguientes razones:

- NO SE COMBINAN CON EL RESTO DE COMPUESTOS ORGÁNICOS DEL OEMII (cuerpo humano).

- SU NÚMERO ESTÁ MUY REDUCIDO (contamos 16 lugares)

Algunos se encuentran en el LÓBULO TEMPORAL DEL TÁLAMO, en el HIPOTÁLAMO y en otras áreas de la CORTEZA CEREBRAL.

Diagrama de flujos neuropáticos

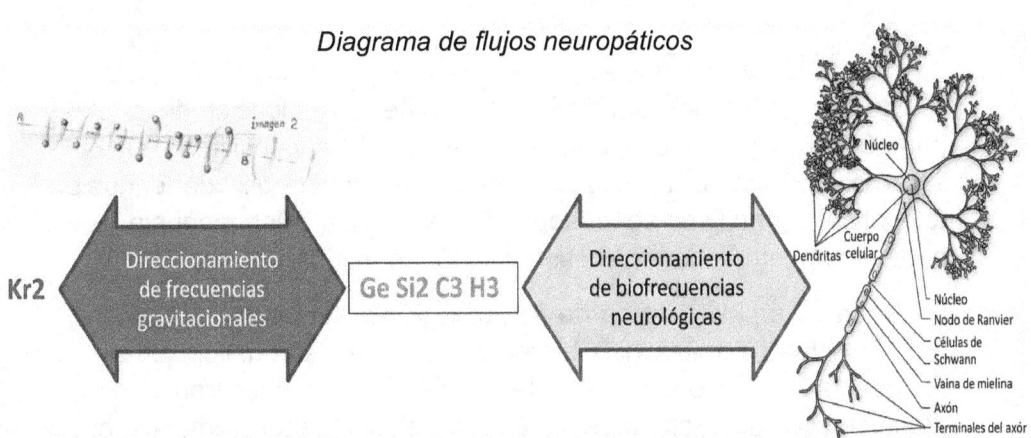

D45: Son los impulsos nerviosos que, gracias a los diferentes átomos de carbono y helio cuyos estados CUÁNTICOS han sido excitados, modifican por resonancia los estados ordinarios de frecuencia cero (onda plana) de cada átomo KRYPTON por el efecto OWEEU OMWAA. Así, los mensajes de la memoria, por ejemplo, se codificarán en estos átomos en forma de ONDES.

Los impulsos nerviosos que llamamos BUUAWE BIEE, cada uno dura 0.000 138 segundos. Son una especie de mensaje telegráfico que se envía a través de uno de los átomos de Krypton.

La biofrecuencia de codificación de flujos neuro-telepáticos es, por lo tanto, 1 / 0.000 138 51 o un poco menos de 7 220 Khz.

Una función periódica en forma de onda cuadrada: esto es lo que captura nuestro BUUAWAA (alma).

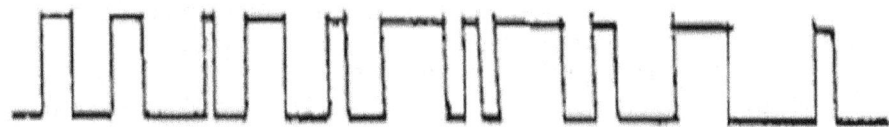

LA TELEPATÍA DE LOS UMMITAS

Con respecto a los Ummitas, la forma de comunicación de la telepatía OANNEAOIYOYOO, transmite mensajes que consisten en ideas simples y de actualidad. No hay indicios de ningún tipo de lenguaje telepático específico, se puede comunicar cualquier lenguaje que necesariamente genere representaciones mentales.

Dada su rápida pérdida de fonación y sus demandas dialécticas, creo que los Ummitas han recreado su lenguaje fonético teniendo en cuenta el funcionamiento telepático. También buscaron hacerlo confiable, con una comunicación basada en conceptos primarios, que corresponden a los componentes básicos de las imágenes mentales de su lenguaje de primer nivel DU-OI-OIYOO. Estos ladrillos básicos fonéticos se transmiten fácilmente de forma secuencial inequívoca.

El origen y el aprendizaje de la telepatía para nuestros amigos de UMMO :

La telepatía es un paso natural en el proceso evolutivo que resulta del aumento continuo de la masa cortical y la complejación de las conexiones sinápticas y neuronales. La arquitectura cortical específica de la telepatía, en OYAGAAOEMMII, existe en un nivel primario, en el nivel de los grupos neuronales-gliales específicos del lenguaje que conectan el giro angular y el área de Broca. Sin embargo, la complejidad requerida para la funcionalidad completa solo se logra para la porción restringida de la población OYAGAA que ha sufrido la mutación M130 (haplogrupo C del ADN del cromosoma Y). El desarrollo de estos grupos neurogliales sigue siendo insuficiente en la mayoría de los otros grupos raciales, especialmente en individuos con haplogrupo predominante de tipo R (caucásico), excepto en casos de mutación individual favorable. OEMMII OYAGAA también tiene la desventaja de la unilateralidad de las áreas del cerebro dedicadas al lenguaje. Sin embargo, sigue siendo posible una capacidad limitada para la telepatía, mediante un ejercicio riguroso, gracias a la plasticidad de estas áreas del cerebro y la naturaleza multimodal de las neuronas involucradas en el proceso.

La capacidad telepática se desarrolla desde el comienzo de la adolescencia, practicando un ejercicio constante que requiere mucha calma, concentración e intimidad con un padre afectivo cercano. Es un proceso de aprendizaje psicodinámico que, en UMMO, requiere varios meses terrestres para obtener una conexión reproducible sistemáticamente mediante el fortalecimiento progresivo de los circuitos sinápticos efectores. Esto es para el único padre con el que el niño hace ejercicio durante esta primera fase. El proceso continúa, cada vez más rápido, con todos los miembros de la familia inmediata.

La capacidad telepática de los niños se prueba durante los 40 XII (UMMO) días de orientación antes de la integración con OUNAWO OUI (universidad) a la edad de 64.67 XEE (13.7 años). Esta capacidad continuará desarrollándose, a través de la emulación y la afinidad, entre los jóvenes que viven lado a lado.

También se puede observar que la oxitocina, una hormona peptídica sintetizada por los núcleos paraventricular y supraóptico del hipotálamo y secretada por la glándula pituitaria posterior (neurohipófisis), promueve el aprendizaje de la telepatía.

El REMOTE VIEWING

La visualización remota es probablemente antediluviana y se experimentó en la década de 1930 con experimentos de J. B. Rhine, Upton Sinclair o Rene Warcollier. Este trabajo continuó en la década de 1970 en la American Society for Psychical Research y SRI-International, con el trabajo del físico Hal Puthoff. Las agencias de inteligencia de las principales potencias han desarrollado esta investigación, a veces oficialmente como la CIA y la Agencia de Inteligencia de Defensa (DIA) con el programa Star Gate.

Estas son comunicaciones telepáticas que se explican por este marco cosmológico. El visor remoto se conecta a la persona objetivo o recupera una conexión sin siquiera conocer a la persona. Esto sirve como cámara y transmite información que el televidente siente con mas o menos claridad.

CUIDADO REMOTO

La práctica del cuidado remoto está cerca de la visualización remota. Hemos visto que el aura y el cuerpo están en interacción fuerte. Creemos que la práctica del cuidado a distancia utiliza el canal telepático.

Esto de muchas maneras posibles. Ya sea influyendo secundariamente en el aura del paciente, o en el subconsciente del paciente, de modo que causa un efecto psicosomático.

CONCLUSIÓN

La evolución neurológica del hombre hacia las posibilidades de acceso a la comunicación telepática puede no ser tan remota como podría pensarse a primera vista.

De hecho, es un hecho comprobado hoy que las estructuras neuronales se pueden reconfigurar de forma dinámica y duradera mediante prácticas de gimnasia mental comúnmente llamadas meditación. Esto ha sido demostrado por varios tipos de experimentos, en particular por Matthieu Ricard y Richard J. Davidson. Esto nos da perspectivas de uso de todas estas aptitudes ...

Aquí está el diagrama de síntesis del flujo telepático:

Emisor de alma -> criptón -> Cerebro -> criptón -> WAAM-UU -> criptón -> receptores encefálicos ...

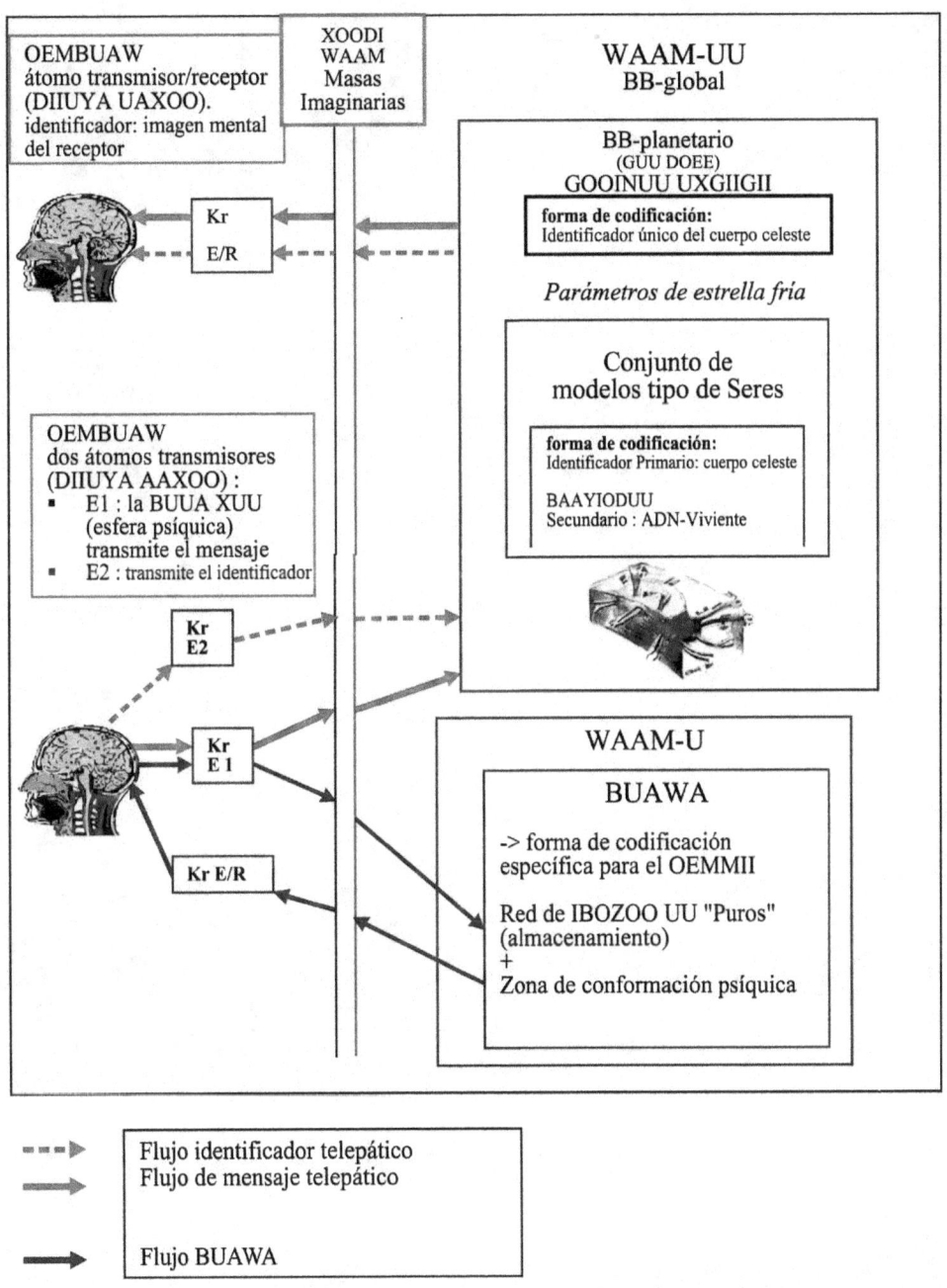

OEMBUAW
átomo transmisor/receptor
(DIIUYA UAXOO).
identificador: imagen mental
del receptor

XOODI
WAAM
Masas
Imaginarias

WAAM-UU
BB-global

BB-planetario
(GUU DOEE)
GOOINUU UXGIIGII

forma de codificación:
Identificador único del cuerpo celeste

Parámetros de estrella fría

Conjunto de
modelos tipo de Seres

forma de codificación:
Identificador Primario: cuerpo celeste

BAAYIODUU
Secundario : ADN-Viviente

Kr

E/R

OEMBUAW
dos átomos transmisores
(DIIUYA AAXOO) :
• E1 : la BUUA XUU
  (esfera psíquica)
  transmite el mensaje
• E2 : transmite el identificador

Kr
E2

Kr
E 1

Kr E/R

WAAM-U

BUAWA

-> forma de codificación
específica para el OEMMII

Red de IBOZOO UU "Puros"
(almacenamiento)
+
Zona de conformación psíquica

- - - ▶   Flujo identificador telepático
       Flujo de mensaje telepático

━━━▶   Flujo BUAWA

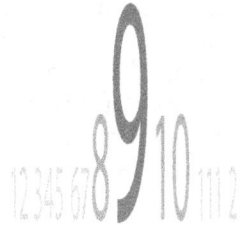

COMUNICACIÓN CON ESPÍRITUS

SÍ-JA, los platos giratorios se conocen como prácticas espiritistas. Los raros experimentos científicos concluyen que el sujeto realiza movimientos musculares inconscientes llamados efecto ideomotor. Lo cual es perfectamente correcto, pero no explica las causas de estos movimientos inconscientes, o por qué las ideas inconscientes generan acciones precisas y concretas ...

La hipótesis es que un flujo telepático, consciente o no, de un nivel suficiente puede apuntar no a un humano vivo, sino a las estructuras de información del meta-cerebro planetario BB y las almas BUAWA interconectadas con el BB- planetario. El resultado sería un retorno de información, consciente o no, capaz de ser transpuesta por los humanos receptores a través de una matriz de YES-JA, por ejemplo.

U. - Estamos en contacto con el B.B. a través de nuestro subconsciente. En estas condiciones, la comunicación es posible, pero en la práctica es difícil de saber (verificar).

Los fenómenos de mediumnicos de la comunicación no siempre son reales, pero pueden serlo. Se deduce que es difícil saber si han pasado por el canal telepático, y uno puede estar equivocado.

D731: Sabemos que a nuestra muerte habrá una fusión, una integración, una conexión cercana de la psique, de nuestra mente (ni material ni inmaterial, sino matriz de toda la información de nuestra vida) con la psique colectiva universal.

Podremos conectarnos más intensamente con los seres queridos, comunicarnos con los espíritus de otros hermanos fallecidos, participar en el conocimiento global de toda la biosfera, no solo de los OEMII que acaban de morir, sino también con todos los humanos desde que nació la vida. en OYAAUMMO (y, por supuesto, para ti, desde el Homo habilis hasta el último de tus hermanos). También es posible conocer el mundo real, incluidos los seres vivos, ya que B.B. está informado de todo el proceso de vida de los seres que aún no han muerto. Esto significa que el OEMMII fallecido, a través de su Psique, puede influir de alguna manera en sus seres más queridos a través del inconsciente y, hasta cierto punto, las cosas a su alrededor, a medida que cambia la biosfera. El entorno físico circundante a través de los seres vivos.

B.B. es el psiquismo colectivo. También podemos llamarlo subconsciente o inconsciente colectivo, en la medida en que su contenido sea operativo, pero no se haga conciente para nosostros los SERES – VIVOS.

El psiquismo de un hermano fallecido puede, y de hecho a veces lo hace, ayudar, proteger y a veces interactuar MUY ACTIVO ...

- ¿Puede un ALMA en el B.B ver el futuro de la Tierra?

U. - NO.

El acceso a las estructuras de información del meta-cerebro planetario BB puede explicar por qué los participantes de SI-JA a veces pueden expresar información que les era desconocida. Alguien ha enviado la información del BB planetario, existe y es potencialmente accesible. Por contra, no hay posibilidad de intentar consultar el BB planetario para obtener los siguientes números de la lotería, ¡porque la información no existe!

Como hemos visto en los capítulos anteriores, se pueden sublimar cantidades infinitesimales de materia en enormes cantidades de energía, son efectos LEIYO de los cambios dimensionales del eje OAWOO. Si impulsamos el razonamiento de nuestra hipótesis, podemos imaginar que el flujo proveniente de BB puede activar un estado psíquico creador de microefectos LEIYO de cambios dimensionales, capaces de impactar el material del marco tridimensional actual. Tal vez a través de biofrecuencias escalares, altamente enérgicas.

En otras palabras, el flujo proveniente de BB transmitido por las antenas receptoras humanas OEMBUAWA, podría activar en el cerebro de personas predispuestas, la capacidad de emitir biofrecuencias generando microefectos de cambios dimensionales. En los objetos, esto produciría diferentes efectos dependiendo de la torsión de los ejes dimensionales OAWOO. Como discutimos en el capítulo La inclinación de los ejes angulares del capítulo *Un nuevo paradigma cosmológico*, estos cambios de eje dimensional pueden ser totales o parciales. Los ejes de las masas y los volúmenes se pueden torcer, lo que produce una pérdida de masa o una desaparición de los volúmenes, y a menudo ambos al mismo tiempo ...

Así iluminaremos misteriosos fenómenos paranormales usando el modelo cosmológico y estas implicaciones concretas. Presentaremos los diferentes escenarios que permiten racionalizar estos fenómenos.

PRECOGNICIÓN O VISIÓN DEL FUTURO

Las nociones de precognición o visión mediática del futuro están vinculadas a los llamados fenómenos de sueños premonitorios o visiones mediumnicas.

¿ Existe el futuro real?

Hemos visto que las potencialidades del Absoluto Real se realizan parcialmente. La realidad absoluta interpretada por la humanidad, el AIIODI, se crea constantemente de manera dinámica, mientras que el conjunto de potencialidades es un depósito casi infinito, pero estático. Por lo tanto, podemos cambiar la evolución de nuestra realidad al pensar de manera diferente sobre nuestro futuro ... Por lo tanto, el futuro real no existe. Tenga en cuenta que si el futuro realmente existiera, el presente o el pasado no tendrían sentido. El tiempo no existiría, todo sería estático.

¿Debemos considerar que los millones de personas que hacen sueños premonitorios todos los días resultan de la mera casualidad? ¿Y las previsiones mediumnicas?

Tenga en cuenta que los sujetos bajo hipnosis tienen mayores capacidades psíquicas y medianas en general y en términos de precognición en particular.

Por otro lado, los estudios realizados por Louisa Rhine han demostrado que las visiones precognitivas son, en su mayoría, trágicas, las premoniciones de eventos desafortunados son cuatro veces más numerosas que las de eventos felices. También se debe tener en cuenta que las poblaciones de culturas donde existen prácticas del orden del chamanismo tuvieron mejores resultados en las pruebas de percepciones extrasensoriales generales que Louisa Rhine se dio cuenta. Los investigadores sobre este tema son muy numerosos, sería difícil nombrarlos a todos, ya que el escritor John White, el parapsicólogo Stanley Krippner, los físicos Harold Puthoff y Russel Targ, el psiquiatra David Loye, son muy depistados y están faltando una teoría satisfactoria, asi se satisfechan con la teoría de la mente holográfica desarrollada por Bohm y Pribram. Esta trae ninguna respuesta concreta a esta pregunta.

Comencemos con un caso concreto, que me fue expuesto por un amigo, Marc. Este niño que había pasado más de un año en una cama de hospital por problemas de columna había tenido tiempo de desarrollar sus habilidades de meditación. Unos meses después de su convalecencia, Marc tuvo un sueño o más bien una pesadilla que lo despertó. Estaba conduciendo por una pequeña carretera en el sur de Francia y al final de una curva salió un vehículo a la derecha para cruzar la carretera cortando la carretera. La colisión ocurrió mientras causaba su muerte. El sueño había sido de un realismo apoyado. El auto blanco golpeó, un Peugeot 206, el conductor un hombre en los años 70, con ropa clara, beige, blanco ... Pero, un simple mal sueño, rápidamente olvidado ...

Una semana más tarde, Marc toma su automóvil para ir a una cita. Este pequeño camino provenzal que conduce a él comienza a recordarle algo, pero ¿qué? Entonces, es la chispa. El mal sueño de la semana pasada. Sí, !él reconoce el sitio! Marc frena de inmediato. El tiene razon. Un Peugeot 206 blanco corta el camino para cruzar en la otra dirección. Marc toca la bocina y le hace señas al conductor, quien estaciona su vehículo un poco más. Marc se une a él, es un hombre de unos 70 años, con ropa clara ...

Para reanudar la diatriba de Louis Jouvet en la película «Drama divertido», es raro, raro ...

Aquí está mi interpretación de este estudio de caso que es generalizable a todos los casos de este tipo.

Sabemos que el meta-cerebro BB es informado por la psique del hombre de blanco que piensa llevar su auto Peugeot 206 blanco. Esto es rutinario o porque el hombre de blanco lo pensó en un momento dado : «No tengo más de este bueno rosado de Provence, lo compraré la próxima semana en mi viticultor favorito ...»

Es lo mismo para Marc y todas las personas relacionadas con el evento. El meta-cerebro BB es informado por las psiques humanas de sus intenciones. Esto a veces mucho antes ...

Es fácil para el meta-cerebro BB predecir lo que sucederá. El pronóstico de colisión es calculado por el meta-cerebro BB. El meta-cerebro BB no quiere perder a estos 2 buenos clientes que lo respaldan llenos de buena información sobre Provenza, y que ciertamente no han terminado su trabajo en el planeta Tierra ... Entonces, el meta-cerebro BB envía un mensaje de alerta Probablemente para toda la humanidad, pero solo el subconsciente de las partes interesadas lo tendrá en cuenta. Marc en particular, será despertado por este mal sueño, que le permitirá recordar ...

Es el poder informático del meta-cerebro BB lo que le permite predecir situaciones futuras. Individualmente, cada uno de los actores humanos del evento tiene solo una fracción de la información y no puede hacer tales predicciones. Por lo tanto, cuando finalmente se enfrentan al evento, les parece que su sueño fue premonitorio ...

Del mismo modo, ciertos mediumes pueden percibir este tipo de información del meta-cerebro BB. A priori, esto con una anticipación que no está limitada en el tiempo. Los únicos límites para la anticipación predictiva son los límites mismos de la potencia informática del meta-cerebro BB.

TRANSCOMUNICACIÓN

En la década de 1960, Marie-Louise Aucher (1908-1994), músico y cantante, descubre correspondencias vibratorias entre los sonidos y el cuerpo humano: cada sonido corresponde a una parte del esqueleto. Ella entiende que el cuerpo humano tiene funciones de transmisor /

receptor cuando se emite un sonido a la frecuencia de resonancia de ciertas partes del esqueleto.

Un instrumento que produce una frecuencia dada puede resonar con una parte del cuerpo y, a la inversa, la voz humana puede resonar con un instrumento. Es psicofonía. Existen muchos fenómenos de resonancia y sus efectos son a veces misteriosos y sorprendentes ...

La transcomunicación tiene una analogía con la psicofonía en la frecuencia del sonido, la diferencia es el rango y la naturaleza de las frecuencias de la transcomunicación. Friedrich Jürgenson descubrió el fenómeno en 1959 y Ernst Senkowski, profesor de física, inventó el concepto de transcomunicación.

Raymond Bayless, Attila Szalay y Konstantin Raudive fueron los pioneros de la experimentación en este tema. El Pr. Marcello Bacci juega con la tecla de sintonización de un receptor de radio con tubos entre 7 y 9 Mhz. Entre los mensajes escuchados: *«La energía de la mente, adecuadamente modulada, se transfiere al receptor que la transforma, con su cerebro, en ondas electromagnéticas que dan lugar a la transmisión de radio».*

Friedrich Jürgenson habría escuchado un mensaje sobre una frecuencia en ondas medias, alrededor de 1480 kHz y Hans Otto König, dos indicaciones de frecuencias en onda corta: 10 MHz y 7 MHz.

```
U. - Las psicofonías [Transcomunicación] son produ-
cidas por radiación electromagnética. Es un fenó-
meno FÍSICO, porque el aparato de grabación puede,
bajo ciertas condiciones, convertirse en un recep-
tor. Una inducción, una bobina, conectada a un
condensador, forma un circuito oscilante capaz de
recibir las ondas electromagnéticas de un trans-
misor. En el transmisor que fabrica, se fabrica,
bajo ciertas condiciones, una resonancia en el
circuito oscilante. Si otro circuito oscilante
tiene las mismas características ... es decir que
la inducción tiene el mismo número de mili hen-
rys, la capacidad el mismo número de faradays o,
combinación de los dos, la inducción de capacidad
al mismas características ... bajo estas condi-
ciones, la transmisión y la recepción de frecuen-
cias electromagnéticas es posible porque los dos
circuitos están en resonancia. En una grabadora de
cinta, a veces se producen efectos de resonancia
con una emisión electromagnética cuya frecuencia
```

se detecta. Aunque la grabadora no fue diseñada para captar ondas electromagnéticas, puede capturarlas. Es en estas condiciones que recibimos psicofonía.

Un elemento capaz de emitir ondas electromagnéticas también puede emitir una PSICOFONIA ... y ser recogido por una grabadora ... La mayoría de las psicofonías [transcomunicaciones] se capturan a través de oscilaciones electromagnéticas.

La transcomunicación instrumental opera con resonancias entre dispositivos electrónicos y dispositivos electromagnéticos inductivos, y frecuencias emitidas por la actividad cerebral humana. La comunicación telepática no consciente se transforma en una frecuencia electromagnética por la persona que se transmite en este rango de frecuencia, y si el dispositivo inductivo resuena, la frecuencia es procesada normalmente por el aparato para producir sonido o grabación.

Esto puede ser una resonancia con el cabezal de grabación de la grabadora, algunos componentes del circuito de amplificación de la radio, o incluso los bobinados del propio altavoz ...

Diagrama de flujo de la SIJA

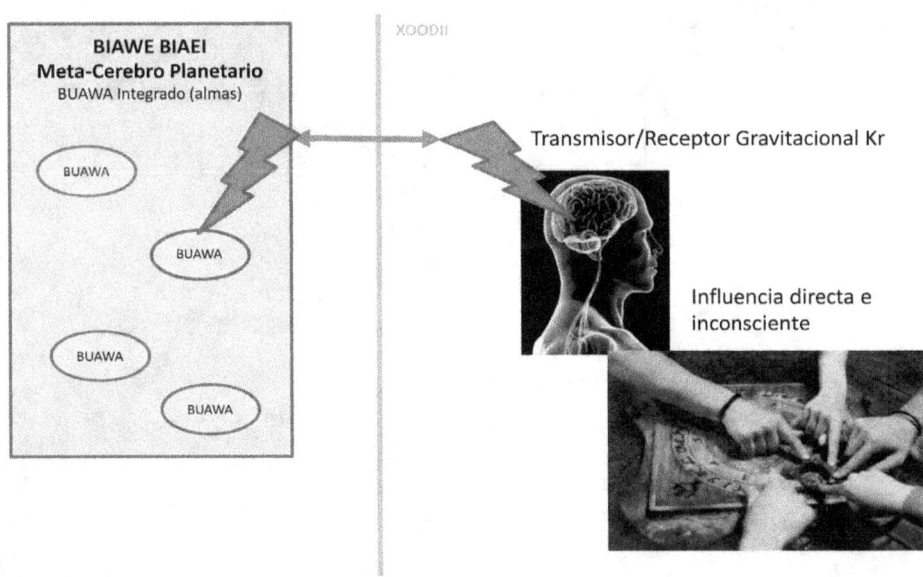

Diagrama de flujo de la Transcomunicación Instrumental

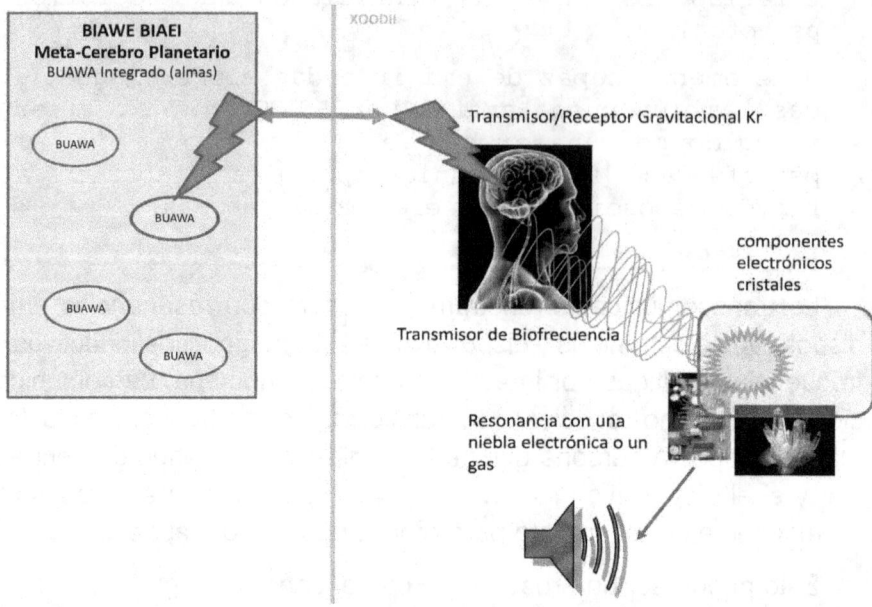

El calentamiento de un taburete por SIJA, acumula energía térmica que excita las capas electrónicas y las hace más sensibles a las biofrecuencias, se deduce que el efecto LEIYO de la proyección sobre el taburete es más rápido que sin calefacción.

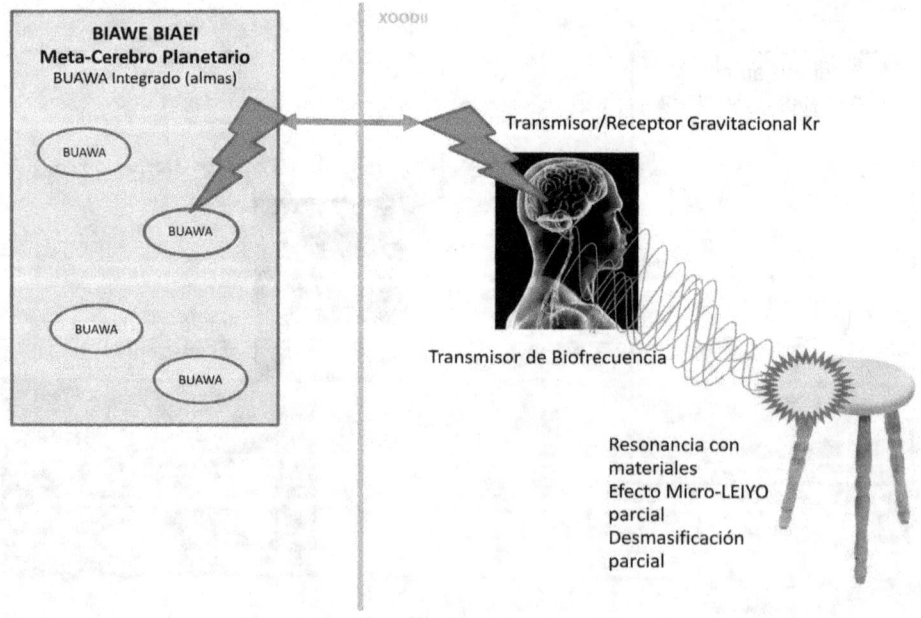

194

OIR LAS VOCES DEL MÁS ALLÁ

El análisis de las voces

El timbre de las voces del más allá es distinto del de los humanos. En la década de 2000, las mediciones de grabaciones realizadas por Michel Marcel para C.E.R.P.I. (Centro de Estudios e Investigación sobre Fenómenos Inexplicables) indican que son aproximadamente 16 veces más rápidos que la propagación del sonido en el aire. Esto tiene el efecto de ser una voz muy distorsionada en comparación con las voces producidas por un conjunto de cuerdas vocales. Lo que los distingue inequívocamente de las voces humanas. Para ser realmente audibles y entendibles por todos, requieren un procesamiento de señal. Las voces grabadas no tienen una frecuencia fundamental, sino solo armónicos y esto en el campo de las bajas frecuencias (10 Hz a 20 Khz) casi siempre de bajo nivel.

La asociacion CROPS y Michel Marcel nos han enviado amablemente varias grabaciones que contienen sonidos que los presentes no percibieron en el campo de sonido. Las grabaciones se realizaron en medios de cinta magnética convertidos a digital o directamente en grabadoras digitales.

Utilizamos la experiencia de un vocoder experto en musicología, Hervé Noury, para analizar estas grabaciones.

Las primeras grabaciones de la serie fueron realizadas por Michel Marcel en presencia del medium Jean-Jacques Poirier.

En la primera grabación, vimos una especie de bramido, que parece una queja. Las diferentes transposiciones y la desaceleración no permitieron escuchar mejor los componentes de este sonido.

Las otras grabaciones dejan en claro algunas de las letras.

La conversación «¿Quién me habla?» deja en claro un «Soy yo» y «Sí», pero no fue posible escuchar mejor el pasaje o esa voz habría dicho su nombre. Del mismo modo, escuchamos un «sí yo puedo» en la conversación que invita a la creación de un centro de investigación.

La grabación realizada por el CROPS no puedo responder explícitamente a una pregunta del otro medium Monique Aubergier.

En todos los casos, las inflexiones tonales del sonido, así como la modificación permanente de los formantes son las que generalmente producen una voz. Tenga en cuenta que en ningún caso, estas voces han sido modificadas por medios acústicos (caja, máscara auditiva, partición ...) o electrónicas (filtros, codificadores de voz, saturación ...). Escuchando, estas voces suenan como si hubiéramos tratado la voz humana con un codificador de voz que modula el ruido blanco (sonido de soplo continua), pero que ha preservado las inflexiones tonales de la voz original. Por alguna razón desconocida, pero no discriminatoria, estos sonidos no tienen fundamentos. No es posible saber si esto se debe a un elemento técnico o si la fuente en sí no contenía ningún elemento fundamental.

Ciertamente, no entendemos realmente las consonantes, sino las vocales, lo que se confirma mediante el análisis ecográfico de las grabaciones. Las frecuencias bajas dominan, hay pocas frecuencias agudas características de las consonantes. Entonces, en el sonograma, observamos que las frecuencias altas están ausentes, de ahí la imposibilidad de comprender las consonantes.

Marcadores de identificaciones electrónicas de «voces»

Mi amigo Thierry Wilson, de TCI-France, hizo un avance importante. Como ingeniero de sonido, analizó miles de grabaciones de voz en transcomunicación. Descubrió que casi todas estas grabaciones contenían lo que él llamó «marcadores» al principio y al final de la grabación. Estas fueron secuencias compactadas que contenían la estructura, el ritmo, la plantilla y la secuencia del mensaje de voz.

Pero, ¿qué pasa con las grabaciones raras de voces de transcomunicación donde no había tales marcadores?

Durante nuestros intercambios, encontramos, en resumen, que estas grabaciones se referían a un contexto específico. Las personas que transmiten la transcomunicación no estaban en relación con el fallecido.

Solo las personas que transmiten transcomunicación en relación con una persona fallecida producen grabaciones con marcadores de identificaciones electrónicas de «voces». Este es un comienzo de prueba y reconocimiento sistemático para diferenciar el origen y la naturaleza de los flujos registrados.

La estructura de flujo contiene secuencias compactadas antes y después de la secuencia de mensajes de voz. Estos marcadores determinan los parámetros estructurales necesarios para la reproducción vocal del mensaje. Es probable que los marcadores codifiquen los sonidos a producir con: la frecuencia o tesitura; intensidad; el timbre que depende de las frecuencias contenidas en un sonido que se superponen; la tasa de retorno de la voz; prosodia o entonación.

Estos parámetros estructurales o mensajes de marcadores identificadores siempre están en línea con la naturaleza del medio de grabación. Es decir, si el medio de grabación hace posible grabar en este o aquel rango de frecuencia, entonces el mensaje se restaurará en el rango de frecuencia apropiado. Los parámetros estructurales de los mensajes tienen en cuenta de forma inteligente la naturaleza del medio de grabación para el que está destinado.

Interpretación en el entorno cosmológico

En todos los casos pudimos eliminar categóricamente los gritos de animales o las firmas de ruido. Todos los sonidos grabados están compuestos de formantes característicos de una voz humana, aunque estos formantes no fueron percibidos en el campo de sonido por los presentes. Los marcadores de identificaciones electrónicas de «voces» prueban que la naturaleza de las voces de transcomunicación es muy específica de la naturaleza del origen del flujo.

Estudiemos las causas de este fenómeno... El flujo de estos datos desde el espacio exterior es a través de un cosmos de naturaleza totalmente diferente. De hecho, estas voces son principalmente datos almacenados en el Alma-BUAWA del difunto que se ha integrado en el Meta-Cerebro planetario. El flujo de esta alma-BUAWA, unidimensional y atemporal, transita en el espacio penta-dimensional de la velocidad fotónica infinita que es el Planetario Meta-Cerebro BB. Es él quien realmente apoya el flujo y lo maneja, y no el BUAWA incorporado del difunto. El Alma-BUAWA integrado establece así el mismo tipo de comunicación telepática que para un enlace humano a humano a través del Meta-Cerebro Planetario BB. Hemos visto el flujo de frecuencias gravitacionales que llegan a los átomos de criptón de OEMBUAWE y salen en biofrecuencias de 7.2 KHz en el lado humano. El compuesto de germanio-silicio, que hablemos antes, actuaría como un transformador condensador de flujo.

La diferencia en la naturaleza de los flujos y las transformaciones en serie explican que puede haber una diferencia de 16 veces entre la velocidad de una voz humana y los flujos de salida finales graba-dos del difunto. Tampoco hay una frecuencia fundamental de flujo de BUAWA a través del Meta-Cerebro BB Planetario.

El Alma-BUAWA es atemporal, como hemos visto, está hecho para transferir información siguiendo el hilo del tiempo. Esto es muy dife-rente de una secuencia de palabras o imágenes. Esta conexión no es entre dos cerebros del mismo tipo que pueden intercambiar imágenes mentales codificadas en el mismo formato. El formato de datos del Soul-BUAWA es un tren de impulsos para procesos cerebrales sub-conscientes, pero no una representación mental que codifica direc-tamente el sonido o la imagen inteligible directamente por las zonas cerebrales del humano terrestre. El humano terrestre no está conec-tado para eso, el flujo de BUAWA permanece subconsciente. Para ser inteligible, debe transformarse en frecuencias que nuestros órganos neurorreceptores puedan captar. Las biofrecuencias humanas se pue-den utilizar como modulador de frecuencia del flujo del BUAWA del difunto que se comunica a través del Meta-Cerebro BB Planetario. Estas biofrecuencias en modulación podrán capturarse con receptores electrónicos, cristales, etc.

Cuando el Alma-BUAWA integrado establece una comunicación telepática para un humano a través del Meta-Cerebro BB Planetario, que estructura de manera inteligente el flujo para que se pueda repre-sentar con una voz humana comprensible. Esta estructura de flujo contiene secuencias compactadas antes y después de la secuencia de mensajes de voz. Estos marcadores determinan los parámetros estructurales necesarios para la reproducción vocal del mensaje. Es probable que los marcadores codifiquen los sonidos a producir con: la frecuencia o tesitura; intensidad; el timbre que depende de las frecuen-cias contenidas en un sonido que se superponen; la tasa de retorno de la voz; prosodia o entonación.

Por lo tanto, las voces del más allá no son voces humanas, sino la expresión de un flujo de datos que finalmente se transforma en fre-cuencias de sonido, de acuerdo con sus marcadores de identificación que codifican los sonidos que se producirán.

El hecho de que los parámetros estructurales o los marcadores de identificación tengan en cuenta de forma inteligente la naturaleza del medio de grabación, me respalda en la idea de que el Meta-Cerebro

BB Planetario está en el origen de la configuración del flujo de los mensajes.

Nos parece que los paquetes y las tramas de estos flujos tienen una arquitectura muy similar a las utilizadas en las redes de computadoras de las cuales aquí hay una hipótesis explicativa (ver también los esquemas del modelo teórico de paquetes de información en formato de frecuencia).

Hipótesis de análisis de una comunicación sonora en la Tierra (TCI)

¿Cómo podría un «difunto», cuya alma está integrada en el BB Meta-Cerebro, comunicar un mensaje de sonido en la Tierra (TCI)?

Cuando un «fallecido» desea comunicar un mensaje de sonido en la Tierra en modo TCI, envía secuencias de mensajes correspondientes a las palabras que desea comunicar. Estas secuencias de mensajes codifican en binario cada sílaba de cada palabra que el difunto desea pronunciar. Cada mensaje corresponde a una palabra de una o más sílabas.

Cada mensaje en sí está estructurado con varios paquetes.

Un paquete de encabezado que se describe a sí mismo la estructura de los otros paquetes del mensaje. Por lo tanto, del segundo paquete al penúltimo se codifican en sílabas binarias de la palabra deseada.

Un paquete final homólogo al paquete inicial cierra el paquete.

El flujo proveniente del Meta-Cerebro BB es, por lo tanto, un campo binario que evoluciona a una velocidad infinita. Este tramo binario está estructurado por secuencias de mensajes, compuestos por un encabezado de inicio, paquetes silábicos y un paquete de fin de mensaje para el final de la palabra. El tramo de inicio podría comenzar con una palabra de sincronización (término en inglés) que permita al receptor adaptarse a la modulación de amplitud, ajustar las variaciones de velocidad de la señal y sincronizar el tramo.

Es necesario que el mensaje binario que sale a la velocidad infinita del Meta-Brain BB, se transforme en un mensaje que ingresa al cerebro humano a la velocidad de la luz. Son los átomos de criptón los que realizan la conversión emitiendo ondas gravitacionales.

Como hemos visto en la sección de biofrecuencias del capítulo LOS FLUJOS DE INFORMACIÓN DE UNA ESPECIE VIVA, la hipótesis es que el compuesto GeSi2C3H3 desempeña un papel de modulador-demodulador en varias longitudes de onda. En particular, transformando estas ondas gravitacionales en diferentes frecuencias necesarias para la sincronización de los orgánulos intracelulares.

La hipótesis complementaria es que el compuesto GeSi2C3H3 también juega un papel en la decodificación de mensajes binarios de Meta-Cerebro BB. El transmisor receptor de cerebro humano está atravesado por una multitud de radiofrecuencias de cualquier tipo, incluidas las radiofrecuencias que rebotan en la ionosfera.

La idea es que el mensaje binario de Meta-Cerebro BB sea transformado por el compuesto GeSi2C3H3, en una señal analógica que contenga las radiofrecuencias de las sílabas de la palabra del mensaje del «difunto».

Por lo tanto, el compuesto GeSi2C3H3 está atravesado por una multitud de frecuencias de radio de todo tipo, incluidas las frecuencias de radio que rebotan en la ionosfera. En el GeSi2C3H3 compuesto, el paquete de encabezado se decodifica con sus descriptores de los otros paquetes silábicos del mensaje. Para lograr esto, el compuesto GeSi2C3H3 utiliza las frecuencias de radio que lo atraviesan de forma natural. Filtra y pasa en el flujo saliente, los bits de radiofrecuencias correspondientes a estos descriptores, en otras palabras, deja salir en la corriente las radiofrecuencias correspondientes a las sílabas de la palabra que el «difunto» desea pronunciar.

Los bits de radiofrecuencia, que transitan permanentemente en el cerebro humano, en el compuesto GeSi2C3H3, que corresponden a los descriptores silábicos, se ensamblan, paquete por paquete.

Por lo tanto, se constituye un tramo analógico de radiofrecuencia. Este nuevo tramo analógico puede ser proyectado por inducción de resonancia por el «medio» en diferentes medios, magnéticos o de otro tipo. En última instancia, esto dará como resultado la grabación de una frecuencia de voz compuesta, resultante de las múltiples frecuencias de radio que formaron un tramo analógico así constituida.

El método de detección y la configuración del descriptor son una invención del Meta-Cerebro BB, adaptado al contexto operativo terrestre. Un otro Meta-Cerebro BB con humanos aptos para la telepatía podría haber funcionado de manera diferente ...

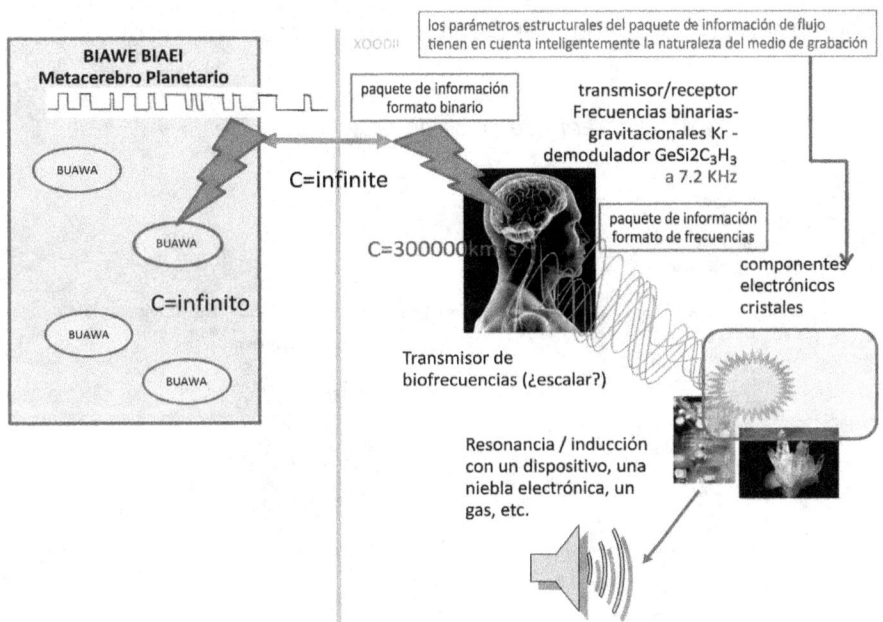

Modelo teórico de un paquete de información en formato de frecuencia				
trama de inicio	1- Secuencia de sonido	2- Secuencia de sonido	3- Secuencia de sonido	trama de final
Parámetros -1- Secuencia de sonido				Parámetros -1- Secuencia de sonido
Parámetros -2- Secuencia de sonido				Parámetros -2- Secuencia de sonido
Parámetros -3- Secuencia de sonido				Parámetros -3- Secuencia de sonido

La trama de inicio podría comenzar con una palabra de sincronización (*en*) permitiendo al receptor adaptarse a la modulación de amplitud, ajustarse a las variaciones de velocidad de la señal y para la sincronización de tramas.

Como hemos visto, la proyección de biofrecuencias puede influir en los ejes de las masas para demasificar un objeto por resonancia. Pero a la inversa, las torsiones en los ejes de las masas pueden generar masa, esto independientemente del material mismo.

Diagrama de flujos de proyección masica

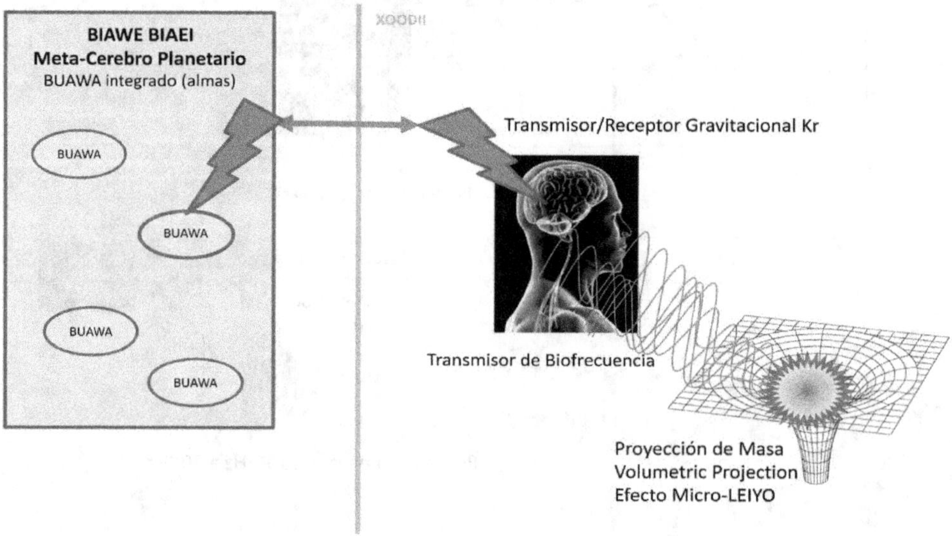

BIAWE BIAEI
Meta-Cerebro Planetario
BUAWA integrado (almas)

XOODH

BUAWA

BUAWA

Transmisor/Receptor Gravitacional Kr

BUAWA

BUAWA

Transmisor de Biofrecuencia

Proyección de Masa
Volumetric Projection
Efecto Micro-LEIYO

En un volumen dado que puede ser un gas o un objeto sólido, el receptor proyectará biofrecuencias que producirán un efecto de giro micro-LEIYO en los ejes de masa, creando en este caso masa en un volumen cualquiero.

Del mismo modo, el receptor proyectará biofrecuencias que producirán un efecto de torsión micro-LEIYO en los ejes de los volúmenes, creando en este caso un volumen sin masa. Este es el caso de apariciones fantasmales estrictamente relacionadas con el relé que es la persona destinataria. Veremos que se pueden producir efectos similares de otra manera.

Efectos similares con diferentes causas dificultan el análisis, de ahí la necesidad de comprender claramente la totalidad del marco cosmológico que subyace a estos fenómenos.

Estos fenómenos pueden acumularse de acuerdo con las habilidades del receptor. Por lo tanto, las proyecciones pueden superponer volúmenes y masas. Esto permitiría la proyección de lo que a menudo se llaman egregores, fantasmas percibidos casi como personas vivas y capaces de intercambiar un flujo telepático vocal que el oyente experimentará como un intercambio de palabras normales. Veremos fenómenos similares en el capítulo *Secuestros y manipulaciones mentales*.

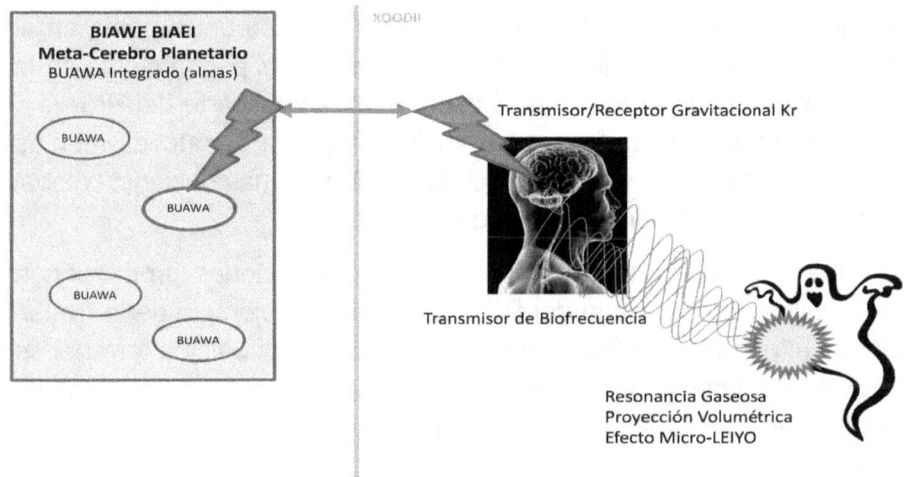

Diagrama de flujos de proyección voluminal holográfica

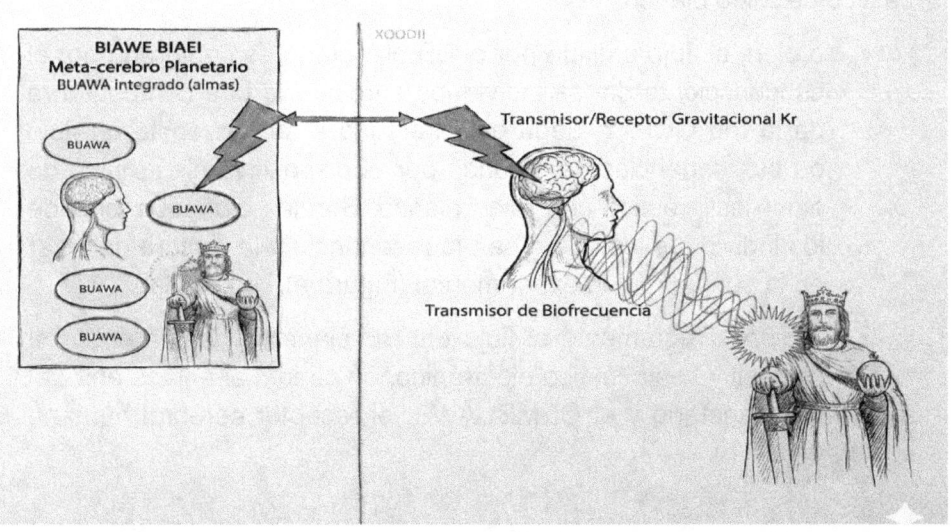

THE GLOBAL CONSCIOUSNESS PROJECT

Además de los programas especiales de Visión Remota, los estudios de investigadores civiles como Charles Honorton de los Laboratorios de Investigación Psicofísica (PRL) y el Laboratorio de Investigación de Anomalías de Ingeniería de Princeton (PEAR) y el trabajo de Peter von Buengner condujeron a la identificación de la interacción psíquica entre máquinas o computadoras con un diodo de ruido blanco incorporado que crea una niebla electrónica como producto intermedio. La niebla electrónica es una emisión de frecuencia que cubre todo el espectro electromagnético.

El vínculo entre el hombre y la máquina, una computadora, por ejemplo, se realiza de forma inalámbrica y se basa únicamente en el hecho de que la persona se concentra mediante el pensamiento en la comunicación con la máquina. Desde 1998, como parte del Proyecto de Conciencia Global, Roger Nelson se pregunta si muchas mentes humanas, en resonancia, no reaccionarían como una conciencia global a los eventos que afectan al mundo.

Nuestras suposiciones sobre flujos y proyecciones proporcionan una explicación detallada del PCG. En el primer ejemplo de la transición al año 2000, una hora antes de que toda la población terrenal se prepare febrilmente para el evento. Las conexiones al BB planetario se concentran en esta información y culminan en la alegría del día de Año Nuevo.

Dos flujos pueden afectar el dispositivo electrónico de diodo estocástico de ruido blanco:

- o bien, el flujo emitido por el BB planetario es capturado por el subconsciente de los individuos cercanos a una computadora de la red GCP. Y luego esta persona a su vez emite un flujo de biofrecuencias capturadas por el dispositivo electrónico de diodo estocástico con ruido blanco. Son las biofrecuencias de los individuos las que crean la resonancia y la ruptura del azar en la configuración experimental (Figura a).

- o bien, directamente el flujo del BB planetario actúa sobre el dispositivo estocástico electrónico, en cuanto al enlace entre el BB planetario y el OEMBUAWE, el receptor cerebral humano (figura b).

Esquemas:

a) en el caso del día del año 2000, los flujos pasan a través del OEMBUAWE (transmisor / receptor del cerebro humano) y esta persona a su vez emite una corriente de biofrecuencias o es directamente el flujo de BB-planetario que actúa sobre el dispositivo electrónico estocástico?

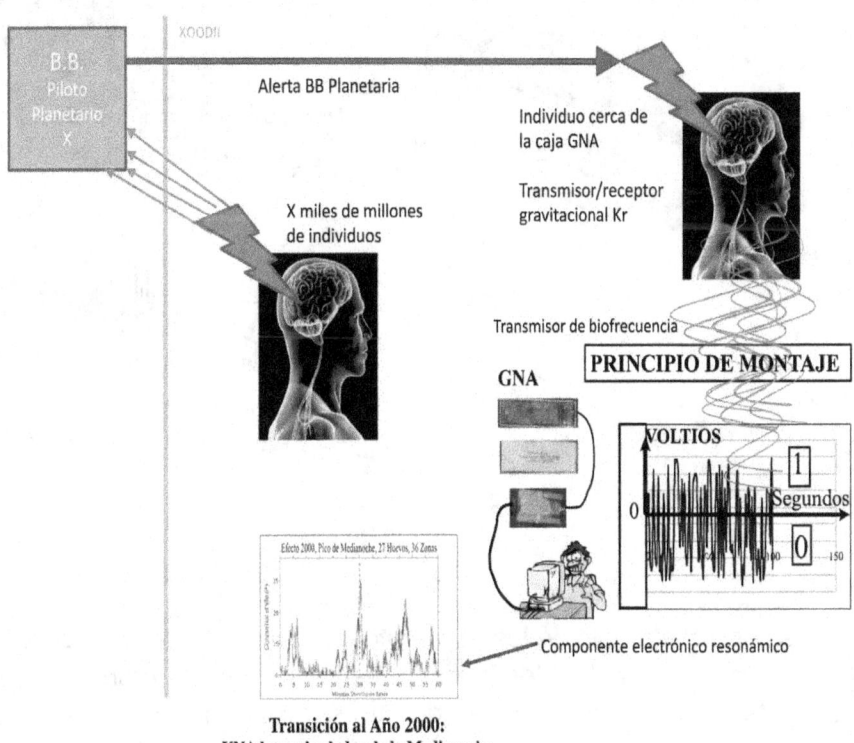

Transición al Año 2000:
UNA hora alrededor de la Medianoche

*b) en el caso de un terremoto, los flujos pasan a través del BAAYIODUU
(transmisor / receptor genómico-cósmico) de los animales y el flujo del planetario BB que actúa sobre el dispositivo electrónico estocástico*

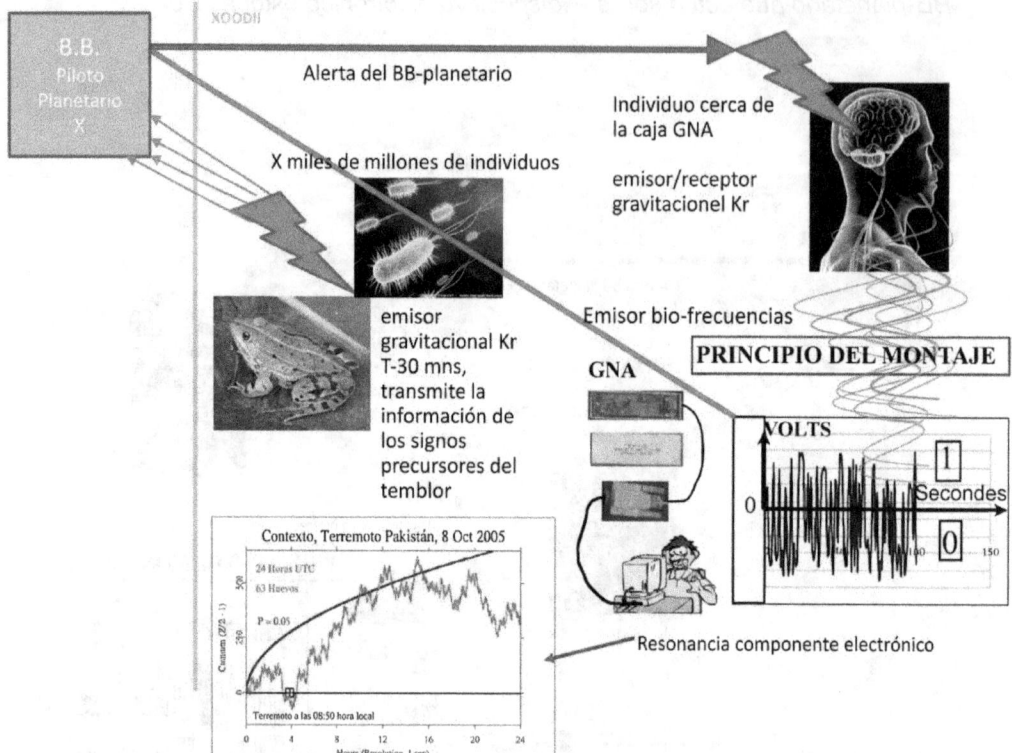

Veamos el ejemplo de los terremotos (Figura b). Estos son percibidos por varios animales desde los primeros signos. La información se
transmite al BB planetario antes de que el evento se manifieste a los
humanos. Aquí nuevamente encontramos la oportunidad en el dispositivo experimental.

Para estos flujos telepáticos, el papel del BB planetario es registrar
y transferir la información. En ningún caso el BB planetario altera el
contenido del flujo. Una alerta lanzada por una bacteria será interpretable por otras bacterias y el BB planetario. Aunque los humanos
reciben esta alerta de las bacterias, no es interpretable por ellos.

Esto nos lleva a concluir que es directamente el flujo del planetario
BB el que actúa sobre el dispositivo estocástico electrónico, en cuanto
al enlace entre el planetario BB y el OEMBUAWE, el receptor cerebral
humano (figura b).

c) en el caso del World Trade Center, los flujos pasan a través del OEMBUAWE (transmisor / receptor cerebroespinal) de los humanos y el flujo del planetario BB que actúa sobre el dispositivo electrónico estocástico

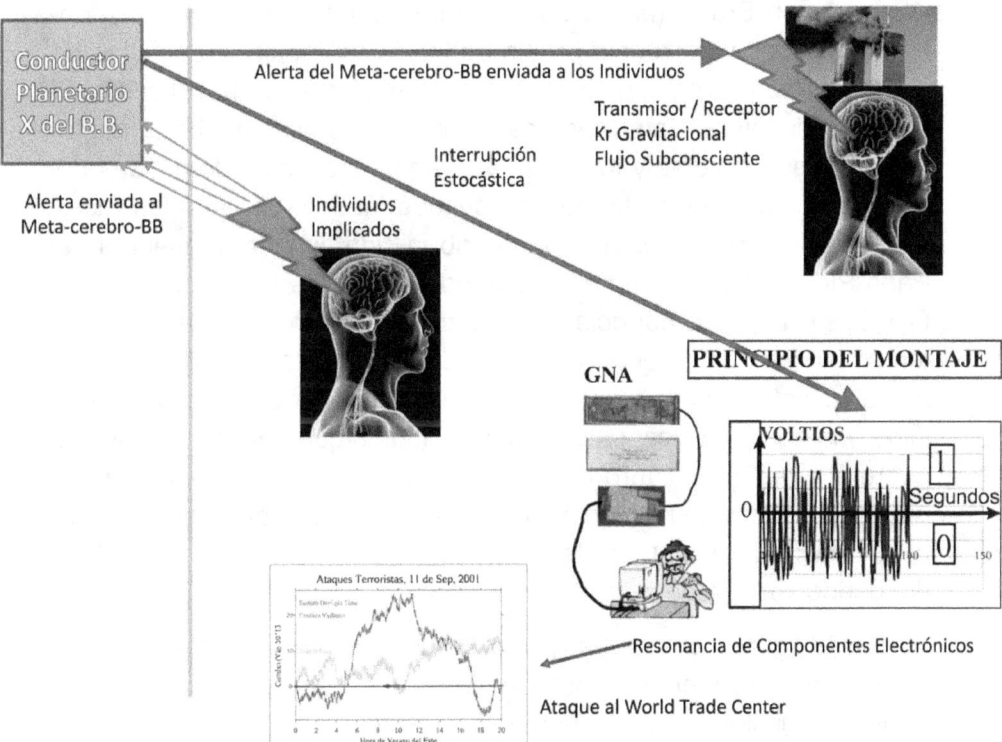

En el caso del World Trade Center, el BB planetario ya estaba alarmado a las 4 am, así que casi cinco horas antes del impacto del primer avión (8:45) y seis horas y media antes de la llegada del segundo avión (10:30). Como los medios no lo mencionaron antes de las 8:45, el planetario BB reaccionó en el dispositivo electrónico estocástico desde el momento en que aquellos que fueron informados de lo que estaba sucediendo habían comenzado a ejecutar su plan. . El BB planetario está informado y puede calcular los eventos que ocurrirán. Algunos médiums tienen sueños premonitorios, otros tienen visiones del desastre, antes de que realmente suceda. Esto nos lleva a concluir que el BB planetario mismo ha «calculado», se ha enterado, los eventos que ocurrirían y por sí solo ha alertado al subconsciente de los humanos (Figura c).

EL CRONOVISOR

Un dispositivo llamado cronovisor, desarrollado hace medio siglo por un equipo de científicos. Fermi (especialista en física atómica) y Wernher von Braun (padre del programa espacial de EE. UU.) fueron implicados y se reunieron alrededor de un monje benedictino de Venecia, Padre Ernetti, especialista en cantos gregorianos, licenciado en física cuántica. Esta máquina habría funcionado en 1972, capturando rangos de olas y logrando visualizar escenas holográficas del pasado: discurso de Napoleón, Quousque tándem Catilina de Cicero, ascenso del Gólgota ... Todo esto habría sido filmado, presentado al Papa Pío XII y a las más altas autoridades civiles italianas. El padre François Brune, que conocía bien al padre Ernetti, relata que los caracteres holográficos no eran muy grandes, como el tamaño de nuestras pantallas catodicas de televisión. Puede configurar el dispositivo en el lugar y la hora que desee. Se elegia a alguien que querían seguir. Era sobre él que se configuró el dispositivo y luego lo siguió automáticamente. El cronoviso ha sido descrito como un gran gabinete con antenas, conectado a un tubo de rayos catódicos. (Ver artículo detallado del periódico Morpheus, marzo de 2012)

Las imágenes producidas por el cronovisor no son copia y pegado de imágenes existentes. Esto también se muestra mediante análisis de fotos digitales de proyecciones holográficas realizadas por Nancy Talbott de BLT Research.

Así, la escultura de Jesucristo del Santuario de Collevalenza, Italia, realizada en España en 1931 por el escultor Lorenzo Valera Cullot se archiva en los datos de BB-Planetario. La imagen proyectada por el cronovisor es fiel, pero de ninguna manera idéntica a la original de la escultura.

La suposición es que las antenas o la máquina en sí contenían elementos basados en germanio y silicio.

Padres Gemelli y Ernetti están conectados al BB planetario, como todos los demás, y capturan información subconsciente. Al centrarse en la imagen mental de una persona crucificada, ejercen un filtro selectivo de las imágenes mentales correspondientes en el BB planetario. Las biofrecuencias se transmiten y amplifican en el cronovisor.

Cuando se identifica a la persona objetivo, el operador bloquea la frecuencia del cronovisor. Solo las imágenes mentales correspondientes a esta frecuencia son proyectadas holográficamente por el dispositivo.

La cámara proyecta imágenes que resultan del BB planetario, pero transformadas por las proyecciones mentales de los operadores de acuerdo con su propia capacidad para producirlas. Si otras personas hubieran investigado a Jesucristo con el cronovisor, es probable que las proyecciones resultantes hayan sido diferentes.

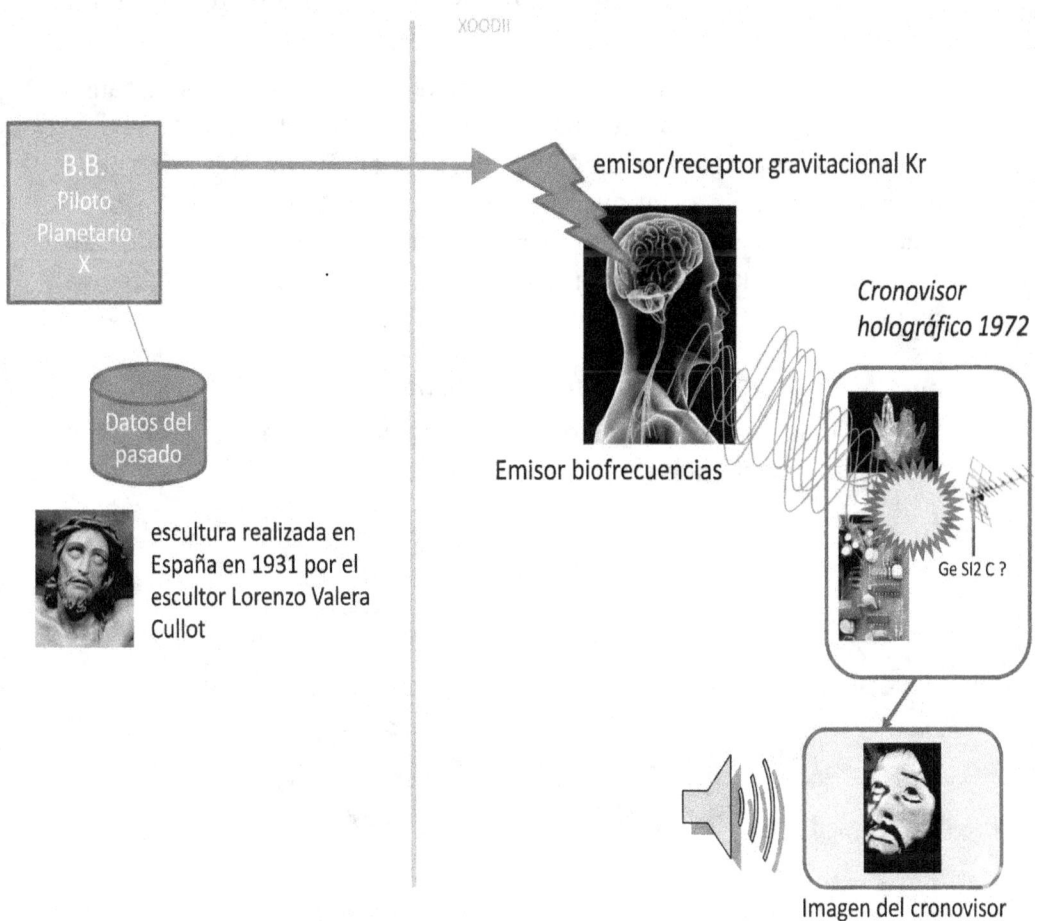

Hemos visto 6 casos típicos del modelo de explicación desde el marco cosmológico. Todas las combinaciones posibles de estas configuraciones pueden producir efectos similares con diferentes causas.

Presentamos los modelos de efectos cuyas causas tienen en común que todos requieren uno o más receptores que transforman y proyectan el flujo recibido. Todos estos fenómenos de proyecciones se expresan bajo el mismo término de fantasmas o manifestaciones paranormales.

También hay todos los casos de manifestaciones donde la causa del fenómeno se debe directamente al Aura residual. El Aura residual del difunto proyecta directamente estas frecuencias en el aparato electrónico, que habla o produce varios efectos sobre el asunto. Todos estos fenómenos también se expresan bajo el mismo término de fantasmas. Los lugares embrujados suelen ser manifestaciones directas de uno o más residuos de auras.

AURA Y ARRASTRE DEL ESPACIO-TIEMPO

Con la muerte del hombre espacio-temporal, esta serpiente larga pierde su cabeza, que es el cuerpo físico del hombre.

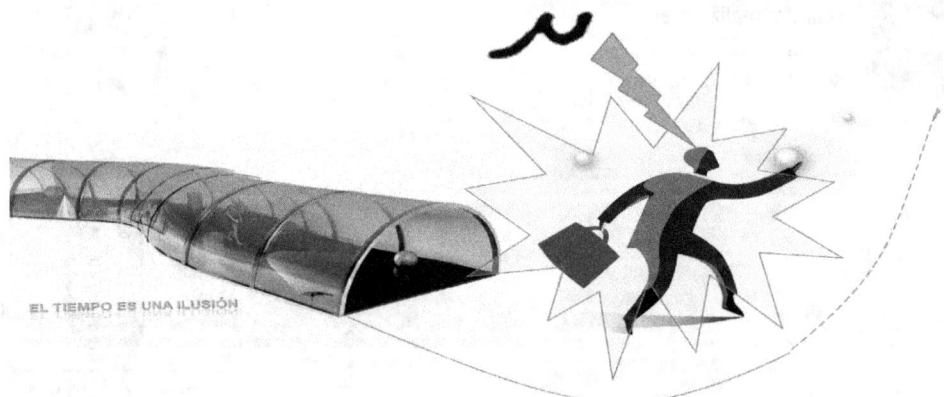

EL TIEMPO ES UNA ILUSIÓN

el Hombre-espaciotemporal ligado a su Aura de bio-frecuencias y su BUAWA

El arrastre espacio-temporal grabado por el OEMMII todavía existe en los IBODSOO cósmicos, pero detiene su progresión temporal en el marco tridimensional. En su vida, el hombre emite múltiples frecuencias biológicas en forma de aura. Este aura es tan inseparable del

210

hombre espacio-temporal como el cuerpo físico. En condiciones normales, el aura desaparece con el cuerpo físico.

La hipótesis es que bajo ciertas condiciones, un Aura residual permanece en el camino espacio-temporal. Este aura residual es una nube electrónica, probablemente un plasma frío. Este aura residual podría evolucionar de diferentes maneras, según el caso. Los dos grandes casos:

- el Aura residual se absorbe cuando el Alma se integra en el Meta-cerebro BB
- el Aura residual queda en el rastro espacio-temporal

INCIDENTES DE INTEGRACIÓN DE ALMAS-BUAWA

El vínculo OEMII-cuerpo / Alma-BUAWA se rompe con la muerte del individuo. Por un efecto LEIYO, el Alma-BUAWA se conecta al BB planetario del que depende.

La hipótesis es que este efecto LEIYO absorbe algunos de los campos de energía humana, las biofrecuencias, del aura del cuerpo humano antes de la ruptura del enlace OEMII-cuerpo / Alma-BUAWA. En otras palabras, en un caso normal, parte de la energía del aura del difunto ayuda a iniciar el proceso del efecto de integración LEIYO de Alma-BUAWA.

Según algunos mediumes, este Aura promediaría 4 días terrestres para ser absorbido parcialmente en el efecto LEIYO y el resto se dispersaría como cualquier campo electromagnético.

Cuando una persona muere en gran angustia psíquica, su Aura emite un alto nivel de biofrecuencias anormalmente altas.

Este Aura anormalmente energética impregna un cierto nivel de energía en el marco 10D-OAWOO en el último segmento del rastro espacio-temporal grabado por el difunto. El Aura residual del difunto permanece atrapado en el rastro espacio-temporal.

LA AURA RESIDUAL

El aura residual del fallecido se bloquea en el arrastre espacio-temporal y, por otro lado, también se detiene el proceso de integración del BUAWA. El Aura residual permanece vinculado a BUAWA. Aunque la integración del Alma está bloqueada, es probable que el Aura residual también esté vinculado al BB planetario, pero sin integración.

La hipótesis es que el efecto LEYIO de integrar BUAWA en el BB planetario no se realiza correctamente. En lugar de conectarse al BB planetario, la conexión se realiza con la niebla electrónica producida por el residuo de Aura sobre energizado por el cuerpo humano durante el incidente traumático.

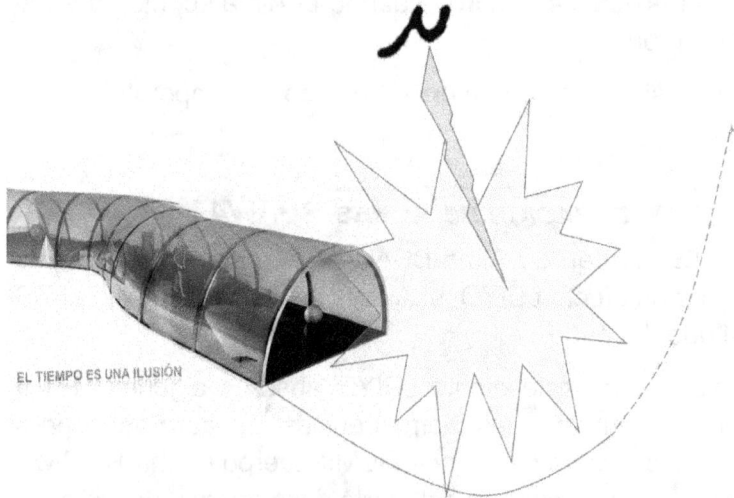

El aura residual del difunto permanece bloqueada en la estela espacio-temporal. La BUAWA no ha sido integrada al BB-planetario, permanece conectada al aura residual y la controla.

El enlace del BB planetario con el Aura-residual

El proceso de integración de BUAWA también se ha detenido. El Aura residual permanece vinculado a BUAWA. Aunque la integración del Alma está bloqueada, es posible que el Aura residual también esté vinculado al BB planetario. Sin embargo, este enlace está bloqueado o congelado ...

Esto explicaría que el proceso de integración de BUAWA en el BB planetario puede relanzarse más tarde.

El efecto de antena con el XOODII

Como hemos visto en el experimento del Proyecto de Conciencia Global, la niebla electrónica es una emisión de frecuencia que cubre todo el espectro electromagnético y crea un efecto de antena con el XOODII. Es este tipo de dispositivo que probablemente se utilizó para el cronovisor.

También se puede configurar otro arreglo para los experimentos de recepción de transcomunicación utilizando un viejo televisor analógico sin antena y conectado a una cámara. La televisión produce una niebla, la nieve en la pantalla, y la cámara filma en reinjeyecion que empañan la televisión. Este bucle larsene podrá desplegarse hasta el infinito y capturar flujos del BB planetario (en conexión con el BUAWA integrado) transmitido a través del XOODII hasta el televisor.

Sin embargo, no se excluye que un Aura residual pueda interferir produciendo una resonancia, directamente en el bucle larsene ...

Vida de fantasma

El Aura residual permanece atado al BUAWA, siempre que el Alma-BUAWA no reciba la energía necesaria para su integración en el BB planetario ...

El plasma frío que probablemente sea Aura residual debe mantener su nivel de energía mediante la absorción de energía asimilada por él: biofrecuencias humanas. Es el fantasma activo del difunto.

Podríamos decir que el par Aura-residual / BUAWA es una especie de OEMMII AÏOOYA AMMIÈ, un humano incorpóreo. Si tiene suficiente energía, este fantasma puede continuar evolucionando fuera del camino grabado por el OEMMII en el espacio-tiempo.

El par Aura-residual / BUAWA bloqueado en el espacio-tiempo podrá aprovechar una antena, un OEMMII medium, para mostrarse en varias proyecciones. Puede hacer proyecciones masicas, de volúmenes, holográficas o ambos en casos extremos ...

Las proyecciones en modo de ahorro de energía serán una de las formas posibles de producir un ORB (*consulte el subcapítulo ORBS*).

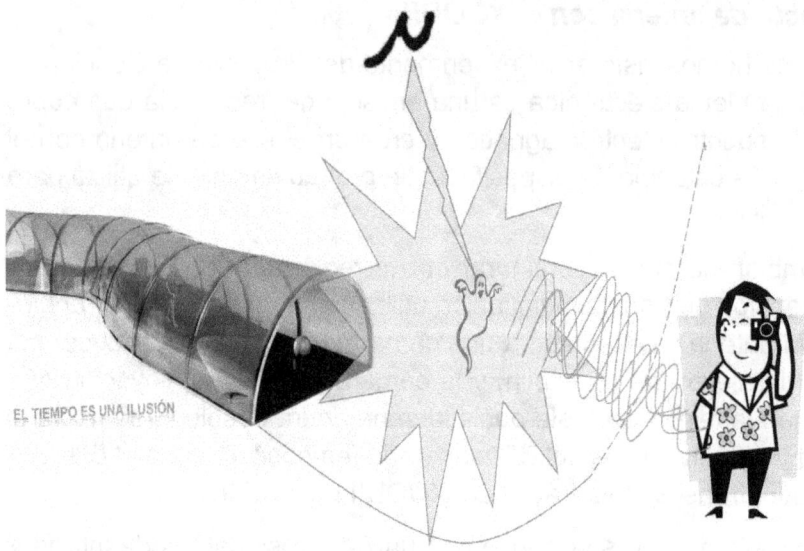

El aura residual vinculada a la BUAWA aumenta su nivel energético mediante la absorción de biofrecuencias humanas. Este es el 'fantasma' activo del difunto.

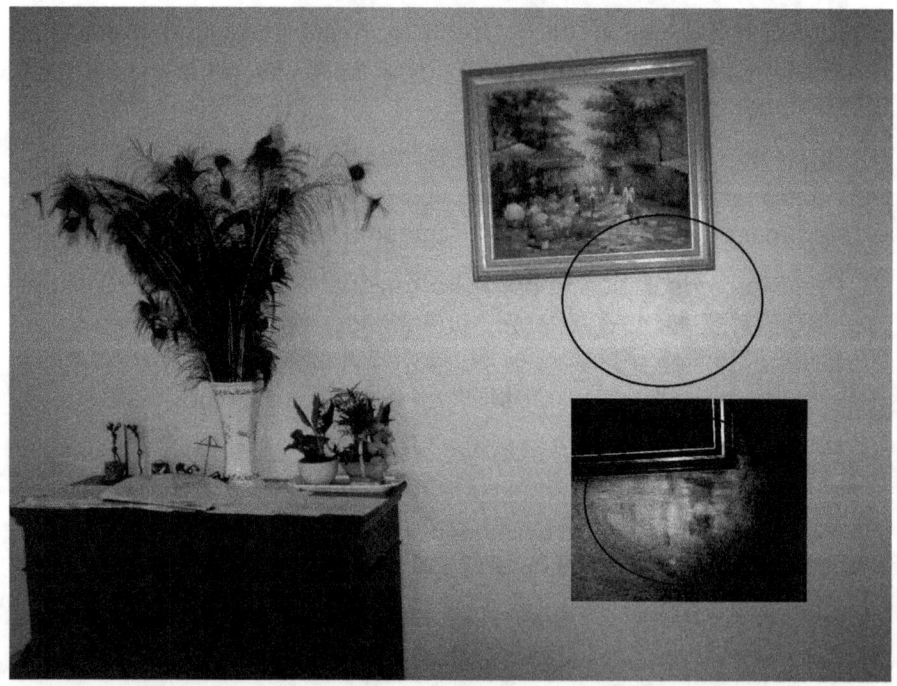

La Penne sur Huveaune — Francia — foto © Michel Marcel

Esta foto aparentemente inocuo no lo es. el flash reverbera una tarea que solo es visible en la foto digital. Una simple mejora del contraste y el brillo muestra que la anomalía proviene de la pared detrás del tablero.

El examen de la superficie de la pared es perfectamente suave, la luz de pastoreo no tiene efecto, las mediciones a posteriori en el infrarrojo y en el ultravioleta no darán resultado, no se detectará ningún campo electromagnético.

La historia comenzó con la solicitud a un médium por parte del dueño del lugar. Estaba preocupado de notar regularmente que las sillas de la casa se habían movido durante la noche ... En la casa, el médium indica estar conectado con el espíritu de una persona martirizada y arrojada a un pozo al final de la segunda Guerra Mundial. El pozo se identificará bajo una losa de la bodega de la casa. Se enciende una grabadora en una habitación de la casa, luego el medium trabaja para desconectar el Aura residual en el sótano. La grabación entregará un mensaje de agradecimiento al medium. El ingeniero investigador en electrónica y mediciones físicas, Michel Marcel, será empujado inconscientemente a irse sin ninguna razón racional en la sala de estar del propietario para tomar la foto presentada al lado.

INTERPRETACIÓN DEL CASO

Este hermoso estudio de caso clásico, tratado perfectamente en el campo es ampliamente generalizable a muchos eventos similares, se puede explicar con la teoría propuesta. Parece que el Aura residual tiene suficiente energía para moverse y hacer proyecciones sobre las sillas haciendo demasificación por efecto leiyo para señalar su presencia al propietario. Este reacciona bien y juiciosamente solicita la ayuda de un médium.

La intervención del medium trae suficiente energía para reiniciar el proceso de integración del Alma-BUAWA al BB planetario. Esto tiene la consecuencia de desconectar el Aura residual de la zona de impregnación inicial y mueve al salon antes del proceso de integración.

Las mediciones se realizan después de la integración del Aura residual o después de salir del salon. Esto puede explicar que las otras mediciones no dan resultado.

ORBS Y PROYECCIONES DE ANIMALES

A veces, los ORBS parecen presentar figuras de animales o informes de proyecciones holográficas de mascotas. Según las indicaciones de los Ummitas, los animales no tienen conexión con un BUAWA. Sin embargo, indirectamente, integran el Meta-Cerebro BB planetario.

El BUUAWE BIAEEI global contiene información sobre las percepciones y procesos mentales de los seres superiores humanos OEMMII. Un humano unido a un animal doméstico volverá al Meta-Cerebro BB planetario con su Alma-BUAWA con enormes cantidades de información que caracteriza a la mascota, su imagen, sus sonidos, sus percepciones afectivas, etc.

Cuando el Alma-BUAWA del humano fallecido integra el Meta-Cerebro, encontrará toda la información de este entorno, incluida la de la mascota ...

La inteligencia del animal es puramente neurocortical, que llega hasta los primates australopitecinos, por lo que ya está muy evolucionada ... En el caso del perro, su información de percepción ambiental se encuentra en el Meta-Cerebro BB Planetario a través de los transmisores de criptón intracelular.

El animal que ha vuelto a ensamblar corrientes de percepciones ambientales a través de los BAYODUU de sus celulas. Este flujo se completa con la información transmitida por el dueño del animal. La agregación de información personal del Alma-BUAWA integrada del maestro fallecido, acumulada con la información complementaria múltiple, hace que su maestro fallecido pueda ver un Alma del perro seudo-integrada.

El Alma-BUAWA integrado del maestro fallecido continuará acumulando información para siempre. Mientras que los datos del perro estarán completos y terminados dentro del BB planetario.

POSESIONES

A veces, durante las sesiones de SIJA en particular, el flujo proveniente de un Alma-BUAWA permanece conectado a la persona que lo recibe. Las tradiciones populares hablan de posesión.

La ruptura del flujo requiere un suministro energético que parece ser capaz de prodigar a ciertas personas, generalmente llamadas exorcistas. Es una contribución de violentas bio-frecuencias de energía. Otras personas que están más calificadas como médiums operan mediante una contribución de bio-frecuencias de energía blanda a través de encantamientos u oraciones.

En el caso de que el Aura residual permanezca vinculado al BUAWA, la ruptura del enlace permitirá la reconexión del BUAWA al BB planetario. Desaparición del aura residual por dispersión energética como cualquier campo electromagnético.

EL POLTERGEIST

El poltergeist es principalmente un efecto sobre las masas que parece ser generado por un aura residual.

Como hemos visto con los efectos de la transcomunicación instrumental, funciona mediante resonancias e inducciones electromagnéticas. Esto entre dispositivos electrónicos y dispositivos electromagnéticos inductivos o resonancias con frecuencias emitidas por la actividad cerebral humana, o incluso por la emisión de frecuencias de Aura-residual. Por lo tanto, este Aura residual podría generar este tipo de resonancias e inducciones electromagnéticas, y tal vez también un microefecto LEIYO que generó una relativa demasificación, es decir, un efecto de resonancia gravitacional en el objeto objetivo. Esto gracias a diferencias de potencial muy altas.

Específicamente, el Aura-residual produce un rango de frecuencias, más o menos pulsadas, que resuenan con un objeto o simplemente producen una descarga electromagnética o electrostática. Hace que se mueva o produzca ruido por deformación local de una estructura rígida. Estos son efectos de torsión de los ejes de las masas, como ya hemos presentado.

EL CASO DE LAS AURAS RESIDUALES EN LA ISLA DE PASCUA

Durante un viaje a la Isla de Pascua en 2014, el magnetista Gilbert Attard y Monique Aubergier se enfrentan a fenómenos atípicos que describen en el sitio de la asociación CROPS.

Frente a algunos MOAI, están sujetos a poderosos flujos telepáticos. A través de estos flujos, los MOAI les transmiten mucha información relacionada con la cultura ancestral de los Pascuans, y afirman que ellos mismos, los MOAI, están vivos y que se comunican entre sí. Los flujos de información se realizarán telepáticamente en francés y se canalizarán en Pascuan durante la presencia de la guía Pascuan. Gilbert Attard vocalizará directamente el flujo mental recibido en este idioma que no conoce ...

Mi suposición es que cada MOAI está rodeado o contiene un Aura residual.

Pero, no se trata de auras residuales de humanos terrestres .

Por el hecho, serían auras residuales de una exocivilización. Estos, muy enérgicos, podrían emitir flujos directamente sobre las auras humanas y así llegar a los centros de conexión mental. Es una conexión de auras residuales de una exocivilización con las auras de los humanos Gilbert Attard y Monique Aubergier. Es probable que el flujo también se pueda realizar a través de un canal telepático como en el caso de la canalización. Estos son auras residuales de la antigua exocivilización presentada y descrita anteriormente en la tradición Pascuane y los petroglifos de gigantes con cráneos largos.

Posiblemente, algunos individuos decidieron morir sin integrar el Meta-cerebro y dejar su Aura residual para mantener el lugar.

Esta hipótesis se ve reforzada por la experiencia de la cueva Vai Teka donde Gilbert Attard y Monique Aubergier detectarán auras residuales de esta exocivilización también protegen este lugar.

Las auras residuales de la exocivilización de los gigantes de cráneo largo parecen tener habilidades bastante diferentes de las auras residuales de los humanos terrestres. De hecho, un MOAI particular, el MOAI con los ojos, proyecta un flujo importante en Monique Aubergier. Esto tiene el efecto de aumentar su agudeza, probablemente en las frecuencias de los rayos UV altos y le permite a Monique Aubergier visualizar dispositivos extraterrestres. Ve múltiples ovnis que otros turistas del grupo no ven ...

Es probable que estos dispositivos estén encapsulados por un campo de derivación fotónica en las frecuencias del humano visible, para hacerlos invisibles para los humanos terrestres o una ligera torsion de aje de masas. Al aumentar la agudeza de Monique Aubergier, el MOAI en los ojos quería darle la oportunidad de ver estas máquinas. En este caso, 3 exocivilizaciones separadas están presentes actualmente en la Isla de Pascua.

LONGITUD DE ONDA DE LOS FANTASMAS

Sin hacer una historia exhaustiva de técnicas e investigaciones sobre biofrecuencias relacionadas con el aura humana, déjenos dar una pequeña idea. Fue en 1936 que las investigaciones de Roy Davis y Walter C. Rawls los llevaron a identificar el biomagnetismo humano. Muchos estudios y desarrollos tratarán este campo de biofrecuencias, pero hay otros. En 1939, el soviético Semyon Kirlian y su esposa Valentina toman fotografías que muestran un halo luminoso alrededor de un objeto sometido a alto voltaje.

Este halo luminoso se explica por el llamado efecto corona de la ionización gaseosa generada en las inmediaciones del objeto inmerso en un fuerte campo eléctrico continuo o alterno. Luego se crea un plasma y las cargas eléctricas se propagan al pasar iones a moléculas de gas neutro, el fluido se ioniza y se convierte en un plasma conductor. Este efecto también depende del diámetro del objeto, su condición de superficie, su densidad y la humedad del aire circundante. No se excluye que las resonancias de Schumann de 3 a 30 Hz del campo electromagnético terrestre también tengan un impacto en el efecto corona ...

En 1983, los investigadores indios Kejariwal, Chattopadhya y Choudhury mostraron que el efecto corona se produce fácilmente con frecuencias superiores a 100 kHz y un voltaje entre 15 y 20 kV.

Se han inventado muchos dispositivos para medir las frecuencias de los campos eléctricos humanos. La frecuencia normal de actividad eléctrica del cerebro está entre 0 y 100 Hz con máximos en el primer tercio de la banda. La de los músculos aumenta con frecuencia alrededor de 225 Hz, y las mediciones tomadas en el corazón dan alrededor de 250 Hz, pero este es el techo de esta actividad eléctrica asociada con las funciones biológicas. Tenga en cuenta que en peces eléctricos las frecuencias también son del orden de 250 Hz.

Como mencionamos anteriormente, Valérie Hunt utilizó un electromiógrafo, que es una técnica de diagnóstico que utiliza corrientes eléctricas. Las biofrecuencias del Aura oscilaron entre 100 y 1600 Hz. Además, en lugar de emanar del cerebro, corazón o músculo, esta actividad eléctrica se intensificó en áreas tradicionalmente asociadas con los chakras. También descubrió que cada color detectado en el aura de una persona correspondía a una curva de frecuencia que aprendió a asociar con él y cuyo osciloscopio dio una traducción en la pantalla. Además, ocho medios podrían comparar simultáneamente sus percepciones con las de sus colegas y la trama generada por el osciloscopio.

La emisión y transmisión de información a través de biofrecuencias humanas también es un hecho establecido en múltiples longitudes de onda. En 1962, la profesora Anna Gurwitsch, gracias al uso del fotomultiplicador confirma la existencia de biofotones. Las obras continúan con Terence Quickenden, Shane Que Hee en 1974. Fritz-Albert Popp, inventor del término, define los biofotones por la intensidad de su emisión en la superficie del tejido vivo, que es del orden de 10 a 1000 fotones por centímetro cuadrado y por segundo. La magnitud típica de los biofotones está en los espectros visible y ultravioleta, y los biofotones están involucrados en el metabolismo intracelular.

Es posible que los flujos de información intracelular, química, magnética, eléctrica, escalar y fotónica sean más o menos redundantes para el funcionamiento seguro de todo este metabolismo altamente sofisticado, que requiere una gran cantidad de interacciones coordinadas ... Estos mecanismos resilientes generalmente se utilizan en control industrial y tecnologías de control ...

Imagenes de las auras residuales pueden ser capturados por cámaras digitales. Además, en general, la energía producida por las auras residuales inhibe los flashes de fotorresistencia de sulfuro de cadmio. Esto significa que estos hologramas devuelven frecuencias en ultravioleta o infrarrojo.

Los niños ven las proyecciones de características más fácilmente que los adultos. La curva de eficiencia espectral de los niños de 2 meses de edad en comparación con la de los adultos (Dobson 1976) muestra que el bebé tiene una mayor sensibilidad a las longitudes de onda cortas (de 400 a 500 nm) de 0.3 unidades logarítmicas. que en adultos

Parece que los perros y gatos que ven en el Ultravioleta, también perciben la energía producida por las auras residuales.

Espectros infrarrojos y ultravioleta de fotorresistencias en cámaras digitales

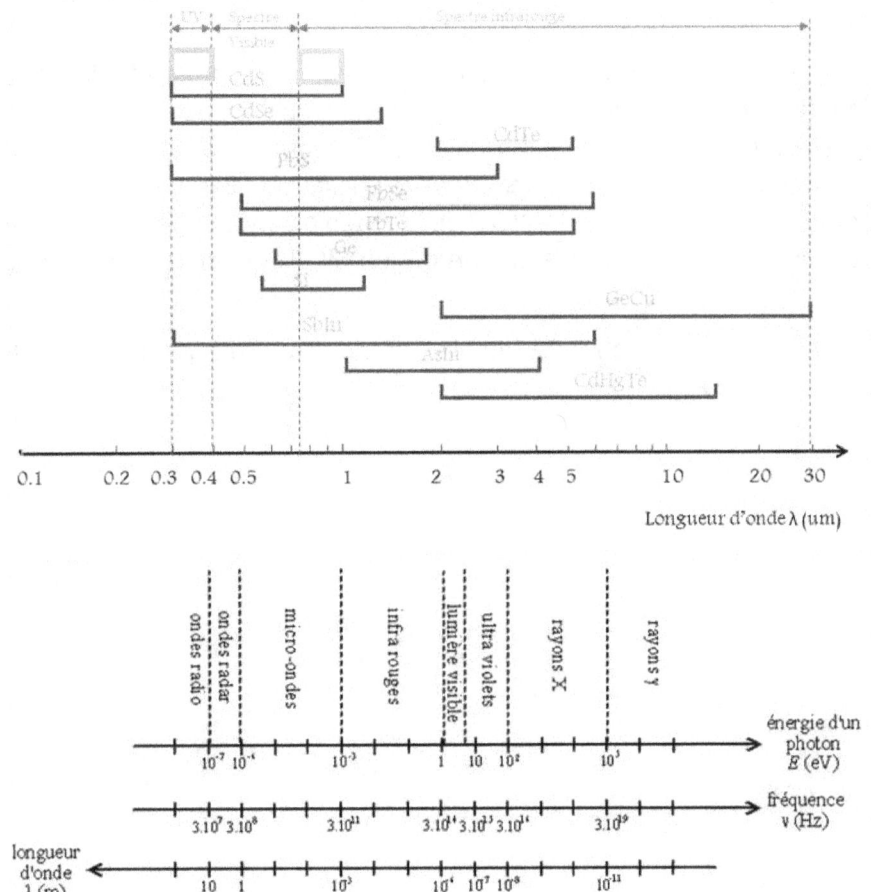

Biofrecuencias escalares?

Por lo tanto, vemos con estos sistemas de medición múltiple que el aura humana y el aura residual son al menos parcialmente detectables y medibles.

Sospechamos que estos residuos de Auras también producen biofrecuencias escalares, cuyos efectos son llamados LEIYO por nuestros amigos de UMMO. Estas biofrecuencias escalares permitirían que las torsiones o la inclinación de los ejes dimensionales causen diversos fenómenos, como la demasificación de los objetos, generalmente llamada psicoquinesis, etc.

En el caso que mencionamos anteriormente sobre Gilbert Attard y Monique Aubergier en la Isla de Pascua, la tradición Pascuane afirma que los MOAI se mudaron de la cantera del volcán a su lugar de instalación, ellos solos y de pie.

Mi idea es que los Pascuans hicieron canciones rituales que sirvieron como portadores para la emisión de biofrecuencias escalares. Lo que llaman el Mana. Algunos Pascuans lo tienen. Debido a los ritmos de los salmos, las biofrecuencias escalares resonarían y producirían giros del eje OAWOO de la masa del MOAI, permitiendo su movimiento en pequeños saltos. Algunos MOAI pesan 250 toneladas ...

Cabe señalar que Mana también es una facultad conocida y utilizada en África.

Almacenar información en el camino espacio-temporal es poten-cialmente eterno. El aura residual puede permanecer atrapado por mucho tiempo. La información emitida por las biofrecuencias de una persona, cualquiera que sea su estado, también puede almacenarse potencialmente en las estructuras cristalinas de los minerales. El alma-cenamiento es muy estable, se puede mantener durante períodos muy largos.

Diagrama de flujos holográficos: almacenamiento y lectura.

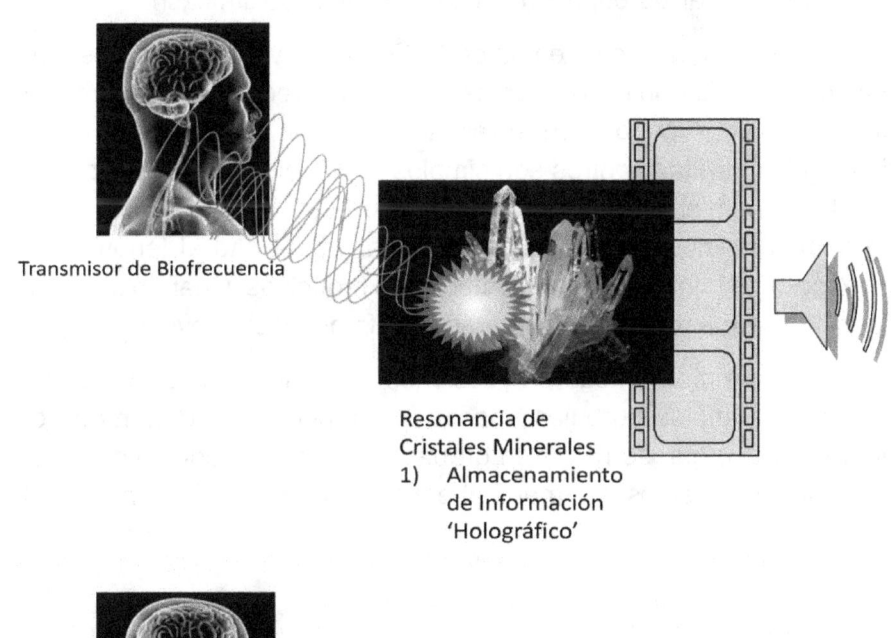

Transmisor de Biofrecuencia

Resonancia de
Cristales Minerales
1)   Almacenamiento
      de Información
      'Holográfico'

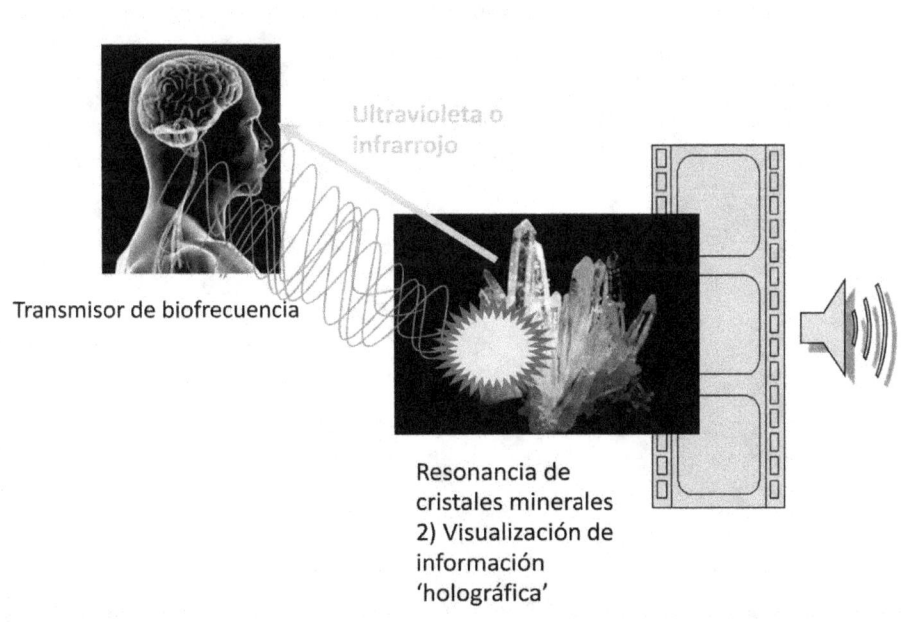

Transmisor de biofrecuencia

Ultravioleta o
infrarrojo

Resonancia de
cristales minerales
2) Visualización de
información
'holográfica'

Los ORBs

La llegada de cámaras con sensores digitales ha sido acompañada por fenómenos de reverberación de la luz sobre el polvo y diversas aberraciones cromáticas. Sin embargo, estas causas no explican la naturaleza de todas las observaciones.

Por ejemplo, en un área cerrada, sin la presencia de polvo en las fotos tomadas en una habitación vacía, no hay ORB. Cuando en la sala hay personas que realizan actividades psíquicas compatibles, puede manifestar burbujas en los disparos incluso sin flash.

La hipótesis es que este tipo de ORB son proyecciones que se forman de acuerdo con los diferentes tipos de proyecciones presentadas anteriormente. Algunos son el resultado de una proyección a través de un relé individual y otros son simples proyecciones holográficas de un almacenamiento de minerales ... Pero estas proyecciones tienen en común tener un bajo nivel de energía. Esto limita el fenómeno a proyecciones mínimas, a manifestaciones reducidas. Cuando se usa el flash, la energía reverberada impregna el fotosensor y revela su forma.

Encontraremos ambas proyecciones que dan caras de baja definición que simples burbujas opacas, pero incluso en este modo de ahorro de energía, se registran grabaciones de transcomunicaciones TCI y algunos medios informan haber estado en conexión con el ORB.

Ejemplo de varias proyecciones - la del centro se amplía - septiembre de 2012 en la Capilla de San Jaume en Carcès - Francia -

foto © Mylène Marcel

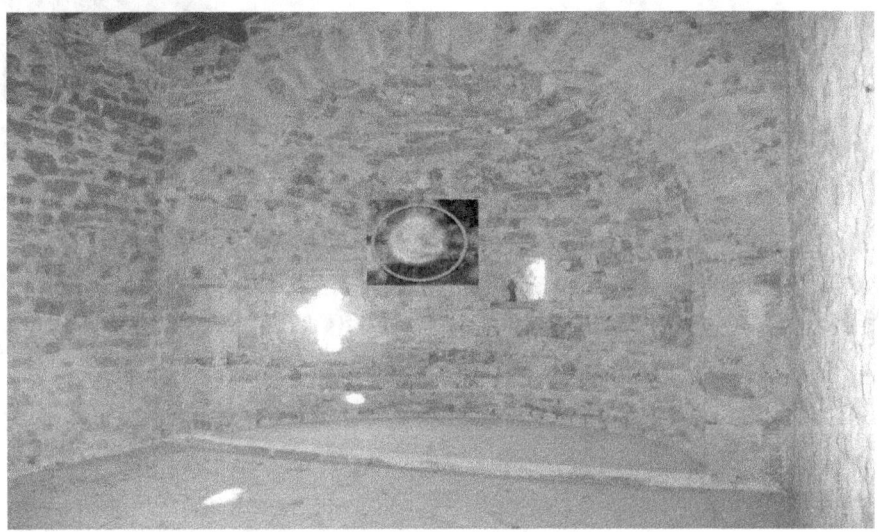

CÍRCULO DE CULTIVOS Y FANTASMAS

Mis amigos Nancy Talbott y Chris Cooper se pusieron en contacto conmigo para colaborar en los casos de Crop Circle, después de un caso de fotografías de varios hologramas con varios personajes, incluidos los de un E.T. índigo azul y una nave espacial.

¿Estos hologramas fueron hechos por nuestros amigos del espacio exterior? Por ejemplo, ¿los creadores de Crop Circles que identificamos en Presence, UFOs, Crop Circles y Exocivilizations?

¿Hubo alguna conexión con cristales de hidromagnesita pura o dolomita encontrados en algunas formaciones?

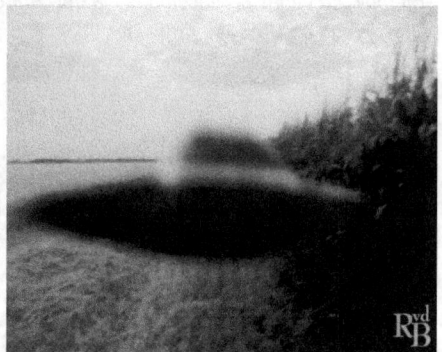

www.robbertvandenbroeke.com et www.bltresearch.com

Todas las fotos que se muestran aquí fueron tomadas con la cámara de Nancy Talbott en compañía del médium Robbert van den Broeke.

Por lo tanto, supuse que los hologramas resultan del almacenamiento de información en cristales de hidromagnesita. Pero, solo un lugar estaba en este caso. Luego, asumimos que los hologramas estaban relacionados con los Círculos de Cultivo. Pero muchas fotos están bien fuera de las formaciones. Le pedí a los especialistas de nuestro equipo que analizaran y compararan la imagen azul índigo de E.T. y la de los fabricantes de Crop Circles que identificamos en Presence, UFOs, Crop Circles y Exocivilizations. Pero no son los mismos personajes.

Concluyo que es la presencia del medio Robbert van den Broeke la causa de estas proyecciones. Entonces no hay conexión con el Crop Circle, ni con nuestros amigos del espacio exterior.

EXPERIMENTA LA MUERTE INMINENTE O NDE

Las EMI o Near Dead Experience es una prueba del modelo cosmológico propuesto.

En este estado, las biofrecuencias cerebrales se detienen, pero el complejo de átomos de criptón OEMBUAWA continúa recibiendo suficiente energía para continuar funcionando y comienza un flujo de integración LEIYO de Alma-BUAWA a BB. A partir de la explicación de un caso concreto, veremos que pueden ocurrir dos fenómenos distintos.

En 1991, en Phoenix, Arizona, el caso de Pamela Reynolds fue completamente documentado durante un procedimiento quirúrgico que la colocó en un estado de muerte clínica durante más de una hora. El Dr. Spetzler establece un paro circulatorio hipotérmico a 15,5 ° C y drena la sangre para tratar el aneurisma. En estas condiciones, el cuerpo normalmente puede sobrevivir entre 30 y 60 minutos.

Pamela Reynolds informa estar fuera de su cuerpo y ver toda la escena desde arriba. El cirujano Robert Spetzler testifica: en este momento de la operación, Pamela Reynolds estaba clínicamente muerta ... pero el complejo de átomos de criptón OEMBUAWA continúa recibiendo suficiente energía para continuar funcionando.

Al principio, el aura de Pamela Reynolds se separa de su cuerpo. Su Aura permanece conectada a su Alma-BUAWA y BB-planetario. El aura captura un conjunto de frecuencias, incluidas las biofrecuencias del médico y las personas de la plataforma técnica quirúrgica. El aura ve, escucha y transmite los datos a su Alma-BUAWA y al BB planetario.

En una segunda vez, el aura comienza la integración del Alma-BUAWA del sujeto al planetario BB del que depende. El Alma-BUAWA puede entonces comenzar a intercambiar información con otros Alma-BUAWA ya integrados en el planetario BB.

El BB planetario decide qué información quiere integrar. Cuando ya no hay una biofrecuencia cerebral, pero a pesar de todo el complejo de átomos de criptón del OEMBUAWA todavía está operativo, es posible que el BB planetario rechace la conexión a un Alma-BUAWA e intente para reconectarla a su cuerpo. Si la reconexión tiene éxito es porque el cuerpo ha recuperado suficiente energía y las estructuras neurológicas del cerebro están operativas, el sujeto reanudará su conciencia terrenal. De lo contrario, desafortunadamente el sujeto seguirá siendo vegetativo con un OEMBUAWA operativo, pero las estructuras cerebrales no funcionarán.

Algún tiempo después de la muerte de su padre, mi amigo Frédéric comienza a sufrir la cadera izquierda. Tanto es así, que en poco tiempo solo se mueve dolorosamente con un bastón y un corsé. No tiene 40 años y los exámenes médicos exhaustivos que aprueba son formales: no tiene absolutamente nada en la cadera y está en perfecto estado de salud ...

¿Es un dolor psicosomático debido a la muerte de su padre?

El dolor es real e incapacitante. Philippe Douillet, nuestro amigo experto en geometría, también tiene habilidades para percibir auras y residuos de auras. Encuentra que una Aura-residual está conectada a la cadera izquierda de Frédéric. También emana de esta aura residual información. Esta sería la manifestación de una persona que murió durante la Guerra de Crimea alrededor de 1853-1854. Según los informes, el fallecido era un soldado de la fuerza expedicionaria enviada por Louis-Napoleón Bonaparte, que recibió una explosión de uno de los primeros proyectiles huecos y explosivos disparados en esta ocasión. Un destello habría golpeado a la víctima en la cadera izquierda y le habría causado la muerte.

El aura residual tenía la forma de un quiste conmemorativo que emanaba de la parte posterior de la cadera izquierda de Frédéric. Philippe lo describe como un hongo de moho, un hongo de 70 a 80 cm de largo con una cabeza en su extremo, tan grande como 2 puños ... Aunque impalpable, Philip dice que la cabeza parece una madeja compacta de cuerdas pequeñas oscuro (color entre el betún y el chocolate muy oscuro), tan duro como una bola de hilo, pero hecho de muchas piezas. Cada pieza parece ser un recuerdo, un evento mal vivido. En la cultura védica esto también se llama residuo kármico.

Mi hipótesis es que la muerte violenta del soldado ha detenido clásicamente la integración del Alma en el BB. Pero, un contexto emocional particular, cuyos parámetros aún no se han establecido, habría estructurado el Aura residual en forma de un quiste de memoria. Este último está vinculado al alma del difunto y la conexión con BB se detuvo en su proceso de integración.

Aunque no tenemos información precisa sobre este tema, podemos imaginar que el aura residual del soldado podría haber permanecido en el campo de batalla, y por casualidad, habría encontrado una aura transportista. Tal vez un compañero que sobrevivió y luego se puso en contacto con la familia del difunto. Al hacerlo, el aura residual así transportada puede conectarse a un ser vivo familiar ... Pasando a través de las generaciones de una cerca a otra, este aura residual se uniría al padre de Frederic. En el momento de la muerte de este último, el Aura residual habría cambiado de portador. Frederic confirmará más tarde que uno de sus tíos bisabuelos murió durante la Guerra de Crimea ...

Finalmente, Philippe Douillet pudo transmitir suficiente energía a este Aura residual para que se separe de Frédéric y se desintegre en un proceso de reconexión normal del alma de este difunto. Philippe usará cuencos tibetanos cuyos armónicos servirán como ondas transportadoras por su capacidad de proyectar ondas bioescalares en el quiste conmemorativo cuyo trauma se reconoce y se libera al absorber suficiente energía para reiniciar su proceso de integración final en BB.

Cuando intuitivamente encontré el tazón correcto, el buen sonido de este tazón, la posición correcta, el ángulo correcto ... el quiste conmemorativo comenzó a desmoronarse. Para volverse menos compacto, menos opaco. Los diversos trozos de cuerda comenzaron a desmoronarse. De inmediato para tomar más espacio y volverse menos oscuro. El fenómeno continuó, las cuerdas divergían más y más entre sí, tomando más y más volumen ... Pero sin cambiar de posición una con respecto a la otra.

Y también se volvieron más y más luminosas.

Al principio, el quiste conmemorativo era tan grande como 2 puños, luego como un globo. Pasó del balonmano al baloncesto y la pelota de playa... Los cordones se volvieron no solo brillantes, sino también más transparentes. Al final, todo se vuelve tan grande y transparente que desaparece.

CONCLUSIÓN

La comunicación con los espíritus representados como un sujeto paranormal o metafísico se racionaliza utilizando el marco cosmológico descrito en los documentos del archivo UMMO.

Creemos que el núcleo amigdalar, la glándula pineal y los núcleos subtalicos son las zonas cerebrales clave en las conexiones de nuestro Ame-BUAWA con el planetario BB y con la emisión de biofrecuencias humanas.

Habría 3 clases principales de fenómenos:

• conexiones de las almas-BUAWA de los muertos integradas en el planetario BB que están en el origen de las proyecciones de biofrecuencia resonante

• Manifestaciones de auras residuales que también producen efectos de resonancia, producen los principales fantasmas y poltergeist.

• el almacenamiento holográfico en minerales que es visible por los efectos de radar de las biofrecuencias humanas, produce algunos ORBS y fantasmas

Todos los modelos de proyección son el resultado de los efectos LEIYO de la torsión del eje dimensional AOWOO. Proyecciones de masas, volúmenes o acumulativos. Todos estos fenómenos de proyecciones se expresan bajo el mismo término de fantasmas.

Los pocos modelos estándar que imaginé por prospectiva me han permitido dar un significado racional a todos los casos que me han sido presentados hasta ahora. Algunos casos son verdaderamente extraordinarios, se necesita una buena dosis de paciencia para mantener una mente abierta, tanto crítica como constructiva, para estudiar estos casos. Un marco de pensamiento racionalizado a través de la cosmología permite este enfoque de análisis. Al final, no es DIOS quien crea al Hombre a su imagen, sino el Hombre que llena el Meta-Cerebro Planetario con sus imágenes.

Podemos esperar que en las próximas décadas podamos tener los medios técnicos de experimentación de estas tesis en un marco público y civil ...

⊠

10

1 2 3 4 5 6 7 8 9 **10** 11 12

SECUESTROS Y MANIPULACIONES MENTALES

DIOS Y LAS EXOCIVILIZACIONES

En *Presence 1 - UFOs, Crop Circle y Exocivilizations* en 2007, presentamos una tabla de resumen detallada que describe 18 exocivilizaciones. Dado que la información adicional, también confirmada por nuestros amigos de UMMO, llegó a enriquecer nuestro conocimiento sobre este tema y desarolladas en *Presencia 4 - Hacia Un Nuevo Mundo ... Con Las Exocivilizaciones.*

En 2015, tenemos 23 exocivilizaciones instaladas en la Tierra o en la Luna. Como explicamos en la Presencia 1, sus visitas tienen varios objetivos científicos, como parte de una Pax Galactica que está en funcionamiento. Esto está garantizado por una (al menos) exocivilización muy antigua y altamente evolucionada (mucho más que las 23 exocivilizaciones que nos visitan) y garantiza nuestra seguridad cósmica general. En otras palabras, ninguna exocivilización puede invadir la Tierra o ejercer actividades bélicas hacia los terrícolas, ni hacia todo el planeta.

Como hemos visto parcialmente y siguiendo a nuestros amigos de UMMO, entre estos 23 ex-visitantes, los objetivos experimentales de nuestros visitantes son muy variados, y su impacto en la Tierra también.

Incluso si su comportamiento está dentro de los límites éticos permitidos en el marco de Pax Galactica, las percepciones de estos límites dependen de la psicología de nuestros visitantes.

El comportamiento de nuestros visitantes también dependerá en parte de su fisiología. Por ejemplo, algunos de ellos pueden tener una fisiología que absorbería las biofrecuencias humanas, haciendo que su contacto físico sea potencialmente peligroso para nosotros. Podríamos descargar como pilas vulgares ...

Pero, los efectos potencialmente más dañinos son más temibles de una psicología que resulta de un no dominio o reconocimiento del conjunto de objetos de la cosmología universal.

De hecho, todas las exocivilizaciones que controlan el panorama cosmológico que presentamos, necesariamente entendieron las interdependencias entre las exocivilizaciones. Esto se puede resumir como: Todo lo que es malo para nosotros es malo para otras exocivilizaciones.

Sin embargo, entre nuestras 23 razas de visitantes del espacio exterior, 3 de ellas no reconocen todos los objetos de esta cosmología. Veamos las implicaciones:

Como hemos visto en detalle, el conocimiento de la estructura del cosmosmos WAAM-WAAM es esencial para controlar el viaje interestelar. Pero eso no tiene un impacto obvio en la psique de nuestros visitantes.

Con respecto a WOA, DIOS, entre la infinidad de las ondas que este transmite en el Universo a través de los Meta-cerebros planetarios, difunde las leyes éticas. No reconocer esta entidad trascendente probablemente disminuye su impacto, pero no la percepción general de la ética que subyace. Por lo tanto, nuestros visitantes tienen su ética específica resultante del marco general. Es cierto que las 19 exocivilizaciones benevolentes que se encuentran en nuestro suelo se adhieren a este concepto. La mayoría de estos parecen practicar una metafísica o religión ritualizada en torno al concepto de Dios, probablemente en relación con su historia cultural. Esta es la evolución lógica para todos los humanos ... de todo el cosmos.

El conocimiento de AIIODII, el Absoluto Real, del XOODII WAAM, el cinturón intercósmico probablemente esté implícito en las civilizaciones itinerantes del cosmos. Por ejemplo, sin esto, los diversos sistemas de medición no podrían desarrollarse a un nivel avanzado.

El conocimiento de WAAM-UU, el Meta-Cerebro Cósmico y el cerebro planetario BUUAWE BIAEEI es un punto sensible. Permite en particular tener en cuenta las interacciones positivas o negativas de una civilización en otra a nivel cósmico. No dominar este aspecto, podría sugerirle a una exocivilización que sus acciones son independientes de los demás y, por lo tanto, que las experiencias en los demás no las impactan. Percibimos allí el riesgo de patinar ... Un desconocimiento de WAAM-U, el cosmos de Souls y BUAWA, Soul obviamente tendría los mismos riesgos ...

Por lo tanto, es uno de estos casos que concierne a 3 exocivilizaciones «hostiles» en nuestro suelo. Para 2 de ellos, pudimos sintetizar información más precisa. Primero veremos el caso de GOHOiens que están involucrados en un programa científico que incluye secuestros de tierras bajo acuerdos secretos, ilegales e ilegítimos con el Ejército de los EE. UU.

En el capítulo 12 de The Anunnaki and the Reptilians, discutiremos el papel probable de los 2— iens, a menudo mencionados en la confusión de rumores y desinformación bajo el término Reptilians.

Desarollaremos todavia mas este en *Presencia 4 —Hacia Un Nuevo Mundo ... Con Las Exocivilizaciones*.

LOS SECUESTROS

En *Presence 1 - Ovnis, Crop Circle y Exocivilisation*, informamos información de secuestro. La exocivilización de GOHOiens se realizó desde 1948, un estudio de fisiología y psicología en humanos terrestres, en gran parte en el territorio de los Estados Unidos. Desde entonces, parece que algunas otras exocivilizaciones tienen prácticas similares.

El estudio de fisiología en humanos terrestres se realizó sin lesiones en los sujetos. A diferencia de otras exocivilizaciones, los GOHOiens parecen no tener medios tecnológicos suficientes para llevar a cabo estudios fisiológicos con medios de análisis remoto. Esta doble experimentación en fisiología y psicología a largo plazo no pasó desapercibida, por las consecuencias del estudio psicológico realizado sobre los sujetos.

Ella está relacionada a través de numerosos testimonios relacionados con una exocivilización de cabeza pequeña con cabeza grande y ojos grandes. Sobre la base de la *Presencia 1: ovnis, Crop Circle y exocivilizaciones*, podemos estimar aproximadamente que el 70% de las exocivilizaciones son individuos pequeños o grandes. No pienso que sea la especie descrita por Budd Hopkins.

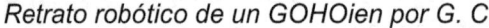

Retrato robótico de un GOHOien por G. C.

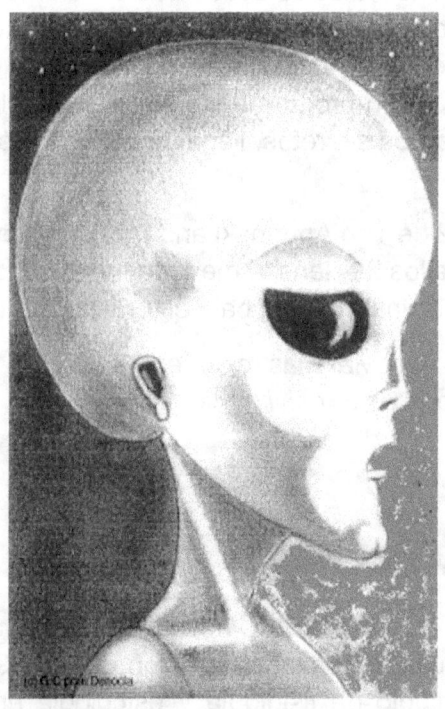

Sobre alrededor de mil casos, un número significativo de sujetos informa haber presenciado una observación de ovnis.

La hipnoterapeuta Yvonne Smith muestra que los sujetos tienen memorias estandarizadas.

Si bien el OVNI generalmente se describe como de unas pocas docenas de metros de diámetro, el sujeto describe una situación en la que habría sido conducido a enormes laboratorios dentro de la nave espacial. Los otros temas recurrentes son los del análisis médico y la creación de seres híbridos.

En un absoluto teórico, la compresión de volúmenes es posible para viajes intercósmicos, en condiciones muy particulares, pero los secuestrados están en nuestro marco dimensional terrestre convencional respondiendo a las leyes físicas clásicas.

La incoherencia del contenido de la memoria estandarizada con las dimensiones reales del tamaño de la máquina puede llevarnos a pensar que parte de la experiencia psíquica pudo haber sido transferir falsos recuerdos al cerebro del sujeto.

Podemos pensar que algunos de estos experimentos consisten principalmente en probar las habilidades de análisis crítico del sujeto en situaciones que plantean preguntas éticas ...

Esta implantación de falsos recuerdos estandarizados, esta memoria impregnada, se borra de la memoria consciente del sujeto después del experimento. Falta de suerte para los experimentadores del espacio exterior, las técnicas de hipnosis revelaron abducción y manipulación psíquica.

En casos puntuales, la memoria impregnada transmite al sujeto nuevos conocimientos o habilidades: habilidades para producir logros electrónicos atípicos mientras que la persona nunca ha tenido ningún conocimiento sobre este tema, habilidades para producir dibujos muy elaborados que antes, la persona nunca tuvo esta habilidad ...

Los secuestros verdaderos son probablemente menos numerosos de lo que muchos testimonios pueden sugerir, pero la impregnacion de la memoria parece ser utilizado con mucha frecuencia por varias exocivilizaciones. Aquí hay algunos ejemplos.

MEMORIA IMPREGNADA DE CONOCIMIENTOS

En 1996, Soissons en Francia, una estafette de la gendarmería realiza un recorrido nocturno por el campo. La estafette se para en el camino, incapaz de avanzar o retroceder, cerca de una potente luz detrás de un arbusto. Todos los gendarmes dicen que han permanecido conscientes, pero paralizados. Solo uno de ellos, Jean-François deja el vehículo y se va detrás del arbusto. No recordará nada, pero según sus colegas dejó al menos 30 minutos. A partir de ese momento, su vida ha cambiado, se ha sentido atraído por tecnologías que no conocía en absoluto: electrónica, motor, y parece haber adquirido espontáneamente el conocimiento de estas técnicas, sin ningún tipo de entrenamiento. ... Hizo ensamblajes electrónicos casi tomando componentes al azar, sin saber nada al respecto, sin saber por sí mismo por qué lo hacía. ¡Pero funcionó! Este gendarme neófito de ciencia y tecnología presentará varias patentes en el INPI. Perfeccionará de manera excepcional el motor Pantone con 87% de agua - ¡gasolina 13%! Patente No. 0902947 comprada y rápidamente enterrada por un fabricante de automóviles, que caerá en el dominio público en 2020 ... tal vez (preguntar a Papa Noel).

MEMORIA IMPREGNADA DE HABILIDADES

La Ciotat en Francia, 1976, Claude G. conduce en automóvil cerca de la montaña Lure en la noche. En la cima de una colina, una pelota muy luminosa despega cerca de su vehículo causando una sacudida y afectando al conductor con fuertes hormigueos y temblores. El conductor dice que simplemente continuó su camino.

Algún tiempo después, Claude está en su lugar de trabajo, a los 50 años sufre un problema de hernia de disco y no puede levantar cargas de más de 30 kg. Esta mañana, en el taller, con sus colegas, organiza una carga de bridas. Son ligeros, piensa, y los lleva a la punta de sus dedos en pares. Los otros colegas se detuvieron para guardar las bridas y mirarlo de manera extraña: cada brida pesa 34.5 kg. Claude lleva sin esfuerzo 138 kg de yemas de los dedos ... ¡Durante dos meses y medio, el sujeto podrá, concentrando unos segundos, levantar masas de hasta 950 kg!

Indicará que se forma una imagen en su cabeza y que comprende que puede levantar a las masas. Sus colegas mencionarán que Claude aparece en otro lugar cuando se da cuenta de estas acciones y él mismo no siempre recuerda claramente lo que hizo en sus presencia.

Al experimentar con la torsión de una barra de hierro de 26 mm de diámetro y hacer que un joven colega lo pruebe, descubrirán que Claude emite una fuerza que permitirá que su compañero de trabajo también gire la barra de metal.

Creemos que este fenómeno del «objeto de goma» es inducido por la demasificación parcial producida por las biofrecuencias emitidas por el sujeto.

No se encuentra ninguna explicación médica que explique las habilidades imposibles del sujeto..

MEMORIA IMPREGNADA DE CONOCIMIENTOS Y HABILIDADES

En una zona rural alrededor de Salers en Francia, 1994, Gerard C. y su familia observaron repetidamente máquinas esféricas cerca de sus hogares. Poco después, aunque no estudió botánica, Gerard descubre, sin explicar por qué, que conoce el nombre de cualquier planta ... Mejor, inconscientemente siente exactamente dónde crece la planta. a pocos kilómetros de distancia ...

Gerard, su esposa y sus hijos contarán sueños u observaciones extraños durante varios años, algunos similares en todos los aspectos con Budd Hopkins, John Mack o Yvonne Smith.

ESTADOS DE CONCIENCIA MODIFICADOS

Una primera dificultad es que diferentes fenómenos se designan con el mismo término OBE revoltijo (experimento fuera del cuerpo):

• fenómenos endógenos, producidos solo por el cerebro

• Fenómenos exógenos con datos del Meta-cerebro o Alma-BUAWA que interfieren

• o bien, fenómenos relacionados con el Aura

Según mi amigo Christopher Blake, él mismo confrontado con experiencias desestabilizadoras, muchos casos de secuestro no están relacionados con exocivilizaciones. La persona vive una experiencia para la cual no tiene referencias personales o conocimiento para analizar el fenómeno y colocarlo en un ambiente seguro, y ponerle fin. La experiencia se informa al comienzo del sueño (parálisis hipnagógica) o al momento del despertar (parálisis hipnopómpica), por lo que está presente en momentos de despertar y dormir. La persona está paralizada, incapaz de realizar movimientos voluntarios y al mismo tiempo consciente de estar en esta situación. Para vivir esto, no es necesario presentar trastornos clínicos, son condiciones bastante comunes, pero la intensidad varía según las personas. Estos estados son comunes porque están relacionados con el desarrollo del sistema nervioso y el cerebro, un fenómeno de fisiología cerebral y glandular.

En este estado particular de estar entre la vigilia y el sueño, la persona percibirá su habitación y escuchará sonidos, sentirá respiraciones, sensaciones de elevación, vibraciones, hormigueo eléctrico, luces, etc. Lo más perturbador serán las sensaciones donde sentimos que las sábanas se mueven, que la cama puede moverse, una presencia percibida como una amenaza, sensaciones de tocar el cuerpo y / o el cuerpo, fuertes presiones, como si alguien se acostaria sobre nosotros mismos, o que queria entrar en nosotros mismos, incluso ver intentos o relaciones sexuales. Todos los sentidos son estimulados. Su vivacidad y duración lo distinguen de un sueño habitual y forman una experiencia que cuestiona. Según el escenario, las variaciones de la experiencia irán del miedo al pánico, al estado de éxtasis o placer para los más agradables. Es muy difícil que una persona no se asuste por esta experiencia tan real y, por lo tanto, inevitablemente traumática. Por lo tanto, la consulta con un terapeuta puede presentar el diagnóstico de una experiencia traumática.

Encontramos todo este panel de observaciones en estados modificados de conciencia, las famosas experiencias fuera del cuerpo o OBE (Experimento fuera del cuerpo). Estas experiencias también se experimentan en el momento de conciliar el sueño, despertar o experimentar durante el sueño de lo que se llama sueño lúcido. Estos fenómenos se conocen desde hace cientos de años en diferentes tradiciones espirituales y especialmente en las prácticas del yoga del sueño y la clara luz del budismo tibetano y Dzogchen Bon. Algunos practicantes los buscan como un juego o como una práctica indispensable en los caminos de la iluminación o la alquimia interna, que requieren precisamente un trabajo en los niveles de conciencia. El sueño asocia funciones endocrianas, tiroideas y nerviosas relacionadas con los ritmos cerebrales. Según el Dr. Lefebure, las salidas fuera del cuerpo se explican por la fisiología cerebral, ejercicios especiales que permiten la sincronización entre hemisferios, algunos de los cuales actúan en los centros de despertar y dormir, lo que permite experimentar este doble estado de conocimiento. Soñamos, actuamos en consecuencia y también vivimos fuera del cuerpo. Este término es inapropiado ya que en realidad es una exploración de niveles de conciencia de los cuales nuestra realidad es parte. Entonces no estás afuera, sino adentro.

La dificultad del análisis radica en la extrema dificultad que tenemos al determinar si estos procesos cognitivos son pura y estrictamente endógenos, producidos únicamente por el cerebro y las funciones endocrinas, o si los datos del Meta-cerebro o Alma-BUAWA interfieren ...

En cuanto a mí, tomo en consideración el término OBE (Experimento fuera del cuerpo) solo para designar la desconexión del Aura del cuerpo, especialmente durante la ECM / NDE.

CONCLUSIÓN

La impregnacion de la memoria parece ser utilizado por varias exocivilizaciones para experimentos psíquicos que desafortunadamente contribuyen a mantener una psicosis comprensible y una sensación de xenofobia contra las exocivilizaciones.

Estas prácticas experimentales son reprensibles e inmorales. Sin embargo, no debemos perder de vista el hecho de que estas son solo manipulaciones psíquicas con recuerdos falsos con fines experimentales sin intención de dañar.

El principal problema es especialmente que se trata de los programas científicos de secuestros terrestres en el marco de acuerdos secretos, ilegales e ilegítimos, con el brazo armado del sistema oligárquico, el ejército estadounidense. Al final, los terrícolas así vendidos representan aproximadamente el 95% de los casos de secuestro.

No hay duda de que algunas exocivilizaciones tienen las capacidades técnicas o mentales para realizar manipulaciones psíquicas extremadamente poderosas.

Sin embargo, según mi apreciación personal, creo que estas impregnaciones de memoria de origen exógeno son muy menores en comparación con las numerosas alteraciones psíquicas de origen terrestre, como lo son, por ejemplo, los sueños lúcidos que son muy frecuentes ...

Por lo tanto, el análisis de los testimonios de quienes describen un fenómeno de abducción debe hacerse teniendo en cuenta los mecanismos psíquicos endógenos naturales y los recuerdos falsos de las impregnaciones de memoria. Esto cambia enormemente la percepción general de este tema ...

☒

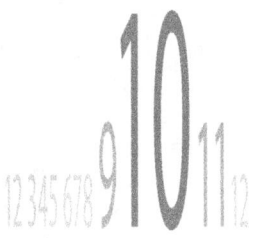

Aparición y evolución del hombre

Dadas las hipótesis sobre el surgimiento de los vivos, debemos necesariamente reconsiderar nuestra visión del surgimiento del hombre. Hay Hombre cuando el encéfalo de un homínido puede conectarse a su BUAWA, una especie de contenedor externo del perfil psíquico, capaz de capturar las leyes morales cosmicas UAA emitidas por la entidad WOA e implementadas por el BB- planetario. El OEMII, es decir, el hombre tomado en su única dimensión fisiológica, está asociado con su BUAWA y se convierte en un OEMMII involucrado en el gran ciclo cibernético de la Evolución del Cosmos.

El surgimiento de Homo Habilis

Tenemos una indicación clara sobre la aparición del primer OEMMII que condujo al Homo sapiens, es el Homo habilis. Antes, ningún hombre, sino simples homínidos.

En ausencia de medios técnicos de análisis para identificar la presencia de un BAYIODUU en el cerebro del Homo habilis, solo podemos suponer que su conexión con BUAWA y su receptividad a las leyes cósmicas de la UAA indujeron un comportamiento deísta.

Entre aproximadamente 1 millón de años y hace 300,000 años, el Homo erectus, el probable descendiente del Homo habilis, deja rastros de probables rituales de canibalismos que generalmente están relacionados con una teología.

En cuanto al Homo sapiens neanderthalensis, su naturaleza OEMMII es clara con ritos funerarios bien identificados.

Puedes verlo en el gráfico. Si, en OYAAGAA, una rama de protomamíferos se ha ramificado en ramas sucesivas de mamíferos, si uno de estos filamentos se transformó en primates, si de ellos derivaron los diversos homínidos hasta que llegaron a Homo habilis y ramas posteriores, esto se debió a que los mecanismos y patrones de selección BB aceleraron la transformación en esta derivación del genotipo.

Tarde o temprano, los otros animales habrían terminado convirtiéndose en seres muy similares al Homo sapiens. En otras palabras: si los OEMII de la Tierra desaparecieran junto con los pongides, cercopithecus, platyrrhinians e incluso el resto de los mamíferos, las clases restantes eventualmente se cristalizarían (gracias a una ramificación más acelerada al principio) en otros nuevos OEMII.

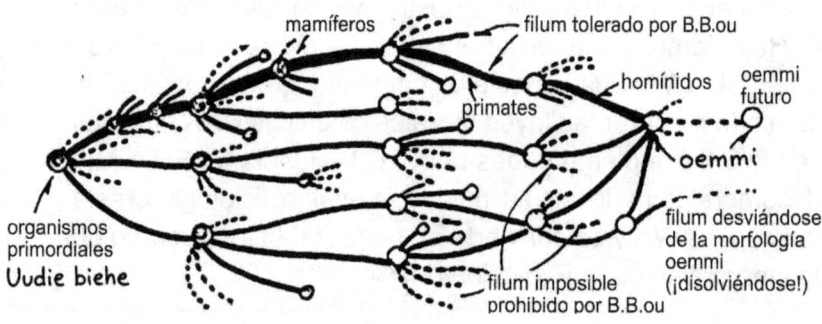

Desde 2003, la mayoría de los científicos consideran dos especies separadas: Homo sapiens y Homo neanderthalensis. Sin embargo, en Europa, según un estudio de 2010 realizado por el Proyecto del Genoma de Neanderthal, un mestizaje muy parcial entre sapiens y neanderthalensis hace 50 000 a 100 000 años, lo que permite a este último participar del 1 al 4% en el genoma de los europeos actuales. Entre los últimos 100,000 años y los últimos 10,000 años de cultura protohistórica, el conocimiento de la evolución del Homo sapiens es muy desigual y poco conocido. Como resultado, se han formulado muchas hipótesis sobre la posible interferencia de exocivilizaciones en la evolución del Homo sapiens.

Hemos visto en la Presencia 1 - Ovnis, Círculo de Cultivos y Exocivilizaciones los elementos de la ética cósmica que hemos llamado Pax Galactica que excluyen la ingerencia sociocultural que no es vital o inadecuada con la civilización receptora. Además, la estructura cosmológica de las interconexiones entre el planetario BB hace que la cosmobiofísica sea interdependiente de todos los OEMMII humanos del cosmos. Entonces, el vínculo entre una humanidad y su planetario BB excluye definitivamente la posibilidad de una interferencia en la estructura genética de otra humanidad con fines de hibridación, por ejemplo ...

Sin embargo, no hay nada que impida intercambios culturales muy puntuales y localizados en el pasado entre exocivilizaciones y pueblos de la tierra, si pudieran recibir cierta información adaptada a su estado de desarrollo.

Es desgarrador ver cuánto es fuerte la idea recibida de que el viejo Homo sapiens era una estúpida piel de animal. Por el contrario, es bastante probable que muchas culturas ancestrales hayan sido mucho más maduras en ciertos aspectos de su desarrollo en comparación con las culturas del mundo actual ...

La mitología sumeria ha dado lugar a numerosos escritos que evocan a los ANUNNAKI, los reptilianos, el planeta Nibiru, los Pleyadianos. Algunos escritos evocan estos temas seriamente mientras respetan los escritos sumerios originales, otros bajo las fantasías de algunos escritores ...

La popularización de estos temas también los ha convertido en temas inspiradores para literatura fantástica o ciencia ficción ... Esto crea mucha confusión para el público en general, que realmente no sabe qué hay en el campo de la escritura seria y bien argumentada. comprobable científico e histórico, o lo que es solo mistificación y engaño ... Todo esto para deleite de los Servicios Especiales a cargo de la información errónea ... Además, aclaremos algunos puntos de este tema nebuloso ...

¿Qué se demuestra realmente hoy en los escritos sumerios?

¿Qué hipótesis se pueden desarrollar seriamente?

¿SON LOS ANUNNA EXTRATERRESTRES?

La mitología sumeria describe dioses llamados ANUNNA que son criaturas del cielo. El término Anunna es el término genérico para algunos de los dioses, mientras que ANUNNAKI es el nombre de los Anunna instalados en la Tierra (KI). Encontramos estos dos términos en los textos sumerios, se refieren a un verdadero mito sumerio ... Está atestiguado a través de documentos históricos, tabletas con escritos cuneiformes.

Muchos autores considerarán que las deidades son en última instancia seres extraterrestres. Estos seres extraterrestres con los que nadie ha podido identificar sus origine, ni a través de los documentos históricos, ni a través de los fragmentos de información que tenemos sobre las exocivilizaciones ...

Los errores de análisis de muchos autores, las mistificaciones y la desinformación activa de los Servicios Especiales, llevaron a la creación de una nueva mitología ufológica contemporánea ... Pero, por todo eso, debemos excluir la posibilidad de que los sumerios y otros pueblos antiguos. podría haber estado en contacto con exocivilizaciones?

¿No existe el riesgo de tener un enfoque demasiado simplista y existe el riesgo de tirar al bebé con el agua del baño?

¿LOS ANUNNA HABRÍAN CREADO AL HOMBRE TERRENAL?

Las deidades sumerias ANUNNAKI hubieran considerado transformar al ser humano, presente antes de la llegada de los Anunna, para hacer esclavos a sus servicio.

Un autor estadounidense llamado Zecharia Sitchin, se embarcó en una larga serie de fabricaciones pseudocientíficas a través de diversas obras e hizo que este humano fuera descrito en los textos sumerios, un mono transformado, según él, en un esclavo humano por el Anunnaki. Los textos de Kharsag, cuidadosamente traducidos por Anton Parks y publicados en su libro Eden, muestran que era un hombre. En cuanto a los medios de transformación de este hombre salvaje en un esclavo dócil, se deben explorar múltiples posibilidades ...

Al igual que Zecharia Sitchin, muchos autores sin escrúpulos afirmaron categóricamente que ANUNNA eran extraterrestres que manipulaban genéticamente a la especie humana para alienarla. Algunos venal iluminados, hicieron religiones jugosas, para deleite de los desacreditadores institucionales ...

Suponiendo que los elementos de la mitología sumeria traducen aquí una verdad histórica, una exocivilización tiene muchos medios de control doméstico de una población humana salvaje, sin tener que modificarla genéticamente.

Una intervención sobre el genoma humano a partir de una exocivilización es una hipótesis simple de interpretación de la noción sumeria de transformación de la población humana salvaje. En cualquier caso, tal eventualidad en su afirmación razonable se referiría solo a modificaciones epigenéticas reversibles después de unas pocas generaciones, o modificaciones genómicas infinitesimales. Esto en la hipótesis de que una exocivilización antigua y experimentada consideraría que tiene derecho a intervenir en el genoma de una especie humana nativa. Esta hipótesis, basada en una visión eugenésica e intervencionista, me parece estar en contradicción con la necesaria madurez intelectual de una exocivilización capaz de hacer viajes intermedios, perfectamente conscientes de la interdependencia de todas las especies humanas del cosmos. Además, esta hipótesis también está en contradicción con los documentos de Ummitas que les dan fe de una deontología de las exocivilizaciones humanas del cosmos y las reglas supervisadas por los humanos más evolucionados del cosmos. Según los Ummitas, otros visitantes observarían activamente nuestra planeta y participarían en un vasto dispositivo de observación y protección de la Tierra. Este dispositivo incluye múltiples grupos étnicos, aseguraría el papel de coordinación y arbitraje, para que las misiones científicas de diferentes razas de extraterrestres vinieran a observarnos.

```
Por lo tanto, existe una raza de OEMMII cuya tec-
nología está más allá de nuestra comprensión y que
parece monitorear diferentes planetas al sondear a
las OUEWA (naves interplanetarias) que están incur-
sionando. (NR13, 14/04/2003).
```

En conclusión, el simple sentido común de un humano terrestre nos tendría, si nosotros mismos fuéramos exiliados a un planeta con nativos que nos gustaría subyugar de una manera inteligente, es probable que recurramos a un control con medios psicotrónicos ... ya disponibles en todos los buenos rayos de los Servicios Especiales Terrestres ... Esta es una solución mucho más simple y mucho más efectiva que la manipulación genética en una especie desconocida, cuyos efectos pueden ser altamente impredecibles ....

En la mitología sumeria, este proyecto para transformar al ser humano en esclavos aborta gracias a la intervención de un personaje llamado ENKI, que brindará a los humanos los medios para recuperar su libertad al educarlos y comunicarse con ellos un gran secreto. Este gran secreto parece haber sido el conocimiento de la metalurgia (ver el *Despertar del Fénix y el Edén* por Anton Parks).

Enki será ayudada por varias mujeres de su clan, como su madre Mamitu-Nammu y Ninmah, la matriarca de la ciudad de Kharsag. No se menciona en ningún texto que Enki sea un dios Anunna. Enki era un ser aparte, como su creador An.

En las mentes de los sumerios, los planetas de los dioses ANUNNA eran montañas del cielo. La colina sagrada o montaña sagrada de Dukù (DU-KÙ) es el punto de origen de los Anunna. Es en este planeta que los dioses ANUNNA fueron creados por An (el padre de Enki) y eso comenzará la gran rebelión de los jóvenes dioses ANUNNA contra los antiguos dioses representados por Tiamat, la reina suprema. Enki encabezó un clan llamado Nungal (o Igigi en acadio) que estaba en conflicto con los Anunna. Estos jóvenes dioses ANUNNA tendrían una génesis para decir lo menos complejo. En cuanto a Enki, su naturaleza sigue siendo muy misteriosa, incluso en las tabletas sumerias ... Los Nungals eran los Vigilantes de la Biblia y, según Anton Parks, eran los siguientes de Osiris y Horus en Egipto. Los seguidores de Osiris y Horus se llaman Shemsu en egipcio (de la palabra egipcia Shms seguir, acompañar). Se dividieron en varios grupos. En los textos apócrifos serían gigantes. El Shemsu egipcio medía aproximadamente 2,10 m, mientras que el tamaño humano normal era de entre 1,50 my 1,65 m. Estaban allí para proteger al rey Osiris y luego a Horus. Anton Parks ha demostrado en sus obras que Enki era en realidad Osiris en Egipto.

Las diferencias de tamaño pueden resaltar diferentes grupos étnicos o razas. El hombre de Neanderthal, por ejemplo, tenía una altura promedio mucho mayor (aproximadamente 1.85 m) que el tamaño promedio del Homo Sapiens que era contemporáneo para él (aproximadamente 1.60 m). Del mismo modo, el hombre de Flores tenía un tamaño promedio muy pequeño de aproximadamente un metro. Esto hace muy plausible que los Shemsu egipcios fueran un grupo étnico específico. ¿Podría el Shemsu egipcio haber sido un clan extraterrestre llamado Nungal? Esta es una hipótesis que también debe ser estudiada entre las demás ...

LOS ANUNNAKI Y NIBIRU

Para vengar su fracaso, los ANUNNAKI pro-esclavitud prohibió a ENKI que huyó. Como Anton Parks explica en sus libros, ninguna tableta dice que Enki huyó a un planeta llamado Nibiru. Ni que un planeta llamado Nibiru sea el de los Anunna. Es una invención pura de Zecharia Sitchin que encontramos entre otras cosas en su libro *El libro perdido de Enki* y en el que se habla de una serie de tabletas que no existen en absoluto ...

Zecharia Sitchin atrajo a sus lectores con esta historia e inventó estas tabletas para traer la prueba falsa de la existencia de Nibiru, tesis que construyó en su primer libro, *The Twelfth Planet.* El libro perdido de Enki es una estafa monumental. Desde muchos medios, las revistas han tomado esta idea de Nibiru, el planeta Anunna. Como señala Anton Parks, el único lugar celestial mencionado en las tabletas como Anunna es el Dukù y, en la mitología sumeria, Enki no huye en Nibiru, sino en África, y particularmente en Egipto. En Sumer, el templo secreto y acuático de Enki se llama Abzu, mientras que en Egipto el templo de agua de Osiris estaba en la ciudad sagrada Abdju (Abydos). Anton Parks pudo hacer una cronología del Nungal-Shemsu en su libro *The Awakening of the Phoenix*.

Obviamente tampoco hay relación entre este falso planeta Nibiru y el planeta real Eris (ex-Xena), que está más allá de Plutón. Pero la ironía del azar está en otra parte, en los documentos Ummans. De hecho, como explicamos en el documental Presence: UFOs, Crop Circle y Exocivilizations, el planeta Eris descubierto en 2003 por astrónomos terrestres, se informó hace 25 años, más allá de Plutón, desde 1979, en documentos que supuestamente la exocivilización del planeta Ummo ... ¿casualidad simple? ¿Pura especulación? El planeta Xena tiene una eclíptica muy atípica que hizo que su descubrimiento fuera muy difícil. Sin embargo, estos mismos documentos de Ummitas dan 25 años antes del descubrimiento de la existencia de este planeta, la posición orbital promedio de este planeta desconocido ... Una simple evaluación probabilística hace que tal nivel de previsibilidad sea totalmente imposible ... un cuarto de siglo antes del descubrimiento del planeta Eris (*Presencia 2, El lenguaje y el misterio del planeta UMMO revelado*).

LOS ANUNNAKI Y LA CONSTELACIÓN DE LAS PLÉYADES

Las Pléyades y los supuestos Pleyadianos también son productos derivados y pastel de crema que traducen una desinformación profunda, mezclando como siempre lo verdadero y lo falso. Para un ojo humano, las Pléyades representan 7 estrellas. Para un astrónomo, es un grupo de varios miles de estrellas ... Esta agrupación de unos 3000 soles, ubicada a unos 450 años luz de distancia, probablemente incluirá estrellas con sistemas solares donde viven exocivilizaciones.

Esto es muy probable. Pero, desde un punto de vista semántico, hablar de los Pléïadiens no tiene absolutamente ningún sentido ... ¿De qué exocivilización de esta constelación se hablaría? Por lo tanto, las referencias a los Pleïadiens deben tomarse con mucho cuidado ... Si nos referimos a la información contenida en los documentos Ummitas, podemos ver que las exocivilizaciones más remotas que nos visitan, no se encuentran más de 150 años -luz. Lo que con los medios habituales de nuestros visitantes y las limitaciones cosmológicas, supone ya viajes muy largos de unos 10 años. Un viaje de 450 AL supone un viaje de unos 30 años. Sin embargo, incluso si tal viaje sigue siendo posible, tal duración, cualquiera que sea la longevidad de los seres humanos involucrados, hace que sea muy difícil, incluso para nuestros amigos del espacio exterior ...

Entre estas múltiples exocivilizaciones de las Pléyades, aunque es muy probable que tengan un fenotipo humanoide, es mucho menos probable que este fenotipo pueda confundirse con los del Homo sapiens terrestre. Pregunta simple de probabilidad...

Con respecto a las tabletas sumerias, ninguna tableta conocida declara explícitamente las Pléyades. Sin embargo, varios sellos de arcilla asocian a los dioses Anunna con las 7 estrellas visibles que uno asocia con la constelación de las Pléyades. Según Anton Parks, el Dukù estaba en las Pléyades. Más tarde, cuando los dioses se asentaron en la Tierra, le dieron a su ciudad construida en las montañas de Tauro el nombre de Dukù (o Dukug) en homenaje a su lugar de origen (ver tabletas traducidas en el libro Edén) . Los Anunna y Nungal se habrían encontrado en la Tierra, al final de la batalla contra su reina Tiamat (ver texto de Enuma Elish). Los ANUNNAKI serían un grupo de guerreros expatriados a la Tierra debido a la guerra.

A primera vista, no tenían nada más que el equipo básico que había en sus carros voladores. Los exiliados con tan rudimentario significa que deben recurrir a mano de obra local ...

ANUNNAKI Y REPTILIANOS

En la mitología de la desinformación de los ovnis, los extraterrestres Anunna serían de forma humana, y los Illuminati podrían ser sus descendientes. Según los documentos Ummitas (D1378) podemos entender que nuestro planeta está en manos de los 3 principales grupos humanos oligárquicos (occidentales, rusos y chinos) peligrosos, cínicos y corruptos.

La hipótesis de los orígenes extraterrestres de estos grupos oligárquicos me parece más que fantasmagórica. Tengo la sensación de que, una vez más, la información errónea está funcionando y busca ocultar estos peligrosos grupos oligárquicos bien terrestres, detrás de una cortina de humo llamado Illuminatis, supustos hibridos extraterrestres ...

Esto todavía da una buena razón para dar plenos poderes a estos peligrosos grupos oligárquicos que podrían tener la buena idea de querer proteger a los humildes ciudadanos terrestres de los malvados extraterrestres ... Una dictadura global sería la apoteosis de una maniobra en el puro respeto de los preceptos de Maquiavelo que enseña que *el Príncipe debe ser temido, pero no debe ser odiado. Si es odiado, vuelve a la gente contra él, si solo se le teme, mantiene su autoridad y su poder. Desde este punto de vista, es una buena política mantener el miedo, sin convertirlo en odio. Un pueblo atemorizado permanece callado. No se atreve a enfrentarse al poder. Un pueblo que comienza a odiar a su soberano buscará derrocarlo y seguirá a aquellos que lo llevarán a la revuelta.*

Todos los tiranos que la humanidad a creado lo sabían. Existe una habilidad maquiavélica calculada y astuta para manipular la inseguridad y usar el miedo.

En cuanto a los reptilianos que también encarnan personajes inquietantes, Zecharia Sitchin había discutido sobre eso con David Icke. Zecharia Sitchin ha ignorado conscientemente los diversos documentos sumerios donde podemos ver a muchos dioses con forma de cocodrilo o por extrapolación de reptiles. Zecharia Sitchin quería que su tesis fuera lo más cercana posible a la Biblia. ¡Para él, los dioses no podían tener la forma de la Serpiente Bíblica! Pero al no ver ninguna duda de que la ola reptiliana estaba ganando impulso, no insistió demasiado y finalmente evitó el tema, para surfear precisamente en esta ola.

Se pueden avanzar varias hipótesis para explicar por qué los dioses ANUNNA a veces se representan con una forma de cocodrilo.

La primera hipótesis es que las referencias a animales del género reptiliano y, posiblemente, su vínculo con la raza humana son las reminiscencias de una memoria colectiva distante transmitida a través de los siglos. (ver el libro de Anton Parks *EDEN* p53)

Los textos de la primera Biblia de Jerusalén parecen estar claramente basados en los escritos sumerios. Es probable que ellos mismos fueran los primeros vectores de una transposición escrita de una larga tradición oral. La memoria del conocimiento tradicional parece haber transmitido a lo largo de los siglos que los reptiles eran anteriores a los mamíferos. Este conocimiento ancestral, es confirmado globalmente por las ciencias modernas del siglo XX, incluso en la evolución del cerebro con la primera teoría en este sentido del cerebro trino de Paul Mac Lean en 1969. Esto resalta, de paso, que nuestros antepasados, lejos de ser estúpido animal desollado con un palo, por el contrario, eran muy buenos en sus observaciones del mundo y en sus análisis ... Si ese no hubiera sido el caso, la humanidad no estaría de todos modos no llegó a la etapa actual de desarrollo ...

Sin embargo, uno puede objetar esta primera hipótesis, formular la segunda hipótesis. Las disimetrías raciales destacan diferentes grupos étnicos. El hombre de Neanderthal, por ejemplo, tenía una altura promedio mucho mayor (aproximadamente 1.85 m) que el tamaño promedio del Homo Sapiens que era contemporáneo para él (aproximadamente 1.60 m). Del mismo modo, el hombre de Flores tenía un tamaño promedio muy pequeño de aproximadamente un metro. Esto hace muy plausible que los Shemsu egipcios fueran un grupo étnico específico. Los sumerios se refieren a serpientes gigantes con mandíbulas despiadadas. ¿Encontraron fósiles de dinosaurios suficientemente evocadores del pasado carnívoro de estos animales? ¿O podrían tener otras fuentes de información? Entonces, también podemos preguntarnos cómo y cómo estos dragones furiosos podrían haberse transformado para convertirse en los Dioses. ¿Podría el Shemsu egipcio haber sido un clan extraterrestre llamado Nungal? Esta es una hipótesis que también debe ser estudiada entre las demás ...

Desarollaremos todavia mas estos temas en *Presencia 4 - Hacia Un Nuevo Mundo ... Con Las Exocivilizaciones*.

NUEVAS HIPÓTESIS SOBRE LA MITOLOGÍA SUMERIA

Si las tesis de Zecharia Sitchin tenían un gran entusiasmo, es porque inicialmente comenzó una verdadera investigación científica. Esta investigación científica se basó en el análisis de textos hebreos de los sumerios y las interpretaciones de documentos cuneiformes en sumerio. Por lo tanto, desde una buena base, nuestro investigador se ha embarcado en traducciones de palabras hebreas y textos sumerios, que no dominó el significado. De hecho, Zecharia Sitchin cometió enormes errores de traducción, incluso hasta el punto de dudar de que pudiera traducir sumerio ... En ningún momento dice en uno de sus libros, aquí está mi traducción de este texto ..., o algo así. Sus traducciones salen de la nada, a menudo sin ninguna referencia. Tanto por sus traducciones del hebreo que no dominó en profundidad, como por los sumerios, donde los errores son aún más penosos para la comprensión real de los textos ... El nivel de errores de interpretación y especulación que Zecharia Sitchin cometió. Es tal que, en última instancia, construyó una hermosa historia ... lejos de la realidad de los textos originales. Las lucubraciones de Zecharia Sitchin han llevado a la creación de una nueva mitología ufológica contemporánea que es una fuente de deleite para los Servicios a cargo de la desinformación ...

Pero, por todo eso, ¿deberíamos excluir la posibilidad de que los sumerios y otros pueblos antiguos pudieran haber estado en contacto con exocivilizaciones?

¿No existe el riesgo de tener un enfoque demasiado simplista y existe el riesgo de tirar al bebé con el agua del baño?

Los sumerios y los pueblos del Indo de este período (alrededor de 6000 a. C. a 5000 a. C.) tenían culturas muy desarrolladas para interesar a los visitantes del espacio exterior ... ¿Cuáles serían los elementos que podrían revelar un potencial contacto con exocivilizaciones?

La mitología sumeria menciona en sentido figurado a las deidades ANUNNAKI como seres cocodrilos homínidos en ciertos sellos (pequeños sellos sumerios o acadios en arcilla, impresos en pedazos de arcilla). Los dioses sumerios están representados con una apariencia de reptil, pero esto nunca se dice realmente en los textos. Algunos textos de Kharsag traducidos por Anton Parks en EDEN muestran a Enki y Ninmah con nombres relacionados con reptiles con algunas descripciones físicas de cocodrilos, así como algunas referencias donde, por ejemplo, los personajes Inanna-Ishtar y su amante Dumuzi poseen la cara o el aspecto de un Umshumgal (gran dragón). Por extensión imaginativa, el homínido de cocodrilo se llama reptiliano ...

Como hemos descrito en Presencia, ovnis, círculos de cultivos y exocivilizaciones, los documentos de Ummitas mencionan la visita de seres hominoides con piel escamosa. Obviamente, esto es muy similar a la denominación de un físico reptiliano, pero una piel escamosa no prejuzga de ninguna manera el tipo de ser vivo. Los seres hominoides con piel escamosa pueden ser perfectamente como mamíferos ... ¡o peces!

En 2007, en PRESENCE Ovnis, Crop Circles and Exocivilisations presentamos 18 exocivilizaciones permanentemente presentes en la Tierra. En 2015, ahora tienen 23 años.

Las más numerosas, 19 exocivilizaciones, son benévolas y actúan positivamente sobre el futuro de la humanidad terrestre. Algunos pueden considerarse amorales en sus prácticas, quizas es el caso de GOHOiens.

Sigue siendo el caso muy especial que también habíamos mencionado en trabajos anteriores, 2 - iens.

Otro elemento perturbador que también podría respaldar la hipótesis de que los sumerios pueden haber tenido contacto con dichos visitantes desde el espacio exterior, es la cronología mencionada en los documentos Ummitas. Su presencia en la Tierra ha sido atestiguada por más de 30 000 años. Que es compatible con un antiguo contacto con sumerios o acadios ...

Los 2 - iens son grandes, entre 2 y 3 metros. Como señaló Anton Parks, seguidores de Enki, el Shemsu egipcio medía alrededor de 2,10 m, mientras que el tamaño humano normal era de entre 1,50 my 1,65 m.

Los amigos de UMMO conocen los 2-iens por su piel escamosa y lívida, su cabeza de serpiente y su silbido que difunde los rumores de muchos reptiles.

Tampoco debemos descuidar el hecho de que la tradición sumeria presenta a las Serpientes como seres de poder y conocimiento. Viven en las altas montañas de Kurdistán, desde donde descendieron para traer a los hombres los beneficios de la civilización.

En conclusión, a pesar de muchas historias al respecto que son totalmente espeluznantes, con fines de lucro y probablemente para desinformar sobre la gravedad de la información en sí misma ... uno no debe excluir la posibilidad real y seria de que los sumerios o Los Acadios podrían haber estado en contacto con los 2 - iens que todavía están presentes en la Tierra ...

Desarollaremos todavia mas estos temas en *Presencia 4 - Hacia Un Nuevo Mundo ... Con Las Exocivilizaciones*.

INDIOS ASHIWI Y EXOCIVILIZACIONES

¿Podrían los contactos éticos entre terrestres y exocivilizaciones haber dejado huellas culturales en las culturas indígenas? Hay evidencia de que los indios Ashiwi pueden haber estado en contacto con la exocivilización hace unos 3.000 años.

En la primera presentación de mi investigación en los EE. UU. en febrero de 2010, en el Congreso de Ovnis de Laughlin, tuve una visita increíble. El jefe chamán de la tribu Zuni. O más bien los Ashiwi como se llaman a sí mismos, el nombre oficial de Zunis fue dado por los españoles. El jefe chamán Clifford Mahooty vino a verme como si me hubiera conocido desde siempre, e inmediatamente me señaló como un hermano... Esto me sorprendió mucho, ya que nunca le habia encontrado antes, pero nuestra simpatía mutua no fue negada durante nuestras reuniones, por el contrario, las convergencias de puntos de vista y nuestros intercambios fueron más ricos ...

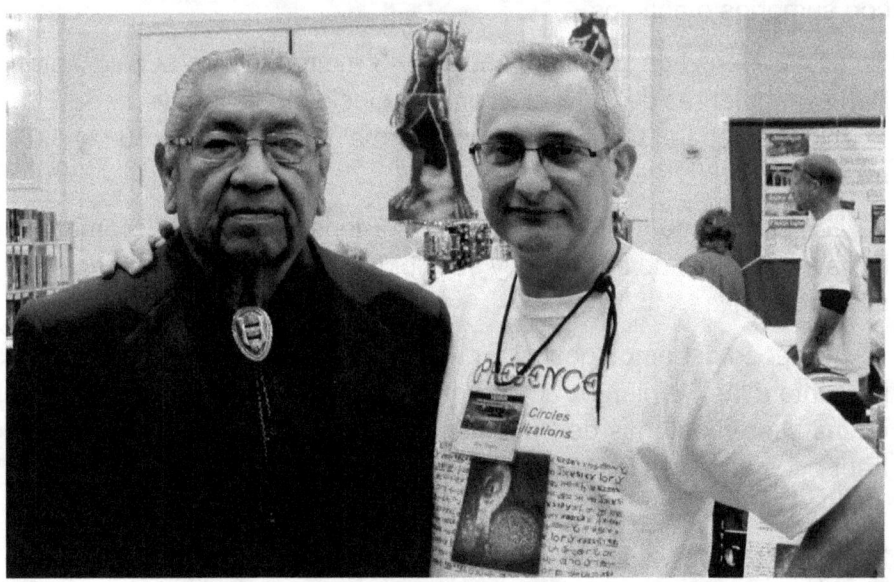

El chamán Clifford Mahooty y Denis Roger DENOCLA
Congreso de ovnis Laughlin Nevada EE.UU. 2010

El territorio de los Ashiwi, es decir, «aquellos donde cada uno es específico», se encuentra al suroeste de la ciudad de Albuquerque. Esta área está atravesada por el Cañón Zuni que conduce al Gran Cañón, más al oeste. Clifford Mahooty me informa rápidamente que el territorio Zuni es muy activo para los ovnis desde los años 60. Las visitas de equipo nocturno con los desplazamientos hieráticos y relámpagos son realmente numerosas, de 1 a 2 veces por mes aproximadamente. A menudo llegan por el sur del cañón Zuni. A veces a plena luz del día. En varias ocasiones, las máquinas se han estacionado cerca del suelo. Como en 2001, cuando una sonda automática de unos 3 metros de diámetro aterrizó a unas decenas de metros de su hogar en un área de cultivo de maíz. Desde entonces, en este lugar la vegetación está atrofiada y el maíz no crece en absoluto.

Varios otros indios de la tribu, incluido Dan un arqueólogo Zuni, una tarde de 2005 en una carretera cerca de la aldea estaban cara a cara con una máquina de más de quince metros de diámetro flotando a nivel del suelo . Uno de los indios asustados quería dispararle a la máquina con un rifle de caza de gran calibre, pero mi amigo Dan, el arqueólogo Zuni, lo disuadió ... Se quedaron a cierta distancia hasta que la máquina salió con algunas oscilaciones y una velocidad vertiginosa ...

Aquí hay algunos ejemplos de encuentros que se pueden realizar en el territorio Zuni, y todos los habitantes conocen el fenómeno. Para una gran parte de ellos, esto es normal, especialmente porque el jefe chamán de la tribu Zuni me contará la historia y la mitología de la tribu. Esto es claramente diferente de la versión oficial ... En esta mitología, la génesis de la cultura del pueblo Zuni proviene de las Kachinas. Las Kachinas están representadas por personajes coloridos y enmascarados que encarnan durante los bailes rituales, no solo las mentes como sugeriría lo políticamente correcto. Pero todos los grandes principios culturales de la sociedad Ashiwi, desde un ángulo muy particular ...

Tomemos el ejemplo de una Kachina habitual del tipo de «hijos de incesto» que son personajes feos y locos que simbolizan los efectos peligrosos de las posibles relaciones de incesto y consanguinidad. Cada familia se encarga de transmitir la memoria oral de un tipo de Kachina con todo su simbolismo. Lo que no sabemos es que para la mayoría de estas Kachinas, el origen de cada uno de estos símbolos está asociado con ... un pueblo del cosmos!

Otro punto totalmente desconocido es que los Kachinas gigantes están en el origen de la base de la cultura Zuni, de estos valores morales y sociales. Muy claramente, Clifford Mahooty me explica que los Zunis han estado en contacto con una civilización extraterrestre que les habría dado mucho conocimiento. Clifford me dice en particular que, en el campo de la astronomía, los Zunis siempre han conocido la existencia de ciertas nebulosas totalmente desconocidas antes de la aparición de telescopios potentes. Para mí, las gigantes Kachinas que estarían en la raíz de la cultura Zuni, evocan de inmediato algo muy específico ...

De hecho, llamo la atención de Clifford sobre el cuadro de razas extraterrestres que publiqué en Presencia, OVNIS, Círculos en los cultivos y Exocivilizaciones. En la terminología de los Ummitas, los IOXianos son extraterrestres grandes, de unos 3 metros de altura, que comenzaron sus visitas a la Tierra en 896 a. C., ¡una presencia iniciada hace unos 3.000 años! La hipótesis de que los Kachinas gigantes son los IOXianos parece muy plausible para Clifford Mahooty, tanto cronológica como moralmente. Porque las fuentes de Oummain especifican que los IOXiens están dotados de una gran inteligencia y una moralidad estricta. Por lo tanto, son buenos candidatos para difundir pautas morales a los Zuni, y a los Hopi que son misma tribua original.

Esta exocivilización anterior habría ocurrido mucho antes de la Pax Galactica de los años 80, en un momento en que el nivel de aceptación de la tierra era fácilmente manejable por nuestros visitantes, y luego infrecuente. Esto nos da una buena hipótesis para esta antigua exocivilización.

Pero, ¿por qué tanta actividad ovni desde los años 60?
Le pregunto al jefe chamán cuáles son para mí los puntos clave lógicos cruciales. ¿Está al tanto de los rumores de instalaciones nucleares secretas en territorio Zuni? Tales instalaciones en los años sesenta no habrían fallado en generar una vigilancia activa de exocivilizaciones. Clifford no excluye esta hipótesis, el trabajo podría haberse hecho de noche o de subterránea sin el conocimiento de la tribu.

El territorio Zuni incluye una zona volcánica inactiva. Este tipo de actividad geológica interesa a muchas exocivilizaciones y podría ser una fuente de curiosidad y estudio para nuestros visitantes. Sin embargo, esta actividad volcánica no es contemporánea y no puede correlacionarse con el período de los años 60. Por otro lado, sugiero a Clifford que esta actividad volcánica y el alivio típico de los cañones monumentales, podría haber sido uno de los motivos que podrían haber tenido podría motivar a IOXiens a venir a la región hace 3.000 años.

Aunque la suposición de sitios nucleares civiles o militares es con frecuencia la causa de una zona activa de ovnis, tengo en cuenta un dato particular. El de la historia de la relación entre los Zunis y los probables IOXiens. Esta antigua relación puede haber requerido el establecimiento de una infraestructura logística IOXIENNE. Esta base IOXIENNE puede ser siempre una base activa, incluso para otras exocivilizaciones. O de nuevo, esta base IOXIENNE podría ser un lugar exohistórico, una especie de Mont-Saint-Michel ... Esta hipótesis también llama la atención de Clifford, quien me dice que también conoce la existencia de petroglifos que nunca se han estudiado en esta difícil área de acceso.

CONCLUSIÓN SOBRE LA INFLUENCIA DE LAS EXOCIVILIZACIONES

En conclusión, debemos tener cuidado con las conclusiones apresuradas y simplistas, y desafiar las ideas recibidas transmitidas perniciosamente para revolver las cartas ... ¿Quién se beneficia del crimen?

Si las exocivilizaciones han tenido buenas razones para entrar en contacto con humanos terrestres, el requisito de autenticidad histórica debe buscarse con tenacidad, incluso a través de mitos y leyendas.

A pesar de que la mitología sumeria solo tenía fundamentos históricos tenues, es sin embargo una mitología fundacional de los grandes textos religiosos de Oriente Medio. Esto ya socava, en gran medida estos dogmas religiosos y la simple suposición de que esta mitología también puede estar estrechamente vinculada a una exocivilización podría ser un golpe de gracia para los dogmas antropocéntricos ...

LA POSIBLE EVOLUCIÓN FUTURA DEL HOMBRE

El generador de WOA parece haber tenido la buena idea de generar un cuasi-infinito de cosmos que sigue los mismos modos de estructuración con variantes, pero en última instancia siempre con seres capaces de desempeñar el papel cibernético esperado. Según los cálculos de los Ummitas, habría 10^{30} razas de humanos en el Multicosmos WAAM-WAAM. En cuanto a las formas de los seres vivos, solo unos pocos millones de billones de formas serían posibles en cada planeta-OYAA.

Normalmente, un nodo de un filo (árbol) puede dar lugar a alrededor de doscientos veinte mil (en promedio) nuevas ramas o filos a través de una mutación dirigida, es decir, controlada. En algunos nodos (aproximadamente) se han detectado 18,376,000 posibilidades de mutaciones toleradas por el BB planetario.

¿Podemos estudiar la posible filogenia en las diferentes OYAA (astros fríos) de WAAM-WAAM? ¡Obviamente no! Es posible que los posibles seres vivos se cuenten por billones o cuadrillones. Calculamos que el WAAM podría codificar hasta 5.2×10^{18} modelos, pero la inexactitud del cálculo hace sospechar que podrían ser mucho más. De estos patrones primarios se pueden derivar miles de millones (individuos o copias), de modo que el orden de magnitud para todos los WAAM-WAAM alcanzaría una cantidad de copias posibles diferentes de 10^{526} (orden de magnitud)

Las indicaciones contenidas en los documentos Ummitas nos explican claramente las principales líneas de evolución de los seres vivos y el Hombre.

- Primera etapa: un organismo que tiene reflejos simples y reacciona directamente al estímulo del entorno físico.
- Segunda etapa: una organización capaz de procesar información y llevar a cabo su conducta de manera determinista no solo en virtud del medio, sino también por la información almacenada.
- Tercera etapa : Cuerpo (OEMII) (Hombre) cuyo cerebro ha experimentado un salto cuántico que le permite ser consciente, relativamente libre y conectado a BUAWAA (Psique), a BUAWEE BIAEII y cuya conducta contribuye a dar forma al WAAM-WAAM
- Cuarta etapa: OIXIOOWOA. La probabilidad de que una mutación OIXIOOWOA (solo una en un cerebro determinado) y dentro de los primeros diez millones de años de una red OEMMII sea muy alta (probabilidad cercana a una) y alcance la unidad si Han pasado al menos trece millones de años. Es muy raro que, durante un período de quince a veinte millones de años (si la humanidad sobrevive), ocurra una mutación idéntica (Nota 4).

[Nota 4] - La ley de distribución de frecuencia en el tiempo sigue una función muy singular, un gráfico que luego exponemos. En cada red social de cualquier astro frío, un solo individuo de esta especie llamado OEMMIIWOA, se genera por casualidad por primera vez. Luego transcurre un gran intervalo de tiempo sin que ocurra el fenómeno, cuya eclosión no volverá a ocurrir hasta después de millones de años. Por lo tanto, la mutación OIXIOOWOA genera un tipo de cerebro radicalmente diferente del del OEMII del que procede. El OEMIIWOA así conformado, es una nueva especie biológica con un genoma distinto. [Nota final 4]

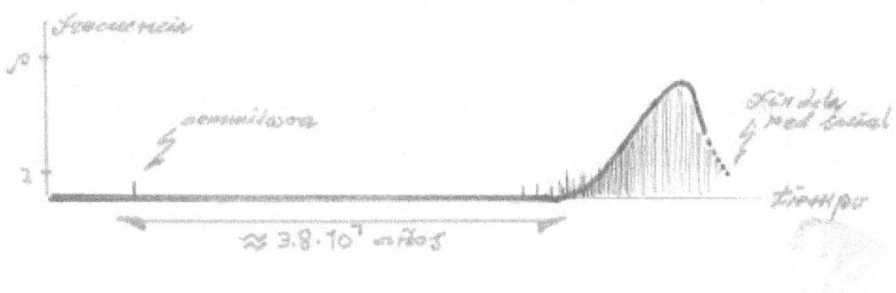

Después de treinta y ocho millones de años, hay un sorprendente fenómeno biológico-físico. Casi todos los cerebros han mutado. Sin embargo, seis millones de años antes de eso, cientos de miles de seres OEMII habían experimentado con esta mutación que los convirtió en el cerebro OIXIOOWOA. Después de unos años (no más de cincuenta años), el cuerpo humano que alberga este cerebro desapareció. (Tenga en cuenta que no decimos que muere, sino que desaparece). Pero está claro que si toda la población de personas que la estrella fría llega a esta etapa, la humanidad deja de existir.

Hemos visto en libros anteriores que muchas exocivilizaciones, esencialmente benévolas, estuvieron presentes en la Tierra, a veces durante decenas de miles de años. En el contexto de la evolución humana de la Tierra, todos los ciudadanos de nuestro planeta pueden hacerse legítimamente las siguientes preguntas:

¿Cómo se organizan nuestros visitantes en sus planetas?

¿Cómo manejan su planeta?

¿Cuál es su organización política?

¿Qué estructura económica tienen?

Tantas preguntas que nos pueden hacer pensar en nuestro propio desarrollo socioeconómico.

¿Qué pasa con la demografía, el socialismo, la etocracia?

¿Qué tipo de sociedad podríamos imaginar para mañana?

Este es el tema de la discusión que tendremos en

PRESENCIA 4 Hacia un mundo nuevo ... con las exocivilizaciones.

☒

11

CONCLUSIÓN GENERAL

A través de la teoría cosmobiofísica de 3 tercios, traté de presentar elementos de respuestas a las grandes preguntas tradicionales de la humanidad. ¿De dónde venimos, cuál es el lugar del hombre en el universo, cuál puede ser nuestro futuro?

Por lo tanto, estas hipótesis proponen nuevas explicaciones mucho más allá de los límites de nuestro conocimiento actual.

Nuestro Universo, al menos decadimensional, por lo tanto, consistiría en láminas de pares de cosmos, impulsados por un BB-global. Las estrellas están conectadas y conducidas por su BB planetario específico, gracias a un efecto LEIYO sobre el criptón que ocurriría en el umbral de la constante criptónica. Esto iniciaría un proceso que conducirá a la emergencia de los vivos de la materia inerte. Por lo tanto, la cadena de criptón de BAAYIODUU pilota los grupos de aminoácidos para formar ARN arcaicos, que se encapsularán rápidamente para crear las primeras entidades de autorreproducción vivas.

El gran ciclo de una Evolución por una gran parte, Orientada, se inicia bajo el control de la cadena de criptón de BAAYIODUU, sigue las leyes cosmobiológicas de la filogenia y la ortogénesis que conducirán a los seres humanos OEMMII en el cosmos. Estos están parcialmente bajo el control de la entidad informativa autónoma de la psique BUAWA.

Este nuevo marco cosmológico hace posible racionalizar muchos temas que pertenecieron a lo paranormal o metafísico. Más que nunca, la ciencia y la conciencia están unidas para ayudarnos a avanzar hacia un mundo que todos queremos más justo, pacífico y feliz.

En una perspectiva distante, quizás nos uniremos a las civilizaciones humanas más sabias que evolucionan hacia una especie cuyo nivel de complejidad será equivalente a su piloto cosmológico, el BB planetario ...

Algunas de estas hipótesis podrían ser probadas experimentalmente hoy en día. La inspiración de estas hipótesis se debe a documentos reclamados por una exocivilización, que le da a la marcha un carácter fuera de lo común y una extrema dificultad psicológica de lectura y aceptación. Pero estos son los hechos.

Entonces, al depositar mi confianza en la Historia, la apuesta más atrevida que puedo hacer hoy es que las hipótesis de la *Teoría cosmobiofísica de los 3 tercios* simplemente se estudian y prueban ...

El autor prohíbe estrictamente la referencia a su

investigación con fines religiosos.

Cuando violamos una norma divina, lo hacemos de acuerdo con una actitud entrópica. Cada pecado social, cada falta contra lo que llamas Caridad (amor) disuelve en menor grado la coordinación de una red social.

Si le hago daño a mi hermano, puedo causar una inhibición de sus funciones de observador, contribuyo en cierto nivel a frenar el plan de captura de información de WAAM, es decir, contribuyo a crear ENTROPIA DE TRASTORNO, ralentizando el progreso del Pluriuniverso.

Esto merece la condena en nombre de todos los OEMII de WAAM-WAAM, ya que nos está causando graves daños.

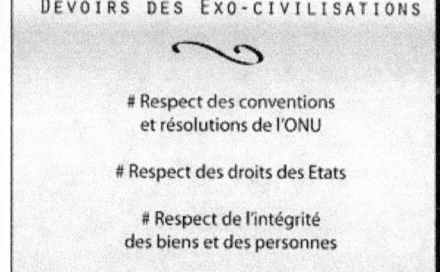

Reconocimiento de las exocivilizaciones en la Constitución;
- Rechazo de la xenofobia contra las exocivilizaciones;
- Rechazo de la militarización, el armamento y la guerra contra las exocivilizaciones;
- Exigir que los líderes políticos rindan cuentas sobre sus relationes y la censura de las exocivilizaciones.

D. R. DENOCLA

Le Savoir pour qui et pourquoi ?

NO OLVIDES DEJAR
TU COMENTARIO EN AMAZON

BIBLIOGRAPHIA

La sources des documents oummains proviennent du site www.ummo-sciences.org et www.ummo-ciencias.org et de D.R. DENOCLA.

Alexandre Oparin L'origine De La Vie, 1938, éditions Masson

Andréï Sakharov Œuvres (scientifiques) complètes Edition Anthropos (ouvrage disparu des catalogues!)

Budd Hopkins' Intruders: The Incredible Visitations at Copley Woods' Three Rivers Press; Édition, 1992

Christian de Duve A l'écoute du vivant, éditions Odile Jacob, 2002

Francis Crick, La vie vient de l'espace, édition Hachette, 1981.

Daniel Verney L'Astrologie et la science futur du psychisme, édition Le Rocher, 1987, Monaco.

Denis Roger DENOCLA Acid Jones et le mystère du temple de la science édition ADDOM, 1990.

Dr. Hyman' The Mischief-Making of Ideomotor Action' in the Fall-Winter 1999 issue of The Scientific Review of Altrnative Medicine, ©1999, Prometheus Books.

Jacques Pazelle, communications personnelles.

John Maynard Smith et Eörs Szathmary, Les origines de la vie, éditions Dunod, 2000

Ludwig Von Bertalanffy : Théorie du système général Edition Dunod, 1993.

Marie-Christine Maurel *La Naissance de la vie*, éditions Dunod, 2003

Michel Marcel, *communications personnelles.*

Percy Seymour' *Astrology: the Evidence of Science'*, Arkana, édition Penguin, 1988, Londres.

Stephen Jay Gould' *Ontogeny and phylogeny'*,1997, editions Belknap Press (janvier 1985)

Stephen Jay Gould, *La structure de la théorie de l'évolution*, 2007, NRF — Gallimard

Tsiang Kan Zheng, *revue AURA — Z n° 3*, 1993

Yvonne Smith' *Chosen. Recollections of UFO abductions through hypnotherapy'*, 2008, éditions Backstage Entertainment.

Webographie :

http://fr.wikipedia.org

http://plato-dialogues.org

http://www.antonparks.com

http://www.astrosurf.org

http://www.cafe.edu

http://www.cropsciences.org

http://www.futura-sciences.com

http://www.gillescosson.com

http://www.mineralinfo.org

http://www.pnas.org

http://www.quackwatch.org

http://www.scedu.umontreal.ca/profs

http://www.sciencedirect.com

http://www.societechimiquedefrance.fr

http://www.quanthomme.free.fr

http://www.morpheus.fr

12

REFERENCIAS

http://www.tci-france.com/

© 2013, UMMO WORLD Publishing
8 Esp. de la Manufacture
92136 Issy-les-Moulineaux

Imprimé par :
Graphic Systems.Com
69 chemin de la Chapelle St Antoine
95300 Ennery

Achevé d'imprimer en septembre 2013
Dépôt légal : septembre 2013
Imprimé en France

www.ingramcontent.com/pod-product-compliance
Lightning Source LLC
Chambersburg PA
CBHW080906170526
45158CB00008B/2006